Be prepared...
Master the test...
Score high...

Get REAdy. It all starts here.
REA's test prep helps get you into
the high school of your choice.

We'd like to hear from you!

*Visit **www.rea.com** to send us your comments*
*or email us at **info@rea.com**.*

Meet the Team Behind...
The Best Test Prep for the Catholic High School Entrance Exams – COOP & HSPT

The *best minds* to help you get the best COOP and HSPT scores

Anita P. Davis of Converse College, Spartanburg, SC; **Mitchel G. Fedak** of Community College of Allegheny County, Monroeville, PA; **Mel Friedman** of Delaware Valley College, Doylestown, PA; **Robert F. Herrmann** of Elmhurst College, Elmhurst, IL; **Rev. Mr. Scott E. McCue** of University of St. Mary of the Lake, Mundelein Seminary, Mundelein, IL; **Michael Modugno** of Piscataway High School, Piscataway, NJ; **George C. Oluikpe** of Friends of Crown Heights Educational Center #2, Brooklyn, NY; **Mark Shapiro** of University of Hartford, West Hartford, CT; **Donna Stelluto** of New Brunswick Public Schools Adult Learning Center, New Brunswick, NJ; **C. Laurie Walsh** of Round Valley Middle School, Lebanon, NJ; **Brian Walsh** of Rutgers University, New Brunswick, NJ; and **Christine Zardecki** of Rutgers University, New Brunswick, NJ.

We also gratefully acknowledge the following for their editorial contributions:
Linda Flint, Regina Gelinas, Robert Gelinas, Lorraine Ghignone, Joyce Kirchin, Joe Mancini, Melissa Pellerano, Dana Petrie, Christopher Pizzino, Peter Sharma, Erin Spanier, and James Quinlan.

Staff Acknowledgments

We would also like to thank **Larry B. Kling,** Vice President, Editorial, for his supervision of editorial production; **Pam Weston,** Vice President, Publishing, for setting the quality standards for production integrity and managing the publication to completion; **Christine Saul** for the cover design; and **Wende Solano** for typesetting the manuscript.

RE**A** *Research & Education Association*

**The Best Test
Preparation for the**

Catholic
High School
Entrance Exams

COOP & HSPT

The Best Test Preparation for the Catholic High School Entrance Exams - COOP & HSPT

Year 2005 Printing

Copyright © 2002 by Research & Education Association, Inc.
All rights reserved. No part of this book may be reproduced in
any form without permission of the publisher.

Printed in the United States of America

Library of Congress Control Number 2001087064

International Standard Book Number 0-87891-095-6

 REA® is a registered trademark of Research & Education Association, Inc.,
Piscataway, New Jersey 08854.

CONTENTS

ABOUT RESEARCH & EDUCATION ASSOCIATION

Founded in 1959, Research & Education Association is dedicated to publishing the finest and most effective educational materials—including software, study guides, and test preps—for students in middle school, high school, college, graduate school, and beyond.

REA's Test Preparation series includes books and software for all academic levels in almost all disciplines. Research & Education Association publishes test preps for students who have not yet completed high school, as well as high school students preparing to enter college. Students from countries around the world seeking to attend college in the United States will find the assistance they need in REA's publications. For college students seeking advanced degrees, REA publishes test preps for many major graduate school admission examinations in a wide variety of disciplines, including engineering, law, and medicine. Students at every level, in every field, with every ambition can find what they are looking for among REA's publications.

REA's practice tests are always based upon the most recently administered exams, and include every type of question that you can expect on the actual exams.

REA's publications and educational materials are highly regarded and continually receive an unprecedented amount of praise from professionals, instructors, librarians, parents, and students. Our authors are as diverse as the fields represented in the books we publish. They are well-known in their respective disciplines and serve on the faculties of prestigious high schools, colleges, and universities throughout the United States and Canada.

Today, REA's wide-ranging catalog is a leading resource for teachers, students, and professionals.

We invite you to visit us at *www.rea.com* to find out how "REA is making the world smarter."

COOP/ HSPT

CHAPTER 1

About this Book

Chapter 1

ABOUT THIS BOOK

This book will provide you with an accurate and complete representation of the Scholastic Testing Service's High School Placement Test (HSPT) and CTB/McGraw-Hill's Cooperative Admissions Examination (COOP). Inside you will find reviews which are designed to provide you with the information and strategies needed to do well on these tests. Two practice tests, based on the official HSPT and COOP exams, are provided as well. The practice tests contain every type of question that you can expect to encounter on test day. Following each of our practice tests, you will find an answer key with detailed explanations designed to help you master the test material.

HOW TO USE THIS BOOK

To thoroughly prepare for the actual tests, it's best to first read over the subject reviews and suggestions for test-taking. Studying the reviews will reinforce the basic skills you need to do well on the test. Be sure to take the practice tests to become familiar with the format and procedures involved with taking the actual COOP or HSPT examinations.

To best utilize your study time, follow our Independent Study Schedule located in the front of this book. Brushing up on areas you did well on wouldn't hurt either.

When Should I Start Studying?

It is never too early to start studying for these exams. The earlier you begin, the more time you will have to sharpen your skills. Do not procrastinate! Cramming is not an effective way to study since it does not allow you the time needed to learn the test material. The sooner you learn the format of the exam you are taking, the more time you will have to familiarize yourself with its content.

THE REVIEW SECTIONS

The reviews in this book are designed to help you sharpen the basic skills needed to approach the HSPT and the COOP, as well as to provide strategies for attacking each type of question. You will also find drills to reinforce what you have learned. By using the reviews in conjunction with the practice tests, you will better prepare yourself for the actual exams themselves.

TIPS FOR TAKING THE HSPT AND COOP

DON'T BE INTIMIDATED

Fear will ruin your chances of doing the best that you can on the test. Studying this book will help you to approach the HSPT or COOP with confidence and poise.

GET TO KNOW THE TEST FORMAT

Our practice tests have been specially designed to reflect the way the actual HSPT and COOP will look. Take some time to get familiar with the different tests that you will be taking. There shouldn't be any surprises for you on test day.

USE THE PROCESS OF ELIMINATION

This is possibly the easiest and quickest way to increase your score. Eliminating answer choices will lead you to the right answer almost every time. Neither CTB McGraw-Hill or STS will deduct points for incorrect answers. This means that even if you can't seem to get an answer, just pick one letter. If you blindly guess, you'll get 1 answer in 5 right. If you can eliminate just 1 answer choice, you'll get 1 answer in 4 right. Either way, you'll raise your score because you don't lose points for leaving an answer blank.

PAY ATTENTION

Be sure that the answer oval that you are marking corresponds to the question number in the test booklet. Otherwise, you run the risk of filling in all of the wrong ovals.

STUDY SCHEDULE

WEEK	ACTIVITY
1	If you are taking the HSPT, Read the "About the HSPT" chapter. Then, take the HSPT Practice Test 1 and use the answer key chart to determine where your weak areas are. If you are taking the COOP, do the same with COOP-related material. Make sure that you study the detailed explanations to gain some initial insight on the problems that you have trouble completing.
2 & 3	Keep in mind the problems that you got wrong. Read and study the Verbal Skills and the Language Skills reviews. Make sure that you answer all of the drill questions. Learn the difference between the correct and incorrect examples. Then, review any material that you answered incorrectly in your practice test.

WEEK	ACTIVITY
4 & 5	Keep in mind the problems that you got wrong in the practice tests. Now study the Reading review. If you are taking the COOP, study the Memory review as well. Answer the drill questions and review any material that you answered incorrectly in your practice test.
6 & 7	Keep in mind the problems that you got wrong. Read and study the Mathematics and Quantitative Skills reviews. Make sure that you answer the drill questions. Pay close attention to the examples given. Now, review any material that you answered incorrectly in your practice test.
8	It's time to see how much you have improved! Take the COOP Practice Test 2 or the HSPT Practice Test 2. Once again, study the detailed explanations to try and gain some insight on the problems that you got wrong. Go back and reread any reviews which pertain to answers that are still unclear.
9	Allow a week for review and taking the optional tests. Review the Mechanical Aptitude Section and take the test. Make sure that you examine all detailed answers.
10	Review the General Science Section and take the test. Make sure that you examine all detailed answers.
11	Review the Catholic Religion Section and take the test. Make sure that you examine all detailed answers.

ABOUT THE HIGH SCHOOL PLACEMENT TEST (HSPT)

ABOUT THE TEST

Who Takes the Test and What Is It Used For?

The HSPT examination is taken by junior high students who plan on applying for admittance to private or parochial high schools. This examination is used to evaluate a student's knowledge and determine if the student has adequate knowledge and understanding in specified subject areas.

Who Administers the Test?

The HSPT is developed and administered by Scholastic Testing Service and is updated each year to ensure test security. The test development process is designed and implemented to also ensure that the content and difficulty level of the test are appropriate.

When Is the HSPT Taken?

Students are required to take the HSPT in the fall of 8th Grade so that they will have another opportunity to take it if they do not pass. Taking our practice tests will familiarize you with the types of questions on and the format of the HSPT exam to eliminate the anxiety of only being able to become familiar with the test as you take it.

When and Where Is the Test Given?

The HSPT is administered in the Fall and once more in the Spring, but you should check with the school you are applying to for the exact date. Also, since the test is used in different ways (again, specific to the school), you will need to take the exam at the school to which you are applying (contact the admissions office of the school for more details).

To receive information on the exam or upcoming administrations of the HSPT, contact Scholastic Testing Service.

Scholastic Testing Service
480 Meyer Road
Bensenville, IL 60106-1617
Phone: (800) 642-6STS
Website: www.ststesting.com

Is There a Registration Fee?

Not exactly. Schools do not actually purchase the HSPT exams; rather, they "rent" them. To ensure test security, all materials provided to a school are returned to STS when the exams are completed. Therefore, your registration costs will most likely be added to the school's admission fees. Since each school is different, you should contact the school(s) in which you are interested to find the exact cost.

FORMAT OF THE HSPT

Section	Questions	Time Length
Verbal	60	16 minutes
Quantitative	52	30 minutes
Reading	62	25 minutes
Mathematics	64	45 minutes
Language	60	25 minutes

OPTIONAL HSPT SECTIONS

Science	40	30 minutes
Mechanical Aptitude	40	30 minutes
Catholic Religion	40	30 minutes

Here is a quick breakdown of the test sections on the HSPT and their subjects.

Verbal Skills—This section tests synonyms, logic, verbal classification, antonyms, and analogies.

Quantitative Skills—This section tests geometric comparisons, non-geometric comparisons, number series, and number manipulations.

Reading Skills—This section tests the ability to recall information from reading material, vocabulary, intuitive thinking (what would happen next), and locating main ideas.

Mathematic Skills—This section tests mathematical concepts and problem solving ability dealing with arithmetic, basic geometry, and elementary algebra.

Language Skills—This section tests an examinee's ability in capitalization, punctuation, word usage, spelling, and composition.

SCORING THE HSPT

Since the HSPT is taken for admittance to private high schools, the score required for admittance varies from institution to institution. HSPT scores are reported on a 200 to 800 scale. Before assigning you a score from the scale, STS first calculates a raw score. The raw score is figured by adding up all of your correct answers. Since STS does not deduct for incorrect answers, it is in your best interest to answer all the questions you can. Your raw scores are scaled to compensate for the slight variations that may arise between different exams.

After you take the actual HSPT examination, the test results you receive will include five different types of scores.

1. The Composite Score—This is the sum of the raw scores you receive on the five parts of the HSPT which is then converted into a standard score (standard scores are a cumulative average of the nation's test-takers per grade).

2. National Percentile Rank (NP)—Your score is ranked on a range from 1 to 99 which compares your HSPT results with that of other students at the same grade level. If a student scored an 81 on the Verbal Section, that student scored above 81% of the students from the national norm sample.

3. Local Percentile Rank (LP)—This evaluates scores much in the same manner as the National Ranking, yet it is focused on a student's comparison with a local group. Local groups are comprised of students who tested at the same school or from the same district.

4. Grade Equivalents—This percentile ranking compares a student's performance with that of other students at different grade levels.

5. Cognitive Skills Quotient—Used to replace the common IQ score, the CSQ serves also to gauge the future academic performance of a student. The CSQ is figured by combining the Verbal and Quantitative Skills scores and comparing them to the test-taker's age when he/she took the test.

HOW DO I SCORE MY PRACTICE TEST?

SCORING WORKSHEET

Use the scoring worksheet below to score each of our two practice tests. The score you earn on each of the test sections is the percentage that you scored correctly. This will help you gauge which sections of the exam on which you need to concentrate more time. Your scores, after you take the actual HSPT, will be prepared by Scholastic Testing Service according to the five divisions mentioned. It would seem logical, however, to realize that the better you score on our sample tests, the better your actual score will be.

Verbal Skills

_____ ÷ 60 × 100 = _____
Questions answered   Total Questions   Percentage
correctly   in Section   Score

Quantitative Skills

_____ ÷ 52 × 100 = _____
Questions answered   Total Questions   Percentage
correctly   in Section   Score

Reading Skills

_____ ÷ 62 × 100 = _____
Questions answered   Total Questions   Percentage
correctly   in Section   Score

Mathematics Skills

_____ ÷ 64 × 100 = _____
Questions answered   Total Questions   Percentage
correctly   in Section   Score

Language Skills

_____ ÷ 60 × 100 = _____
Questions answered   Total Questions   Percentage
correctly   in Section   Score

Optional: Science

_____ ÷ 40 × 100 = _____
Questions answered   Total Questions   Percentage
correctly   in Section   Score

Optional: Mechanical Aptitude

_____ ÷ 40 × 100 = _____
Questions answered   Total Questions   Percentage
correctly   in Section   Score

Optional: Catholic Religion

_____ ÷ 40 × 100 = _____
Questions answered   Total Questions   Percentage
correctly   in Section   Score

ABOUT THE COOPERATIVE ADMISSIONS EXAMINATION (COOP)

ABOUT THE TEST

Who Takes the Test and What Is It Used For?

The COOP examination is taken by junior high students who plan on applying for admittance to parochial (Catholic) high schools. This examination is used to evaluate a student's knowledge and determine if he/she has adequate knowledge and understanding in specified subject areas. The test is also used as a means of course placement. Very often, your performance on the COOP will dictate the level of courses that you are assigned upon entrance to the parochial school (if you are accepted). A very important point about the COOP is that it may only be taken once. It is imperative that you take the time to prepare for this exam and study.

Who Administers the Test?

The COOP is developed and administered by CTB/McGraw-Hill Publishers of Monterey, California. For further questions concerning the COOP exam, contact:

> Cooperative Admissions Examination Office
> CTB/McGraw-Hill
> 20 Ryan Ranch Road
> Monterey, CA 93940
> Phone: (800) 569-COOP (800-569-2667)
> http://www.ctb.com/coop/

When Is the COOP Taken?

The COOP examination is usually administered in the Fall of each year (usually in September or October), although the exact date is different for each diocese. Taking our practice tests will familiarize you with the types of questions and format of the COOP exam. This eliminates the anxiety of having to become familiar with the test as you take it.

Where Is the Test Given?

The COOP is offered at most parochial schools. To find out which schools offer the COOP in your area, check the back of the Student Handbook/Registration bulletin for a prospective school's diocese (to receive a Student Handbook, contact the school to which you are interested in applying). While students may take the test at most parochial schools, a student is NOT permitted to take the COOP at a school to which he/she is applying.

To receive specific information about upcoming administrations of the COOP or general information about the exam, contact your local diocese or parochial school.

Is There a Registration Fee?

Yes. The COOP requires a $33.00 nonrefundable registration fee which includes reporting scores to three high schools of your choice. Check your COOP Student Handbook for more information on payment.

FORMAT OF THE COOP

Section	Questions	Time Length
Sequences	20	15 minutes
Analogies	20	7 minutes
Memory	20	17 minutes
Verbal Reasoning	20	15 minutes
Reading Comprehension	40	40 minutes
Mathematics Concepts and Applications	40	35 minutes
Language Expression	40	30 minutes

Here is a quick breakdown of the test sections on the COOP exam and their subjects.

Sequences—This section tests the ability to distinguish various patterns in a series of numbers, figures, or similar arrangements. The examinee is responsible to select the part that will continue the pattern.

Analogies—This section tests the ability to associate a concrete or abstract relationship between two pictures, then select an image to maintain that relationship with another set of words, objects, or phrases.

Memory—This section tests the ability to recall previously presented nonsensical words and their definitions. After reviewing a list of words, the students are tested on their ability to create associations between the definitions and their nonsensical words.

Verbal Reasoning—This section tests the examinee's ability to reason with word relation, multiple word relations, intuitive reasoning on making a statement from known facts, and creating words from parts of nonsensical words.

Reading Comprehension—This section tests an examinee's vocabulary, ability to recall and understand information from a passage, select main ideas, and make suggestions as to what would happen next.

Mathematics Concepts and Applications—This section tests the examinee's ability in basic geometry, arithmetic, elementary algebra, and word problem solving.

Language Expression—This section tests the examinee's ability in sentence structure and language. The examinee is tested on the organization and creation of sentences and passages, and the ability to select writing based on clear and concise main ideas.

Calculator Use

Calculators will not be permitted during the test.

HOW DO I SCORE MY PRACTICE TEST?

Use the scoring worksheet below to score each of our two practice tests. Though the COOP is scored differently from the method below, the score you earn on our practice tests should approximate how well you will perform on the COOP.

SCORING WORKSHEET

Sequences

_____ ÷ 20 × 100 = _____
Questions answered / Total Questions / Percentage
correctly / in Section / Score

Analogies

_____ ÷ 20 × 100 = _____
Questions answered / Total Questions / Percentage
correctly / in Section / Score

Memory

_____ ÷ 20 × 100 = _____
Questions answered / Total Questions / Percentage
correctly / in Section / Score

Verbal Reasoning

_____ ÷ 20 × 100 = _____
Questions answered   Total Questions   Percentage
correctly   in Section   Score

Reading Comprehension

_____ ÷ 40 × 100 = _____
Questions answered   Total Questions   Percentage
correctly   in Section   Score

Mathematics Concepts and Applications

_____ ÷ 40 × 100 = _____
Questions answered   Total Questions   Percentage
correctly   in Section   Score

Language Expression

_____ ÷ 40 × 100 = _____
Questions answered   Total Questions   Percentage
correctly   in Section   Score

COOP/
HSPT

HSPT

Practice Test 1

Subtest 1: Verbal Skills

TIME: 16 Minutes
   60 Questions

```
DIRECTIONS: Select the best answer choice.
```

1. Sunrise is to morning as sunset is to _____

   (A) horizon.   (C) evening.

   (B) afternoon.   (D) moon.

2. Country is to continent as county is to _____

   (A) city.   (C) state.

   (B) capital.   (D) town.

3. Mumps is to swollen glands as measles is to _____

   (A) disease.   (C) fever.

   (B) symptom.   (D) rash.

4. Scissors is to cut as ruler is to _____

   (A) straight.   (C) inches.

   (B) wood.   (D) measure.

5. She is to her as they is to _____

   (A) their.   (C) them.

   (B) theirs.   (D) themselves.

6. Ten is to decade as one hundred is to _____

   (A) century.   (C) dollars.

   (B) millennium.   (D) era.

7. Moat is to surround as canopy is to _____

   (A) top.   (C) around.

   (B) cover.   (D) building.

8. Doctor is to hospital as teacher is to _____

    (A) history.   (C) school.

    (B) classroom.   (D) student.

9. Play is to act as book is to _____

    (A) chapter.   (C) character.

    (B) author.   (D) title.

10. Sidewalk is to concrete as floor is to _____

    (A) kitchen.   (C) table.

    (B) room.   (D) tile.

11. Endure means to

    (A) perish.   (C) tolerate.

    (B) reject.   (D) fail.

12. Pessimism most nearly means

    (A) idealism.   (C) suspicion.

    (B) visionary.   (D) optimism.

13. Skeptical most nearly means

    (A) doubtful.   (C) certain.

    (B) confident.   (D) convinced.

14. Rectify most nearly means

    (A) correct.   (C) dilapidate.

    (B) destroy.   (D) demolish.

15. To retract is to

    (A) uphold.   (C) admit.

    (B) declare.   (D) deny.

16. Protagonist most nearly means

    (A) villain.   (C) professor.

    (B) antagonist.   (D) hero.

17. Revenge most nearly means

    (A) repay.   (C) advocate.

    (B) clerical.   (D) danger.

18. Paranoid most nearly means

    (A) trusting.   (C) suspicious.

    (B) angry.   (D) confident.

19. A martyr is a

    (A) manager.   (C) victor.

    (B) victim.   (D) delinquent.

20. Regime most nearly means

    (A) reign.   (C) luxurious.

    (B) generation.   (D) regimen.

21. Detest most nearly means

    (A) like.   (C) cherish.

    (B) loathe.   (D) idolize.

22. Rational most nearly means

    (A) logical.   (C) unreasonable.

    (B) insane.   (D) foolish.

23. Obscure most nearly means

    (A) unclear.   (C) known.

    (B) distinct.   (D) evident.

24. To dissuade is to

    (A) disapprove.   (C) encourage.

    (B) camouflage.   (D) thwart.

25. Terminate means to

    (A) start.   (C) conclude.

    (B) originate.   (D) initiate.

26. Peter works harder than Patrick. Patrick works harder than Paul. Paul works harder than Victor. If the first two statements are true, the third is

   (A) true.

   (B) false.

   (C) uncertain.

27. Ashley dances better than Diane. Diane dances better than Pamela. Pamela dances better than Alison. If the first two statements are true, the third is

   (A) true.

   (B) false.

   (C) uncertain.

28. Jefferson High School has more students than Roosevelt High School. Roosevelt High School has more students than Lincoln High School. Lincoln High School has more students than Jefferson High School. If the first two statements are true, the third is

   (A) true.

   (B) false.

   (C) uncertain.

29. Mrs. Perez has more children than Mrs. Martin. Mrs. Martin has more children than Mrs. Lee. Mrs. Lee has more children than Mrs. Perez. If the first two statements are true, the third is

   (A) true.

   (B) false.

   (C) uncertain.

30. Every family in Sunrise Village has a car. The Palmers do not have a car. The Palmers do not live in Sunrise Village. If the first two statements are true, the third is

   (A) true.

   (B) false.

   (C) uncertain.

31. Every adult in Beechwood voted in the last presidential election. Mr. Turner did not vote in the last presidential election. Mr. Turner does not live in Beechwood. If the first two statements are true, the third is

(A) true.

(B) false.

(C) uncertain.

32. Wednesday was warmer than Tuesday. Monday was cooler than Tuesday. Monday was cooler than Wednesday. If the first two statements are true, the third is

(A) true.

(B) false.

(C) uncertain.

33. Bill's house is larger than Fred's. Lucille's house is smaller than Fred's. Lucille's house is smaller than Bill's. If the first two statements are true, the third is

(A) true.

(B) false.

(C) uncertain.

34. It's farther to walk from the tennis courts to the beach than from the beach to the swimming pool. It's farther to walk from the beach to the swimming pool than from the swimming pool to the ice cream parlor. It's farther to walk from the swimming pool to the ice cream parlor than from the tennis courts to the beach. If the first two statements are true, the third is

(A) true.

(B) false.

(C) uncertain.

35. It's closer to drive from the supermarket to the library than from the library to the train station. It's closer to drive from the library to the train station than from the train station to the bank. It's closer to drive from the train station to the bank than from the supermarket to the library. If the first two statements are true, the third is

(A) true.

(B) false.

(C) uncertain.

36. Which word does <u>not</u> belong with the others?

(A) Program   (C) Printer

(B) Monitor   (D) Keyboard

37. Which word does <u>not</u> belong with the others?

    (A) Rice   (C) Wheat

    (B) Cereal   (D) Corn

38. Which word does <u>not</u> belong with the others?

    (A) Alleviate   (C) Lessen

    (B) Reduce   (D) Increase

39. Which word does <u>not</u> belong with the others?

    (A) Gold   (C) Emerald

    (B) Diamond   (D) Sapphire

40. Which word does <u>not</u> belong with the others?

    (A) Reptile   (C) Turtle

    (B) Snake   (D) Crocodile

41. Which word does <u>not</u> belong with the others?

    (A) Piano   (C) Cymbals

    (B) Drums   (D) Guitar

42. Which word does <u>not</u> belong with the others?

    (A) Ounce   (C) Gallon

    (B) Pound   (D) Quart

43. Which word does <u>not</u> belong with the others?

    (A) Nitrogen   (C) Helium

    (B) Oxygen   (D) Sodium

44. Which word does <u>not</u> belong with the others?

    (A) Tin   (C) Copper

    (B) Marble   (D) Nickel

45. Which word does <u>not</u> belong with the others?

    (A) Tense   (C) Relaxed

    (B) Anxious   (D) Nervous

46. Which word does <u>not</u> belong with the others?

    (A) Odor

    (B) Smell

    (C) Stench

    (D) Scent

47. Which word does <u>not</u> belong with the others?

    (A) Mother

    (B) Cousin

    (C) Niece

    (D) Sister

48. Which word does <u>not</u> belong with the others?

    (A) Undecided

    (B) Uncertain

    (C) Unsure

    (D) Uncomfortable

49. Which word does <u>not</u> belong with the others?

    (A) Media

    (B) Cactus

    (C) Alumni

    (D) Data

50. Which word does <u>not</u> belong with the others?

    (A) Classroom

    (B) Blackberry

    (C) Lighthouse

    (D) Dreamer

51. Which word does <u>not</u> belong with the others?

    (A) Fraction

    (B) Addition

    (C) Subtraction

    (D) Division

52. Metropolitan does not mean

    (A) urban.

    (B) cosmopolitan.

    (C) antiquated.

    (D) city-like.

53. Miserly does not mean

    (A) generous.

    (B) cheap.

    (C) avaricious.

    (D) stingy.

54. Malign does not mean

    (A) unfavorable.

    (B) malicious.

    (C) benign.

    (D) evil.

55. Impenetrable does not mean

    (A) opaque.   (C) obscure.

    (B) translucent.   (D) thick.

56. Courtly means the opposite of

    (A) dignified.   (C) cultured.

    (B) frivolous.   (D) stately.

57. Melancholy means the opposite of

    (A) sad.   (C) despondent.

    (B) depressed.   (D) ecstatic.

58. Occasional means the opposite of

    (A) alternate.   (C) rhythmical.

    (B) periodic.   (D) incessant.

59. Stalwart means the opposite of

    (A) gallant.   (C) timid.

    (B) valorous.   (D) dauntless.

60. Glowing means the opposite of

    (A) ruddy.   (C) incandescent.

    (B) vivid.   (D) doleful.

Subtest 2: Quantitative Skills

TIME: 30 Minutes
52 Questions

DIRECTIONS: Select the best answer choice.

---

61. Examine (a), (b), and (c) and find the best answer.

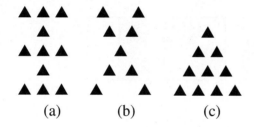

(a)   (b)   (c)

(A)   (a) is greater than (b) and less than (c).

(B)   (b) and (c) are equal.

(C)   (a) and (c) are equal.

(D)   (c) is less than (a) and more than (b).

62. Look at this series: 90, 77, 64, 51,… What numeral should come next?

(A)   42   (C)   36

(B)   38   (D)   40

63. Look at this series: 86, 78, 75, 67, 64,… What numeral should come next?

(A)   56   (C)   58

(B)   57   (D)   61

64. Examine (a), (b), and (c) and find the best answer.

(a) $(3 + 4) \times 5$

(b) $3 + (4 \times 5)$

(c) $(5 + 3) \times 4$

(A)   (a) is greater than (b) and less than (c).

(B)   (a) is greater than (b) and greater than (c).

(C)   (c) is less than (b) and greater than (c).

(D)   (a) is less than (b) and less than (c).

65. What number is 7 more than $\frac{1}{2}$ of 16?

(A)   8   (C)   15

(B)   10   (D)   23

66. Examine the equal rectangles (a), (b), and (c) and find the best answer regarding their shaded parts.

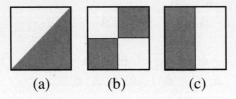

(a)   (b)   (c)

(A)   (a), (b), and (c) are equal.

(B)   (a) is greater than (b) and equal to (c).

(C)   (b) is greater than (c).

(D)   (a) and (b) are equal and both are less than (c).

67. Examine (a), (b), and (c) and find the best answer.

(a) $\frac{1}{2}$ of 24

(b) $\frac{1}{3}$ of 48

(c) $\frac{1}{4}$ of 60

(A)   (a), (b), and (c) are all equal.

(B)   (a) is greater than (b) and less than (c).

(C)   (c) is greater than (a) and less than (b).

(D)   (b) is greater than (c) and less than (a).

68. Look at this series: 20, 24, 30, 35, 42,... What numeral should come next?

(A)   49   (C)   45

(B)   48   (D)   50

69. What number is 4 less than $\frac{2}{3}$ of 21?

    (A) 10   (C) 14

    (B) 18   (D) 3

70. What number is 10 more than $\frac{1}{5}$ of 35?

    (A) 15   (C) 10

    (B) 17   (D) 21

71. Examine the equal rectangles (a), (b), and (c) and find the best answer regarding their shaded parts.

    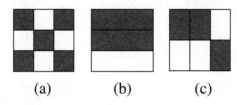

         (a)   (b)   (c)

    (A) (a) is greater than (b) and greater than (c).

    (B) (a) is greater than (b) and less than (c).

    (C) (a) is less than (b) and greater than (c).

    (D) (a), (b), and (c) are equal.

72. Look at this series: 200, 180, 164, 152, 144,…What numeral should come next?

    (A) 144   (C) 136

    (B) 140   (D) 132

73. What number subtracted from 22 leaves $\frac{1}{10}$ of 90?

    (A) 9   (C) 16

    (B) 13   (D) 20

74. What number squared is half of 72?

    (A) 3   (C) 9

    (B) 6   (D) 12

75. Look at this series: 35, 44, 48, 57, 61,…What numeral should come next?

(A) 68   (C) 70

(B) 69   (D) 72

76. Look at this series: 2008, 1995, 1982, 1969,…What numeral should come next?

(A) 1960   (C) 1957

(B) 1958   (D) 1956

77. What number multiplied by 7 is 3 more than 95?

(A) 14   (C) 21

(B) 18   (D) 28

78. Look at this series: 8, 17, 26, ___ , 44, 53,…What numeral should fill in the blank?

(A) 32   (C) 34

(B) 33   (D) 35

79. Examine (a), (b), and (c) and find the best answer.

(a) $\dfrac{11}{20}$

(b) 60%

(c) .5

(A) (a) is greater than (b) and greater than (c).

(B) (b) is greater than (a) and greater than (c).

(C) (c) is greater than (a) and greater than (b).

(D) (c) is greater than (b) and less than (a).

80. What number divided by 3 leaves 5 less than 18?

(A) 13   (C) 39

(B) 33   (D) 42

81. Examine the equilateral (equal-sided) triangle and find the best answer.

(A) AD is equal to AB.   (C) AD is greater than BC.

(B) AD is less than AC.   (D) AD is less than CD.

82. What number multiplied by itself is 20 less than 45?

(A) 5   (C) 6

(B) 10   (D) 3

83. Examine (a), (b), and (c) and find the best answer.

(a) $\dfrac{7}{16}$

(b) $\dfrac{3}{8}$

(c) $\dfrac{13}{32}$

(A) (c) is greater than (a) and greater than (b).

(B) (b) is greater than (a) and greater than (c).

(C) (a) is greater than (b) and greater than (c).

(D) (a), (b), and (c) are equal.

84. Examine the circle with center E and find the best answer.

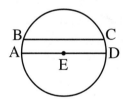

(A) BC is equal to AB.   (C) AD is equal to BC.

(B) AE is equal to DE.   (D) BC is equal to CD.

85. What number divided by 20 leaves 20 less than 30?

(A) 100   (C) 300

(B) 200   (D) 400

86. Look at this series: 512, 128, 32, 8,…What numeral should come next?

(A) 6   (C) 2

(B) 4   (D) 1

87. Look at this series: 90, 30, 27, 9, 6,…What numeral should come next?

    (A) 1   (C) 3
    (B) 2   (D) 4

88. Three-fourths of what number is $\frac{1}{3}$ of 36?

    (A) 12   (C) 16
    (B) 15   (D) 18

89. Look at this series: XX, XXV, XXX, XXXV,…What numeral should come next?

    (A) XXVX   (C) LX
    (B) XXXVI   (D) XL

90. Look at this series: 53, 45, 41, 33, 29, 21,…What numeral should come next?

    (A) 17   (C) 13
    (B) 15   (D) 11

91. One-sixth of what number is 4 multiplied by itself?

    (A) 18   (C) 144
    (B) 60   (D) 96

92. Examine (a), (b), and (c) and find the best answer.

    (a) $(16 \div 8) \times 2$

    (b) $(16 \div 2) \times 8$

    (c) $16 \div (8 \times 2)$

    (A) (a), (b), and (c) are all equal.

    (B) (a) is less than (b) and less than (c).

    (C) (b) is less than (a) and less than (c).

    (D) (c) is less than (a) and less than (b).

93. Look at this series: 61, 63, 70, __ , 79, 81, 88,…What numeral should fill in the blank?

    (A) 90   (C) 72
    (B) 95   (D) 59

94. What number divided by 6 is $\frac{1}{8}$ of 32?

    (A) 12   (C) 18
    (B) 24   (D) 36

95. Look at this series: 13, 9, 18, 14, 28, 24,…What number should come next?

    (A) 32   (C) 56
    (B) 20   (D) 48

96. Examine (a), (b), and (c) and find the best answer.

     = 10
     = 5

    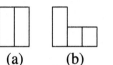
    (a)   (b)   (c)

    (A) (a) is greater than (b) and greater than (c).
    (B) (b) is greater than (a) and greater than (c).
    (C) (c) is greater than (a) and greater than (b).
    (D) (a), (b), and (c) are all equal.

97. What number subtracted from 30 leaves 4 more than $\frac{5}{6}$ of 30?

    (A) 26   (C) 5
    (B) 1   (D) 6

98. Examine (a), (b), and (c) and find the best answer.

    (a) $2x + 3y$
    (b) $6xy$
    (c) $3x + 2y$
    (A) (a) = (b) = (c)
    (B) (a) = (b), (b) ≠ (c)
    (C) (a) ≠ (b), (b) ≠ (c), (a) ≠ (c)
    (D) (a) ≠ (b), (b) = (c)

99. Look at this series: 53, 49, 60, 56, 67, 63,…What two numerals should come next?

    (A) 69, 65   (C) 70, 66

    (B) 74, 70   (D) 71, 67

100. Examine (a), (b), and (c) and find the best answer.

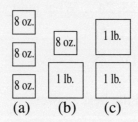

    (A) (a) is equal to (b).

    (B) (a) is equal to (c).

    (C) (b) is equal to (c).

    (D) (a) is equal to (b) and equal to (c).

101. What number added to 10 is twice the product of 5 and $\frac{1}{2}$ of 8?

    (A) 10   (C) 25

    (B) 20   (D) 30

102. Look at this series: 68, 109, 72, 101, 76,…What numeral should come next?

    (A) 105   (C) 103

    (B) 80   (D) 93

103. Examine (a), (b), and (c) and find the best answer.

    (a) 2^4

    (b) 3^3

    (c) 4^2

    (A) (a) is equal to (b).

    (B) (a) is equal to (c).

    (C) (b) is equal to (c)

    (D) (a) is equal to (b) is equal to (c).

104. Examine the graph and find the best answer.

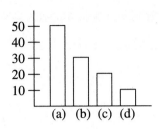

(A)   (a) minus (b) equals (c) minus (d).

(B)   (a) minus (c) equals (b) minus (d).

(C)   (a) minus (d) equals (b) plus (d).

(D)   (b) plus (c) equals (a) plus (d).

105. Look at this series: 84, 81, 27, 24, 8,…What numeral should come next?

(A)   5   (C)   6

(B)   7   (D)   3

106. What number multiplied by 2 is 3 times $\frac{1}{2}$ of 16?

(A)   4   (C)   15

(B)   12   (D)   20

107. What number added to $\frac{5}{9}$ of 36 is $\frac{2}{3}$ of 42?

(A)   8   (C)   14

(B)   12   (D)   20

108. Examine (a), (b), and (c) and find the best answer.

(a) $.3 \times .4$

(b) $.6 \times .2$

(c) 1×1.2

(A)   (a) is equal to (b) is equal to (c).

(B)   (a) is equal to (b) which is greater than (c).

(C)   (a) is equal to (b) which is less than (c).

(D)   (a) is greater than (b) and greater than (c).

109. Examine the parallelogram and find the best answer.

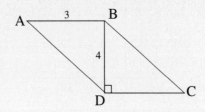

(A) The perimeter of the parallelogram is 12.

(B) The area of the parallelogram is 12.

(C) The perimeter of triangle ABD is 13.

(D) The area of triangle ABD is 5.

110. Look at this series: 42, 47, 46, 52, 49, 56, 51,...What three numerals should come next?

(A) 59, 52, 61   (C) 57, 53, 61

(B) 60, 54, 62   (D) 62, 60, 68

111. One-third of what number subtracted from 10 is 2 times $\frac{1}{4}$ of 12?

(A) 6   (C) 15

(B) 12   (D) 18

112. Look at this series: 51, 57, 63, 60, 66, 72,...What numeral should come next?

(A) 76   (C) 70

(B) 74   (D) 69

Subtest 3: Reading

TIME: 25 Minutes
62 Questions

Comprehension

> **DIRECTIONS:** Read the following passages and then select the best answer choice.

Questions 113–117 are based on the following passage.

In medieval times, an almanac was a chart showing the movements of the stars over a period of several years. Eventually, almanacs were printed in book form and included information which was especially useful to farmers. In the sixteenth century, almanacs began to be <u>issued</u> every year and included predictions of the weather based on previous weather patterns. At about the same time, almanacs included elaborate calendars that listed church feast days. In the seventeenth century, almanacs included jokes and short accounts of humorous incidents. Benjamin Franklin continued this tradition with *Poor Richard's Almanac*, which was published from 1732–1758. In Germany, almanacs of the eighteenth century included sophisticated, contemporary poetry by serious authors. The almanacs printed in the United States from 1835–1856 were called "Davy Crockett" almanacs because they included many frontier tall tales based mainly on oral tradition.

113. What appeared in almanacs a century after church holidays were included?

    (A) Weather predictions   (C) Jokes and humor

    (B) Star movements   (D) Elaborate calendars

114. Based on the passage, which of the following is TRUE?

    (A) The almanac included extra days for farmers.

    (B) Benjamin Franklin invented the almanac.

    (C) Almanacs are now printed every ten years.

    (D) *Poor Richard's Almanac* was published from 1732–1758.

115. The word <u>issued</u> as underlined and used in the passage most nearly means

    (A) dated.   (C) available.

    (B) given.   (D) numbered.

116. The poetry included in eighteenth century German almanacs was

(A) written by farmers.

(B) placed next to frontier tall tales.

(C) sophisticated.

(D) humorous.

117. In the sixteenth century, almanacs began to include

(A) weather predictions.   (C) jokes.

(B) "Davy Crockett."   (D) church feast days.

Questions 118–121 are based on the following passage.

Six members of a local university basketball team walked off the court during practice last week. They later said they were protesting unfair treatment by the head coach. The day after walking off the court, the players held a meeting with the university president to discuss their complaints. They met the Director of Athletics two days later and expressed their <u>concerns</u>. They also met with the assistant coach. After refusing to practice for four days, the team apologized to the fans, returned to practice, and promised to play the next scheduled game that season. The players also stated that their opinion of the head coach had not changed, but that they thought the assistant coach was fair.

118. According to the passage, how did the head coach feel about the protest?

(A) Angry

(B) Confused

(C) Unjustly accused

(D) Not enough information is given to answer this question.

119. The next game the team will play will be

(A) when a new head coach is found.

(B) the next scheduled game in the season.

(C) when the assistant coach is promoted.

(D) next season.

120. The word <u>concerns</u> as underlined and used in the passage most nearly means

(A) problems.   (C) anxiety.

(B) caring.   (D) playing.

121. Based on the passage, which of the following is TRUE?

    (A) The five members will play the next game.

    (B) The players apologized to the head coach.

    (C) The players apologized to the assistant coach.

    (D) The players continued to practice despite their concerns.

Questions 122–126 are based on the following passage.

The issue of adult literacy has finally received recognition as a major social problem. Unfortunately, the issue is usually presented in the media as a "women's interest issue." Numerous governors' wives and even Barbara Bush have publicly expressed concern about literacy. As well-meaning as the politicians' wives may be, it is more important that the politicians themselves recognize the seriousness of the problem and support increased funding for literacy programs.

Literacy education programs need to be directed at two different groups of people with very different needs. The first group is composed of people who have very limited reading and writing skills. These people are complete illiterates. A second group is composed of people who can read and write but whose skills are not sufficient to meet their needs. This second group is called functionally illiterate. Successful literacy programs must meet the needs of both groups.

Instructors in literacy programs have three main responsibilities. First, the educational needs of the illiterates and functional illiterates must be met. Second, the instructors must approach the participants in the program with empathy, not sympathy. Third, all participants must experience success in the program and must perceive their efforts as worthwhile.

122. According to the passage, some politicians

    (A) have expressed great concern over adult literacy.

    (B) are more concerned with complete illiterates than with functional illiterates.

    (C) need to recognize the problem's seriousness and support it with increased funding.

    (D) know the correct elements of literacy programs.

123. The goal of adult literacy programs is

    (A) to help the functionally illiterate only.

    (B) to teach people to be able to read and write for their needs.

    (C) to be empathetic.

    (D) to be sympathetic.

124. By stating that politicians' wives, rather than the politicians themselves, are discussing adult literacy, the author is concerned that

    (A) more women than men will be literate.

    (B) it is a social, not real, problem.

    (C) politicians aren't women.

    (D) it is not viewed as a serious problem.

125. The responsibilities of literacy programs as mentioned in this passage emphasize

    (A) the self-esteem of the participants.

    (B) political support.

    (C) books.

    (D) magazines.

126. The functional illiterate may

    (A) not be able to meet his or her needs.

    (B) be helped by a literacy program.

    (C) have trouble writing.

    (D) All of the above.

Questions 127–131 are based on the following passage.

The price of cleaning up the environment after oil spills is on the increase. After the massive Alaskan spill that created miles of sludge-covered beach, numerous smaller spills have occurred along the Gulf Coast and off the coast of California. Tides and prevailing winds carried much of this oil to shore in a matter of days. Workers tried to contain the oil with weighted, barrel-shaped plastic tubes stretched along the sand near the water. They hoped to minimize the damage. Generally, the barriers were successful, but there remained many miles of oil-covered sand. Cleanup crews shoveled the oil-covered sand into plastic bags for removal.

Coastal states are responding to the problem in several ways. California is considering the formation of a department of oceans to oversee protection programs and future cleanups. Some states have suggested training the National Guard in cleanup procedures. Other states are calling for the creation of an oil spill trust fund large enough to cover the costs of a major spill. Still other states are demanding federal action and funding. Regardless of the specific programs that may be enacted by the various states or the federal government, continued offshore drilling and the shipping of oil in huge tankers creates a constant threat to the nation's shoreline.

127. Which of the following would not pose a problem for cleaning the environment?

    (A) Offshore drilling

    (B) Weighted, barrel-shaped plastic tubes

    (C) Coastal winds

    (D) Tides

128. The cost of oil spill cleanups is paid for by

    (A) the oil companies.

    (B) the coastal states.

    (C) the National Guard.

    (D) Not enough information is given.

129. Some states want

    (A) the creation of an oil spill trust fund.

    (B) an end to offshore drilling.

    (C) plastic barrels.

    (D) oil companies.

130. After several recent oil spills, workers

    (A) tried to minimize the damage.

    (B) removed sand.

    (C) A and B.

    (D) None of the above.

131. The price of cleaning up the environment after oil spills

    (A) is decreasing.

    (B) is increasing as the number of spills increases.

    (C) is staying the same as workers clean up.

    (D) doesn't cost anything.

Questions 132–136 are based on the following passage.

It is estimated that over six million Americans suffer from diabetes. This disease, which often runs in families, is the result of insufficient amounts of insulin made by the body to meet its needs. Insulin is produced by the pancreas and is used by the body to take glucose from the blood for use as fuel. A deficiency results in high blood levels and low tissue levels of glucose.

There are two types of diabetes. The first type appears early in life and is the result of abnormal cells in the pancreas so that little or no insulin is made. This is juvenile diabetes. The standard treatment for juvenile diabetes is insulin replacement therapy. The second type of diabetes occurs later in life, usually during a person's fifties or sixties. In this type of diabetes the pancreatic beta cells are normal and produce normal amounts of insulin. However, for some unexplained reason, the tissues in the body have become resistant to the action of insulin. This second type of diabetes is more common in obese people than lean people.

Diet is very important in the treatment of both forms of diabetes. High levels of fat in the blood, which interfere with the absorption of insulin, are often associated with diabetes. A person who has either form of diabetes should reduce the total amount of fat to 20–25 percent of the total calories consumed and increase the amount of carbohydrates to approximately 40 percent. Simple sugars should be kept to 10–15 percent of all calories, and protein should not exceed 24 percent.

132. A person with diabetes should have a total diet of approximately

    (A) 80% fat; 40% carbohydrates; 10–15% sugar; and 24% protein.

    (B) 40% fat; 40% carbohydrates; 10–15% sugar; and 20% protein.

    (C) 30–35% fat; 10% carbohydrates; 50% sugar; and 14% protein.

    (D) 20–25% fat; 40% carbohydrates; 10-15% sugar; and 24% protein.

133. Insulin replacement therapy is standard treatment for

    (A) adult diabetes.   (C) both.

    (B) juvenile diabetes.   (D) neither.

134. A deficiency of insulin results in

    (A) high blood levels and low tissue levels of glucose.

    (B) abnormal pancreatic cells.

    (C) obesity in adults.

    (D) obesity in juveniles.

135. High levels of fat in the blood

    (A) cause adult diabetes.

    (B) are a sign of high glucose levels.

    (C) are found in six million Americans.

    (D) interfere with insulin absorption.

136. Diabetes is usually detected or develops

    (A) when the person is a juvenile.

    (B) when a person is 50–70 years old.

    (C) when a person is 60–80 years old.

    (D) A and B.

Questions 137–141 are based on the following passage.

There's no room on the football field for "dumb jocks." Athletes who cannot consistently maintain a 2.0 grade-point average should not be permitted to participate in any sports. Athletes must realize that the purpose of school is to produce scholars, not professional ball players. If, by chance, an athlete is able to acquire a place in the professional ranks of sports, good! But the primary objective of school is the manufacturing and nurturing of productive citizens who can make worthwhile contributions to society. It is irritating to observe <u>star</u> quarterbacks who can't read, to observe star infielders who can't write, to observe star point guards who can't speak, and to observe outstanding pitchers who can't add, subtract, or multiply.

137. The word <u>star</u>, as used in this passage, most nearly means

    (A) constellation.   (C) successful.

    (B) pointed.   (D) athletic.

138. According to the author, what should the minimum requirement be for people who want to play sports in school?

    (A) They should be able to read and write.

    (B) They should be able to speak.

    (C) They should maintain a 2.0 grade-point average.

    (D) They should be able to subtract and multiply.

139. Which of the following sports is NOT alluded to in the passage?

    (A) Football   (C) Baseball

    (B) Basketball   (D) Hockey

140. Based on the passage, the author values

    (A) professional teachers over professional athletes.

    (B) professional students over professional athletes.

(C) productive citizens over scholars.

(D) educated athletes over uneducated athletes.

141. The author views athletics as

(A) an important part of school.

(B) important in training to be a professional.

(C) a part of adolescence.

(D) None of the above.

Questions 142–147 are based on the following passage.

A big toxic spill took place on the upper Sacramento River in California on July 13, 1991 at about 10 P.M. when a slow moving Southern Pacific train derailed north of the town of Dansmuir. A tank car containing 19,500 gallons of pesticide broke open and spilled into the river. This pesticide is used to kill soil pests. Since the spill, thousands of trout and other fish were poisoned along a 45-mile stretch of river. In addition, 190 people were treated at a local hospital for respiratory and related illnesses. Residents along the river have been warned to stay away from the tainted water. Once this water reaches Lake Shasta, a source of water for millions of Californians, samples will be taken to assess the quality of the water.

142. The pesticide was intended to

(A) be diluted and entered into the river.

(B) treat land pests.

(C) be taken to a dump for disposal.

(D) be banned by the government.

143. The water in Lake Shasta

(A) is undrinkable.

(B) sent 190 people to the hospital.

(C) will be tested.

(D) is fine for drinking.

144. The spill definitely affected

(A) 45 miles of river.   (C) A and B.

(B) Lake Shasta.   (D) None of the above.

145. The word <u>toxic</u>, as underlined and used in this passage, most nearly means

    (A) poisonous.

    (B) plastic.

    (C) beneficial.

    (D) huge.

146. How much pesticide was contained in the tank car?

    (A) 190 gallons

    (B) 45 thousand gallons

    (C) 10 thousand gallons

    (D) 19,500 gallons

147. Residents of the area have

    (A) been warned to avoid the river.

    (B) killed thousands of fish.

    (C) been drinking poisoned lake water.

    (D) None of the above.

Questions 148–152 are based on the following passage.

Lead poisoning is considered by health authorities to be the most common and devastating environmental disease of young children. According to studies made, it affects 15% to 20% of urban children and from 50% to 75% of inner-city, poor children. As a result of a legal settlement in July 1991, all of California's Medicaid-eligible children, ages one through five, will now be routinely screened annually for lead poisoning. Experts estimate that more than 50,000 cases will be detected in California because of the newly mandated tests. This will halt, at an early stage, a disease that leads to learning disabilities and life-threatening <u>disorders</u>.

148. The best title for this passage is

    (A) "Lead Poisoning and How to Stop It."

    (B) "Lead Poisoning and California."

    (C) "The History of Lead Poisoning."

    (D) "World Wide Lead Poisoning."

149. The word <u>disorders,</u> as used in this passage, most nearly means

    (A) chaos.

    (B) toxic.

    (C) ailments.

    (D) confusion.

150. How many cases of lead poisoning are predicted to be found due to annual screening in California?

(A) 75%   (C) 19,000

(B) 50,000   (D) 20,000

151. How often will California's Medicaid-eligible children from the ages of 1–5 be tested for lead poisoning?

(A) Every five years   (C) Every other year

(B) 15%   (D) Every year

152. Lead poisoning is

(A) the most common environmental disease of young children.

(B) a disease that leads to life-threatening disorders.

(C) A and B.

(D) None of the above.

Vocabulary

> **DIRECTIONS:** Choose the word that means the same or about the same as the underlined word.

153. a <u>vigilant</u> guard

(A) watchful   (C) lazy

(B) reckless   (D) powerful

154. a known <u>parable</u>

(A) teacher   (C) stronghold

(B) tale   (D) strength

155. a <u>buoyant</u> spirit

(A) scary   (C) supernatural

(B) depressed   (D) light-hearted

156. a <u>gracious</u> host

(A) elegant   (C) courteous

(B) beautiful   (D) extravagant

157. pay <u>homage</u> to the winner

    (A) prizes   (C) insult

    (B) honor   (D) wages

158. a <u>grievous</u> burden

    (A) joyous   (C) disturbing

    (B) grave   (D) serious

159. the <u>incessant</u> noise

    (A) brief   (C) pleasant

    (B) loud   (D) constant

160. the <u>invincible</u> army

    (A) unconquerable   (C) feeble

    (B) invisible   (D) minute

161. a <u>portly</u> figure

    (A) sloppy   (C) heavy

    (B) well-groomed   (D) slim

162. the <u>ornate</u> furnishings

    (A) simple   (C) cheap

    (B) expensive   (D) elaborate

163. <u>encumbered</u> his movements

    (A) restricted   (C) lightened

    (B) encouraged   (D) watched

164. an <u>avid</u> fan

    (A) uncontrollable   (C) lifeless

    (B) ardent   (D) gloomy

165. to <u>vie</u> for a championship

    (A) wait   (C) advertise

    (B) compete   (D) survive

166. an <u>ample</u> supply

    (A) inexpensive   (C) equal

    (B) insufficient   (D) abundant

167. to <u>devise</u> a formula

    (A) eliminate   (C) choose

    (B) create   (D) delineate

168. a <u>chronic</u> ailment

    (A) small   (C) brief

    (B) perpetual   (D) unknown

169. a <u>haggard</u> expression

    (A) scrawny   (C) cautious

    (B) dirty   (D) haggle

170. to creep <u>stealthily</u>

    (A) openly   (C) randomly

    (B) quickly   (D) secretly

171. a <u>pathetic</u> sight

    (A) miserable   (C) ruthless

    (B) undesirable   (D) frustrating

172. a <u>verbose</u> speech

    (A) resignation   (C) persuasive

    (B) short   (D) wordy

173. <u>savor</u> a meal

    (A) enjoy   (C) prepare

    (B) save   (D) serve

174. a <u>rigid</u> person

    (A) warm-hearted   (C) tedious

    (B) unyielding   (D) loud

Subtest 4: Mathematics

TIME: 45 Minutes
   64 Questions

Concepts

DIRECTIONS: Select the best answer choice.

175. Round off 3.47 to the nearest tenth

   (A) 3.4   (C) 3.47

   (B) 3.5   (D) 34.7

176. Add together: $3n + 4m - 6$ and $3m - 4n + 6$

   (A) $7m - n$ (C) $6m$

   (B) $7m + n$ (D) $6n$

177. Which of the following pairs of numbers is represented by the point, P, in the graph?

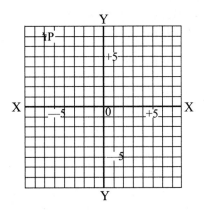

   (A) (6, 7)   (C) (7, 6)

   (B) (–6, 7)   (D) (–7, 6)

178. The sum of two consecutive whole numbers is 55. What are the two numbers?

   (A) 25, 30   (C) 27, 28

   (B) 26, 29   (D) 28, 29

179. If $x = 2$, $y = -5$ and $z = 0$, then $3x - 2y + 5z =$

   (A) −4   (C) 16

   (B) 1   (D) 21

180. Simplify: $12\frac{3}{4} + 5\frac{1}{3}$.

   (A) $8\frac{1}{12}$ (C) $17\frac{4}{7}$

   (B) $17\frac{1}{12}$ (D) $18\frac{1}{12}$

181. A prime number has no factors other than 1 and the number itself. Which of the following numbers is prime?

   (A) 36   (C) 38

   (B) 37   (D) 39

182. To compute the area of any rectangle, Rose applied the formula:

   Area = length × width.

   After computing the areas of four rectangles, including one square, Rose lost the paper from which she copied the figures. Remember that the length and width of a square are equal. Which of the following numbers represents the area of the square?

   (A) 42   (C) 49

   (B) 45   (D) 51

183. Simplify: $3(2 + 5) - 12$

   (A) −9   (C) 1

   (B) −1   (D) 9

184. Simplify: $5\frac{1}{4} \times 2\frac{1}{3}$

   (A) $12\frac{1}{4}$ (C) $1\frac{1}{2}$

   (B) $2\frac{1}{4}$ (D) $\frac{4}{9}$

185. What mixed number is the same as $5.\overline{3}$?

    (A) $5\dfrac{1}{3}$ (C) $5\dfrac{3}{100}$

    (B) $5\dfrac{3}{10}$ (D) $5\dfrac{3}{30}$

186. What percent of 60 is 75?

    (A) 1.25%   (C) 80%

    (B) 15%   (D) 125%

187. Rewrite $2\dfrac{1}{2}$ as a percent.

    (A) 250%   (C) 25%

    (B) 50%   (D) 2.5%

188. $q(r-s) =$

    (A) $q + r - s$ (C) $r - qs$

    (B) $qr - s$ (D) $qr - qs$

189. The sum of the measures of any two sides of a triangle is always greater than the measure of the third side of that triangle. Which of the following sets of sticks can be joined together, end-to-end, to form a triangle?

    (A) 3, 4, 5   (C) 5, 5, 12

    (B) 2, 5, 7   (D) 2, 4, 6

190. The sum of the measures of the three interior angles of a triangle is always 180 degrees. Which of the following sets of numbers represents the measures of interior angles of a triangle?

    (A) 60, 60, 90   (C) 60, 70, 80

    (B) 55, 65, 75   (D) 30, 75, 75

191. The following table shows the areas of the four classrooms and the number of students in each room in one small school.

Classroom	Area (in square ft.)	Number of students
A	770	22
B	960	24
C	540	18
D	627	19

Judging by the figures in this table, which of the four classrooms is the <u>least</u> crowded?

(A) A

(B) B

(C) C

(D) D

The graph below shows the average rainfall (in inches) in a small town for a 5-month period. Use the information in the graph to answer questions 192 and 193.

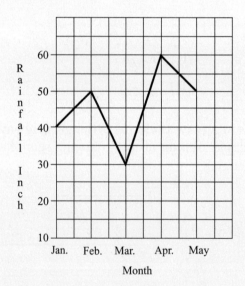

192. How much more rain fell in the wettest month than during the driest month for this period?

(A) 5 in.

(B) 30 in.

(C) 50 in.

(D) 60 in.

193. What was the average rainfall for the five months?

(A) 30 in.

(B) 46 in.

(C) 50 in.

(D) 60 in.

The graph below shows Matthew's mathematic performance scores for 12 months in a year-round school. Use the information in this graph to answer questions 194 to 195 that follow. Please note that each point on the graph represents the average exam score for each month.

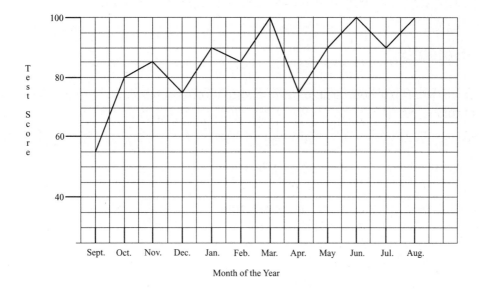

194. Which month's average shows the greatest gain compared to the prior month's average?

   (A)   October   (C)   June

   (B)   March   (D)   August

195. By how many points did Matthew's score improve between January and March?

   (A)   5   (C)   15

   (B)   20   (D)   10

196. The '3' in 54,362 is in the hundreds place. In what place is the '3' in 29.536?

   (A)   hundredths   (C)   singles

   (B)   tenths   (D)   hundreds

197. Which of the following is an acute triangle?

   (A)   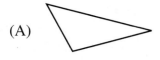   (C)

   (B)   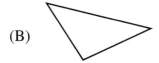   (D)

198. In this right triangle, find the value of *x*:

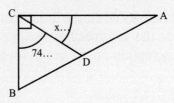

    (A) 90°

    (B) 74°

    (C) 26°

    (D) 16°

Problem-Solving

199. Carol earns $9.50 per hour as a teller in a neighborhood bank. How much does she earn in 8 hours at this rate?

    (A) $17.50

    (B) $76.00

    (C) $175.00

    (D) $760.00

200. The population of a small town increased from 360 to 468 in 9 years. What was the percent increase?

    (A) 12%

    (B) 30%

    (C) 77%

    (D) 108%

201. The formula for the area of a rectangle is:

    Area = length × width.

The cost of carpeting a floor is $1.50 per square foot. What is the cost of carpeting a floor measuring 18 feet by 15 feet?

    (A) $27.00

    (B) $40.50

    (C) $270.00

    (D) $405.00

202. A bee flies 45 m in 10 seconds. At this rate, how far would this bee fly in 2 minutes?

    (A) 90 m

    (B) 450 m

    (C) 540 m

    (D) 900 m

203. Rhonda, Paula, and Brenda jointly own a small business. Rhonda owns $\frac{1}{2}$ of the business, while Paula owns $\frac{2}{5}$ of it. What fraction of the business does Brenda own?

    (A) $\frac{1}{10}$

    (B) $\frac{1}{2}$

    (C) $\frac{3}{5}$

    (D) $\frac{9}{10}$

204. The value of a car decreases at the rate of 14% per year. If a new car cost $15,000.00, how much would it be worth at the end of the first year?

    (A) $12,900.00   (C) $14,986.00

    (B) $14,914.00   (D) $17,100.00

205. The marked price for a sofa is $460. If Alice buys this sofa with a 25% discount, how much does she pay for it?

    (A) $345.00   (C) $485.00

    (B) $435.00   (D) $575.00

206. Mrs. Smith left Starttown at 6:00 p.m. and drove non-stop to Endcity, 81 miles away. If Mrs. Smith arrived at Endcity at 7:30 p.m., what was her average speed per hour?

    (A) 50   (C) 60

    (B) 54   (D) 65

207. Jack cut one long strip of wood into 4 pieces and then joined these pieces end-to-end, as shown, to make a rectangle. What was the length of the original strip before Jack cut it up?

25 ft

35 ft

    (A) 60 ft.   (C) 437.5 ft.

    (B) 120 ft.   (D) 875 ft.

208. A rabbit may weigh up to 7 kg, while an adult harvest mouse weighs only 7 g. How many harvest mice would together weigh as much as one rabbit?

    (A) 1   (C) 100

    (B) 10   (D) 1,000

209. The Goliath beetle is 5 in. long and the fairy fly is only 1/100 in. long. What is the ratio of the length of a fairy fly to the length of a Goliath beetle?

    (A) 500:1   (C) 100:500

    (B) 1:100   (D) 1:500

210. A full grown ostrich weighs up to 156 kg. If the bee hummingbird weighs only 2 g, what fraction of an ostrich's weight is the bee hummingbird's weight?

(A) $\dfrac{1}{78,000}$ (C) $\dfrac{1}{780}$

(B) $\dfrac{1}{7,800}$ (D) $\dfrac{1}{78}$

211. An adult elephant may weigh up to 6,600 kg. If the blue whale weighs 200,000 kg, by how many kilograms is the blue whale heavier than the elephant?

(A) 294,400   (C) 19,340

(B) 293,400   (D) 193,400

212. Mrs. Knights cut a loaf of bread into 16 equal slices. Her children ate $\dfrac{5}{8}$ of the whole bread. How many slices of bread did they eat?

(A) 5   (C) 8

(B) 6   (D) 10

213. A book dealer sold a book for $30, making a profit of 20%. How much did the book dealer pay for the book?

(A) $10   (C) $25

(B) $24   (D) $50

214. A farmer has 3,000 acres of farm land. If he cultivates 18% of this land each year, how many acres are left uncultivated?

(A) 540   (C) 2,912

(B) 2,460   (D) 2,982

215. The flea is only $\dfrac{1}{8}$ in. long and can jump 13 in. The Goliath beetle is 5 in. long. If jumping strength is directly proportional to its height, how far can a Goliath beetle jump?

(A) 40 in.   (C) 104 in.

(B) 65 in.   (D) 520 in.

Use the diagram on the following page to answer questions 216 and 217.

216. What fraction of this rectangle is <u>not</u> shaded?

(A) $\dfrac{3}{5}$ (C) $\dfrac{5}{9}$

(B) $\dfrac{2}{5}$ (D) $\dfrac{4}{9}$

217. What percent of the rectangle is shaded?

(A) 76%   (C) 40%

(B) 60%   (D) 24%

218. Alice scored 82, 79, 91, and 85 points on the first 4 science tests during one year. If her total score on 5 tests was 425, what was her score on the fifth test?

(A) 88   (C) 337

(B) 80   (D) 90

219. The clear portions in this picture are quarter-circles. Find the area of the shaded region in the picture.

The area of a circle may be calculated from the formula:

Area = $3.14 \times r^2$, where r = measure of radius of circle.

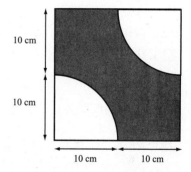

(A) 400 cm²   (C) 157 cm²

(B) 243 cm²   (D) 86 cm²

220. The picture shows a wire bent into the shape of a semi-circle. What is the length of this wire?

You may compute the circumference of a circle from the formula:

Circumference = $3.14 \times d$, where d = measure of diameter of circle.

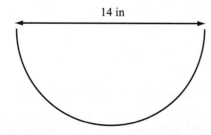

(A) 21.98 in.   (C) 17.14 in.

(B) 47.96 in.   (D) 10.14 in.

221. Find the area of the parallelogram on the following page.

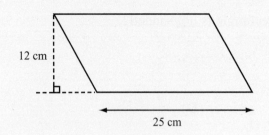

(A) 300 cm²   (C) 74 cm²

(B) 150 cm²   (D) 37 cm²

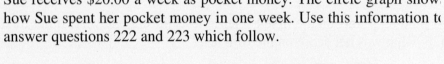

Sue receives $20.00 a week as pocket money. The circle graph show how Sue spent her pocket money in one week. Use this information to answer questions 222 and 223 which follow.

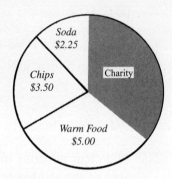

222. How much money did Sue donate to charity that week?

(A) $10.75   (C) $5.75

(B) $9.25   (D) $6.00

223. What percent of Sue's pocket money did she spend on chips?

(A) 3.5%   (C) 35%

(B) 46.25%   (D) 17.5%

224. Rhonda made 'cool aid' with 1.2 liters of iced tea and 300 milliliters of lemon juice. What percent of the drink is tea?

(A) 80%   (C) 25%

(B) 40%   (D) 2.5%

225. The ratio of boys to girls in a school is 52 to 48. If there are 500 students in the school, how many are boys?

(A) 260   (C) 52

(B) 240   (D) 480

226. Mike Smith earned $899.60 during one week by working overtime. Assume that he earned a basic hourly rate for the first 40 hours and an overtime rate for each hour after 40 hours. If he worked a total of 48 hours, what was his overtime rate? Assume overtime rate = (1.5) (basic rate).

(A) $17.30   (C) $25.95

(B) $18.74   (D) $28.11

227. Laura Brown decides to invest $6,000 into an account which pays 13% per year simple interest. How much money should she invest into a second account paying 16.25% per year simple interest, so that the total interest for the year is $1,348.75?

    (A) $3,500.00   (C) $4,267.50

    (B) $3,883.75   (D) $4,651.25

228. How many ounces of pure water should be added to 50 ounces of a water-based solution which is 12% salt in order to produce a solution which is 4% salt?

    (A) 50   (C) 150

    (B) 100   (D) 200

229. In 31 years, Alice will be three times as old as she was last year. How old is she now?

    (A) 18   (C) 16

    (B) 17   (D) 15

230. Working together, Dave and Wendy can complete an assignment in 4 hours. Working alone, Dave would require 6 hours. How many hours would Wendy require if she worked alone?

    (A) 6   (C) 10

    (B) 8   (D) 12

231. What is the measure of the angle formed by the minute and hour hands of a clock at 3:20?

    (A) 5°   (C) 20°

    (B) 10°   (D) 30°

232. The length of a rectangle is 6 times its width. If its area is 37.5, what is its perimeter?

    (A) 40   (C) 30

    (B) 35   (D) 25

233. What is the area of a sector in a circle of radius 4 for which the central angle is 72°?

    (A) $1.6\,\pi$ (C) $3.2\,\pi$

    (B) $2.4\,\pi$ (D) $4.0\,\pi$

234. In the figure on the right, $\overline{AB}$ and $\overline{AC}$ are radii of a circle and are perpendicular to each other. $\overline{BC}$ is an arc of that circle. If $\overline{AB}$ is an arc of a circle for which $\overline{AB}$ is a diameter, what is the ratio of the shaded area to the unshaded area?

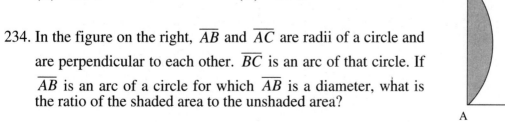

(A) $\dfrac{4}{\pi}$ (C) $\dfrac{3}{\pi}$

(B) $\dfrac{1}{1}$ (D) $\dfrac{1}{\pi}$

235. A gum-ball dispenser is filled with exactly 900 pieces of gum. The gum balls are always dispensed in the following order: 2 red, 3 yellow, 4 green, and 5 white. What is the color of the last gum ball to be dispensed?

(A) green   (C) white

(B) red   (D) yellow

236. Maria Jones earned a score of 75% on a calculus exam. If she had gotten 3 more correct answers, her score would have been 80%. Assuming each problem counted equally, how many actual problems did Maria answer correctly?

(A) 54   (C) 48

(B) 51   (D) 45

237. If 70% of the workers in an office are non-smokers, what is the ratio of smokers to non-smokers?

(A) 3:7   (C) 10:7

(B) 7:10   (D) 7:3

238. The marked price on a sofa is $520. After the first week, the price is marked down 20%. After the second week, the price is marked down an additional 30% and sold. What is the selling price?

(A) $124.80   (C) $291.20

(B) $260.00   (D) $426.40

Subtest 5: Language Skills

TIME: 25 Minutes
　　60 Questions

Punctuation, Capitalization, and Usage

<u>**DIRECTIONS:**</u> Look for errors of punctuation, capitalization, or usage in the following sentences. If there are no mistakes, mark "D."

239. (A) Tony walked across the lawn.

　　(B) John eats dinner last night.

　　(C) Traci danced with her friends.

　　(D) No mistakes.

240. (A) Luis is looking for martha.

　　(B) Please check your work.

　　(C) Dan is playing football.

　　(D) No mistakes.

241. (A) George wants to watch television.

　　(B) The book is on the table next to the lamp.

　　(C) Cindy is looking for my watch.

　　(D) No mistakes.

242. (A) My family went to Pittsburgh last summer.

　　(B) "What can I do for you?" she asked.

　　(C) I bought notebooks pens and a pencil for school.

　　(D) No mistakes.

243. (A) Laura went to visit her friend at the hospital.

　　(B) The black car drove past us.

　　(C) My uncle baked a lot of food for the holidais.

　　(D) No mistakes.

244. (A) I feed our fishes every day.

    (B) His birthday is January 12, 1965.

    (C) April is my favorite month.

    (D) No mistakes.

245. (A) Lou finished the assignment on time.

    (B) Jason walked into the room with a smile on his face.

    (C) Bob a good friend is famous.

    (D) No mistakes.

246. (A) Jennifer do a good job on this painting.

    (B) Mike will be in the concert on Saturday.

    (C) We are going to the movies tomorrow night.

    (D) No mistakes.

247. (A) They walked over to the store.

    (B) Are you going to the library after school.

    (C) We are playing soccer later.

    (D) No mistakes.

248. (A) I need to by some milk later.

    (B) Sal is playing tennis with us later.

    (C) We are going on vacation next month.

    (D) No mistakes.

249. (A) My mother wants to have lunch with me.

    (B) I didn't have time to finish reading the book.

    (C) Our cat's name is Max.

    (D) No mistakes.

250. (A) Tanya moved to Wisconsin.

    (B) What time is it? "Joy asked."

    (C) My sister has a splinter in her hand.

    (D) No mistakes.

251. (A) Paul is a very good photographer.

    (B) We usually get something to drink after school.

    (C) Everything is alright.

    (D) No mistakes.

252. (A) I would like some cookies to.

    (B) My father wants me to come home now.

    (C) Let's go to the dance later.

    (D) No mistakes.

253. (A) The phone is ringing.

    (B) I checked to see if the mail arrived yet.

    (C) Their going to meet us later for dinner.

    (D) No mistakes.

254. (A) We wanted to see the museum later.

    (B) Her close were all over the floor.

    (C) Mike will go away next year.

    (D) No mistakes.

255. (A) I looked for a new skateboard yesterday.

    (B) All he thinks about is basketball.

    (C) She is going to Florida to visit her grandparents.

    (D) No mistakes.

256. (A) I like that song alot.

    (B) We have band practice after school tomorrow.

    (C) Something is going to happen.

    (D) No mistakes.

257. (A) Nancy is going to call me later.

    (B) John likes to watch shows about penguins.

    (C) I left your wallet in the table.

    (D) No mistakes.

258. (A) If you find out what time we should meet, let me know.

     (B) We took a lot of pictures at the show.

     (C) How many money do you have?

     (D) No mistakes.

259. (A) If we were in class, I'd be home sleeping.

     (B) Yesterday, my brother went to the park.

     (C) They talked loudly before the movie began.

     (D) No mistakes.

260. (A) Shelly's little sister broked the vase.

     (B) Ian wrote a really good story.

     (C) Sam wants to use the computer.

     (D) No mistakes.

261. (A) She has done many strange things.

     (B) We went on a boat on lake erie.

     (C) Did you ever think about talking to her?

     (D) No mistakes.

262. (A) My aunt sent us some magazines to read.

     (B) We saw the following people at the park Marie, John, and his aunt.

     (C) Tomorrow we are going to the beach.

     (D) No mistakes.

263. (A) Please bring that newspaper article tomorrow.

     (B) We watched the sun set.

     (C) Mrs. Dodson came over to visit my mother.

     (D) No mistakes.

264. (A) After we brought home the dog my dad started to smile.

     (B) My cousins live at the beach.

     (C) Evan started to sing.

     (D) No mistakes.

265. (A) My baseball team has practice on Tuesdays.

     (B) The bottles of milk, and not the cereal, goes in the refrigerator.

     (C) She asked a very important question.

     (D) No mistakes.

266. (A) They painted the house a strange blue color.

     (B) We walked around the lake and played on the swings.

     (C) I wanted to borrow Judys bike.

     (D) No mistakes.

267. (A) I wanted to get that roll in the school play.

     (B) We watched the news on television last night.

     (C) The store sells different kinds of bread.

     (D) No mistakes.

268. (A) Saturday we are going to the dance.

     (B) The home team won the game.

     (C) My teacher really likes my writting.

     (D) No mistakes.

269. (A) What time are you going to the fair?

     (B) I paints a good picture.

     (C) We walked all the way to the park yesterday.

     (D) No mistakes.

270. (A) Phil likes to play video games.

     (B) There are thirty-nine students in my math class.

     (C) Marc watched the fireworks at the river.

     (D) No mistakes.

271. (A) Karen wants to go to England.

     (B) Joanna was on the phone all night long.

     (C) after I talked to Dana, I went to sleep.

     (D) No mistakes.

272. (A) After last night's performance, he was a little embarressed.

    (B) The letter arrived in yesterday's mail.

    (C) Of course, I forgot my homework.

    (D) No mistakes.

273. (A) I broke my leg skiing last winter.

    (B) Four feet of snow fell last night.

    (C) Who's book is this?

    (D) No mistakes.

274. (A) My aunt was born on a leap day.

    (B) Afterwards, she lead us to the farm.

    (C) The clouds started to get darker.

    (D) No mistakes.

275. (A) She gave me some very important advice.

    (B) The dentist told me that I have three cavities.

    (C) Basicly, he wanted me to go camping with him.

    (D) No mistakes.

276. (A) We went to a very good restaurant last night.

    (B) Why are you always late?

    (C) Its time for us to go home.

    (D) No mistakes.

277. (A) Can we see a menu?

    (B) He lie the book on the counter.

    (C) I tried to find it, but the library was closed.

    (D) No mistakes.

278. (A) He dances good.

    (B) The rain leaked through the roof.

    (C) I went to the doctor for an eye exam.

    (D) No mistakes.

Spelling

DIRECTIONS: Choose the sentence that contains a spelling error. If there are no errors, choose "D."

279. (A) The weather forecaster predicted rain for tomorow.
   (B) The musician played the piccolo in the orchestra.
   (C) The students were permitted to use calculators on the mathematics examination.
   (D) No mistakes.

280. (A) The sailors were stranded on a dessert island.
   (B) Several mourners gathered at the cemetery.
   (C) His fatigue may be caused by a vitamin deficiency.
   (D) No mistakes.

281. (A) The retired English professor volunteers at the library on Wednesdays.
   (B) He canceled his dental appointment.
   (C) Max's guidance counseler advised him to take Spanish.
   (D) No mistakes.

282. (A) There are alot of vehicles in line at the inspection station.
   (B) My niece Jennifer performed in a dance recital yesterday.
   (C) The elderly gentleman preferred to travel by train.
   (D) No mistakes.

283. (A) A committee meeting was scheduled for 7:30 on February 1st.
   (B) His secretary's habitual tardiness cost her a promotion.
   (C) The investigator figured out the criminal's elaborate scheme.
   (D) No mistakes.

284. (A) Self-confidence is a valuable asset.
   (B) The reporter's constant interruptions were unnecessary.
   (C) The sophmore class assembled in the cafeteria.
   (D) No mistakes.

285. (A) The personnel manager interviewed the candidate.

   (B) The accomodations at the new waterfront hotel are luxurious.

   (C) We viewed the French countryside from a hot air balloon.

   (D) No mistakes.

286. (A) The politician delivered a lengthy campaign speech.

   (B) The optimistic job seeker submitted an application.

   (C) The high school principle addressed the student body.

   (D) No mistakes.

287. (A) Ann handed the police officer her license, registration, and insurance card.

   (B) Her patient exhibited signs of depression.

   (C) The signature on the perscription is illegible.

   (D) No mistakes.

288. (A) All roads in the vicinity of the accident were closed.

   (B) Nine planets revolve around the sun in our solar system.

   (C) Gossip is truly a waste of time and energy.

   (D) No mistakes.

Composition

DIRECTIONS: Select the best answer choice.

289. Choose the correct word to join the thoughts together.
   Tony's car registration had expired, _____ the police officer didn't give him a ticket.

   (A) but   (C) so

   (B) and   (D) None of these.

290. Choose the correct word to join the thoughts together.
   I needed my friend's address at summer camp, _____ I called his parents.

   (A) but   (C) for

   (B) so   (D) None of these.

291. Choose the correct word to join the thoughts together.
Adriana set her alarm clock for one hour earlier than usual last night _____ she had to study for a science test.

   (A) although   (C) because

   (B) if   (D) None of these.

292. Choose the correct word to join the thoughts together.
Mary put on the sunscreen she bought _____ she had been at the beach for three hours.

   (A) while   (C) after

   (B) before   (D) None of these.

293. Choose the group of words that best completes the sentence.
Alyssa's bus was late; however, _____.

   (A) she was late for school.

   (B) she was on time for school.

   (C) she was never on time for school.

   (D) she had band practice before school.

294. Choose the group of words that best completes the sentence.
John wants to do well on the math test; therefore, _____.

   (A) math is his favorite subject.

   (B) he has not studied.

   (C) he has been studying all week.

   (D) it is the last test before the final exam.

295. Which of these expresses the idea most clearly?

   (A) Jim went to Florida on vacation several people told me.

   (B) To Florida on vacation, several people told me Jim went.

   (C) Several people told me Jim went to Florida on vacation.

   (D) Several people told me to Florida Jim went on vacation.

296. Which of these expresses the idea most clearly?

   (A) Phyllis decided to invite some friends over on Saturday to celebrate her birthday.

(B)   On Saturday to celebrate her birthday, Phyllis decided to invite some friends over.

(C)   To celebrate her birthday, to invite some friends over Phyllis decided on Saturday.

(D)   Phyllis decided on Saturday to celebrate her birthday to invite some friends over.

297. Which of these expresses the idea most clearly?

(A)   I asked my friend to return my new baseball bat in time for the game.

(B)   To return my new baseball bat I asked my friend in time for the game.

(C)   In time for the game, I asked my friend to return my new baseball bat.

(D)   I asked my friend in time for the game to return my new baseball bat.

298. Which of these expresses the idea most clearly?

(A)   On the table, our parents were surprised to find dinner when they came home.

(B)   Our parents were surprised to find dinner when they came home on the table.

(C)   To find dinner on the table our parents were surprised when they came home.

(D)   When they came home, our parents were surprised to find dinner on the table.

STS HSPT

PRACTICE TEST 1

ANSWER KEY

Question Number	Correct Answer	If You Answered this Question Incorrectly, Refer to...

Subtest 1: Verbal Skills

1.	(C)	P. 194
2.	(C)	P. 191
3.	(D)	P. 194
4.	(D)	P. 194
5.	(A)	P. 194
6.	(A)	P. 194
7.	(B)	P. 190
8.	(C)	P. 191
9.	(A)	P. 191
10.	(D)	P. 192
11.	(C)	P. 247
12.	(C)	P. 197
13.	(A)	P. 197
14.	(A)	P. 197
15.	(D)	P. 197
16.	(D)	P. 197
17.	(A)	P. 197
18.	(C)	P. 197
19.	(B)	P. 197
20.	(A)	P. 197

21.	(B)	P. 197
22.	(A)	P. 197
23.	(A)	P. 197
24.	(D)	P. 197
25.	(C)	P. 197
26.	(C)	P. 186
27.	(C)	P. 186
28.	(B)	P. 186
29.	(B)	P. 186
30.	(A)	P. 186
31.	(A)	P. 186
32.	(A)	P. 186
33.	(A)	P. 186
34.	(B)	P. 188
35.	(B)	P. 188
36.	(A)	P. 195
37.	(B)	P. 195
38.	(D)	P. 195
39.	(A)	P. 195
40.	(A)	P. 195
41.	(D)	P. 195
42.	(B)	P. 195
43.	(D)	P. 195
44.	(B)	P. 195
45.	(C)	P. 195
46.	(C)	P. 195
47.	(B)	P. 195
48.	(D)	P. 195
49.	(B)	P. 195
50.	(D)	P. 195
51.	(A)	P. 195
52.	(C)	P. 196
53.	(A)	P. 196
54.	(C)	P. 196

55.	(B)	P. 196
56.	(B)	P. 196
57.	(D)	P. 196
58.	(D)	P. 196
59.	(C)	P. 196
60.	(D)	P. 196

Subtest 2: Quantitative Skills

61.	(D)	P. 404
62.	(B)	P. 404
63.	(A)	P. 401
64.	(B)	P. 407
65.	(C)	P. 328, 409
66.	(A)	P. 404
67.	(C)	P. 328, 409
68.	(B)	P. 401
69.	(A)	P. 328, 409
70.	(B)	P. 328, 409
71.	(C)	P. 404
72.	(B)	P. 401
73.	(B)	P. 328, 409
74.	(B)	P. 328, 373, 409
75.	(C)	P. 401
76.	(D)	P. 401
77.	(A)	P. 409
78.	(D)	P. 401
79.	(B)	P. 328, 353, 382, 407
80.	(C)	P. 328, 409
81.	(B)	P. 404
82.	(A)	P. 409
83.	(C)	P. 328, 407
84.	(B)	P. 404
85.	(B)	P. 409
86.	(C)	P. 401

87.	(B)	P. 401
88.	(C)	P. 328, 409
89.	(D)	P. 401
90.	(A)	P. 401
91.	(D)	P. 328, 409
92.	(D)	P. 369
93.	(C)	P. 401
94.	(B)	P. 328, 409
95.	(D)	P. 401
96.	(D)	P. 404
97.	(B)	P. 328, 409
98.	(C)	P. 407
99.	(B)	P. 401
100.	(A)	P. 404
101.	(D)	P. 328, 409
102.	(D)	P. 401
103.	(B)	P. 373, 407
104.	(C)	P. 404
105.	(A)	P. 401
106.	(B)	P. 328, 409
107.	(A)	P. 328, 409
108.	(C)	P. 360, 407
109.	(B)	P. 377, 404
110.	(A)	P. 401
111.	(B)	P. 328, 409
112.	(D)	P. 401

Subtest 3: Reading Comprehension

113.	(C)	P. 272
114.	(D)	P. 272
115.	(C)	P. 282
116.	(C)	P. 272
117.	(A)	P. 272
118.	(D)	P. 272

119.	(B)	P. 272
120.	(A)	P. 282
121.	(D)	P. 272
122.	(C)	P. 272
123.	(B)	P. 272
124.	(D)	P. 272
125.	(A)	P. 272
126.	(D)	P. 272
127.	(B)	P. 272
128.	(D)	P. 272
129.	(A)	P. 272
130.	(C)	P. 272
131.	(B)	P. 272
132.	(D)	P. 272
133.	(B)	P. 272
134.	(A)	P. 272
135.	(D)	P. 272
136.	(D)	P. 272
137.	(C)	P. 282
138.	(C)	P. 272
139.	(D)	P. 274
140.	(D)	P. 275
141.	(D)	P. 272
142.	(B)	P. 275
143.	(C)	P. 272
144.	(A)	P. 272
145.	(A)	P. 282
146.	(D)	P. 272
147.	(A)	P. 272
148.	(B)	P. 270
149.	(C)	P. 282
150.	(B)	P. 272
151.	(D)	P. 272
152.	(C)	P. 272

Vocabulary

153.	(A)	P. 197, 286
154.	(B)	P. 197, 286
155.	(D)	P. 197, 286
156.	(C)	P. 197, 286
157.	(B)	P. 197, 286
158.	(C)	P. 197, 286
159.	(D)	P. 197, 286
160.	(A)	P. 197, 286
161.	(C)	P. 197, 286
162.	(D)	P. 197, 286
163.	(A)	P. 197, 286
164.	(B)	P. 197, 286
165.	(B)	P. 197, 286
166.	(D)	P. 197, 286
167.	(B)	P. 197, 286
168.	(B)	P. 197, 286
169.	(A)	P. 197, 286
170.	(D)	P. 197, 286
171.	(A)	P. 197, 286
172.	(D)	P. 197, 286
173.	(A)	P. 197, 286
174.	(B)	P. 197, 286

Subtest 4: Mathematics Concepts

175.	(B)	P. 354
176.	(A)	P. 409
177.	(B)	P. 404
178.	(C)	P. 315
179.	(C)	P. 409
180.	(D)	P. 331, 334
181.	(B)	P. 320
182.	(C)	P. 378

183.	(D)	P. 370
184.	(A)	P. 331, 345
185.	(A)	P. 330
186.	(D)	P. 383
187.	(A)	P. 382
188.	(D)	P. 370
189.	(A)	P. 391
190.	(D)	P. 391
191.	(B)	P. 378
192.	(B)	P. 404
193.	(B)	P. 371, 404
194.	(A)	P. 404
195.	(D)	P. 404
196.	(A)	P. 354
197.	(C)	P. 391
198.	(D)	P. 391

Problem-Solving

199.	(B)	P. 360
200.	(B)	P. 383, 395
201.	(D)	P. 360, 378
202.	(C)	P. 320, 323
203.	(A)	P. 334
204.	(A)	P. 396
205.	(A)	P. 371
206.	(B)	P. 371
207.	(B)	P. 377
208.	(D)	P. 320, 323
209.	(D)	P. 320, 323
210.	(A)	P. 320, 323
211.	(D)	P. 317
212.	(D)	P. 328
213.	(C)	P. 383
214.	(B)	P. 385

215.	(D)	P. 320, 396, 402
216.	(B)	P. 328
217.	(B)	P. 382
218.	(A)	P. 315, 317
219.	(B)	P. 391
220.	(A)	P. 391
221.	(A)	P. 378
222.	(B)	P. 356, 358
223.	(D)	P. 383
224.	(A)	P. 382
225.	(A)	P. 385
226.	(C)	P. 360, 409
227.	(A)	P. 382, 409
228.	(B)	P. 382
229.	(B)	P. 409
230.	(D)	P. 409
231.	(C)	P. 391
232.	(B)	P. 377
233.	(C)	P. 391
234.	(B)	P. 391
235.	(D)	P. 315, 323
236.	(D)	P. 382, 409
237.	(A)	P. 382
238.	(C)	P. 396

Subtest 5: Language Skills
Punctuation, Capitalization, and Usage

239.	(B)	P. 211
240.	(A)	P. 244
241.	(D)	P. 212, 244
242.	(C)	P. 228
243.	(C)	P. 252
244.	(A)	P. 249
245.	(C)	P. 232

246.	(A)	P. 211
247.	(B)	P. 228
248.	(A)	P. 249
249.	(D)	P. 237
250.	(B)	P. 239
251.	(D)	P. 250
252.	(A)	P. 249
253.	(C)	P. 217
254.	(B)	P. 250
255.	(D)	P. 212
256.	(A)	P. 250
257.	(C)	P. 214
258.	(C)	P. 204
259.	(A)	P. 204
260.	(A)	P. 211
261.	(B)	P. 245
262.	(B)	P. 236
263.	(D)	P. 244, 250
264.	(A)	P. 229
265.	(B)	P. 212
266.	(C)	P. 237
267.	(A)	P. 253
268.	(C)	P. 249
269.	(B)	P. 212
270.	(D)	P. 212
271.	(C)	P. 244
272.	(A)	P. 251
273.	(C)	P. 254
274.	(B)	P. 249
275.	(C)	P. 249
276.	(C)	P. 237
277.	(B)	P. 211
278.	(A)	P. 224

Spelling

279.	(A)	P. 254
280.	(A)	P. 251
281.	(C)	P. 251
282.	(A)	P. 250
283.	(D)	P. 249
284.	(C)	P. 253
285.	(B)	P. 250
286.	(C)	P. 253
287.	(C)	P. 253
288.	(D)	P. 249

Composition

289.	(A)	P. 207
290.	(B)	P. 207
291.	(C)	P. 207
292.	(C)	P. 207
293.	(B)	P. 207
294.	(C)	P. 207
295.	(C)	P. 204
296.	(A)	P. 204
297.	(A)	P. 204
298.	(D)	P. 204

Subtest 1: Verbal Skills

DETAILED EXPLANATIONS
OF ANSWERS

1. **(C)** A *sunset* occurs in the *evening* as a *sunrise* occurs in the *morning*.

2. **(C)** A *county* is part of a *state* as a *country* is part of a *continent*.

3. **(D)** A *rash* is a visible symptom of *measles* as *swollen glands* are visible symptoms of *mumps*. Although an elevated body temperature, or *fever* (C), is a symptom of an infection, it is not the correct answer because it is not a visible symptom like a *rash*.

4. **(D)** A *ruler* is used to *measure* as *scissors* are used to *cut*.

5. **(A)** *Her* is the possessive form of the third person singular pronoun *she*; *their* is the possessive form of the third person plural pronoun *they*. *Theirs* (B) is also a possessive form of the pronoun *they*; however, it is not the correct answer. Unlike *her* and *their*, which must be followed by nouns (*her* blanket; *their* children), *theirs* stands alone. (The new black car is *theirs*.)

6. **(A)** A *century* is one hundred years as a *decade* is ten years. A *millennium* (B) is 1,000 years.

7. **(B)** A *canopy covers* as a *moat surrounds*.

8. **(C)** A *teacher* works in a *school* as a *doctor* works in a *hospital*. Although a *teacher* does teach in a *classroom* (B), the *school* or the building is analogous to a *hospital*, not a single room.

9. **(A)** A *book* is divided into *chapters* as a *play* is divided into *acts*.

10. **(D)** A *floor* can be made of *tile* as a *sidewalk* can be made of *concrete*.

11. **(C)** *Endure* means to *tolerate* (C). The two words are similar and are synonyms. The word *perish* (A) means to *pass away*. The word *reject* (B) means to *discard* or *lay aside*, and the word *fail* (D) means to *fall short*. Neither (A), (B), nor (D) is a synonym of the word *endure*. Since *tolerate* (C) means the same as *endure*, it is the best answer.

12. **(C)** *Pessimism* most nearly means *distrust* or *suspicion* (C). *Pessimism* does not mean

idealism (A), *visionary* (B), or *optimism* (D); these words suggest a positive outlook and hope. They are opposites of *pessimism*. The best choice for a synonym of *pessimism* is *suspicion* (C).

13. **(A)**   *Skeptical* most nearly means *unbelieving* or *doubtful* (A). The words *confident* (B) and *convinced* (D) imply that something is believed. They are not synonymous with the word *skeptical*. The word *certain* (C) is the opposite of *skeptical*. The best answer for a synonym of *skeptical* is *doubtful* (A).

14. **(A)**   *Rectify* most nearly means to *right*, to *correct* (A), to *make better*, or to *ameliorate*. The best answer is (A). The word *rectify* does not mean to *destroy* (B), to *dilapidate* (C), or to *demolish* (D)—words which imply ruination. The word most nearly like *rectify* is the synonym *correct* (A).

15. **(D)**   To *retract* is to *take back*, to *reconsider*, to *deny* (D). *Retract* is the opposite of *uphold* (A), *declare* (B), or *admit* (C). To *admit* (C) is to *clear up*, to *make clear*, to *explain*; this term is not synonymous with *retract*. The best answer for a synonym of *retract* is (D)—*deny*.

16. **(D)**   *Protagonist* most nearly means *hero* (D). The *protagonist* is the opposite of the *villain* (A), the *antagonist* (B), or the "bad guy." Although the *protagonist* might be a *professor* (C), the word *professor* (C) is not necessarily a synonym of the word *protagonist*. *Hero* (D) is the synonym the test-taker is seeking.

17. **(A)**   *Revenge* means to *get even*, to *repay* (A). The word *revenge* may suggest the word *rector* and *clerical* (B) to some test-takers, but the religious rector or cleric is not synonymous with *revenge*. To *advocate* (C) or to *suggest* is not the same as to *repay* or to *retaliate*. Neither (B) nor (C) is the correct answer. *Danger* (D) does not necessarily mean *revenge*; (D) is not the best synonym. The best choice as a synonym of *revenge* is *repay* (A).

18. **(C)**   *Paranoid* most nearly means *suspicious* (C), *uneasy*, *mistrustful*. *Paranoid* is the opposite of *trusting* (A); the test-taker, however, is seeking a synonym, not an antonym. The word *angry* (B) is not a word which means the same as *paranoid*. The word *confident* (D) is also an antonym of *paranoid*. The best choice is *suspicious* (C).

19. **(B)**   A *martyr* is a *victim* (B). In fact, the martyr often loses his life. A *martyr* is not a *victor* (C), or one who wins. A *martyr* is not necessarily a *manager* (A) or an *overseer*. A *delinquent* (D) is the antonym of *martyr*. The best choice for a synonym of *martyr* is clearly *victim* (B).

20. **(A)**   *Regime* most nearly means the *reign* (A) or the *rule* of a particular period or person. The *regime* may last a *generation* (B) or longer—or shorter; the time span of a *generation* is not necessarily a component of *regime* and is not a synonym of the term. *Luxurious* (C) means *elegant*; (C) is not the best choice as a word meaning the same as *regime*. The test-taker who selected *regimen* (D) as the synonym of *regime* probably confused the shape of the words. The best word to express a similar meaning to a *regime* is *reign* (A).

21.   **(B)**   *Detest* most nearly means *loathe* (B). The words *like* (A), *cherish* (C), and *idolize* (D) are antonymns of the word *detest*. These words suggest *love* or *appreciation*. The best answer for a synonym of *detest* is *loathe* (B).

22.   **(A)**   *Rational* most nearly means *logical* (A) or *sensible*. The words *insane* (B), *unreasonable* (C), and *foolish* (D) are opposite from the word *rational*. The best answer is (A).

23.   **(A)**   *Obscure* means *unclear* (A). The two words are synonyms. The words *distinct* (B) and *evident* (D) imply *clarity* and *clearness*. The word *known* (C) means the opposite of *obscure*. The best answer for a synonym of *obscure* is *unclear* (A).

24.   **(D)**   To *dissuade* is to *deter, hinder, obstruct,* or *thwart* (D). The best synonym for *dissuade* is choice (D)—*thwart*. *Disapprove* (A) is similar in shape—not meaning—to *dissuade*. *Camouflage* (B) means to *mask*, to *cover*, or to *hide*. Choice (B) is not a similar word to *dissuade* and is not a good choice. *Encourage* (C) is an antonym or an opposite word from *dissuade*. Again, (A), (B), and (C) are not acceptable answers. The best synonym is (D).

25.   **(C)**   *Terminate* is to *finish* or *conclude* (C). These are synonyms. The words *start* (A), *originate* (B), and *initiate* (D) are antonymns of the word *terminate*. They refer to a beginning, while *terminate* refers to an end. The best answer is (C).

26.   **(C)**   **Uncertain** is correct. The truth of the third statement is uncertain because the first two statements, which we know are true, give us no information about Victor.

27.   **(C)**   **Uncertain** is correct. The truth of the third statement is uncertain because the first two statements, which we know are true, give us no information about Alison.

28.   **(B)**   **False** is correct. If Jefferson High School has more students than Roosevelt High School, and Roosevelt has more students than Lincoln High School, then Lincoln cannot have more than Jefferson.

29.   **(B)**   **False** is correct. If Mrs. Perez has more children than Mrs. Martin, and Mrs. Martin has more children than Mrs. Lee, then Mrs. Lee cannot have more children than Mrs. Perez.

30.   **(A)**   **True** is correct. If every family in Sunrise Village has a car, and the Palmers do not have a car, then the Palmers cannot live in Sunrise Village.

31.   **(A)**   **True** is correct. If every adult in Beechwood voted in the last presidential election, and Mr. Turner didn't vote, then Mr. Turner cannot live in Beechwood.

32.   **(A)**   **True** is correct. If Wednesday was warmer than Tuesday, and Monday was cooler than Tuesday, then Monday also must have been cooler than Wednesday.

33.   **(A)**   **True** is correct. If Bill's house is larger than Fred's, and Lucille's house is smaller than Fred's, then Lucille's house also must be smaller than Bill's.

34. **(B)**   **False** is correct. If the first two statements are true, then the opposite of the third statement is true: The swimming pool is *closer* to the ice cream parlor than the tennis courts are to the beach.

35. **(B)**   **False** is correct. If the first two statements are true, then the opposite of the third statement is true: The train station is *farther* from the bank than the supermarket is from the library.

36. **(A)**   A *program* is computer software, while a *monitor*, a *printer*, and a *keyboard* are computer hardware.

37. **(B)**   *Rice*, *wheat*, and *corn* are all kinds of *cereals*, or grains, that can be eaten.

38. **(D)**   *Alleviate*, *reduce*, and *lessen* have nearly the same meaning, while *increase* has the opposite meaning.

39. **(A)**   *Gold* is a precious metal, while *diamonds*, *emeralds*, and *sapphires* are precious gemstones.

40. **(A)**   *Snakes*, *turtles*, and *crocodiles* are all kinds of *reptiles*.

41. **(D)**   A *guitar* is classified as a stringed instrument, while the *piano*, *drums*, and *cymbals* are classified as percussion instruments.

42. **(B)**   A *pound* is a unit of dry measurement, while an *ounce*, a *gallon*, and a *quart* are units of liquid measurement. Although an *ounce* can also be used in dry measurement, *pound* is the correct answer because it is never used for liquid measurement.

43. **(D)**   *Sodium* is solid, while *nitrogen*, *oxygen*, and *helium* are gases.

44. **(B)**   *Marble* is a kind of stone, while *tin*, *copper*, and *nickel* are metals.

45. **(C)**   *Tense*, *anxious*, and *nervous* have nearly the same meaning, while *relaxed* has the opposite meaning.

46. **(C)**   *Odor*, *smell*, and *scent* have nearly the same meaning. *Stench* is also a smell, but it is only an unpleasant smell; the other words can be either pleasant or unpleasant.

47. **(B)**   A *mother*, a *niece*, and a *sister* are female relatives; a *cousin* can be either male or female.

48. **(D)**   All of the words begin with the prefix *un-*, which means *not*. However, *uncomfortable* has a different meaning from *undecided*, *uncertain*, and *unsure*, which are synonyms.

49. **(B)**   *Cactus* is a singular form of a word, while *media*, *alumni*, and *data* are plural forms.

50. **(D)** *Classroom*, *blackberry*, and *lighthouse* are all compound words, that is, words that are formed by joining two words. *Dreamer* is not a compound word.

51. **(A)** *Addition*, *subtraction*, and *division* are all mathematical operations; however, a *fraction* is a way to express a number.

52. **(C)** *Metropolitan* means *urban* (A), *cosmopolitan* (B), *city-like* (D), and *current* or *up-to-date*. The word does NOT mean *old* or *antiquated* (C). Because *antiquated* is the opposite of *current*, it is an antonym. The best answer for an opposite word is *antiquated* (C).

53. **(A)** *Miserly* means *saving*, *cheap* (B), *avaricious* (C), or *stingy* (D). It does not mean *generous* (A) or *open-handed*. The best of the choices for a word opposite of *miserly* is *generous* (A).

54. **(C)** *Malign* means *unfavorable* (A), *malicious* (B), or *evil* (D). *Malign* does not mean *good*, *gracious*, *kind*, *harmless*, or *benign* (C). The opposite word, then, is (C).

55. **(B)** *Impenetrable* means *not penetrable*, *not pervious*, *not transparent*. An impenetrable paint is *thick* (D), heavy; because one cannot see through impenetrable paint, it is *opaque* (A), or *nontransparent*. Something that is difficult to understand or to see through easily is *obscure* (C). *Impenetrable*, then, is opposite of *translucent*, which means thin or almost transparent. The best choice for an antonym of *impenetrable* is *translucent* (B).

56. **(B)** *Courtly* means *sophisticated*, *dignified* (A), *cultured* (C), and *stately* (D). It is the opposite (the antonym) of *frivolous* (B), which means *unimportant* or *trivial*. The word *frivolous* (B) is the best answer as an antonym to *courtly*.

57. **(D)** *Melancholy* means *sad* (A) or *depressed* (B); it can also be a synonym of *dejected*, *gloomy*, or *despondent* (C). It is the opposite of *happy* or *ecstatic* (D). The antonym of *melancholy* is (D).

58. **(D)** *Occasional* means *alternate* (A), *periodic* (B), or *rhythmical* (C). *Incessant* (D) means *nonstopping*. It is the opposite of *occasional*. The antonym of *occasional* is (D).

59. **(C)** *Stalwart* means *gallant* (A), *valorous* (B), or *dauntless* (D). It does not mean *cowardly*, *fearful*, or *timid* (C). The opposite of the word *stalwart* is (C).

60. **(D)** *Glowing* means *ruddy* (A), *vivid* (B), or *incandescent* (C). It does not mean *doleful* (D), *sad*, or *dismal*. The right choice for the antonym of *glowing* is *doleful* (D).

Subtest 2: Quantitative Skills

DETAILED EXPLANATIONS OF ANSWERS

For each problem, the answer will be given first. Then we will name the type of question—Series, Comparison, or Pre-algebra.

For Series questions, we will show the pattern on the list of numbers, state the rule, and get the answer.

For Comparison questions, we will give the quantities associated with (a), (b), and (c) or the picture, and, if necessary, explain how to get them. The correct choice of (A), (B), (C), or (D) will then be obvious.

For Pre-algebra questions, we will use the word method to arrive at the correct answer. Remember: You may want to use trial-and-error for some or all of the Pre-algebra questions.

61. **(D)** (c) is less than (a) and more than (b). Comparison. (a) = 11, (b) = 9, and (c) = 10. Count items.

62. **(B)** 38. Series.

$$
\begin{array}{ccccccc}
& -13 & & -13 & & -13 & & -13 = \underline{38} \\
& \diagup \diagdown & \diagup \diagdown & \diagup \diagdown & \diagup \\
90 & & 77 & & 64 & & 51
\end{array}
$$

Rule: Subtract 13. Answer: $51 - 13 = 38$.

63. **(A)** 56. Series.

$$
\begin{array}{ccccccccc}
& -8 & & -3 & & -8 & & -3 & & -8 = \underline{56} \\
& \diagup \diagdown & \diagup \diagdown & \diagup \diagdown & \diagup \diagdown & \diagup \\
86 & & 78 & & 75 & & 67 & & 64
\end{array}
$$

Rule: Subtract 8, then subtract 3. Answer: $64 - 8 = 56$.

64. **(B)** (a) is greater than (b) and greater than (c). Comparison. (a) = $7 \times 5 = 35$, (b) = $3 + 20 = 23$, and (c) = $8 \times 4 = 32$.

65. **(C)**   15. Pre-algebra. $\frac{1}{2}$ of 16 = $\frac{1}{2} \times 16 = 8$;   7 more than 8 = 8 + 7 = 15.

66. **(A)**   (a), (b), and (c) are equal. Comparison. Each shaded area represents $\frac{1}{2}$ of the rectangle.

67. **(C)**   (c) is greater than (a) and less than (b). Comparison. (a) = 12, (b) = 16, and (c) = 15. Multiplication of fractions.

68. **(B)**   48. Series.

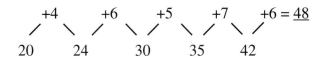

Rule: Add a number, add 2 more than the previous number, add 1 less than the previous, add 2 more than the previous, etc. 42 + 6 = 48.

69. **(A)**   10. Pre-algebra. $\frac{2}{3}$ of 21 = $\frac{2}{3} \times 21 = 14$. 4 less than 14 = 14 − 4 = 10.

70. **(B)**   17. Pre-algebra. $\frac{1}{5}$ of 35 = $\frac{1}{5} \times 35 = 7$. 10 more than 7 = 7 + 10 = 17.

71. **(C)**   (a) is less than (b) and greater than (c). Comparison. (a) = $\frac{5}{9} = \frac{10}{18}$, (b) = $\frac{2}{3} = \frac{12}{18}$, and (c) = $\frac{1}{2} = \frac{9}{18}$. Find a common denominator: 18.

72. **(B)**   140. Series.

$$
\begin{array}{ccccccccc}
& -20 & & -16 & & -12 & & -8 & & -4 = \underline{140} \\
& \diagup\diagdown & & \diagup\diagdown & & \diagup\diagdown & & \diagup\diagdown & \diagup \\
200 & & 180 & & 164 & & 152 & & 144
\end{array}
$$

Rule: Subtract 20, then amounts that drop by 4 each time. 144 − 4 = 140.

73. **(B)** 13. Pre-algebra. $\frac{1}{10}$ of $90 = \frac{1}{10} \times 90 = 9$. The number sub-tracted from 22 to give 9 is $22 - 9$, or 13.

74. **(B)** 6. Pre-algebra. Half of $72 = \frac{1}{2} \times 72 = 36$. The number which multiplied by itself gives 36 is 6.

75. **(C)** 70. Series.

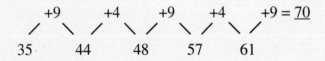

Rule: Add 9, then add 4. $61 + 9 = 70$.

76. **(D)** 1956. Series.

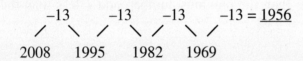

Rule: Subtract 13. $1969 - 13 = 1956$.

77. **(A)** 14. Pre-algebra. 3 more than $95 = 95 + 3 = 98$. The number multiplied by 7 to give 98 is $98 \div 7$, or 14.

78. **(D)** 35. Series.

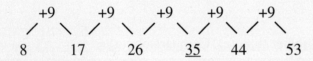

Rule: Add 9. $26 + 9 = 35$.

79. **(B)** (b) is greater than (a) and greater than (c). Comparison. (a) = .55, (b) = .60, and (c) = .50. Convert to the same form of fraction. You could also use ratios or percents.

80. **(C)** 39. Pre-algebra. 5 less than $18 = 18 - 5 = 13$. The number divided by 3 to yield 13 is 3 times 13, or 39.

81. **(B)** *AD* is less than *AC*. Comparison. Since the triangle is equilateral, all sides are equal in length. The altitude or height (*AD*) in an equilateral triangle is shorter than the sides, but greater than half a side.

82. **(A)** 5. Pre-algebra. 20 less than 45 = 45 – 20 = 25. The number multiplied by itself to give 25 is 5.

83. **(C)** (a) is greater than (b) and greater than (c). Comparison. (a) = $\frac{7}{16}$ = $\frac{14}{32}$, (b) = $\frac{3}{8}$ = $\frac{12}{32}$, and (c) = $\frac{13}{32}$. Find a common denominator: 32.

84. **(B)** *AE* is equal to *DE*. Comparison. As the circle is drawn, the only thing we can be sure of is that the radii, *AE* and *DE*, are equal in length. As shown in the picture, the other relationships do not appear to be true.

85. **(B)** 200. Pre-algebra. 20 less than 30 = 30 – 20 = 10. The number divided by 20 that gives 10 is 20 × 10, or 200.

86. **(C)** 2. Series.

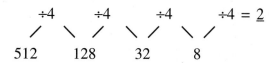

Rule: Divide by 4. 8 ÷ 4 = 2.

87. **(B)** 2. Series.

$$\begin{array}{ccccccccc} & \div3 & & -3 & & \div3 & & -3 & & \div3 = \underline{2} \\ 90 & & 30 & & 27 & & 9 & & 6 \end{array}$$

Rule: Divide by 3, then subtract 3. 6 ÷ 3 = 2.

88. **(C)** 16. Pre-algebra. $\frac{1}{3}$ of 36 = $\frac{1}{3} \times 36$ = 12. If $\frac{3}{4}$ of a number is 12, the number must be $\frac{4}{3}$ of 12. $\frac{4}{3}$ of 12 = $\frac{4}{3} \times 12$ = 16

89. **(D)** XL. Series.

$$\begin{array}{ccccccc} & +5 & & +5 & & +5 & & +5 = \underline{40} \text{ or } \underline{\text{XL}} \\ \text{XX} & & \text{XXV} & & \text{XXX} & & \text{XXXV} \end{array}$$

Rule: Add 5. 35 + 5 = 40, which is written XL in Roman numerals.

90. **(A)** 17. Series.

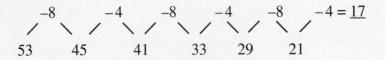

Rule: Subtract 8, subtract 4. 21 − 4 = 17.

91. **(D)** 96. Pre-algebra. 4 multiplied by itself = 4 × 4 = 16. If $\frac{1}{6}$ of a number is 16, the number must be 6 × 16, or 96.

92. **(D)** (c) is less than (a) and less than (b). Comparison. (a) 16 ÷ 8 = 2, and 2 × 2 = 4, (b) 16 ÷ 2 = 8, and 8 × 8 = 64, and (c) 8 × 2 = 16, and 16 ÷ 16 = 1.

93. **(C)** 72. Series.

$$
\begin{array}{ccccccccccccc}
 & +2 & & +7 & & +2 & & +7 & & +2 & & +7 & \\
\diagup & & \diagdown\diagup & & \diagdown\diagup & & \diagdown\diagup & & \diagdown\diagup & & \diagdown\diagup & & \diagdown \\
61 & & 63 & & 70 & & \underline{72} & & 79 & & 81 & & 88
\end{array}
$$

Rule: Add 2, then add 7. 70 + 2 = 72.

94. **(B)** 24. Pre-algebra. $\frac{1}{8}$ of 32 = $\frac{1}{8}$ × 32 = 4. The number divided by 6 to get 4 is 6 times 4, or 24.

95. **(D)** 48. Series.

$$
\begin{array}{ccccccccccccc}
 & -4 & & \times 2 & & -4 & & \times 2 & & -4 & & \times 2 = \underline{48} \\
\diagup & & \diagdown\diagup & & \diagdown\diagup & & \diagdown\diagup & & \diagdown\diagup & & \diagdown\diagup \\
13 & & 9 & & 18 & & 14 & & 28 & & 24
\end{array}
$$

Rule: Subtract 4, then multiply by 2.   24 × 2 = 48.

96. **(D)** (a), (b), and (c) are all equal. Comparison. Each part of the picture graph represents 20. (a) = 2 × 10 = 20, (b) = 10 + 5 + 5 = 20, and (c) = 4 × 5 = 20.

97. **(B)** 1. Pre-algebra. $\frac{5}{6}$ of 30 = $\frac{5}{6}$ × 30 = 25. 4 more than 25 = 25 + 4 = 29. The number subtracted from 30 to give 29 must be 30 − 29, or 1.

98. **(C)** (a) ≠ (b), (b) ≠ (c), (a) ≠ (c). Comparison. None of the three algebraic expressions are equal.

99. **(B)** 74, 70. Series.

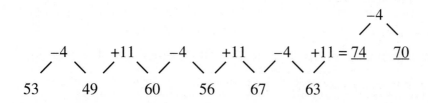

Rule: Subtract 4, then add 11.   63 + 11 = 74, 74 − 4 = 70.

100. **(A)** (a) is equal to (b). Comparison. (a) = 24 ounces, or $1\frac{1}{2}$ pounds, (b) = 24 ounces or $1\frac{1}{2}$ pounds, and (c) = 2 pounds, or 32 ounces. We must know that 1 pound is equal to 16 ounces.

101. **(D)** 30. Pre-algebra. $\frac{1}{2}$ of 8 = $\frac{1}{2}$ × 8 = 4, the product of 5 and 4 = 5 × 4 = 20, twice 20 = 2 × 20 = 40. The number added to 10 to get 40 is 40 − 10, or 30.

102. **(D)** 93. Series.

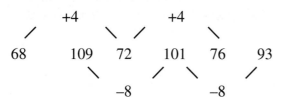

Rule: Use every other number. For 68, 72, 76, add 4. For 109, 101, subtract 8. 101 − 8 = 93. It is possible to do this using one number after the other, but the rule is more complicated: the number you subtract is 4 less than the previous number that you added, and the number you add is 8 less than the previous number that you subtracted.

103. **(B)** (a) is equal to (c). Comparison. (a) = 2^4 = 2 × 2 × 2 × 2 = 16, (b) = 3^3 = 3 × 3 × 3 = 27, and (c) = 4^2 = 4 × 4 = 16. The exponent tells the number of times the base number must be written before it is multiplied.

104. **(C)** (a) minus (d) equals (b) plus (d). Comparison. Here, the length of the bar on the bar graph gives the size. (a) = 50, (b) = 30, (c) = 20, and (d) = 10.

105. **(A)** 5. Series.

$$\overset{-3}{\diagup\diagdown}\ \overset{\div 3}{\diagup\diagdown}\ \overset{-3}{\diagup\diagdown}\ \overset{\div 3}{\diagup\diagdown}\ \overset{-3}{\diagup\diagdown}$$

84   81   27   24   8

Rule: Subtract 3, then divide by 3. $8 - 3 = 5$.

106. (B)   12. Pre-algebra. $\frac{1}{2}$ of $16 = \frac{1}{2} \times 16 = 8$. 3 times $8 = 3 \times 8 = 24$. The number multiplied by 2 to give 24 is $24 \div 2$, or 12.

107. (A)   8. Pre-algebra. $\frac{2}{3}$ of $42 = \frac{2}{3} \times 42 = 28$, $\frac{5}{9}$ of $36 = \frac{5}{9} \times 36 = 20$. The number added to 20 to get 28 is $28 - 20$, or 8.

108. (C)   (a) is equal to (b) which is less than (c). Comparison. (a) $= .3 \times .4 = .12$, (b) $= .6 \times .2 = .12$, and (c) $= 1 \times 1.2 = 1.2$. When numbers are multiplied, add the number of decimal places in the factors to get the number of decimal places in the answer.

109. (B)   The area of the parallelogram is 12. Comparison. This is more of a geometry question. The area of a parallelogram is given by multiplying the base times the height, in this case 3×4, which equals 12. We can figure out the lengths of the slanting sides in the parallelogram using the Pythagorean Theorem: $a^2 + b^2 = c^2$. $3^2 + 4^2 = 9 + 16 = 25$, and $5^2 = 25$, so the other side is 5. Because b is the correct answer, we don't actually need to know this length for this problem.

110. (A)   59, 52, 61. Series.

$$\overset{-7}{\diagup\diagdown}\ \overset{+9}{\diagup\diagdown}$$

+5   −1   +6   −3   +7   −5   +8 =   <u>59</u>   <u>52</u>   <u>61</u>

$$\diagup\diagdown\diagup\diagdown\diagup\diagdown\diagup\diagdown\diagup\diagdown\diagup\diagdown\diagup$$

42   47   46   52   49   56   51

Rule: Add, then subtract, then add, etc. The amount we add increases by 1. The amount we subtract increases by 2. $51 + 8 = 59$, $59 - 7 = 52$, and $52 + 9 = 61$.

111. (B)   12. Pre-algebra. $\frac{1}{4}$ of $12 = \frac{1}{4} \times 12 = 3$. 2 times $3 = 2 \times 3 = 6$. The number subtracted from 10 to give 6 is $10 - 6$, or 4. $\frac{1}{3}$ of a number equals 4, so the number must be 3×4, or 12.

112. **(D)**   69. Series.

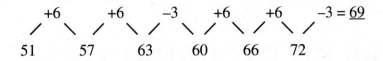

Rule: Add 6, add 6, subtract 3. 72 − 3 = 69.

Subtest 3: Reading

DETAILED EXPLANATIONS
OF ANSWERS

Comprehension

113. **(C)**   According to the passage, star movements (B) appeared in the medieval almanac. Church feast days and elaborate calendars (D) were added in the sixteenth century, as were weather predictions (A). Jokes and humor (C) appeared in the seventeenth century.

114. **(D)**   The almanac did not include extra days (A). Contemporary almanacs are not discussed in this passage (C). The passage discusses almanacs from medieval times, so Franklin could not have invented the almanac (C); however, Franklin published his *Poor Richard's Almanac* from 1732–1758 (B).

115. **(C)**   Choices (A), (B), and (D) are not supported by the passage.

116. **(C)**   The passage states that almanacs in Germany included "sophisticated, contemporary poetry by serious authors."

117. **(A)**   The passage describes how almanacs in the sixteenth century began to be issued every year and included weather predictions.

118. **(D)**   The passage does not describe how the coach felt about the protest.

119. **(B)**   The passage describes how the players promised to play the next scheduled game that season.

120. **(A)**   The players met with the Director of Athletics to discuss their reasons for walking off of the court. The word "problems" best expresses this.

121. **(D)**   The passage does state that the members of the team will play again; however, there were six members who walked off and not five (A). It did not mention any apologies (B, C). But it did state that the six members would practice despite their concerns.

122. **(C)**   This passage does not support choices (A), (B), or (D).

123. **(B)**   While it is expressed that a literacy program needs to be empathetic towards its participants (C), the overall goal is to teach its participants to read and write (B). The program

should not be sympathetic (D) but should meet the needs of both functional (A) and complete illiterates.

124. **(D)** The author is concerned that the issue of adult literacy is not viewed as a serious problem (D) since politicians do not seem to be addressing it. Calling adult literacy a "women's interest issue" does not mean that more women are affected by it (A). Being a social problem does not make it less real (B). Many women are politicians (C).

125. **(A)** The emphasis placed on empathy and on ensuring that the participants experience success shows how the self-esteem of the participants is an important responsibility for literacy programs (A). Political support is not the responsibility of the program (B). Books and magazines (C, D) are not mentioned as part of a literacy program's responsibilities.

126. **(D)** The passage describes how a functionally illiterate person can read and write a little (A and C) and can be helped by a literacy program (B). The correct answer is (D), all of the above.

127. **(B)** Weighted, plastic barrel-shaped tubes were used to help clean up the environment (B). Offshore drilling can result in oil spills (A) and coastal winds and tides (C and D) carry the oil to the shore quickly.

128. **(D)** The passage does not describe who pays the cost of oil spill cleanups (D).

129. **(A)** The passage says some states want to help cover the cost of cleaning up oil spills.

130. **(C)** The passage describes how the workers tried to minimize the damage caused by the oil spill by using the weighted, barrel-shaped tubes (A) and by shoveling oil-covered sand into plastic bags for removal (B). The correct answer is (C).

131. **(B)** The opening sentence states that the price of cleaning up after oil spills is increasing, and the passage continues to describe how numerous spills have occurred.

132. **(D)** The last paragraph of the passage states the breakdown of a proper diet for a person with diabetes (D).

133. **(B)** The second paragraph states that the standard treatment for juvenile diabetics is insulin replacement therapy (B).

134. **(A)** The first paragraph of the passage describes how diabetes is the result of insufficient amounts of insulin made by the body. Insulin is used by the body to take glucose from the blood for fuel; a deficiency in insulin results in high blood levels and low tissue levels of glucose (A). The presence of abnormal pancreatic cells causes juvenile diabetes (B). Adult diabetes is more common in obese adults (C). Obese juveniles (D) are not discussed in the passage.

135. **(D)**   The third paragraph details how high levels of fat in the blood interfere with insulin absorption (D).

136. **(D)**   Diabetes is usually detected when the person is a juvenile (A) or when the person is 50–70 years old (B). The correct answer is (D).

137. **(C)**   "Successful" (C) is the best choice to mean "star" as in "star quarterback."

138. **(C)**   The author states in the second paragraph that students who cannot maintain a 2.0 grade-point average should not be permitted to participate in any sports (C). The other choices describe the opposite of what the author finds irritating in athletes.

139. **(D)**   Hockey is the only sport not described; football ("quarterbacks") (A), basketball ("point guard") (B), and baseball ("infielders") (C) are described.

140. **(D)**   The passage describes how the author does not like to see uneducated athletes; it does not describe how the author prefers teachers or students over athletes (A and B), or how the author prefers citizens over scholars (C).

141. **(D)**   The author does not describe athletics as any of the mentioned choices.

142. **(B)**   The passage describes how the pesticide is used to kill soil pests (B).

143. **(C)**   The passage describes how once the river water reaches Lake Shasta, the lake will have to be tested for poison (C). We do not know the safety status of the water from this passage.

144. **(A)**   The passage states how thousands of trout and other fish were poisoned along a 45-mile stretch of river after the oil spill.

145. **(A)**   Poisonous is the best choice.

146. **(D)**   The passage states how the train was carrying 19,500 gallons (D) of the pesticide.

147. **(A)**   The passage states how residents around the Sacramento River in California were warned to stay away from the tainted water (A).

148. **(B)**   The passage describes lead poisoning and legislation in California to test for it (B). It does not describe how to stop it entirely (A), its history (C), or its effects around the world (D).

149. **(C)**   The word disorders refers to the life-threatening ailments (C) that result from lead poisoning.

150. **(B)**   The passage states that 50,000 cases will be detected in California as a result of the newly mandated tests (B).

151. **(D)**   Children from the ages of 1–5 will be tested annually, which means every year (D).

152. **(C)**   The beginning of the passage describes how health authorities consider lead poisoning to be the most common and devastating environmental disease of young children. The end of the passage describes how lead poisoning, if undetected, can result in life-threatening disorders. The correct answer is (C).

Vocabulary

153. **(A)**   The word *vigilant* means *watchful* (A) or observant. *Reckless* (B) means rash and careless and would be incorrect since it is closer to being an antonym of *vigilant*. *Lazy* (C) means inactive or slothful and would also be the wrong answer. *Powerful* (D) means strong and does not imply watchfulness.

154. **(B)**   The word *parable* is a kind of *tale* (B) or morality story. A *teacher* (A) might be the sort of person who would tell a *parable* to instruct others, but this answer choice is incorrect since a teacher is not a parable. A *stronghold* (C) is a domain in which a person may have security or safety; this choice is also incorrect. Choice (D), *strength*, means power and is not a synonym of the word *parable*.

155. **(D)**   A *buoyant* spirit is one that is joyful or *light-hearted* (D). A *scary* (A) spirit is one that inflicts fear or dread—which is incorrect. Choice (B), *depressed*, means gloomy or sad and is an antonym of *buoyant*. *Supernatural* (D) means abnormal and would not be a synonym for *buoyant*.

156. **(C)**   The word *gracious* describes someone who is thoughtful or *courteous* (C). This word does not mean *elegant* (A), since elegant describes a person's refinement. It does not mean *beautiful* (B), since beauty refers to a person's attractiveness. Nor does it mean *extravagant* (D), which describes something's luxury.

157. **(B)**   When you pay *homage* to someone, you bestow *honor* (B) upon them. *Prizes* (A) or gifts may accompany *homage*, but *homage* is the act of reverence. An *insult* (C) or slander would be incorrect since they are antonyms of *homage*. *Wages* (D) are a person's salary or pay and are not related in giving honor to someone.

158. **(C)**   A *grievous* burden is *disturbing* (C) or sad. Answer choice (A), *joyous*, which means bright or happy, is an antonym of *grievous* and incorrect. If something were *grave* (B) or *serious* (D), it would be important and would not necessarily be *grievous* which makes both answer selections incorrect.

159. **(D)**   An *incessant* noise is *constant* (D). It is not *brief* (A) or periodic; those selections would be the word's antonyms. Though an *incessant* noise could be *loud* (B), loudness measures the noise's intensity, whereas an *incessant* noise describes its duration. Likewise, answer choice (C) is incorrect since *pleasant*, which means good or favorable, does not even relate to the word *incessant*.

160. **(A)**   When an *invincible* army is not able to be defeated, it is *unconquerable* (A). An-

swer choice (B), *invisible*, may relate to why the army was so powerful, but it does not relate to whether it is *invincible* or not. Answer choice (C), *feeble*, is incorrect since *feeble* is an antonym of *invincible*. *Minute* (D) means small or insignificant and does not relate to *invincible*.

161. **(C)** The word *portly* means *heavy* (C) or stocky. Answer choice (A), *sloppy*, means messy or careless and (B), *well-groomed*, means clean and ordered; these words are opposites and would not be correct choices. The last answer choice, *slim* (D), which means thin or lean, is the antonym of *portly* and would also be incorrect.

162. **(D)** *Ornate* furnishings are *elaborate* (D) and lavish. They are not *simple* (A), which means easy or basic, the antonym of *ornate*. Answer choice (B), *expensive*, which means costly or valuable, and (C), *cheap*, which means budget or flimsy, could only describe the cost of the furnishings and would not be correct answer choices.

163. **(A)** Movements that are *encumbered* are not able to move freely, they are *restricted* (A). Answer choice (B) would not be correct since *encourage* means to assure or advocate. *Lighten* (C) means to ease or unburden and is incorrect. Choice (D), *watched*, means viewed or examined and is also incorrect.

164. **(B)** An *avid* fan is someone who is enthusiastic, excited, or *ardent* (B) about his/her interest. Though a fan may become *uncontrollable* (A), to be enthusiastic about something is much different than being *uncontrollable*. A *lifeless* (C) fan would be the antonym of the *avid* fan—dull and lifeless. Answer choice (D), *gloomy*, which means sad or depressed, would be incorrect also.

165. **(B)** When you *vie* for something, you need to contend or *compete* (B) for it. You might be required to *wait* (A), which means to anticipate, but this answer choice is incorrect. Answer choice (C), *advertise*, means to publicize or broadcast and is not a synonym for *vie*. You might choose the last answer choice, *survive* (D), which means to endure or persevere, since a connection might be made to the word—in that you hope to *survive* the competition—but it is not correct.

166. **(D)** When you have an *ample* supply of something, you have more than you need; the amount is *abundant* (D). Answer choice (A), *inexpensive*, means reasonable or low-priced, and is not the correct answer choice. *Insufficient* (B), which means lacking or scanty, would be the antonym of *ample*. Lastly, *equal* (C), which means even or uniform, would also be an incorrect answer choice.

167. **(B)** The word *devise* means to *create* (B). Answer choice (A), *eliminate*, which means to exterminate (an antonym of *devise*) is an incorrect answer choice. Choice (C), which means to select, is also incorrect as is choice (D), *delineate*, which means to depict or portray.

168. **(B)** A *chronic* ailment is unceasing or *perpetual* (B) throughout a person's life. Answer choice (A), *small*, meaning little or tiny is an incorrect choice. *Brief* (C), which means tempo-

rary, would be incorrect since it is the antonym of *chronic*. Choice (D), *unknown*, is also incorrect since it means strange or hidden.

169. **(A)** The word *haggard* means starved or *scrawny* (A). It does not mean *dirty* (B), which means filthy or unclean, *cautious* (C), which means careful, or *haggle* (D) which means to bargain or argue.

170. **(D)** The word *stealthily* means slyly or *secretly* (D). *Openly* (A), which means candidly or out in the open, would be incorrect because it is an antonym of *stealthily*. Answer choice (B), *quickly*, means quick or immediate and (C), *randomly*, means by chance, and are both incorrect answer choices.

171. **(A)** The word *pathetic* means *miserable* (A) or pitiful. If something is *miserable*, it might be *undesirable* (B), which means unwanted, but this is not a correct answer choice in this context. Answer choice (C), *ruthless*, which means merciless and choice (D), *frustrating*, are also wrong answer choices.

172. **(D)** A speech is *verbose* if it is *wordy* (D) or long-winded. Answer choice (A), *resignation*, would be a wrong answer choice. *Short* (B), which means little or small, would be incorrect since it is an antonym of verbose. *Persuasive* (C), which means convincing or compelling, would also be a wrong answer choice.

173. **(A)** The word *savor* means to appreciate or *enjoy* (A). It does not mean *save* (B), which means to preserve or maintain, *prepare* (C), which means to arrange or make, or *serve* (D), which means to aid or help.

174. **(B)** The word *rigid* means *unyielding* (B). It does not mean *loud* (D), which means noisy, or *tedious* (C), which means dull. It is the opposite of *warm-hearted* (A).

Subtest 4: Mathematics

DETAILED EXPLANATIONS OF ANSWERS

Concepts

175. **(B)**   The digit that comes immediately after the tenths place is 7, which is greater than 5. So we add 1 to the digit in the tenths place: $3.47 \cong 3.5$.

176. **(A)**   Arrange like terms vertically and add:

$$\begin{array}{r} 3n + 4m - 6 \\ -4n + 3m + 6 \\ \hline -n + 7m + 0 \end{array}$$

Rearrange terms: $7m - n$

177. **(B)**   P is 6 spaces to the left of the Y-axis, so the first number in the pair is –6. P is also 7 spaces above the X-axis, so the second number is 7. Therefore, the position of P is represented by (–6, 7).

178. **(C)**   Let x represent the smaller number, so the larger number must be $(x + 1)$. Then the sum of the two numbers must be: $x + (x + 1) = 2x + 1 = 55$. To solve this equation,

add –1 to both sides:

$$\begin{array}{r} 2x + 1 = 55 \\ -1 \quad -1 \\ \hline \end{array}$$

divide both sides by 2: $2x = 54$ $x = 27$.

The smaller number is $x = 27$ and the larger number is $x + 1 = 27 + 1 = 28$.

179. **(C)**   Replace x with 2, y with –5, and z with 0: $3x - 2y + 5z$
$= 3(2) - 2(-5) + 5(0)$
Simplify: $= 6 + 10 + 0 = 16$

180. **(D)** $12\dfrac{3}{4} + 5\dfrac{1}{3} = (12 + 5) + \dfrac{3}{4} + \dfrac{1}{3} = 17 + \dfrac{9+4}{12} = 17 + \dfrac{13}{12} = 18\dfrac{1}{12}.$

181. **(B)**   All the numbers listed have factors, except 37. So 37 is a prime number.

182. **(C)**   Since width of square = length of square, the number representing the area of a square must be a perfect square number. That is, the number must have two identical factors.

Here is one way to test for identical factors:

$42 = 2 \times 21 = 3 \times 14 = 6 \times 7$. (no pair of identical factors)
$45 = 3 \times 15 = 5 \times 9$. (no pair of identical factors)
$49 = 7 \times 7$. (one pair of identical factors)
$51 = 3 \times 17$. (no pair of identical factors)
The answer must be 49.

183. **(D)** $\quad 3(2 + 5) - 12 = (3 \times 7) - 12 = 21 - 12 = 9.$

184. **(A)** $\quad 5\frac{1}{4} \times 2\frac{1}{3} = \frac{21}{4} \times \frac{7}{3} = \frac{49}{4} = 12\frac{1}{4}.$

185. **(A)** $\quad 5.\bar{3} = 5.333 \ldots$ To change this number to a mixed number, let $n = 5.3$ . . . . (1)
Append the repeating digit (3) once to obtain a modified equation, $n = 5.33$ . . . . (2)
Since there is only one repeating digit, multiply both sides of the equation by 10:
$10n = 53.3$ . . . . (3)
Subtract equation (2) from equation (3): $\quad\begin{aligned} 10n &= 53.3 \\ n &= \underline{\ 5.3} \\ 9n &= 48 \end{aligned}$

Divide both sides by 9: $\dfrac{48}{9} = 5\dfrac{3}{9} = 5\dfrac{1}{3}.$

186. **(D)** $\quad$ To express 75 as a percent of 60, write: $\dfrac{75}{60} \times \dfrac{100}{1} = 125\%.$

187. **(A)** $\quad 2\dfrac{1}{2} = 2.5.$ So $2\dfrac{1}{2} = 2.5 \times 100 = 250\%$

188. **(D)** $\quad q(r - s) = qr - qs.$

189. **(A)** $\quad$ One of the most efficient methods is to add only the measures of the shortest sticks:
(a) $(3 + 4) = 7$ and $7 > 5$.

It would be possible to join sticks measuring 3 units, 4 units, and 5 units, end-to-end to form a triangle. This must be the right set. [Just to verify, we may try the sticks in sets (b), (c), and (d). For example, for set (b), $(2 + 5) = 7$ and $7 = 7$. There is no way to join these three sticks end-to-end to form a triangle.]

190. **(D)** $\quad$ If we add the three numbers in each set, we find that the only set that adds to exactly 180 is set (d).

191. **(B)** $\quad$ To determine which is the least crowded classroom, we must first find out how

many square feet of space each child has in each classroom:
In classroom A, each child has $770 \div 22 = 35$ ft^2 of space.
In classroom B, each child has $960 \div 24 = 40$ ft^2 of space.
In classroom C, each child has $540 \div 18 = 30$ ft^2 of space.
In classroom D, each child has $627 \div 19 = 33$ ft^2 of space.

Classroom B has the most space per student; so it is the <u>least</u> crowded.

192. **(B)** The wettest month was April, with 60 in. of rain. The driest month was March, with only 30 in. of rainfall. The difference is $(60 - 30) = 30$ in. of rainfall.

193. **(B)** The total rainfall for the five months was $(40 + 50 + 30 + 60 + 50) = 230$ in. The average rainfall for the 5 months was $230 \div 5 = 46$ in.

194. **(A)** Notice that each space on the test scale represents 5 points. Matthew scored 55 points in September and 80 points in October. So his score rose by 25 points in October. If we check the months of November, January, March, May, June and August, his score rose by fewer points in each of these months than in October.

195. **(D)** Matthew scored 90 in January and 100 in March, so his score improved by $(100 - 90) = 10$ points.

196. **(A)** The '3' in 29.536 is in the hundredths position.

197. **(C)** An acute triangle is one that has exactly three acute triangles. The triangle in (c) is the only one that has exactly 3 acute angles.

198. **(D)** The small box signifies that angle ACB is a right angle (90°), so the sum of angles ACD and BCD is 90°. Then the measure of angle ACD must be $(90° - 74°) = 16°$.

Problem-Solving

199. **(B)** To determine Carol's earnings for 8 hours, multiply the hourly earning by 8: $9.50 \times 8 = \$76.00$

200. **(B)** The increase in population is $(468 - 360) = 108$. Express 108 to a percent of 360:
$\frac{108}{360} \times \frac{100}{1} = 30\%$.

201. **(D)** First, find the area of the floor, using the given formula: Area $= 18 \times 15 = 270$ ft^2. To find the cost of carpeting the floor, multiply the cost of carpeting 1 square foot by the area of the floor: $\$1.50 \times 270 = \$405$.

202. **(C)** First, convert 2 minutes to seconds, to make computation easy: 2 min. $= 2 \times 60 =$

120 seconds. If in 10 seconds the bee travels 45 m, then in 1 second it must travel $45 \div 10 = \dfrac{45}{10}$ meters. In 120 seconds, it must travel $\dfrac{45}{10} \times \dfrac{120}{1} = 540$ meters.

203. (A) Rhonda and Paula together own $\dfrac{1}{2} + \dfrac{2}{5} = \dfrac{5+4}{10} = \dfrac{9}{10}$. Then Brenda owns $1 - \dfrac{9}{10} = \dfrac{1}{10}$.

204. (A) At the end of the year, the value of the car decreases to $100 - 14 = 86\%$. Find 86% of the value of a new car:

$\dfrac{86}{100} \times \dfrac{15,000}{1} = \$12,900$.

205. (A) With a discount of 25%, Alice would have to pay only $(100 - 25) = 75\%$ of the marked price. 75% of $460 = \dfrac{75}{100} \times \dfrac{460}{1} = \$345$.

206. (B) From 6:00 p.m. to 7:30 p.m. is 1 hour 30 minutes $= 1\dfrac{1}{2}$ hours. Since, in $1\dfrac{1}{2}$ hours, Mrs. Smith traveled 81 miles, in 1 hour she must have traveled $81 \div 1\dfrac{1}{2} = \dfrac{81}{1} \div \dfrac{3}{2} = \dfrac{81}{1} \times \dfrac{2}{3} = 54$ miles.

207. (B) In a rectangle, the opposite sides are equal in measure. So there are two sides each measuring 35 ft. and two sides each measuring 25 ft. So the four pieces that make up the given rectangle must add up to $(35 + 35) + (25 + 25) = 120$ ft.

208. (D) Convert 7 kg to grams: 7 kg $= 7 \times 1,000 = 7,000$ g. To find the number of harvest mice that would weigh as much as 1 rabbit, divide: $7,000 \div 7 = 1,000$.

209. (D) 1/100 in. = 1 hundredth of an in. So the fairy fly is 1 hundredth of an inch long. The Goliath beetle is 5 in. long. Convert 5 in. to hundredths of an inch, so we can deal with only hundredths of an inch: 5 in. $= 5 \times 100 = 500$ hundredths of an inch. The ratio of the length of a fairy fly to the length of a Goliath beetle is 1 to 500, that is, 1:500.

210. (A) Convert 156 kg to g, so we can work with g only: 156 kg $= 156 \times 1,000 = 156,000$ g. The required fraction is $\dfrac{2}{156,000} = \dfrac{1}{78,000}$.

211. **(D)** The blue whale is heavier than an elephant by $(200,000 - 6,600) = 193,400$ kg.

212. **(D)** There are 16 slices of bread. $\frac{5}{8}$ of $16 = \frac{5}{8} \times \frac{16}{1} = 10$ slices.

213. **(C)** $30 represents $(100 + 20) = 120\%$ of the cost price. The cost price must be $\frac{30}{120} \times \frac{100}{1} = \$25$.

214. **(B)** Since the farmer cultivates 18% of the land, then $(100 - 18) = 82\%$ must lie uncultivated. 82% of $3,000 = \frac{82}{100} \times \frac{3,000}{1} = 2,460$ acres.

215. **(D)** For every $\frac{1}{8}$ in. of body length, an insect jumps 13 in. For every full inch, the insect must jump $13 \div \frac{1}{8} = \frac{13}{1} \times \frac{8}{1}$ in. For 5 in. of body length, the insect would jump $\frac{13}{1} \times \frac{8}{1} \times 5 = 520$ in.

216. **(B)** The rectangle has a total of 60 small squares, of which 24 are not shaded. The fraction of the rectangle that is not shaded is $\frac{24}{60} = \frac{2}{5}$.

217. **(B)** 36 of the 60 small squares are shaded. This represents $\frac{36}{60} \times \frac{100}{1} = 60\%$.

218. **(A)** Alice's total score on the first 4 tests must be $(82 + 79 + 91 + 85) = 337$. Her total score on the first five tests was 425; this included her score on the fifth test. So her score on the fifth test must be $(425 - 337) = 88$.

219. **(B)** The rectangle in the picture is a square, since each side measures $(10 + 10) = 20$ cm. The area of the square must be $20 \times 20 = 400$ cm^2. The area of each clear region is one-quarter of a full circle with the same radius. The area of such circle is $(3.14 \times 10^2) = 314$ cm^2. The area of each clear region must be $314 \div 4 = 78.5$ cm^2. The combined areas of the two quarter circles must be $78.5 \times 2 = 157$ cm^2. The area of the unshaded region must be $(400 - 157) = 243$ cm^2.

220. **(A)** The wire is shaped like a half circle. The circumference of a full circle with the same diameter would be $(3.14 \times 14) = 43.96$ in. Since the wire is only a half circle, its length must be $43.96 \div 2 = 21.98$ in.

221. **(A)**   The area of the parallelogram would be the same as that of a rectangle with the same length and height. That is, $12 \times 25 = 300$ cm^2.

222. **(B)**   The total amount that Sue spent on food and drink is ($2.25 + $3.50 + $5.00) = $10.75. The remainder from $20.00 must be ($20.00 − $10.75) = $9.25. This is the amount she donated to charity.

223. **(D)**   Sue spent $3.50 on chips. Express this as a percent of $20.00: $\dfrac{3.50}{20.00} \times \dfrac{100}{1} =$ 17.5%.

224. **(A)**   It would be most convenient to work with similar units, so convert 1.2 liters to milliliters: 1.2 liters = $(1.2 \times 1{,}000) = 1{,}200$ milliliters. The 'cool aid' consisted of $(1{,}200$ milliliters + 300 milliliters) = 1,500 milliliters. Now express 1,200 as a percent of 1,500: $\dfrac{1{,}200}{1{,}500}$ $\times \dfrac{100}{1} = 80\%$.

225. **(A)**   The ratio of boys to girls may be written as 52:48 and the sum of the terms is $(52 + 48) = 100$. What per 500 is equivalent to 52 per 100? Let n represent the unknown number. Then we can write: $52:100 = n:500$ or $\dfrac{52}{100} = \dfrac{n}{500}$. So $100 \times n = 52 \times 500 = 26{,}000$ and $n = 260$.

226. **(C)**   Let x = basic rate and 1.5x = overtime rate. The 48 hours total consists of 40 hours at the basic rate and 8 hours at the overtime rate. Then $40x + (8)(1.5x) = \$899.60$. Simplifying, $52x = 899.60$, so x = $17.30. The overtime rate, denoted by $1.5x = (1.5)(\$17.30) = \$25.95$.

227. **(A)**   Let x = amount to be invested into a second account. To determine the simple interest for one year, multiply the amount invested by the corresponding percent. Then ($6,000)(.13) + (x)(.1625) = $1,348.75. Simplifying, $780.00 + .1625x = $1,348.75. Solving, x = $3,500.00.

228. **(B)**   Let x = number of ounces of pure water. The amount of salt in each of the 3 solutions becomes 0x, (.12)(50), and (.04)(x + 50). Then 0x + (.12)(50) = .04(x + 50). This becomes $0 + 6 = .04x + 2$. So, $4 = .04x$ and thus x = 100.

229. **(B)**   Let x = her present age. Then x − 1 = last year's age and x + 31 is her age in 31 years. So, x + 31 = 3(x − 1); then 2x = 34, and x = 17.

230. **(D)**   Let x = Wendy's time alone. In 1 hour, Wendy does $\dfrac{1}{x}$ of the work, Dave does $\dfrac{1}{6}$ of the work, and $\dfrac{1}{4}$ of the work is finished. Then $\dfrac{1}{x} + \dfrac{1}{6} = \dfrac{1}{4}$. Simplifying, $\dfrac{1}{x} = \dfrac{1}{4} - \dfrac{1}{6} = \dfrac{1}{12}$.

Solving, $x = 1 / \dfrac{1}{12} = 12$.

231. **(C)** At 3:20, the minute hand faces the 4, and the hour hand has moved $\dfrac{20}{60} = \dfrac{1}{3}$ of the distance between the 3 and the 4. Now, the two hands lie $\dfrac{2}{3}\left(1-\dfrac{1}{3}\right)$ of the distance between the numbers 3 and 4. In angular measure, the distance between these two numbers $= \dfrac{1}{12}(360°) = 30°$. Now, the angular measure between the two hands $= \left(\dfrac{2}{3}\right)(30°) = 20°$.

232. **(B)** Let x = width, 6x = length. The area is given by $(6x)(x) = 6x^2 = 37.5$, so $x^2 = 6.25$ and $x = \sqrt{6.25} = 2.5$. The width = 2.5 and the length = (6)(2.5) = 15. The perimeter = (2)(15) + (2)(2.5) = 35.

233. **(C)** The area of the entire circle = $(\pi)(4^2) = 16\pi$. The area of a sector with a 72° central angle $= \left(\dfrac{72}{360}\right)(16\pi) = 3.2\pi$.

234. **(B)** Let 1 = length of $\overline{AC} = \overline{AB}$. The quarter-circle for which $\overline{AC}$ is the radius has an area of $\left(\dfrac{1}{4}\right)(\pi)(1^2) = \dfrac{1}{4}\pi$. For the shaded area, the half-circle for which $\overline{AB}$ is the diameter has an area of $\left(\dfrac{1}{2}\right)(\pi)(.5^2) = \dfrac{1}{8}\pi$. Then the unshaded area $= \dfrac{1}{4}\pi - \dfrac{1}{8}\pi = \dfrac{1}{8}\pi$. Finally, $\dfrac{1}{8}\pi / \dfrac{1}{8}\pi = \dfrac{1}{1}$.

235. **(D)** A complete cycle of dispensed gum balls is 2 red, 3 yellow, 4 green, 5 white, which is 14 gum balls. Now $900 \div 14 = 64$ and a remainder of 4. This means that 64 cycles could be completed with (64)(14) = 896 gum balls. The last 4 gum balls are red, red, yellow, and yellow.

236. **(D)** Let x = actual number of questions on the exam. Then .75x = number of correct answers. By getting 3 more right, .75x + 3 is equivalent to .80x. Solving, .75x + 3 = .80x, we get x = 60. Thus, the number of questions answered correctly = (.75)(60) = 45.

237. **(A)** Since 70% are non-smokers, 100% − 70% = 30% are smokers. The required ratio is 30:70 or 3:7.

238. **(C)** After the first week, the price is $520 − (.20)($520) = $416. After the second week, the price becomes $416 − ($416)(.30) = $291.20.

Subtest 5: Language Skills

DETAILED EXPLANATIONS OF ANSWERS

Punctuation, Capitalization, and Usage

239. **(B)**   The sentence should read "John ate dinner last night" to match the tense of "to eat" with "last night."

240. **(A)**   The proper noun "Martha" needs to be capitalized.

241. **(D)**   There are no mistakes.

242. **(C)**   The list of objects in this example needs to be separated by commas: "I bought notebooks, pens, and a pencil for school."

243. **(C)**   "Holidays" is spelled incorrectly in this example.

244. **(A)**   The plural of "fish" is "fish," not "fishes."

245. **(C)**   The phrase "a good friend" should be separated by commas: "Bob, a good friend, is famous."

246. **(A)**   The phrase "Jennifer do" should be "Jennifer did" for proper agreement.

247. **(B)**   Since "Are you going to the library after school" is a question, it should end in a question mark.

248. **(A)**   The correct word should be the verb "buy" rather than its homonym "by."

249. **(D)**   There are no mistakes.

250. **(B)**   The quotation marks are incorrectly placed. The sentence should read, "What time is it?" Joy asked.

251. **(D)**   There are no mistakes.

252. **(A)**   The word "too," meaning "also," should be used.

253. **(C)** The word "they're," which is the contraction for "they are," should be used rather than the possessive pronoun "their."

254. **(B)** "Close" is a verb; the noun "clothes" is needed.

255. **(D)** There are no mistakes.

256. **(A)** "A lot" should be written as two words.

257. **(C)** The correct preposition should be "on" rather than "in" the table.

258. **(C)** "Much," which generally refers to an amount or quantity, is the proper adjective for this example.

259. **(A)** The speaker could not be in class and be home sleeping at the same time. The sentence should read "If I weren't in class, I'd be home sleeping."

260. **(A)** The correct form of the irregular verb "to break" in this example is "broke."

261. **(B)** "Lake Erie" is a proper noun and should be capitalized.

262. **(B)** A colon should be placed before the list begins. The sentence should read "We saw the following people at the park: Marie, John, and his aunt."

263. **(D)** There are no mistakes.

264. **(A)** Introductory clauses should be separated with a comma: "After we brought home the dog, my dad started to smile."

265. **(B)** The verb "to go" needs to agree with the plural subject bottles. The sentence should read: "The bottles of milk, and not the cereal, go in the refrigerator."

266. **(C)** An apostrophe should be added to show possession: "Judy's bike."

267. **(A)** A "role," rather than a "roll," is a character in a play.

268. **(C)** The word "writing" is incorrectly spelled in this example.

269. **(B)** The verb "paint" needs to agree with the subject "I."

270. **(D)** There are no mistakes.

271. **(C)** A sentence must start with a capital letter.

272. **(A)** The word is spelled "embarrassed."

273. **(C)** The possessive form of "who" is needed: "Whose book is this?" "Who's" is a contraction of "who is."

274. **(B)** This sentence requires the past tense of the verb: "Afterwards, she led us to the farm."

275. **(C)** The word is spelled "basically."

276. **(C)** This sentence requires the contraction "It's" or the phrase "It is."

277. **(B)** The verb in this sentence should be "lays," which means to put something down, rather than "lie," which means to rest or to recline.

278. **(A)** The adverb "well" is needed to describe the verb "dances." "Good" is an adjective used to describe nouns.

Spelling

279. **(A)** *The weather forecaster predicted rain for **tomorow**.* The correct spelling is **tomorrow**.

280. **(A)** *The sailors were stranded on a **dessert** island.* The correct spelling is **desert**.

281. **(C)** *Max's guidance **counseler** advised him to take Spanish.* The correct spelling is **counselor**.

282. **(A)** *There were **alot** of vehicles in line at the inspection station.* The correct spelling is **a lot**. "A lot" is two words.

283. **(D)** There are no misspelled words.

284. **(C)** *The **sophmore** class assembled in the cafeteria.* The correct spelling is **sophomore**.

285. **(B)** *The **accomodations** at the new waterfront hotel are luxuri-ous.* The correct spelling is **accommodations**.

286. **(C)** *The high school **principle** addressed the student body.* The correct spelling is **principal**.

287. **(C)** *The signature on the **perscription** is illegible.* The correct spelling is **prescription**.

288. **(D)** There are no misspelled words.

Composition

289. **(A)** All of the answer choices are coordinating conjunctions, which are used to connect independent clauses. The two independent clauses in the sentence express contrasting ideas. ***But***

is the correct choice because it is the only word of the three choices that is used to join contrasting ideas.

290. **(B)**   All of the answer choices are coordinating conjunctions, which are used to connect independent clauses. The two independent clauses in the sentence express a cause and effect relationship. *So* is the correct choice because it is the only word of the three choices that is used to join a cause to an effect.

291. **(C)**   All of the answer choices are subordinating conjunctions, which are used to connect independent and dependent clauses. The clauses express a cause and effect relationship. ***Because*** is the correct choice since it is the only word of the three choices used to join a cause to an effect.

292. **(C)**   All of the answer choices are subordinating conjunctions, which are used to connect independent and dependent clauses. In addition, all three of the choices are used to show a time relationship. *After* is the only answer choice that makes sense.

293. **(B)**   **However** is a conjunctive adverb used to connect contrasting ideas. Of the four answer choices, *she was on time for school*, is the only choice that contrasts the first independent clause, *Alyssa's bus was late.*

294. **(C)**   **Therefore** is a conjunctive adverb used to show a cause and effect relationship. Of the four answer choices, *he has been studying all week* is the only choice that expresses the effect, or result, of the first independent clause, *John wants to do well on the math test*. The first clause expresses the cause or reason; the second clause expresses the effect, or result.

295. **(C)**   Sentence (C) expresses the idea most clearly.

296. **(A)**   Sentence (A) expresses the idea most clearly.

297. **(A)**   Sentence (A) expresses the idea most clearly.

298. **(D)**   Sentence (D) expresses the idea most clearly.

COOP/ HSPT

COOP

Practice Test 1

Test 1: Sequences

TIME: 15 Minutes
20 Questions

DIRECTIONS: Study the sequences and then choose the best answer from the choices given.

---

1. ○○□□|○□○□|○□□○| ___

   (A) □□○○   (C) □○□○

   (B) □○○□   (D) ○□○□

2. TY↑|Y↑↑| ↑↑ | ↑↑↑ ___

   (F) ↑T   (H) ↑Y

   (G) ↑↑   (J) ↑Y

3. ▫▪|▫▪|▫▫|▫▪| ___

   (A) ▫▪   (C) ▯▯

   (B) ▫▪   (D) ▫▫

4. △○□◇|○△□◇|○□△◇| ___

   (F) □△○◇   (H) ○◇□△

   (G) ○□◇△   (J) ○△◇□

5. ◪◪◪◪|◪◪◪◪|◪◪◪◪| ___

   (A) ◪◪◪◪   (C) ◪◪◪◪

   (B) ◪◪◪◪   (D) ◪◪◪◪

6. □□□□|△□□□| ___ |△△△□

   (F) △□△□   (H) □□□△

   (G) △△□□   (J) □△□□

109

7. ○△△□ | ○□△△ | ○△△□ | ○□△△ | ____

   (A) ○□△△   (C) ○△△□

   (B) △△○□   (D) ○△□△

8. WVU | SRQ | ONM | ____ | GFE

   (F) DCB   (H) JIH

   (G) LKJ   (J) KJI

9. PQR | QRS | RST | ____ | TUV

   (A) STU   (C) TVU

   (B) SUT   (D) STV

10. ABEF | EFIJ | IJMN | ____

    (F) MNOP   (H) OPQR

    (G) MNQR   (J) OPST

11. PEAL | LEAN | ____ | TEAL

    (A) DEAL   (C) NEAL

    (B) NEAT   (D) LEAP

12. $Y_3 X_2 T_1$ | $Y_3 X_2 T_2$ | $Y_3 X_3 T_2$ | ____ | $Y_4 X_3 T_3$

    (F) $Y_3 X_3 T_3$ (H) $Y_4 X_3 T_1$

    (G) $Y_3 X_3 T_1$ (J) $Y_4 X_3 T_2$

13. $R S_3 T_3$ | $R S_3 T_2$ | $R S_2 T_2$ | ____ | $R S_1 T_1$

    (A) $R S_2 T_1$ (C) $R S_3 T_2$

    (B) $R S_3 T_1$ (D) $R S_1 T_2$

14. $A_1 B_2 C$ | $A_2 B_2 C$ | $A_2 B_3 C$ | ____ | $A_3 B_4 C$

    (F) $A_2 B_4 C$ (H) $A_3 B_3 C$

    (G) $A_3 B_2 C$ (J) $A_4 B_3 C$

15. 4 2 12 | 8 6 36 | 10 __ 48

    (A) 4   (C) 8

    (B) 12   (D) 6

16. 88 90 30 | 28 30 10 | 58 60 __

    (F) 10   (H) 40

    (G) 20   (J) 30

17. 81 9 27 | $\frac{1}{2}$ $\frac{1}{18}$ $\frac{1}{6}$ | 27 3 9 | $\frac{1}{3}$ ____

    (A) $\frac{1}{27}$ $\frac{1}{9}$ (C) $\frac{1}{24}$ $\frac{1}{8}$

    (B) $\frac{1}{12}$ $\frac{1}{6}$ (D) $\frac{1}{21}$ $\frac{1}{7}$

18. 33 27 24 | 28 27 19 | 21 27 12 | 18 __ __

    (F) 24 9   (H) 27 10

    (G) 24 10   (J) 27 9

19. 2 3 5 8 | 3 5 8 13 | 5 8 13 21 | __ __ __ __

    (A) 13 21 34 55   (C) 13 21 43 64

    (B) 8 13 21 33   (D) 8 13 21 34

20. 8 32 20 | 15 60 48 | 32 128 116 | 24 __ __

    (F) 48 36   (H) 72 60

    (G) 96 84   (J) 106 94

Test 2: Analogies

TIME: 7 Minutes
20 Questions

DIRECTIONS: For numbers 1-20, choose the picture that would go in the empty box so that the bottom two pictures are related in the same way the top two are related.

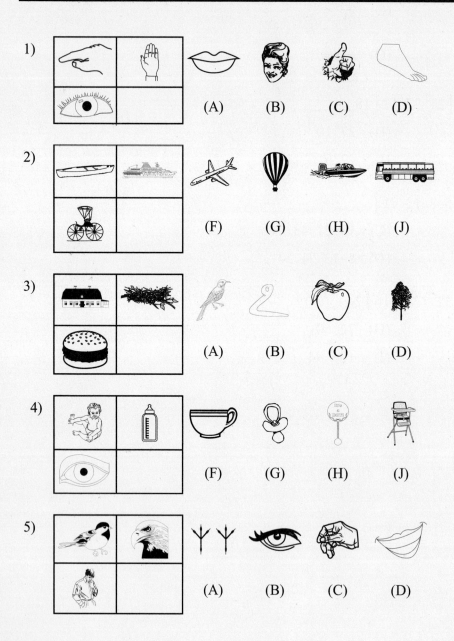

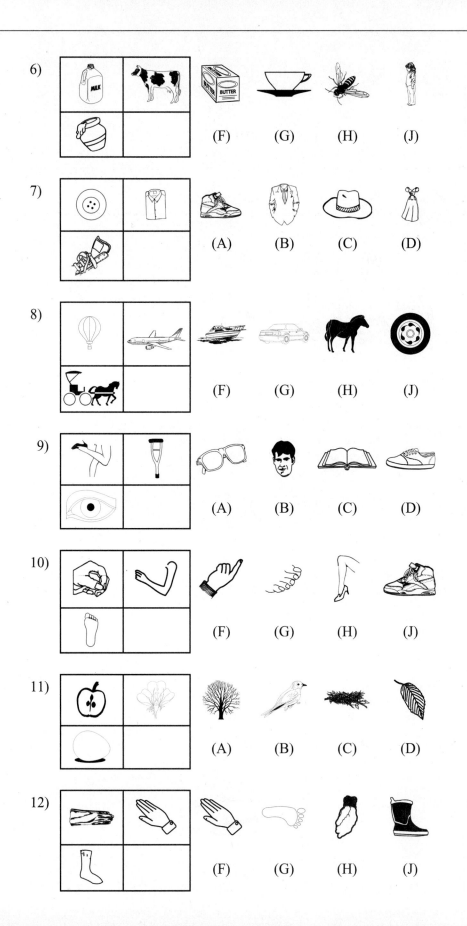

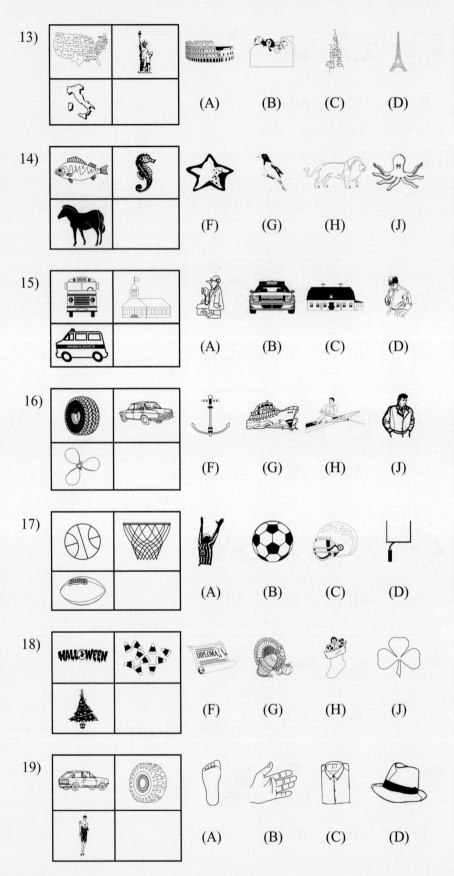

20)

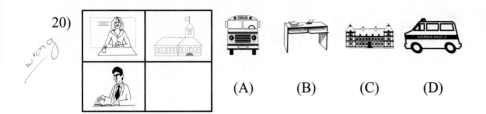

wrong

(A)　　(B)　　(C)　　(D)

Test 3: Memory

TIME: 17 Minutes
20 Questions

DIRECTIONS: Study the list below, then answer the questions that follow.

---

1. A **mulag** is a branch of a tree.
2. **Dotmic** means to act like a baby.
3. **Wazur** means to confuse.
4. A **balligag** is a high wall.
5. A **sirot** is a pet.
6. A **winlot** is a rainstorm.
7. **Pollma** means to be different.
8. A **cesy** is a shout.
9. A **shamel** is a bruise.
10. **Dentalog** means to remove.
11. **Hammasure** means to be very quiet.
12. **Gradem** means to chirp like a bird.
13. A **chimra** is a piece of clothing.
14. A **winuim** is a glass bottle.
15. **Flamom** means to be like ice.
16. **Blancum** means to be rocky.
17. **Tuckel** means to smell like flowers.
18. A **refub** is a house.
19. A **blum** is a wheel.
20. **Stelin** means to speak.

1. Which word means <u>a pet</u>?

   (A) wazur   (D) stelin

   (B) mulag   (E) winuim

   (C) sirot

2. Which word means <u>to be very quiet</u>?

   (F) pollma   (J) flamom

   (G) wazur   (K) hammasure

   (H) winlot

3. Which word means <u>a glass bottle</u>?

   (A) chimra   (D) stelin

   (B) refub   (E) balligag

   (C) winuim

4. Which word means <u>to be like ice</u>?

   (F) cesy   (J) tuckel

   (G) blancum   (K) hammasure

   (H) flamom

5. Which word means <u>to smell like flowers</u>?

   (A) dotmic   (D) tuckel

   (B) mulag   (E) blum

   (C) gradem

6. Which word means <u>a house</u>?

   (F) dentalog   (J) refub

   (G) cesy   (K) pollma

   (H) shamel

7. Which word means <u>to speak</u>?

   (A) pollma   (D) blum

   (B) shamel   (E) stelin

   (C) gradem

8. Which word means <u>a wheel</u>?

   (F) cesy   (J) blum

   (G) balligag   (K) tuckel

   (H) dotmic

9. Which word means <u>a high wall</u>?

   (A) mulag   (D) balligag

   (B) dotmic   (E) sirot

   (C) wazur

10. Which word means <u>a rainstorm</u>?

(F) winlot

(J) chimra

(G) pollma

(K) tuckel

(H) cesy

11. Which word means <u>a branch of a tree</u>?

(A) flamom

(D) dentalog

(B) blum

(E) mulag

(C) stelin

12. Which word means <u>to be different</u>?

(F) pollma

(J) refub

(G) hammasure

(K) stelin

(H) dotmic

13. Which word means <u>a shout</u>?

(A) blum

(D) cesy

(B) flamom

(E) winlot

(C) shamel

14. Which word means <u>a bruise</u>?

(F) dentalog

(J) winuim

(G) gradem

(K) sirot

(H) shamel

15. Which word means <u>to remove</u>?

(A) flamom

(D) balligag

(B) pollma

(E) dotmic

(C) dentalog

16. Which word means <u>to chirp like a bird</u>?

(F) winlot

(J) blancum

(G) refub

(K) tuckel

(H) gradem

17. Which word means <u>a piece of clothing</u>?

    (A) shamel   (D) hammasure

    (B) mulag   (E) chimra

    (C) stelin

18. Which word means <u>to be rocky</u>?

    (F) dentalog   (J) blancum

    (G) sirot   (K) pollma

    (H) winlot

19. Which word means <u>to confuse</u>?

    (A) mulag   (D) gradem

    (B) sirot   (E) wazur

    (C) cesy

20. Which word means <u>to act like a baby</u>?

    (F) flamom   (J) dotmic

    (G) refub   (K) balligag

    (H) blum

Test 4: Verbal Reasoning

TIME: 15 Minutes
20 Questions

DIRECTIONS: For numbers 1-6, find the word that names a necessary part of the underlined word.

1. <u>egg</u>

    (A) bacon   (C) shell

    (B) breakfast   (D) hatch

2. <u>car</u>

    (F) driver's license   (H) map

    (G) passenger   (J) engine

3. <u>highway</u>

    (A) cars   (C) toll

    (B) pavement   (D) bridge

4. <u>fireplace</u>

    (F) fire   (H) chimney

    (G) logs   (J) matches

5. <u>language</u>

    (A) voice   (C) Spanish

    (B) speak   (D) vocabulary

6. <u>dinner</u>

    (F) fork   (H) food

    (G) table   (J) napkin

DIRECTIONS: For numbers 7-12, the words in the top row are related in some way. The words in the bottom row are related in the same way. For each item, find the word that completes the bottom row of words.

7. peas   lettuce   cucumbers

    cherry   strawberry

    (A) apple   (C) banana

    (B) orange   (D) peach

8. transportation   car   Mustang

    food   vegetable

    (F) fruit   (H) corn

    (G) dinner   (J) garden

9. London   Paris   Munich

    New York   San Francisco

    (A) Montreal   (C) California

    (B) Texas   (D) England

10. paint   canvas   brushes

    nails   wood

    (F) hammer   (H) carpenter

    (G) furniture   (J) hardware store

11. walk   jog   sprint

    giggle   laugh

    (A) chuckle   (C) shout

    (B) guffaw   (D) cry

12. sand   glass   window

    tree   lumber

    (F) plank   (H) deck

    (G) oak   (J) knot

DIRECTIONS: For numbers 13-17, find the statement that is true according to the given information.

13. Alfred couldn't wait to go to the zoo. When he got there, he raced straight to the reptile house and went inside. There, he began to describe each reptile to his mom in great detail. His mom was impressed.

    (A) Alfred's mom was afraid of reptiles.

    (B) Alfred was afraid of reptiles.

    (C) Alfred goes to the zoo every week.

    (D) Alfred knew quite a bit about reptiles.

14. As she was leaving for school one morning, Jesse stepped outside and then quickly ran back inside again, dripping wet. She ran upstairs and grabbed an umbrella from her closet and then went to catch the bus.

    (F) It looked like it might rain.

    (G) Jesse forgot her homework and ran back inside to get it.

    (H) It was raining outside.

    (J) Jesse doesn't like school.

15. Max got home from work late one night. He didn't feel like eating spaghetti since that was what he had last night, and there weren't any hamburgers. So, even though he doesn't really like hot dogs, he cooked some for dinner.

    (A) Max doesn't like hamburgers.

    (B) Max is a good cook.

    (C) There was nothing else in the house to eat except hot dogs.

    (D) Max had hot dogs for dinner.

16. On the way home, Jill stopped and picked tulips, pansies, and daisies from her friend's garden. She did not pick any roses.

    (F) Jill doesn't like roses.

    (G) Jill's friend doesn't grow roses.

    (H) Jill is allergic to roses.

    (J) Jill picked three kinds of flowers.

17. Jane currently has two pets. She used to have a dog named Rover. She now has a cat named Mittens.

(A) Rover ran away.

(B) Jane now has two cats.

(C) Jane has never had a rabbit.

(D) Jane now has at least one cat.

DIRECTIONS: For numbers 18-20, find the correct answer.

---

18. Here are some words translated from an artificial language.

    Turfimablinty means anyhow.
    Turfimsblints means somehow.
    Refitablinty means anywhere.

    Which word means somewhere?

    (F) turfim   (H) ablinty

    (G) refitasblints   (J) ablintyturfim

19. Here are some words translated from an artificial language.

    Miffizacken means crack.
    Mossizacken means shatter.
    Miffidrospen means drizzle.

    Which word means pour?

    (A) miffimossi   (C) drospenmossi

    (B) zackendrospen   (D) mossidrospen

20. Here are some words translated from an artificial language.

    Zolterfen means tell.
    Rosterfen means sell.
    Erzolterfen means told.

    Which word means sold?

    (F) errosterfen   (H) rosterfenfen

    (G) erzolterfener   (J) errosterfener

Test 5: Reading Comprehension

TIME: 40 Minutes
40 Questions

DIRECTIONS: Each passage is followed by questions based on its content. After reading the passage, choose the best answer to each question. Answer all questions based on what is indicated or implied in that passage.

Questions 1–4 are based on the following passage.

Spa water quality is maintained through a filter to ensure cleanliness and clarity. Wastes such as perspiration, hairspray, and lotions which cannot be removed by the spa filter can be controlled by shock treatment or super chlorination every other week. Although the filter traps most of the solid material to control bacteria and algae and to oxidize any organic material, the addition of disinfectants such as bromine or chlorine is necessary.

As all water solutions have a pH which controls corrosion, proper pH balance is also necessary. A pH measurement determines if the water is acid or alkaline. Based on a 14-point scale, a pH reading of 7.0 is considered neutral while a lower reading is considered acidic, and a higher reading indicates alkalinity or basic. High pH (above 7.6) reduces sanitizer efficiency, clouds water, promotes scale formation on surfaces and equipment, and interferes with filter operation. When pH is high, add a pH decreaser such as sodium bisulphate (e.g., Spa Down). Because the spa water is hot, scale is deposited more rapidly. A weekly dose of a stain and scale fighter will also help to control this problem. Low pH (below 7.2) is equally damaging, causing equipment corrosion, water which is irritating, and rapid sanitizer dissipation. To increase pH add sodium bicarbonate (e.g., Spa Up).

The recommended operating temperature of a spa (98°-104°) is a fertile environment for the growth of bacteria and viruses. This growth is prevented when appropriate sanitizer levels are continuously monitored. Bacteria can also be controlled by maintaining a proper bromine level of 3.0 to 5.0 parts per million (ppm) or a chlorine level of 1.0-2.0 ppm. As bromine tablets should not be added directly to the water, a bromine floater will properly dispense the tablets. Should chlorine be the chosen sanitizer, a granular form is recommended, as liquid chlorine or tablets are too harsh for the spa.

1. Who is the intended audience for this passage?

    (A) scientists

    (B) home-spa owners

    (C) spa manufacturers

    (D) spa salespeople

2. The main purpose of the passage is

    (F) to convince shoppers to buy a spa.

    (G) to convince shoppers not to buy a spa.

    (H) to explain why spas are dangerous.

    (J) to instruct spa owners on how to care for their spa.

3. According to the passage, why is the use of sanitizer important?

    (A) Sanitizer keeps the pH balanced.

    (B) Sanitizer can be used instead of a filter.

    (C) Sanitizer keeps the spa from developing bacteria and viruses in the warm water.

    (D) Sanitizer helps maintain the right temperature.

4. Why is the use of a spa filter important?

    (F) The filter maintains the water quality by trapping most solid material.

    (G) The filter keeps the pH balanced.

    (H) The filter maintains the right temperature.

    (J) The filter removes perspiration, hairspray, and other lotions from the water.

Questions 5–8 are based on the following passage.

The relationship of story elements found in children's generated stories to reading achievement was analyzed. Correlations ranged from .61101 (p=.64) at the beginning of first grade to .83546 (p=.24) at the end of first grade, to .85126 (p=.21) at the end of second grade, and to .82588 (p=.26) for fifth/sixth grades. Overall, the correlation of the story elements to reading achievement appeared to indicate a high positive correlation trend even though it was not statistically significant.

Multiple regression equation analyses dealt with the relative contribution of the story elements to reading achievement. The contribution of certain story elements was substantial. At the beginning of first grade, story conventions added 40 percent to the total variance while the other increments were not significant. At the end of first grade, story plot contributed 44 percent to the total variance, story conventions contributed 20 percent, and story sources contributed 17 percent. At the end of second grade, the story elements contributed more equal percentages to the total partial correlation of .8513. Although none of the percentages were substantial, story plot (.2200), clausal connectors (.1858), and T-units (.1590) contributed the most to the total partial correlation. By the fifth and sixth grades three other story elements—T-units (.2241), story characters (.3214), and clausal connectors (.1212)—contributed most to the total partial correlation. None of these percentages were substantial.

5. This passage is most likely intended for

   (A) young readers.

   (B) first through fifth graders.

   (C) researchers or scientists.

   (D) parents.

6. The main idea of this passage is that

   (F) there is a direct relationship between the sophistication level of the stories children make up and their reading level.

   (G) there is a direct relationship between children's IQs and their reading levels.

   (H) children who want to improve their reading should watch less TV.

   (J) children who watch more TV tend to be better storytellers.

7. Which elements were used to analyze the children's stories?

   (A) story conventions and T-units

   (B) story plot and story characters

   (C) story sources and causal connectors

   (D) All of the above.

8. The study focused on

   (F) pre-school and kindergarten aged children.

   (G) children in grades K-8.

   (H) children in public school.

   (J) children in grades 1-6.

Questions 9–13 are based on the following passage.

Mark Twain has been characterized as "an authentic American author" and as "a representative American author." These descriptions seem to suit the man and his writings. He was born Samuel Clemens in 1835, when Missouri and Louisiana were the only states west of the Mississippi River. His birthplace was less than fifty miles from the river. His father, John Clemens, a lawyer and merchant, was rarely far from financial disaster. When Samuel Clemens was four, the family settled in Hannibal, Missouri, and it was there beside the great river that Samuel lived out the adventurous life he describes in his best-loved novels. Samuel traveled extensively and tasted life as no other author had done. He said of his life, "Now then: as the most valuable capital, or culture, or education usable in the building of novels is personal experience, I ought to be well equipped for that trade." He acquired a wealth of personal experiences for his novels. As a boy of twelve he was apprenticed to the printer of his brother's newspaper in Hannibal. Six years later, in 1853, he set out to see the world as a printer in St. Louis, then in Chicago, Philadelphia, Keokuk, and Cincinnati. In 1857 he impulsively apprenticed himself to Horace Bixby, a riverboat pilot, and traveled all 1,200 miles of the Mississippi River. He said of his years on the river, "I got personally and familiarly acquainted with all the different types of human nature that are to be found in fiction, biography, or history."

The Civil War ended his steamboating and he served briefly in a Confederate militia company. Following his stint in the military, he set out with his brother, Orion, by stagecoach over the Rockies. While in the West he tried prospecting and speculating, but found his true calling in journalism. He was greatly influenced by the literary comedians and local colorists of the period, Bret Harte and Artemus Ward. He became more skillful than his teachers in developing his rich characterizations. In 1865 he attained national fame using his pseudonym, Mark Twain, with his story "The Celebrated Jumping Frog of Calaveras County." He also discovered a new vocation as a popular lecturer in San Francisco, keeping his audiences convulsed with tales of his adventures. Full public recognition came with the publishing of *Innocents Abroad* (1869), a wild and rollicking account of his invasion of the Old World, much of which would seem quite languid by today's standards. Some of his finest writings were three works filled with lively adventures on the Mississippi River and based on his boyhood: *Tom Sawyer* (1876), *Old Times on the Mississippi* (1883), and *Huckleberry Finn* (1884). Throughout his career Twain preferred to display his flair for journalistic improvisation rather than maintain the artist's concern for form. In his artfully told stories, Mark Twain conveyed his keen powers of observation and perception, his broad understanding of human nature, and his refreshing sense of humor.

9. The author of the passage considers Samuel Clemens to be an authentic and representative American author because

   (A) he traveled throughout the United States.

   (B) he set all of his stories in the United States.

   (C) his style was humorous and informal.

   (D) Both (A) and (C).

10. The passage describes Twain's novel *Innocents Abroad* as an "account of his invasion of the Old World." By "invasion of the Old World," the author means

   (F) Twain's visit to a museum.

(G) Twain's journey on the Mississippi.

(H) Twain's travels in Europe.

(J) Twain's travels in the United States.

11. Mark Twain was at some time in his life all of the following EXCEPT

(A) a newspaper editor.   (C) a printer.

(B) a militiaman.   (D) a lecturer.

12. The author's attitude toward Mark Twain is

(F) negative.   (H) confused.

(G) admiring.   (J) sentimental.

13. Mark Twain stopped working on the steamboat because

(A) he became a popular writer.

(B) he joined the Confederate militia company.

(C) he became editor of his brother's newspaper.

(D) he decided to travel by land throughout the United States.

Questions 14–17 are based on the following passage.

As noted by Favat in 1977, the study of children's stories has been an ongoing concern of linguists, anthropologists, and psychologists. The past decade has witnessed a surge of interest in children's stories from researchers in these and other disciplines. The use of narratives for reading and reading instruction has been commonly accepted by the educational community. The notion that narrative is highly structured and that children's sense of narrative structure is more highly developed than expository structure has been proposed by some researchers.

Early studies of children's stories followed two approaches for story analysis: the analysis of story content or the analysis of story structure. Story content analysis has centered primarily on examining motivational and psychodynamic aspects of story characters as noted in the works of Erikson and Pitcher and Prelinger in 1963 and Ames in 1966. These studies have noted that themes or topics predominate and that themes change with age.

Early research on story structure focused on formal models of structure such as story grammar and story schemata. These models specified basic story elements and formed sets of rules similar to sentence grammar for ordering the elements.

The importance or centrality of narrative in a child's development of communicative ability has been proposed by Halliday (1976) and Hymes (1975). Thus, the importance of narrative for language communicative ability and for reading and reading instruction has been well documented. However, the question still remains about how these literacy abilities interact and lead to conventional reading.

14. What was the main purpose of the author in writing this passage?

    (F)   to suggest that existing research on children's literature is incorrect

    (G)   to suggest that more research be done on whether stories are important to children's communication

    (H)   to give a brief overview of existing research on children's stories

    (J)   to explain why researchers are interested in children's stories

15. The word "narrative" as used in this passage means

    (A)   content.   (C)   structure.

    (B)   analysis.   (D)   story.

16. The studies of children's stories the author discusses analyzed which two elements?

    (F)   story content and story structure

    (G)   literacy abilities and conventional reading

    (H)   communicative ability and conventional reading

    (J)   reading and reading instruction

17. Why does the author say that "the question still remains about how these literacy abilities interact and lead to conventional reading"?

    (A)   The author failed in his/her research about this point.

    (B)   The author suggests that this could be a question for future research.

    (C)   The author believes the past research was wrong.

    (D)   The author believes the past research was not important.

Questions 18–21 are based on the following passage.

Seldom has the American school system not been the target of demands for change to meet the social priorities of the times. This theme has been traced through the following significant occurrences in education: Benjamin Franklin's advocacy in 1749 for a more useful type of education; Horace Mann's zealous proposals in the 1830s espousing the tax-supported public school; John Dewey's early twentieth century attack on traditional schools for not developing the child effectively for his or her role in society; the post-Sputnik pressure for academic rigor; the prolific criticism and accountability pressures of the 1970s, and the ensuing disillusionment and continued criticism of schools until this last decade of the twentieth century. Indeed, the waves of criticism about American education have reflected currents of social dissatisfaction for any given period of this country's history.

As dynamics for change in the social order result in demands for change in the American educational system, so in turn has insistence developed for revision of teacher education (witness the more recent Holmes report (1986)). Historically, the education of American teachers has reflected evolving attitudes about public education. With slight modifications the teacher education pattern established following the demise of the normal school during the early 1900s has persisted in most teacher preparation programs. The pattern has been one requiring certain academic and professional (educational) courses often resulting in teachers teaching as they had been taught.

18. The main purpose of this passage is to

(F) argue for further changes to the school system.

(G) argue against further changes to the school system.

(H) show that changes in the school system and teacher education are linked to popular concerns of American society.

(J) show that changes in the school system and teacher education occur independently of the concerns of American society.

19. The passage describes all of the following reforms EXCEPT

(A) increasing academic rigor.

(B) paying for public schools with tax money.

(C) increasing the "usefulness" of education.

(D) creating normal school programs.

20. According to the passage, why is the education of teachers revised?

(F) Changes in society lead to the revision of teacher education.

(G) Teachers tend to teach as they have been taught.

(H) Teachers need to learn new methods of teaching to compete with television.

(J) Public- and private-school teachers are dissatisfied with the way they have been taught and demand revisions to teacher education.

21. According to the passage, teachers are prone to teaching as they have been taught because

   (A) the normal schools were replaced.

   (B) other teachers take the same educational courses.

   (C) the education of teachers reflects public opinion.

   (D) teachers try to keep pace with other teachers.

Questions 22–25 are based on the following passage.

Frederick Douglass was born Frederick Augustus Washington Bailey in 1817 to a white father and a slave mother. Frederick was raised by his grandmother on a Maryland plantation until he was eight. It was then that he was sent to Baltimore by his owner to be a servant to the Auld family. Mrs. Auld recognized Frederick's intellectual acumen and defied the law of the state by teaching him to read and write. When Mr. Auld warned that education would make the boy unfit for slavery, Frederick sought to continue his education in the streets. When his master died, Frederick was returned to the plantation to work in the fields at age sixteen. Later, he was hired out to work in the shipyards in Baltimore as a ship caulker. He plotted an escape but was discovered before he could get away. It took five years before he made his way to New York City and then to New Bedford, Massachusetts, eluding slave hunters by changing his name to Douglass.

At an 1841 anti-slavery meeting in Massachusetts, Douglass was invited to give a talk about his experiences under slavery. His impromptu speech was so powerful and so eloquent that it thrust him into a career as an agent for the Massachusetts Anti-Slavery Society.

Douglass wrote his autobiography in 1845 primarily to counter those who doubted his authenticity as a former slave. This work became a classic in American literature and a primary source about slavery from the point of view of a slave. Douglass went on a two-year speaking tour abroad to avoid recapture by his former owner and to win new friends for the abolition movement. He returned with funds to purchase his freedom and to start his own anti-slavery newspaper. He became a consultant to Abraham Lincoln and throughout Reconstruction fought doggedly for full civil rights for freedmen; he also supported the women's rights movement.

22. Why, most probably, did some people doubt that Frederick Douglass was a former slave?

   (F) He was inexperienced at plantation work.

   (G) He was such a powerful and eloquent speaker and writer.

   (H) He knew several trades.

   (J) He wrote his own autobiography.

23. Which of the following jobs did Frederick Douglass NOT work as?

    (A) Agent for an anti-slavery society

    (B) Consultant to the President of the United States

    (C) Lawyer for anti-slavery causes

    (D) Publisher of an anti-slavery newspaper

24. It can be inferred from the passage that Frederick Douglass sought to continue his education in the streets because

    (F) Mr. Auld probably forbid Mrs. Auld to teach Douglass further.

    (G) Mrs. Auld had taught him all she knew.

    (H) Douglass needed to find a teacher with more experience in writing books.

    (J) Douglass began to work in the shipyards and no longer lived with the Aulds.

25. According to the passage, which of the following did Douglas support?

    (A) Civil rights

    (B) The women's rights movement

    (C) Both (A) and (B).

    (D) Neither (B) nor (A).

Questions 26–30 are based on the following passage.

> Passive-aggressive personality disorder has as its essential characteristic covert noncompliance to ordinary performance demands made in social and occupational situations. To a greater extent than in other personality disorders, this pattern may be context dependent, appearing only in certain situations.
>
> Aggressive impulses and motives are expressed by passivity. These represent its primary dynamic and may take the form of inaction, inefficiency, procrastination, or obstructionism. It is an interpersonal disorder, the recognition of which depends on the seemingly unjustified frustration and hostility others feel toward such individuals. By the use of verbal expressions indicating compliance or agreement, the passive-aggressive person conceals his/her actual noncompliance and the secret sadistic satisfaction he/she derives from the frustration he/she thereby causes. This dynamic is distinguished from that associated with masochism, in which self-punitive actions are used to control others or to evoke protective responses from them. It is also distinguished from the ambivalence and indecision of obsessive-compulsive persons, who may appear passive and obstructionistic, but are not motivated by a wish to evoke frustration in others.

26. What was the main purpose of the author in writing this passage?

(F)   To describe passive-aggressive personality disorder

(G)   To discuss treatments for passive-aggressive personality disorder

(H)   To list situations that may cause passive-aggressive behavior

(J)   To list clinics where patients can be treated for passive-aggressive behavior

27. Which of the following statements is supported by the passage?

(A)   Passive-aggressive personality disorder is probably a genetic disorder.

(B)   Passive-aggressive behavior is more common in men than women.

(C)   Passive-aggressive behavior may be triggered by certain situations and not by others.

(D)   Passive-aggressive behavior is more common in children than in adults.

28. According to the passage, one can recognize that a person has a passive-aggressive personality disorder by

(F)   taking a blood sample.

(G)   the frustrated reactions of others around that person.

(H)   giving the person a personality test.

(J)   having a psychologist evaluate the person.

29. How is passive-aggressive personality disorder defined in the passage?

(A)   The person often gets in fights with others.

(B)   The person can't make decisions and constantly changes his/her mind.

(C)   The person says he/she agrees with others, but then acts contrary to that agreement, thereby frustrating other people.

(D)   By punishing him/herself, the person controls others.

30. As used in the first sentence of the passage, the word "covert" most nearly means

(F)   aggressive.   (H)   open.

(G)   secretive.   (J)   evoke.

Questions 31–35 are based on the following passage.

Instructions for Absentee Voting

These instructions describe conditions under which voters may register for or request absentee ballots to vote in the November 5 election.

(1)   If you moved on or prior to October 7 and did not register to vote at your new address, you are not eligible to vote in this election.

(2)   If you move after this date, you may vote via absentee ballot or at your polling place, using your previous address as your address of registration for this election.

(3)   You must register at your new address to vote in future elections.

(4)   The last day to request an absentee ballot is October 29.

(5)   You must be a registered voter in the county.

(6)   You must sign your request in your own handwriting.

(7)   You must make a separate request for each election.

(8)   The absentee ballot shall be issued to the requesting voter in person or by mail.

31. What is the main purpose of this passage?

(A) to instruct voters at the polls

(B) to instruct vote-counters on how to count absentee ballots

(C) to instruct people interested in using an absentee ballot

(D) to explain how to work a voting machine

32. According to the passage, when is the deadline for getting an absentee ballot?

(F) November 5   (H) October 28

(G) October 7   (J) October 29

33. This passage was most likely written by

(A) an organization that encourages people to vote.

(B) the United States government.

(C) voters who have used absentee ballots before.

(D) the League of Women Voters.

34. In number two of this passage, the word "via" most nearly means

(F) without.   (H) by.

(G) over.   (J) not.

35. If a person moved on October 8, and did not register to vote at the new address, how could he/she vote?

(A)   at his/her old polling place

(B)   with an absentee ballot

(C)   at the nearest polling place in his/her new county

(D)   Either (A) or (B), but not (C).

Questions 36–40 are based on the following passage.

One of the many tragedies of the Civil War was the housing and care of prisoners. The Andersonville prison, built by the Confederates in 1864 to accommodate 10,000 Union prisoners, was not completed when prisoners started arriving. Five months later the total number of men incarcerated there had risen to 31,678.

The sounds of death and dying were not diminished by surrender of weapons to a captor. Chances of survival for prisoners in Andersonville were not much better than in the throes of combat. Next to overcrowding, inadequate shelter caused unimaginable suffering. The Confederates were not equipped with the manpower, tools, or supplies necessary to house such a population of captives; prisoners themselves gathered lumber, logs, anything they could find to construct some sort of protection from the elements. Some prisoners dug holes in the ground, risking suffocation from cave-ins, but many hundreds were left exposed to the wind, rain, cold, and heat.

Daily food rations were exhausted by the sheer numbers they had to serve, resulting in severe dietary deficiencies. The overcrowding, meager rations, and deplorable unsanitary conditions resulted in rampant disease and a high mortality rate. The consequences of a small scratch or wound could result in death in Andersonville. During the prison's thirteen-month existence, more than 12,000 prisoners died and were buried in the Andersonville cemetery. Most of the deaths were caused by diarrhea, dysentery, gangrene, and scurvy that could not be treated due to inadequate staff and supplies.

36.   What is the main idea of this passage?

(F)   The Union prisons were better than the Confederate prisons.

(G)   The chances of survival for prisoners were about the same as for soldiers in combat.

(H)   Many Union prisoners suffered and died at Andersonville prison because the Confederates could not provide enough shelter and supplies.

(J)   The food in prisons is very unhealthy.

37.   According to the passage, which of the following problems did Andersonville prison have?

(A)   Prison doctors couldn't handle emergencies.

(B) Prisoners did not get enough exercise.

(C) Prisoners did not have enough food.

(D) All of the above.

38. According to the passage, how long did the prison stay open?

(F) five months   (H) thirteen months

(G) one year   (J) two years

39. According to the passage, prisoners died from all the following EXCEPT

(A) gangrene.   (C) dermatitis.

(B) scurvy.   (D) dysentery.

40. This passage was most likely taken from

(F) a textbook.   (H) prison records.

(G) a government report.   (J) journals kept by prisoners.

Test 6: Mathematics Concepts and Applications

TIME: 35 Minutes
    40 Questions

DIRECTIONS: Select the best answer choice.

---

1. What is the value of x in the equation: $3x - 6 = 15$?

    (A) 21   (C) 7

    (B) 9   (D) 3

2. Albert bought a jacket for $50 from pocket money he had collected from five of his relatives. He received $12.00 from his aunt, $8.25 from his uncle, $12.50 from his mother, and $7.50 from his father. His grandfather made up the rest. How much did Albert's grandfather give him?

    (F) $50.00   (H) $10.25

    (G) $10.75   (J) $9.75

3. Sara drank 7 oz. of milk on Monday, 6 oz. on Tuesday, 5 oz. on Wednesday, an unknown amount on Thursday, and 5 oz. on Friday. If Sara drank an average of 6 oz. per day for the five days, how much did she drink that Thursday?

    (A) 3 oz.   (C) 5 oz.

    (B) 4 oz.   (D) 7 oz.

4. In the number 534.0024, what is the value of the 2?

    (F) 2   (H) 2 hundredths

    (G) 2 tenths   (J) 2 thousandths

5. Instead of multiplying a certain number by 100, Tina divided it by 100. If her answer was 37625.45, what should be the correct answer?

    (A) 376254500   (C) 376.2545

    (B) 3762545   (D) 3.762545

6. One day, when Janet was trying to use a new calculator to add 54 to a certain number, she pressed the minus button (–) instead of the plus (+) button. The calculator showed –13. If Janet had pressed the correct button, what should have been the answer?

   (F)   108

   (G)   95

   (H)   67

   (J)   41

7. Arrange the following quantities in order, from <u>smallest to greatest</u>:

   83% 0.78 $\dfrac{13}{16}$

   (A) $0.78, \dfrac{13}{16}, 83\%$

   (C) $\dfrac{13}{16}, 0.78, 83\%$

   (B) $0.78, 83\%, \dfrac{13}{16}$

   (D) $\dfrac{13}{16}, 83\%, 0.78$

8. Mrs. Fraser took her class of 18 students to lunch at a restaurant. If she spent $4.93 on each student, how much did the students' lunches cost her?

   (F) $936.70

   (G) $887.40

   (H) $93.67

   (J) $88.74

9. If $x = 3$ and $y = -2$, what is the value of $2x + 3y$?

   (A)   –12

   (B)   –1

   (C)   0

   (D)   12

10. If $y = 6$ and $z = -2$, find the value of $\dfrac{3y}{z}$.

   (F)   –9

   (G)   –3

   (H)   3

   (J)   9

11. Alice can arrange all her cards in exactly 5 sets of 7, with 4 left over. How many cards does Alice have?

   (A)   39

   (B)   35

   (C)   28

   (D)   20

12. Cathy packs 357 video cassettes in boxes designed to hold 15 cassettes. How many additional cassettes does she need in order to fill the last box?

(F)   345

(H)   12

(G)   23

(J)   3

13. The sum of two consecutive multiples of 4 is 12 less than the product of 8 and 9. Find the smaller of the two multiples of 4?

(A)   44

(C)   32

(B)   40

(D)   28

14. In the picture, $\overline{OD} \perp \overline{AB}$. Find the value of x.

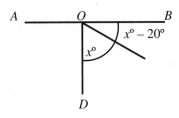

(F)   110

(H)   65

(G)   60

(J)   55

15. Find the value of y in the figure.

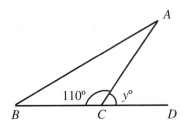

(A)   110

(C)   70

(B)   80

(D)   60

16. In the figure, *ABC* is a right triangle. What is the value of x?

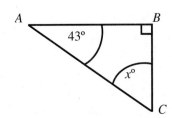

(F) 43   (H) 47

(G) 45   (J) 57

17. Two sets of straws are shown, with the measures of their lengths. Which straw in set 2 would you combine with the three straws in set 1 so they can be joined end-to-end to form a rectangle?

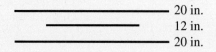

Set 1
20 in.
12 in.
20 in.

(A) ————————— 20 in.

(B) ————— 16 in.

Set 2

(C) ——— 12 in.

(D) ————— 22 in.

18. Two sets of rods are shown, with the measures of their lengths. Which rod in set 2 would you combine with the two rods in set 1 so they can be joined end-to-end to form a scalene triangle?

————— 15 in.
—— 6 in.

Set 1

(F) ———— 10 in.

(G) ——— 9 in.

Set 2

(H) —— 6 in.

(J) ———— 15 in.

19. Xena is 2 years older than her sister, Yvonne, who is 5 years younger than their elder brother Steve. Let x stand for Xena's age. Which one of the following expressions best represents Steve's age?

(A) $2x + 3$ (C) $x + 5$

(B) $x - 2$ (D) $x + 3$

20. Edith earned the same amount of money for each of her first 9 months on the job. For the next 3 months, she earned $15 less per month due to frequent absences. Let d represent Edith's earnings per month for each of the first 9 months. Which one of the following expressions accurately describes her total earnings for the 12 months?

(F) $12d + 45$ (H) $9d - 15$

(G) $12d - 45$ (J) $3d - 15$

21. Find the product of $(3n + 4)$ and $(n - 2)$?

(A) $3n^2 + 10n - 8$ (C) $3n^2 + 2n - 8$

(B) $3n^2 - 2n - 8$ (D) $3n^2 - 10n - 8$

22. Simplify $24 \div 6 + 2 \times 8$.

(F)   20   (H)   48

(G)   24   (J)   50

23. Divide 20% of 90 by 25% of 36.

(A)   2   (C)   18

(B)   9   (D)   36

24. Find 210% of 420.

(F)   882   (H)   630

(G)   840   (J)   88.2

25. Plywood is sold in sheets of 4 ft. by 8 ft. What is the smallest number of sheets that a carpenter must buy in order to build a temporary fence 40 ft. by 7 ft.?

(A)   8   (C)   10

(B)   9   (D)   12

Information for questions 26 to 29

Seven of Mr. Lee's students did poorly on their final examination. Mr. Lee decided to give them a chance to improve their test scores. Here are the students' scores on the two tests. Someone misplaced Tamara's score on Test 2.

Student's name	Test 1	Test 2
Nancy	64	70
Rhoda	71	69
Clara	58	65
Gregory	49	58
Jerome	56	67
Bill	60	58
Tamara	65	x

26. Which one of the students improved the most, from the first to the second test?

    (F) Gregory (H) Rhoda

    (G) Nancy (J) Jerome

27. If the two tests are combined, which student did the worst?

    (A) Bill (C) Gregory

    (B) Clara (D) Rhoda

28. What was the average score for the seven students on the first test?

    (F) 64 (H) 58

    (G) 61 (J) 56

29. If the average score for the 7 students on the second test was 66, what was Tamara's score on this test?

    (A) 64 (C) 69

    (B) 66 (D) 75

30. Wong drove from Alphatown to Betatown in 4 hours at an average of 45 mph, then from Betatown to Chetatown in 5 hours at an average of 54 mph. What was Wong's average speed for the entire journey?

    (F) 49 mph (H) 50 mph

    (G) 49.5 mph (J) 50.5 mph

31. A certain printer makes the dot over the letter "i" approximately 0.0012 inch in diameter. A magnifying glass enlarges this dot by a factor of 10,000. What is the diameter of the dot in the magnifying glass?

    (A) 0.000012 (C) 12

    (B) 0.00012 (D) 120

32. Solve for x: $3x - 6 = 42$.

    (F) 48 (H) 16

    (G) 36 (J) 12

33. Find the slope of the line in the graph.

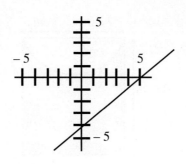

(A) $-\dfrac{4}{5}$ (C) $-\dfrac{5}{4}$

(B) $\dfrac{4}{5}$ (D) $\dfrac{5}{4}$

34. The sum of the 5 interior angles of a pentagon is 540°. If angles *A* and *E* are right angles, find the value of the remaining angles.

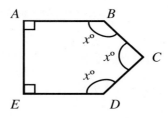

(F) 90   (H) 240

(G) 120   (J) 360

35. Find the total area of the 3 visible faces of the box shown in the figure.

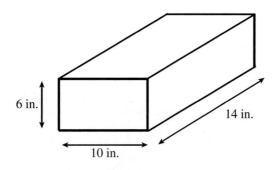

(A) 284 in²   (C) 568 in²

(B) 420 in²   (D) 840 in²

36. The formula for the area of a circle is πr^2, where r^2 stands for the radius of the circle. Find the area of the shaded portion of the figure below, if $\pi = 3.14$.

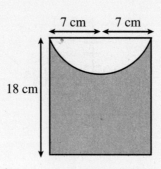

(F) 252 cm²

(H) 154 cm²

(G) 175 cm²

(J) 98 cm²

37. If one kilogram is equal to 2.2 pounds, how many pounds is equal to 150 kilograms?

(A) 33

(C) 330

(B) 68

(D) 3,300

38. The finance charge for a $25,000 car is $3,000. At the same rate, what is the finance charge for a $30,000 car?

(F) $3,800

(H) $4,200

(G) $3,600

(J) $4,400

Information for questions 39 and 40

The graph shows the average temperature, in degrees Fahrenheit, in a certain city, from January to August of the same year.

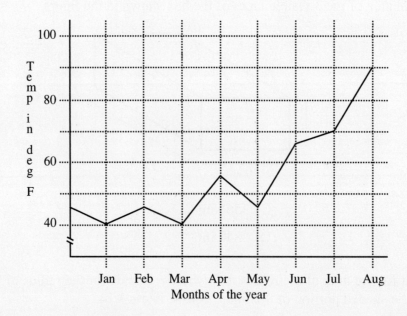

39. Between which two-month interval did the temperature rise the most steeply?

    (A) February – April   (C) April – June

    (B) March – May   (D) May – July

40. What was the average temperature rise between March and August?

    (F) 40°   (H) 10°

    (G) 35°   (J) 7°

Test 7: Language Expression

TIME: 30 Minutes
40 Questions

DIRECTIONS: For numbers 1-6, choose the word or words that best completes the sentence.

---

1. I really don't know where Ms. Jasper's coat has gone. She _____ it when we left the museum.

   (A) is carrying
   (B) will be carrying it
   (C) will have been carrying
   (D) was carrying

2. The pumpkin on the right is the _____ of the two being judged.

   (F) heavier
   (G) heaviest
   (H) most heavy
   (J) heavy

3. Because they want to go fishing on Saturday, Maggie and her sister Cassie _____ to finish all their schoolwork on Friday night.

   (A) plans
   (B) plan
   (C) is planning
   (D) was planning

4. The movie we watched last night was the _____ of all those we watched over the vacation.

   (F) scarier
   (G) scariest
   (H) more scary
   (J) scary

5. By the time we get to Aunt Harriet's, you _____ all of the chocolates in that box.

   (A) ate
   (B) have eaten
   (C) will have eaten
   (D) will have been eating

6. Beth set the table for dinner in the dining room. _____, her brother made the mashed potatoes in the kitchen.

   (F) Anyway
   (G) Regardless
   (H) Meanwhile
   (J) In spite of this

DIRECTIONS: Choose the sentence that is complete and that is written correctly.

7. (A) Janice brushed her hair she was going to a party.

   (B) Going to the party while Janice brushed her hair.

   (C) As she was brushing her hair for the party.

   (D) Janice brushed her hair because she was going to a party.

8. (F) While he went to the store and bought soup and bread.

   (G) Going to the store, the bread and soup were bought.

   (H) He bought the soup and bread when he went to the store.

   (J) He went to the store he bought soup and bread.

9. (A) Before the accident when he saw the lights of the oncoming car.

   (B) When he saw the lights of the oncoming car before the accident.

   (C) He saw the lights of the oncoming car before the accident.

   (D) He saw the lights of the oncoming car then he had the accident.

10. (F) Mom took Dad's car when she went to work.

    (G) Mom went to work she took Dad's car.

    (H) When Mom took Dad's car as she went to work.

    (J) Taking Dad's car to work this morning.

11. (A) Playing the trombone in the marching band, the football game was played.

    (B) Allen played the trombone in the band he marched at the football game.

    (C) Marching in the band and playing the trombone at the football game.

    (D) Allen played the trombone in the marching band at the football game.

12. (F) Dotty and Kim are on the phone all the time they are best friends.

    (G) Because they are best friends and are talking on the phone all the time.

    (H) Dotty and Kim, who are best friends, are on the phone all the time.

    (J) Talking on the phone all the time and being best friends.

13. (A) The snow was really deep in Rachel's neighborhood, so we brang our sleds to her house and played all afternoon.

    (B) The school bus pulled up in front of my house, and we race for the front door to get warm.

    (C) Whenever Michael comes to my house for dinner, he ate more food than anyone else.

    (D) These last few weeks have been very stressful, so I'm looking forward to our spring vacation.

14. (F) They came to the party on time, but they wasn't supposed to leave so early.

    (G) Next summer we are going camping in Virginia, so my brother is saving his money for a new tent.

    (H) New Jersey, my home state, and Pennsylvania, the state to our west, is part of the Mid-Atlantic states.

    (J) Not wearing his helmet could of been the reason that Jake didn't survive the crash.

15. (A) For three days we waited for the rafts to rescue us; then we took our chances and swam for the island in the distance.

    (B) When he turned the corner onto 14th Street, Andy sees a man breaking into the drug store.

    (C) Mannie lifts weights for three years before he became the champion at our high school.

    (D) The snow had been falling for hours when he finally calls to me he's running late.

16. (F) Swimming and ballroom dancing is a good way to keep fit.

    (G) When I get back from the grocery store, I will expect you to have started making dinner.

    (H) My snow board was buried in the garage somewhere because it hasn't yet snowed this winter.

    (J) Jackie and Neil leaved my house at 6:00, so they should be home soon.

17. (A) By the time my mother got home, I had picked up all the mess from the party.

    (B) George studies his French every day, but he didn't get any better.

    (C) You and Will haven't gave me the money for the tickets yet.

    (D) Before she can buy any new clothes, Carrie had to get a part-time job.

DIRECTIONS: For numbers 18-21, choose the underlined part that is the simple subject of the sentence.

18. Sitting in the <u>kitchen</u> as if <u>nothing</u> had happened was <u>my</u> <u>mother</u>.
               F   G   H J

19. <u>When</u> I think about all the <u>aggravation</u> <u>you</u> put me through, <u>I</u> could scream.
   A   B   C   D

20. In the <u>middle</u> of the <u>floor</u> stood a paper <u>bag</u> full of caramel <u>popcorn</u>.
            F   G   H   J

21. My <u>mind</u> raced as <u>I</u> wondered <u>who</u> was coming up the <u>stairs</u>.
      A   B   C   D

DIRECTIONS: For numbers 22-24, choose the underlined part that is the simple predicate (verb) of the sentence.

22. Yolanda <u>felt</u> a <u>sense</u> of total <u>defeat</u> by the end of the tennis <u>match</u>.
       F   G   H   J

23. My parents <u>encourage</u> me <u>always</u> to <u>do</u> my <u>best</u> in all things.
               A   B   C   D

24. The <u>extreme</u> <u>heat</u> in the cabin <u>caused</u> the captain's <u>drowsiness</u> and the terrible accident.
       F   G   H   J

25. To <u>give in</u> to a bully <u>leads</u> to more <u>bullying</u> <u>later</u> on.
      A   B   C   D

DIRECTIONS: For numbers 26-28, read the underlined sentences. Choose the sentence that best combines those sentences into one.

26. <u>Many of the children in my neighborhood will be celebrating Chanukah during December.</u>
<u>Chanukah is the Jewish festival of lights.</u>

  (F)   Chanukah, the Jewish festival of lights, will be celebrated by many children in my neighborhood during December.

  (G)   Because many children in my neighborhood will be celebrating Chanukah during December, it is the Jewish festival of lights.

  (H)   During Chanukah, which is the Jewish festival of lights, many children in my neighborhood will be celebrating in December.

  (J)   Celebrating Chanukah, many children in my neighborhood are Jewish and will celebrate the festival of the lights in December.

27. <u>We drove to Maine to go camping last summer. We came home early because the weather was terrible.</u>

    (A) When we drove to Maine to go camping last summer, we came home early because the weather was terrible.

    (B) We came home early last summer when the weather was terrible because we drove to Maine to go camping.

    (C) Because the weather in Maine was so terrible last summer, we came home early from our camping trip.

    (D) Even though the weather in Maine was terrible last year, we came home early from our camping trip.

28. <u>Trail mix can be made of many different ingredients. Some of them are peanuts, raisins, and chocolate chips.</u>

    (F) Trail mix can be made of many different ingredients and some of them are peanuts, raisins, and chocolate chips.

    (G) Peanuts, raisins, and chocolate chips are some of the many ingredients that can be used to make trail mix.

    (H) Even though peanuts, raisins, and chocolate chips are used to make trail mix, there are many more ingredients.

    (J) Trail mix is made of peanuts, raisins, and chocolate chips.

DIRECTIONS: In numbers 29-31, choose the topic sentence that best fits the paragraph.

---

29. _____. Most people recognize the names Siamese, Persian, Burmese, and Manx as popular breeds of cats. There are actually nearly 40 distinctive breeds of cats grouped into two categories: the Persian and the domestic shorthair. What many people do not realize is that until 100 years ago, cats interbred freely all over the world, and few distinctive breeds were recognized. As cat fanciers came to value certain qualities or features in their pets, they interbred similar cats until all litters all had similar offspring. When this occurred, they were said to have "bred true," and a new breed was established.

    (A) Purebred cats make wonderful pets.

    (B) Cats have been companions for centuries and now are becoming more popular.

    (C) Some breeds of cats are more valuable than others because of their distinctive qualities.

    (D) Although cat fanciers may take pride in their purebred pets, the idea of distinctive breeds of cats is a relatively new one.

30. _____. Many common beetles from our woodlands are black or brown with patterns or markings that help them blend in with the wood or soil around them. Others from rain forests and jungles may be orange, red, yellow, or even metallic green or blue. This helps them blend in with the brilliant flowers in their surroundings. Beetles may have huge ornate antennae, large hooked jaws or mandibles, or even horns protruding from their foreheads.

   (F) Beetles come in many colors and can be fascinating to study.

   (G) Beetles come in a variety of colors and shapes that may help them blend in with their environment.

   (H) Beetles can easily be identified by their many shapes and sizes.

   (J) Beetles are identified by their colors and shapes and are designed to do various important jobs in the world.

31. _____. It is the largest and most populated of all the world's continents. It has the highest mountains, most of the longest rivers, and the largest deserts in the world. The countries of Asia include some of the poorest and some of the richest in the world, and while several of the world's largest cities are in Asia, most of its people are rural farmers working with simple tools. Birthplace of some of the world's oldest cultures, Asian nations compete on the cutting edge of modern technology.

   (A) Asia contains many contrasts in geography, economy, and technology.

   (B) Asia has many interesting geographical qualities.

   (C) Asia is different from the other continents of the world.

   (D) Asia combines the old and the new in its many nations.

DIRECTIONS: In numbers 32-34, choose the answer that best develops the topic sentence.

---

32. A flower is composed of four major organs: sepals, petals, the stamen, and the pistil.

   (F) Flowers are often brightly colored to attract insects.

   (G) The calyx and the corolla together form the perianth.

   (H) Sepals make up the cup-like calyx of the flower, which surrounds the base of the petals.

   (J) Insects carry pollen from the flower and fertilize other plants.

33. Snowflakes are made up of many ice crystals; their size and shape is determined primarily by the temperature of the air when they form and by the amount of water vapor in the air.

   (A) Snowflakes are usually hexagonal in shape because of the hydrogen and oxygen atoms in the crystalline water.

(B)   Snowflakes form as droplets of water vapor that cling to tiny dust or dirt particles in the air.

(C)   When the air is warmer and can hold more water vapor, crystals tend to grow quickly and have more branches clumping together to form large snowflakes.

(D)   Sleet and hail are also formed by freezing water or water vapor.

34.   All many-celled organisms, regardless of the species, reproduce by way of the one-celled ovum commonly called the egg.

(F)   An ovum contains an embryo fed by a yolk, which can be large or small depending on the length of time required for full development and on other sources of nourishment.

(G)   Eggs can be large or small, shelled or unshelled, single or in batches of up to 6 million in a single breeding season.

(H)   Whales produce only one offspring every two years.

(J)   Mammal ovum have small yolk sacs because the primary nourishment for the embryo comes from the mother's body.

DIRECTIONS: In numbers 35-37, choose the sentence that does not belong to the paragraph.

---

35.   1. The United States Marines are soldiers trained to serve on land, sea, and in the air but always in operations related to naval campaigns. 2. Although they became well known during World War II as they landed on islands in the Pacific, the Marines have been serving our country since July 11, 1798. 3. They prefer, however, to recognize the date of November 10, 1775, when the Continental Congress sanctioned the first two battalions of Marines. 4. Perhaps one of their most historically significant contributions to our history was their support of General George Washington and his troops as they crossed the Delaware to defeat the Hessians on Christmas Day, 1776.

(A)   Sentence 1   (C)   Sentence 3

(B)   Sentence 2   (D)   Sentence 4

36.   1. Influenza C, often confused with the common cold, is an airborne viral infection that causes fever, chills, headache, muscle ache, and sore throat. 2. It is most commonly contracted in the winter months when the weather is cold because people are indoors with poor air circulation and in closer proximity to one another. 3. The incubation period for the flu is 2 to 3 days, and it takes 7 to 10 days to run its course. 4. In 1918, the Spanish flu killed 20 million people in only a few months.

(F)   Sentence 1   (H)   Sentence 3

(G)   Sentence 2   (J)   Sentence 4

37. 1. The Great Depression had a devastating and long-term effect on the economy of the United States. 2. The collapse of the stock market in 1929 caused banks to fail and businesses to close. 3. The drought in the rural midwest created the 1930's Great Plains Dust Bowl, which damaged an already weak agricultural economy. 4. Wages for the lucky workers who were still employed fell as competition for work increased.

(A) Sentence 1   (C) Sentence 3

(B) Sentence 2   (D) Sentence 4

DIRECTIONS: In numbers 38-40, read the paragraph. Choose the sentence that best fills the blank in the paragraph.

---

38. _____. Solid matter has definite size and shape regardless of where it is put. A liquid, however, takes on the shape of the container in which it is placed even though it has definite size known as volume. A gas expands to fill the container in which it is placed, dispersing its molecules evenly and changing its relative density.

(F) A fourth state of matter where electrons are knocked free of their nuclei is called plasma.

(G) All matter is made of molecules, which are in turn made of atoms.

(H) Matter comes in three main forms: solid, liquid, and gas.

(J) The law of the Conservation of Matter says that matter cannot be destroyed.

39. During the Middle Ages in Germany, a medieval play about Adam and Eve used a tree hung with apples as part of its scenery. The tree, which represented the Garden of Eden, was called the "Paradise Tree" and was set up on December 24th, the feast day of Adam and Eve. It was hung with wafers, which represented communion hosts, and later with candles, which represented the light of Christ. As time passed, cookies and sweets replaced wafers, and the tree merged with a pyramidal ornament also popular at the time that was decorated with figures and topped with a star. _____.

(A) It is easy to see how these early decorations developed into the Christmas tree we know today.

(B) Prince Albert, the German husband of Queen Victoria, brought the tradition of the Christmas tree to England.

(C) Electric lights and more durable ornaments make our modern Christmas trees safer and more enjoyable than those of the past.

(D) Christmas was not celebrated as an important Christian holiday until several centuries after Jesus' birth.

40. The nine planets of our solar system orbit the sun, which holds them in our solar system by

its gravity, while also providing them with heat and light. _____. Mercury and Venus are sometimes classified as inferior planets because their orbits are smaller in diameter than that of Earth. The rest of the planets, Mars, Jupiter, Saturn, Uranus, Neptune, and Pluto, are considered superior planets because of the large diameter of their orbits.

(F)   There are several different methods of classifying the planets.

(G)   One method of classifying the planets is by the size of their orbits.

(H)   It is difficult to determine a single method of classifying these diverse bodies.

(J)   The terrestrial planets are often called the inner planets.

COOP

PRACTICE TEST 1

ANSWER KEY

Question Number	Correct Answer	If You Answered this Question Incorrectly, Refer to...

Test 1: Sequences

1.	(C)	P. 401
2.	(F)	P. 401
3.	(A)	P. 401
4.	(G)	P. 401
5.	(D)	P. 401
6.	(G)	P. 401
7.	(C)	P. 401
8.	(J)	P. 401
9.	(A)	P. 401
10.	(G)	P. 401
11.	(B)	P. 401
12.	(J)	P. 401
13.	(A)	P. 401
14.	(H)	P. 401
15.	(C)	P. 401
16.	(G)	P. 401
17.	(A)	P. 401
18.	(J)	P. 401
19.	(D)	P. 401
20.	(G)	P. 401

Test 2: Analogies

1.	(B)	P. 189
2.	(J)	P. 189
3.	(B)	P. 189
4.	(F)	P. 189
5.	(D)	P. 189
6.	(H)	P. 189
7.	(A)	P. 189
8.	(G)	P. 189
9.	(A)	P. 189
10.	(H)	P. 189
11.	(B)	P. 189
12.	(F)	P. 189
13.	(A)	P. 189
14.	(H)	P. 189
15.	(C)	P. 189
16.	(G)	P. 189
17.	(D)	P. 189
18.	(H)	P. 189
19.	(A)	P. 189
20.	(H)	P. 189

Test 3: Memory

1.	(C)	P. 415
2.	(K)	P. 415
3.	(C)	P. 415
4.	(H)	P. 415
5.	(D)	P. 415
6.	(J)	P. 415
7.	(E)	P. 415
8.	(J)	P. 415
9.	(D)	P. 415
10.	(F)	P. 415
11.	(E)	P. 415

12.	(F)	P. 415
13.	(D)	P. 415
14.	(H)	P. 415
15.	(C)	P. 415
16.	(H)	P. 415
17.	(E)	P. 415
18.	(J)	P. 415
19.	(E)	P. 415
20.	(J)	P. 415

Test 4: Verbal Reasoning

1.	(C)	P. 198
2.	(J)	P. 198
3.	(B)	P. 198
4.	(H)	P. 198
5.	(D)	P. 198
6.	(H)	P. 198
7.	(A)	P. 198
8.	(H)	P. 198
9.	(A)	P. 198
10.	(F)	P. 198
11.	(B)	P. 198
12.	(H)	P. 198
13.	(D)	P. 275
14.	(H)	P. 275
15.	(D)	P. 275
16.	(J)	P. 275
17.	(D)	P. 275
18.	(G)	P. 189
19.	(D)	P. 189
20.	(F)	P. 189

Test 5: Reading Comprehension

1.	(B)	P. 275
2.	(J)	P. 270
3.	(C)	P. 272
4.	(F)	P. 272
5.	(C)	P. 275
6.	(F)	P. 270
7.	(D)	P. 272
8.	(J)	P. 272
9.	(D)	P. 272
10.	(H)	P. 282
11.	(A)	P. 274
12.	(G)	P. 280
13.	(B)	P. 272
14.	(H)	P. 270
15.	(D)	P. 282
16.	(F)	P. 272
17.	(B)	P. 275
18.	(H)	P. 270
19.	(D)	P. 274
20.	(F)	P. 272
21.	(B)	P. 272
22.	(G)	P. 275
23.	(C)	P. 274
24.	(F)	P. 275
25.	(C)	P. 272
26.	(F)	P. 270
27.	(C)	P. 272
28.	(G)	P. 272
29.	(C)	P. 272
30.	(G)	P. 282
31.	(C)	P. 270
32.	(J)	P. 272
33.	(B)	P. 275

34.	(H)	P. 282
35.	(D)	P. 272
36.	(H)	P. 270
37.	(C)	P. 272
38.	(H)	P. 272
39.	(C)	P. 274
40.	(F)	P. 275

Test 6: Mathematics Concepts and Applications

1.	(C)	P. 409
2.	(J)	P. 356
3.	(D)	P. 371
4.	(J)	P. 354
5.	(A)	P. 360, 363
6.	(G)	P. 315, 317
7.	(A)	P. 328, 353, 382
8.	(J)	P. 360
9.	(C)	P. 320, 409
10.	(F)	P. 320, 323, 409
11.	(A)	P. 320
12.	(J)	P. 323
13.	(D)	P. 320
14.	(J)	P. 391
15.	(C)	P. 391
16.	(H)	P. 391
17.	(C)	P. 377
18.	(F)	P. 377, 391
19.	(D)	P. 409
20.	(G)	P. 409
21.	(B)	P. 409
22.	(F)	P. 369
23.	(A)	P. 363, 385
24.	(F)	P. 385
25.	(B)	P. 377

26.	(J)	P. 317
27.	(C)	P. 315
28.	(G)	P. 371
29.	(D)	P. 371
30.	(H)	P. 371
31.	(C)	P. 391
32.	(H)	P. 409
33.	(B)	P. 409
34.	(J)	P. 391
35.	(A)	P. 377
36.	(G)	P. 391
37.	(C)	P. 320
38.	(G)	P. 320, 323
39.	(D)	P. 404
40.	(H)	P. 371, 404

Test 7: Language Expression

1.	(D)	P. 211
2.	(F)	P. 225
3.	(B)	P. 211
4.	(G)	P. 225
5.	(C)	P. 211
6.	(H)	P. 207
7.	(D)	P. 207
8.	(H)	P. 211
9.	(C)	P. 207
10.	(F)	P. 206
11.	(D)	P. 206
12.	(H)	P. 206, 229
13.	(D)	P. 211
14.	(G)	P. 211
15.	(A)	P. 211, 234
16.	(G)	P. 211
17.	(A)	P. 212

18.	(J)	P. 212
19.	(D)	P. 212
20.	(H)	P. 212
21.	(A)	P. 212
22.	(F)	P. 212
23.	(A)	P. 212
24.	(H)	P. 212
25.	(B)	P. 212
26.	(F)	P. 206, 230
27.	(C)	P. 206, 230
28.	(G)	P. 206, 230
29.	(D)	P. 270
30.	(G)	P. 270
31.	(A)	P. 270
32.	(H)	P. 270
33.	(C)	P. 270
34.	(G)	P. 270
35.	(A)	P. 270
36.	(J)	P. 270
37.	(C)	P. 270
38.	(H)	P. 270
39.	(A)	P. 270
40.	(G)	P. 270

Test 1: Sequences

DETAILED EXPLANATIONS
OF ANSWERS

1. **(C)** The squares move right to left, one at a time.

2. **(F)** The first figure in each set is removed; the second becomes the first; the third becomes the second; a new figure becomes the third.

3. **(A)** The dots move above the squares, then move back into the squares.

4. **(G)** The triangle switches with the figure to its right.

5. **(D)** The last figure becomes the first; the other figures move one position to the right.

6. **(G)** The number of triangles increases from the left in each set.

7. **(C)** The first and third sets are the same; the second and fourth sets are the same; the fifth must be the same as the first and third since they alternate.

8. **(J)** This is a section of the alphabet in reverse order with one letter missing between each set of three letters.

9. **(A)** The first letter in each set is removed; the next two letters in each set move one position to the left; the next letter in the alphabet becomes the third letter.

10. **(G)** Each set is missing in the middle two letters in alphabetical order. The last two letters of each set become the first two in the next set.

11. **(B)** The two middle letters are always EA; the last letter of each set becomes the first letter of the next set.

12. **(J)** The subscripts increase by one, from right to left, one at a time.

13. **(A)** The subscripts decrease by one, from right to left, one at a time.

14. **(H)** The subscripts increase by one, from left to right, one at a time.

15. **(C)** The second number in each set is 2 less than the first number; the third number is six times the second number.

16. **(G)** The second number in each set is 2 more than the first number; the third number is the second number divided by three.

17. **(A)** The second number in each set is the first number divided by 9; the third number is 3 times the second.

18. **(J)** The second number in each set is always 27; the third number is 9 less than the first number.

19. **(D)** The third number in each set is the sum of the first and second numbers; the fourth is the sum of the second and third numbers; the first three numbers of a set are the last three numbers of the previous set.

20. **(G)** The second number in each set is 4 times the first number; the third number is 12 less than the second number.

Test 2: Analogies

DETAILED EXPLANATIONS
OF ANSWERS

1.   **(B)**   A finger is part of the hand, just as an eye is part of the face, choice (B). Choice (A), mouth, is another part of the face, but the relationship is part to whole. Thumb, choice (C), is another part of the hand, but does not belong listed in the second relationship. Foot, choice (D), is another body part, but does not complete the relationship with eye.

2.   **(J)**   In the same way that an ocean liner can transport more people by sea than a canoe, so can a bus, choice (J), transport more people by land than a buggy. (F) and (G), an airplane and a hot air balloon, are similar to a buggy because they are used for travel, but these two choices travel in the air and not the ground as a buggy does. (H), a boat, is another mode of transportation, like the bus, but boats travel by water.

3.   **(B)**   A house is a home for humans and a nest is a home for birds, just as a hamburger is a meal for humans and a worm (B) is a meal for birds. A bird, choice (A), uses the nest, but the relationship is that of SYNONYMS. An apple, choice (C), could be food for birds; however, worm is a better choice. A tree, choice (D), does not complete the relationship and would be incorrect.

4.   **(F)**   A baby primarily drinks from a bottle, just as a child usually drinks from a cup. Choice (G), pacifier, (H), rattle, and (J), highchair, are all items used by a baby. In addition, these words do not have any relation to bottle in their usage. The word needed to complete the analogy would have to be an object used by a child. The cup, answer choice (F), can be used by a child for drinking (just like a bottle).

5.   **(D)**   A part of a bird is its beak, and the relating part of a person is his/her mouth, choice (D). Choice (A), bird legs, would be incorrect since the missing word would have to be a body part of a human and relate to beak. Choice (B), eye, is incorrect for the same reason; it is a body part, but it does not relate to the bird's beak. Hand, choice (C), is part of a person, but it also does not relate to a bird's beak.

6.   **(H)**   Just as milk is produced by a cow, honey is produced by a bee, choice (H). Choice (F), butter, and (G), tea cup are incorrect because the missing word would need to be the producer of honey. Butter and tea cups are not even animate objects! Choice (J), child, may be thought to be correct, but a child does not produce honey.

7.   **(A)**   A button is part of a shirt that keeps it closed, just as shoe laces are the part of shoes that keep them closed. A coat, choice (B), hat, choice (C), and dress, choice (D) are not kept closed with shoe laces.

8.   **(G)**   A hot air balloon is an old-fashioned mode of traveling by air, and an airplane is a modern mode of air travel, just as a horse and buggy is an old-fashioned mode of ground travel, and a car is a modern way of traveling by ground. Choice (F), boat, is incorrect since it is a mode of traveling by water. Choice (H), horse, is a method of ground transportation, but it is not one that is contemporary. A tire, choice (J), is part of a car, and alone is not a method of travel.

9.   **(A)**   A weak or damaged leg can be assisted by a crutch, just as weak or damaged eyes can be assisted by glasses. Choice (B), face, is related to the word eye, but it is not an aiding device that would relate to crutch. Eye might relate to choice (C), book, since most people use their eyes to read, but the relationship would be completed with glasses (which relates to crutch much better). Choice (D), shoe, is related to a foot, not an eye—and would be incorrect.

10.   **(H)**   A hand is found at the end of an arm, just as a foot is found at the end of a leg (H). Choice (F), finger, and choice (G), toes, are related to this analogy since they are further extremities of a hand and foot. However, the word that is necessary to complete this relationship would need to compare with arm, and choices (F) and (G) are the incorrect body parts. Choice (J), shoe, would go on a foot, but the missing word would need to show what the foot is at the end of (not what goes on the end of a foot).

11.   **(B)**   A young flower emerges from a seed, just as a young bird (B) emerges from an egg. If the observation is made that a flower emerges from a seed, then answer choices (A) tree, (C) nest, and (D) leaf are incorrect since the answer choices do not emerge from eggs. The only answer choice that emerges from an egg is choice (B), the bird.

12.   **(F)**   A glove is placed over a hand, just as a sock is put on over a foot (F). Though you might think answer choices (G) and (J) are relevant, socks are not put on over shoes or boots. Answer choice (H), mitten, would not complete the analogy since socks are not normally placed over mittens.

13.   **(A)**   The United States is where the Statue of Liberty is located, just as Italy is where the Roman Colosseum (A) is located. (A) is correct since the completed analogy required a monument/landmark that was within Italy. Answer choice (B), Mount Rushmore, is located in the US, and would be incorrect. Choice (C), castle, is too broad. There are many castles located in many different countries, so it is not the best choice. Lastly, choice (D), Eiffel Tower, is located in France.

14.   **(H)**   A fish and a sea horse are found in the water, just as a horse and a lion (H) are found on land. Answer choices (F) and (J), star fish and octopus, are incorrect since they are primarily found in water, not land. Choice (G), bird, can be found on land, but is generally associated with the sky.

15. **(C)**   A school bus is used to take people to school, just as an ambulance is used to take people to a hospital (C). Choice (A), doctor, is one of the reasons why people are brought to the hospital, but choice (B), police car, is incorrect since it is another mode of transportation and not the destination of ambulances. Person, choice (D), is too vague, but would be incorrect for the same reason as choice (A).

16. **(G)**   A tire is part of a car that aids in its movement, just as the propeller of a ship (G) aids its movement. This analogy deals with propulsion and answer choice (F), anchor, helps a ship stop or remain stationary. Answer choice (H), would be incorrect since a crew boat does not have a propeller—it is moved by oars. Person, choice (J), would also be incorrect since people do not have propellers attached to them to move around—just ships.

17. **(D)**   A basketball is thrown in the air through a basketball hoop to score points, just as a football is kicked in the air through the uprights to score points. Answer choice (A), umpire, officiates sports games and is not involved in scoring points. Soccer ball, answer choice (B), is not used in the game of football or basketball and would not be the correct answer in this analogy. Choice (C), football helmet could be a good match with a football for a component relationship. However, the word that is needed serves as the goal through which the first word must pass in order for a team to score points.

18. **(H)**   Halloween is closely associated with trick-or-treating and candy, just as the Christmas holiday is associated with gift-giving and presents. Answer choice (F), diploma, is connected to graduations and not to the aforementioned holidays. While turkey, choice (G), is a common meal during many holidays, it is most closely associated with Thanksgiving. Shamrocks (J) are symbols of Ireland and the holiday of St. Patrick's Day. Answer choice (H), stockings/presents, is the best answer choice to relate with Christmas.

19. **(A)**   An automobile drives with the use of the tire as a person walks with the use of his/her foot. A shirt (C) and a hat (D) are connected with accessories and are not essential to moving. The hand (B) is not as essential to walking as the foot is.

20. **(H)**   A teacher works at a school, just as a doctor works at a hospital (H). Since the analogy requires a location to complete itself, answer choice (F), school bus, would be incorrect. The same is true for answer choice (G), desk. Though it is associated with the teacher and school, it is incorrect. Though an ambulance, choice (J), is associated with doctors, it is also (with the same reasoning as choice (F)) incorrect. Hospital, choice (H), is the appropriate answer selection since it is the place where most doctors work.

Test 3: Memory

DETAILED EXPLANATIONS OF ANSWERS

1. **(C)** Sirot means a pet. One way you may have connected the word sirot to its definition is to notice that the last three letters of si**rot** match a common pet bird, the par**rot**.

2. **(K)** Hammasure means to be very quiet. For strategies on how to connect the word hammasure to its definition, refer to the techniques presented in the Memory Review.

3. **(C)** Winuim means a glass bottle. One way you may have connected the word winuim to its definition is to notice that the first three letters in **win**uim match those in the word **win**dow. The connection is that windows are made of glass, like glass bottles.

4. **(H)** Flamom means to be like ice. For strategies on how to connect the word flamom to its definition, refer to the techniques presented in the Memory Review.

5. **(D)** Tuckel means to smell like flowers. For strategies on how to connect the word tuckel to its definition, refer to the techniques mentioned in the Memory Review.

6. **(J)** Refub means a house. One way you may have connected the word refub to its definition is to notice that refub is close to the word refurbish, which means to renovate. The association then can be made that houses are commonly refurbished.

7. **(E)** Stelin means to speak. For strategies on how to connect the word stelin to its definition, refer to the techniques offered in the Memory Review.

8. **(J)** Blum means a wheel. For strategies on how to connect the word blum to its definition, refer to the techniques presented in the Memory Review.

9. **(D)** Balligag means a high wall. One way you may have connected the word balligag to its definition is to notice that the letters "b" and "l" in the word **bal**ligag mimic the height of the wall in the definition.

10. **(F)** Winlot means a rainstorm. One way that you may have connected the word winlot to its definition is to notice that the letters "win" in **win**lot also match the letters in the word **win**d. The connection is made in that during rainstorms, there are often rough winds.

11. **(E)** Mulag means a branch of a tree. One way that you may have connected the word mulag to its definition is to associate the "lag" part of mu**lag** with the similar sounding "log." The connection is made that logs are made of wood—or more generally, trees.

12. **(F)** Pollma means to be different. For strategies on how to connect the word pollma to its definition, refer to the techniques presented in the Memory Review.

13. **(D)** Cesy means a shout. For strategies on how to connect the word cesy to its definition, refer to the techniques presented in the Memory Review.

14. **(H)** Shamel means a bruise. One way that you may have connected the word shamel to its definition is to associate the word shamel and **sham**bles, which means in ruins or bad shape. The connection is that if a person were in shambles, he/she might have bruises on him/herself.

15. **(C)** Dentalog means to remove. One way that you may have connected the word dentalog to its definition is to associate the first part of **dent**alog with **dent**ist. The association is made that dentists often remove teeth from people.

16. **(H)** Gradem means to chirp like a bird. For strategies on how to connect the word gradem to its definition, refer to the techniques presented in the Memory Review.

17. **(E)** Chimra means a piece of clothing. For strategies on how to connect the word chimra to its definition, refer to the techniques offered in the Memory Review.

18. **(J)** Blancum means to be rocky. For strategies on how to connect the word blancum to its definition, refer to the techniques offered in the Memory Review.

19. **(E)** Wazur means to confuse. For strategies on how to connect the word wazur to its definition, refer to the techniques offered in the Memory Review.

20. **(J)** Dotmic means to act like a baby. For strategies on how to connect the word dotmic to its definition, refer to the techniques offered in the Memory Review.

Test 4: Verbal Reasoning

DETAILED EXPLANATIONS OF ANSWERS

1. **(C)** Shell. Every egg has a shell (C); it is the part that holds an egg in its form. The shell is a necessary part of an egg. Bacon is often eaten with eggs for breakfast. Bacon (A) and breakfast (B) are associated with an egg, not parts of a whole. Hatch (D) is what some eggs do. However, not all eggs hatch, so that is not a necessary part of an egg.

2. **(J)** Engine. Without an engine, a car will go nowhere. A car must have an engine in order to be useful; an engine is a necessary part of a car. One needs a driver's license (F) to operate a car, but it is not considered a part of a car. A person can be a passenger and consider a car quite useful, even without a license. A passenger (G) uses a car but is not a part of a car. A car sitting in a driveway is without passengers, but it is still a perfectly functioning car. A map (H) can be helpful when in a car. However, it is only a tool to help one who is using a car; it is not a necessary part of a car. A person can certainly use a car without a map.

3. **(B)** Pavement. Highways are paved; it is this pavement that creates the highway. Without it, there would be no highway, just a dirt road, so pavement is a necessary part of a highway. Cars (A) utilize a highway, but if you take away the cars, the highway still exists. Cars are not a necessary part of a highway. Some highways have bridges (D) and some have tolls (C). They are sometimes part of a highway, but if you took away the tolls or the bridges, you could still have a highway; they are not a necessary part of all highways.

4. **(H)** Chimney. In order to be able to use a fireplace, there must be a chimney for ventilation. In order for it to function properly, a chimney is a necessary part of a fireplace. Sometimes there is a fire (F) in a fireplace, and sometimes there is not. A fire might be considered a part of a fireplace, but it is not a necessary part. The fireplace still exists in the same form, even when there is no fire. In order to create a fire in the fireplace, one must use some sort of fuel (like logs (G)) and something to start the fire (like matches (J)). However, like the fire, these things might be commonly associated with a fireplace, but they are not necessary parts. Again, the fireplace still exists in the same form, even when there is no fire (or logs or matches).

5. **(D)** Vocabulary. To use a language, one must know the vocabulary or words. Vocabulary is a necessary part of language. Voice (A) is used to speak (B) a language, but language is also written. There can also be language without voice, such as sign language. Spanish (C) is one example of language; it is not a part of language.

6. **(H)** Food. An essential component of dinner is food. While dinner may be eaten at a table (G), with a fork (F), or accompanied by a napkin (J), the necessary part is food (H).

7. **(A)** Apple. The relationship between peas/lettuce/cucumbers is that they are all green vegetables. Cherry/strawberry/apple are all red fruits. All of the items are connected based on their color and type. The other choices (B), (C), and (D) are all fruits, but none is red.

8. **(H)** Corn. The relationship between transportation/car/Mustang is that each word is more specific than the previous word. Car is more specific than transportation—it is a mode of transportation. Mustang is more specific than car—it is a type of car. Vegetable is more specific than food, and corn is more specific than vegetable. All of the items are connected by going from general to specific. Fruit (F) is another food group like vegetables. It is not a specific type of vegetable. Dinner (G) may be associated with food and vegetables, but it is not a specific type of vegetable. A garden (J) may be associated with vegetables because it is a place where vegetables grow, but it is not a specific type of vegetable.

9. **(A)** Montreal. The relationship between London/Paris/Munich is that they are cities in Europe. New York/San Francisco/Montreal are all cities in North America. All of the cities are connected based on their location. Answers (B), (C), and (D) are states or countries, not cities.

10. **(F)** Hammer. The relationship between paint/canvas/brushes is that they are tools used by a painter. Nails/wood/hammer are all tools used by a carpenter. All of the items are connected based on who uses them. A carpenter makes furniture (G), like an artist makes a painting, but this does not convey the same relationship as brush and hammer. There is not enough information given about carpenter (H) and the hardware store (J) to establish a relationship.

11. **(B)** Guffaw. The relationship between walk/jog/sprint is that they show an increase in intensity. Jog is faster than walk, and sprint is stronger than jog. Giggle/laugh/guffaw also show an increase in intensity. Laugh is stronger than giggle, and guffaw is stronger than laugh. All of the items are connected based on an increase in intensity. Chuckle (A) is softer than laugh, not stronger. That would show a decreased intensity. Shout (C) and cry (D) are other actions a person can do, but they are not the same type of action as giggle and laugh.

12. **(H)** Deck. The relationship between sand/glass/window is that glass is made from sand, and windows are made from glass. Tree/wood/deck shows the same relationship. Wood is made from a tree, and a deck is made from wood. All of these items are connected based on material and use. A plank (F) is a specific size piece of lumber, not what one would create out of the lumber. Oak (G) is just a type of tree. It has nothing to do with the use of lumber. A knot (J) is part of a tree or lumber. The connection needs to be based on use, not the relation of a part to a whole.

13. **(D)** Alfred knew quite a bit about reptiles. If Alfred or his mom were afraid (A) and (B), they probably would not go to the reptile house to begin with. Also, there is nothing indicating that they were afraid. There is nothing indicating whether Alfred goes to the zoo every week (C). He might, but we can't know for sure, so it is not the best answer.

14. **(H)**   It was raining outside. Jesse was dripping wet when she came back for the umbrella. Most likely she got wet from the rain (H), so (H) is the best choice for this question. Since Jesse got wet, it is safe to assume it is already raining (F), not that it might in the future. There is no mention of homework. Also, since she grabbed an umbrella (not her homework (G)), it seems that she probably came back for that. There is also nothing indicating whether Jesse likes school (J). She may or may not.

15. **(D)**   Max had hot dogs for dinner. Since it states that Max cooked hot dogs for dinner, we can guess that that's what he ate. Max looked for hamburgers so we can guess he probably likes them; even if we don't guess that, there isn't anything indicating that he doesn't like them (A). Although he is able to make hamburgers, spaghetti, and hot dogs, there is nothing indicating whether he is actually a good cook (B). He may or may not be. This is not likely to be the best answer. We know that there weren't any hamburgers, but there was spaghetti, and there may or may not have been anything else (C).

16. **(J)**   Jill picked three kinds of flowers. Count up the types of flowers, and you can see that Jill picked at least three types of flowers, making (J) the best answer. All we know for sure is that Jill did not pick any roses, but we have no idea why. Whether she doesn't like them (F), her friend doesn't grow them (G), or whether she is allergic to them (H) are all possibilities, but we do not know for sure. There is nothing indicating whether any of these things is true.

17. **(D)**   Jane now has at least one cat. Jane has two pets, and one is definitely a cat. The other pet may or may not be a cat. We're not sure, but we know she has at least one cat (Mittens). We have no idea whether she has a rabbit (C) or whether Rover ran away (A). Neither rabbits nor what happened to Rover is mentioned, so we cannot make guesses. We only know Jane has two pets (B), and one of them is a cat. We do not know anything about the second pet; it may or may not be another cat.

18. **(G)**   Refitasblints. Look at <u>turfim</u>ablinty meaning any<u>how</u> and <u>turfim</u>sblints meaning some<u>how</u>. Turfim must mean how. That leaves ablinty to mean any and sblints to mean some. Look at refitablinty meaning <u>any</u>where. Ablinty means any, so refit must mean where. So refitasblints must mean somewhere.

19. **(D)**   Mossidrospen. A crack is a smaller break; whereas, shatter is a large break. Compare miffizacken and mossizacken, both types of breaks. Zacken must be the root, meaning a type of break. Since a crack is smaller and a shatter is bigger, miffi must indicate little, and mossi must indicate big. If miffidrospen is a small amount of liquid, mossidrospen must be a larger amount of liquid.

20. **(F)**   Errosterfen. To create the past tense of "to tell" (zolterfen), one must add "er" at the beginning. So to create the past tense of "to sell" (rosterfen), one must also add "er" to the beginning of the word, making errosterfen.

Test 5: Reading Comprehension

DETAILED EXPLANATIONS OF ANSWERS

1.   **(B)**   The passage gives directions on how to use a spa and explains how to take care of a spa; therefore, we can tell that the passage is directed toward spa owners (B), not scientists (A), spa manufacturers (C), or spa salespeople (D).

2.   **(J)**   The passage focuses on giving directions for spa care, thereby assuming that the reader already owns one, making (F) and (G) false. The passage does not say spas are dangerous (H).

3.   **(C)**   The third paragraph of the passage says that the growth of bacteria and viruses is prevented with sanitizer. Sanitizer doesn't control the pH (A), doesn't affect water temperature (D), and cannot be used instead of a filter (B).

4.   **(F)**   The first paragraph of the passage describes the work of the filter. The filter does not control the pH (G) or temperature (H), and the passage explicitly states that it cannot remove the items listed in (J).

5.   **(C)**   The technical language and statistics show that this passage is intended for researchers. The passage is too technical to be intended for children (A) and (B) or parents (D).

6.   **(F)**   The entire passage reports the findings of a study on the relationship between children's reading levels and the stories they make up. The passage does not mention I.Q. levels (G) or television (H) and (J).

7.   **(D)**   All of the elements were used in the study according to the passage.

8.   **(J)**   The passage only discusses the findings about children in grades 1-6. The passage does not mention any other grades (F) and (G). The passage says nothing about public or private school (H).

9.   **(D)**   Twain's travels in the U.S. and his writing style are reasons the author gives for Twain's Americanness. Twain did not set all of his stories in the United States (B), as *Innocents Abroad* is set in Europe.

10.   **(H)**   Europe is sometimes called "the Old World" and by Twain's account of his inva-

sion of the Old World, the author means Twain's travels in Europe as an American. A museum (F), the Mississippi (G), and the United States (J) are not known as "the Old World."

11. **(A)**   Twain did not work as a newspaper editor, although he did work as a printer's apprentice (C), a lecturer (D), and was in the Confederate militia (B).

12. **(G)**   From the very beginning of the passage, an admiring tone is used to describe Twain's life. The author is definitely not negative (F) and is neither confused (H) nor sentimental (J) about the details of Twain's life.

13. **(B)**   The first sentence of the second paragraph tells us that the Civil War ended Twain's steamboating and that he served in a Confederate militia company. Twain was never a newspaper editor (C), and although he did travel in the U.S. (D) and did become a popular writer (A), these elements had nothing to do with ending his steamboating career.

14. **(H)**   This passage gives a brief overview of research on children's stories. The author does not disagree with the findings (F) or explain why researchers are interested in this topic (J). Although the last sentence of the passage suggests a possible area for more research, there is nothing in the paragraph about children's communication (G).

15. **(D)**   The word "narrative" means "story." Content (A), analysis (B), and structure (C) are all parts of a story, but they do not mean narrative.

16. **(F)**   The first sentence of the second paragraph lists the two approaches to analyzing children's stories. Although the elements listed in (G), (H), and (J) are discussed in the passage, they are not described as approaches.

17. **(B)**   In the last sentence of the passage, the author suggests a direction for future research. The author does not conduct any research (A), he/she is only summarizing past research, which he/she does not believe is wrong (C) or unimportant (D).

18. **(H)**   From the very first sentence this passage asserts that demands for changes in the school system are a result of the changing concerns of American society, not the opposite (J). The passage does not argue for (F) or against (G) more changes.

19. **(D)**   The passage mentions the end of the normal school during the early 1900s but does not discuss its creation. The passage does discuss the reforms listed in (A), (B), and (C).

20. **(F)**   The second paragraph of the passage is about the revision of teacher education and how it reflects changes in society. Although the paragraph states that teachers tend to teach as they have been taught, this is an effect, rather than a cause, of change. The passage does not discuss television (H) or teacher dissatisfaction (J).

21. **(B)**   The last sentence of the passage explains that teachers tend to teach as they have been taught because they take the same educational courses. (A) and (C) are both true in and of

themselves, but they are not causes of teachers teaching as they have been taught. The passage does not mention teachers trying to keep pace with other teachers (D).

22. **(G)** Douglass was such a good speaker that some people didn't believe that he could have been a slave. He wrote his autobiography after they doubted him, in order to prove them wrong (J). His plantation (F) and work experience (H) did not cause people to doubt that he was a former slave.

23. **(C)** According to the passage, Douglass worked against slavery as an agent (A), a consultant to the President (B), and as a publisher (D), but the passage does not say he was a lawyer (C).

24. **(F)** The passage states that Douglass had to continue his education in the streets because Mr. Auld warned Mrs. Auld that education would make Douglass unfit for being a slave. We can assume that Mr. Auld was in control of everyone in the household and was able to keep Mrs. Auld from continuing to teach Douglass. (G) and (H) are false because Douglass could certainly have continued to learn from Mrs. Auld. Mrs. Auld was forced to stop teaching Douglass before Douglass moved and began working in a shipyard (J).

25. **(C)** The passage states that Douglass worked to get both civil rights for freed men (A) and rights for women (B).

26. **(F)** This passage describes passive-aggressive personality disorder but does not list the situations that cause it (H), discuss treatments (G), or list clinics (J).

27. **(C)** The first paragraph of the passage says that this disorder "may be context dependent, appearing only in certain situations." The passage does not discuss causes of the disorder (A), nor does it discuss the distribution of the disease (B) and (D).

28. **(G)** The second paragraph of the passage says that the disorder is recognized by the "seemingly unjustified frustration and hostility others feel toward such individuals." The passage does not mention a blood sample (F), a personality test (H), or a psychiatrist (J).

29. **(C)** The first sentence of the passage defines the disorder. Choice (A) is the exact opposite of passive-aggressive behavior, as fighting is open aggression. The passage does not mention indecision (B). Choice (D) describes masochism, not passive-aggressive disorder.

30. **(G)** Covert means hidden or secretive. Open (H) is the opposite of covert. Aggressive (F) and evoke (J) are unrelated to covert.

31. **(C)** This passage tells the reader how to use an absentee ballot and when it can be used. If a voter were at the poll, he/she would have no use for these instructions (A). The passage does not explain how to work a voting machine (D) or how to count ballots (B).

32. **(J)** Condition four explains that the last day to request an absentee ballot is October 29.

The passage gives the dates of choices (F) and (G) for other deadlines. The date of choice (H) is not in the passage at all.

33.   **(B)**   "Instructions for Absentee Voting" is probably a government publication because the government controls voting. The instructions are not by previous absentee voters (C) because the instructions are formal in tone and seem official. There is no evidence in the passage to support the idea that the passage was authored by the League of Women Voters (D) or any other organization (A).

34.   **(H)**   "Via" means "by way of." Choices (F), (G), and (J) are unrelated to via.

35.   **(D)**   According to condition two, the person could vote at his/her old polling place (A) or with an absentee ballot (B). The person could not vote somewhere where he/she isn't registered (C).

36.   **(H)**   The passage describes the suffering and death of the Union prisoners at Andersonville prison due to the lack of shelter and supplies. The passage doesn't discuss Union prisons (F). The passage mentions the chances of survival (G) and the lack of food (J), but neither of these is the main idea of the passage.

37.   **(C)**   The first sentence of the last paragraph states that the prisoners didn't get enough food. The passage does not mention doctors (A) or lack of exercise (B); in fact, the passage discusses the physical work done by the prisoners.

38.   **(H)**   The last paragraph states that the prison was open thirteen months.

39.   **(C)**   The last sentence of the passage lists the causes from which the prisoners died; the list includes the diseases of choices (A), (B), and (D).

40.   **(F)**   This passage was probably taken from a textbook because it is a formal overview. This indicates that there is some distance between the event and the writers of the passage. A government report (G) would probably have been more technical and given more statistics. Prison records would not have given a detached summary of the conditions of the prison. Journals kept by prisoners (J) would have been personal stories full of details about their lives.

Test 6: Mathematics Concepts
and Applications

DETAILED EXPLANATIONS
OF ANSWERS

1. **(C)** Add 6 to both sides of the equation: $3x - 6 + 6 = 15 + 6$, $3x = 21$. Divide both sides by 3: $\dfrac{3x}{3} = \dfrac{21}{3}$; so $x = 7$.

2. **(J)** The total amount Albert collected from his aunt, uncle, mother, and father was ($12.00 + $8.25 + $12.50 + $7.50) = $40.25. So the amount he received from his grandfather must be $50.00 − $40.25 = $9.75.

3. **(D)** The total amount of milk that Sara drank is $(7 + 6 + 5 + 5) = 23$ oz. The total amount of milk she drank for the 5 days is $(6 \times 5) = 30$ oz. The missing amount of milk (for Thursday) must be $30 - 23 = 7$ oz.

4. **(J)** The "2" is the third digit to the right of the decimal point. So it must be 2 thousandths.

5. **(A)** To multiply a number by 100 results in shifting the decimal point 2 places to the right. Dividing by 100 results in shifting the decimal point 2 places to the left. When the decimal point is shifted 2 places to the left instead of 2 places to the right, it results in the decimal point being 4 places to the left of where it should have been. To correct this, we shift the decimal point 4 places to the right:

$$37625.4500$$

6. **(G)** If Janet had pressed the plus button, the original number would have increased by 54. By pressing the minus button, she caused the number to decrease by 54. So she lost 54 twice. To make up for this double loss, we must add $(54 + 54) = 108$ to the result. Janet obtained $-13 + 108 = 95$.

7. **(A)** We begin by converting the given numbers to similar expressions. Here it is best to convert to decimal fractions: $83\% = 0.83$, $\dfrac{13}{16} = 0.8125$, and 0.78 is already a decimal fraction. Now we see that the correct order is 0.78, 0.8125, 0.83. This is the same as 0.78, $\dfrac{13}{16}$, 83%.

8. **(J)**   The total cost of the students' lunches must be $4.93 × 18 = $88.74.

9. **(C)**   If we replace x with 3 and y with –2, we obtain $2x + 3y = 2(3) + 3(-2) = 6 - 6 = 0$.

10. **(F)**   If we replace y with 6 and z with –2, we obtain $\dfrac{3y}{z} = \dfrac{3(6)}{-2} = -9$.

11. **(A)**   5 sets of 7 result in $5 × 7 = 35$. If we include the 4 that were left over, we obtain $35 + 4 = 39$.

12. **(J)**   Divide 357 by 15: $357 ÷ 15 = 23$, remainder 12. So there are already 23 full boxes, and the 24th box would need $15 - 12 = 3$ cassettes to fill it.

13. **(D)**   Let m represent the smaller multiple of 4. Then the next higher multiple of 4 must be $m + 4$. The sum of these two multiples of 4 must be $m + (m + 4) = 2m + 4$. The product of 8 and 9 is $8 × 9 = 72$. The number that is 12 less than the product of 8 and 9 is $72 - 12 = 60$. So, to rephrase the original story, we may say $2m + 4 = 60$. Now, add -4 to both sides: $2m + 4 - 4 = 60 - 4$, so $2m = 56$. Divide both sides by 2: $\dfrac{2m}{2} = \dfrac{56}{2}$, so $m = 28$.

14. **(J)**   Since $\overline{OD} \perp \overline{AB}$, the measure of angle DOB must be 90°. So $x° + (x° - 20°) = 90°$. Now combine like terms (ignoring the degree sign): $2x - 20 = 90$. Add 20 to both sides: $2x - 20 + 20 = 90 + 20$, so $2x = 110$. Divide both sides by 2: $\dfrac{2x}{2} = \dfrac{110}{2}$, so $x = 55$.

15. **(C)**   [In the figure, we do not need to pay attention to the triangle.] $\overline{AC}$ meets straight line $\overline{BC}$ at C, making angles BCA and ACD complementary (their sum is 180°). That is: $y + 110 = 180$ (ignoring the degree sign). Subtract 110 from both sides: $y + 110 - 110 = 180 - 110$, so $y = 70$.

16. **(H)**   Recall that the sum of the two acute angles of a right triangle is 90°. That is: $x + 43 = 90$ (again ignoring the degree sign). Add -43 to both sides: $x + 43 - 43 = 90 - 43$, so $x = 47$.

17. **(C)**   A rectangle must contain two pairs of congruent sides. In set 1, we already have two straws, measuring 20 in. each. We needed to find a match for the 12-in. side.

18. **(F)**   A scalene triangle has 3 unequal sides. So we cannot choose (H) or (J). We must also bear in mind that the sum of the measures of any two sides of a triangle must be greater than the measure of the third side. So we cannot choose (G), since $9 + 6 = 15$. The correct choice is (F). [Check: (1) 15, 6, and 10 are mutually unequal, and (2) $6 + 10 > 15$.]

19. **(D)**   If we let x represent Xena's age, then Yvonne's age must be $x - 2$. Since Yvonne is 5 years younger than Steve, his age must be $(x - 2) + 5$, that is, $x + 3$.

20. **(G)** At d dollars per month for 9 months, Edith would earn $9d$. For the next 3 months, she earned $d - \$15$ per month. So for the last 3 months, she earned $3(d - 15)$ (we can safely ignore the dollar sign). For the 12 months, she would earn a total of $9d + 3(d - 15)$. Clear brackets: $9d + 3(d - 15) = 9d + 3d - 45 = 12d - 45$.

21. **(B)** Multiply each term in $(3n + 4)$ by each term in $(n - 2)$ and simplify: $(3n + 4)(n - 2) = 3n^2 - 2n - 8$.

22. **(F)** Although it is not absolutely necessary, it would help to group the numbers, as a reminder of the operations that must be performed first: $24 \div 6 + 2 \times 8 = (24 \div 6) + (2 \times 8) = 4 + 16 = 20$.

23. **(A)** First, find 20% of 90: $\dfrac{20 \times 90}{100} = 18$. Next, find 25% of 36: $\dfrac{25 \times 36}{100} = 9$. Finally, divide 18 by 9: $18 \div 9 = 2$.

24. **(F)** 210% of 420 is $\dfrac{210 \times 420}{100} = 882$.

25. **(B)** First, compute the area of 1 sheet of plywood $4 \times 8 = 32$ ft^2. Next, compute the area of the fence: $40 \times 7 = 280$ ft^2. Then, divide the area of the fence by the area of 1 sheet of plywood: $280 \div 32 = 8.75$. Since plywood is sold only in whole sheets, the carpenter must buy 9 sheets.

26. **(J)** Gregory improved his score by $58 - 49 = 9$; Nancy improved hers by $70 - 64 = 6$; Jerome improved his by $67 - 56 = 11$; and Rhoda actually decreased. Jerome showed the most improvement.

27. **(C)** First, compute the total score for each of these four students: Bill: $60 + 58 = 118$, Clara: $58 + 65 = 123$, Gregory: $49 + 58 = 107$, and Rhoda: $71 + 69 = 140$. We see that Gregory did the worst.

28. **(G)** The average score for the 7 students on the first test was $(64 + 71 + 58 + 49 + 56 + 60 + 65) \div 7 = 423 \div 7 = 60.43$. The nearest number given is 61.

29. **(D)** If the average score for the 7 students on the second test was 66, then the total score must be $66 \times 7 = 462$. The subtotal from the first 6 students is $(70 + 69 + 65 + 58 + 67 + 58) = 387$. So the missing score must be $462 - 387 = 75$.

30. **(H)** First, compute the distance between Alphatown and Betatown: $45 \times 4 = 180$ miles. Next, calculate the distance between Betatown and Chetatown: $54 \times 5 = 270$ miles. So Wong's total driving time was $4 + 5 = 9$ hours, for a total distance of $180 + 270 = 450$ miles. His average speed must be $450 \div 9 = 50$ mph.

31. **(C)** Multiply 0.0012 by 10,000: $0.0012 \times 10,000 = 12$.

32. **(H)** Add 6 to both sides of the equation: $3x - 6 + 6 = 42 + 6$, so $3x = 48$. Divide both sides by 3: $\dfrac{3x}{3} = \dfrac{48}{3}$; so $x = 16$.

33. **(B)** The line intersects the y-axis at 4 units from 0 and intersects the x-axis 5 units from 0. So the slope of the line is $\dfrac{4}{5}$. Since we can clearly see that the line is right-inclined (runs from lower left to upper right), the slope is positive. (This is why we could safely ignore the signs of the x- and y-intercepts.)

34. **(J)** The sum of angles A and E is $90° + 90° = 180°$. The sum of the three remaining angles must be $540° - 180° = 360°$. These three angles may may have different values, but they must equal $360°$.

35. **(A)** Compute the area of the front face: $6 \times 10 = 60$ in². Compute the area of the top face: $10 \times 14 = 140$ in². Compute the area of the side face: $6 \times 14 = 84$ in². Add these three areas together: 60 in² $+ 140$ in² $+ 84$ in² $= 284$ in².

36. **(G)** The width of the rectangle containing a semicircle is $(7 \text{ cm} + 7 \text{ cm}) = 14$ cm. The area of the complete rectangle is $18 \times 14 = 252$ cm². The area of the semicircle is half the area of a complete circle with the same radius; the radius of the circle is 7, so its area is $3.14 \times 7^2 = 3.14 \times 7 \times 7 = 153.86$ cm². The area of the semicircle must be 153.86 cm² $\div 2 = 76.93$ cm². The area of the shaded region of the rectangle must be 252 cm² $- 76.93$ cm² $= 175.07$ cm², which is close to 175 cm².

37. **(C)** If 1 kg $= 2.2$ lbs, then 150 kg $= 2.2 \times 150 = 330$ lbs.

38. **(G)** One way to answer this question is to begin by expressing \$3,000 as a fraction of \$25,000: $\dfrac{3000}{25000} = 0.12$. Then multiply \$30,000 by 0.12: $\$30,000 \times 0.12 = \$3,600$.

39. **(D)** Here we are interested in the <u>net rise</u>, that is, temperature at the end of a period minus temperature at the beginning of that period. So the temperature rises are: February – April $= 10°$, March – May $= 5°$, April – June $= 10°$, and May – July $= 25°$.

40. **(H)** We need the <u>net rise</u>. The easiest way to compute the average temperature rise between March and August is as follows: find the difference between the temperature readings for the two months. The temperature in August was $90°$, while in March it was $40°$. So the net rise was $90° - 40° = 50°$. This is a 5-month interval; hence, the average temperature rise must be $50° \div 5 = 10°$.

Test 7: Language Expression

DETAILED EXPLANATIONS
OF ANSWERS

1. **(D)**   It is the only choice that is in the past tense.

2. **(F)**   When comparing two items, heavier is the correct adjective.

3. **(B)**   Together, Maggie and Carrie are "they" and this requires the word "plan."

4. **(G)**   When comparing three or more items, the superlative "scariest" is used.

5. **(C)**   Because it relates to an action that will be completed in the future, "will have eaten," which is future perfect, is used.

6. **(H)**   Because it refers to an action that is taking place at the same time as another, "meanwhile" is the correct choice.

7. **(D)**   (A) is two sentences without punctuation, and (B) and (C) are dependent clauses.

8. **(H)**   (F) is a dependent clause; (G) contains a dangling participle, and (J) is two sentences.

9. **(C)**   (A) and (B) are dependent clauses, and (D) is two sentences.

10. **(F)**   (G) is two sentences, and (H) and (J) are dependent clauses.

11. **(D)**   (A) has a dangling participle; (B) is two sentences, and (C) is only participial phrases.

12. **(H)**   (F) is two sentences; (G) is a dependent clause, and (J) is a participial phrase.

13. **(D)**   (A) uses "brang," and (B) has inconsistent tenses, as does (C).

14. **(G)**   (F) uses "wasn't" for "weren't"; (H) has a compound subject and needs "are;" and (J) uses "could of" for "could have."

15. **(A)**   (B), (C), and (D) have inconsistent tenses.

16. **(G)** (F) has a compound subject and requires "are," and (H) and (J) have inconsistent tenses.

17. **(A)** (B) and (D) have inconsistent tenses, and (C) uses "haven't gave" for "haven't given."

18. **(J)** Mother is the one sitting.

19. **(D)** The first part is an adverbial clause. "I could scream" is the independent clause.

20. **(H)** The bag stood in the middle of the floor.

21. **(A)** The mind is what is racing.

22. **(F)** "Felt" is the verb. "Defeat" and "match" are nouns in this sentence.

23. **(A)** "Encourage" is the verb. "To do" is an infinitive used as a noun.

24. **(H)** "Heat caused" is the simple sentence.

25. **(B)** "Leads" is the verb. "To give in" is an infinitive used as the subject of the sentence.

26. **(F)** (G) assumes a non-existent cause and effect; (H) is a muddled mess; and (J) is just plain awkward.

27. **(C)** (A) sounds as though they came home when they drove there; (B) infers that the weather was terrible because they drove there; and (D) states that they would have liked to stay despite the terrible weather.

28. **(G)** (F) would be barely acceptable even with a comma; (H) makes incorrect use of "even though"; and (J) infers that these three are the only ingredients.

29. **(D)** The main idea of the paragraph is not related to cats as good pets, cats being popular, or the value of certain breeds.

30. **(G)** There is no mention of beetles being fascinating to study or of ways of identifying them. There is also no mention of the jobs that they do.

31. **(A)** The paragraph discusses more than geography; no other continents are described, and the last option does not cover geography.

32. **(H)** (F) is too general; (G) names parts unrelated to the sentence before it, and (J) is unrelated to the parts of the flower.

33. **(C)**   (A) is unrelated to the previous sentence, as is (D). (B) is related to the topic, but does not expand the idea of temperature as the cause of size and shape.

34. **(G)**   (F) is too specific to the purpose of the yolk sac, as is (J). (H) is too specific to one species.

35. **(A)**   Sentence 1 does not address the history of the Marines.

36. **(J)**   Sentence 4 relates a statistic out of the context of a paragraph that gives general information on flu and flu symptoms.

37. **(C)**   Although the information on the drought is related to the topic, it is out of place in a paragraph focusing on banks and business.

38. **(H)**   The paragraph is focusing on the differences between the three most common states of matter.

39. **(A)**   Prince Albert is an interesting fact; the safety of Christmas trees is not being discussed; and background into the date of the first Christmas celebrations does not belong with a history of the Christmas tree.

40. **(G)**   No method other than that of orbits is discussed; they have been classified, and inner and outer planets are not the actual topic.

COOP/
HSPT

CHAPTER 2

Verbal Skills
Review

Chapter 2

VERBAL SKILLS REVIEW

    I.   **ANALYTICAL REASONING QUESTIONS**

    II.   **ANALOGY QUESTIONS**

   III.   **VERBAL REASONING QUESTIONS**

   IV.   **ANTONYM QUESTIONS**

    V.   **SYNONYM QUESTIONS**

   VI.   **OTHER TEST-TAKING POINTERS**

As you probably noticed on the practice tests, there are several types of problems on the HSPT and the COOP that require a solid command of verbal skills. Furthermore, as you get ready to take the actual *Verbal Skills* subtest of the HSPT or the *Analogies* test on the COOP, you'll need to be aware of the following question types:

- Analogies

- Synonyms

- Antonyms

- Verbal Classification

- Verbal Reasoning

- Analytical Reasoning

A prospective test-taker should carefully consider each type of problem.

I. ANALYTICAL REASONING QUESTIONS

TYPES OF QUESTIONS IN THE VERBAL SKILLS SECTION OF THE HSPT

An analytical reasoning question requires the test-taker to break a passage into parts and to study or analyze carefully **the parts** of the passage. **The arrangement problem** and **the spatial relationship problem** are two distinct types of analytical reasoning questions on the verbal skills section of the HSPT.

THE ARRANGEMENT OR ORDERING PROBLEMS

Arrangement problems involve ordering persons, places, or things into a set position. Test-takers must rank, sort chronologically, or assign a physical position on these questions. The arrangements may be linear—as on a time line—or even nonlinear—as around a banquet table. These arrangement problems may involve attributes, conditional statements, ordering and spatial relations, or time assignments.

Some of the ordering or arrangement questions may include a set of conditions. In answering some of the questions, it may be useful to draw a rough diagram before choosing the response that most accurately and completely answers the question and blackening the corresponding space on the answer sheet.

Below are tips on answering the arrangement or ordering questions:

Tip 1: Determine the problem type. Because there are several types of problems on the HSPT, the test-taker must, first of all, determine the kind of problem.

Tip 2: If you decide the problem is an analytical (ordering or arrangement) type of problem, you must look carefully at the parts and determine what you have to do with the information.

Tip 3: Read the question and as you read,

a) summarize,

b) take notes, and/or

c) diagram.

Tip 4: Make any deductions you can.

Tip 5: Compare your answer to the answer choices on the HSPT to find the best selection.

Let's see how these tips work with an actual problem.

First, you must determine the problem type. Consider the following question:

1. Bernice weighs more than Winneka. Winneka weighs more than Nicole. Nicole weighs more than Bernice. If the first two statements are true, then the third statement is

(A)   true.

(B)   false.

(C)   uncertain.

Is the question an **analogy question**—which means does it ask for a relationship such as, "Big is to little as fat is to_____."? Is it an **antonym question** requiring the reader to select words that are opposite? Is the question a **synonym question** requiring the reader to select words that are similar in meaning? Does the problem involve **verbal reasoning**, which requires one to choose a word that does not belong? Is it an **analytical reasoning** question—which means does it ask the test-taker to look carefully at the individual parts of a passage?

Question 1 above requires the reader to study each part of the passage carefully and to analyze the parts. This means that the question is an analytical reasoning question. The reader must determine if the response is 1) to draw a map (spatial relationship) or 2) to arrange the parts in a specific order. (The question above seems to be an ordering or arrangement question.)

Second, once you decide the question is an arrangement or ordering question, you may wish to try reading the question at the end of the passage and the answers before you read the first part of the passage. Some test-takers find this preview helpful to determine what they have to do with the information. For instance, consider question number 1 above.

1.   Bernice weighs more than Winneka. Winneka weighs more than Nicole. Nicole weighs more than Bernice. If the first two statements are true, then the third statement is

(A)   true.

(B)   false.

(C)   uncertain.

The question asks the status of the third sentence if the first two sentences are true. This tells you that the third sentence may or may not be true. If you are making a diagram of this question, you may not want to enter the third sentence into your diagram as permanent or true information at this time.

Third, you should summarize, take notes, and diagram as you read. The following guides will save you time on the test and help you to improve your score on the HSPT.

1.   Summarize and take notes as you read.

a)   Abbreviate. It is helpful if you use a single letter to record the facts. If the characters in the paragraph are Bob, Charles, Dedo, and Elbert, abbreviate the facts by using B, C, D, and E. If their names are Barnard, Beld, and Bill, use BA, BE, and BI. With the previous question you can use B, N, and W.

b)   Relationship. You might find it helpful to use some of the symbols you used in math classes to speed your diagramming and to prevent your having to re-read the passage. You might diagram "Chief weighs less than Ace" as C<A. You might consider drawing a continuum with the largest size, number, age, etc. at the right-hand side and the smallest number at the left-hand side.

```
        –              +
Chief........<...........Ace
```

c) The equal sign. To show that two persons must stand next to each other, you might use the equal sign. You might represent "Ace must always stand next to Anita" by AC = AN.

2. Diagram as you read.

Some diagrams are simple to construct. Consider the arrangement problem you saw earlier:

Bernice weighs more than Winneka. Winneka weighs more than Nicole. Nicole weighs more than Bernice. If the first two statements are true, then the third statement is

(A) true.

(B) false.

(C) uncertain.

Your diagram might look like this:

B ...... > .... W .... > .... N

Fourth, make your deductions after you read. Ask yourself what the question asks you about the remaining information. (Can Nicole weigh more than Bernice?)

You have a key deduction: Nicole cannot simultaneously weigh both more than Bernice and less than Winneka.

Fifth, look at the question that you must answer. In this case the question asks if the third sentence is

(A) true.

(B) false.

(C) uncertain.

Sixth, make your final deduction.

Notice how in this case all the statements are helpful to you in determining that the answer is false. You cannot say Nicole weighs less than Winneka and weighs more than Bernice. Choice (B) is the best answer.

SPATIAL RELATIONSHIP PROBLEMS

In spatial relationship problems, you will have to determine the position of objects. The following is an example of such a question. Carefully read through the passage, the conditions/clues, and the questions.

PASSAGE: I must walk east from my house on Elm Street to the mall, the grocery store, and the church; all three are on Elm Street. 1) It is farther to walk from my house to the mall than to walk from my house to the grocery store. 2) It is farther to walk west from the mall to the church than to walk west from the grocery store to the church. 3) It is closer to walk west from the mall to the church than to walk east from the house to the mall. If the first two statements are true, the third is

(A) true.

(B) false.

(C) uncertain.

After you have read through the passage and conditions or clues, you can more easily determine if you are dealing with a spatial relationship question. If so, the next step you should take is to indicate, on paper, the relationships expressed in the conditions/clues. You may want to draw a diagram that expresses the spatial relationship expressed in the conditions/clues.

In the question on the previous page, the first condition concerns the walk from my house to the mall and the walk from my house to the grocery store.

House————————————Grocery————————————Mall

The second condition states it is farther to walk west from the mall to the church than to walk west from the grocery store to the church. You can add that information to the map you are making. The diagram for these conditions follows.

House—————Church—————Grocery—————Mall

The third condition states that it is closer to walk west from the mall to the church than to walk east from the house to the mall. (Observe your diagram above.)

The question the reader must answer is if the first two sentences are true, is the third sentence true, false, or uncertain? The third sentence reads that it is closer to walk west from the mall to the church than to walk east from the house to the mall.

It is easy after the quick diagramming to determine that the final sentence is true.

Tips on the spatial relationship questions:

Tip 1: Read through each condition.

Tip 2: Do one part of the diagram at a time.

Tip 3: Do not impose your own assumptions or beliefs on the conditions or clues.

II. ANALOGY QUESTIONS

Analogies are an important part of the Verbal Review for the HSPT. An analogy is a comparison between items that are basically different but that have some similarities. An analogy is similar to a math proportion. In math you might say that, "4 to 1 is the same as 8 to _____." A **verbal analogy question** asks for a relationship. An example might be, "Big is to little as fat is to _____."

Both accuracy and speed are important parts of the HSPT. The key to completing analogies is to identify the pattern in a timely manner. There are several types of analogies which one often sees on the HSPT.

ANALOGY QUESTION TYPE ONE: WORD TO DEFINITION, SYNONYM, OR ANTONYM

The HSPT may ask the test-taker to identify patterns. These patterns might include the word and its definition, the word and its synonym, or the word and its antonym. Consider the examples below:

A. Pattern one: *Word-Definition*

Example: Regurgitate is to disgorge as incorporate is to _____.

  (A) merge

  (B) dissuade

  (C) separate

  (D) segregate

Because *regurgitate* means to throw up or to disgorge, the analogy or pattern is word to definition. *Incorporate* means to combine; the correct answer is *merge*, which also means to meld or combine.

B. Pattern two: *Word-Antonym*

Example: Meld is to separate as dissuade is to _____.

  (A) withhold

  (B) preclude

  (C) prevent

  (D) encourage

Because the opposite of *meld* (join) is to *separate*, the test-taker must choose the opposite of *dissuade* (hinder). The word *encourage* is the best choice as an antonym.

C. Pattern three: *Word-Synonym*

Example: Captivate is to entice as overestimate is to _____.

  (A) exaggerate

  (B) understate

  (C) postpone

  (D) alliterate

Captivate is similar to *entice*; the pattern seems to be similarity, or synonym. The word *overestimate* means to *exaggerate*. Choice (A) is the best choice because the relationship between the two is the same as that in the first part of the analogy: synonym.

ANALOGY QUESTION TYPE TWO: PART-TO-WHOLE ANALOGY

With part-to-whole analogy, the part comes first and the whole comes second. The reader should try to express the relationship in the first example in a sentence. (See Tips below.)

An example of a part-to-whole analogy is the following:

Notes are to music as chapters are to _____.

(A) sentences

(B) words

(C) books

(D) letters

Tip 1: First try to find the type of relationship.

Notes are to music as chapters are to _____.

(A) sentences

(B) words

(C) books

(D) letters

In the example above, the sequence is from part (notes) to whole (music).

Tip 2: Use sentences to help you express the relationship.

For instance, you might simply say, "Notes make up music as chapters make up _____."

Tip 3: Watch out for mirror relationships.

Often the answers will include a choice that is the opposite pattern from the example; this opposite, a reverse, or "mirror," answer should not mislead you. Watch out for it!

In the example above, for instance, *chapter* to *sentences* or *chapter* to *words* or *chapter* to *letters* is the opposite from part to whole. The pattern, if the test-taker falls for the incorrect pattern, is a whole-to-part—not part-to-whole—relationship. It is the opposite (a mirror image) of the example that the reader should choose.

ANALOGY QUESTION TYPE THREE: WHOLE-TO-PART ANALOGY

Consider the following: Seam is to stitch as paragraph is to sentences. The pattern of the analogy above is whole to part. Some simple tips will help you with this type of analogy.

Tip 1: First, try to find the type of relationship.

Libraries are to books as skeletons are to _____.

(A) muscles

(B)   tendons

(C)   bones

Tip 2: Use sentences to help you express the relationship.

In the example above, the sequence is from whole to part. For instance, you might make up a sentence which says, "Libraries are made up of books as skeletons are made up of _____."

Tip 3: Watch out for mirror relationships.

As with part-to-whole analogies, the answers will often include a choice that is the opposite pattern from the example; this opposite, reverse, or "mirror" answer should not mislead you. Watch out for it!

ANALOGY QUESTION TYPE FOUR: USER-TO-TOOL ANALOGY

Consider the following: Carpenter is to hammer as cook is to pot.

Just as a carpenter uses a hammer as a primary tool, a cook uses a pot as a primary tool; the preceding example illustrates a user-to-tool analogy. Below are some tools and the person who often uses the implement:

Tool	User	Tool	User
awl	leather-maker	anvil	blacksmith
pliers	electrician	screwdriver	mechanic
knife	surgeon	ball	ballplayer
chalk	teacher	helmet	race car driver

Some of the previous tips hold true with tool-to-user analogy questions.

Tip 1: First try to find the type of relationship.

Consider the following example:

Telephones are to operators as salad bowls are to _____.

(A)   tongs

(B)   lettuce

(C)   chef

In the example above, the sequence is from an object to a person. The category is tool to user.

Tip 2: Use sentences to help you express the relationship.

You might make up a sentence which says, "Telephones are used by operators; salad bowls are used by _____."

Tip 3: Watch out for incorrect relationships.

Often the answers will include a choice that is closely related but is not the same pattern as the example.

For example, in the problem above, *lettuce* does go in a salad bowl but the pattern sought is tool-to-user pattern. Again, tongs are often associated with salad bowls, but the analogy is tool-to-user.

ANALOGY QUESTION TYPE FIVE: GROUP-TO-MEMBER

Flock is to sheep as school is to _____.

(A)   teacher

(B)   fish

(C)   learn

Just as a flock is a group of sheep, a school is a group of fish; the preceding is an example of a group-to-member analogy. Because the HSPT uses some of the group-to-member analogies regularly, you might want to look over the following list:

Group	Animal	Group	Animal
covey	quail	pride	lions
flock	geese	group	people
herd	cattle	school	fish
swarm	bees	sleuth	bears
hover	trout	knot	toads
army	caterpillars	exaltation	larks
bed	clams	pod	whales
smack	jellyfish	litter	kittens

Tip 1: First try to find the type of relationship.

Consider the following example:

Flock is to geese as school is to _____.

(A)   teacher

(B)   fish

(C)   learn

In the example above, the sequence is from group to animal.

Tip 2: Use sentences to help you express the relationship.

You might make up a sentence which says, "A flock is a group of geese; a school is a group of _____."

Tip 3: Watch out for incorrect relationships.

A school does have a teacher and over a period of time one can get a complete education in a school. The relationship with the first part of the analogy, however, is group to individual animal.

ANALOGY QUESTION TYPE SIX: CAUSE-AND-EFFECT

Drought is to famine as school is to _____.

(A)   teacher

(B)   education

(C)   learning

The preceding example illustrates cause and effect.

Just as a *drought* causes or results in *famine*, *school* has the effect (usually) of causing one to *learn*. Choice (B) is a better choice than (C) for several reasons. Notice the form of the words: *education* and *learning*. Notice that one ends in *-ing* and the other does not. Because the pattern the test-taker must replicate ("Drought is to famine") does not have any *-ing* words, the comparative analogy will normally follow the same form. Choice (C) is a gerund ending in *-ing*; (B) is the best answer.

Because there are numerous types of possible analogies, the following tips may help the test-taker.

Tip 1: Make up a sentence that shows the connection between the first two words in the analogy. Establishing this sentence is often the difference between a low and a high score on the analogy section on the HSPT.

Tip 2: The parts of speech must match. If the first pair is NOUN to NOUN, the correct answer must also be NOUN to NOUN; if the first pair is NOUN to VERB, the correct answer must also be NOUN to VERB. For example, consider the following analogy: SWIM is to FISH as WADDLE is to _____. The pattern is VERB to NOUN. If one's answer choices were DUCK, WALK, AWKWARD, and FEET, one could immediately see that the correct answer should be a noun. The only correct noun choice is DUCK.

Tip 3: The answer must be in the same order as the example. For instance, in the analogy ARTIST is to PAINTING, the test-taker might make a sentence like, "An artist makes a painting." Possible answers might read:

(A)   skyscraper is to blueprint

(B)   music is to composer

(C)   novel is to writer

(D)   carpenter is to house

It is clear to the test-taker that (A) is incorrect because it is not a pattern of "one who makes" to "what is made." The three remaining answer choices (music is to composer, novel is to writer, carpenter is to house) all include the names of "producers" and the "products" they make. The order varies. Only choice (D) has the same pattern as the example analogy: producer-product. (D) is the best answer.

III. VERBAL REASONING QUESTIONS

The verbal reasoning questions on the HSPT require the student taking the test to choose the word in a list which does not belong with the others. The test-taker must look at the words and choose the pattern of the choices. For example, a test-taker might find the following list of words:

(A) paper

(B) pencil

(C) eraser

(D) teacher

The item that is different is (D) teacher. The other items are inanimate and are all connected with school; the teacher also is connected with school, but a teacher is a person while the others are objects. The test-taker must try to figure out the relationship of three of the four things. The remaining item is the answer.

Consider the following list of words:

(A) Sahara

(B) Nile

(C) Congo

(D) Mississippi

(E) Missouri

Items (B), (C), (D), and (E) are all the names of rivers. Item (A) is a desert and does not belong. A student may have selected (D) Mississippi since the first three choices are outside the United States. However, places within the United States and outside the United States cannot be used as the criteria since both (D) and (E) are within the United States.

Look at the following:

(A) cat

(B) catfish

(C) dog

(D) whale

(E) elephant

The difference is not size because both the elephant and whale are huge. The difference is not land-dwellers and water-dwellers because both (B) and (D) are water dwellers. The classification of mammals and fish is the difference; only item (B) is a fish. The rest are mammals.

IV. ANTONYM QUESTIONS

Antonym questions are those which require the test-taker to identify an answer choice that is most nearly opposite in meaning to the word in the question *stem*, or statement of the question. Some test-taking tips will help you to score high on this section.

Tip 1: Read the question stem carefully.

Tip 2: Note the qualifier in the question stem. (A *qualifier* is a word that tells you to find the *opposite* of the word in the stem. With the synonym questions in the next section of this review, you will be asked to find words that are the *same*.) You should **circle** the qualifying word; this heavy black circle will remind you what you are looking for in the question. Circling the qualifier will remind you that your task is to find the opposite meaning and ensure that you distinguish antonym questions from synonym questions.

Tip 3: Watch out for incorrect relationships.

Often the answers will include a choice that is related closely but is not the same pattern as the example. For example, a synonym or synonyms might be in the answer choices. If the test-taker has not read the question stem correctly and noted the qualifying word(s), the first instinct might be to circle the word that is similar in meaning.

Now try the following:

1. Chasm does not mean _____.

   (A)   ravine

   (B)   abyss

   (C)   canyon

   (D)   mount

The word *chasm* means *a gully, a gorge, a ravine* (A), *an abyss* (B), or *a canyon* (C). The word *mount* (D) is the opposite or the antonym of a *chasm*. The word *mount* implies a peak—the opposite of *chasm*. The antonym of *chasm* is *mount* (D).

2. The opposite of procrastinate is _____.

   (A)   prolong

   (B)   stall

   (C)   delay

   (D)   hasten

The word *procrastinate* means *to prolong* (A), *to stall* (B), *to delay* (C). The opposite of *to procrastinate, to prolong* (A), *to stall* (B), or *to delay* (C) is *to speed up* or *to hasten* (D). Choice (D) is the best selection of an antonym for procrastinate.

V. SYNONYM QUESTIONS

Synonym questions are those that require the test-taker to identify a word in the choices that is similar in meaning to the word in the question *stem*, or statement of the question. Some test-taking tips will help you to score high on this section.

Tip 1: Read the question stem carefully. Reasoning questions, analogies, synonyms, antonyms, and analytical questions are "mixed in" together. In other words, the questions are not separated according to type. Again, you must read the directions for each question carefully to make certain you answer the question appropriately.

Tip 2: Note any qualifier in the question stem. (A *qualifier* is a word that tells you in a synonym question to find *the word that means the same*, *the word that most nearly means the same*, etc. With the antonym questions in the previous section of this review, for example, you were asked to find words that are the *opposite*.) With the synonym section, you will be finding similar words or words that mean almost the same. You should **circle** the qualifying word(s); this heavy black circle will remind you what you are looking for in the question. If the previous question was an antonym question, for example, it is easy to answer the following question in the same way. If you have to come back to this question, it is easy to forget what you are to do. The heavy circle will be an instant reminder to you! You will not have to use precious time re-reading the question.

Tip 3: Watch out for incorrect relationships.

Often the answers will include a choice that is closely related but is not the same pattern as the example. For example, an antonym or antonyms might be in the choices. If the test-taker has not read the question stem correctly and noted the qualifying word(s), the first instinct might be to circle the word that is similar in meaning.

Try these questions:

1. Frantic means most nearly _____.

    (A) calm

    (B) ignorant

    (C) excited

    (D) frisk

Frantic means (C) *excited, wild*, or *distraught*. *Frantic* does not mean *calm* (A), *ignorant* (B), or *frisk* (D). The best choice is (C).

2. Construct most nearly means _____.

    (A) erect

    (B) wreck

    (C) destroy

    (D) raze

To construct means most nearly *to erect* (A), *to form*, *to build*, or *to assemble*. The antonym or opposite of *construct* or to build is *to wreck* (B), *to destroy* (C), or *to raze* (D).

3. Coddle most nearly means to _____.

   (A) pamper

   (B) reject

   (C) tolerate

   (D) fail

The word *coddle* means *to pamper* (A), *to baby*, *to humor*, or *to spoil*. The opposite of *coddle* is *reject* (B); choice (B) is not the best answer for a synonym. *To tolerate* (C) implies *to endure*, *to accept*, or *to abide*; choice (C) is not a synonym for *coddle*. *To fail* (D), *to displease* is not the same as *to coddle*; choice (D) is not an appropriate synonym.

VI. OTHER TEST-TAKING POINTERS

Some general test-taking pointers are helpful for anyone attempting a standardized test.

POINTER 1: Spend some time taking practice tests. Make the environment as much like a real testing situation as you can when you try the test. Take the phone off the hook. Time yourself. Do not peek at the answers until you finish. Work your way through the entire test.

POINTER 2: Take several number 2 pencils with you to the test. There is nothing more frustrating than to have a pencil point break and to have to waste valuable test time in securing another pencil. Lay several sharpened pencils on the desk in front of you to save time.

POINTER 3: Mark in your test booklet. If you have a question about one of the questions, put a large "?" in the margin of the book. If you have time, you can come back to that question.

POINTER 4: Be sure that you are clear on whether wrong answers will count against your score on the test administration you are attending. In other words, be sure you know if the scorer will count off a full point or a portion of a point for each incorrect answer you have. This will certainly make a difference in how you answer the questions. BE CERTAIN YOU ARE CLEAR ON THE PROCEDURE FOR THE TEST ADMINISTRATION **YOU ARE ATTENDING** BECAUSE THE PROCEDURE MAY VARY FROM TEST TO TEST. For instance:

a) If incorrect answers count against you on the test administration, your method of answering the questions will differ from your method if wrong answers do not count against you.

If wrong answers count against you,

   i)   do not guess if you have no idea what the right answer is. Instead, put a "?" in the margin. Come back to that question if you have time.

   ii) guess if you can narrow your choice down from three choices to two choices. You have a better chance of getting the answer correct (1 out of 2—not 1 out of 3). Put a "?" in the margin, but mark out the choice you know is wrong on the test booklet. If you have time to review the section, you will not have to read all the choices.

b) If wrong answers do not count against you,

    i)   GUESS!

    ii)   you will want to indicate in the margin by a "?" any item you may want to review again if time permits.

    iii) do not leave any question blank.

POINTER 5: Take a watch with you to the test. Continue to watch your time and pace yourself accordingly. Do not trust the test center to have a clock available for you. Take your own watch.

POINTER 6: Review, review, review. Looking over the sample tests ahead of time and reviewing the form of the test will make you feel more confident and will prevent surprises. Remember the best surprise on the HSPT is to find no surprise at all when you go to take the test.

Study hard and best wishes! As those in show business say, "Break a leg!"

COOP/ HSPT

CHAPTER 3

Language Skills Review

Chapter 3

LANGUAGE SKILLS REVIEW

I.   SENTENCE STRUCTURE SKILLS

II.   VERBS

III.   PRONOUNS

IV.   ADJECTIVES AND ADVERBS

V.   PUNCTUATION

VI.   CAPITALIZATION

VII.   SPELLING

The HSPT's *Language Skills* and the COOP's *Language Expression* cover a variety of topics in language. To succeed on these tests, you will need knowledge in the following areas:

- Punctuation
- Capitalization
- Usage
- Spelling
- Composition

I. SENTENCE STRUCTURE SKILLS

PARALLELISM

Parallel sentences contain a series of words or phrases that have the same grammatical structure. Parallel words or phrases can be structured like any of the following:

Phrases:

The squirrel ran *along the fence*, *up the tree*, and *into his burrow* with a mouthful of acorns.

Adjectives:

The job market is flooded with *very talented*, *highly motivated*, and *well-educated* young people.

Nouns:

You will need a *notebook*, *pencil*, and *dictionary* for the test.

Clauses:

The children were told to decide *which toy they would keep* and *which toy they would give away*.

Verbs:

The farmer *plowed*, *planted*, and *harvested* his corn in record time.

Verbals:

Reading, *writing*, and *calculating* are fundamental skills that all of us should possess.

Correlative conjunctions:

Either you will do your homework *or* you will fail.

Structural signals:

(such as articles, auxiliaries, prepositions, and conjunctions)

INCORRECT: I have quit my job, enrolled in school, and looking for a reliable babysitter.

CORRECT: I *have quit* my job, *have enrolled* in school, and *am looking* for a reliable babysitter.

Note: Repetition of prepositions is considered formal and is not necessary.

You can travel *by car, by plane, or by train*; it's all up to you.

OR

You can travel *by car, plane, or train*; it's all up to you.

When a sentence contains items in a series, check for both punctuation and sentence balance. When you check for punctuation, make sure the commas are used correctly. When you check for parallelism, make sure that each item in the series has the same grammatical structure.

MISPLACED AND DANGLING MODIFIERS

A misplaced modifier is one that is in the wrong place in the sentence. Misplaced modifiers come in all forms—words, phrases, and clauses. Sentences containing misplaced modifiers are often very comical: *Mom made me eat the spinach instead of my brother.* Misplaced modifiers, like the one in this sentence, are usually too far away from the word or words they modify. This sentence should read: *Mom made me, instead of my brother, eat the spinach.*

Modifiers like *only*, *nearly*, and *almost* should be placed next to the word they modify and not in front of some other word, especially a verb, that they are not intended to modify.

A modifier is misplaced if it appears to modify the wrong part of the sentence or if we cannot be certain what part of the sentence the writer intended it to modify. To correct a misplaced modifier, move the modifier next to the word it describes.

    INCORRECT: She served hamburgers to the men on paper plates.

    CORRECT: She served hamburgers on paper plates to the men.

Split infinitives also result in misplaced modifiers. Infinitives consist of the marker *to* plus the plain form of the verb. The two parts of the infinitive make up a grammatical unit that should not be split. Splitting an infinitive is placing an adverb between *to* and the verb.

    INCORRECT: The weather service expects temperatures to not rise.

    CORRECT: The weather service expects temperatures not to rise.

Sometimes a split infinitive may be natural and preferable, though it may still bother some readers.

    EX: Several U.S. industries expect *to* more than *triple* their use of robots within the next decade.

A squinting modifier is one that may refer to either a preceding or a following word, leaving the reader uncertain about what it is intended to modify. Correct a squinting modifier by moving it next to the word it is intended to modify.

    INCORRECT: Snipers who fired on the soldiers often escaped capture.

    CORRECT: Snipers who often fired on the soldiers escaped capture.

    OR   Snipers who fired on the soldiers escaped capture often.

A dangling modifier is a modifier or verb in search of a subject: the modifying phrase (usually an *-ing* word group, an *-ed* or *-en* word group, or a *to* + *a verb* word group—participle phrase or infinitive phrase respectively) either appears to modify the wrong word or has nothing to modify. It is literally dangling at the beginning or the end of a sentence. The sentences often look and sound correct: *To be a student government officer, your grades must be above average.* However, the verbal modifier has nothing to describe. Who is *to be a student government* *officer*? Your grades? Questions of this type require you to determine whether a modifier has a headword or whether it is dangling at the beginning or the end of the sentence.

To correct a dangling modifier, reword the sentence by either: 1) changing the modifying phrase to a clause with a subject, or 2) changing the subject of the sentence to the word that should be modified. The following are examples of a dangling gerund, a dangling infinitive, and a dangling participle:

INCORRECT: Shortly after leaving home, the accident occurred.

Who is <u>leaving home</u>, the accident?

CORRECT: Shortly after we left home, the accident occurred.

INCORRECT: To get up on time, a great effort was needed.

<u>To get up</u> needs a subject.

CORRECT: To get up on time, I made a great effort.

FRAGMENTS

A fragment is an incomplete construction which may or may not have a subject and a verb. Not all fragments appear as separate sentences. Often, fragments are separated by semicolons.

INCORRECT: Traffic was stalled for ten miles on the freeway. Because repairs were being made on potholes.

CORRECT: Traffic was stalled for ten miles on the freeway because repairs were being made on potholes.

INCORRECT: It was a funny story; one that I had never heard before.

CORRECT: It was a funny story, one that I had never heard before.

RUN-ON/FUSED SENTENCES

A run-on or fused sentence is not necessarily a long sentence or a sentence that the reader considers too long. Often it may be two short sentences: *Dry ice does not melt it evaporates*. A run-on results when the writer fuses or runs together two separate sentences without any correct mark of punctuation separating them.

INCORRECT: Knowing how to use a dictionary is no problem each dictionary has a section in the front of the book telling how to use it.

CORRECT: Knowing how to use a dictionary is no problem. Each dictionary has a section in the front of the book telling how to use it.

Even if one or both of the fused sentences contains internal punctuation, the sentence is still a run-on.

INCORRECT: Bob bought dress shoes, a suit, and a nice shirt he needed them for his sister's wedding.

CORRECT: Bob bought dress shoes, a suit, and a nice shirt. He needed them for his sister's wedding.

COMMA SPLICES

A comma splice is the incorrect use of a comma to combine what really is two separate sentences.

INCORRECT: One common error in writing is incorrect spelling, the other is the occasional use of faulty diction.

CORRECT: One common error in writing is incorrect spelling; the other is the occasional use of faulty diction.

Both run-on sentences and comma splices may be corrected in one of the following ways:

RUN-ON: Neal won the award he had the highest score.

COMMA SPLICE: Neal won the award, he had the highest score.

Separate the sentences with a period:

Neal won the award. He had the highest score.

Separate the sentences with a comma and a coordinating conjunction *(and, but, or, nor, for, yet, so)*:

Neal won the award, for he had the highest score.

Separate the sentences with a semicolon:

Neal won the award; he had the highest score.

Separate the sentences with a subordinating conjunction such as *although, because, since, if*:

Neal won the award because he had the highest score.

SUBORDINATION, COORDINATION, AND PREDICATION

Suppose, for the sake of clarity, you wanted to combine the information in these two sentences to create one statement:

I studied a foreign language. I found English quite easy.

How you decide to combine this information should be determined by the relationship you'd like to show between the two facts. *I studied a foreign language, and I found English quite easy* seems rather illogical. The **coordination** of the two ideas (connecting them with the coordinating conjunction *and*) is ineffective. Using **subordination** instead (connecting the sentences with a subordinating conjunction) clearly shows the degree of relative importance between the expressed ideas:

After I studied a foreign language, I found English quite easy.

When using a conjunction, be sure that the sentence parts you are joining are in agreement.

INCORRECT: She loved him dearly but not his dog.

CORRECT: She loved him dearly but she did not love his dog.

A common mistake that is made is to forget that each member of the pair must be followed by the same kind of construction.

INCORRECT: They complimented them both for their bravery and they thanked them for their kindness.

CORRECT: They both complimented them for their bravery and thanked them for their kindness.

While refers to time and should not be used as a substitute for *although*, *and*, or *but*.

INCORRECT: While I'm usually interested in Fellini movies, I'd rather not go tonight.

CORRECT: Although I'm usually interested in Fellini movies, I'd rather not go tonight.

Where refers to location and should not be used as a substitute for *that*.

INCORRECT: We read in the paper where they are making great strides in DNA research.

CORRECT: We read in the paper that they are making great strides in DNA research.

After words like reason and explanation, use *that*, not *because*.

INCORRECT: His explanation for his tardiness was because his alarm did not go off.

CORRECT: His explanation for his tardiness was that his alarm did not go off.

☞ Drill: Sentence Structure Skills

DIRECTIONS: Choose the sentence that expresses the thought most clearly and that has no error in structure.

1.   (A)   Many gases are invisible, odorless, and they have no taste.

     (B)   Many gases are invisible, odorless, and have no taste.

     (C)   Many gases are invisible, odorless, and tasteless.

     (D)   Many gases are invisible and odorless and have no taste.

2.   (A)   Everyone agreed that she had neither the voice or the skill to be a speaker.

     (B)   Everyone agreed that she had neither the voice nor the skill to be a speaker.

     (C)   Everyone agreed that she had either the voice nor the skill to be a speaker.

     (D)   Everyone agreed that she had not the voice nor the skill to be a speaker.

3. (A) The mayor will be remembered because he kept his campaign promises and because of his refusal to accept political favors.

    (B) The mayor will be remembered because he kept his campaign promises and because he refused to accept political favors.

    (C) The mayor will be remembered because of his refusal to accept political favors and because he kept his campaign promises.

    (D) The mayor will be remembered because of his refusal to accept political favors and that he kept his campaign promises.

4. (A) While taking a shower, the doorbell rang.

    (B) While I was taking a shower, the doorbell rang.

    (C) While taking a shower, someone rang the doorbell.

    (D) The doorbell rang, while taking a shower.

5. (A) He swung the bat, while the runner stole second base.

    (B) The runner stole second base while he swung the bat.

    (C) While he was swinging the bat, the runner stole second base.

    (D) The runner was stealing second base while he was swinging the bat.

DIRECTIONS: Choose the correct option.

---

6. Nothing grows as well in Mississippi as <u>cotton. Cotton</u> being the state's principal crop.

    (A) cotton, cotton   (C) cotton cotton

    (B) cotton; cotton   (D) No change is necessary.

7. It was a heartwrenching <u>movie; one</u> that I had never seen before.

    (A) movie and   (C) movie. One

    (B) movie, one   (D) No change is necessary.

8. Traffic was stalled for three miles on the <u>bridge. Because</u> repairs were being made.

    (A) bridge because   (C) bridge, because

    (B) bridge; because   (D) No change is necessary.

9. The ability to write complete sentences comes with <u>practice writing</u> run-on sentences seems to occur naturally.

    (A) practice, writing   (C) practice and

    (B) practice. Writing   (D) No change is necessary.

10. Even though she had taken French classes, she could not understand native French <u>speakers</u> <u>they</u> all spoke too fast.

    (A) speakers, they   (C) speaking

    (B) speakers. They   (D) No change is necessary.

II. VERBS

VERB FORMS

This section covers the principal parts of some irregular verbs including troublesome verbs like *lie* and *lay*. The use of regular verbs like *look* and *receive* poses no real problem to most writers because the past and past participle forms end in *-ed*; it is the irregular forms that pose the most serious problems—for example, *seen*, *written*, and *begun*.

Irregular Verbs

Irregular verbs are words that have past tense and past participle forms that do not end in -ed or -d. Although a standard pattern does not exist, most irregular verbs are commonly known.

> The lightning almost struck the tree by my house.

> He had run all the way to the store.

In reviewing the table below, remember that the action being described in the past tense has occurred entirely in the past; it does not take a helping verb. Past participles take a helping verb.

> Yesterday, Alex drew a picture of my mother. (past tense)

> If you look on the table, you will see the portrait drawn by my friend. (past participle)

Frequently Used Irregular Verbs

Infinitive	Past Tense	Past Participle
to be	was/were	been
to begin	began	begun
to break	broke	broken
to buy	bought	bought
to come	came	come
to do	did	done
to eat	ate	eaten
to fly	flew	flown
to give	gave	given
tp get	got	gotten
to go	went	gone
to lay	laid	laid
to lie	lay	lain
to see	saw	seen

to seek	sought	sought
to sit	sat	sat
to swim	swam	swum
to throw	threw	thrown
to use	used	used
to wear	wore	worn
to write	wrote	written

Verb Tenses

In grammar, the word "tense" refers to the time an action takes place.

Use present tense

in statements of universal truth:

> I learned that the sun *is* ninety-million miles from the earth.

in statements about the contents of literature; other published works; or art work:

> In this book, Sandy *becomes* a nun and *writes* a book on psychology.

Use past tense

for action that occurred in some past time:

> He *wrote* his first book in 1949, and it *was published* in 1952.

Use present perfect tense

for an action that began in the past but continues into the future:

> I *have lived* here all my life.

Use past perfect tense

for an earlier action that is mentioned in a later action:

> Cindy ate the apple that she *had picked.*

(First she picked it, then she ate it.)

Use future perfect tense

for an action that will have been completed at a specific future time:

> By May, I *shall have graduated.*

Use a present participle

for action that occurs at the same time as the verb:

> As Ray and I *were speeding* down the interstate, I saw a cop's flashing lights.

Use a perfect participle

for action that occurred before the main verb:

> *Having read* the directions, I started the test.

Use the subjunctive mood

to express a wish or state a condition contrary to fact:

> *If it were not raining*, we could have a picnic.

in *that* clauses after verbs like *request, recommend, suggest, ask, require*, and *insist*; and after such expressions like *it is important* and *it is necessary*:

> It is necessary that all papers *be* submitted on time.

Subject-Verb Agreement

Agreement is the grammatical correspondence between the subject and the verb of a sentence: All verbs must agree with their subjects in person and number. If the subject is first person singular (I) the verb must also be first person singular: *I do, I say, I walk*. If the subject is third person singular, the verb form must agree: *he does, he says, he walks*.

Study these rules governing subject-verb agreement:

A verb must agree with its subject not with any other phrase in the sentence such as a prepositional or verbal phrase. Ignore such phrases.

> Your *copy* of the rules *is* on the desk.

> Ms. Craig's *record* of community service and outstanding teaching *qualifies* her for promotion.

In an inverted sentence, which begins with a prepositional phrase, the verb still agrees with its subject.

> At the end of the summer *come* the best *sales*.

> Under the house *are* some old Mason *jars*.

Prepositional phrases beginning with compound prepositions such as *along with, together with, in addition to,* and *as well as* should be ignored. They do not affect subject-verb agreement.

> *Gladys Knight*, as well as the Pips, *is* riding the midnight train to Georgia.

A verb must agree with its subject and not its subject complement. A subject complement is a word or phrase that follows a linking verb and describes the subject of a sentence.

> *Taxes are* a problem.

> A *problem is* taxes.

> His main *source* of pleasure *is* cycling and tennis.

> *Tennis and cycling are* his main source of pleasure.

The words *there, here,* or *it* are considered expletives when they are used at the beginning of a clause and the subject is not in its usual position before the verb. In such sentences, the verb should still agree with the subject and not the expletive.

> Surely, there *are* several *alumni* who would be interested in forming a group.

> There *are* 50 *students* in my English class.

> There *is* a horrifying *study* on child abuse in *Psychology Today*.

Indefinite pronouns, which refer to a non-specific person or thing, include *each, either, one, everyone, everybody,* and *everything* and are singular.

> *Somebody* in Detroit *loves* me.
>
> *Does either* [one] of you have a pencil?
>
> *Neither* of my brothers *has* a car.

Indefinite pronouns such as *several, few, both,* and *many* are plural.

> *Both* of my sorority sisters *have* decided to live off-campus.
>
> *Few seek* the enlightenment of transcendental meditation.

Indefinite pronouns such as *all, some, most,* and *none* may be singular or plural depending on their referents.

> *Some* of the food *is* cold.
>
> *Some* of the vegetables *are* cold.
>
> I can think of some retorts, but *none seem* appropriate.
>
> *None* of the children *is* as sweet as Sally.

Fractions such as *one-half* and *one-third* may be singular or plural depending on what is being described.

> *Half* of the mail *has* been delivered.
>
> *Half* of the letters *have* been read.

Subjects joined by *and* take a plural verb unless the subjects are thought to be one item or unit.

> *Jim and Tammy were* televangelists.
>
> *The Cure is* my favorite group.

In cases when the subjects are joined by *or, nor, either . . . or,* or *neither . . . nor,* the verb must agree with the subject closer to it.

> Either the teacher or the *students are* responsible.
>
> Neither the students nor the *teacher is* responsible.

Relative pronouns, such as *who, which,* or *that,* introduce adjective clauses within a sentence. When the relative pronoun describes a plural subject, the verb should be plural. Relative pronouns describing singular subjects should take singular verbs.

> She is one of the girls *who cheer* on Friday nights.
>
> She is the only cheerleader *who has* a broken leg.

Subjects preceded by *every, each,* and *many a* are singular.

> *Every* man, woman, and child *was* given a life preserver.
>
> *Each* undergraduate *is* required to pass a proficiency exam.
>
> *Many a* tear *has* to fall before one matures.

Nouns that name a group of persons or objects, such as *audience, faculty, jury,* etc., are collective nouns. Collective nouns require a singular verb when the group is regarded as a whole, and a plural verb when the members of the group are regarded as individuals.

> The *jury has* made its decision.

> The *faculty are* preparing their grade rosters.

Subjects preceded by *the number of* or *the percentage of* are singular, whereas subjects preceded by *a number of* or *a percentage of* are plural.

> *The number of* vacationers in Florida *increases* every year.

> *A number of* vacationers *are* young couples.

Titles of books, companies, name brands, and groups are singular or plural depending on their meaning.

> *Great Expectations is* my favorite novel.

> The *Rolling Stones are* performing in the Super Dome.

Certain nouns of Latin and Greek origin have unusual singular and plural forms.

Singular	Plural
criterion	criteria
alumnus	alumni
datum	data
medium	media

> The *data are* available for inspection.

> The only *criterion* for membership *is* a high GPA.

Some nouns such as *deer, shrimp,* and *sheep* have the same spellings for both their singular and plural forms. In these cases, the meaning of the sentence will determine whether they are singular or plural.

> *Deer are* beautiful animals.

> The spotted *deer is* licking the sugar cube.

Some nouns like *scissors* and *jeans* have plural forms but no singular counterparts. These nouns almost always take plural verbs.

> The *scissors are* on the table.

> My new *jeans fit* me like a glove.

Words used as examples, not as grammatical parts of the sentence, require singular verbs.

> *Can't is* the contraction for "cannot."

> *Cats is* the plural form of "cat."

Mathematical expressions of subtraction and division require singular verbs, while expressions of addition and multiplication take either singular or plural verbs.

Ten *divided* by two *equals* five.

Five *times* two *equals* ten.

OR: Five *times* two *equal* ten.

Nouns expressing time, distance, weight, and measurement are singular when they refer to a unit and plural when they refer to separate items.

Fifty yards is a short distance.

Ten years have passed since I finished college.

Expressions of quantity are usually plural.

Nine out of ten dentists *recommend* that their patients floss.

Some nouns ending in *-ics*, such as *economics* and *ethics*, take singular verbs when they refer to principles or a field of study; however, when they refer to individual practices, they usually take plural verbs.

Ethics is being taught in the spring.

His unusual business *ethics are* what got him into trouble.

Some nouns like *measles*, *news*, and *calculus* appear to be plural but are actually singular in number. These nouns require singular verbs.

Measles is a very contagious disease.

Calculus requires great skill in algebra.

Gerund and infinitive verbs can be used as nouns. A gerund is a verb ending in *-ing*, such as *running*, *sitting*, *reading*. An infinitive is the word *to* plus a verb, such as *to be*. Gerunds and infinitives are considered verbal nouns, and are treated as singular even if the object of the verbal phrase is plural.

Hiding your mistakes *does* not make them go away.

To run five miles *is* my goal.

A noun phrase or clause acting as the subject of a sentence requires a singular verb.

What I need is to be loved.

Whether there is any connection between them is unknown.

Clauses beginning with *what* may be singular or plural depending on the meaning, that is, whether *what* means "the thing" or "the things."

What I want for Christmas is a new motorcycle.

What matters are Clinton's ideas.

Appositives are nouns or pronoun phrases that rename the nouns or pronouns and have the same function as the words they describe.

When the girls throw a party, *they* each bring a *gift*.

The *board*, all ten members, *is* meeting today.

☞ Drill: Verbs

DIRECTIONS: Choose the correct option.

1. If you <u>had been concerned</u> about Marilyn, you <u>would have went</u> to greater lengths to ensure her safety.

   (A) had been concern . . . would have gone

   (B) was concerned . . . would have gone

   (C) had been concerned . . . would have gone

   (D) No change is necessary.

2. Susan <u>laid</u> in bed too long and missed her class.

   (A) lays   (C) lied

   (B) lay   (D) No change is necessary.

3. The Great Wall of China <u>is</u> fifteen hundred miles long; it <u>was built</u> in the third century B.C.

   (A) was . . . was built   (C) has been . . . was built

   (B) is . . . is built   (D) No change is necessary.

4. Joe stated that the class <u>began</u> at 10:30 a.m.

   (A) begins   (C) was beginning

   (B) had begun   (D) No change is necessary.

5. The ceiling of the Sistine Chapel <u>was</u> painted by Michelangelo; it <u>depicted</u> scenes from the Creation in the Old Testament.

   (A) was . . . depicts   (C) has been . . . depicting

   (B) is . . . depicts   (D) No change is necessary.

6. After Christmas <u>comes</u> the best sales.

   (A) has come   (C) is coming

   (B) come   (D) No change is necessary.

7. The bakery's specialty <u>are</u> wedding cakes.

   (A) is   (C) be

   (B) were   (D) No change is necessary.

8. Every man, woman, and child <u>were given</u> a life preserver.

   (A) have been given   (C) was given

   (B) had gave   (D) No change is necessary.

9. Hiding your mistakes <u>don't</u> make them go away.

    (A) doesn't   (B) do not

    (C) have not   (D) No change is necessary.

10. The Board of Regents <u>has recommended</u> a tuition increase.

    (A) have recommended   (C) had recommended

    (B) has recommend   (D) No change is necessary.

III. PRONOUNS

PRONOUN CASE

Nominative case (also called subjective) pronouns function as subjects or subject complements in a sentence. Objective case pronouns function as objects in a sentence.

Nominative Case	Objective Case
I	me
he	him
she	her
we	us
they	them
who	whom

This review section answers the most frequently asked grammar questions: when to use *I* and when to use *me*; when to use *who* and when to use *whom*. Some writers avoid *whom* altogether, and instead of distinguishing between *I* and *me*, many writers incorrectly use *myself*.

Use the nominative case (subject pronouns)
    for the subject of a sentence:

        We students studied until early morning for the final.

        Alan and *I* "burned the midnight oil," too.

    for pronouns that rename nouns or pronouns and have the same meaning or function as the words they rename (also called in apposition).

        Only two students, Alex and *I*, were asked to report on the meeting.

    for words that follow a linking verb and describe the subject of a sentence (subject complement):

        The actors nominated for the award were *she* and *I*.

    for the subject in a comparison (Note: think of the words missing from the sentence: Molly is more experienced than *he* is.):

Molly is more experienced than *he.*

for the subject of a clause that cannot stand on its own (subordinate clause):

Robert is the driver *who* reported the accident.

as part of a direct object comprised of a infinitive verb and a pronoun.

I would not want to be *he.*

Use the objective case (object pronouns)

for the direct object of a sentence:

Mary invited *us* to her party.

for the object of a preposition:

The books that were torn belonged to *her.*

Just between you and *me,* I'm bored.

for the indirect object of a sentence:

Walter gave a dozen red roses to *her.*

for the appositive of a direct object:

The committee elected two delegates, Barbara and *me.*

for the object of an infinitive:

The young boy wanted to help *us* paint the fence.

for the object of a gerund:

Enlisting *him* was surprisingly easy.

for the object of a past participle:

Having called the other students and *us,* the secretary went home for the day.

for a pronoun that precedes an infinitive (the subject of an infinitive):

The supervisor told *him* to work late.

for the complement of an infinitive with an expressed subject:

The fans thought the best player to be *him.*

for an object of a comparison (Note: think of the words missing from the sentence. Bill tackled Joe harder than he tackled me.)

Bill tackled Joe harder than *me.*

for the object of a verb in apposition:

Charles invited two extra people, Carmen and *me,* to the party.

When a conjunction connects two pronouns or a pronoun and a noun, remove the "and" and the other pronoun or noun to determine what the correct pronoun form should be:

Mom gave ~~Tom and~~ myself a piece of cake.

Mom gave ~~Tom and~~ I a piece of cake.

Mom gave ~~Tom and~~ me a piece of cake.

Removal of these words reveals what the correct pronoun should be:

Mom gave *me* a piece of cake.

The only pronouns that are acceptable after *between* and other prepositions are: *me, her, him, them,* and *whom.*

When deciding between *who* and *whom,* try substituting *he* for *who* and *him* for *whom;* then follow these easy transformation steps:

1. Isolate the *who* clause or the *whom* clause:

   whom we can trust

2. Invert the word order, if necessary. Place the words in the clause in the natural order of an English sentence, subject followed by the verb:

   we can trust whom

3. Read the final form with the *he* or *him* inserted:

   We can trust ~~whom~~ him.

When a pronoun follows a comparative conjunction like *than* or *as,* complete the elliptical construction to help you determine which pronoun is correct.

EX: She has more credit hours than me [do].

She has more credit hours than I [do].

PRONOUN-ANTECEDENT AGREEMENT

An antecedent is a noun or pronoun to which another noun or pronoun refers. Questions on pronoun-antecedent agreement test your knowledge of using an appropriate pronoun to agree with its antecedent in number (singular or plural form) and gender (masculine, feminine, or neuter).

Here are the two basic rules for pronoun reference-antecedent agreement:

1. Every pronoun must agree with its antecedent in number, gender, and person.

2. Every pronoun must have a conspicuous antecedent.

When an antecedent is one of dual gender like *student, singer, artist, person, citizen,* etc., use *his or her.* Some careful writers change the antecedent to a plural noun to avoid using the sexist, singular masculine pronoun his:

INCORRECT: Everyone hopes that he will win the lottery.

CORRECT: Most people hope that they will win the lottery.

Ordinarily, the relative pronoun *who* is used to refer to people, *which* to refer to things and places, *where* to refer to places, and *that* to refer to places or things. The distinction between *that* and *which* is a grammatical distinction (see the section on Word Choice Skills).

Many writers prefer to use *that* to refer to collective nouns.

    EX: A family *that* traces its lineage is usually proud of its roots.

Many writers, especially students, are not sure when to use the reflexive case pronoun and when to use the possessive case pronoun. The rules governing the usage of the reflexive case and the possessive case are quite simple.

Use the possessive case

before a noun in a sentence:

Our friend moved during the semester break.

My dog has fleas, but *her* dog doesn't.

before a gerund in a sentence:

Her running helps to relieve stress.

His driving terrified her.

as a noun in a sentence:

Mine was the last test graded that day.

to indicate possession:

Karen never allows anyone else to drive *her* car.

Brad thought the book was *his,* but it was someone else's.

Use the reflexive case

as a direct object to rename the subject:

I kicked *myself.*

as an indirect object to rename the subject:

Henry bought *himself* a tie.

as an object of a prepositional phrase:

Tom and Lillie baked the pie for *themselves.*

as a predicate pronoun:

She hasn't been *herself* lately.

Do not use the reflexive in place of the nominative pronoun:

    INCORRECT: Both Randy and *myself* plan to go.

    CORRECT: Both Randy and *I* plan to go.

    INCORRECT: *Yourself* will take on the challenges of college.

    CORRECT: *You* will take on the challenges of college.

INCORRECT: Either James or *yourself* will paint the mural.

CORRECT: Either James or *you* will paint the mural.

Watch out for careless use of the pronoun form:

INCORRECT: George *hisself* told me it was true.

CORRECT: George *himself* told me it was true.

——————————————————

INCORRECT: They washed the car *theirselves*.

CORRECT: They washed the car *themselves*.

Notice that reflexive pronouns are not set off by commas:

INCORRECT: Mary, *herself*, gave him the diploma.

CORRECT: Mary *herself* gave him the diploma.

INCORRECT: I will do it, *myself*.

CORRECT: I will do it *myself*.

PRONOUN REFERENCE

Writing without pronouns would sound dull. For example: "Jack finished Jack's homework before Jack went to bed" is a very repetitive sentence. Using pronouns to replace some of those nouns makes the sentence flow better: "Jack finished his homework before he went to bed." The pronoun "his" and "he" are used to replace "Jack." In grammatical terms, "Jack" is known as the antecedent, the word to which the pronouns refer. It is important to make sure that the antecedent to which the pronoun refers is conspicously clear or obvious to the reader. It is also important to be sure that pronouns refer only to another noun or pronoun and not to an idea or a sentence.

Pronoun reference problems occur

when a pronoun refers to either of two antecedents:

INCORRECT: Joanna told Julie that *she* was getting fat.

CORRECT: Joanna told Julie, "I'm getting fat."

when a pronoun refers to a remote antecedent:

INCORRECT: A strange car followed us closely, and *he* kept blinking his lights at us.

CORRECT: A strange car followed us closely, and its driver kept blinking his lights at us.

when *this*, *that*, and *which* refer to the general idea of the preceding clause or sentence rather than the preceding word:

INCORRECT: The students could not understand the pronoun reference handout, which annoyed them very much.

CORRECT: The students could not understand the pronoun reference handout, a fact that annoyed them very much.

OR: The students were annoyed because they could not understand the pronoun reference handout.

when a pronoun refers to an unexpressed but implied noun:

INCORRECT: My husband wants me to knit a blanket, but I'm not interested in it.

CORRECT: My husband wants me to knit a blanket, but I'm not interested in knitting.

when *it* is used at the beginning of a clause and the subject of the sentence is not before the verb.

INCORRECT: It says in today's paper that the newest shipment of cars from Detroit, Michigan, seems to include outright imitations of European models.

CORRECT: Today's paper says that the newest shipment of cars from Detroit, Michigan, seems to include outright imitations of European models.

INCORRECT: The football game was canceled because it was bad weather.

CORRECT: The football game was canceled because the weather was bad.

when *they* or *it* is used to refer to something or someone nonspecific:

INCORRECT: At the job placement office, they told me to stop wearing ripped jeans to my interviews.

CORRECT: At the job placement office, I was told to stop wearing ripped jeans to my interviews.

when the pronoun does not agree with its antecedent in number, gender, or person:

INCORRECT: Any graduate student, if they are interested, may attend the lecture.

CORRECT: Any graduate student, if he or she is interested, may attend the lecture.

OR: All graduate students, if they are interested, may attend the lecture.

INCORRECT: Many Americans are concerned that the overuse of slang and colloquialisms is corrupting the language.

CORRECT: Many Americans are concerned that the overuse of slang and colloquialisms is corrupting their language.

INCORRECT: The Board of Regents will not make a decision about a tuition increase until their March meeting.

CORRECT: The Board of Regents will not make a decision about a tuition increase until its March meeting.

when a noun or pronoun has no clear antecedent:

INCORRECT: In the President's address to the union, he promised no more taxes.

CORRECT: In his address to the union, the President promised no more taxes.

☞ Drill: Pronouns

DIRECTIONS: Choose the correct option.

1. My friend and <u>myself</u> bought tickets for *Cats*.

    (A) I

    (B) me

    (C) us

    (D) No change is necessary.

2. Alcohol and tobacco are harmful to <u>whomever</u> consumes them.

    (A) whom

    (B) who

    (C) whoever

    (D) No change is necessary.

3. Everyone is wondering <u>whom</u> her successor will be.

    (A) who

    (B) whose

    (C) who'll

    (D) No change is necessary.

4. Rosa Lee's parents discovered that it was <u>her who</u> wrecked the family car.

    (A) she who

    (B) she whom

    (C) her whom

    (D) No change is necessary.

5. A student <u>who</u> wishes to protest <u>his or her</u> grades must file a formal grievance in the Dean's office.

    (A) that . . . their

    (B) which . . . his

    (C) whom . . . their

    (D) No change is necessary.

6. One of the best things about working for this company is that <u>they pay</u> big bonuses.

    (A) it pays

    (B) they always pay

    (C) they paid

    (D) No change is necessary.

7. Every car owner should be sure that <u>their</u> automobile insurance is adequate.

    (A) your

    (B) his or her

    (C) its

    (D) No change is necessary.

8. My mother wants me to become a teacher, but I'm not interested in <u>it</u>.

    (A) this

    (B) teaching

    (C) that

    (D) No change is necessary.

9. Since I had not paid my electric bill, <u>they</u> sent me a delinquent notice.

    (A) the power company

    (B) he

    (C) it

    (D) No change is necessary.

10. Margaret seldom wrote to her sister when <u>she</u> was away at college.

    (A) who   (C) her sister

    (B) her   (D) No change is necessary.

IV. ADJECTIVES AND ADVERBS

CORRECT USAGE

Adjectives are words that modify nouns or pronouns by defining, describing, limiting, or qualifying those nouns or pronouns.

Adverbs are words that modify verbs, adjectives, or other adverbs and that express ideas such as time, place, manner, cause, and degree.

EX:	The old man's speech was *eloquent*.	ADJECTIVE
	Mr. Brown speaks *eloquently*.	ADVERB
	Please be *careful*.	ADJECTIVE
	Please drive *carefully*.	ADVERB

Good or well

Good should be used as an adjective; not as an adverb.

    INCORRECT: He plays *good*.

    CORRECT: He looks *good* to be an eighty-year-old.

                    The quiche tastes very *good*.

Well may be either an adverb or an adjective. As an adjective, *well* means "in good health."

CORRECT:	He plays *well*.	ADVERB
	My mother is not *well*.	ADJECTIVE

Bad or badly

Bad is an adjective used after sense verbs such as *look*, *smell*, *taste*, *feel*, or *sound*, or after linking verbs (*is, am, are, was, were*).

    INCORRECT: I feel *badly* about the delay.

    CORRECT: I feel *bad* about the delay.

Badly is an adverb used after all other verbs.

    INCORRECT: It doesn't hurt very *bad*.

    CORRECT: It doesn't hurt very *badly*.

Real or really

Real is an adjective meaning "genuine." *Really* is an adverb meaning "very."

INCORRECT:	He writes *real* well.
CORRECT:	This is *real* leather.
INCORRECT:	This is *really* diamond.
CORRECT:	Have a *really* nice day.

EX:	This is a *real* amethyst.	ADJECTIVE
	This is *really* difficult.	ADVERB
	This is a *real* crisis.	ADJECTIVE
	This is *really* important.	ADVERB

Sort of and kind of

Sort of and *kind of* are often misused in written English by writers who actually mean *rather* or *somewhat*.

INCORRECT:	Jan was *kind of* saddened by the results of the test.
CORRECT:	Jan was *somewhat* saddened by the results of the test.

FAULTY COMPARISONS

Sentences containing a faulty comparison often sound correct because their problem is not one of grammar but of logic. Read these sentences closely to make sure that like things are being compared, that the comparisons are complete, and that the comparisons are logical.

When comparing two persons or things, use the comparative (better, older), not the superlative (best, oldest), form of an adjective or an adverb. The superlative form is used only for comparison of more than two persons or things. Use *any*, *other*, or *else* when comparing one thing or person with a group of which it, he, or she is a part.

Most one- and two-syllable words form their comparative and superlative degrees with *-er* and *-est* suffixes. Adjectives and adverbs of more than two syllables form their comparative and superlative degrees with the addition of *more* and *most*.

Positive	Comparative	Superlative
good	better	best
old	older	oldest
friendly	friendlier	friendliest
lonely	lonelier	loneliest
talented	more talented	most talented
beautiful	more beautiful	most beautiful

A double comparison occurs when the writer incorrectly adds both *-er* and *more* or *-est* and *most* to the adjective or adverb.

INCORRECT: He is the *most nicest* brother.

CORRECT: He is the *nicest* brother.

INCORRECT: She is the *more meaner* of the sisters.

CORRECT: She is the *meaner* sister.

Illogical comparisons occur when there is an implied comparison between two things that are not actually being compared or that cannot be logically compared.

INCORRECT: The interest at a loan company is higher *than* a bank.

CORRECT: The interest at a loan company is higher *than* that *at* a bank.

OR: The interest at a loan company is higher *than at* a bank.

Ambiguous comparisons occur when elliptical words (those omitted) create for the reader more than one interpretation of the sentence.

INCORRECT: I like Mary better than you. (than you *what*?)

CORRECT: I like Mary better than I like you.

OR: I like Mary better than you do.

Incomplete comparisons occur when the basis of the comparison (the two categories being compared) is not clearly stated.

INCORRECT: Skywriting is *more* spectacular.

CORRECT: Skywriting is *more* spectacular *than* billboard advertising.

Do not omit the words *other, any,* or *else* when comparing one thing or person with a group of which it, he, or she is a part.

INCORRECT: Joan writes better *than any* student in her class.

CORRECT: Joan writes better *than any other* student in her class.

Do not omit the second *as* of *as . . . as* when making a point of equal or superior comparison.

INCORRECT: The University of West Florida is *as large* or larger than the University of North Florida.

CORRECT: The University of West Florida is *as large as* or larger than the University of Northern Florida.

Do not omit the first category of the comparison, even if the two categories are the same.

INCORRECT: This is one of the best, if not the best, college in the country.

CORRECT: This is one of the best colleges in the country, if not the best.

The problem with the incorrect sentence is that *one of the best* requires the plural word *colleges*, not *college*.

☞ Drill: Adjectives and Adverbs

1. Although the band performed <u>badly</u>, I feel <u>real bad</u> about missing the concert.

   (A) badly . . . real badly   (C) badly . . . very bad

   (B) bad . . . badly   (D) No change is necessary.

2. These reports are <u>relative simple</u> to prepare.

   (A) relatively simple   (C) relatively simply

   (B) relative simply   (D) No change is necessary.

3. He did <u>very well</u> on the test although his writing skills are not <u>good</u>.

   (A) real well . . . good   (C) good . . . great

   (B) very good . . . good   (D) No change is necessary.

4. Shake the medicine bottle <u>good</u> before you open it.

   (A) very good   (C) well

   (B) real good   (D) No change is necessary.

5. Though she speaks <u>fluently</u>, she writes <u>poorly</u> because she doesn't observe <u>closely</u> or think <u>clear</u>.

   (A) fluently, poorly, closely, clearly

   (B) fluent, poor, close, clear

   (C) fluently, poor, closely, clear

   (D) No change is necessary.

6. (A) Los Angeles is larger than any city in California.

   (B) Los Angeles is larger than all the cities in California.

   (C) Los Angeles is larger than any other city in California.

   (D) Los Angeles is larger than the cities in California.

7. (A) Art history is as interesting as, if not more interesting than, music appreciation.

   (B) Art history is as interesting, if not more interesting than, music appreciation.

    (C)   Art history is as interesting as, if not more interesting, music appreciation.

    (D)   Art history is as interesting as, if not more interesting as, music appreciation.

8.   (A)   The baseball team here is as good as any other university.

    (B)   The baseball team here is as good as all the other universities.

    (C)   The baseball team here is as good as any other university's.

    (D)   The baseball team here is as good as the other universities.

9.   (A)   I like him better than you.

    (B)   I like him better than I like you.

    (C)   I like him better.

    (D)   I like him more than you.

10.   (A)   You are the most stingiest person I know.

    (B)   You are the most stingier person I know.

    (C)   You are the stingiest person I know.

    (D)   You are the more stingiest person I know.

V. PUNCTUATION

COMMAS

Commas should be placed according to standard rules of punctuation for purpose, clarity, and effect. The proper use of commas is explained in the following rules and examples.

In a series

When more than one adjective describes a noun, use a comma to separate and emphasize each adjective. The comma takes the place of the word *and* in the series.

> the long, dark passageway
>
> another confusing, sleepless night
>
> an elaborate, complex, brilliant plan
>
> the old, gray, crumpled hat

Some adjective-noun combinations are thought of as one word. In these cases, the adjective in front of the adjective-noun combination needs no comma. If you inserted *and* between the adjective-noun combination, it would not make sense.

a stately oak tree

an exceptional wine glass

my worst report card

a china dinner plate

The comma is also used to separate words, phrases, and whole ideas (clauses); it still takes the place of *and* when used this way.

an apple, a pear, a fig, and a banana

a lovely lady, an elegant dress, and many admirers

She lowered the shade, closed the curtain, turned off the light, and went to bed.

The only question that exists about the use of commas in a series is whether or not one should be used before the final item. It is standard to do so, although many newspapers and magazines have stopped using the final comma. Occasionally, the omission of the comma can be confusing.

CORRECT: She ate lunch with Susan, saw a movie with Harold and Joan, and had coffee with Gregory.

With a long introductory phrase

Usually if a phrase of more than five or six words or a clause that cannot stand alone as a sentence (a dependent clause) precedes the subject at the beginning of a sentence, a comma is used to set it off.

After last night's fiasco at the party, she couldn't bear the thought of looking at him again.

Whenever I try to talk about politics, my wife leaves the room.

Provided you have said nothing, they will never guess who you are.

It is not necessary to use a comma with a short sentence.

In January she will go to Switzerland.

After I rest I'll feel better.

During the day no one is home.

If an introductory phrase includes a verb form that is being used as another part of speech (a *verbal*), it must be followed by a comma.

INCORRECT: When eating Mary never looked up from her plate.

CORRECT: When eating, Mary never looked up from her plate.

―――――――――――――

INCORRECT: Because of her desire to believe her faith in James wavered.

CORRECT: Because of her desire to believe, her faith in James wavered.

―――――――――――――

INCORRECT: Having decided to leave Mary James wrote her a letter.

CORRECT: Having decided to leave Mary, James wrote her a letter.

To separate sentences with two main ideas

To understand this use of the comma, you need to be able to recognize compound sentences. When a sentence contains more than two subjects and verbs (clauses), and the two clauses are joined by a conjunction (*and, but, or, nor, for, yet*), use a comma before the conjunction to show that another clause is coming.

> I thought I knew the poem by heart, but he showed me three lines I had forgotten.
>
> Are we really interested in helping the children, or are we more concerned with protecting our good names?
>
> He is supposed to leave tomorrow, but he is not ready to go.
>
> Jim knows you are disappointed, and he has known it for a long time.

If the two parts of the sentence are short and closely related, it is not necessary to use a comma.

> He threw the ball and the dog ran after it.
>
> Jane played the piano and Michael danced.

Be careful not to confuse a sentence that has a compound verb and a single subject with a compound sentence. If the subject is the same for both verbs, there is no need for a comma.

> INCORRECT: Charles sent some flowers, and wrote a long letter explaining why he had not been able to attend.
>
> CORRECT: Charles sent some flowers and wrote a long letter explaining why he had not been able to attend.

> INCORRECT: Last Thursday we went to the concert with Julia, and afterwards dined at an old Italian restaurant.
>
> CORRECT: Last Thursday we went to the concert with Julia and afterwards dined at an old Italian restaurant.

> INCORRECT: For the third time, the teacher explained that the literacy level for high school students was much lower than it had been in previous years, and, this time, wrote the statistics on the board for everyone to see.
>
> CORRECT: For the third time, the teacher explained that the literacy level for high school students was much lower than it had been in previous years and this time wrote the statistics on the board for everyone to see.

In general, words and phrases that stop the flow of the sentence or are unnecessary for the main idea are set off by commas.

Abbreviations after names

> Did you invite John Paul, Jr., and his sister?
>
> Martha Harris, Ph.D., will be the speaker tonight.

Interjections (an exclamation without added grammatical connection)

Oh, I'm so glad to see you.

I tried so hard, alas, to do it.

Hey, let me out of here.

Direct address

Roy, won't you open the door for the dog?

I can't understand, Mother, what you are trying to say.

May I ask, Mr. President, why you called us together?

Hey, lady, watch out for that car!

Tag questions

I'm really hungry, aren't you?

Jerry looks like his father, doesn't he?

Geographical names and addresses

The concert will be held in Chicago, Illinois, on August 12.

The letter was addressed to Mrs. Marion Heartwell, 1881 Pine Lane, Palo Alto, California 95824.

(Note: No comma is needed before the zip code, because it is already clearly set off from the state name.)

Transitional words and phrases

Transitional words and phrases serve as a bridge between sentence parts and complete sentences, such as *"as a matter of fact, for example, however."*

On the other hand, I hope he gets better.

In addition, the phone rang constantly this afternoon.

I'm, nevertheless, going to the beach on Sunday.

You'll find, therefore, that no one is more loyal than I am.

Parenthetical words and phrases

Parenthetical words and phrases are expressions that interrupt the flow of a sentence with extra information.

You will become, I believe, a great statesman.

We know, of course, that this is the only thing to do.

In fact, I planted corn last summer.

The Mannes affair was, to put it mildly, a surprise.

Unusual word order

The dress, new and crisp, hung in the closet.

Intently, she stared out the window.

With nonrestrictive elements

Parts of a sentence that modify other parts are sometimes essential to the meaning of the sentence and sometimes not. When a modifying word or group of words is not vital to the meaning of the sentence, it is set off by commas. Since it does not restrict the meaning of the words it modifies, it is called "nonrestrictive." Modifiers that are essential to the meaning of the sentence are called "restrictive" and are not set off by commas.

ESSENTIAL: The girl *who wrote the story* is my sister.

NONESSENTIAL: My sister, *the girl who wrote the story*, has always loved to write.

———————————

ESSENTIAL: The cup *that is on the piano* is the one I want.

NONESSENTIAL: The cup, *which my brother gave me last year*, is on the piano.

———————————

ESSENTIAL: The people *who arrived late* were not seated.

NONESSENTIAL: George, *who arrived late*, was not seated.

To set off direct quotations

Most direct quotes or quoted materials are set off from the rest of the sentence by commas.

"Please read your part more loudly," the director insisted.

"I won't know what to do," said Michael, "if you leave me."

The teacher said sternly, "I will not dismiss this class until I have silence."

Who was it who said "Do not ask for whom the bell tolls; it tolls for thee"?

Note: Commas always go inside the closing quotation mark, even if the comma is not part of the material being quoted.

Be careful not to set off indirect quotes or quotes that are used as subjects or complements.

"To be or not to be" is the famous beginning of a soliloquy in Shakespeare's *Hamlet*. (subject)

She said she would never come back. (indirect quote)

Back then my favorite poem was "Evangeline." (complement)

To set off contrasting elements

Her intelligence, not her beauty, got her the job.

Your plan will take you a little further from, rather than closer to, your destination.

It was a reasonable, though not appealing, idea.

He wanted glory, but found happiness instead.

In dates

Both forms of the date are acceptable.

She will arrive on April 6, 1998.

He left on 5 December 1980.

In January 1967, he handed in his resignation.

On October 22, 1992, Frank and Julie were married.

After Subordinate Clauses

Subordinate clauses are comprised of a subject and a verb that cannot stand alone as a sentence. When these clauses appear at the beginning of a sentence, they should be separated with a comma.

If we hurry, we can still make the early movie.

Unless my mom changes her mind, I won't be able to go to the concert.

Listed below are several subordinate conjunctions, which are words that are used to join subordinate clauses to independent clauses in a sentence. If one of these words begins a clause that is an incomplete thought and it begins the sentence, the clause should be followed by a comma.

after	since
although	so that
as	though
as if	till
because	unless
before	until
even though	when
if	whenever
inasmuch as	while

SEMICOLONS

Questions testing semicolon usage require you to be able to distin-guish between the semicolon and the comma, and the semicolon and the colon. This review section covers the basic uses of the semicolon: (1) to separate independent clauses not joined by a coordinating conjunction, (2) to separate independent clauses separated by a conjunctive adverb, and (3) to separate items in a series with internal commas. It is important to be consistent; if you use a semicolon between *any* of the items in the series, you must use semicolons to separate *all* of the items in the series.

Usually, a comma follows the conjunctive adverb. A conjunctive adverb is an adverb that connects independent clauses in a sentence or group of sentences.

My teeth were chattering and feet were freezing. Nonetheless, I still wanted to continue skiing.

Note also that a period can be used to separate two sentences joined by a conjunctive adverb. Some common conjunctive adverbs are:

accordingly	nevertheless
besides	next
consequently	nonetheless
finally	now
furthermore	on the other hand
however	otherwise
indeed	perhaps
in fact	still
moreover	therefore

Note: *Then* is also used as a conjunctive adverb, but it is not usually followed by a comma.

Use the semicolon
to separate independent clauses that are not joined by a coordinating conjunction:

I understand how to use commas; the semicolon I have not yet mastered.

to separate two independent clauses connected by a conjunctive adverb:

He took great care with his work; *therefore*, he was very successful.

to combine two independent clauses connected by a coordinating conjunction if either or both of the clauses contain other internal punctuation:

Success in college, some maintain, requires intelligence, industry, and perseverance; *but* others, fewer in number, assert that only personality is important.

to separate items in a series when each item has internal punctuation:

I bought an old, dilapidated chair; an antique table that was in beautiful condition; and a new, ugly, blue and white rug.

Call our customer service line for assistance: Arizona, 1-800-555-6020; New Mexico, 1-800-555-5050; California, 1-800-555-3140; or Nevada, 1-800-555-3214.

Do not use the semicolon
to separate a dependent and an independent clause:

INCORRECT: You should not make such statements; even though they are correct.

CORRECT: You should not make such statements even though they are correct.

to separate an appositive phrase or clause from a sentence:

INCORRECT: His immediate aim in life is centered around two things; becoming an engineer and learning to fly an airplane.

CORRECT: His immediate aim in life is centered around two things: becoming an engineer and learning to fly an airplane.

to precede an explanation or summary of the first clause:

Note: Although the sentence below is punctuated correctly, the use of the semicolon provides a miscue, suggesting that the second clause is merely an extension, not an explanation, of the first clause. The colon provides a better clue.

WEAK: The first week of camping was wonderful; we lived in cabins instead of tents.

BETTER: The first week of camping was wonderful: we lived in cabins instead of tents.

to substitute for a comma:

INCORRECT: My roommate also likes sports; particularly football, basketball, and baseball.

CORRECT: My roommate also likes sports, particularly football, basketball, and baseball.

to set off other types of phrases or clauses from a sentence:

INCORRECT: Being of a cynical mind; I should ask for a recount of the ballots.

CORRECT: Being of a cynical mind, I should ask for a recount of the ballots.

INCORRECT: The next meeting of the club has been postponed two weeks; inasmuch as both the president and vice-president are out of town.

CORRECT: The next meeting of the club has been postponed two weeks, inasmuch as both the president and vice-president are out of town.

Note: The semicolon is not a terminal mark of punctuation; therefore, it should not be followed by a capital letter unless the first word in the second clause ordinarily requires capitalization.

COLONS

Although it is true that a colon is used to precede a list, one must also make sure that a complete sentence precedes the colon. The colon signals the reader that a list, explanation, or restatement of the preceding will follow. It is like an arrow, indicating that something is to follow. The difference between the colon and the semicolon and between the colon and the period is that the colon is an introductory mark, not a terminal mark. Look at the following examples:

The Constitution provides for a separation of powers among the three branches of government.

government. The period signals a new sentence.

government; The semicolon signals an interrelated sentence.

government, The comma signals a coordinating conjunction followed by another independent clause.

government: The colon signals a list.

The Constitution provides for a separation of powers among the three branches of *government*: executive, legislative, and judicial.

Use the Colon

To introduce a list:

> I hate this one course: English.

Note: One item may constitute a list:

> Three plays by William Shakespeare will be presented in repertory this summer at the University of Michigan: *Hamlet, Macbeth,* and *Othello.*

To introduce a list preceded by *as follows* or *the following*:

> The reasons he cited for his success are as follows: integrity, honesty, industry, and a pleasant disposition.

To separate two independent clauses, when the second clause is a restatement or explanation of the first:

> All of my high school teachers said one thing in particular: college is going to be difficult.

To introduce a word or word group that is a restatement, explanation, or summary of the first sentence:

> These two things he loved: an honest man and a beautiful woman.

To introduce a formal appositive:

> I am positive there is one appeal that you can't overlook: money.

To separate the introductory words from a long or formal quotation:

> The actor then stated: "I would rather be able to adequately play the part of Hamlet than to perform a miraculous operation, deliver a great lecture, or build a magnificent skyscraper."

The colon should only be used after statements that are grammatically complete.

Do *not* use a colon after a verb:

> INCORRECT: My favorite holidays are: Christmas, New Year's Eve, and Halloween.
>
> CORRECT: My favorite holidays are Christmas, New Year's Eve, and Halloween.

Do *not* use a colon after a preposition:

> INCORRECT: I enjoy different ethnic foods such as: Greek, Chinese, and Italian.
>
> CORRECT: I enjoy different ethnic foods such as Greek, Chinese, and Italian.

Do *not* use a colon interchangeably with the dash:

INCORRECT: Mathematics, German, English: these gave me the greatest difficulty of all my studies.

CORRECT: Mathematics, German, English—these gave me the greatest difficulty of all my studies.

Information preceding the colon should be a complete sentence regardless of the explanatory information following the clause.

Do *not* use the colon before the words *for example, namely, that is,* or *for instance* even though these words may be introducing a list.

INCORRECT: We agreed to it: namely, to give him a surprise party.

CORRECT: There are a number of well-known American women writers, for example, Nikki Giovanni, Phyllis Wheatley, Emily Dickinson, and Maya Angelou.

APOSTROPHES

Apostrophe questions require you to know when an apostrophe has been used appropriately to make a noun possessive, not plural. Remember the following rules when considering how to show possession.

Add *'s* to singular nouns and indefinite pronouns:

> Tiffany's flowers
>
> a dog's bark
>
> everybody's computer
>
> at the owner's expense
>
> today's paper

Add *'s* to singular nouns ending in *s*, unless this distorts the pronunciation:

> Delores's paper
>
> the boss's pen
>
> Dr. Yots' class
>
> for righteousness' sake
>
> Dr. Evans's office OR Dr. Evans' office

Add *an apostrophe* to plural nouns ending in *s* or *es*:

> two cents' worth
>
> ladies' night
>
> thirteen years' experience
>
> two weeks' pay

Add *'s* to plural nouns not ending in *s*:

> men's room
>
> children's toys

Add *'s* to the last word in compound words or groups:

>   brother-in-law's car
>
>   someone else's paper

Add *'s* to the last name when indicating joint ownership:

>   Joe and Edna's home
>
>   Julie and Kathy's party
>
>   women and children's clinic

Add *'s* to both names if you intend to show individual ownership:

>   Joe's and Edna's trucks
>
>   Julie's and Kathy's pies
>
>   Ted's and Jane's marriage vows

Possessive pronouns do not require the addition of an apostrophe:

>   her, his, hers
>
>   your, yours
>
>   their, theirs
>
>   it, its

Use the possessive form of a noun when it precedes a gerund:

>   His driving annoys me.
>
>   My bowling a strike irritated him.
>
>   Do you mind our stopping by?
>
>   We appreciate your coming.

Add *'s* to words and initials to show that they are plural:

>   no if's, and's, or but's
>
>   the do's and don't's of dating
>
>   three A's
>
>   IRA's are available at the bank.

Add *s* to numbers, symbols, and letters to show that they are plural:

>   TVs
>
>   VCRs
>
>   the 1800s
>
>   the returning POWs

QUOTATION MARKS AND ITALICS

These kinds of questions test your knowledge of the proper use of quotation marks with other marks of punctuation, with titles, and with dialogue. These kinds of questions also test your knowledge of the correct use of italics and underlining with titles and words used as sample words (for example, *the word is is a common verb*).

The most common use of double quotation marks (", ") is to set off quoted words, phrases, and sentences.

> "If everybody minded their own business," said the Duchess in a hoarse growl, "the world would go round a great deal faster than it does."
>
> "Then you would say what you mean," the March Hare went on.
>
> "I do," Alice hastily replied: "at least—at least I mean what I say—that's the same thing, you know."
>
> —from Lewis Carroll's Alice in Wonderland

Single quotation marks are used to set off quoted material when it appears within another set of quotes.

> "Shall I bring 'Rime of the Ancient Mariner' along with us?" she asked her brother.
>
> Mrs. Green said, "The doctor told me, 'Go immediately to bed when you get home!'"
>
> "If she said that to me," Katherine insisted, "I would tell her, 'I never intend to speak to you again! Goodbye, Susan!'"

When writing dialogue, begin a new paragraph each time the speaker changes.

> "Do you know what time it is?" asked Jane.
>
> "Can't you see I'm busy?" snapped Mary.
>
> "It's easy to see that you're in a bad mood today!" replied Jane.

Use quotation marks to enclose words used as words (sometimes italics are used for this purpose).

> "Judgment" has always been a difficult word for me to spell.
>
> Do you know what "abstruse" means?
>
> "Horse and buggy" and "bread and butter" can be used either as adjectives or as nouns.

If slang is used within more formal writing, the slang words or phrases should be set off with quotation marks.

> Harrison's decision to leave the conference and to "stick his neck out" by flying to Jamaica was applauded by the rest of the conference attendees.

When words are meant to have an unusual or specific significance to the reader, for instance irony or humor, they are sometimes placed in quotation marks.

> For years, women were not allowed to buy real estate in order to "protect" them from unscrupulous dealers.
>
> The "conversation" resulted in one black eye and a broken nose.

To set off titles of TV shows, poems, stories, and book chapters, use quotation marks. (Book, motion picture, newspaper, and magazine titles are underlined when handwritten and italicized when printed.)

The article "Moving South in the Southern Rain," by Jergen Smith in the *Southern News*, attracted the attention of our editor.

The assignment is "Childhood Development," Chapter 18 of *Human Behavior*.

My favorite essay by Montaigne is "On Silence."

"Happy Days" led the TV ratings for years, didn't it?

You will find Keats' "Ode to a Grecian Urn" in Chapter 3, "The Romantic Era," in Lastly's *Selections from Great English Poets*.

Errors to avoid:

Be sure to remember that quotation marks always come in pairs. Do not make the mistake of using only one set.

INCORRECT: "You'll never convince me to move to the city, said Thurman. I consider it an insane asylum."

CORRECT: "You'll never convince me to move to the city," said Thurman. "I consider it an insane asylum."

INCORRECT: "Idleness and pride tax with a heavier hand than kings and parliaments," Benjamin Franklin is supposed to have said. If we can get rid of the former, we may easily bear the latter."

CORRECT: "Idleness and pride tax with a heavier hand than kings and parliaments," Benjamin Franklin is supposed to have said. "If we can get rid of the former, we may easily bear the latter."

When a quote consists of several sentences, do not put the quotation marks at the beginning and end of each sentence; put them at the beginning and end of the entire quotation.

INCORRECT: "It was during his student days in Bonn that Beethoven fastened upon Schiller's poem." "The heady sense of liberation in the verses must have appealed to him." "They appealed to every German." —John Burke

CORRECT: "It was during his student days in Bonn that Beethoven fastened upon Schiller's poem. The heady sense of liberation in the verses must have appealed to him. They appealed to every German." —John Burke

Instead of setting off a long quote with quotation marks, if it is longer than four lines you may want to indent and single space it. If you do indent, do not use quotation marks.

In his *First Inaugural Address,* Abraham Lincoln appeals to the war-torn American people:

> We are not enemies, but friends. We must not be enemies. Though passion may have strained, it must not break, our bonds of affection. The mystic chords of memory, stretching from every battlefield and patriot grave to every living heart and hearthstone all over this broad land, will yet swell the chorus of the Union when again touched, as surely they will be, by the better angels of our nature.

Be careful not to use quotation marks with indirect quotations.

INCORRECT: Mary wondered "if she would get over it."

CORRECT: Mary wondered if she would get over it.

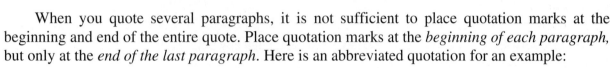

INCORRECT: The nurse asked "how long it
had been since we had visited
the doctor's office."

CORRECT: The nurse asked how long it had
been since we had visited the doctor's
office.

When you quote several paragraphs, it is not sufficient to place quotation marks at the beginning and end of the entire quote. Place quotation marks at the *beginning of each paragraph,* but only at the *end of the last paragraph.* Here is an abbreviated quotation for an example:

> "Here begins an odyssey through the world of classical mythology, starting with the creation of the world . . .
>
> "It is true that themes similar to the classical may be found in any corpus of mythology . . . Even technology is not immune to the influence of Greece and Rome . . .
>
> "We need hardly mention the extent to which painters and sculptors . . . have used and adapted classical mythology to illustrate the past, to reveal the human body, to express romantic or antiromantic ideals, or to symbolize any particular point of view."

Remember that commas and periods are *always* placed inside the quotation marks even if they are not actually part of the quote.

INCORRECT: "Life always gets colder near the summit", Nietzsche is purported to have said,
"—the cold increases, responsibility grows".

CORRECT: "Life always gets colder near the summit," Nietzsche is purported to have said,
"—the cold increases, responsibility grows."

INCORRECT: "Get down here right away", John cried. "You'll miss the sunset if you don't."

CORRECT: "Get down here right away," John cried. "You'll miss the sunset if you don't."

INCORRECT: "If my dog could talk", Mary mused, "I'll bet he would say, 'Take me for a walk
right this minute'".

CORRECT: "If my dog could talk," Mary mused, "I'll bet he would say, 'Take me for a walk
right this minute'."

Other marks of punctuation, such as question marks, exclamation points, colons, and semicolons, go inside the quotation marks only if they are part of the quoted material. If they are not part of the quotation, they go outside the quotation marks. Be careful to distinguish between the guidelines for the comma and period, which always go inside the quotation marks, and those for other marks of punctuation.

INCORRECT: "I'll always love you"! he exclaimed happily.

CORRECT: "I'll always love you!" he exclaimed happily.

INCORRECT: Did you hear her say, "He'll be there early?"

CORRECT: Did you hear her say, "He'll be there early"?

INCORRECT: She called down the stairs, "When are you going"?

CORRECT: She called down the stairs, "When are you going?"

INCORRECT: "Let me out"! he cried. "Don't you have any pity"?

CORRECT: "Let me out!" he cried. "Don't you have any pity?"

Remember to use only one mark of punctuation at the end of a sentence ending with a quotation mark.

INCORRECT: She thought out loud, "Will I ever finish this paper in time for that class?".

CORRECT: She thought out loud, "Will I ever finish this paper in time for that class?"

INCORRECT: "Not the same thing a bit!", said the Hatter. "Why, you might just as well say that 'I see what I eat' is the same thing as 'I eat what I see'!".

CORRECT: "Not the same thing a bit!" said the Hatter. "Why, you might just as well say that 'I see what I eat' is the same thing as 'I eat what I see'!"

☞ Drill: Punctuation

DIRECTIONS: Choose the correct option.

1. Indianola, <u>Mississippi, where B.B. King and my father grew up,</u> has a population of less than 50,000 people.

   (A) Mississippi where, B.B. King and my father grew up,

   (B) Mississippi where B.B. King and my father grew up,

   (C) Mississippi; where B.B. King and my father grew up,

   (D) No change is necessary.

2. John Steinbeck's best known novel *The Grapes of Wrath* is the story of the <u>Joads an Oklahoma family</u> who were driven from their dustbowl farm and forced to become migrant workers in California.

   (A) Joads, an Oklahoma family

   (B) Joads, an Oklahoma family,

(C) Joads; an Oklahoma family

(D) No change is necessary.

3. All students who are interested in student teaching next <u>semester, must submit an application to the Teacher Education Office.</u>

(A) semester must submit an application to the Teacher Education Office.

(B) semester, must submit an application, to the Teacher Education Office.

(C) semester: must submit an application to the Teacher Education Office.

(D) No change is necessary.

4. Whenever you travel by <u>car, or plane, you</u> must wear a seatbelt.

(A) car or plane you   (C) car or plane, you

(B) car, or plane you   (D) No change is necessary.

5. Wearing a seatbelt is not just a good <u>idea, it's</u> the law.

(A) idea; it's   (C) idea. It's

(B) idea it's   (D) No change is necessary.

6. Senators and representatives can be reelected <u>indefinitely; a</u> president can only serve two terms.

(A) indefinitely but a   (C) indefinitely a

(B) indefinitely, a   (D) No change is necessary.

7. Students must pay a penalty for overdue library <u>books, however, there</u> is a grace period.

(A) books; however, there (C) books: however, there

(B) books however, there   (D) No change is necessary.

8. Among the states that seceded from the Union to join the Confederacy in 1860–1861 <u>were:</u> Mississippi, Florida, and Alabama.

(A) were   (C) were.

(B) were;   (D) No change is necessary.

9. The art exhibit displayed works by many famous <u>artists such as:</u> Dali, Picasso, and Michelangelo.

(A) artists such as;   (C) artists. Such as

(B) artists such as   (D) No change is necessary.

10. The National Shakespeare Company will perform <u>the following plays:</u> *Othello*, *Macbeth*, *Hamlet*, and *As You Like It*.

    (A) the following plays,   (C) the following plays

    (B) the following plays;   (D) No change is necessary.

VI. CAPITALIZATION

When a word is capitalized, it calls attention to itself. This attention should be for a good reason. There are standard uses for capital letters. In general, capitalize (1) all proper nouns, (2) the first word of a sentence, and (3) the first word of a direct quotation.

WORDS YOU SHOULD ALSO CAPITALIZE

Names of ships, aircraft, spacecraft, and trains:

Apollo 13	*Mariner IV*
DC-10	S.S. *United States*
Sputnik 11	Boeing 707

Names of deities:

God	Jupiter
Allah	Holy Ghost
Buddha	Venus
Jehovah	Shiva

Geological periods:

Neolithic age	Cenozoic era
late Pleistocene times	Ice Age

Names of astronomical bodies:

Mercury	Big Dipper
the Milky Way	Halley's comet
Ursa Major	North Star

Personifications:

Reliable Nature brought her promised Spring.

Bring on Melancholy in his sad might.

She believed that Love was the answer to all her problems.

Historical periods:

the Middle Ages	World War I
Reign of Terror	Great Depression
Christian Era	Roaring Twenties
Age of Louis XIV	Renaissance

Organizations, associations, and institutions:

Girl Scouts	North Atlantic Treaty Organization
Kiwanis Club	League of Women Voters
New York Yankees	Unitarian Church
Smithsonian Institution	Common Market
Library of Congress	Franklin Glen High School
New York Philharmonic	Harvard University

Government and judicial groups:

United States Court of Appeals	Senate
Committee on Foreign Affairs	Parliament
New Jersey City Council	Peace Corps
Arkansas Supreme Court	Census Bureau
House of Representatives	Department of State

A general term that accompanies a specific name is capitalized only if it follows the specific name. If it stands alone or comes before the specific name, it is put in lowercase:

Washington State	the state of Washington
Senator Dixon	the senator from Illinois
Central Park	the park
Golden Gate Bridge	the bridge
President Clinton	the president
Pope John XXIII	the pope
Queen Elizabeth I	the queen of England
Tropic of Capricorn	the tropics
Monroe Doctrine	the doctrine of expansion
the Mississippi River	the river
Easter Day	the day
Treaty of Versailles	the treaty
Webster's Dictionary	the dictionary
Equatorial Current	the equator

Use a capital to start a sentence:

> Our car would not start.
>
> When will you leave? I need to know right away.
>
> Never!
>
> Let me in! Please!

When a sentence appears within a sentence, start it with a capital letter:

> We had only one concern: When would we eat?
>
> My sister said, "I'll find the Monopoly game."
>
> He answered, "We can only stay a few minutes."

The most important words of titles are capitalized. Those words not capitalized are conjunctions (*and*, *or*, *but*) and short prepositions (*of*, *on*, *by*, *for*). The first and last word of a title must always be capitalized:

A Man for All Seasons	*Crime and Punishment*
Of Mice and Men	*Rise of the West*
Strange Life of Ivan Osokin	"Sonata in G Minor"
"Let Me In"	"Ode to Billy Joe"
"Rubaiyat of Omar Khayyam"	"All in the Family"

Capitalize newspaper and magazine titles:

> *U.S. News & World Report*
>
> *National Geographic*
>
> The *New York Times*
>
> *Sports Illustrated*

Capitalize radio and TV station call letters:

ABC	NBC
WNEW	WBOP
CNN	HBO

Do not capitalize compass directions or seasons:

west	north
east	south
spring	winter
autumn	summer

Capitalize regions:

the South	the Northeast
the West	Eastern Europe

BUT: the south of France

         the east part of town

Capitalize specific military units:

      the U.S. Army

      the 7th Fleet

      the German Navy

      the 1st Infantry Division

Capitalize political groups and philosophies:

Democrat	Communist
Marxist	Nazism
Whig	Federalist
Existentialism	Transcendentalism

BUT: do not capitalize systems of government or individual adherents to a philosophy:

democracy	communism
fascist	agnostic

☞ Drill: Capitalization

DIRECTIONS: Choose the correct option.

---

1. Mexico is the southernmost country in <u>North America</u>. It borders the United States on the north; it is bordered on the <u>south</u> by Belize and Guatemala.

   (A) north America...South

   (B) North America...South

   (C) North america...south

   (D) No change is necessary.

2. (A) Until 1989, Tom Landry was the only Coach the Dallas cowboys ever had.

   (B) Until 1989, Tom Landry was the only coach the Dallas Cowboys ever had.

   (C) Until 1989, Tom Landry was the only Coach the Dallas Cowboys ever had.

   (D) Until 1989, Tom Landry was the only Coach The Dallas Cowboys ever had.

3. The <u>Northern Hemisphere</u> is the half of the <u>earth</u> that lies north of the <u>Equator.</u>

   (A) Northern hemisphere...earth...equator.

    (B)   Northern hemisphere . . . Earth . . . Equator.

    (C)   Northern Hemisphere . . . earth . . . equator.

    (D)   No change is necessary.

4.   (A)   My favorite works by Ernest Hemingway are "The Snows of Kilamanjaro," *The Sun Also Rises,* and *For Whom the Bell Tolls.*

    (B)   My favorite works by Ernest Hemingway are "The Snows Of Kilamanjaro," *The Sun Also Rises,* and *For Whom The Bell Tolls.*

    (C)   My favorite works by Ernest Hemingway are "The Snows of Kilamanjaro," *The Sun also Rises,* and *For whom the Bell Tolls.*

    (D)   My favorite works by Ernest Hemingway are "The Snows of Kilamanjaro," *The Sun also Rises*, and *For Whom the Bell Tolls.*

5.   Aphrodite (<u>Venus in Roman Mythology</u>) was the <u>Greek</u> goddess of love.

    (A)   Venus in Roman mythology . . . greek

    (B)   venus in roman mythology . . . Greek

    (C)   Venus in Roman mythology . . . Greek

    (D)   No change is necessary.

6.   The <u>Koran</u> is considered by <u>Muslims</u> to be the holy word.

    (A)   koran . . . muslims   (C)   Koran . . . muslims

    (B)   koran . . . Muslims   (D)   No change is necessary.

7.   (A)   The freshman curriculum at the community college includes english, a foreign language, Algebra I, and history.

    (B)   The freshman curriculum at the community college includes English, a foreign language, Algebra I, and history.

    (C)   The Freshman curriculum at the Community College includes English, a foreign language, Algebra I, and History.

    (D)   The freshman curriculum at the community college includes english, a foreign language, algebra I, and history.

8.   At the <u>spring</u> graduation ceremonies, the university awarded over 2,000 <u>bachelor's</u> degrees.

    (A)   Spring . . . Bachelor's   (C)   Spring . . . bachelor's

    (B)   spring . . . Bachelor's   (D)   No change is necessary.

9. The fall of the <u>Berlin wall</u> was an important symbol of the collapse of <u>Communism</u>.

    (A) berlin Wall . . . communism.

    (B) Berlin Wall . . . communism.

    (C) berlin wall . . . Communism.

    (D) No change is necessary.

10. A photograph of <u>mars</u> was printed in <u>the *New York Times*</u>.

    (A) Mars . . . *The New York Times*.

    (B) mars . . . *The New York times*.

    (C) mars . . . *The New York Time*s.

    (D) No change is necessary.

VII. SPELLING

Spelling questions test your ability to recognize misspelled words. This section reviews spelling tips and rules to help you spot incorrect spellings. Problems such as the distinction between *to* and *too* and *lead* and *led* are covered under the Word Choice Skills section of this review.

- Remember, *i* before *e* except after *c*, or when sounded as "a" as in *neighbor* and *weigh*.

- There are only three words in the English language that end in **-ceed**:

    proceed, succeed, exceed

- There are several words that end in *-cede*:

    secede, recede, concede, precede

- There is only one word in the English language that ends in *-sede*:

    supersede

Many people learn to read English phonetically; that is, by sounding out the letters of the words. However, many English words are not pronounced the way they are spelled, and those who try to spell English words phonetically often make spelling *errors*. It is better to memorize the correct spelling of English words rather than relying on phonetics to spell correctly.

FREQUENTLY MISSPELLED WORDS

The following list of words are frequently misspelled. Study the spelling of each word by having a friend or teacher drill you on the words. Then mark down the words that you misspelled and study those select ones again. (The words appear in their most popular spellings.)

a lot
ability
absence
absent
abundance
accept
acceptable
accident
accommodate
accompanied
accomplish
accumulation
accuse
accustomed
ache
achieve
achievement
acknowledge
acquaintance
acquainted
acquire
across
address
addressed
adequate
advantage
advantageous
advertise
advertisement
advice
advisable
advise
advisor
aerial
affect
affectionate
again
against
aggravate
aggressive
agree
aisle
all right
almost

already
although
altogether
always
amateur
American
among
amount
analysis
analyze
angel
angle
annual
another
answer
antiseptic
anxious
apologize
apparatus
apparent
appear
appearance
appetite
application
apply
appreciate
appreciation
approach
appropriate
approval
approve
approximate
argue
arguing
argument
arouse
arrange
arrangement
article
artificial
ascend
assistance
assistant
associate

association
attempt
attendance
attention
audience
August
author
automobile
autumn
auxiliary
available
avenue
awful
awkward
bachelor
balance
balloon
bargain
basic
beautiful
because
become
before
beginning
being
believe
benefit
benefited
between
bicycle
board
bored
borrow
bottle
bottom
boundary
brake
breadth
breath
breathe
brilliant
building
bulletin
bureau

burial
buried
bury
bushes
business
cafeteria
calculator
calendar
campaign
capital
capitol
captain
career
careful
careless
carriage
carrying
category
ceiling
cemetery
cereal
certain
changeable
characteristic
charity
chief
choose
chose
cigarette
circumstance
citizen
clothes
clothing
coarse
coffee
collect
college
column
comedy
comfortable
commitment
committed
committee
communicate

company
comparative
compel
competent
competition
compliment
conceal
conceit
conceivable
conceive
concentration
conception
condition
conference
confident
congratulate
conquer
conscience
conscientious
conscious
consequence
consequently
considerable
consistency
consistent
continual
continuous
controlled
controversy
convenience
convenient
conversation
corporal
corroborate
council
counsel
counselor
courage
courageous
course
courteous
courtesy
criticism
criticize

crystal
curiosity
cylinder
daily
daughter
daybreak
death
deceive
December
deception
decide
decision
decisive
deed
definite
delicious
dependent
deposit
derelict
descend
descent
describe
description
desert
desirable
despair
desperate
dessert
destruction
determine
develop
development
device
dictator
died
difference
different
dilemma
dinner
direction
disappear
disappoint
disappointment
disapproval

disapprove
disastrous
discipline
discover
discriminate
disease
dissatisfied
dissection
dissipate
distance
distinction
division
doctor
dollar
doubt
dozen
earnest
easy
ecstasy
ecstatic
education
effect
efficiency
efficient
eight
either
eligibility
eligible
eliminate
embarrass
embarrassment
emergency
emphasis
emphasize
enclosure
encouraging
endeavor
engineer
English
enormous
enough
entrance
envelope
environment

equipment
equipped
especially
essential
evening
evident
exaggerate
exaggeration
examine
exceed
excellent
except
exceptional
exercise
exhausted
exhaustion
exhilaration
existence
exorbitant
expense
experience
experiment
explanation
extreme
facility
factory
familiar
fascinate
fascinating
fatigue
February
financial
financier
flourish
forcibly
forehead
foreign
formal
former
fortunate
fourteen
fourth
frequent
friend

frightening	incidental	laid	momentous
fundamental	increase	language	monkey
further	independence	later	monotonous
gallon	independent	latter	moral
garden	indispensable	laugh	morale
gardener	inevitable	leisure	mortgage
general	influence	length	mountain
genius	influential	lesson	mournful
government	initiate	library	muscle
governor	innocence	license	mysterious
grammar	inoculate	light	mystery
grateful	inquiry	lightning	narrative
great	insistent	likelihood	natural
grievance	instead	likely	necessary
grievous	instinct	literal	needle
grocery	integrity	literature	negligence
guarantee	intellectual	livelihood	neighbor
guess	intelligence	loaf	neither
guidance	intercede	loneliness	newspaper
half	interest	loose	newsstand
hammer	interfere	lose	niece
handkerchief	interference	losing	noticeable
happiness	interpreted	loyal	o'clock
healthy	interrupt	loyalty	obedient
heard	invitation	magazine	obstacle
heavy	irrelevant	maintenance	occasion
height	irresistible	maneuver	occasional
heroes	irritable	marriage	occur
heroine	island	married	occurred
hideous	its	marry	occurrence
himself	it's	match	ocean
hoarse	itself	material	offer
holiday	January	mathematics	often
hopeless	jealous	measure	omission
hospital	journal	medicine	omit
humorous	judgment	million	once
hurried	kindergarten	miniature	operate
hurrying	kitchen	minimum	opinion
ignorance	knew	miracle	opportune
imaginary	knock	miscellaneous	opportunity
imbecile	know	mischief	optimist
imitation	knowledge	mischievous	optimistic
immediately	labor	misspelled	origin
immigrant	laboratory	mistake	original

oscillate
ought
ounce
overcoat
paid
pamphlet
panicky
parallel
parallelism
particular
partner
pastime
patience
peace
peaceable
pear
peculiar
pencil
people
perceive
perception
perfect
perform
performance
perhaps
period
permanence
permanent
perpendicular
perseverance
persevere
persistent
personal
personality
personnel
persuade
persuasion
pertain
picture
piece
plain
playwright
pleasant
please

pleasure
pocket
poison
policeman
political
population
portrayal
positive
possess
possession
possessive
possible
post office
potatoes
practical
prairie
precede
preceding
precise
predictable
prefer
preference
preferential
preferred
prejudice
preparation
prepare
prescription
presence
president
prevalent
primitive
principal
principle
privilege
probably
procedure
proceed
produce
professional
professor
profitable
prominent
promise

pronounce
pronunciation
propeller
prophet
prospect
psychology
pursue
pursuit
quality
quantity
quarreling
quart
quarter
quiet
quite
raise
realistic
realize
reason
rebellion
recede
receipt
receive
recipe
recognize
recommend
recuperate
referred
rehearsal
reign
relevant
relieve
remedy
renovate
repeat
repetition
representative
requirements
resemblance
resistance
resource
respectability
responsibility
restaurant

rhythm
rhythmical
ridiculous
right
role
roll
roommate
sandwich
Saturday
scarcely
scene
schedule
science
scientific
scissors
season
secretary
seize
seminar
sense
separate
service
several
severely
shepherd
sheriff
shining
shoulder
shriek
siege
sight
signal
significance
significant
similar
similarity
sincerely
site
soldier
solemn
sophomore
soul
source
souvenir

special	sweat	treasury	view
specified	sweet	tremendous	village
specimen	syllable	tries	villain
speech	symmetrical	truly	visitor
stationary	sympathy	twelfth	voice
stationery	synonym	twelve	volume
statue	technical	tyranny	waist
stockings	telegram	undoubtedly	weak
stomach	telephone	United States	wear
straight	temperament	university	weather
strength	temperature	unnecessary	Wednesday
strenuous	tenant	unusual	week
stretch	tendency	useful	weigh
striking	tenement	usual	weird
studying	therefore	vacuum	whether
substantial	thorough	valley	which
succeed	through	valuable	while
successful	title	variety	whole
sudden	together	vegetable	wholly
superintendent	tomorrow	vein	whose
suppress	tongue	vengeance	wretched
surely	toward	versatile	
surprise	tragedy	vicinity	
suspense	transferred	vicious	

☞ Drill: Spelling

DIRECTIONS: Identify the misspelled word in each set.

1. (A) probly
   (B) accommodate
   (C) acquaintance
   (D) among

2. (A) auxiliary
   (B) atheletic
   (C) beginning
   (D) awkward

3. (A) environment

   (B) existence

   (C) Febuary

   (D) daybreak

4. (A) ocassion

   (B) occurrence

   (C) omitted

   (D) fundamental

5. (A) perspiration

   (B) referring

   (C) priviledge

   (D) kindergarten

DIRECTIONS: Choose the correct option.

---

6. <u>Preceding</u> the <u>business</u> session, lunch will be served in a <u>separate</u> room.

   (A) preceeding . . . business . . . seperate

   (B) proceeding . . . bussiness . . . seperate

   (C) proceeding . . . business . . . seperite

   (D) No change is necessary.

7. Monte <u>inadvertently</u> left <u>several</u> of his <u>libary</u> books in the cafeteria.

   (A) inadverdently . . . serveral . . . libery

   (B) inadvertently . . . several . . . library

   (C) inadvertentely . . . several . . . librery

   (D) No change is necessary.

8. Sam wished he had more <u>liesure</u> time so he could <u>persue</u> his favorite hobbies.

   (A) leisure . . . pursue   (B) Liesure . . . pursue

   (C) leisure . . . persue   (D) No change is necessary.

9. One of my <u>favrite charecters</u> in <u>litrature</u> is Bilbo from *The Hobbit*.

   (A) favrite . . . characters . . . literature

(B)   favorite . . . characters . . . literature

(C)   favourite . . . characters . . . literature

(D)   No change is necessary.

10.   Even <u>tho</u> Joe was badly hurt in the <u>accidant</u>, the company said they were not <u>lible</u> for damages.

(A)   though . . . accidant . . . libel

(B)   though . . . accident . . . liable

(C)   though . . . acident . . . liable

(D)   No change is necessary.

LANGUAGE SKILLS REVIEW

ANSWER KEY

Drill: Sentence Structure Skills

1.	(C)	3.	(B)	5.	(A)	7.	(B)	9.	(B)
2.	(B)	4.	(B)	6.	(A)	8.	(C)	10.	(B)

Drill: Verbs

1.	(C)	3.	(D)	5.	(A)	7.	(A)	9.	(A)
2.	(D)	4.	(A)	6.	(B)	8.	(C)	10.	(D)

Drill: Pronouns

1.	(A)	3.	(A)	5.	(D)	7.	(B)	9.	(A)
2.	(C)	4.	(A)	6.	(A)	8.	(B)	10.	(C)

Drill: Adjectives and Adverbs

1.	(C)	3.	(D)	5.	(A)	7.	(A)	9.	(B)
2.	(A)	4.	(C)	6.	(C)	8.	(C)	10.	(C)

Drill: Punctuation

1.	(D)	3.	(A)	5.	(A)	7.	(A)	9.	(B)
2.	(A)	4.	(C)	6.	(D)	8.	(A)	10.	(D)

Drill: Capitalization

1.	(D)	3.	(C)	5.	(C)	7.	(B)	9.	(B)
2.	(B)	4.	(A)	6.	(D)	8.	(D)	10.	(A)

Drill: Spelling

1.	(A)	3.	(C)	5.	(C)	7.	(B)	9.	(B)
2.	(B)	4.	(A)	6.	(D)	8.	(A)	10.	(B)

DETAILED EXPLANATIONS OF ANSWERS

Drill: Sentence Structure Skills

1. **(C)** Choice (C) is correct. Each response contains items in a series. In choices (A), (B), and (D) the word group after the conjunction is not an adjective like the first words in the series. Choice (C) contains three adjectives.

2. **(B)** Choice (B) is correct. Choices (A) and (C) combine conjunctions incorrectly. Choice (D) incorrectly uses the adverb *not*.

3. **(B)** Choice (B) is correct. Choices (A) and (C) appear to be parallel because the conjunction *and* connects two word groups that both begin with *because*, but the structure on both sides of the conjunction are very different. Choice (D) has the same structural problem as both (A) and (C) and it uses the conjunction *that* unnecessarily. *Because he kept his campaign promises* is a clause; *because of his refusal to accept political favors* is a prepositional phrase. Choice (B) connects two dependent clauses.

4. **(B)** Choice (B) is correct. Choices (A), (C), and (D) contain the elliptical clause *While . . . taking a shower*. It appears that the missing subject in the elliptical clause is the same as that in the independent clause—the *doorbell* in choice (A) and *someone* in choice (C), neither of which is a logical subject for the verbal *taking a shower*. Choice (B) removes the elliptical clause and provides the logical subject.

5. **(A)** Choice (A) is correct. Who swung the bat? Choices (B), (C), and (D) imply that it is the runner who swung the bat. Only choice (A) makes it clear that as *he* swung the bat, someone else (the *runner*) stole second base.

6. **(A)** Choice (A) is correct. The punctuation in the original sentence and in choice (B) creates a fragment. *Cotton being the state's principal crop* is not an independent thought because it lacks a complete verb—*being* is not a complete verb.

7. **(B)** Choice (B) is correct. The punctuation in the original sentence and in choice (A) creates a fragment. Both the semicolon and the period should be used to separate two independent clauses. The word group *one that I have never seen before* does not express a complete thought and therefore is not an independent clause.

8. **(C)** Choice (C) is correct. The dependent clause *because repairs were being made* in choices (B) and (C) is punctuated as if it were a sentence. The result is a fragment.

9. **(B)** Choice (B) is correct. Choices (A) and (C) do not separate the complete thoughts in the independent clauses with the correct punctuation.

10. **(B)** Choice (B) is correct. Choices (A) and (C) do not separate the independent clauses with the correct punctuation.

Drill: Verbs

1. **(C)** Choice (C) is correct. The past participle form of each verb is required because of the auxiliaries (helping verbs) *had been* (concerned) and *would have* (gone).

2. **(D)** Choice (D) is correct. The forms of the irregular verb meaning *to rest* are *lie (rest),* *lies (rests), lay (rested),* and *has lain (has rested).* The forms of the verb meaning *to put* are *lay (put), lays (puts), laying (putting), laid (put),* and *have laid (have put).*

3. **(D)** Choice (D) is correct. The present tense is used for universal truths and the past tense is used for historical truths.

4. **(A)** Choice (A) is correct. The present tense is used for customary happenings. Choice (B), *had begun,* is not a standard verb form. Choice (C), *was beginning,* indicates that 10:30 a.m. is not the regular class time.

5. **(A)** Choice (A) is correct. The past tense is used for historical statements, and the present tense is used for statements about works of art.

6. **(B)** Choice (B) is correct. The subject of the sentence is the plural noun *sales,* not the singular noun *Christmas,* which is the object of the prepositional phrase.

7. **(A)** Choice (A) is correct. The subject *specialty* is singular.

8. **(C)** Choice (C) is correct. Subjects preceded by *every* are considered singular and therefore require a singular verb form.

9. **(A)** Choice (A) is correct. The subject of the sentence is the gerund *hiding,* not the object of the gerund phrase *mistakes. Hiding* is singular; therefore, the singular verb form *does* should be used.

10. **(D)** Choice (D) is correct. Though the form of the subject *Board of Regents* is plural, it is singular in meaning.

Drill: Pronouns

1. **(A)** Choice (A) is correct. Do not use the reflexive pronoun *myself* as a substitute for I.

2. **(C)** Choice (C) is correct. In the clause *whoever consumes them, whoever* is the subject. *Whomever* is the objective case pronoun and should be used only as the object of a sentence, never as the subject.

3. **(A)** Choice (A) is correct. Use the nominative case pronoun *who* as the subject complement after the verb *is*.

4. **(A)** Choice (A) is correct. In this sentence use the nominative case/subject pronouns *she who* as the subject complement after the *be* verb *was*.

5. **(D)** Choice (D) is correct. *Student* is an indefinite, genderless noun that requires a singular personal pronoun. While *his* is a singular personal pronoun, a genderless noun includes both the masculine and feminine forms and requires *his or her* as the singular personal pronoun.

6. **(A)** Choice (A) is correct. The antecedent *company* is singular, requiring the singular pronoun *it*, not the plural *they*.

7. **(B)** Choice (B) is correct. Choice (A) contains a person shift: *Your* is a second person pronoun, and *his* and *her* are third person pronouns. The original sentence uses the third person plural pronoun *their* to refer to the singular antecedent *every car owner*. Choice (B) correctly provides the masculine and feminine forms *his or her* required by the indefinite, genderless *every car owner*.

8. **(B)** Choice (B) is correct. The implied antecedent is *teaching*. Choices (A) and (C) each contain a pronoun with no antecedent. Neither *it* nor *this* are suitable substitutions for *teacher*.

9. **(A)** Choice (A) is correct. The pronoun *they* in the original sentence has no conspicuous antecedent. Since the doer of the action is obviously unknown (and therefore genderless), choice (B), *he*, is not the correct choice.

10. **(C)** Choice (C) is correct. The original sentence is ambiguous: the pronoun *she* has two possible antecedents; we don't know whether it is Margaret or her sister who is away at college.

Drill: Adjectives and Adverbs

1. **(C)** Choice (C) is correct. *Bad* is an adjective; *badly* is an adverb. *Real* is an adjective meaning *genuine* (*a real problem*, *real leather*). To qualify an adverb of degree to express how bad, how excited, how boring, etc., choose *very*.

2. **(A)** Choice (A) is correct. Use an adverb as a qualifier for an adjective. *How simple? Relatively simple.*

3. **(D)** Choice (D) is correct. *Good* is an adjective; *well* is both an adjective and an adverb. As an adjective, *well* refers to health; it means "not ill."

4. **(C)** Choice (C) is correct. All the other choices use *good* incorrectly as an adverb. *Shake* is an action verb that requires an adverb, not an adjective.

5. **(A)** Choice (A) is correct. The action verbs *speaks*, *writes*, *observe*, and *think* each require adverbs as modifiers.

6. **(C)** Choice (C) is correct. The comparisons in choices (A), (B), and (D) are illogical: these sentences suggest that Los Angeles is not in California because it *is larger than any city in California.*

7. **(A)** Choice (A) is correct. Do not omit the second *as* of the correlative pair *as . . . as* when making a point of equal or superior comparison, as in choice (B). Choice (C) omits *than* from "if not more interesting [than]." Choice (D) incorrectly uses *as* instead of *than.*

8. **(C)** Choice (C) is correct. Choice (A) illogically compares *baseball team* to a *university,* and choices (B) and (D) illogically compare *baseball team* to *other universities.* Choice (C) logically compares the baseball team here to the one at any other university, as implied by the possessive ending on university—*university's.*

9. **(B)** Choice (B) is correct. Choices (A), (C), and (D) are ambiguous; because these sentences are too obscure, the reader does not know where to place the missing information.

10. **(C)** Choice (C) is correct. Choice (A) is redundant; there is no need to use *most* with *stingiest.* Choice (B) incorrectly combines the superlative word *most* with the comparative form *stingier.* Choice (D) incorrectly combines the comparative word *more* with the superlative form *stingiest.*

Drill: Punctuation

1. **(D)** Choice (D) is correct. Nonrestrictive clauses, like other nonrestrictive elements, should be set off from the rest of the sentence with commas.

2. **(A)** Choice (A) is correct. Use a comma to separate a nonrestrictive appositive from the word it modifies. "An Oklahoma family" is a nonrestrictive appositive.

3. **(A)** Choice (A) is correct. Do not use unnecessary commas to separate a subject and verb from their complement. Both choices (B) and (C) use extra punctuation.

4. **(C)** Choice (C) is correct. Do not separate two items in a compound with commas. The original sentence incorrectly separates "car or plane." Choice (A) omits the comma after the introductory clause.

5. **(A)** Choice (A) is correct. Use a semicolon to separate two independent clauses/sentences that are not joined by a coordinating conjunction, especially when the ideas in the sentences are interrelated.

6. **(D)** Choice (D) is correct. Use a semicolon to separate two sentences not joined by a coordinating conjunction.

7. **(A)** Choice (A) is correct. Use a semicolon to separate two sentences joined by a conjunctive adverb.

8. **(A)**   Choice (A) is correct. Do not use a colon after a verb or a preposition. Remember that a complete sentence must precede a colon.

9. **(B)**   Choice (B) is correct. Do not use a colon after a preposition, and do not use a colon to separate a preposition from its objects.

10. **(D)**   Choice (D) is correct. Use a colon preceding a list that is introduced by words such as *the following* and *as follows*.

Drill: Capitalization

1. **(D)**   Choice (D) is correct. *North America*, like other proper names, is capitalized. *North, south, east*, and *west* are only capitalized when they refer to geographic regions (*the Southwest, Eastern Europe*); as compass directions, they are not capitalized.

2. **(B)**   Choice (B) is correct. Although persons' names are capitalized, a person's title is not (*coach*, not *Coach* since it stands alone). Capitalize the complete name of a team, school, river, etc. (as in Dallas Cowboys). *The* is not part of the official title. Therefore, it is never capitalized when it appears in text.

3. **(C)**   Choice (C) is correct. Capitalize all geographic units, and capitalize *earth* only when it is mentioned with other planets. *Equator* is not capitalized.

4. **(A)**   Choice (A) is correct. Capitalize the first and last words in a title and all other words in a title except articles, prepositions with fewer than five letters, and conjunctions.

5. **(C)**   Choice (C) is correct. Capitalize proper adjectives (proper nouns used as adjectives): *Greek* goddess, *Roman* mythology.

6. **(D)**   Choice (D) is correct. Capitalize all religious groups, books, and names referring to religious deities.

7. **(B)**   Choice (B) is correct. Do not capitalize courses unless they are languages (English) or course titles followed by a number (Algebra I).

8. **(D)**   Choice (D) is correct. Do not capitalize seasons unless they accompany the name of an event such as *Spring Break*. Do not capitalize types of degrees (*bachelor's degrees*); capitalize only the name of the degree (*Bachelor of Arts degree*).

9. **(B)**   Choice (B) is correct. As a landmark, *Berlin Wall* is capitalized; however, do not capitalize systems of government or individual adherents to a philosophy, such as *communism*.

10. **(A)**   Choice (A) is correct. The names of planets, as well as the complete names of newspapers and other periodicals, are capitalized.

Drill: Spelling

1. **(A)**   The correct spelling of choice (A) is "probably."

2. **(B)**   The correct spelling is "athletic."

3. **(C)**   Choice (C) should be spelled "February."

4. **(A)**   The correct spelling of this word is "occasion."

5. **(C)**   Choice (C) should be spelled "privilege."

6. **(D)**   Choice (D) is the best response. *Business* has only three *-s's*. Separate has an *-e* at the beginning and the end, not in the middle.

7. **(B)**   Choice (B) is the best response. *Library* has two *r's*.

8. **(A)**   Choice (A) is the best response. *Leisure* is one of the few English words that does not follow the *i* before *e* except after *c* rule. *Pursue* has two *u's* and only one *e*.

9. **(B)**   Choice (B) is the best response. "Favorite," "characters," and "literature" are commonly mispronounced, and when someone who mispronounces them tries to spell them phonetically, he or she often misspells them.

10. **(B)**   Choice (B) is the best response. Advertisements often misspell words to catch the consumer's eye (*lite* for light, *tho* for though, etc.), and these misspellings are becoming more common in student writing. "Accident" and "liable" are examples of words that are not pronounced the way they are spelled.

COOP/
HSPT

CHAPTER 4

Reading
Review

Chapter 4

READING REVIEW

I. READING COMPREHENSION
II. VOCABULARY

The following review will give you some techniques and strategies that will increase your reading comprehension skills and help you get better scores on the *HSPT: Subtest 3* or the *COOP: Test 5.*

Both of these tests require a strong understanding of reading skills. You will improve your performance on the *Reading* subtest of the HSPT or *Reading Comprehension* COOP test if you know and prepare for three things.

- How do you read effectively?

- What are the six basic questions commonly asked?

- Do you have a good understanding of the English vocabulary?

I. READING COMPREHENSION

EFFECTIVE READING TIPS

While the following proven strategies and techniques will improve your overall comprehension in any reading situation, they are particularly effective in helping you find the type of information needed to answer the reading questions on the HSPT.

Let's look at each and decide how and why it works.

Step 1: Skim the Passage and the Questions

Skimming is a quick technique that takes only seconds. It gives a general idea of the passage. You can understand a passage better if you know the general subject

it will discuss before you read it. You can also answer questions with more success if you have a basic idea of what will be asked before you read. When you skim the questions, you read ONLY the questions and not the answer choices. You want to know the general information they will ask for. You don't need to remember them exactly; that will come later. Knowing the general subject and the general questions gives you a head start.

Skimming is a simple way to find the important ideas that will be discussed. It can also help you to identify the major idea of the passage. There are two different ways to skim a passage, depending on its structure. The reading passages have two basic structures: One long paragraph or two or more shorter paragraphs.

If the passage is constructed in *one long paragraph*, read:

The first two sentences and the last sentence of the paragraph.

Then skim the questions.

If the passage is constructed of *two or more paragraphs*, read:

The first sentence of each paragraph.

Then skim the questions.

Step 2: Read the Passage

This is simple. This is where the real comprehension occurs. There are a number of techniques to improve both comprehension and test scores.

1. **PACE YOURSELF.** There are usually 4 to 6 passages with questions in the reading portion of the test. Try to spend no more than a few minutes to complete each passage and its questions. And remember the first passage may be easier than the second and so on. Extra time will be needed for the later passages.

2. **READ IDEAS NOT JUST WORDS.** Read sentences. Read ideas. Try to hear your own voice inside your head speaking naturally. If you don't understand a sentence, read it again. Try varying the phrasing of the sentence. Ask yourself "Who or what is this sentence about?" to find the subject. Look for action words and results. Ask yourself "What is this about?" to find main ideas. "How do I know?" to find supporting ideas. Try to see how they are organized.

3. **USE CONTEXT CLUES TO UNDERSTAND DIFFICULT WORDS.** Many times when you read a passage, you will find words whose meanings are not clear. Luckily, the sentence that the word is in and the other sentences in the passage will often provide context clues—information that helps to explain what that word means. There are many types of context clues and with them you can increase your understanding of particular words and thereby increase your general understanding of the passage.

NOTE: A full discussion of context clues is given in the vocabulary review section.

Step 3: Scan to Answer Questions

Once you have completed steps 1 and 2, you are ready to deal with the questions.

Scanning is a quick way of finding specific words in a passage. Those specific words mark the location in the passage where you can find the information you need to answer a question. Scanning is not reading! When you scan, your eyes move very quickly through the sentences and paragraphs. You have only one purpose: find the key word. Once you have found the key word, begin to read for the information you need to answer the question. Let's look at a passage:

There are many important resort areas in the state of New Jersey. They include popular ski areas in the northern part of the state and the river and forest wilderness of the Pinelands in the central region, but both of these areas draw a relatively small number of tourists compared to the coastal resorts which attract millions each year to their beaches for sand, sea, and sun. Probably the best known of these resorts are Long Beach Island, which provides activity for the whole family; Atlantic City, whose casinos provide the excitement of gambling and nightlife; and Cape May, a small town which has carefully preserved its rich history and architecture, and which is today home to some of the finest restaurants in the country.

Key words in the questions [we've put them in boldface] will indicate where to look for the answers!

1. The **Pinelands** is famous for what physical features?

2. A **family man** would probably choose which beach resort?

3. A **gourmet** would probably choose which beach resort?

Scan quickly through the passage to find where the key words are located. The information needed to answer each question is nearby. Repeat the key word in your mind as you scan.

Let's look at the passage again. The key words are in boldface and the essential information is <u>underlined</u>.

There are many important resort areas in the state of New Jersey. They include popular ski areas in the northern part of the state and the <u>river and forest wilderness</u> of the **Pinelands** in the central region, but both of these areas draw a relatively small number of tourists compared to the coastal resorts which attract millions each year to their beaches for sand, sea, and sun. Probably the best known of these resorts are <u>Long Beach Island</u>, which provides activity for **the whole family**; Atlantic City, whose casinos provide the excitement of gambling and nightlife; and <u>Cape May</u>, a small town which has carefully preserved its rich history and architecture, and which is today home to some of the finest **restaurants** in the country.

QUESTION #1:   Once we find the key word "Pinelands," we can quickly find the answer. "Physical features?"

ANSWER: "river and forest wilderness"

QUESTION #2:   A "family man" wants a resort which provides activities for the "whole family."

ANSWER: "Long Beach Island"

QUESTION #3: The first two questions were fairly easy to answer, but the last question required you to know what a "gourmet" is. The key word "gourmet" is never mentioned in the passage, but if you know that the word means, "a person who is an expert in fine food and dining," then scanning still provides the answer. We see "the finest restaurants" and we know these would interest a gourmet.

ANSWER: "Cape May… home to some of the finest restaurants"

These three basic techniques will help you to read with greater speed and comprehension, and they will provide you with effective ways to answer the questions which the reading portion of the HSPT will ask. But to be fully prepared for this section of the test, you need to understand and be familiar with the types of questions you will be asked so that you can practice our reading techniques on them.

BASIC QUESTIONS

Let's look at six basic questions asked on the test.

Basic Question 1

What is the main idea of the passage?

Good writing is carefully organized around an important idea. This idea controls all of the other ideas within the passage. Sometimes this main idea is clearly stated in one or two sentences in the passage BUT not always. Sometimes it is not directly mentioned in the passage at all.

Let's look at an example:

Marge sure knows how to have a party. I got there at nine o'clock and the place was already jumping. People were laughing and shouting as waiters ran back and forth from the kitchen with trays loaded down with lobster and caviar. A mariachi band was performing on the patio and a long line of people were doing the "conga." I didn't see who was the first person to jump into the pool, but before long everyone at the party had joined in. People tell me it was around midnight when the circus performers showed up, but I really couldn't tell you for sure.

One main idea controls all of the facts, examples, and discussion in this passage:

Marge's party was a lot of fun.

In this passage the first sentence ("Marge sure knows how to have a party.") gives us a very clear indication of what that main idea is, but it is not exactly the main idea. Marge's general ability to plan and give parties is not the central idea. The main idea of a passage will *sometimes* be stated in the first or second sentence of the passage.

Many times the main idea is not directly stated in the passage. But even without that first sentence the main idea is clear. Look at the examples presented:

...the place was jumping...people laughing and shouting...trays loaded with lobster and caviar...a mariachi band...people dancing...people jumping into the pool...and circus performers too.

All of these examples point to only one central idea: The party was fun.

Let's look at another example:

Life in Colorado was changed overnight by the Gold Rush of 1859. Miners needed supplies and, at first, depended upon the foodstuffs imported from the Midwest. Flour cost as much as $50 a barrel, but hungry miners were willing to pay these inflated prices. Further, because many of these Fifty-niners had farming backgrounds, they turned to agriculture after they were unable to survive in the mines. These people found the land fertile and began to farm the land. They did not plant crops for survival but rather to sell. At this point agriculture in Colorado changed from subsistence to commercial farming.

The first sentence of this paragraph gives us important information about the central idea, but it is not the central idea. The first sentence is too general. Read the passage again and try to decide what idea controls the discussion.

Yes, "Life in Colorado was changed overnight by the gold rush," but the passage does not discuss all the ways "life" was changed. The passage discusses only one aspect of life in Colorado which changed: agriculture. The controlling idea is

Farming in Colorado was changed suddenly by the gold rush.

Let's look at the **important supporting ideas.**

Life in Colorado was changed overnight by the Gold Rush of 1859. Miners needed supplies and, at first, **depended upon the foodstuffs** imported from the Midwest. **Flour cost** as much as $50 a barrel, but **hungry miners were willing to pay** these inflated prices. Further, because many of **these Fifty-niners had farming backgrounds**, they **turned to agriculture** after they were unable to survive in the mines. These people found the **land fertile** and **began to farm** the land. They did not **plant crops** for survival but rather to sell. At this point **agriculture in Colorado changed** from subsistence to **commercial farming**.

All of these supporting ideas point in only one direction.

NOT: Life in Colorado

NOT: The Gold Rush

NOT: Farming in Colorado

BUT: ... **How farming was changed by the Gold Rush in Colorado**

Remember: The first and last sentences of each paragraph are very important. They usually point towards the main idea.

Once we know what the main idea is, we will be able to answer many questions. The HSPT reading comprehension section uses information connected to the main idea to ask many different types of questions.

Examples:

1. What would be a good title for this passage?

    (A) Farming in Colorado

    (B) The Gold Rush of '59

    (C) The Real Gold Grew Out of the Ground

    (D) Go West, Young Man

All of these ideas are connected to the passage, but only one is a good title. To choose the best answer we must know that the main idea is neither farming nor the Gold Rush but the relationship between the two. The best title is (C) because it mentions both.

2. What is the author's main purpose?

    (A) To discuss Colorado's interesting history

    (B) To show that farming is sometimes better than mining

    (C) To show that the Gold Rush was an exciting time to be alive

    (D) To show the effects of the Gold Rush upon agriculture in
        Colorado

All of these ideas were in the passage, but only one of them was the main purpose. The author's main purpose is always to clearly express and to support his main idea. The main purpose of this passage is (D).

Related Questions:

> What is the subject of the passage?
> What is the topic of the passage?
> What is the emphasis of the passage?
> What is the controlling idea?

The answer to all of these questions can be found in the main idea.

Basic Question 2

What specific facts were stated in the passage?

Let's look at an example:

Coral reef communities are normally classified in two ways: live bottom or patch reef. The live bottom community, also known as hardground, is generally found closest to shore in tidal passes, under bridges, and short distances seaward of the intertidal zone. It usually occupies fossil reef formations, limestone, and other rocky substrates. Animal and plant life are not consistent from reef to reef but are usually visually dominated by octocorals, algae, and sponges.

This passage appears to be quite difficult. The reason it appears so difficult is because of the technical words which it uses. It is not necessary to know every word in a passage in order to understand it.

Read the passage again and see if you can answer these questions.

1. What is the general subject of the discussion?

2. How many types of reef communities are there?

3. Which type of reef community is discussed?

4. Where is this type of reef found?

5. What does it occupy?

6. What plants and animals dominate?

To read with understanding it is necessary to understand how a basic sentence in written English works.

There is a SUBJECT and there is a VERB.

The SUBJECT is	a person	The VERB is	an action
	a place		a state of being
	a thing		
	an idea		

To put it simply: SOMEONE OR SOMETHING **DOES** SOMETHING!

or

SOMEONE OR SOMETHING **IS** SOMETHING!

"Bob eats hamburgers."

Subject   BOB

Verb   EATS

"Bob is a policeman."

Subject   BOB

Verb   IS

Every sentence contains at least one idea. To understand that idea, you must know what the subject is and what the subject does.

Let's look at the passage again. The subjects will be shown in **boldface** and the verbs will be underlined.

Coral reef communities are normally classified in two ways: live bottom or patch reef. The **live bottom community,** also known as hardground, is generally found closest to shore in tidal passes, under bridges, and short distances seaward of the intertidal zone. **It** usually occupies fossil reef formations, limestone, and other rocky substrates. **Animal and plant life** are not consistent from reef to reef, but are usually visually dominated by octocorals, algae, and sponges.

Understanding this passage is much easier now even with the technical vocabulary. Try answering these questions:

1. How are reef communities classified?

2. Where is the live bottom community found?

3. What does it usually occupy?

4. What types of plants and animals visually dominate the reefs?

If you understand the subject and the verb of each sentence, the information that follows is easier to understand even when the vocabulary is very difficult.

Let's look at the passage again. This time look for the important information which follows the verbs. The verbs will be <u>underlined</u> and the factual information will be in **boldface**.

Coral reef communities <u>are</u> normally <u>classified</u> in two ways: **live bottom or patch reef.** The live bottom community, also known as hardground, <u>is</u> generally <u>found</u> closest to shore **in tidal passes, under bridges, and short distances seaward of the intertidal zone.** It usually <u>occupies</u> **fossil reef formations, limestone, and other rocky substrates.** Animal and plant life <u>are</u> **not consistent** from reef to reef, but <u>are</u> usually visually <u>dominated</u> by **octocorals, algae, and sponges.**

1. How are reef communities classified?

   Live bottom or patch reef

2. Where is the live bottom community found?

   In tidal passes, under bridges, and seaward of the intertidal zone

3. What does it usually occupy?

   Fossil reef formations, limestone, and rocky substrates

4. What types of plants and animals visually dominate the reefs?

   Octocorals, algae, and sponges

By understanding the structure and organization of a sentence, you can understand the idea it expresses even when the meanings of many words in that sentence are unclear.

BE CAREFUL OF REVERSE QUESTIONS!

Many times the questions will ask not only what was discussed but also **what wasn't discussed.** Let's look at an example:

Chicago, the windy city, as it is sometimes called, has always possessed its own unique style. Its citizens are justly proud of its long, glorious, and slightly notorious history. Its reputation, deservedly or not, is known throughout the world. Mention Al Capone, prohibition, or a mobster with a machine gun and only one city comes to mind.

A reverse question might ask:

According to the passage, Chicago's history has **NOT** been

(A) developed over many years.   (B)   filled with glory.

(C) somewhat notorious.   (D)   carefully recorded.

Our key word is "history." When we scan quickly for the word, we see that it is described as "long, glorious, and slightly notorious." The choices we are given have been slightly changed, but we can see (A), (B), and (C) are used in the passage to describe Chicago's history. (D) "Carefully recorded" has NOT been mentioned. It is the correct choice.

Here's another example:

According to the passage, Chicago quickly comes to mind to people all over the world EXCEPT when you mention

(A) windy city.   (B)   Al Capone.

(C) prohibition.   (D)   mobsters.

The key words in this question are "all over the world." Three examples are mentioned after this phrase. They are (B), (C), and (D). (A) "windy city" is mentioned at the beginning of the passage, but it is not a specific example which causes people throughout the world to think of Chicago. (A) is correct.

Basic Question 3

What new ideas can be inferred from the passage?

In question 2 we were asked to find facts, data, and other types of information which were stated in the passage. But in basic question 3 we have to take the next step. We have to develop new ideas which are based upon the facts that we have read. These new ideas are called inferences.

Let's look at an example:

FACT: Oliver Twist was having his ninth birthday.

FACT: He was pale and thin.

You know this information is correct.

When you make an inference, you have to study the facts carefully and decide what new idea can be formed.

From the facts that you know, decide which inference concerning Oliver Twist's birthday would be most reasonable.

INFERENCE 1: Oliver has not eaten properly up to his ninth birthday.

INFERENCE 2: Oliver probably has not eaten properly up to his ninth birthday.

INFERENCE 3: As Oliver has grown, he has become thin.

The only difference between 1 and 2 is the word "probably." If you chose 2, then you are correct. What's wrong with 1? Well....do you know for sure that the reason Oliver was thin was that he had not eaten? NO! The problem with one is that it leaves no room for questions or possibilities, and there are both.

Inference 2 is a good inference because it uses the correct word "probably" to describe the relationship between the facts.

Inference 3, "As Oliver has grown, he has become thin," was a trick! It is not really an inference. Inference 3 does not give you any new information. It only gives you the facts that you already knew. An inference must give new information.

Now read the whole story.

In this excerpt from Dickens' *Oliver Twist*, we read the early account of Oliver's birth and the beginning of his life.

It cannot be expected that this system of farming would produce any very extraordinary or luxuriant crop. Oliver Twist's ninth birthday found him a pale thin child, somewhat diminutive in stature, and decidedly small in circumference. But nature or inheritance had implanted a good sturdy spirit in Oliver's breast. It had plenty of room to expand, thanks to the spare diet of the establishment; and perhaps to this circumstance may be attributed his having any ninth birthday at all.

When you look at a statement of fact, you can say that it is either true or false. But when you look at an inference, you have to judge it in a different way. You can say that it is:

ALMOST CERTAIN   The world will not end tomorrow.

VERY PROBABLE   It will rain in New York this summer.

PROBABLE   You will lose you car keys someday.

POSSIBLE   You will meet a movie star.

UNLIKELY   You will live to be 90 years old.

VERY UNLIKELY   You will live to be 100 years old.

ALMOST IMPOSSIBLE You will win the lottery this week.

Let's look at several inferences connected to the passage and decide if they are weak or strong.

INFERENCE:	Oliver's guardians are not concerned with Oliver's well-being.
PROBABLE	WHY? You know from the passage that the "establishment" that he resides in provides him with a "spare diet." And you know that Oliver appears very small in size.
INFERENCE:	The fact that Oliver was able to survive for this long should be credited to the kind of food that he did eat.
UNLIKELY	WHY? The last two sentences explain that while he did have a "spare diet," Oliver was able to develop "a good sturdy spirit." His "spirit" is what enabled him to survive.

> **DIRECTIONS:** Look at the inferences listed below and decide if they are weak or strong. Find clues from the passage to support your ideas.

1. Oliver would be a good person to have with you in a time of emergency.

2. We can be fairly sure that Oliver liked living in the conditions that he had.

3. Oliver will have a very productive life.

4. People were surprised with the way that Oliver looked.

5. Oliver got his outlook on life from his parents.

Let's discuss each inference and the information from the passage which shows it to be weak or strong.

Inferences:

1. PROBABLE: It seems clear to the reader that despite his life's hardship, he has used this misfortune to grow and become more hopeful. Perhaps, one can infer that Oliver was a very resourceful child. It can even be inferred that it was mainly because of this hardship that he got this far in life.

2. POSSIBLE: In this passage, we are given information that could point in two different directions. The opening sentence stresses that nobody can be expected to thrive in a place like this, yet we are told that he does. There is really never any specific reference to Oliver's feelings on the matter. We don't know if he thrives out of anger, spiritual fulfillment, or something else. This inference is possible, but you can't be sure.

3. PROBABLE/VERY PROBABLE: Having made it through life this far with his diet, one could logically surmise he would be productive in whatever he chooses. He will probably be able to accomplish this feat whether he likes the way his life feels or not.

4. UNLIKELY: Immediately, the reader is told that "it cannot be expected that his system of farming would be a luxuriant crop." It also states the effects of this "farming." It says that he was "small in circumference" and "diminutive in stature." It is unlikely that people were surprised by him.

5. POSSIBLE: There is only one small clue to indicate where Oliver gets his outlook from. The passage says that "nature or inheritance" had given him his spirit. We aren't sure if this was given to him by nature or his family because the passage isn't sure either. Therefore, there is no way for us to determine this.

Basic Question 4

What might be discussed before or after the passage?

This is a very difficult question for most students to answer. The reason why it is so difficult is that most students never ask themselves this question. Their major problem is understanding the passage, which is difficult enough without thinking about "What might come before?" or "What might come next?" But it's not hard if you know what to look for. The secret to answering this type of question is to recognize the structure of the passage.

The purpose of writing is to express ideas. Many times those ideas are complicated. Good writers know that their ideas have to be carefully organized.

Once the pattern of the organization is understood, it is easy to know what would come before and what would come after. There are many ways to organize these ideas. Let's look at some examples:

Order of importance

PROBLEM: Imagine you have a brother whom you love very much but whom you haven't seen for many years. In the years you have been away, you have become very rich. You are flying home for his birthday party, and you have decided to buy him three presents:

(A) a beautiful watch

(B) a trip to Hawaii

(C) a brand new Mercedes-Benz 540 sport coupe

You want him to enjoy his party and you want him to appreciate each of his presents, but you can't decide which gift to give him first, which second, and which last.

There is only one **effective** way to give him the presents. Decide which present should be given first and so on.

Remember: You want him to appreciate all three gifts.

The gifts must be organized this way:

> First the watch
>
> Second the trip
>
> Last the Mercedes

What happens if you give the trip first? Your brother will love it. But how will he feel when he gets the watch next? He will feel let down because the first gift was better than the second. The pattern has to follow from good to better to best. This pattern is called order of importance. In this example it moves from least important to most important.

Process

PROBLEM: Your Aunt Mary went to Florida to see her sister. Uncle Harry, her husband, is having his boss come over for dinner. Unfortunately, Uncle Harry is a terrible cook. He calls you for help. You know a wonderful way to make lasagna. How do you explain it to him so he can prepare it properly? How do we organize the steps?

Making lasagna is a PROCESS. There is only one way to organize a process: STEP BY STEP.

> What is done first?
>
> What is done second?
>
> What is done next?
>
> And so on until the process is complete.

General to Specific

PROBLEM: The year is 2345 and you are visiting a faraway planet. You have met a resident of this planet and you have become friends. You want to tell him about your hometown. His only knowledge of earth is its general location in the universe. Where do you begin your discussion?

Begin with the general and move to the specific.

1. Solar system

2. Planet

3. Continent

4. Country

5. State

6. City

7. Street

8. House

9. Room

If the passage is moving from GENERAL TO SPECIFIC, then you can determine what would be discussed before and after the passage.

A passage discussing California would probably have a discussion about the United States coming before it, and the passage would probably be followed by a discussion of cities in California.

Cause and effect

This is another common method of organization. It would follow this pattern:

| *General Discussion of Problem or Situation* | *Discussion of Causes* | *Discussion of Effects* | *Discussion of Solutions* |

If the subject of the passage is the "effects of drug abuse," then a discussion of its causes would have come before and possible solutions would be discussed after the effects.

Compare and contrast

Usually you don't have one without the other. When you **compare**, you examine how two things are similar or the **same**. When you **contrast**, you examine how two things are **different**.

| Usual Pattern: | *Discussion of similarities* | *then* | *Discussion of differences* |

Because there are many different ways to organize information, we have only discussed the most common methods. The other methods all follow a pattern. The pattern will be logical. It will make sense. Listed below are some other common patterns.

Most to Least	Far to Near
Least to Most	Near to Far
Large to Small	Left to Right
Small to Large	Morning to Evening

Basic Question 5

What is the author's attitude toward a subject?

The author, like any person, has an opinion about a subject. He or she might consider it to be right or wrong, good or bad, sad or happy, or wise or silly. Very seldom do you have an opinion of something without having some emotional feeling concerning the same subject. The emotional feeling can be strong or weak or anywhere in between.

An author's attitude is this combination: OPINION and EMOTION.

How can you recognize the author's attitude?

There are two types of clues:

1. The selection of specific facts mentioned in the passage.

2. Choice of specific words used in the passage.

Let's look at an example:

Roger and Mary were married for many years. Their children were all grown and had moved out of the house. With the children gone, Mary felt bored and lonely. Mary had been thinking about getting a job for years now, and Roger said that he thought it was a good time to get started. While Roger earned a good living, he believed that Mary's new job would add significantly to the household income. Sitting around the house all day with nothing to do but watch television, Mary began to work on her resume. Roger helped her organize all her employment history. Additionally, Mary began to look on the Internet each day before dinner for ads. While Roger spent long hours at work, he made phone calls around town for Mary every day. Eventually, Mary discovered a job online and accepted it. Now, Roger works less time and the family makes more money. Mary seems energetic and is more content with her new job. Roger half-jokingly takes all the credit for Mary's new-found employment and their renewed happiness. Mary says that it has nothing to do with him. Who should take credit?

MARY'S OPINION: Roger should not get credit.

ROGER'S OPINION: Mary should not get credit.

There are facts to support each opinion, but a writer will select certain facts to show his opinion is strong. Here are some facts. Look at them carefully and decide which opinion they support.

FACTS:

1. Mary was spending time on the Internet each day before dinner.

2. Roger prompted Mary to start looking for a job.

3. Roger helped Mary organize her employment history.

4. Mary discovered the job.

5. Mary had been thinking about getting a job for years.

6. While Roger was at work, he made phone calls for Mary.

These facts don't change but each side in the argument selects only those facts which support its opinion.

MARY'S OPINION: 1, 4, 5   ROGER'S OPINION: 2, 3, 6

Authors have many words to choose from when stating their ideas. Their attitudes toward a subject will determine which words they will select.

DIRECTIONS: Look at the following examples and decide what each author's attitude is concerning the same subject: **SNAKES**.

Peter: "Like a thin ribbon of many colors, it glides softly through the grass and calmly disappears before our eyes."

Paul: "The cold beady eyes of the deadly assassin are watchful. It lurks hidden, ready to strike and devour its prey."

George: "This limbless, scaled reptile has a long, tapering body. One of its many unusual characteristics is that it is known to exist in all types of habitat except for the polar regions."

Who hates snakes?

Who loves snakes?

Who considers them an interesting subject for study?

Read the sentences again and notice the highlighted words.

Peter: "Like a **thin ribbon** of **many colors,** it **glides softly** through the grass and **calmly disappears** before our eyes."

Paul: "The **cold beady eyes** of the **deadly assassin** are watchful. It **lurks hidden,** ready to **strike and devour** its prey."

George: "This **limbless scaled reptile** has a **long tapering body.** One of its many **unusual characteristics** is that it is known to **exist** in all types of **habitat** except for the polar regions."

Each author chose different words to refer to the snake.

Peter: **thin ribbon**

Paul: **deadly assassin**

George: **limbless scaled reptile**

Each author described the snake differently.

Peter: **many colors...glides softly...calmly disappears**

Paul: **cold beady eyes...lurks hidden...strike and devour**

George: **long tapering body...unusual characteristics... exists...habitat**

Peter chose words to show that the snake is a beautiful creature with graceful movements.

"thin ribbon...many colors...glides softly...calmly disappears"

Attitude: Snakes are wonderful creatures.

Paul chose words to make the snake appear dangerous and evil.

"cold beady eyes...deadly assassin...lurks hidden...strike and devour"

Attitude: Snakes are terrible creatures.

George gave scientific facts. The only opinion given is that the snake has "many unusual characteristics" which can indicate that he finds snakes interesting.

Attitude: Snakes are scientifically interesting.

Remember: By examining the author's choice of words and facts, you can determine his attutide.

Basic Question 6

What is the meaning of the word or phrase?

The reading portion of the HSPT will ask you questions related to the meaning of specific words in the passages. The questions will ask you to choose a suitable replacement for a word or phrase.

Let's look at a passage:

Mr. Brown's odious habits were disgusting to strangers and even more so to his coworkers who, day after day, were forced to watch and listen as he scratched, belched, and spit. He was a walking collection of nasty gestures and poor manners. In addition to this, he was an insult to the olfactory sense of anyone who by bad luck happened to have a nose.

A replacement question might ask:

1. In the first sentence, the word "odious" could best be replaced by which of the following?

    (A) Unpleasant   (C) Hateful

    (B) Evil   (D) Foul smelling

Vocabulary questions such as the one above can be answered in two different ways:

1. Using our knowledge of vocabulary.

2. Using context clues to discover the meaning of an unknown word.

You might know simply by looking at the word "odious" that it means: deserving hatred or repugnance. But this will *not* usually be the case. The meaning of many words will be unclear to you, but there are ways to solve this problem. Context clues given in the passage can help you to understand what the word means. Context clues can come from the facts and the grammar which surround the word.

Let's look at the passage again, this time with context clues in boldface:

Mr. Brown's <u>odious</u> habits were **disgusting** to strangers and even more so to his coworkers who, day after day, were forced to watch and listen as he **scratched, belched, and spit.** He was a walking collection of **nasty gestures and poor manners.** In addition to this, he was an insult to the olfactory sense of anyone who by bad luck happened to have a nose.

The grammatical structure of the first sentence shows us that "odious" is an adjective which modifies "habits." If you know something about these "habits," you will have a good clue towards understanding "odious."

What specifically were the habits of Mr. Brown?

1. Scratched

2. Belched

3. Spit

How would you describe these habits?

How would you feel if you had to watch someone doing this every day?

By answering these questions you begin to see that these habits are "not nice." But when you look at the answer choices, you see that all of the choices are "not nice." You need to be more specific and more exact.

In the first sentence, his habits are described as "disgusting to strangers and coworkers." The second sentence calls them, "nasty gestures."

Now when you look at the answer choices, you are able to eliminate certain ones:

(D) Foul smelling. At the end of the passage there is a discussion about how Mr. Brown smells but this is not related to his habits and has nothing to do with "odious." It is incorrect.

(B) Evil. This choice is **too strong.** "Evil" causes harm or injury to others. His habits cause unhappiness to those around him but they do not cause harm or injury. It is incorrect.

Next you have to decide which word is best: unpleasant or hateful. Both are related to "odious" in meaning but one is a much better replacement. The most important context clues are "disgusting and nasty" and the examples themselves. A disgusting and nasty habit, such as spitting, is more than "unpleasant"; the correct answer is "hateful."

Try another example on your own.

In the last sentence of the passage, what does the word "olfactory" mean? There are several context clues to help you understand its meaning. Read the sentence carefully.

This is only a brief discussion of how you can use context clues to discover the meaning of words. In the Vocabulary Review section, we will discuss with explanations and examples all of the various context clues.

ADDITIONAL TIPS

It is impossible to include in any review a discussion of all the problems which a student may face during the HSPT, but there are elements in the test that are sure to appear.

Two different ideas are often joined together in one sentence. The word that joins these two ideas expresses their relationship to one another. To increase comprehension, it is essential to understand that relationship, but that can only be done when you understand the meaning of the connecting word.

SIMPLE CONNECTORS: The most simple of the two types of connectors are called *coordinating conjunctions*. Most students will easily recognize and understand the meaning of these basic connectors:

AND	OR	BUT
FOR	SO	YET
NOR		

"AND" means the addition of both ideas.

Example: Bob **and** Sally went to the party. (These two people went to the party.)

"OR" means there is a choice of only one.

Example: Bob **or** Sally will go to the party. (Only one person will go.   If Bob, then not Sally. If Sally, then not Bob.)

"BUT" and **"YET"** have the same basic meaning. They both are used to show the differences in the ideas being joined.

Example: Fred has a lot of money, but his car is very old. (We know that Fred has a lot of money. We expect his car to be new. His car is not new. These ideas contrast with one another. They are different ideas.)

"FOR" and **"SO"** are opposites which are used to show the correct relationship between a cause and an effect. There are two possibilities:

CAUSE	"SO"	EFFECT
EFFECT	"FOR"	CAUSE

Example: <u>Marta broke her leg</u> so <u>she went to the hospital</u>.

CAUSE	EFFECT

Example: <u>Jose worked day and night</u> **for** <u>he needed money badly</u>.
              EFFECT   CAUSE

    "NOR" performs the same basic function as "AND" but it is used with negative ideas.

Example: Bob will go home and Mary will too.

Example: Bob will not go home nor will Mary.

CONFUSING CONNECTORS: While most students recognize and understand coordinating conjunctions, they are often confused by the connectors called *conjunctive adverbs*. An easy way to understand what they mean is to know that most of them share a common meaning with one of the seven basic conjunctions. For example, the connector "nevertheless" serves the same basic function as "but."

    The lists below will group the confusing connectors which share a common meaning with one of the simple connectors.

AND	BUT/YET	SO
ALSO	HOWEVER	CONSEQUENTLY
BESIDES	NEVERTHELESS	HENCE
FURTHERMORE	NONETHELESS	THEREFORE
MOREOVER	STILL	THUS
IN ADDITION	ALTHOUGH	ACCORDINGLY

MODALS: Modals are auxiliary verbs that are used with the base form of another verb to express differences in mood. Auxiliary verbs include words such as can, could, may, might, shall, should, will, would, and must. A clear understanding of how modals function to change the meaning of a sentence is essential for developing your reading comprehension.

    Let's look at a basic sentence and see how it and its meaning will change with the addition of a modal.

BASIC SENTENCE: ERIC FLIES AIRPLANES.

Ability: Eric **can** fly an airplane.

Possibility: Eric **could** fly an airplane.

Slight Possibility: Eric **may** fly an airplane.

Slight Possibility: Eric **might** fly an airplane.

Permission: **Can** Eric fly the airplane?

                       Could Eric fly the airplane?

	May Eric fly the airplane?
	Might Eric fly the airplane?
Obligation:	Eric **should** fly an airplane.
	Eric **ought** to fly an airplane.
Necessity:	Eric **must** fly the airplane.
	Eric **has to** fly the airplane.
Prohibition:	Eric **must not** fly the airplane.
No Necessity:	Eric **does not have** to fly the airplane.
Inference:	Eric **must** fly an airplane since he is a pilot.
Preference:	Eric **would rather** fly an airplane than drive a bus.
Past habit:	Eric **would** fly his airplane every Saturday before the accident happened.
Advisability:	Eric **had better** fly his plane before the storm comes.

II. VOCABULARY

Your knowledge of English vocabulary will be tested within the reading comprehension section of the HSPT. All of the questions will deal with vocabulary to some degree. Vocabulary is the base for all reading comprehension because the reader must understand the meaning of the words before the meaning of the passage can be learned.

Sometimes, the meaning of a word will be clear to you, but many times the meaning of a word will not be clear. To solve this problem, use context clues inside the sentence. Not every sentence will provide enough clues to allow you to determine the meaning of the words, but many times they will.

PROBLEM SITUATIONS

Following are four main problem situations, along with discussions, explanations, and strategies that can be used to manage them. The strategies presented below will help you answer those questions faster and with more accuracy.

Situation 1: *You are familiar with the word. You are familiar with the answer choices. You think you know the correct choice.*

You have to be careful. A single word can have many meanings. Often, these meanings will be very similar to one another, but only one will be correct.

Let's look at examples using the word "collect."

Example **1:** Many animals <u>collect</u> seeds and nuts for the winter.

(A) pick up   (C) store

(B) organize   (D) need

Example **2:** She wanted to <u>collect</u> her thoughts before she spoke to
her boss.

(A) pick up   (C) store

(B) organize   (D) need

The correct answer for Example 1 is (A) "pick up." It would be very easy to choose (C) "store" because animals store food after they collect it, but it is not the best replacement. They (D) "need" seeds and nuts to survive the winter, but "need" and "collect" are not synonyms. (B) "organize" makes no sense in the context of the sentence.

The correct answer for Example 2 is (B) "organize." Her thoughts need to be arranged and organized before she speaks to her boss. In this example, the word does **not** mean "pick up" as it did in the first example.

Situation 2: *You understand the meaning of the word, but you are not sure which answer choice is correct.*

When there are no context clues to help you understand the meaning of answer choices, you need to deal with them quickly and to take your chances. Follow these simple rules:

1. Eliminate the choices you know are incorrect.

2. Don't choose a word because it looks like or sounds like the word. These words are often used to confuse or trick you. They are usually not the correct choice.

3. After going through steps one and two, make your best guess. Many times, your first choice will be the best.

4. Don't waste valuable time.

Situation 3: *The meaning of the word is not clear, but you are familiar with the answer choices and their meanings.*

Use context clues in the sentence to help you discover the meaning of a word. This is probably the most common situation you will face, and there are many ways to manage it which are explained on the following pages.

Situation 4: *You don't understand the meaning of the word. You don't know the meanings of the answer choices.*

You can often discover the meaning of a word by using context clues, but if you have no idea what an answer choice means, you face an unsolvable problem. Waste no time! Take a guess and move to the next question.

CONTEXT CLUES

Context clues come in many shapes and forms. They include examples, synonyms, antonyms, grammatical structures, and the general idea of a sentence or passage. What type of clues they are doesn't matter. What matters is being able to use whatever information you are given to discover the meaning.

> **DIRECTIONS:** Read the examples below and underline what you think are context clues. Then try to write a definition for the italicized word.

1. The war caused tremendous *turmoil* but, eventually, order and calm were restored to the nation.

2. The drug was widely used and was considered *innocuous*; however, recent studies indicate many harmful side effects can occur with its usage.

3. She had been *sterilized* as a young girl, so now it was impossible for her to have children even if she wanted to.

4. There was no *malice* in her heart towards the murderer, for she had forgiven him years before.

In the examples above, the connecting words give you information about the relationship between ideas. If you understand the relationship and you understand one idea, then you can often understand the other idea. Important context clues are in **boldface** below that help to define the italicized word.

1. The war caused tremendous *turmoil* **but**, eventually, **order and calm were restored** to the nation.

2. The drug was widely used and was considered *innocuous*; **however**, recent studies **indicate many harmful side-effects can occur with its usage.**

3. She had been *sterilized* as a young girl, **so** now **it was impossible for her to have children** even if she wanted to.

4. There was no *malice* in her heart towards the murderer, **for** she **had forgiven** him years before.

DISCUSSION

In sentence 1, the connector "but" indicates ideas that contrast or are different. The second idea is "order and calm." The first idea must be different or opposite. "Turmoil" means disorder, chaos, or confusion.

In sentence 2, the word "however" functions the same way as "but," so again there are contrasting ideas. On one side are "harmful side effects," so on the other side you can assume there is no harm or danger. "Innocuous" means harmless.

In sentence 3, the connector "so" shows a relationship of cause-and-effect. The result or effect is that she can't have children. The cause is something that prevents having children. "Sterilized" is a medical procedure which prevents a woman from becoming pregnant.

In sentence 4, "for" indicates a cause-and-effect relationship, but it is the opposite of "so." After "so" you have the result. After "for" you have the cause. What is the result of having "forgiven him"? No malice. Malice means anger, ill will, or bad intentions towards someone.

Let's look at some more sentences.

DIRECTIONS: Again, look for context clues and then try to write a definition for the underlined word.

---

1. <u>Vulgar</u> habits, such as spitting, belching, or wiping your nose without a handkerchief, are considered most inappropriate in public.

2. The state's most impressive <u>attractions</u>, including the Empire State Building, Radio City Music Hall, and the Museum of Modern Art, are the recipients of millions of eager tourists each year.

These two sentences include examples of the underlined words.

1. <u>Vulgar</u> habits, **such as spitting, belching, or wiping your nose without a handkerchief,** are considered most inappropriate in public.

2. The city's most impressive <u>attractions</u>, **including the Empire State Building, Radio City Music Hall, and the Museum of Modern Art,** are the recipients of millions of eager tourists each year.

DISCUSSION

By looking at the examples that follow the underlined word, you get a good idea of what that word means.

1. "Vulgar" is an adjective that modifies "habits." The specific habits that are considered "vulgar" in public are spitting, belching, or wiping your nose without a handkerchief. These are not considered to be proper actions when done in public. Someone who does them in public does not have good manners. "Vulgar" means having the qualities of being rude, unpleasant, or disgusting.

2. The examples that follow "attractions," the Empire State Building, Radio City Music Hall, and the Museum of Modern Art, give important clues. When you put these clues together with "eager tourists," you can guess that "attractions" are famous places where tourists go.

Another important source of information can come from **adjective clauses.** An easy way to spot them is to look for the relative pronouns that introduce them: **who, whom, which, that,** and **whose.** Relative clauses provide information about the noun they modify.

Let's look at some examples.

> **DIRECTIONS:** Find the key words that introduce the clause. Underline the clause. What information does it give about the italicized noun in front of it? Try to write a definition.

1. The *gizmo*, which regulates the valves and the choke mechanism, must be carefully installed.

2. The *benefactress*, who gave huge sums of money to schools and hospitals in our city, died recently.

DISCUSSION

1. What kind of thing "regulates the valves and the choke mechanism?"

Answer: Some kind of mechanical device.

2. What kind of person "gave huge sums of money to schools and hospitals"?

Answer: Someone who is very generous with her money.

There are many different types of context clues. Look at the information that surrounds the words. It can help you understand the word's meaning.

VOCABULARY WORD LIST

The following list consists of commonly used words that may help you during the reading comprehension section of the HSPT. Study these words and then complete the following 25 exercises.

There are a few ways to go about studying this section. Choose the one with which you feel most comfortable.

1. Study 25 words a day for three weeks.

2. Study the words in the list that you consider to be difficult words.

3. Study each word and example sentence. Make up your own sentence using the word.

4. Try to use words from the list in conversations with your friends and family every day before the day of the test.

abandon, *v.* to leave alone or to give up. *The baby wolf was abandoned in the woods when its mother was killed.*

abate, *v.* to decrease or diminish. *For three terrible days, the heat of the sun never abated.*

abet, *v.* to help or aid. *The stranger abetted the lost child by taking him to the police station.*

abhor, *v.* to hate something. *Everyone abhors war and the loss of life it causes.*

abject, *adj.* hopeless or miserable. *Many charities have been started as a result of the abject poverty existing in many countries.*

absorbent, *adj.* having the quality of holding water. *The paper towels were almost as absorbent as the sponge.*

abundance, *n.* a greater amount than needed. *There is an abundance of oil in Saudi Arabia.*

accessory, *n.* an extra or added part. *A beautiful handbag is an important accessory to a woman's wardrobe.*

accommodation, *n.* something supplied for convenience. *Temporary accommodations were provided to the refugees.*

accomplice, *n.* someone who helps another to break the law. *The bank robber claims to have acted alone, but the police believe he had an accomplice.*

accomplish, *v.* to achieve. *Everyone wishes to accomplish something important in his life.*

accost, *v.* to bother or threaten. *A person walking alone in the city can be accosted at any time.*

accrue, *v.* to build up over time. *As a result of his wise investments in stocks and bonds, he had accrued a fortune by the age of 80.*

accumulate, *v.* to build up, to collect. *If a room is not used, dust begins to accumulate.*

acrid, *adj.* having an unpleasant, irritating quality. *The acrid smoke from the chemicals burned his eyes.*

acuity, *n.* sharpness of perception. *Visual acuity is important to an airline pilot.*

adapt, *v.* to change. *Many wild animals cannot adapt to life in a zoo.*

admonish, *v.* to advise or to warn against. *Parents must admonish their children about the use of drugs.*

adroitly, *adv.* with easy skill and ability. *A great soccer player like Pele could adroitly pass the ball to a teammate.*

advantage, *n.* benefit. *One advantage of not smoking is that you save a lot of money.*

advocate, *v.* to propose or to support. *Many doctors advocate a balanced diet that includes only a small amount of red meat.*

affluent, *adj.* rich or wealthy. *From the size of our large homes, people assume we live in an affluent society.*

aggravate, *v.* to make worse. *He aggravated his sore elbow by trying to play tennis.*

agile, *adj.* able to move quickly and easily. *A deer in the woods is the most agile of runners.*

agitate, *v.* to cause trouble and upset. *The students agitated the teacher by talking during class.*

ailment, *n.* physical or mental problem. *Coughing is a common ailment for people who work in coal mines.*

akin, *adj.* like or similar to. *Although ice skating is akin to roller skating, it is often more difficult for some people.*

alleviate, *adj.* to fix or remedy a problem or condition. *Winning a million dollars in the lottery would alleviate many of his financial problems.*

allure, *n.* the ability to strongly attract. *The allure of easy money and little work attracts many to a life of crime.*

amateur, *n.* a nonprofessional. *An amateur should never try to fix a problem that concerns electrical wiring.*

ambiguous, *adj.* unclear. *The clues found by the detective were so ambiguous that he had no idea who had committed the crime.*

amicable, *adj.* friendly. *An amicable man like Joe has many friends and belongs to many clubs.*

ample, *adj.* more than enough. *We had ample time to answer all of the questions and to finish the test with ease.*

analyst, *n.* person who carefully studies data in order to reach a conclusion. *The analyst studied the decline in church attendance.*

anchor, *v.* to hold in position. *Only a steel chain with a great weight can anchor a large ship.*

anguish, *n.* great worry or concern. *Moving away from his friends caused the young man great anguish.*

angular, *adj.* to have sharp, pointed angles. *His long pointed nose and chin gave his face a very angular appearance.*

antique, *adj.* old or old-fashioned. *The antique chair had been made in 1745.*

apex, *n.* the highest point. *At the apex of his career, he had great wealth and power.*

apparatus, *n.* device or machine. *A chemistry lab is equipped with an apparatus to allow students to perform experiments.*

appreciable, *adj.* noticeable or substantial. *For weeks, there was no appreciable change in his illness until doctors began to administer antibiotics.*

approximate, *adj.* not exact but close to the amount or number. *No one knows for sure exactly how many people live in China, but the approximate number is one billion.*

arduous, *adj.* difficult. *Sailing alone across an ocean is an arduous task.*

argue, *v.* to strongly support an idea. *He argued that the money should be spent for health care and not for weapons.*

arouse, *v.* to excite. *Sharks are aroused by the smell of blood in water.*

arrogance, *n.* offensive display of superiority; overbearing pride. *The man showed his arrogance by pushing his way to the front of the line and demanding that he be served first.*

artifact, *n.* object made in the past. *Archaeologists dig through the ruins of ancient cities in order to find artifacts.*

aspire, *v.* to desire or to long for. *The young actor aspired to someday be a famous movie star.*

assert, *v.* to say that something is true or correct. *Columbus asserted that the world was round and not flat as most people believed in his time.*

assuage, *v.* to ease or to relieve. *His mother tried to assuage his fears by holding his hand and whispering that everything would be all right.*

atop, *prep.* on top of. *A radio tower was placed atop the building.*

attain, *v.* to reach a goal or position. *We can attain our dreams with hard work and dedication.*

audacious, *adj.* bold, daring, willing to risk danger. *Many believed that Lindbergh's audacious plan to cross the Atlantic alone in a single-engine plane was impossible.*

augment, *v.* to add to. *He had to take a second job at night to augment his low salary.*

authentic, *adj.* real. *The jewels in her necklace were so large that many believed they were not authentic.*

automaton, *n.* machine which performs jobs normally done by humans. *Automatons will be used in space flights to distant planets because of the many years the journeys will take.*

aversion, *n.* dislike. *She has a strong aversion to most insects, but she hates flies most of all.*

ban, *v.* to make illegal. *Many drugs have been banned after it was found that they caused dangerous side-effects.*

barricade, *v.* to be surrounded with walls for protection. *The soldiers built a barricade to keep their enemies out.*

basis, *n.* the foundation, what we build upon. *A good education is the basis for a successful career.*

behavior, *n.* conduct or actions. *The student's rude and noisy behavior was unacceptable to his teacher.*

bewilder, *v.* to confuse. *He was bewildered by many of the difficult questions asked in the test.*

blame, *n.* guilt or fault. *A careless cigarette smoker was to blame for the forest fire.*

blight, *n.* disease or curse, or a run-down condition. *The blight of many of our inner cities is caused by poor economic conditions.*

blunder, *n.* a bad mistake. *Trying to cheat on the test was a blunder that caused him to fail the course.*

bribe, *n.* the illegal act of giving money to someone in order to influence their actions. *The man tried to give the policeman a bribe so that he wouldn't get a speeding ticket.*

brittle, *adj.* easily broken. *When we grow older, our bones may become brittle.*

callous, *adj.* having no feeling. *Her callousness kept her from making a donation to the charity.*

canal, *n.* structure designed to carry liquids. *A canal was built across the desert to provide water for the new city.*

capacious, *adj.* having a large area. *It was a huge house and the capacious dining room could seat 100 guests.*

captive, *n.* one who is held hostage or imprisoned. *The lion was held captive before it could be released in the wild.*

castigate, *v.* to strongly criticize. *The politician was castigated for having lied about his love affair.*

category, *n.* division or class within a larger group. *Snakes are usually divided into two categories, poisonous or nonpoisonous.*

cessation, *n.* an ending or completion. *With the cessation of the war, refugees returned to their homes and began to rebuild.*

chaos, *n.* total confusion. *The effects of the earthquake created chaos in the city.*

characteristic, *n.* an aspect or feature. *Most employers look for characteristics such as motivation, dedication, and a good attitude in their prospective employees.*

chasm, *n.* a deep hole. *The explosion caused a chasm in the side of the mountain.*

chore, *n.* a small job or an unpleasant task. *Washing the dishes each night after supper is a real chore if you have worked all day.*

clumsy, *adj.* awkward in actions or movements. *Everyone appears clumsy the first time they ice-skate.*

coerce, *v.* to try to force one to do or say something against his/her will. *She felt coerced by her friends who promised never to talk to her again if she didn't help them cheat on the test.*

cogent, *adj.* convincing or persuasive. *His speech was so powerful and his ideas so cogent that everyone agreed that his plan was best.*

commerce, *n.* the activity of business and trade. *Commerce between the two countries has increased because of the new trade policy.*

compassion, *n.* sympathy for the problems of others. *The nurse's compassion for her patients made them love her.*

composite, *n.* something formed by the combination of different elements or substances. *Salt is a composite of sodium and chloride.*

compulsory, *adj.* required, necessary, or mandatory. *Compulsory education in the U.S. requires that every child attend school until the age of 16.*

concentration, *n.* a gathering or collection. *The highest concentration of big-game animals can be found in national parks.*

concoct, *v.* to create by mixing things together. *He concocted a bad-tasting drink by mixing milk and apple juice.*

condone, *v.* to approve of or to forgive an action. *The judge condoned the woman's actions by saying she acted in self-defense.*

confidant, *n.* one to whom secrets can be told. *She was not only his wife but also his closest confidant, and therefore, knew all of his deepest secrets.*

confide, *v.* to tell someone a secret or personal information. *The boy confided to his mother that he had broken the window by accident.*

confine, *v.* to limit or restrict movement. *After the accident, he was confined to a wheelchair for many weeks.*

confiscate, *v.* to take or seize goods because of criminal activity. *The police confiscated the robber's gun once he was arrested.*

congeal, *v.* to change from liquid to solid. *The milk that was left in the glass overnight slowly began to congeal.*

congenial, *adj.* friendly and pleasant to be with. *They were such congenial people that everyone wished to attend their parties.*

conscientious, *adj.* careful to fulfill responsibilities. *Since the lives of many people are in their hands, doctors and airline pilots have to be conscientious.*

consequence, *n.* results of an action. *There is strong evidence to indicate that there are many harmful consequences of smoking cigarettes.*

consummate, *v.* to perfect or complete. *Their long romance was consummated in marriage.*

contaminate, *v.* to make dirty or impure. *Water in the bay was contaminated by oil leaking from the ship.*

contingent, *adj.* likely but not certain to happen. *Payment of the money was contingent upon delivery of the goods.*

conventional, *adj.* common or usual. *In Japan, wood is the conventional material used to build houses.*

core, *n.* the center, the heart. *We eat most of the apple, but we usually leave the core.*

corroborate, *v.* to confirm or support what someone else has said. *Mr. Brown's explanation of what caused the accident was corroborated by a policeman who saw it happen.*

create, *v.* to make for the very first time. *The Bible says that God created the world in six days and then rested on the seventh.*

credulous, *adj.* trusting or unsuspecting. *A credulous person is often the first to be robbed or cheated.*

creed, *n.* one's belief or faith. *The creed that we follow helps us to determine which actions are good and which are evil.*

cruel, *adj.* lacking human kindness, mean or vicious. *The cruel man refused to help the lost couple.*

cryptic, *adj.* difficult to understand. *The note that was found in the bottle was too cryptic to understand.*

dangle, *v.* to hang down. *The windstorm knocked over trees and utility poles; the electric wires that dangled down were a real danger.*

decade, *n.* period of ten years. *The 1980s was a decade of economic prosperity.*

decency, *n.* the moral state of good behavior. *Decency demands that we do the right thing whether we want to or not.*

decrepit, *adj.* old and in poor condition. *The house was so decrepit that it would be cheaper to tear it down and start again rather than try to repair it.*

defect, *n.* a flaw or imperfection. *His job was to find any product with a defect and see that it was corrected.*

deficiency, *n.* something needed but not present. *In the past, sailors who had no fresh vegetables suffered from vitamin deficiencies and became ill.*

deliberately, *adv.* to do something on purpose with a clear understanding of the consequences. *He deliberately slammed the door in his boss's face.*

dependable, *adj.* can be relied upon. *American cars are very dependable and seldom break down.*

depict, *v.* to describe or characterize. *In the movie, he was depicted as kind and gentle.*

deprecate, *v.* to criticize or belittle. *Thomas Edison's efforts to create a light bulb were deprecated by many experts as impossible until he achieved success.*

deprive, *v.* to prevent from having. *A child whose parents have died is often deprived of the love that he needs.*

deride, *v.* to strongly criticize. *Critics derided the writer's new book as being poorly written and filled with lies.*

desire, *v.* a strong wish or want. *Everyone desires health, happiness, and sometimes, a piece of chocolate.*

destiny, *n.* fate or the future. *A fortune-teller claims to be able to know our destiny.*

detect, *v.* to notice or to find. *The doctors gave her a blood test, but they could not detect any signs of disease.*

deterioration, *n.* the state of declining or decaying. *The deterioration of the old church prompted the community to raise money to rebuild it.*

determinant, *n.* important factor that affects the result. *Exercise is a major determinant in losing weight.*

deviate, *v.* to change course. *If we never deviate from our normal activities, our lives will be boring.*

devise, *v.* to conceive, design, or create. *He devised a new method to change sea water to fresh water.*

diagnosis, *n.* the conclusion reached by a doctor as to the cause of an illness. *After a thorough examination, the doctor's diagnosis was that the patient had the flu.*

digress, *v.* to turn away from the main subject of attention. *To be an effective writer, you must organize your thoughts and never digress too far from your main idea.*

diligent, *adj.* hard-working. *The diligent way he performed his work earned him many promotions.*

diminutive, *adj.* small. *The problem was so diminutive that no one was concerned about it.*

discern, *v.* to discover or to be able to tell the difference between two things. *Only an expert could discern which painting was the original.*

discontinue, *v.* to stop. *The sale of many toys has been discontinued because of their danger to children.*

disposal, *n.* having the property to get rid of or to eliminate. *The garbage disposal unit failed to operate as the salesman promised it would.*

dissect, *v.* to cut something up in order to study it. *Sandy refused to dissect the frog, and as a result, failed the biology course.*

disseminate, *v.* to send out. *His job as a mailman is to disseminate the mail.*

dissolvable, *adj.* the ability to break down and disappear in a liquid. *Instead of swallowing them, Denise put the dissolvable tablets in her glass of water.*

divulge, *v.* to give secret or personal information. *Mrs. Haddy was angry that her sister Sylvia divulged her secrets to the neighborhood gossip.*

documentation, *n.* written evidence or proof. *Sarah's documentation showed that she was an official member of the club.*

dominant, *adj.* strongest or most powerful. *Jack's talkative nature made him the dominant member of the discussion group.*

drought, *n.* a long period of time with little or no rainfall. *Because of the long drought and dry conditions in the western states, many homes have been destroyed by fire.*

dubious, *adj.* doubtful or uncertain. *Fred was not hired for the position because of his dubious reputation.*

durable, *adj.* able to last a long time. *The label on the uniform stated that the fabric was durable and stain resistant.*

eccentric, *adj.* odd or unusual. *Jonathan was considered by the local community to be an eccentric inventor whose creations were useless.*

ecosystem, *n.* the complex of living things and their environment which functions as a single unit or a whole. *Many local scientists have warned about the effects of pollution on the fragile ecosystem of the bay.*

effects, *n.* the results or consequences. *The effects of his recent medical treatments are not yet known.*

elicit, *v.* to draw out. *The inspector was determined to elicit as much information as he could from each suspect.*

elucidate, *v.* to explain or clarify. *Marcus was always proud of his ability to elucidate the more difficult passages in the chemistry book.*

elusive, *adj.* difficult to find, catch, or see. *The Zodiac Killer had remained elusive to the New York City Police Department for months.*

emerge, *v.* to come out of. *Maria has emerged as one of the most talented female basketball players the school has ever had.*

emit, *v.* to send out. *The residents of Pleasant Park have been complaining about the foul odors being emitted by the new recycling center in town.*

emulate, *adj.* to copy or to follow. *Many children like to emulate their parents in some ways.*

energetically, *adv.* to act with vigor. *When Billy's father promised him ten dollars to rake the fall leaves, Billy energetically completed the task.*

enhance, *v.* to make better or clearer. *The attractive pink eyeglass frames enhanced the color of her eyes.*

ensnare, *v.* to trap or entangle. *As the township administrator, she had no intention of becoming ensnared in the local corruption scandal.*

ensue, *v.* to follow. *With the help of his college counselor, Carlos was determined to ensue the career path he had chosen.*

enterprise, *n.* a business venture. *The dream of launching the enterprise soon collapsed when the two businessmen realized the amount of money that would be needed.*

enticement, *n.* something which attracts or lures. *The enticement of winning a vacation in Hawaii for two weeks caused Lisa to fill out 15 entry forms for the contest.*

equivocal, *adj.* uncertain or vague. *Sharice's equivocal response did not tell me whether she liked the idea or not.*

erosion, *n.* the process of wearing away caused by wind or water. *The retired couple could not fulfill their dream of building a home near the beach because of erosion along the coast.*

essential, *adj.* necessary or most important. *It is essential that each student pass every exam in order to receive credit for the course.*

esteem, *n.* honor or respect. *General Tindal was held in high esteem by the soldiers because of his courage.*

evidence, *n.* facts or data which support an idea. *Enough evidence was gathered to indict three employees with illegally tampering with government documents.*

evolve, *v.* to change. *His ideas on life in the twentieth century evolved into one of the most complex philosophies she had ever read.*

exacting, *adj.* carefully precise. *The professor's exacting instructions made the assignment lengthy and complicated.*

examiner, *n.* one who carefully inspects. *The claims examiner rejected the customer's request for payment of medical treatment due to restrictions in the policy.*

exasperate, *v.* to annoy a person until he/she reaches a state of confusion or anger. *Manny's wife exasperated him so much that he backed into a neighbor's fence with his car.*

excessive, *adj.* more than is needed. *Eating a whole bag of candy after trick-or-treating is a bit excessive.*

exempt, *v.* to release from a commitment. *Jimmy was exempted from gym class for a week after running into the fence while playing baseball.*

exhaust, *v.* to tire out or to use up completely. *The gambler exhausted his family's savings and sold their house to pay off his debts.*

exist, *v.* to be alive. *Scholars consider William Faulkner to be one of the greatest American writers who ever existed.*

exorbitant, *adj.* extremely high priced. *They were selling hot dogs for the exorbitant price of $10 apiece.*

exotic, *adj.* unusual or uncommon. *Mary always considered her friend Susan's taste in clothing to be exotic.*

expensive, *adj.* costly or high priced. *When the Martins heard how expensive the new house was, they were shocked and decided not to buy it.*

explicit, *adj.* clear and specific. *Norma considered her instructions explicit and could not understand why her husband kept overcooking the pasta for dinner.*

explore, *v.* to investigate or to search through new territory. *He explored the passages of the cave.*

expose, *v.* to uncover or to reveal. *The political scandal was exposed on Friday, and by Saturday morning it was on the front page of every newspaper in the city.*

extensive, *adj.* covering a large area or amount. *The Pacific Ocean covers an extensive portion of Earth.*

extinct, *adj.* no longer in existence. *Dinosaurs have been extinct for millions of years.*

extravagant, *adj.* excessive or lavish. *Owning a house with 24 bedrooms is extravagant, even for a rich person.*

facile, *adj.* easy or simple. *For some complex problems, there are no facile solutions.*

facilitate, *v.* to aid or assist. *Automatic doors facilitate the movement of handicapped people who use wheelchairs.*

fail, *v.* unable to succeed. *He was sure that his plan could not fail.*

falter, *v.* to stumble or to momentarily hesitate. *At first he was winning the race, but as the pain in his leg increased, he began to falter.*

fascinate, *v.* to strongly attract someone's interest. *Children are fascinated by toys and games.*

feebleness, *n.* weakness. *With old age comes a gradual loss of hearing and a general state of feebleness.*

feud, *n.* an argument or quarrel which has lasted a long time. *The two families had a feud for so long that no one was quite sure how the argument had started.*

flee, *v.* to try to escape from some danger. *The war in Vietnam caused thousands of farmers to flee their homes.*

flimsy, *adj.* weak, easily broken. *A kite is a flimsy toy which can be easily damaged by a high wind.*

follow, *v.* to come after. *A dinner party later that afternoon will follow the wedding ceremony.*

foremost, *adj.* first or most important. *Water is of foremost importance when traveling across a desert.*

foresee, *v.* to see what will happen in the future. *Fortune tellers claim to foresee the future, but most simply want our money.*

forfeit, *v.* to lose or to surrender. *If you don't vote, then you are forfeiting your rights to participate in our democratic process of elections.*

foster, *v.* to help to grow with care and support. *Sunlight and water help to foster the growth of plants.*

fraction, *n.* a part of the whole. *The Christian population in Egypt makes up only a small fraction of the total population there.*

fraud, *n.* the attempt to cheat people with lies and deception. *If someone tries to sell you a watch on the street, be careful it isn't a fraud.*

fret, *v.* to worry. *Don't fret over how you will do on the test; study hard and hope for the best.*

fugitive, *n.* someone trying to escape the law. *Sometimes it takes years, but most fugitives are eventually caught and sent back to jail.*

futile, *adj.* useless or hopeless. *He made a futile attempt to put out the fire, but the building burned to the ground.*

genealogy, *n.* study of one's family and relatives in the past. *Many people study their genealogy to see if they are related to famous people.*

generic, *adj.* common or general. *A generic brand of aspirin is much cheaper than one with a brand name, even though they are the same product.*

genuinely, *adv.* honestly. *Even after he apologized for the insults, she didn't believe that he was genuinely sorry for his behavior.*

germinate, *v.* to begin to grow. *It takes two weeks after the seeds have been planted for them to begin to germinate.*

gist, *n.* the essential part or a summary. *He told her he didn't have time for all the details; he just wanted the gist of the story.*

glitter, *v.* to sparkle with light, to shine. *On a clear night, the stars glitter like diamonds.*

globose, *adj.* shaped like a globe or a sphere. *The shape of the fat man's stomach was globose.*

greed, *n.* the extreme desire to possess more than is needed. *The man's greed for money and power caused him to lose his friends.*

grievance, *n.* a complaint or an objection. *If a worker has a grievance, he should discuss it with his supervisor before he files a written complaint.*

group, *n.* a collection of things. *Many animals live in groups in order to survive.*

grudge, *n.* a feeling of resentment caused by an action in the past. *Even though the man had forgiven her, the girl still felt as though he was holding a grudge.*

guarantee, *n.* an assurance for the fulfillment of a condition. *The VCR came with a 12-month guarantee on all parts and service.*

hamper, *v.* to bother or hinder. *Rain and snow hampered the construction of the new building.*

handicap, *n.* problem or disability that limits actions. *Being unable to hear is a handicap that many people have to overcome.*

haphazard, *adj.* in a careless or disorganized fashion. *She was such a haphazard driver that she had four accidents in four days.*

harsh, *adj.* hard or cruel. *Without any concern for her feelings, the policeman yelled at the woman in a harsh manner.*

hectic, *adj.* confused or chaotic. *Traffic is most hectic at 5:00 p.m. when everyone is leaving work.*

hold, *v.* to argue or propose. *Many geographers held that the world was flat until Columbus proved that it was round by sailing to America.*

hilarious, *adj.* extremely funny or humorous. *The audience in the theater thought the movie was so hilarious that they couldn't stop laughing.*

hoax, *n.* a joke or deception meant to fool people. *Mary's boyfriend pretended to be a policeman, but she knew it was a hoax when she heard his voice.*

humid, *adj.* weather condition of very wet or moist air. *Summer is more humid than winter because warm air can carry more moisture than cold air.*

hypothesis, *n.* prediction or guess. *With careful experiments, scientists can usually determine if a hypothesis is correct or not.*

ignorant, *adj.* lacking knowledge. *People who do not go to school are ignorant of the many cultures and societies that exist in the world.*

illuminate, *v.* to brighten with light or to clarify. *Street lights help to illuminate dark roads.*

imaging, *n.* the process of producing a picture or image. *The powerful imaging produced by the telescope allowed the scientists to see the planet in much clearer detail.*

immature, *adj.* not yet adult or fully grown. *An immature bird can't fly.*

imminent, *adj.* approaching, near, about to happen. *The residents who remained in the city were in imminent danger from the approaching storm.*

impede, *v.* to hinder, restrict, or delay. *Doctors had to operate to remove the obstacle which impeded the flow of blood to his heart.*

impediment, *n.* obstacle or barrier. *Nervousness is often an impediment to learning to speak a new language.*

impinge, *v.* to impact, make an impression on. *The long hours he spent at work impinged upon his relationship with his family.*

inaugurate, *v.* to begin. *A ceremony took place to inaugurate the opening of the new bridge.*

inception, *n.* the beginning. *At the inception of the company there were only two employees; a year later, there were a hundred.*

incessant, *adj.* constant or continuous. *He had to leave the city to escape the incessant noise of the traffic.*

incisive, *adj.* a clear, sharp understanding. *His incisive ideas helped them to find a solution to the problems.*

inconsequential, *adj.* of no real importance. *We do a thousand inconsequential actions each day which our minds quickly forget after having done them.*

index, *v.* to put into a list or catalog. *Every magazine purchased by the library was carefully indexed.*

indict, *v.* to be brought to trial and accused. *The wife, who was found holding the gun, was indicted for the murder of her husband.*

induce, *v.* to cause to happen. *Doctors often prescribe drugs that induce sleep.*

inept, *adj.* lacking the necessary skill or ability. *She was a skillful writer, but her nervousness made her totally inept as a speaker.*

infamous, *adj.* famous for bad actions. *Hitler was an infamous dictator who caused the death of millions of people.*

inferior, *adj.* lower in degree or rank. *Shoppers prefer fresh vegetables rather than frozen ones which are inferior in taste.*

infest, *v.* to occupy or spread over in a troubling way. *The apartment was infested with bugs and had to be sprayed before the people could move in.*

inflammable, *adj.* having the ability to burn easily. *Petroleum is an inflammable substance.*

inhabit, *v.* to normally live in or occupy a particular place. *Camels inhabit the dry regions of the earth because of their ability to go long periods without water.*

injustice, *n.* a wrong action done to someone. *To purposely damage or destroy the property or goods of others is an injustice.*

inquisitive, *adj.* curious. *Children are inquisitive because they want to know why and how things happen.*

integrate, *v.* to combine with or to unite together. *In the early 1960s, schools in America were integrated so that black and white children could attend classes together.*

intentionally, *adv.* done on purpose. *The fire was no accident; it had been started intentionally.*

interactive, *adj.* acting with or in response to another. *An interactive exchange of ideas between countries is the best way to prevent wars.*

intrepid, *adj.* adventurous or fearless. *Early American pioneers had to be intrepid to face the dangers of the wilderness.*

intricate, *adj.* complex or complicated. *A wristwatch is a very intricate machine.*

intruder, *n.* a person who enters without permission. *An intruder broke the lock on their back door and entered their house while they were sleeping.*

invalid, *n.* one unable to live normally because of an illness or handicap. *The invalid had been confined to a wheelchair since the car accident.*

investment, *n.* money used for income or profit. *He bought land in Florida in hopes that it would increase in value, but his investment never paid off.*

irritation, *n.* an annoyance or problem. *A piece of sand in your eye can be a painful irritation.*

jilt, *v.* to abandon one's lover. *After waiting an hour in a restaurant for her boyfriend to appear, she knew she had been jilted.*

lack, *n.* the absence of something. *The lack of rain caused the grass to die.*

lament, *v.* to express great sorrow, to cry and moan. *For many years, the mother lamented the death of her son.*

lapses, *n.* periods of omissions or errors. *The lapses in his memory were caused by a blow to the head.*

leisure, *adj.* free time. *He likes to swim and play golf in his leisure time.*

lengthwise, *adv.* in relation to something's length (end to end). *The tree, measured lengthwise, was 100 feet long.*

license, *n.* legal document which allows an action to be performed. *To be legally married, a young couple must first apply for a marriage license.*

limb, *n.* an arm or leg on a person, or a branch on a tree. *In the storm, a limb of the tree fell down.*

dirty with trash or garbage. *People who litter our streets with trash cost the state lars each year to collect that trash.*

ate or despise. *George loathes broccoli since he was forced to eat it as a child.*

xist in a particular spot. *Paris is located in France.*

adj. moving from top to bottom. *The ship was moving in a longitudinal direction south.*

l. *When the electricity went out, people began to loot the shops along the darkened street.*

luminous, *adj.* filled with light. *The full moon was so luminous that the night seemed like day.*

maintain, *v.* to keep in current condition. *A car has to be maintained to stay in good condition.*

malign, *v.* to injure someone by saying bad things about him or her. *His good name was maligned by the story in the newspaper which called him a liar.*

masonry, *n.* blocks or bricks jointed together with cement. *The masonry of ancient Egyptians can be seen in their pyramids.*

massive, *adj.* very large, huge. *A whale is a massive mammal.*

mature, *adj.* adult or fully grown. *Grapes are picked as soon as they are mature.*

meddle, *v.* to interfere in the business of others. *The young husband told his mother-in-law not to meddle in his affairs.*

melancholy, *adj.* sad or unhappy. *The play was so melancholy that it made the audience cry.*

menace, *n.* a threat or threatening. *Air pollution is a menace to our health.*

merge, *v.* to join or combine together. *The two small companies merged to form one large company.*

metabolism, *n.* the processes by which energy is provided for life. *Our metabolism slows when we go to sleep.*

meticulous, *adj.* precise and careful about even the smallest detail. *She was so meticulous with her house that she even scrubbed and waxed the garage floor.*

migrate, *v.* to travel from place to place. *Every year, the photography club gathers at the state park to photograph birds that migrate south for the winter.*

morbid, *adj.* psychologically unhealthy. *Sally was so morbid at times that many of her friends stopped calling her.*

mundane, *adj.* common or ordinary. *The professor always tried to persuade his students from living a mundane life.*

mutual, *adj.* in conjunction with another. *A mutual feeling of resentment and anger built up between the couple after only two years of marriage.*

nadir, *n.* the lowest point. *He considered the six months he lived in New York City without a job or a decent place to live as the nadir of his existence.*

neglect, *v.* to fail to provide what is needed. *Rita caught the flu and her doctor admonished her for neglecting to eat and rest properly during the winter months.*

negligent, *adj.* responsible for improper actions. *Dan's electricity was turned off yesterday because he was negligent in paying his monthly bill.*

negligible, *adj.* unimportant or insignificant. *At the office meetings, Debbie felt her opinions were considered negligible by her coworkers, and so she decided not to speak up any more.*

nomadic, *adj.* having the characteristic of moving from place to place without a fixed pattern. *As a child, Howard resented his family's nomadic lifestyle because he was never able to develop lasting friendships.*

notorious, *adj.* famous for wrong actions. *Luiz was notorious for borrowing money and failing to pay it back.*

objective, *n.* goal or purpose. *Her main objective was to find her own apartment to live in as soon as possible.*

obscure, *adj.* not well known. *Alex always enjoyed the obscure writings of the early philosophers.*

obsolete, *adj.* no longer of any use. *The customer knew the record player would soon become obsolete, but he bought it anyway.*

occurrence, *n.* event or happening. *The repeated occurrence of missing funds at the bank baffled the investigators.*

ominous, *adj.* menacing or threatening. *The large black clouds looked ominous, and so the baseball game was canceled.*

omit, *v.* to leave out. *Betty was hurt when she heard her name was omitted from Ana's wedding invitation list.*

orbit, *n.* circular pattern of movement around another object. *Christopher won second prize at the science fair for his detailed diagram of the orbit of the planets.*

ordeal, *n.* a painful or difficult experience. *Mr. Thompson considered his visit to the dentist such a frightening ordeal that he vowed never to go back.*

origin, *n.* the source or cause. *Cindy was determined to find the origin of the rumors circulating about her in the office.*

ostensibly, *adv.* as it appears, apparently. *Ostensibly, he was honest about his past, but she didn't trust him.*

output, *n.* what was produced. *The production manager was troubled over the recent drop in output by his employees.*

pact, *n.* an agreement. *Before Jerry moved, he made a pact with his best friend that they would meet at Hadley's Park on Jerry's eighteenth birthday.*

palatable, *adj.* eatable or good tasting. *Mike and Sara agreed that their dinner at the new restaurant was just about palatable.*

paralyze, *v.* to cause something to be unable to move. *Some predators will paralyze their prey with poison and then devour them.*

parasitic, *adj.* the quality of living off others. *This parasitic species of fish was called "blood-sucker" by local fisherman.*

patent, *n.* legal right of ownership. *Tom was advised to obtain a patent for his latest invention.*

penetrable, *adj.* can be entered. *The commander realized the fort was penetrable and ordered his troops to attack the weak point.*

penetrate, *v.* to enter into. *Since the spilled wine penetrated the upholstery, Lydia decided to purchase a new couch.*

perforated, *adj.* filled with holes. *The bucket of water was found empty since the boy hadn't noticed that it was perforated.*

perish, *v.* waste away, disappear, to die. *Abe watched Loretta's love letters perish as he placed each one of them into the fireplace.*

perpetual, *adj.* lasting forever. *Margaret hoped that her neighbor's sunrise visits would not become a perpetual problem.*

persist, *v.* to continue an action despite obstacles. *Mr. Price persisted in eating a breakfast of eggs and sausage every morning in spite of his high cholesterol readings.*

pessimist, *n.* one who expects the worst will happen. *Mary came to be known as the pessimist in her family because she always found something to worry about.*

petition, *n.* a written request. *Many angry residents circulated a petition to repeal the large tax increases in the state.*

phenomenon, *n.* an unusual event or occurrence. *Many consider the aurora borealis to be a spectacular phenomenon of nature.*

phlegmatic, *adj.* showing no feeling or energy. *Having studied for two straight days without stopping to sleep, he appeared phlegmatic as he sat at his desk with the test before him.*

placate, *v.* to make peace with an enemy. *He tried to placate his angry wife by bringing her flowers.*

plea, *n.* a request, usually with strong emotion. *The Red Cross made an urgent plea for blood donors to aid the victims of the fire.*

plethora, *n.* a large amount of variety. *She said it was just a dinner party, but when he saw the plethora of food and drink, he knew it was a real feast.*

pollute, *v.* to make dirty. *Exhaust from cars pollutes our air.*

ponder, *v.* to think carefully. *Great men often ponder the eternal questions of why we were born and why we must die.*

postpone, *v.* to delay an action until a later time. *The class picnic had to be postponed because of the heavy rain.*

precede, *v.* to come before. *Fall precedes winter.*

predator, *n.* a creature that survives by attacking and eating another creature. *The most feared of all marine predators is the great white shark.*

predetermine, *v.* to decide the outcome or result before it occurs. *She hoped to predetermine the questions she would be asked in the test so that she would be better prepared.*

prelude, *n.* what comes before. *The dark skies and the sound of distant thunder were a prelude to the storm.*

premise, *n.* an unproven idea which is the basis for research. *His theory was based on the premise that animals could be taught to speak.*

prescription, *n.* a written order of medicine given by a doctor. *The prescription stated that the antibiotics were to be taken three times a day.*

prevalent, *adj.* common in many areas. *Colds are most prevalent during the winter months.*

prior, *adj.* before or previous. *He graduated from high school three years prior to entering college.*

probe, *n.* a careful study to discover information. *The detective began to probe through the dark house with his flashlight.*

prolific, *adj.* abundant or productive. *He was such a prolific writer that he was able to complete a novel every three weeks.*

prosecute, *v.* to seek punishment for breaking the law. *The banker was prosecuted for stealing money from his own bank.*

prudent, *adj.* careful. *It is considered prudent for a married man to have life insurance.*

purify, *v.* to make pure or clean. *Charcoal filters in the air conditioner were used to purify the air coming into the house.*

quality, *n.* a feature or characteristic. *One quality common to all societies is the love and care given to children.*

random, *adj.* with no pattern or organization. *The numbers for the lottery are chosen at random.*

raze, *v.* to demolish or destroy. *It took the bulldozer only one hour to raze the old building into a pile of bricks.*

recede, *v.* to go back to a previous state. *After the high tide caused by the rain and storm, the water slowly began to recede to its normal level.*

receptive, *adj.* open to new ideas. *His father was very old-fashioned, so he was not receptive to new ideas.*

recite, *v.* to read aloud. *Most children learn the alphabet by reciting it many times.*

recluse, *n.* one who wishes to live alone. *The old recluse lived deep in the woods, ten miles from the nearest neighbor.*

reconcile, *v.* to make peace. *When a husband and wife cannot reconcile their differences, a divorce is likely to occur.*

refine, *v.* to make better by removing impurities. *Petroleum has to be refined before it can be used as fuel.*

remnant, *n.* something left behind. *The only remnant left of the ancient city is a pile of rocks.*

repel, *v.* to fight off. *Fire will repel wild animals.*

repugnant, *adj.* offensive, distasteful, repulsive. *Bad manners are quite repugnant.*

resolute, *adj.* very determined to do something. *A resolute person will endure any hardship to reach his or her goal.*

retard, *v.* to slow down. *The five car pile-up retarded the progress of the other motorists on the highway.*

revenue, *n.* money collected from taxes or by a business. *The government receives the revenue needed to operate by taxing people and companies.*

ridicule, *v.* to make fun of. *The student was ridiculed by his classmates for giving the wrong answer in class.*

ripe, *adj.* mature, fully grown, or ready to eat. *A green banana is usually not ripe enough to eat.*

rivalry, *n.* competition. *In the Olympic Games, there is a rivalry between many nations.*

sagacity, *n.* wisdom or great knowledge. *Through long years of experience and study, the old man had acquired a sagacity about the ways of men.*

savage, *n.* one who is not civilized or educated. *Savages in the jungles of the Amazon use primitive stone tools.*

scarce, *adj.* in short supply, hard to find. *Diamonds and gold have always been scarce; that is part of the reason they are so valuable.*

scatter, *v.* to throw in many directions. *The strong wind scattered the leaves across the yard.*

schedule, *v.* to assign a particular time for an event to occur. *He was scheduled to see the doctor at 10:00 a.m. and the dentist at 1:00 p.m.*

scorn, *v.* to ridicule or to express great contempt. *The man who ran away from the battle was scorned by the other soldiers who had fought.*

scrutiny, *n.* a careful investigation or examination. *The liar hoped that the story he had told the police would pass their scrutiny.*

secure, *adj.* safe. *Until army troops move over the border and away from the city, local citizens will never feel truly secure.*

seemingly, *adv.* apparently. *Seemingly, the stranger had knocked at the door to get directions into town.*

seize, *v.* to quickly grab and hold. *The policeman seized all of the drugs and money found in the apartment.*

selective, *adj.* careful when making a choice. *We have to be very selective when purchasing a used car.*

self-reliance, *n.* to depend upon oneself. *Camping in the woods is a good test of self-reliance.*

senility, *n.* mental condition of confusion caused by old age. *Everyone reaches a state of senility if they live long enough.*

shatter, *v.* to break into many pieces. *The window was shattered by a rock.*

shield, *v.* to protect from outside harm. *A mother bear will shield her young from any danger.*

shrewd, *adj.* very clever. *A shrewd man knows both his strengths and his weaknesses.*

simulate, *v.* to copy or imitate. *Pilots often practice in a machine which simulates the problems they might face when flying.*

situate, *v.* to locate. *Los Angeles is situated in California.*

skeptical, *adj.* unbelieving. *We should always be skeptical when someone tells us they know an easy way to make money.*

sleazy, *adj.* of low quality. *The hotel room was so sleazy that not even the rats wanted to be there.*

sluggish, *adj.* slow in movement. *Bob's mind and actions are very sluggish when he first wakes up in the morning.*

soluble, *adj.* able to dissolve or melt in water or liquids. *Sugar is soluble in water.*

soothe, *v.* to ease or to calm. *Cool water is soothing on a hot day.*

species, *n.* a category of biological classification. *A new species of animal was discovered by the zoologist.*

specific, *adj.* particular or designated. *The judge wanted the defendant to give a specific answer to the question: yes or no.*

spill, *v.* to overturn so that liquid escapes. *Despite his years of experience as a waiter, Walter managed to spill the wine on the customer.*

sporadic, *adj.* occurring at odd intervals. *At sporadic times, the sky was lit by flashes of lightning.*

spurn, *v.* to reject. *She would never forget how her boyfriend had spurned her for another woman.*

squash, *v.* to stop or to destroy. *He squashed the bug with his shoe.*

stable, *adj.* steady and not easily changed. *They couldn't build the skyscraper since the area was not stable enough to support the great weight.*

stagnant, *adj.* not flowing or moving. *Mosquitoes will breed in stagnant water.*

static, *adj.* not changing. *She felt her life had grown too static; she wanted to make some changes.*

stimulate, *v.* to cause action. *The ideas in the book stimulated his imagination.*

strain, *n.* tension or stress. *The worries that he faced each day on his job caused him great strain.*

stun, *v.* to daze or to shock. *He was stunned to find out that his uncle had died and left him a million dollars.*

subject, *v.* to cause to experience or to submit to. *A traveler is subjected to the laws of the country in which he is traveling.*

subordinate, *v.* to put under the control of higher power. *The employees were surprised to hear that the company subordinated Bob, a long-time employee, to Stan, the new employee.*

substance, *n.* matter or material. *Vivian was unsure of the substance in the package, so she threw the package out.*

supercede, *v.* to displace. *Judy Cameron superceded Beatrice Mills as the president of the Women's Club on campus.*

surmise, *v.* to assume. *Many students surmised that the history class would be difficult merely by the stern look on their professor's face.*

surname, *n.* family name. *By changing his surname to Walters, Albert Waltinchizsky thought he could become a famous actor.*

survive, *v.* to continue to live. *No one can survive without food or water.*

symbolize, *v.* to represent or to stand for. *Since the American flag symbolizes freedom to many, Americans are proud to display it on the Fourth of July.*

sympathy, *n.* feelings of understanding for the problems of others. *Many people in the neighborhood like to visit the elderly woman because of her great sympathy and concern for others.*

synchronize, *v.* to align or to match the movement of two. *It took great skill for the two skaters to synchronize their movements during the performance.*

taciturn, *adj.* quiet and stern. *Jean complains that her husband is so taciturn that she can't even have an argument with him.*

tactile, *adj.* related to the sense of touch. *The curators of the state museum were pleased that the tactile activities delighted the children who visited the exhibit.*

tailor, *v.* to design to fit particular needs. *Many passengers on the cruise ship had such a good time that they swore the trip was tailored especially for them.*

tangible, *adj.* touchable or real. *Marissa insisted on some tangible evidence from her friend before she would believe her husband was cheating on her.*

tentative, *adj.* temporary or uncertain. *A tentative schedule was set up for the employees until the new business was fully operational.*

tenuous, *adj.* vague or weak. *She felt her husband's tenuous grasp of their marital problems would lead them to divorce.*

terminate, *v.* to bring to an end or to stop. *Teresa was distraught when she learned her position at the company would be terminated.*

terse, *adj.* short or brief. *She abruptly hung up the phone after Kurt's terse reply.*

therapy, *n.* treatment provided to restore good health. *After the accident, Randy received three weeks of physical therapy and was soon back at his job.*

tolerant, *adj.* open to many ideas. *The class discussions were often lively and controversial due to the instructor's tolerant attitude.*

track, *v.* to follow something's movements. *The hunter's adept ability to silently track the movements of his prey brought him many awards.*

tract, *n.* an area or region. *City officials plan to turn the tract of land along the river into a park.*

tranquility, *n.* a state of complete rest and peace. *Many people spend all their lives seeking peace and tranquility.*

transact, *v.* to engage in or to accomplish. *Simon hated the daily grind of transacting with business leaders, so he quit and became a sculptor.*

transcribe, *v.* to write down what is spoken. *Fortunately, many of the poet's last words were transcribed by his wife.*

trauma, *n.* a severe injury or a state of emotional distress. *The patients in the intensive care unit had been in a car accident and were under heavy trauma.*

traverse, *v.* to cross. *Because the bridge was traversed by so many people traveling into the city, it was finally closed for repairs.*

trivial, *adj.* unimportant. *He thought her complaints were trivial and left the room.*

tumble, *v.* to fall down or to roll. *Mrs. Benthill shrieked as she watched her new vase tumble to the floor and shatter.*

tumult, *n.* chaos or upheaval. *The sudden cancellation of the concert caused such a tumult in the crowd that extra police were called to the site.*

turmoil, *n.* confusion. *The turmoil over her daughter's upcoming wedding gave Mrs. Windman constant headaches.*

ultimate, *adj.* the highest, the best, the most important. *Bernie's ultimate goal was to become president of the company by the age of 40.*

unique, *adj.* unlike anything else. *His paintings were so unique that he was complimented on his imagination and ingenuity.*

unreliable, *adj.* cannot be trusted. *Pete's plumbing business finally went bankrupt because of his unreliable service.*

vacillate, *v.* to hesitate or to waver. *Archie impatiently drummed his fingers on the table as his wife vacillated between ordering chicken or seafood for dinner.*

vary, *v.* to change. *The teacher always varied her lesson plans in order to keep her students stimulated and motivated.*

venture, *n.* a gamble or risk. *Mr. Stanton refused to financially support his son's latest business venture.*

verify, *v.* to check that something is true or correct. *Every statement by the bank teller about the robbery was verified by witnesses standing in the lobby.*

vibrant, *adj.* full of life. *Emma had such a vibrant personality that no one could believe she was 82 years old.*

vibrate, *v.* to move in a back-and-forth motion. *Charlie's washing machine would vibrate so loudly in the spin cycle that his neighbors constantly complained to the landlord.*

vigorously, *adv.* showing great energy or life. *Shirley spent an hour vigorously scrubbing her kitchen floor before her dinner guests arrived.*

volatile, *adj.* explosive or unsteady. *After the shooting of an innocent victim, the crowds in the streets became volatile and citizens were advised to stay at home.*

vulnerable, *adj.* open to danger or damage. *A woman walking alone at night on a deserted street is vulnerable to an attack.*

warranty, *n.* a written guarantee. *Arthur searched and searched through the box but could not find the warranty that was supposed to come with his new car radio.*

wither, *v.* to die slowly because of a lack of water. *On the fifth day of no rain, Bernice's flowers began to wither and die.*

wrath, *n.* great anger. *His wrath was so great that many employees refused to go near his office.*

zone, *n.* a specific region or area. *Because of an attack by a bear on campers, the area was declared a danger zone and visitors were denied access to it.*

COOP/
HSPT

CHAPTER 5

Mathematics
Review

Chapter 5

MATHEMATICS REVIEW

I. **WHOLE NUMBERS**
II. **FRACTIONS**
III. **DECIMALS**
IV. **TOPICS IN MATHEMATICS**
V. **PERCENTS**
VI. **ADVANCED TOPICS**

Take a look back at the *Mathematics* portion of the HSPT practice test 1 or *Mathematics Concepts and Applications* test of the COOP. If you didn't do as well here, you may or may not have to do some more work in the following areas of math:

• Concepts and Computation

• Problem Solving

I. WHOLE NUMBERS

ADDITION OF WHOLE NUMBERS

The easiest way to add whole numbers is to write the numbers in a column with the place values lined up. That is, the ones digits are lined up in one column, the tens digits are lined up in the next column, etc. Then we add the digits down each column, moving from the right to the left to calculate our overall answer. If the sum of a column is ten or more, we place the right-hand digit of the answer column in our overall answer and "carry" the tens (or possibly hundreds) position to the next column. In the following examples we will consider some problems where carrying is necessary.

Examples

Add the following numbers.

(a)   Add 345, 401, and 232.

$$
\begin{array}{r}
345 \\
401 \\
+\,232 \\
\end{array}
\quad\longrightarrow\quad
\begin{array}{r}
345 \\
401 \\
+\,232 \\
\hline
978 \\
\end{array}
$$

By adding the ones column, we get $5 + 1 + 2 = 8$. The tens column gives $4 + 0 + 3 = 7$, and the hundreds column gives $3 + 4 + 2 = 9$. Carrying is not used in this problem. The final answer is 978.

(b)   Add 3,456, 2,589, 3,764, and 4,607.

$$
\begin{array}{r}
3456 \\
2589 \\
3764 \\
+\,4607 \\
\end{array}
\quad\longrightarrow\quad
\begin{array}{r}
\overset{2\,2\,2}{3456} \\
2589 \\
3764 \\
+\,4607 \\
\hline
14416 \\
\end{array}
$$

By adding the ones column, we get $6 + 9 + 4 + 7 = 26$. We can place the 6 in our answer line and carry the 2 to the tens column. (This accounts for the 2 above the 5 in the rewrite.) By adding the tens column, we get $2 + 5 + 8 + 6 + 0 = 21$. We can place the 1 in the answer line and carry the 2 to the hundreds column. (This accounts for the 2 above the 4 in the rewrite.) By adding the hundreds column, we get $2 + 4 + 5 + 7 + 6 = 24$. We can place the 4 in the answer line and carry the 2 to the thousands column. (This accounts for the 2 above the 3 in the rewrite of the problem.) By adding the thousands column, we get $2 + 3 + 2 + 3 + 4 = 14$. Since we have no more columns to add, we can write the 14 in our answer line. The final answer is 14,416.

Drill: Addition of Whole Numbers

Add the following numbers.

1. $245 + 912 + 357$

2. $4,376 + 1,994 + 8,953$

3. $15,274 + 98,407$

4. $4,275 + 7,136 + 3,983 + 5,648$

5. $67,134 + 34,673 + 25,876$

Answers to Drill Questions

1.　1,514

$$
\begin{array}{r}
\mathit{1\,1} \\
245 \\
912 \\
+\ 357 \\
\hline
1514
\end{array}
$$

2.　15,323

$$
\begin{array}{r}
\mathit{2\,2\,1} \\
4376 \\
1994 \\
+\ 8953 \\
\hline
15323
\end{array}
$$

3.　113,681

$$
\begin{array}{r}
\mathit{1\ \ \ 1} \\
15274 \\
+\ 98407 \\
\hline
113681
\end{array}
$$

4.　21,042

$$
\begin{array}{r}
\mathit{2\,2\,2} \\
4275 \\
7136 \\
3983 \\
+\ 5648 \\
\hline
21042
\end{array}
$$

5.　127,683

$$
\begin{array}{r}
\mathit{1\,1\,1\,1} \\
67134 \\
34673 \\
+\ 25876 \\
\hline
127683
\end{array}
$$

SUBTRACTION OF WHOLE NUMBERS

Now that we are "experts" at adding numbers, we want to discuss the other operations that can be used with whole numbers. In this section, we will consider subtraction. As with addition, in subtraction we will write our numbers in column format with the place values lined up. We will subtract the bottom number from the top number (if possible), moving right to left. If the subtraction is not possible, we can borrow one from the next larger column. In the following examples, we will borrow where necessary.

Examples

Subtract the following pairs of numbers.

(a)   4,572 – 3,469

$$
\begin{array}{r}
4572 \\
-\ 3469 \\
\end{array}
\qquad\longrightarrow\qquad
\begin{array}{r}
4\overset{6\,_1}{5}72 \\
-\ 3469 \\
\hline
1103 \\
\end{array}
$$

If we try to subtract the ones column, we see that we have a difficulty (2 – 9 cannot be done using whole numbers). In order to do this subtraction, we need to borrow 1 from the tens column. This would change the 7 to a 6 in the tens position and change 2 into 12 in the ones position. We are now able to subtract the ones column. This will give 12 – 9 = 3. We can write this value on our answer line. By subtracting the tens column, we get 6 – 6 = 0. We can write this value on our answer line. By subtracting the hundreds column, we get 5 – 4 = 1. We can write this value on our answer line. By subtracting the thousands column, we get 4 – 3 = 1. We can write this value on our answer line. The final value is 1,103.

(b)   8,737 – 4,364

$$
\begin{array}{r}
8737 \\
-\ 4364 \\
\end{array}
\qquad\longrightarrow\qquad
\begin{array}{r}
8\overset{6\,_1}{7}37 \\
-\ 4364 \\
\hline
4373 \\
\end{array}
$$

By subtracting the ones column, we get 7 – 4 = 3. We can write this value on our answer line. In order to subtract the tens column, we need to borrow 1 from the hundreds column. The 7 becomes a 6 and the 3 becomes a 13. Therefore, subtracting the tens column gives 13 – 6 = 7. This value can be placed on our answer line. By subtracting the hundreds column, we get 6 – 3 = 3. We can write this value on our answer line. By subtracting the thousands column, we get 8 – 4 = 4. We can write this value on our answer line. The final answer is 4,373.

Drill: Subtraction of Whole Numbers

Subtract the following pairs of numbers.

1.   9,846 – 1,345

2.   4,256 – 2,133

3.   3,457 – 1,246

4.   89,725 – 68,413

5.   2,795 – 1,257

6.   5,637 – 4,258

7.   85,267 – 25,456

Answers to Drill Questions

1.   8,501

    9846
    – 1345
    8501

2.   2,123

    4256
    – 2133
    2123

3.   2,211

    3457
    – 1246
    2211

4.   21,312

    89725
    – 68413
    21312

5.   1,538

    8 1
    2795
    – 1257
    1538

6.   1,379

    5121
    5637
    – 4258
    1379

7.   59,811

    7141
    85267
    – 25456
    59811

MULTIPLICATION OF WHOLE NUMBERS

The next operation that we want to discuss is multiplication. As with addition and subtraction, we will write our problems in a column format. We will begin by multiplying the ones digit in the second number by each digit in the first number. Then, if it exists, we will repeat this process with the tens digit in the second number. This action will continue until we have used each digit in the second number. Remember to carry where necessary. After multiplying the next digits, we need to add in anything carried over from the preceding product. If the second number contains more than one digit, our final step is to add down each column to get our final answer. In the following examples, we will address a variety of problems.

Examples

Multiply the following pairs of numbers.

(a) $3,451 \times 67$

$$
\begin{array}{r} 3451 \\ \times\, 67 \end{array}
\quad \longrightarrow \quad
\begin{array}{r} \overset{3\ 3}{3451} \\ \times\, 67 \\ \hline 24157 \end{array}
$$

$$
\begin{array}{r} \overset{2\ 3}{3451} \\ \times\, 67 \\ \hline 24157 \\ +\, 207060 \end{array}
\quad \longrightarrow \quad
\begin{array}{r} \overset{1\quad 1}{24157} \\ +\, 207060 \\ \hline 231217 \end{array}
$$

We begin by multiplying the 7 and the 1 together, producing 7. We write this value on our answer line. Then we multiply the 7 and the 5 together, getting 35. We can place the 5 on our answer line and carry the 3. (This accounts for the 3 above the 4 in the second rewrite of this problem.) We can continue this process by multiplying the 7 and the 4 together. This results in 28. When we add in the 3 that was carried over, we get 31. We can write the 1 on our answer line and carry the 3. (This accounts for the 3 appearing above the 3 in the second rewrite of the example.) By multiplying the 7 and the 3 together, we get 21. When we add in the 3 that was carried over, we get a result of 24. We can write this value on our answer line. Since the second number contains two digits, we must multiply each digit by the first number. At this point, we have only multiplied the ones digit in the second number by the first number. Now we have to do the same thing with the tens digit of the second number. We have placed a 0 in the ones digit on the answer line for the second step of this problem in order to keep the proper columns. (This is the italicized zero (*0*) appearing in the third rewrite of this example.) We then take 6 and multiply it by 1. This results in 6, and we can place this value on our answer line. Next, we multiply the 6 and the 5. In this case we get 30. We can place the 0 on our answer line and carry the 3. (This accounts for the 3 appearing above the 4 in the third rewrite of the above problem.) Now we can multiply the 6 and the 4 to get 24. When we add in the 3 that was carried over, we get 27. We can write the 7 on our answer line and carry the 2. (This accounts for the 2 appearing above the 3 in the third rewrite of this problem.) When we multiply the 6 and the 3 together, we get 18. When we add in the 2 that was carried over, we get 20. We can place this value on our answer line. The final stage of this problem is to add the two answer lines together. Keep in mind that we also need to carry here when necessary. Our final answer is 231,217.

(b) 736×142

$$
\begin{array}{r} 736 \\ \times\,142 \\ \hline \end{array}
\longrightarrow
\begin{array}{r} \overset{1}{7}36 \\ \times\,142 \\ \hline 1472 \end{array}
\longrightarrow
\begin{array}{r} \overset{12}{7}36 \\ \times\,142 \\ \hline 1472 \\ +\,2944\mathit{0} \end{array}
$$

$$
\longrightarrow
\begin{array}{r} 736 \\ \times\,142 \\ \hline 1472 \\ 29440 \\ +\,736\mathit{00} \end{array}
\longrightarrow
\begin{array}{r} \overset{111}{1}472 \\ 29440 \\ +\,73600 \\ \hline 104512 \end{array}
$$

We begin by multiplying the ones digit in the second number by the first number. In this problem, we would get $736 \times 2 = 1,472$. We place this value on our first answer line. Remember to carry when necessary. We then need to take the tens digit in the second number and multiply it by the first number. In this example, we would get $736 \times 4 = 2,944$. We have placed a zero (0) in the ones position of our second answer line in order to keep the proper columns. Therefore, our second answer line would be 29,44*0*. We now need to take the hundreds digit in the second number and multiply it by the first number. In this example, we would get $736 \times 1 = 736$. We have placed zeros (0) in the ones and tens positions of our third answer line in order to keep the proper columns. Therefore, our third answer line would be 73,6*00*. To finish up this problem, we must add the three answer lines together. If we again remember to carry where needed, we will get a final answer of 104,512. Notice that in the work above we have shown all carried numbers in italics.

(c) 632×113

$$
\begin{array}{r} 632 \\ \times\,113 \\ \hline \end{array}
\longrightarrow
\begin{array}{r} 632 \\ \times\,113 \\ \hline 1896 \end{array}
\longrightarrow
\begin{array}{r} 632 \\ \times\,113 \\ \hline 1896 \\ +\,632\mathit{0} \end{array}
$$

$$
\longrightarrow
\begin{array}{r} 632 \\ \times\,113 \\ \hline 1896 \\ 6320 \\ +\,632\mathit{00} \end{array}
\longrightarrow
\begin{array}{r} \overset{111}{1}896 \\ 6320 \\ +\,63200 \\ \hline 71416 \end{array}
$$

We begin by multiplying the ones digit in the second number by the first number. In this problem, we would get $632 \times 3 = 1,896$. We place this value on our first answer line. Remember to carry when necessary. We then need to take the tens digit in the second number and multiply it by the first number. In this example, we would get $632 \times 1 = 632$. We have placed a zero (*0*) in the ones position of our second answer line in order to keep the proper columns. Therefore, our second answer line would be 6,32*0*. We now need to take the hundreds digit in the second number and multiply it by the first number. In this example, we would get $632 \times 1 = 632$. We have placed (*0*) in the ones and tens positions of our third answer line in order to keep the proper columns. Therefore, our third answer line would be 63,2*00*. To finish up this problem, we must add the three answer lines together. If we again remember to carry where needed, we will get a final answer of 71,416. Notice that in the work above we have shown all carried numbers in italics.

Drill: Multiplication of Whole Numbers

Multiply the following pairs of numbers.

1. $8,157 \times 46$

2. 370×51

3. 607×32

4. 816×79

5. 434×65

Answers to Drill Questions

1. 375,222

$$
\begin{array}{r}
8157 \\
\times\,46 \\
\hline
48942 \\
+\,32628 \\
\hline
375222 \\
\end{array}
$$

2. 18,870

$$
\begin{array}{r}
370 \\
\times\,51 \\
\hline
370 \\
+\,1850 \\
\hline
18870 \\
\end{array}
$$

3. 19,424

          607
    $\times$ 32

         1214
     + 1821

        19424

4. 64,464

          816
    $\times$ 79

         7344
     + 5712

        64464

5. 28,210

          434
    $\times$ 65

         2170
     + 2604

        28210

DIVISION OF WHOLE NUMBERS

The last operation that we want to cover is division. By writing the problems in long division format, we can compare digits. Here we are looking to see how many times a number goes into another. That is, what must a number be multiplied by to get the other? Hopefully, this can be an exact number. If not, we have a **remainder**. In this book, we will write "R" and then the value to denote a remainder. Here we want the largest value possible without exceeding the number. This is a quick overview of the method that we will use. In the examples below, we will refine this technique.

Examples

Divide the following numbers

(a) $4,768 \div 32$

$$32\overline{)4768} \longrightarrow 32\overline{)4768} \atop \begin{array}{r} 1 \\ \hline \end{array}$$

$$\begin{array}{r} 1 \\ 32\overline{)4768} \\ -32 \\ \hline 156 \end{array}$$

$$\rightarrow \quad 32\overline{)\,4768}^{\,14} \quad\rightarrow\quad 32\overline{)\,4768}^{\,149}$$
$$\underline{-\,32}\qquad\qquad \underline{-\,32}$$
$$156\qquad\qquad 156$$
$$\underline{-\,128}\qquad\quad \underline{-\,128}$$
$$288\qquad\qquad 288$$
$$\underline{-\,288}$$
$$0$$

Since it is not possible for 32 to go into 4, we consider how many times 32 goes into 47. Our answer here is 1. By multiplying 32 and 1 together, we get 32. We can place this value under the first number and subtract. Here we get $47 - 32 = 15$ and bring down the next digit (6). We now consider how many times 32 goes into 156. This gives 4, since 32×4 equals 128. When we place this value under the first number and subtract, we get 28. We bring down the next digit (8) and repeat this procedure. We now consider how many times 32 goes into 288. This gives 9, since $32 \times 9 = 288$. If we place this value under the first number and subtract, we get 0. There is no remainder in this problem.

(b) $16,468 \div 46$

$$46\overline{)\,16468} \quad\longrightarrow\quad 46\overline{)\,16468}^{\,3} \quad\longrightarrow$$
$$\underline{-\,138}$$
$$266$$

$$\longrightarrow \quad 46\overline{)\,16468}^{\,35} \quad\longrightarrow\quad 46\overline{)\,16468}^{\,358}$$
$$\underline{-\,138}\qquad\qquad \underline{-\,138}$$
$$266\qquad\qquad 266$$
$$\underline{-\,230}\qquad\qquad \underline{-\,230}$$
$$368\qquad\qquad 368$$
$$\underline{-\,368}$$
$$0$$

Since it is not possible for 46 to go into 1 or 16, we consider how many times 46 goes into 164. Our answer here is 3. By multiplying 46 and 3 together, we get 138. We can place this value under the first number and subtract. Here we get $164 - 138 = 26$ and bring down the next digit (6). We now consider how many times 46 goes into 266. This gives 5, since $46 \times 5 = 230$. When we place this value under the first number and subtract, we get 36. We bring down the next digit (8) and repeat this procedure. We now consider how many times 46 goes into 368. This gives 8, since $46 \times 8 = 368$. If we place this value under the first number and subtract, we get 0. There is no remainder in this problem.

(c) 15,799 ÷ 61

$$61\overline{)15799} \longrightarrow 61\overline{)\overset{2}{15799}} \longrightarrow$$
$$-\,122$$
$$\overline{359}$$

$$\longrightarrow 61\overline{)\overset{25}{15799}} \longrightarrow 61\overline{)\overset{259}{15799}}$$
$$-\,122 \qquad\qquad -\,122$$
$$\overline{359} \qquad\qquad \overline{359}$$
$$-\,305 \qquad\qquad -\,305$$
$$\overline{549} \qquad\qquad \overline{549}$$
$$\qquad\qquad\qquad -\,549$$
$$\qquad\qquad\qquad \overline{0}$$

Since it is not possible for 61 to go into 1 or 15, we consider how many times 61 goes into 157. Our answer here is 2. By multiplying 61 and 2 together, we get 122. We can place this value under the first number and subtract. Here we get 157 − 122 = 35 and bring down the next digit (9). We now consider how many times 61 goes into 359. This gives 5, since 61 × 5 = 305. When we place this value under the first number and subtract, we get 54. We bring down the next digit (9) and repeat this procedure. We now consider how many times 61 goes into 549. This gives 9, since 61 × 9 = 549. If we place this value under the first number and subtract, we get 0. There is no remainder in this problem.

(d) 9,625 ÷ 21 0

$$21\overline{)9625} \longrightarrow 21\overline{)\overset{4}{9625}}$$
$$-\,84$$
$$\overline{122}$$

$$\longrightarrow 21\overline{)\overset{45}{9625}} \longrightarrow 21\overline{)\overset{458\ R\ 7}{9625}}$$
$$-\,84 \qquad\qquad\quad -\,84$$
$$\overline{122} \qquad\qquad\quad \overline{122}$$
$$-\,105 \qquad\qquad -\,105$$
$$\overline{175} \qquad\qquad\quad \overline{175}$$
$$\qquad\qquad\qquad -\,168$$
$$\qquad\qquad\qquad \overline{7}$$

We begin by considering how many times 21 goes into 96. Our answer is 4. Since $21 \times 4 = 84$, we can place this value under the first number and subtract. After subtracting and bringing down the next digit, we get 122. We now consider how many times 21 goes into 122. Our answer here is 5. Since $21 \times 5 = 105$, we can place this value under the first number and subtract. After subtracting and bringing down the next digit, we get 175. We now consider how many times 21 goes into 175. Our answer is 8. Since $21 \times 8 = 168$, we can place this value under the first number and subtract. This subtraction result is 7. Since we have no more digits in the first number, this result (7) becomes our remainder. Our overall answer is 458 R 7.

Drill: Division of Whole Numbers

Divide the following numbers.

1. $7,912 \div 17$

2. $7,799 \div 25$

3. $53,920 \div 43$

4. $122,444 \div 128$

Answers to Drill Questions

1. 465 R 7

$$
\begin{array}{r}
4 \\
17\overline{)7912} \\
-68 \\
\hline
111
\end{array}
\longrightarrow
\begin{array}{r}
46 \\
17\overline{)7912} \\
-68 \\
\hline
111 \\
-102 \\
\hline
92
\end{array}
$$

$$
\longrightarrow
\begin{array}{r}
465\ R\ 7 \\
17\overline{)7912} \\
-68 \\
\hline
111 \\
-102 \\
\hline
92 \\
-85 \\
\hline
7
\end{array}
$$

2. 311 R 24

$$
\begin{array}{r}
3 \\
25\overline{\smash{)}7799} \\
-75 \\
\hline
29
\end{array}
\longrightarrow
\begin{array}{r}
31 \\
25\overline{\smash{)}7799} \\
-75 \\
\hline
29 \\
-25 \\
\hline
49
\end{array}
$$

$$
\longrightarrow
\begin{array}{r}
311 \text{ R } 24 \\
25\overline{\smash{)}7799} \\
-75 \\
\hline
29 \\
-25 \\
\hline
49 \\
-25 \\
\hline
4
\end{array}
$$

3. 1,253 R 41

$$
\begin{array}{r}
1 \\
43\overline{\smash{)}53920} \\
-43 \\
\hline
109
\end{array}
\longrightarrow
\begin{array}{r}
12 \\
43\overline{\smash{)}53920} \\
-43 \\
\hline
109 \\
-86 \\
\hline
232
\end{array}
$$

$$
\longrightarrow
\begin{array}{r}
125 \\
43\overline{\smash{)}53920} \\
-43 \\
\hline
109 \\
-86 \\
\hline
232 \\
-215 \\
\hline
170
\end{array}
\longrightarrow
\begin{array}{r}
1253 \text{ R } 41 \\
43\overline{\smash{)}53920} \\
-43 \\
\hline
109 \\
-86 \\
\hline
232 \\
-215 \\
\hline
170 \\
-129 \\
\hline
41
\end{array}
$$

4.   956 R 76

$$
\begin{array}{r}
9 \\
128 \overline{)122444} \\
-1152 \\
\hline
724
\end{array}
\qquad \longrightarrow \qquad
\begin{array}{r}
95 \\
128 \overline{)122444} \\
-1152 \\
\hline
724 \\
-640 \\
\hline
844
\end{array}
$$

$$
\longrightarrow
\begin{array}{r}
956 \text{ R } 76 \\
128 \overline{)122444} \\
-1152 \\
\hline
724 \\
-640 \\
\hline
844 \\
-768 \\
\hline
76
\end{array}
$$

II. FRACTIONS

INTRODUCTION TO FRACTIONS

As we saw in the last section, whole numbers are just one type of number that can be discussed. Another kind of number is called a fraction. Fractions are expressions that are the quotient of a number expressed a/b (where b does not equal zero). An example of a fraction would be 1/2. Instead of dividing out the numbers and getting a decimal, we leave it in a "fraction format." The number on the top part of the fraction (1 in this case) is referred to as the **numerator**. The bottom part of a fraction (2 in this example) is called the **denominator**. Depending on the operation that we are looking at, each of these parts of a fraction has a significant role.

Example

In the fraction below, determine whether the 5 appears in the numerator or denominator.

$$\frac{3}{5}$$

In this example, the 5 appears in the bottom part of the fraction. From our discussion above, we know that this is the denominator.

Any whole number can be made into a fraction by putting it over 1. We can place the whole number in the numerator of a fraction and place a 1 in the denominator. At this point, we might have a hard time seeing why this would be of any importance. But as we proceed through this section, we will come across examples where this will be needed.

Example

Write the following whole number as a fraction.

3

In order to write this number as a fraction, we can write this value (3) in the numerator and place a one in the denominator. This gives us 3/1.

If we are considering a fraction where the numerator (top part of the fraction) is smaller than the denominator (bottom part of a fraction), then we have a number that is less than one. Some examples are 1/2, 3/9, and 7/11. In each of the above cases, the numerator is less than the denominator. Some of these fractions can be **reduced**. Instead of working with 3/9, we could consider 1/3. Even though these fractions look different, they have the same value. If we would divide each of them out, we would get exactly the same value (0.3333). How did we do this? By looking at the top and the bottom of 3/9, we see that both the numerator and denominator have a similarity. Both of them can be divided by 3. If we divide 3 by 3 and 9 by 3, we would get 1 and 3. These are the same values that we stated above.

$$\frac{3}{9} \quad \begin{matrix} \rightarrow 3 \div 3 = 1 \rightarrow \\ \rightarrow 9 \div 3 = 3 \rightarrow \end{matrix} \quad \frac{1}{3}$$

If we have any fractions where the top and bottom have this type of similarity, we know that we can reduce them. By reducing a fraction, we are rewriting it with smaller values in the numerator and denominator.

Examples

Reduce the following fractions.

(a) $\frac{4}{8}$

In this example, we have a 4 in the numerator and an 8 in the denominator. We can see that they are both divisible by 4. If we divide the numerator and denominator by 4, we get 1/2. Below are the detailed steps.

$$\frac{4}{8} \quad \begin{matrix} \rightarrow 4 \div 4 = 1 \rightarrow \\ \rightarrow 8 \div 8 = 2 \rightarrow \end{matrix} \quad \frac{1}{2}$$

(b) $\frac{5}{20}$

In this example, we have a 5 in the numerator and a 20 in the denominator. We can see that they are both divisible by 5. If we divide the numerator and denominator by 5, we get 1/4. Below are the steps needed for this reduction.

$$\frac{5}{20} \rightarrow \frac{5 \div 5 = 1 \rightarrow}{20 \div 5 = 4 \rightarrow} \frac{1}{4}$$

Example

Simplify the following fraction.

$$\frac{86}{86}$$

In this example, we have an 86 in the numerator and denominator. These values can be divided by 86. This gives us 1/1. Since any whole number can be written as a fraction by placing it over one, we can rewrite this fraction as 1. Below are the details needed to get this answer.

$$\frac{86}{86} \rightarrow \frac{86 \div 86 = 1 \rightarrow}{86 \div 86 = 1 \rightarrow} \frac{1}{1} = 1$$

If the numerator is greater than the denominator, we have a fraction greater than one. These types of fractions are also referred to as **improper fractions** and can be rewritten as **mixed numbers**. A mixed number is a whole number combined with a fraction. Instead of writing the number 11/6, we can also think of it as $1^5/_6$. At first glance this seems strange. But, as we considered above, when the numerator and denominator match, we get 1. If we subtract 6 from 11, we get 5. This accounts for the 5 appearing as the numerator of the fractional part of the mixed number. Notice that the denominator of the fractional part has the same value as the denominator of the original fraction. In the example below, we will discuss converting improper fractions into mixed numbers.

There is another way of approaching improper fractions that some students may find easier.

Take 11/6 from the above example. What we want to do here is take the denominator of the improper fraction and divide it into the numerator. In other words, we want to see how many 6's are in 11. We see that 6 goes into 11 once, with a remainder of 5 (there is only one 6 in 11 with 5 left over). We then place the 5 over the original denominator, 6, and place the 1 (for the amount of times 6 goes into 11) in front of 5/6, to get the mixed number $1^5/_6$.

Examples

Convert these fractions into mixed numbers.

(a) $\dfrac{7}{4}$

In this example, we can see that the numerator is larger than the denominator. This tells us that this fraction has a value larger than 1. By subtracting the denominator from the numerator $(7 - 4 = 3)$, we will get the numerator of the fractional part of our mixed number. Therefore, another way of saying 7/4 is $1^3/_4$.

If we divide, we see 7 is divisible by 4 once with 3 left over or $1^3/_4$.

(b) $\dfrac{9}{7}$

In this example, we can see that the numerator is larger than the denominator. This tells us that this fraction has a value larger than 1. By subtracting the denominator from the numerator (9 − 7 = 2), we will get the numerator of the fractional part of our mixed number. Therefore, another way of saying 9/7 is $1^2/_7$.

Dividing 9 by 7 will give us 1, with 2 left over, or $1^2/_7$.

Since we are able to rewrite improper fractions as mixed numbers, it would make sense that we could also go the other way. Changing mixed numbers into improper fractions is very similar to the above discussion, but in reverse. The next example will demonstrate how this can be done.

Examples

Write the following mixed numbers as improper fractions.

(a) $1\dfrac{1}{2}$

Before, we subtracted the denominator from the numerator to get the fractional part of our answer. In this case, we want to do the opposite. Here we want to think of the whole number 1 as 2/2 (It should be noted that this method only works when the whole number of the mixed number is one). We know that these values are equal. Therefore, by adding the numerator and denominator together (1 + 2 = 3), we will get the numerator of our improper fraction. Another way of saying $1^1/_2$ would be 3/2. Notice that the denominator of the fractional part becomes the denominator of the improper fraction.

Another way to get this answer is to multiply the denominator by the whole number and add that sum to the numerator to get our new numerator. Leaving out the whole number, and keeping the original denominator, we get the improper fraction. Take $1^1/_2$ from above. We multiply 2 and 1 and get 2. We then add this number to our current numerator to get 3. Placing the 3 in the numerator and the 2 in the denominator, we have 3/2.

(b) $2\dfrac{4}{5}$

In this case, we are dealing with a number that has a whole part larger than 1. In order to handle this problem, we can apply the above procedure twice. Each of these procedures will convert one whole number into the corresponding fractional part. First, we want to think of the $2\dfrac{4}{5}$ as 10/5. We know that these values are equal. Therefore, by adding the numerator and denominator together (4 + 10 = 14), we will get the numerator of our improper fraction. Another way of saying $2^4/_5$ would be $1^9/_5$. We can replace the remaining one with its fraction part. We again think of 1 as 5/5. By adding the numerator and denominator together (9 + 5 = 14), we will get the numerator of our improper fraction. Another way of saying $1^9/_5$ would be 14/5. Therefore, we can write $2^4/_5$ as 14/5. Notice that the denominator of the fractional part remains the denominator in the improper fraction.

In previous sections, we discussed the ideas of a number being less than another, two numbers being equal, and a number being greater than another. In the next section we will also discuss this notion using fractions.

Drill: Introduction to Fractions

In the fractions below, determine whether the even number appears in the numerator or denominator.

1. $\dfrac{7}{8}$

2. $\dfrac{10}{13}$

Write the numbers below as fractions.

3. 43

4. 152

Reduce the following fractions as much as possible.

5. $\dfrac{27}{49}$

6. $\dfrac{12}{18}$

Convert these fractions into mixed numbers.

7. $\dfrac{26}{19}$

8. $\dfrac{18}{7}$

Write the following mixed numbers as improper fractions.

9. $2\dfrac{3}{14}$

10. $3\dfrac{1}{2}$

Answers to Drill Questions

1. Denominator

2. Numerator

3. $\dfrac{43}{1}$

4. $\dfrac{152}{1}$

5. $\dfrac{27}{49}$. Cannot be reduced.

6. $\dfrac{2}{3}$

$$\dfrac{12}{18}\dfrac{(\div 6)}{(\div 6)}=\dfrac{2}{3}$$

7. $1\dfrac{7}{19}$

$$\dfrac{26}{19}=1\dfrac{7}{19}$$

8. $2\dfrac{4}{7}$

$$\dfrac{18}{7}=2\dfrac{4}{7}$$

9. $\dfrac{31}{14}$

$$2\dfrac{3}{14}=\dfrac{31}{14}$$

10. $\dfrac{7}{2}$

$$3\dfrac{1}{2}=\dfrac{7}{2}$$

ADDITION OF FRACTIONS

Now that we understand what fractions and mixed numbers are, we want to discuss adding, subtracting, multiplying, and dividing. This section looks at addition. In the following sections, we will address the other operations. We will discover, as we have in previous sections, that working with fractions has similarities to working with whole numbers. These topics are not exactly the same, but we will see how a good understanding of whole numbers will help us here.

The first case of adding fractions that we will consider will be when the denominators are equal. In this case, we just need to add the numerators together and bring the common denominator along for the ride. As we saw in our discussion on mixed numbers, the denominator will play a very important role in addition.

Example

Add the following fractions.

$$\frac{5}{12}+\frac{1}{12}$$

In this example, we notice that the denominators of these fractions have the same value (12). This being the case, we just need to add the numerators together (5 + 1 = 6) and bring the denominator (12) along. Therefore, our answer is 6/12. Below are the detailed steps needed to complete this problem.

$$\frac{5}{12}+\frac{1}{12}=\frac{5+1}{12}=\frac{6}{12}$$

But is this our final answer? Recall our discussions in the previous section. We saw that some fractions can be reduced. In our answer above, both the numerator and denominator can be reduced by 6. When this is accomplished, our final answer will be 1/2. Below are the detailed steps.

$$\frac{6}{12} \rightarrow \begin{matrix} 6 \div 6 = 1 \\ 12 \div 6 = 2 \end{matrix} \rightarrow \frac{1}{2}$$

We now need to look at problems where the denominators are not the same. In order to add fractions, we need to transform the denominator in each fraction into a common value. One way of accomplishing this is by taking the denominators and multiplying them together. We can easily transform each denominator into this value, but in most cases this gives an extremely large value. An example of this would be 6/12 + 7/18. If we multiply the denominators together (12 × 18), we would get 216. This value would work as a common denominator, but is there a smaller value that would also work?

The smallest value possible that could be used is referred to as the **Lowest Common Denominator** or **LCD**. Instead of using large numbers, the LCD allows us to use the smallest value possible. Sometimes this is still a large value but, in most cases, the value we are working with is much more tolerable. The big question now becomes how do we find the LCD. The traditional way to find the LCD is to form factor trees of each denominator and then compare the factors. If we stick with the above problem (6/12 + 7/18), we would break down 12 and 18 into a list of prime numbers multiplied together.

$$
\begin{array}{cc}
12 & 18 \\
\wedge & \wedge \\
2 \times 6 & 2 \times 9 \\
/ \quad \wedge & / \quad \wedge \\
2 \times 2 \times 3 & 2 \times 3 \times 3
\end{array}
$$

In each level of these factor trees, we still have 12 or 18, depending on which tree we are considering. Also, in each level we are breaking down parts of the original number. We began by breaking 12 into 2×6. Since 2 is already prime, we can leave it alone. The 6, on the other hand, is not prime and can be broken down into 2×3. By combining everything together, we get $2 \times 2 \times 3$. We followed similar thinking to get the above factor tree for 18.

We now need to compare the last line of each factor tree. We begin by letting the LCD equal the bottom line of the first factor tree. In this example, we would get LCD = $2 \times 2 \times 3$. We now compare each factor in the bottom line of the other factor tree to this LCD and see what is already there and what needs to be included. We first compare the 2 to the LCD that we already have (LCD = $\underline{2} \times 2 \times 3$). Since we already have a 2 in our LCD line (the underlined 2 in our LCD statement), we do not need to include it again. Now, we compare the next factor (3) to our LCD line. Since we already have a 3 in our LCD line (LCD = $2 \times 2 \times \underline{3}$), we don't need to include it again. The last factor we need to compare to our LCD line is another 3. This time, when we compare the 3 to our LCD line, we see that we have to include another 3 in our LCD line. This is because we have already accounted for the underlined 3. Therefore, our LCD would be $2 \times 2 \times 3 \times 3$ or 36. Even though this value is a bit large, it is nowhere near the 216 that we discussed. Knowing this, we would then transform each fraction into one that has a 36 in the denominator. Once this is done, we can add the fractions.

Even though this method works, we hope that there is an easier way. Surprisingly, there is yet another method that can be used. The main point of this method is reducing a special fraction called the **test fraction**. This test fraction is made up of the denominators in the original problem. Since denominators play such an active role in adding fractions, we want to get them involved as soon as possible. If we consider the problem from above, 6/12 + 7/18, our test fraction would be 12/18. We just put one denominator on the top and the other on the bottom of our test fraction. Can this fraction be reduced? Our answer here is "Yes!" Both 12 and 18 can be divided by 6 evenly. This gives 2/3.

$$
\frac{12}{18} \quad
\begin{array}{l}
\rightarrow 12 \div 6 = 2 \rightarrow \\
\rightarrow 18 \div 6 = 3 \rightarrow
\end{array}
\quad \frac{2}{3}
$$

We can now take this reduced test fraction to get the Lowest Common Denominator (LCD) to appear in both fractions. Since the 2 "corresponds" with the 12 (they are both in the numerator of equal fractions), we want to place this value in both the numerator **and** denominator of the fraction that does **not** have 12 in the denominator, that is 7/18. Therefore,

$$\frac{6}{12}+\frac{7}{18}=\frac{6}{12}+\frac{7\times2}{18\times2}$$

Now we can continue this process by looking at the denominators of the test fraction. Since 3 "corresponds" with the 18 (they are both in the denominator of equal fractions), we want to place this value in both the numerator **and** denominator of the fraction that does **not** have 18 in the denominator, that is, 6/12. Therefore,

$$\frac{6}{12}+\frac{7\times2}{18\times2}=\frac{6\times3}{12\times3}+\frac{7\times2}{18\times2}$$

At first glance, it does not seem to help in any way. But, if we simplify both of these fractions, we will get

$$\frac{6\times3}{12\times3}+\frac{7\times2}{18\times2}=\frac{18}{36}+\frac{14}{36}$$

At this point, we notice the denominators are the same. The surprising thing is that this value (36) is the LCD. Even though this method appears lengthy, all we have to do is reduce our test fraction. Here, we don't need to worry about factor trees (or anything like this). Now that the denominators are the same, we can add the numerators. If we complete this problem, we will get

$$\frac{18}{36}+\frac{14}{36}=\frac{18+14}{36}=\frac{32}{36}$$

Even though we have simplified these fractions, this is not our final answer. As with our test fraction, this answer can also be reduced.

$$\frac{32}{36}\rightarrow\begin{array}{l}32\div4\rightarrow\\36\div4\rightarrow\end{array}\frac{8}{9}$$

At last, we have our answer. Thus, 6/12 + 7/18 = 8/9. Both methods discussed above will always work. Since most students prefer the second one, this will be the one stressed here.

Example

Add the following fractions.

(a) $\dfrac{3}{10}+\dfrac{2}{15}$

Our test fraction in this example is 10/15. This is a must here because the denominators do not match. Our test fraction can be reduced to find out what value must be used for the LCD.

$$\frac{10}{15}\rightarrow\begin{array}{l}10\div5=2\rightarrow\\15\div5=3\rightarrow\end{array}\frac{2}{3}$$

Since the 2 corresponds with the 10, we multiply the numerator and the denominator of the fraction that does not contain the 10 in the denominator by 2.

$$\frac{3}{10} + \frac{2}{15} = \frac{3}{10} + \frac{2 \times 2}{15 \times 2}$$

Likewise, since 3 corresponds to 15, we multiply the numerator and the denominator of the fraction that does not contain the 15 in the denominator by 3.

$$\frac{3}{10} + \frac{2 \times 2}{15 \times 2} = \frac{3 \times 3}{10 \times 3} + \frac{2 \times 2}{15 \times 2}$$

We simplify both of these fractions and see that the denominators now match. This being the case, we are able to add the numerators together.

$$\frac{9}{30} + \frac{4}{30} = \frac{9+4}{30} = \frac{13}{30}$$

Since this answer cannot be reduced or rewritten as a mixed number, we are done with this problem.

(b) $\dfrac{5}{6} + \dfrac{3}{8}$

In order to add these fractions, the denominators must have the same value. To begin with they do not, but we can create our test fraction and use it to determine what value should be used. Here, our test fraction is 6/8.

$$\frac{6}{8} \begin{array}{l} \rightarrow 6 \div 2 = 3 \rightarrow \\ \rightarrow 8 \div 2 = 4 \rightarrow \end{array} \frac{3}{4}$$

Since 3 "corresponds" with the 6 (they are both in the numerator of equal fractions), we want to place this value in both the numerator **and** denominator of the fraction that does **not** have 6 in the denominator. That is, the fraction that has the 8.

$$\frac{5}{6} + \frac{3}{8} = \frac{5}{6} + \frac{3 \times 3}{8 \times 3}$$

Since 4 "corresponds" with the 8 (they are both in the denominator of equal fractions), we want to place this value in both the numerator **and** denominator of the fraction that does **not** have 8 in the denominator. That is, the fraction that has the 6.

$$\frac{5}{6} + \frac{3 \times 3}{8 \times 3} = \frac{5 \times 4}{6 \times 4} + \frac{3 \times 3}{8 \times 3}$$

If we now simplify both of these fractions, we will get 20/24 + 9/24. Since the denominators are finally the same, we can add the two fractions. This will give

$$\frac{20}{24} + \frac{9}{24} = \frac{20+9}{24} = \frac{29}{24}$$

Since our numerator is larger than the denominator, we know that this fraction is larger than one and can be written as a mixed number. By subtracting the denominator from the numerator

(29 − 24 = 5), we will get the numerator of the fractional part of our mixed number. Therefore, another way of saying 29/24 is 1⁵/₂₄.

Now that we are "experts" at adding fractions, we want to consider adding mixed numbers. As we saw earlier in this section, we can rewrite mixed numbers as improper fractions. With this in mind, we want to convert the mixed numbers into fractions, add the fractions as we did above, and then convert our answer back into a mixed number if needed. The examples below show this idea in more detail.

Examples

Add the following numbers.

(a) $1\frac{1}{2}+1\frac{2}{3}$

We begin by converting both of these mixed numbers into improper fractions. This would change the problem into 3/2 + 5/3. Our test fraction in this example is 2/3. Since we cannot reduce this fraction, we have 2/3 = 2/3. We now know that we can multiply the top and bottom of the fraction containing a 3 in the denominator by 2. Likewise, we can multiply the top and bottom of the fraction containing a 2 in the denominator by 3.

$$\frac{3}{2}+\frac{5}{3}=\frac{3\times3}{2\times3}+\frac{5\times2}{3\times2}=\frac{9}{6}+\frac{10}{6}$$

Now that we have matching denominators, we can add the numerators. This gives us the following:

$$\frac{9}{6}+\frac{10}{6}=\frac{9+10}{6}=\frac{19}{6}$$

Again, in this example, our answer is an improper fraction. We know this since the top of our fraction is larger than the bottom. If we subtract the denominator from the numerator (19 − 6 = 13), we see that 19/6 equals 1¹³/₆. We can continue this process a few more times and get 3¹/₆. Therefore, 19/6 is the same as 3¹/₆.

(b) $3\frac{3}{4}+1\frac{5}{6}$

We can begin by converting both of these mixed numbers into improper fractions. This will change the problem into 15/4 + 11/6. Our test fraction in this example is 4/6. Reducing this fraction, we have 4/6 = 2/3. We now know that we can multiply the top and bottom of the fraction containing a 6 in the denominator by 2. Likewise, we can multiply the top and bottom of the fraction containing a 4 in the denominator by 3.

$$\frac{15}{4}+\frac{11}{6}=\frac{15\times3}{4\times3}+\frac{11\times2}{6\times2}$$
$$=\frac{45}{12}+\frac{22}{12}$$

Now that we have matching denominators, we can add the numerators. This gives us the following:

$$\frac{45}{12} + \frac{22}{12} = \frac{45+22}{12} = \frac{67}{12}$$

Again, in this example, our answer is an improper fraction. We know this because the top of our fraction is larger than the bottom. If we divide 67 by 12 we get $5^7/_{12}$ as our answer.

We now want to consider some unusual cases. In the examples below we will look at problems involving fractions and whole numbers, as well as problems with more than two fractions. We will see that in both cases our work is very similar to what we have already done.

Examples

Add the following numbers.

(a) $\frac{1}{2} + 3$

When adding fractions, we know that the denominators must match. In this example, the second number is not a fraction. In order to overcome this situation, we can rewrite this number as a fraction by placing it over 1 (as we did in the previous section). Therefore, we get $1/2 + 3/1$. Now, we need to get the bottoms of these fractions to be the same value. In this case, the LCD is 2. Since the first fraction already has 2 in its denominator, we will leave it alone. In the second fraction, we have to multiply the denominator by 2 to get our LCD to appear. To keep this fraction equal, we must also multiply the numerator by the same value (2).

$$\frac{1}{2} + \frac{3}{1} = \frac{1}{2} + \frac{3\times2}{1\times2} = \frac{1}{2} + \frac{6}{2}$$

Since the denominators are both 2, we can now add the fractions.

$$\frac{1}{2} + \frac{6}{2} = \frac{1+6}{2} = \frac{7}{2}$$

This answer is an improper fraction and we can simplify it to get $3^1/_2$.

(b) $\frac{1}{2} + \frac{3}{4} + \frac{7}{8}$

As with adding two fractions, in order to add three fractions, we also need a common denominator throughout the problem. It is always a good idea to use the LCD whenever possible. This keeps our numbers somewhat small. Our LCD in this example is 8. In order to get an 8 in the denominator of the first fraction, we must multiply both the top and bottom of that fraction by 4. To get an 8 to appear in the denominator of the second fraction, we must multiply the top and bottom of that fraction by 2. Since the third fraction already has 8 appearing in the denominator, we do not need to do anything with this fraction. In the first and second fractions, the numerator is also multiplied by the same value we used in the denominator so that the value of the fractions stays the same. Therefore,

$$\frac{1}{2}+\frac{3}{4}+\frac{7}{8}=\frac{1\times4}{2\times4}+\frac{3\times2}{4\times2}+\frac{7}{8}$$

We can now simplify these fractions and add them together.

$$\frac{4}{8}+\frac{6}{8}+\frac{7}{8}=\frac{4+6+7}{8}=\frac{17}{8}$$

Since the top of the fraction is larger than the bottom, we know that we have an improper fraction. If we subtract the denominator from the numerator, we can see that 17/8 is $2\frac{1}{8}$.

Drill: Addition of Fractions

Add the following fractions.

1. $\frac{15}{31}+\frac{9}{31}$

2. $\frac{5}{7}+\frac{6}{7}$

Add the following numbers.

3. $6\frac{4}{15}+3\frac{1}{60}$

4. $\frac{4}{7}+6$

5. $\frac{3}{4}+\frac{1}{8}+\frac{7}{16}$

Answers to Drill Questions

1. $\frac{24}{31}$

$$\frac{15}{31}+\frac{9}{31}=\frac{24}{31}$$

2. $1\frac{4}{7}$

$$\frac{5}{7}+\frac{6}{7}=\frac{11}{7} \text{ or } 1\frac{4}{7}$$

3. $9\frac{17}{60}$

$$6\frac{4}{15}+3\frac{1}{60}=6\frac{16}{60}+3\frac{1}{60}$$
$$=9\frac{17}{60}$$

4. $6\frac{4}{7}$

$$\frac{4}{7}+6=6\frac{4}{7}$$

Just combine the whole number with the proper fraction.

5. $1\frac{5}{16}$

$$\frac{3}{4}+\frac{1}{8}+\frac{7}{16}=\frac{12}{16}+\frac{2}{16}+\frac{7}{16}$$
$$=\frac{21}{16}=1\frac{5}{16}$$

SUBTRACTION OF FRACTIONS

As we saw before, addition and subtraction are not that much different. In order to subtract fractions, we need to have denominators that are the same. Our test fraction idea that we used when adding fractions will also be used here.

Example

Subtract the following numbers.

$$\frac{21}{25}-\frac{16}{25}$$

We can subtract the numerators right away since the denominators are already the same value. This gives

$$\frac{21}{25}-\frac{16}{25}=\frac{21-16}{25}=\frac{5}{25}$$

If we look closely at our answer, we see that it can be reduced.

$$\frac{5}{25} \quad \begin{array}{l} \rightarrow \quad 5 \div 5 = 1 \rightarrow \\ \rightarrow 25 \div 5 = 5 \rightarrow \end{array} \quad \frac{1}{5}$$

Therefore, our final answer is $\frac{1}{5}$.

Examples

Subtract the following fractions.

(a) $\quad \dfrac{5}{6} - \dfrac{1}{8}$

The first thing we need to do here is to get the denominators to have the same value. We can create our test fraction from the denominators in the original problem. This is 6/8 in this case. We can reduce this fraction to get 3/4. Since 3 corresponds to 6, we multiply the top and bottom of the fraction containing the 8 in the denominator by 3. Since 4 corresponds to 8, we multiply the top and bottom of the fraction containing the 6 in the denominator by 4.

$$\frac{5}{6} - \frac{1}{8} = \frac{5 \times 4}{6 \times 4} - \frac{1 \times 3}{8 \times 3}$$

If we simplify these fractions, we can subtract the numerators.

$$\frac{20}{24} - \frac{3}{24} = \frac{20 - 3}{24} = \frac{17}{24}$$

Since this fraction cannot be reduced, our final answer is 17/24.

(b) $\quad \dfrac{7}{12} - \dfrac{5}{9}$

First we need to use our test fraction idea to change the denominators to the same value. In this case, our test fraction would be 12/9 or 4/3 if we reduce it. Since the 4 corresponds to the 12, we multiply the top and bottom of the fraction containing the 9 by 4. Since the 3 corresponds to the 9, we multiply the top and bottom of the fraction containing 12 by 3.

$$\frac{7}{12} - \frac{5}{9} = \frac{7 \times 3}{12 \times 3} - \frac{5 \times 4}{9 \times 4}$$

Next, we can simplify these fractions and then subtract the numerators. This gives us

$$\frac{21}{36} - \frac{20}{36} - \frac{21 - 20}{36} = \frac{1}{36}$$

Since this fraction cannot be reduced, our final answer is 1/36.

Examples

Subtract the following numbers.

(a) $3\frac{1}{2} - 2\frac{3}{4}$

When dealing with mixed numbers, the first step that we want to do is convert everything into improper fractions. In this example, our problem becomes 7/2 – 11/4. Now we need to get the denominators to have the same value. This can be done using our test fraction idea. Our test fraction is 2/4, or 1/2 if we reduce it. Since the 1 corresponds to the 2, we multiply the top and bottom of the fraction that contains 4 by 1. Since the 2 corresponds to the 4, we multiply the top and bottom of the fraction containing 2 by 2. Therefore,

$$\frac{7}{2} - \frac{11}{4} = \frac{7 \times 2}{2 \times 2} - \frac{11 \times 1}{4 \times 1}$$

If we simplify these fractions, we can then subtract the numerators. Thus,

$$\frac{14}{4} - \frac{11}{4} = \frac{14 - 11}{4} = \frac{3}{4}$$

Since this fraction cannot be reduced, our final answer is 3/4.

(b) $2\frac{1}{6} - 1\frac{7}{8}$

When dealing with mixed numbers, the first step that we want to do is convert everything into improper fractions. In this example, our problem becomes 13/6 – 15/8. Now we need to get the denominators to have the same value. This can be done using our test fraction idea. Our test fraction is 6/8, or 3/4 if we reduce it. Since the 3 corresponds to the 6, we multiply the top and bottom of the fraction that contains 8 by 3. Since the 4 corresponds to the 8, we multiply the top and bottom of the fraction containing 6 by 4. Therefore,

$$\frac{13}{6} - \frac{15}{8} = \frac{13 \times 4}{6 \times 4} - \frac{15 \times 3}{8 \times 3}$$

If we simplify these fractions, we can then subtract the numerators. Thus,

$$\frac{52}{24} - \frac{45}{24} = \frac{52 - 45}{24} = \frac{7}{24}$$

Since this fraction cannot be reduced, our final answer is 7/24.

Drill: Subtraction of Fractions

Subtract the following numbers.

1. $\frac{11}{36} - \frac{5}{24}$

2. $\dfrac{2}{3} - \dfrac{26}{51}$

3. $2\dfrac{1}{3} - 1\dfrac{7}{9}$

4. $5\dfrac{1}{2} - 2\dfrac{5}{16}$

5. $7\dfrac{19}{36} - 5\dfrac{11}{24}$

Answers to Drill Questions

1. $\dfrac{7}{72}$

$$\dfrac{11}{36} - \dfrac{5}{24} = \dfrac{22}{72} - \dfrac{15}{72} - \dfrac{7}{72}$$

Convert each fraction to a denominator of 72, which is the lowest common denominator of 24 and 36.

2. $\dfrac{8}{51}$

$$\dfrac{2}{3} - \dfrac{26}{51} = \dfrac{34}{51} - \dfrac{26}{51} = \dfrac{8}{51}$$

Convert 2/3 to a fraction with a denominator of 51. Subtract in the numerator.

3. $\dfrac{5}{9}$

$$2\dfrac{1}{3} - 1\dfrac{7}{9} = 2\dfrac{3}{9} - 1\dfrac{7}{9}$$

$$= 1\dfrac{12}{9} - 1\dfrac{7}{9} = \dfrac{5}{9}$$

Convert first fractional part to ninths. Change $2^3/_9$ to $1^{12}/_9$. Subtract whole parts and fractional parts separately.

4. $3\dfrac{3}{16}$

$$5\dfrac{1}{2} - 2\dfrac{5}{16} = 5\dfrac{8}{16} - 2\dfrac{5}{16} = 3\dfrac{3}{16}$$

Convert first fractional part to sixteenths. Subtract whole parts and fractional parts separately.

5. $2\dfrac{5}{72}$

$$7\dfrac{19}{36} - 5\dfrac{11}{24} = 7\dfrac{38}{72} - 5\dfrac{33}{72} = 2\dfrac{5}{72}$$

Convert both fractional parts to a denominator of 72, which is the lowest common denominator of 24 and 36. Subtract whole parts and fractional parts separately.

MULTIPLICATION OF FRACTIONS

Now that we understand adding and subtracting fractions, we want to switch gears and discuss multiplying fractions. Even though this topic may sound more involved, it is actually easier. In multiplication, there is no need for a Lowest Common Denominator (LCD). Multiplying fractions is one of the most intuitive operations. For the most part, we just multiply straight across. We multiply the numerators together to get the resulting "answer" numerator, and then multiply the denominators together to get the resulting "answer" denominator. We can then reduce this "answer" (if possible) to get our final answer. As we move through this section, we see a few "short-cuts" that can be used to make the problems more tolerable. Initially, we will just multiply straight across.

Examples

Multiply the following numbers.

(a) $\dfrac{1}{2} \times \dfrac{1}{3}$

When multiplying fractions, we just multiply straight across. We multiply the numerators and then the denominators. In this example, we get $1 \times 1 = 1$ in the numerator and $2 \times 3 = 6$ in the denominator.

$$\dfrac{1}{2} \times \dfrac{1}{3} = \dfrac{1 \times 1}{2 \times 3} = \dfrac{1}{6}$$

Since $^1/_6$ cannot be reduced, our final answer is 1/6.

(b) $\dfrac{4}{7} \times \dfrac{1}{2}$

When multiplying fractions, we just multiply straight across. We multiply the numerators and then the denominators. In this example, we get $4 \times 1 = 4$ in the numerator and $7 \times 2 = 14$ in the denominator.

$$\dfrac{4}{7} \times \dfrac{1}{2} = \dfrac{4 \times 1}{7 \times 2} = \dfrac{4}{14}$$

Notice that this fraction can be reduced. Both the top and the bottom are divisible by 2.

$$\frac{4}{14} \quad \begin{array}{l} \rightarrow 4 \div 2 = 2 \rightarrow \\ \rightarrow 14 \div 2 = 7 \rightarrow \end{array} \quad \frac{2}{7}$$

Therefore, our final answer is 2/7.

Even though the method described above will always work, there is a short-cut that can help us out. A good example of these special problems is example (b) above. Instead of waiting and reducing at the end of the problem, in some problems we are able to reduce in the beginning and work with smaller numbers. In order to do this, we must have a common factor appearing in both a numerator and a denominator. The difference here is that they do not have to be in the same fraction. As long as one is above the fraction bar, one is below the fraction bar, and the operation between the fractions is multiplication, we can do a type of cancellation. Let us reconsider the above problem.

$$\frac{4}{7} \times \frac{1}{2}$$

Notice that a common factor of 2 appears in the numerator of the first fraction and in the denominator of the second fraction. Two can be divided evenly into both 4 and 2. If we do this cancellation, we replace the 4 with a 2 (4/2) and replace the 2 with a 1 (2/2).

$$\frac{4}{7} \times \frac{1}{2} = \frac{\overset{2}{4}}{7} \times \frac{1}{\underset{1}{2}} = \frac{2}{7} \times \frac{1}{1}$$

After this cancellation has been done, we multiply the fractions together as we talked about earlier.

$$\frac{2}{7} \times \frac{1}{1} = \frac{2 \times 1}{7 \times 1} = \frac{2}{7}$$

Since 2/7 cannot be reduced, our answer this time is 2/7. Notice that in both cases (here and example (b)), we get the same value for our answer.

Examples

Multiply the following numbers. Cancel where possible.

(a) $\dfrac{4}{5} \times \dfrac{3}{8}$

Instead of multiplying straight across, we want to consider if cancellation is possible. In this example, notice the top of the first fraction and the bottom of the second fraction. Four can be divided into both 4 and 8 evenly. Therefore, we get

$$\frac{4}{5} \times \frac{3}{8} = \frac{\overset{1}{4}}{5} \times \frac{3}{\underset{2}{8}} = \frac{1}{5} \times \frac{3}{2}$$

Now that we have cancelled where possible, we can multiply the fractions straight across.

$$\frac{1}{5} \times \frac{3}{2} = \frac{1 \times 3}{5 \times 2} = \frac{3}{10}$$

Since 3/10 cannot be reduced, our final answer is 3/10. Notice in this example, by cancelling first, the numbers we multiply together are smaller and easier to deal with.

(b) $\dfrac{5}{6} \times \dfrac{12}{13}$

Instead of multiplying straight across, we first want to consider if cancellation is possible. In this example, notice the bottom of the first fraction and the top of the second fraction. Six can be divided into both 6 and 12 evenly. Therefore, we get

$$\frac{5}{6} \times \frac{12}{13} = \frac{5}{6} \times \frac{\overset{2}{\cancel{12}}}{13} = \frac{5}{1} \times \frac{2}{13}$$

Now that we have cancelled where possible, we can multiply the fractions straight across.

$$\frac{5}{1} \times \frac{2}{13} = \frac{5 \times 2}{1 \times 13} = \frac{10}{13}$$

Since 10/13 cannot be reduced, our final answer is 10/13.

Now that we understand how to multiply fractions, we want to move our discussion to mixed numbers. As we did in the addition and subtraction sections, we will begin by rewriting the mixed number as an improper fraction. Then we can cancel where possible and finally multiply straight across.

Examples

Multiply the following numbers.

(a) $1\dfrac{1}{2} \times 1\dfrac{1}{3}$

We begin by converting both of these mixed numbers into improper fractions. In this example, we have $3/2 \times 4/3$. Instead of multiplying straight across, we want to consider if cancellation is possible. In this example, notice the top of the first fraction and the bottom of the second fraction. Three can be divided into both 3 and 3 evenly. Also, consider the bottom of the first fraction and the top of the second fraction. Two can be divided into both 2 and 4 evenly. Therefore, we get

$$\frac{3}{2} \times \frac{4}{3} = \frac{\overset{1}{\cancel{3}}}{\underset{1}{\cancel{2}}} \times \frac{\overset{2}{\cancel{4}}}{\underset{1}{\cancel{3}}} = \frac{1}{1} \times \frac{2}{1}$$

Now that we have cancelled where possible, we can multiply the fractions straight across.

$$\frac{1}{1} \times \frac{2}{1} = \frac{1 \times 2}{1 \times 1} = \frac{2}{1}$$

Since we can rewrite 2/1 as 2, our final answer is 2.

(b) $3\frac{3}{4} \times 2\frac{2}{5}$

We begin by converting both of these mixed numbers into improper fractions. In this example, we have $15/4 \times 12/5$. Instead of multiplying straight across, we want to consider if cancellation is possible. In this example, notice the top of the first fraction and the bottom of the second fraction. Five can be divided into both 15 and 5 evenly. Also, consider the bottom of the first fraction and the top of the second fraction. Four can be divided into both 4 and 12 evenly. Therefore, we get

$$\frac{15}{4} \times \frac{12}{5} = \frac{\overset{3}{\cancel{15}}}{\underset{1}{\cancel{4}}} \times \frac{\overset{3}{\cancel{12}}}{\underset{1}{\cancel{5}}} = \frac{3}{1} \times \frac{3}{1}$$

Now that we have cancelled where possible, we can multiply the fractions straight across.

$$\frac{3}{1} \times \frac{3}{1} = \frac{3 \times 3}{1 \times 1} = \frac{9}{1}$$

Since we can rewrite 9/1 as 9, our final answer is 9.

Drill: Multiplication of Fractions

Multiply the following numbers.

1. $\frac{7}{13} \times \frac{3}{14}$

2. $\frac{10}{27} \times \frac{3}{20}$

3. $4\frac{2}{7} \times 5\frac{1}{6}$

4. $7\frac{1}{2} \times 1\frac{1}{3}$

5. $3\frac{4}{5} \times 2\frac{9}{38}$

Answers to Drill Questions

1. $\dfrac{3}{26}$

$$\frac{7}{13}\times\frac{3}{14}=\frac{\overset{1}{\cancel{7}}}{13}\times\frac{3}{\underset{2}{\cancel{14}}}=\frac{3}{26}$$

Divide 7 and 14 by 7 to produce 1 and 2. Multiply the numerators, then multiply the denominators.

2. $\dfrac{1}{18}$

$$\frac{10}{27}\times\frac{3}{20}=\frac{\overset{1}{\cancel{10}}}{\underset{9}{\cancel{27}}}\times\frac{\overset{1}{\cancel{3}}}{\underset{2}{\cancel{20}}}=\frac{1}{18}$$

Divide 10 and 20 by 10 to produce 1 and 2. Divide 3 and 27 by 3 to produce 1 and 9. Multiply the numerators, then multiply the denominators.

3. $22\dfrac{1}{7}$

$$4\frac{2}{7}\times 5\frac{1}{6}=\frac{30}{7}\times\frac{31}{6}$$

$$=\frac{\overset{5}{\cancel{30}}}{7}\times\frac{31}{\underset{1}{\cancel{6}}}=\frac{155}{7}=22\frac{1}{7}$$

Convert mixed fractions to improper fractions. Divide 6 and 30 by 6 to produce 1 and 5. Multiply the numerators, then the denominators. Convert the improper fraction to a mixed fraction.

4. 10

$$7\frac{1}{2}\times 1\frac{1}{3}=\frac{15}{2}\times\frac{4}{3}$$

$$=\frac{\overset{5}{\cancel{15}}}{\underset{1}{\cancel{2}}}\times\frac{\overset{2}{\cancel{4}}}{\underset{1}{\cancel{3}}}=\frac{10}{1}=10$$

Convert mixed fractions to improper fractions. Divide 3 and 15 by 3 to produce 1 and 5. Divide 2 and 4 by 2 to produce 1 and 2. Multiply the numerators, then the denominators. Reduce 10/1 to 10.

5. $8\dfrac{1}{2}$

$$3\frac{4}{5} \times 2\frac{9}{38} = \frac{19}{5} \times \frac{85}{38}$$

$$= \frac{\overset{1}{\cancel{19}}}{\underset{1}{5}} \times \frac{\overset{17}{\cancel{85}}}{\underset{2}{\cancel{38}}} = \frac{17}{2} = 8\frac{1}{2}$$

Convert mixed fractions to improper fractions. Divide 19 and 38 by 19 to produce 1 and 2. Divide 5 and 85 by 5 to produce 1 and 17. Multiply the numerators, then the denominators. Convert the improper fraction to a mixed fraction.

DIVISION OF FRACTIONS

As with multiplication, division does not require the use of a Lowest Common Denominator (LCD). In some ways, division is similar to multiplication. In order to divide fractions, we rewrite the first fraction, flip the second fraction, and then multiply. Mathematicians love to change problems into ones that they already know how to simplify. In this case, they change division into multiplication. Instead of "flipping" the second fraction, sometimes this will be referred to as forming the **reciprocal**. Whether we refer to it as forming the reciprocal or flipping, we are just switching the positions of the numerator and denominator.

Examples

Divide the following fractions.

(a) $\dfrac{6}{13} \div \dfrac{12}{5}$

In order to divide these fractions, we rewrite the first fraction, flip the second fraction, and then multiply. In this problem, we have

$$\frac{6}{13} \times \frac{5}{12} = \frac{\overset{1}{6}}{13} \times \frac{5}{\underset{2}{\cancel{12}}}$$

$$= \frac{1}{13} \times \frac{5}{2} = \frac{1 \times 5}{13 \times 2} = \frac{5}{26}$$

Since 5/26 cannot be reduced, our final answer is 5/26. Notice that we cancelled where possible. Remember that we want to reconstruct our problem into multiplication before any cancelling is done.

(b) $\dfrac{5}{9} \div \dfrac{10}{18}$

In order to divide these fractions, we rewrite the first fraction, flip the second fraction, and then multiply. In this problem, we have

$$\dfrac{5}{9} \times \dfrac{18}{10} = \dfrac{\overset{1}{\cancel{5}}}{9} \times \dfrac{\overset{2}{\cancel{18}}}{\underset{2}{\cancel{10}}}$$

$$= \dfrac{1}{1} \times \dfrac{\overset{1}{\cancel{2}}}{\underset{1}{\cancel{2}}} = \dfrac{1 \times 1}{1 \times 1} = \dfrac{1}{1}$$

Since 1/1 can be written as 1, our final answer is 1. Notice that we cancelled where possible. Remember that we want to reconstruct our problem into multiplication before any cancelling is done.

Examples

Divide the following fractions.

(a) $2\dfrac{1}{5} \div 1\dfrac{7}{15}$

As before, we begin by writing the mixed numbers as improper fractions. In this example, we get 11/5 ÷ 22/15. We now rewrite the first fraction, flip the second fraction, and then multiply.

$$\dfrac{11}{5} \times \dfrac{15}{22} = \dfrac{\overset{1}{\cancel{11}}}{5} \times \dfrac{\overset{3}{\cancel{15}}}{\underset{2}{\cancel{22}}}$$

$$= \dfrac{1}{1} \times \dfrac{3}{2} = \dfrac{1 \times 3}{1 \times 2} = \dfrac{3}{2}$$

Since the numerator is larger than the denominator, we know that we are dealing with a number larger than 1. By subtracting the denominator from the numerator, we see that 3/2 equals $1\frac{1}{2}$. Therefore, our final answer is $1\frac{1}{2}$.

(b) $4\dfrac{2}{9} \div 3\dfrac{1}{6}$

As before, we begin by writing the mixed numbers as improper fractions. In this example, we get 38/9 ÷ 19/6. We now rewrite the first fraction, flip the second fraction, and then multiply.

$$\frac{38}{9} \times \frac{6}{19} = \frac{\overset{2}{\cancel{38}}}{\underset{3}{\cancel{9}}} \times \frac{\overset{2}{\cancel{6}}}{\underset{1}{\cancel{19}}}$$

$$= \frac{2}{3} \times \frac{2}{1} = \frac{2 \times 2}{3 \times 1} = \frac{4}{3}$$

Since the numerator is larger than the denominator, we know that we are dealing with a number larger than 1. By subtracting the denominator from the numerator, we see that 4/3 equals 1¹/₃. Therefore, our final answer is 1¹/₃.

Drill: Division of Fractions

Divide the following fractions.

1. $\dfrac{2}{3} \div \dfrac{4}{7}$

2. $\dfrac{5}{9} \div \dfrac{10}{13}$

3. $\dfrac{13}{5} \div \dfrac{26}{50}$

4. $2\dfrac{9}{13} \div 3\dfrac{23}{39}$

5. $5\dfrac{4}{9} \div 1\dfrac{3}{18}$

Answers to Drill Questions

1. $1\dfrac{1}{6}$

$$\frac{2}{3} \div \frac{4}{7} = \frac{2}{3} \times \frac{7}{4} = \frac{2}{3} \times \frac{7}{\underset{2}{\cancel{4}}} = \frac{7}{6} = 1\frac{1}{6}$$

2. $\dfrac{13}{18}$

$$\frac{5}{9} \div \frac{10}{13} = \frac{5}{9} \times \frac{13}{10} = \frac{5}{9} \times \frac{13}{\cancel{10}} = \frac{13}{18}$$

3. 5

$$\frac{13}{5} \div \frac{26}{50} = \frac{13}{5} \times \frac{50}{26}$$

$$= \frac{\cancel{13}}{\cancel{5}} \times \frac{\cancel{50}}{\cancel{26}} = \frac{10}{2} = 5$$

4. $\dfrac{3}{4}$

$$2\frac{9}{13} \div 3\frac{23}{39} = \frac{35}{13} \div \frac{140}{39} = \frac{35}{13} \times \frac{39}{140}$$

$$= \frac{35}{\cancel{13}} \times \frac{\cancel{39}}{\cancel{140}} = \frac{3}{4}$$

5. $4\dfrac{2}{3}$

$$5\frac{4}{9} \div 1\frac{3}{18} = \frac{49}{9} \div \frac{21}{18} = \frac{49}{9} \times \frac{18}{21}$$

$$= \frac{49}{9} \times \frac{\cancel{18}}{\cancel{21}} = \frac{14}{3} = 4\frac{2}{3}$$

III. DECIMALS

INTRODUCTION TO DECIMALS

As we go through life we learn that not all numbers are whole numbers. In some cases, we have "pieces" of a whole number, for example, when we work with money. When visiting a store, we often find prices like $4.99, $10.35, and $1.79. In each of these cases, we have

decimals. The digit or digits to the left of the decimal point (.) is the whole number part of our price and the digit or digits to the right of the decimal point is the decimal part. Working with decimals is very similar to working with whole numbers. Decimal numbers also have place values in the same way as whole numbers. The whole number part of a decimal number has the same place values as we discussed in Section I. The place values for the decimal part are very similar except that instead of the place values ending in "s," the decimal place values end in "ths." If we consider the decimal number below, we can see an example of this.

15.3864

1 is in the tens place

5 is in the ones place

3 is in the ten*ths* place

8 is in the hundred*ths* place

6 is in the thousand*ths* place

4 is in the ten thousand*ths* place

The only confusing part of this discussion is that there is no "oneths" or "onths" place. Except for that, the place values are exactly the same. If we pair the decimal point with the ones place, we can see the similarities better—tens and tenths, hundreds and hundredths, etc.

Example

Write the place value of the 7 in the following numbers.

(a) 29.752

This 7 is in the <u>tenths</u> place.

(b) 6.1275

This 7 is in the <u>thousandths</u> place.

(c) 5.273

This 7 is in the <u>hundredths</u> place.

(d) 0.6597

This 7 is in the <u>ten thousandths</u> place.

Rounding decimal numbers is very similar to rounding whole numbers. Sometimes an approximation can be used instead of working with the exact value. A few examples are listed on the next page.

Examples

Round the following numbers to the appropriate position.

(a) Round 3.467 to the hundredths position.

3.4<u>6</u>7—Since the digit to the right is 7, we would add 1 to the marked digit and drop the remainder of the number: 3.47

(b) Round 14.5299 to the tenths position.

14.<u>5</u>299—Since the digit to the right is 2, we would leave the marked digit alone and drop the remainder of the number: 14.5

(c) Round 0.245789 to the ten thousandths position.

0.245<u>7</u>89—Since the digit to the right is 8, we would add 1 to the marked digit and drop the remainder of the number: 0.2458

(d) Round 7.29342 to the thousandths position.

7.29<u>3</u>42—Since the digit to the right is 4, we would leave the marked digit alone and drop the remainder of the number: 7.293

Drill: Introduction to Decimals

Write the place value of the underlined digit in the following numbers.

1. 234.67<u>8</u>9   _____

2. 8.<u>1</u>24   _____

3. 0.7640<u>2</u>   _____

4. 69.34<u>6</u>56   _____

5. 49.5<u>3</u>561   _____

Round the following numbers to the underlined position.

6. 56.54<u>7</u>8   _____

7. 0.4<u>8</u>36   _____

8. 7.5831<u>3</u>4   _____

9. 67.528<u>4</u>5   _____

10. 0.<u>8</u>64   _____

Answers to Drill Questions

1. Thousandths. The third place value to the right of the decimal point is the thousandths place.

2. Tenths. The first place value to the right of the decimal point is the tenths place.

3. Hundred thousandths. The fifth place value to the right of the decimal point is the hundred thousandths place.

4. Thousandths. The third place value to the right of the decimal point is the thousandths place.

5. Hundredths. The second place value to the right of the decimal point is the hundreths place.

6. 56.54<u>8</u>

7. 0.4<u>8</u>

8. 7.5831<u>3</u>

9. 67.528<u>5</u>

10. 0.<u>9</u>

ADDITION OF DECIMALS

Now that we have a better understanding of decimals, what can we do with them? The same four operations (addition, subtraction, multiplication, and division) can be used here. The following sections will deal with each of these operations in turn.

In order to add decimal numbers, we must write the numbers in a column with the decimal points lined up. To help with spacing and columns, we can use zero (0) as a place holder to block off the problem. The examples below demonstrate this method.

Examples

Add the following numbers.

(a) Add 2.467482, 1.4126, and 3.46571.

$$
\begin{array}{r}
2.467482 \\
1.4126 \\
+\ 3.46571 \\
\hline
\end{array}
\quad \longrightarrow \quad
\begin{array}{r}
^{1}\ ^{111} \\
2.467482 \\
1.412600 \\
+\ 3.465710 \\
\hline
7.345792
\end{array}
$$

(b) Add 7.5189, 5.789, 1.7826, and 2.54799.

$$\begin{matrix} & 2\ 2\,2\,2 \\ 7.5189 & 7.51890 \\ 5.789 & 5.78900 \\ 1.7826 & 1.78260 \\ +\,2.54799 \rightarrow & +\,2.54799 \\ & \overline{17.63849} \end{matrix}$$

(c) 2.45789 + 3.483

$$\begin{matrix} & 1\,1 \\ 2.45789 & 2.45789 \\ +\,3.483 \rightarrow & +\,3.48300 \\ & \overline{5.94089} \end{matrix}$$

(d) 34.6 + 65.856 + 43.68743

$$\begin{matrix} & 12\,11 \\ 34.6 & 34.60000 \\ 65.856 & 65.85600 \\ +\,43.68743 \rightarrow & +\,43.68743 \\ & \overline{144.14343} \end{matrix}$$

Drill: Addition of Decimals

Add the following numbers.

1. 4.57457 + 3.4678

2. 3.4896 + 8.57046 + 3.489861

3. 24.589434 + 56.7257 + 6.76821

4. 8.72566 + 4.5745 + 3.463019

5. 24.5869 + 8.24567 + 452.772

Answers to Drill Questions

1. 8.04237

$$\begin{matrix} 1\ 111 \\ 4.57457 \\ +\,3.4678 \\ \overline{8.04237} \end{matrix}$$

2. 15.549921

    1 2111

    3.4896

    8.57046

    + 3.489861

    15.549921

3. 88.083344

    12 121

    24.589434

    56.7257

    + 6.76821

    88.083344

4. 16.763179

    1 111

    8.72566

    4.5745

    + 3.463019

    16.763179

5. 485.60457

    11 211

    24.5869

    8.24567

    + 452.772

    485.60457

SUBTRACTION OF DECIMALS

As we saw in the previous section, working with decimals is very similar to working with whole numbers. Some of the same ideas that we used in addition also apply to subtraction. We need to begin by lining up the decimal points. Using zeros as place holders can also help keep the columns and place values straight. Recall that sometimes we need to borrow in order to subtract. The examples below demonstrate these topics.

Examples

Subtract the following numbers. Borrow when necessary.

(a) 4.25734 − 3.4857

$$
\begin{array}{r}
4.25734 \\
-\ 3.4857 \\
\hline
\end{array}
\quad\longrightarrow\quad
\begin{array}{r}
{\scriptstyle 111} \\
3.15634 \\
-\ 3.48570 \\
\hline
0.77164
\end{array}
$$

(b) 86.8348 – 34.5786

$$
\begin{array}{r}
86.8348 \\
-\ 34.5786 \\
\hline
\end{array}
\quad\longrightarrow\quad
\begin{array}{r}
{\scriptstyle 11} \\
86.7248 \\
-\ 34.5786 \\
\hline
52.2562
\end{array}
$$

Drill: Subtraction of Decimals

Subtract the following numbers.

1. 9.5867– 4.1571

2. 65.876 – 48.1323

3. 45.892459 – 2.35634

4. 12.3415 – 2.63756

5. 458.9756 – 245.86789

Answers to Drill Questions

1. 5.4296

$$
\begin{array}{r}
{\scriptstyle 7}\;{\scriptstyle 1} \\
9.5867 \\
-\ 4.1571 \\
\hline
5.4296
\end{array}
$$

2. 17.7437

$$
\begin{array}{r}
{\scriptstyle 5}\;\;\;{\scriptstyle 5}\;{\scriptstyle 1} \\
65.8760 \\
-\ 48.1323 \\
\hline
17.7437
\end{array}
$$

3. 43.536119

$$
\begin{array}{r}
{\scriptstyle 8}\;{\scriptstyle 1} \\
45.892459 \\
-\ 2.356340 \\
\hline
43.536119
\end{array}
$$

4. 9.70394

$$\begin{array}{r} \overset{\underset{1}{1}\overset{304}{\underset{1\,1\,1}{\cancel{34150}}}}{12.34150} \\ -\,2.63756 \\ \hline 9.70394 \end{array}$$

5. 213.10771

$$\begin{array}{r} \overset{\overset{645}{\underset{1\,1\,1}{}}}{458.97560} \\ -\,245.86789 \\ \hline 213.10771 \end{array}$$

MULTIPLICATION OF DECIMALS

Now that we are "experts" in addition and subtraction of decimals, we can switch our discussion to multiplication. Multiplying decimals is closer to working with whole numbers than either of the above topics. Here we want to write the numbers in a table format and multiply them together as if the decimal points were not present. After we get a result we must take into account that the original problem was made up of decimal numbers. Next, we must add the decimal places in all the numbers involved in the problem. In order to get the proper placement of the decimal point in the final answer, we count off the correct number of places moving right to left. The examples that follow consider most of the details that might arise.

Examples

Multiply the following numbers.

(a) 5.68×2.3

$$\begin{array}{r} 5.68 \\ \times\,2.3 \\ \hline \end{array} \longrightarrow \begin{array}{r} 568 \\ \times\,23 \\ \hline 1704 \\ +\,11360 \\ \hline 13064 \end{array} \longrightarrow \begin{array}{r} 5.68 \\ \times\,2.3 \\ \hline 13.064 \end{array}$$

(2 decimal places)
(1 decimal place)
(3 decimal places)

(b) 4.564×3.12

$$\begin{array}{r} 4.564 \\ \times\,3.12 \\ \hline \end{array} \longrightarrow \begin{array}{r} 4564 \\ \times\,312 \\ \hline 9128 \\ 45640 \\ +\,1369200 \\ \hline 1423968 \end{array} \longrightarrow \begin{array}{r} 4.564 \\ \times\,3.12 \\ \hline 14.23968 \end{array}$$

(3 decimal places)
(2 decimal places)
(5 decimal places)

(c) 0.258×0.6

0.258		258		0.258	(3 decimal places)
$\times 0.6$	$\longrightarrow$	$\times 6$	$\longrightarrow$	$\times 0.6$	(1 decimal place)
		1548		0.1548	(4 decimal places)

(d) 0.023×0.07

0.023		23		0.023	(3 decimal places)
$\times 0.07$	$\longrightarrow$	$\times 7$	$\longrightarrow$	$\times 0.07$	(2 decimal places)
		161		0.00161	(5 decimal places)

(e) 341.786×6.7

341.786		341786		341.786	(3 decimal places)
$\times 6.7$	$\longrightarrow$	$\times 67$	$\longrightarrow$	$\times 6.7$	(1 decimal place)
		2392502		2289.9662	(4 decimal places)
		+ 20507160			
		22899662			

(f) 0.6045×3.7

0.6045		6045		0.6045	(4 decimal places)
$\times 3.7$	$\longrightarrow$	$\times 37$	$\longrightarrow$	$\times 3.7$	(1 decimal place)
		42315		2.23665	(5 decimal places)
		+ 181350			
		223665			

Drill: Multiplication of Decimals

Multiply the following numbers.

1. 0.9674×0.56

2. 3.1358×0.512

3. 34.7×0.68

4. 2.356×0.971

5. 134.689×2.34

Answers to Drill Questions

1. 0.541744

    | 0.9674 | (4 decimal places) |
    | × 0.56 | (2 decimal places) |
    | 58044 | |
    | + 48370 | |
    | 0.541744 | (6 decimal places) |

2. 1.6055296

    | 3.1358 | (4 decimal places) |
    | × 0.512 | (3 decimal places) |
    | 62716 | |
    | 31358 | |
    | +156790 | |
    | 1.6055296 | (7 decimal places) |

3. 23.596

    | 34.7 | (1 decimal place) |
    | × 0.68 | (2 decimal places) |
    | 2776 | |
    | + 2082 | |
    | 23.596 | (3 decimal places) |

4. 2.287676

    | 2.356 | (3 decimal places) |
    | × 0.971 | (3 decimal places) |
    | 2356 | |
    | 16492 | |
    | + 21204 | |
    | 2.287676 | (6 decimal places) |

5. 315.17226

    | 134.689 | (3 decimal places) |
    | × 2.34 | (2 decimal places) |
    | 538756 | |
    | 404067 | |
    | +269378 | |
    | 315.17226 | (5 decimal places) |

DIVISION OF DECIMALS

We divide decimals in essentially the same way that we divided whole numbers. If we are dividing by a whole number, we just bring the decimal point up to our answer line and then divide as we did in the previous chapter. On the other hand, if we are dividing by a decimal number, we must first move the decimal point of this number to the right as many spaces as needed to make it a whole number. In order to keep our problem equivalent, we must move the decimal point of the number under the division bar by the same number of places. If we move the decimal point two spaces to the right in the number outside, we must also move the decimal point two spaces to the right inside the division bar. In the following examples, we will address both of these situations. Instead of leaving our answer with a remainder, we can use zeros as place holders and continue dividing until our answer works out exactly.

Examples

Divide the following numbers.

(a) $5.8956 \div 17$

$$
\begin{array}{r} . \\ 17\overline{)5.8956} \end{array}
\longrightarrow
\begin{array}{r} 0.3 \\ 17\overline{)5.8956} \\ -5\,1 \\ \hline 79 \end{array}
\longrightarrow
\begin{array}{r} 0.34 \\ 17\overline{)5.8956} \\ -5\,1 \\ \hline 79 \\ -68 \\ \hline 115 \end{array}
\longrightarrow
$$

$$
\longrightarrow
\begin{array}{r} 0.346 \\ 17\overline{)5.8956} \\ -5\,1 \\ \hline 79 \\ -68 \\ \hline 115 \\ -102 \\ \hline 136 \end{array}
\longrightarrow
\begin{array}{r} 0.3468 \\ 17\overline{)5.8956} \\ -5\,1 \\ \hline 79 \\ -68 \\ \hline 115 \\ -102 \\ \hline 136 \\ -136 \\ \hline 0 \end{array}
$$

Since we are dividing by a whole number, we just need to move the decimal point up to our answer line and divide as we did in the last section. How many times will 17 go into 58? Our answer here would be 3. Since $17 \times 3 = 51$, we can place this value under the first number and subtract. If we subtract and bring down the next digit, we get 79. Now we need to consider how many times 17 goes into 79. Our answer is 4. Since $17 \times 4 = 68$, we can place this value under the first number and subtract. If we subtract and bring down the next digit, we get 115. Now we consider how many times 17 goes into 115. Our answer is 6. Since $17 \times 6 = 102$, we can place this value under the first number and subtract. If we subtract and bring down the next digit, we will get 136. Now we consider how many times 17 goes into 136. Our answer is 8. Since $17 \times 8 = 136$, we can place this value under the first number and subtract. Here we get $136 - 136 = 0$. We have no remainder in this problem. Our overall answer would be 0.3468.

(b) $1218.14 \div 49$

$$49\overline{)1218.14} \longrightarrow \begin{array}{r} 2 \\ 49\overline{)1218.14} \\ -98 \\ \hline 238 \end{array} \longrightarrow \begin{array}{r} 24. \\ 49\overline{)1218.14} \\ -98 \\ \hline 238 \\ -196 \\ \hline 42\,1 \end{array}$$

$$\longrightarrow \begin{array}{r} 24.8 \\ 49\overline{)1218.14} \\ -98 \\ \hline 238 \\ -196 \\ \hline 42\,1 \\ -39\,2 \\ \hline 2\,94 \end{array} \longrightarrow \begin{array}{r} 24.86 \\ 49\overline{)1218.14} \\ -98 \\ \hline 238 \\ -196 \\ \hline 42\,1 \\ -39\,2 \\ \hline 2\,94 \\ -2\,94 \\ \hline 0 \end{array}$$

Since we are dividing by a whole number, we just need to move the decimal point up to our answer line and divide as we did in the last section. How many times will 49 go into 121? Our answer is 2. Since $49 \times 2 = 98$, we can place this value under the first number and subtract. If we subtract and bring down the next digit, we will get 238. Now we need to consider how many times 49 goes into 238. Our answer is 4. Since $49 \times 4 = 196$, we can place this value under the first number and subtract. If we subtract and bring down the next digit, we get 421. Now we consider how many times 49 goes into 421. Our answer is 8. Since $49 \times 8 = 392$, we can place this value under the first number and subtract. If we subtract and bring down the next digit, we will get 294. Now we consider how many times 49 goes into 294. Our answer is 6. Since $49 \times 6 = 294$, we can place this value under the first number and subtract. Here we get $294 - 294 = 0$. We have no remainder in this problem. Therefore, our overall answer is 24.86.

(c) $74.36 \div 0.2$

$$0.2\overline{)74.36} \longrightarrow \begin{array}{r} 3 \\ 2\overline{)743.6} \\ -6 \\ \hline 14 \end{array} \longrightarrow \begin{array}{r} 37. \\ 2\overline{)743.6} \\ -6 \\ \hline 14 \\ -14 \\ \hline 3 \end{array}$$

$$\longrightarrow \begin{array}{r} 371. \\ 2\overline{)743.6} \\ -6 \\ \hline 14 \\ -14 \\ \hline 3 \\ -2 \\ \hline 1\,6 \end{array} \longrightarrow \begin{array}{r} 371.8 \\ 2\overline{)743.6} \\ -6 \\ \hline 14 \\ -14 \\ \hline 3 \\ -2 \\ \hline 1\,6 \\ -1\,6 \\ \hline 0 \end{array}$$

We are familiar with dividing a number by 3 or 7, but not by 0.2. By moving the decimal point one place to the right, this value becomes 2. In order to keep this problem equivalent, we must also move the decimal inside the division bar one space to the right. This changes 74.36 into 743.6. Now we divide 2 into 743.6 as we did in the examples above. Two goes into 7 three times. Since $2 \times 3 = 6$, we can place this value under the first number and subtract. This gives 1, and by bringing down the next digit, we get 14. Two goes into 14 seven times. Since $2 \times 7 = 14$, we can place this value under the first number and subtract. This gives 0. When we bring down the next digit, we get 3. Two goes into 3 once. Since $2 \times 1 = 2$, we can place this value under the first number and subtract. This gives 1. When we bring down the next digit, we get 16. Two goes into 16 eight times. Since $2 \times 8 = 16$, we can place this value under the first number and subtract. This gives us 0. Our overall answer is 371.8.

(d) $0.876 \div 0.06$

$$
0.06\overline{\smash{)}0.876} \quad\longrightarrow\quad
\begin{array}{r} 1\;. \\ 6\,\overline{\smash{)}87.6} \\ -6 \\ \hline 27 \end{array}
\quad\longrightarrow\quad
\begin{array}{r} 14. \\ 6\,\overline{\smash{)}87.6} \\ -6 \\ \hline 27 \\ -24 \\ \hline 3\,6 \end{array}
\quad\longrightarrow\quad
\begin{array}{r} 14.6 \\ 6\,\overline{\smash{)}87.6} \\ -6 \\ \hline 27 \\ -24 \\ \hline 3\,6 \\ -3\,6 \\ \hline 0 \end{array}
$$

Since we are dividing by 0.06, we must move the decimal point two places to the right. In order to keep this problem equivalent, we must also move the decimal point under the division bar two places to the right. This changes 0.876 into 87.6. Six goes into 8 once. Since $6 \times 1 = 6$, we can place this value under the first number and subtract. This gives 2. When we bring down the next digit, we get 27. Six goes into 27 four times. Since $6 \times 4 = 24$, we can place this value under the first number and subtract. This will give us 3. When we bring down the next digit, we get 36. Six goes into 36 six times. Since $6 \times 6 = 36$, we can place this value under the first number and subtract. This gives us 0. Therefore, our final answer is 14.6.

(e) $6.1663 \div 0.23$

$$
0.23\overline{\smash{)}6.1663} \quad\longrightarrow\quad
\begin{array}{r} 2\;. \\ 23\,\overline{\smash{)}616.63} \\ -46 \\ \hline 156 \end{array}
\quad\longrightarrow\quad
\begin{array}{r} 26. \\ 23\,\overline{\smash{)}616.63} \\ -46 \\ \hline 156 \\ -138 \\ \hline 18\,6 \end{array}
$$

$$
\longrightarrow\quad
\begin{array}{r} 26.8 \\ 23\,\overline{\smash{)}616.63} \\ -46 \\ \hline 156 \\ -138 \\ \hline 18\,6 \\ -18\,4 \\ \hline 23 \end{array}
\quad\longrightarrow\quad
\begin{array}{r} 26.81 \\ 23\,\overline{\smash{)}616.63} \\ -46 \\ \hline 156 \\ -138 \\ \hline 18\,6 \\ -18\,4 \\ \hline 23 \\ -23 \\ \hline 0 \end{array}
$$

Since we are dividing by 0.23, we must move the decimal point two places to the right. In order to keep this problem equivalent, we must also move the decimal point under the division bar two places to the right. This changes 6.1663 into 616.63. Twenty-three goes into 61 twice. Since $23 \times 2 = 46$, we can place this value under the first number and subtract. This gives 15, and when we bring down the next digit, we get 156. Twenty-three goes into 156 six times. Since $23 \times 6 = 138$, we can place this value under the first number and subtract. This will give us 18, and when we bring down the next digit, we get 186. Twenty-three goes into 186 eight times. Since $23 \times 8 = 184$, we can place this value under the first number and subtract. This gives us 2, and when we bring down the next digit, we get 23. Twenty-three goes into 23 once. Since $23 \times 1 = 23$, we can place this value under the first number and subtract. This gives us 0. Therefore, our final answer is 26.81.

(f) $0.2235 \div 0.06$

```
        .
0.06 ) 0.2235    →    6 ) 22.35    →    6 ) 22.35
                          - 18              - 18
                           4 3               4 3
                                            - 4 2
                                              15

                      3.                3.7
```

```
          3.72                  3.725
     6 ) 22.35      →      6 ) 22.350
        - 18                  - 18
         4 3                   4 3
        - 4 2                  - 4 2
          15                    15
        - 12                  - 12
           3                    30
                              - 30
                                 0
```

Here, we are dividing 0.2235 by 0.06. In order to do this, we must move our decimal points two places to the right. We now have 6 being divided into 22.35. Six goes into 22 three times. Since $6 \times 3 = 18$, we can place this value under the first number and subtract. This will give us 4, and when we bring down the next digit, we get 43. Six goes into 43 seven times. Since $6 \times 7 = 42$, we can place this value under the first number and subtract. This gives 1, and when we bring down the next digit, we get 15. Six goes into 15 twice. Since $6 \times 2 = 12$, we can place this value under the first number and subtract. This will give us 3. If we place a zero after the number and continue our division, we can work this problem out exactly. Six goes into 30 five times. Since $6 \times 5 = 30$, we can place this value under the first number and subtract. This gives us 0. Therefore, our final answer is 3.725.

(g) $1.8629 \div 0.25$

```
         .
0.25 ) 1.8629  →  25 ) 186.29  →  25 ) 186.29  →
                       - 175           - 175
                        11 2            11 2
                                      - 10 0
                                        1 29

                        7.              7.4
```

```
      7.45                  7.451                  7.4516
25 ⌐186.29    ─►   25 ⌐186.290    ─►   25 ⌐186.2900
  − 175               − 175                − 175
  ─────               ─────                ─────
    11 2                11 2                 11 2
  − 10 0              − 10 0               − 10 0
  ─────               ─────                ─────
    1 29                1 29                 1 29
  − 1 25              − 1 25               − 1 25
  ─────               ─────                ─────
      4                   40                   40
                        − 25                 − 25
                        ────                 ────
                          15                  150
                                            − 150
                                            ─────
                                                0
```

In order to divide 1.8629 by 0.25, we must move the decimal points two places to the right. Now we are dividing 186.29 by 25. Twenty-five goes into 186 seven times. Since 25 × 7 = 175, we can place this value under the first number and subtract. This gives 11, and when we bring down the next digit, we get 112. Twenty-five goes into 112 four times. Since 25 × 4 = 100, we can place this value under the first number and subtract. This gives 12, and when we bring down the next digit, we get 129. Twenty-five goes into 129 five times. Since 25 × 5 = 125, we can place this value under the first number and subtract. This gives us 4, and if we bring down the next digit (a zero used as a place holder at the end of the number), we get 40. Twenty-five goes into 40 once. Since 25 × 1 = 25, we can place this value under the first number and subtract. This gives us 15, and when we bring down the next digit (another zero used as a place holder at the end of the number), we get 150. Twenty-five goes into 150 six times. Since 25 × 6 = 150, we can place this value under the first number and subtract. This gives us 0. Our final answer is 7.4516.

Drill: Division of Decimals

Divide the following numbers.

1. 1,135.52 ÷ 47

2. 59.276 ÷ 0.7

3. 35.075 ÷ 0.61

4. 163.1463 ÷ 4.3

5. 0.941196 ÷ 0.123

Answers to Drill Questions

1. 24.16

```
      2 .                    24 .                      24.1                      24.16
47 |1135.52    →    47 |1135.52    →    47 |1135.52    →    47 |1135.52
  − 94                  − 94                   − 94                      − 94
  ─────                 ─────                  ─────                     ─────
   195                   195                    195                       195
                       − 188                  − 188                     − 188
                       ─────                  ─────                      ─────
                         75                     75                        75
                                               − 47                      − 47
                                               ─────                     ─────
                                                282                       282
                                                                        − 282
                                                                        ─────
                                                                           0
```

2.   84.68

```
          .                     8 .                    84.                     84.6                     84.68
0.7 |59.276    →    7 |592.76    →    7 |592.76    →    7 |592.76    →    7 |592.76
                       − 56                   − 56                     − 56                      − 56
                       ─────                  ─────                    ─────                     ─────
                         32                     32                       32                        32
                                              − 28                     − 28                      − 28
                                              ─────                    ─────                     ─────
                                                47                       47                        47
                                                                       − 42                      − 42
                                                                       ─────                     ─────
                                                                         56                        56
                                                                                                 − 56
                                                                                                 ─────
                                                                                                    0
```

3.   57.5

```
             .               5 .                    57.                     57.5
0.61 |35.075    →    .61 |3507.5    →    .61 |3507.5    →    .61 |3507.5
                         − 305                   − 305                     − 305
                         ─────                   ─────                     ─────
                          457                     457                       457
                                                 − 427                     − 427
                                                 ─────                     ─────
                                                   305                       305
                                                                           − 305
                                                                           ─────
                                                                              0
```

4.   37.941

```
              .                    3 .                      37.
4.3 |163.1463    →    43 |1631.463    →    43 |1631.463    →
                          − 129                    − 129
                          ─────                    ─────
                           341                      341
                                                   − 301
                                                   ─────
                                                    404
```

$$
\begin{array}{r}
37.9 \\
43\overline{\smash{)}1631.463} \\
-129 \\
\hline
341 \\
-301 \\
\hline
404 \\
-387 \\
\hline
176
\end{array}
\quad\longrightarrow\quad
\begin{array}{r}
37.94 \\
43\overline{\smash{)}1631.463} \\
-129 \\
\hline
341 \\
-301 \\
\hline
404 \\
-387 \\
\hline
176 \\
-172 \\
\hline
43
\end{array}
\quad\longrightarrow\quad
\begin{array}{r}
37.941 \\
43\overline{\smash{)}1631.463} \\
-129 \\
\hline
341 \\
-301 \\
\hline
404 \\
-387 \\
\hline
176 \\
-172 \\
\hline
43 \\
-43 \\
\hline
0
\end{array}
$$

5. 7.652

$$
\begin{array}{r}
0.123\overline{\smash{)}0.941196}
\end{array}
\quad\longrightarrow\quad
\begin{array}{r}
7. \\
123\overline{\smash{)}941.196} \\
-861 \\
\hline
801
\end{array}
\quad\longrightarrow\quad
\begin{array}{r}
7.6 \\
123\overline{\smash{)}941.196} \\
-861 \\
\hline
801 \\
-738 \\
\hline
639
\end{array}
$$

$$
\begin{array}{r}
7.65 \\
123\overline{\smash{)}941.196} \\
-861 \\
\hline
801 \\
-738 \\
\hline
639 \\
-615 \\
\hline
24
\end{array}
\quad\longrightarrow\quad
\begin{array}{r}
7.652 \\
123\overline{\smash{)}941.196} \\
-861 \\
\hline
801 \\
-738 \\
\hline
639 \\
-615 \\
\hline
246 \\
-246 \\
\hline
0
\end{array}
$$

IV. TOPICS IN MATHEMATICS

SIMPLIFYING EXPRESSIONS

Since we have a good understanding of natural numbers and decimals, we want to move our attention to other topics in mathematics. In this section, we will begin to see how mathematics can be used in physical situations. In order to make our work easier, we first want to discuss the

"Order of Operations." These rules give us a recipe, or **algorithm**, to follow when simplifying mathematical expressions. We start at the top of the list and proceed down until all operations have been completed. The list below sets the order of operations. This order makes sure that we all get the same answer from a problem. Most of these ideas have already been discussed, but a few are new to the section. We will explain in detail those topics that have not already been explained.

Order of Operations

1. Do the operations above and below the fraction bar separately.

2. Work inside the parentheses (innermost first). Note that ( ), [ ], and { } can all be used as grouping symbols and are generally referred to as parentheses.

3. Simplify exponents.

4. Multiply and divide from left to right. Note that multiplication and division are done at the same time as we move left to right.

5. Add and subtract from left to right. Note that addition and subtraction are also done at the same time as we move left to right.

Examples

Simplify the following expressions.

(a) $4 + 2(1 + 6)$

In this example, we must begin inside the parentheses and simplify this part of the expression. Here $1 + 6$ equals 7. If we substitute this value into our expression we get

$4 + 2(7)$

According to our order of operations, the next thing to do is the multiplication (2×7). Even though the multiplication symbol does not appear in the original expression, it is implied. Anytime we have a parenthesis next to another parenthesis or number together without an operation, such as ") (" and "2(," it is understood that multiplication is the operation being indicated. In this example, 2×7 equal 14. Thus, our expression becomes

$4 + 14$

Finally, we can do the addition and get our answer. Here our final answer is 18.

(b) $\dfrac{1 + 2(7 - 5)}{4(9 - 6) + 3}$

In this example, we must simplify the numerator and denominator of this expression separately. Keep in mind that we must follow the order of operations. In simplifying the numerator, we must work inside the parentheses first. This gives

$\dfrac{1 + 2(2)}{4(9 - 6) + 3}$

We then do the multiplication in the numerator.

$$\frac{1+4}{4(9-6)+3}$$

We now do the addition in the numerator, getting

$$\frac{5}{4(9-6)+3}$$

Next, we follow the same ideas with the denominator.

$$\frac{5}{4(3)+3}$$

When we do the multiplication in the denominator, we get

$$\frac{5}{12+3}$$

By doing the addition in the denominator and reducing the fraction, our expression becomes

$$\frac{1}{3} = 0.\overline{3}$$

Therefore, our answer is $0.\overline{3}$ rounded to one decimal place. The short line appearing above the 3 denotes that the value repeats (0.333333333333...).

AVERAGES

Sometimes finding the middle value of a list of numbers is important to us. Mathematically, this is referred to as the **average**. For example, a number of people take a certain standardized test. After the group receives their scores, they want to know the average score. Knowing this, they can compare their scores easily to see how the group did. This can be done by adding the scores together and then dividing by the number of scores (or items). This would be the score of the "typical" student.

Example

Find the average of the following

75, 81, and 99

In order to calculate this average, we must begin by adding the numbers together. In this case, we get 75 + 81 + 99 = 255. Since we are trying to find the average of three numbers, we divide the sum of the scores by 3. Therefore, 255/3 equals 85. This shows that the "typical" student would score 85. We can also look at this as an equation.

$$\frac{75+81+99}{3} = \frac{255}{3} = 85$$

Drill: Simplifying Expressions and Averages

Simplify the following expressions.

1. $11 + 3(7-2)$

2. $4.7 + 2.1(6.5 - 3.9)$

Find the averages of the following numbers.

3. 85, 95, and 97

4. 1, 3, 5, 7, 9, and 9

5. 10, 75, 80, and 92

Answers to Drill Questions

1. 26

    $$11 + 3(7 - 2) = 11 + 3(5)$$
    $$= 11 + 15$$
    $$= 26$$

2. 10.16

    $$4.7 + 2.1(6.5 - 3.9) = 4.7 + 2.1(2.6)$$
    $$= 4.7 + 5.46$$
    $$= 10.16$$

3. $92.3\overline{3}$

    $$
    \begin{array}{r}
    \overset{1}{85} \\
    95 \\
    +\,97 \\
    \hline
    277
    \end{array}
    \qquad
    \begin{array}{r}
    92.33 \\
    3\,\overline{)\,277} \\
    -27 \\
    \hline
    07 \\
    -6 \\
    \hline
    10 \\
    -9 \\
    \hline
    10
    \end{array}
    $$

4. $5.6\overline{6}$

    $$1 + 3 + 5 + 7 + 9 + 9 = 34$$

$$
\begin{array}{r}
5.66 \\
6\overline{)34} \\
-30 \\
\hline
40 \\
-36 \\
\hline
40
\end{array}
$$

5. $\quad$ 64.25

$$
\begin{array}{r}
64.25 \\
10 \\
75 \\
80 \\
+\,92 \\
\hline
257
\end{array}
$$

$$
\begin{array}{r}
6 \\
4\overline{)257} \\
-24 \\
\hline
17
\end{array}
\qquad\longrightarrow\qquad
\begin{array}{r}
64.25 \\
4\overline{)257.00} \\
-24 \\
\hline
17 \\
-16 \\
\hline
10 \\
-8 \\
\hline
20 \\
-20 \\
\hline
0
\end{array}
$$

CUBES AND ROOTS

This section will look at exponents and roots. Exponents can be used to denote repetitive multiplication. The following two expressions mean the same thing.

$$11 \times 11 \times 11 \times 11 \qquad \text{or} \qquad \mathbf{11^4}$$

The second form is the **exponential** form. Since we are multiplying 11 by itself, we use that value as a **base**. Because we are multiplying four 11's together, we place a 4 in the **exponent position**. This is the little number appearing above and to the right of the base. Using exponents condenses the expression. In the next two sets of examples, we will become familiar with switching to and from exponents.

Examples

Rewrite the following as an exponent or equation.

(a) 5×5

Rewrite this as 5^2. The base is 5, so we know that we have a line of 5's being multiplied together. Since our exponent is 2, we know that we will have two 5's multiplied; therefore, we get 5×5. The important point here is being able to convert back and forth between the multiplication form and the exponential form. If we want to or are asked to, we could also multiply this out and get 25.

(b) 2^3

The base is 2, so we know that we have a line of 2's being multiplied together. Since our exponent is 3, we know that we will have three 2's multiplied; therefore, we get $2 \times 2 \times 2$. The important point here is being able to convert back and forth between the multiplication form and the exponential form. If we want to or are asked to, we could also multiply this out and get 8.

Examples

Rewrite the following using exponents.

(a) $7 \times 7 \times 7$

In this example, we are multiplying a line of 7's together. Therefore, our base is 7. Since we have three 7's being multiplied, our exponent is 3. Thus, we get

7^3

(b) 9×9

In this example, we are multiplying a line of 9's together. Therefore, our base is 9. Since we have two 9's being multiplied, our exponent is 2. Thus, we get

9^2

Another related topic is **roots**. We will begin by discussing **square roots**. Later, we will see that **cube roots** are very similar. When asked for the square root of a number, we want to find a number that, when we square it, gives us the original number. Knowing this gives us an immediate check to see if our answer is correct. The symbol for square root is something like a check mark ($\sqrt{}$).

Examples

Find the square root of the following numbers.

(a) $\sqrt{4}$ or the square root of 4 is _____.

When asked to find the square root of 4, we want to find a number that when squared equals 4. After some consideration, we can see that our answer is 2. This is because

$2^2 = 2 \times 2 = 4$

and this is the beginning value.

(b) $\sqrt{25}$ or the square root of 25 is _____.

When asked to find the square root of 25, we want to find a number that when squared equals 25. After some consideration, we can see that our answer is 5. This is because

$$5^2 = 5 \times 5 = 25$$

and this is the beginning value.

(c) $\sqrt{9}$ or the square root of 9 is _____.

When asked to find the square root of 9, we want to find a number that when squared equals 9. After some consideration, we can see that our answer is 3. This is because

$$3^2 = 3 \times 3 = 9$$

and this is the beginning value.

(d) $\sqrt{100}$ or the square root of 100 is _____.

When asked to find the square root of 100, we want to find a number that when squared equals 100. After some consideration, we can see that our answer is 10. This is because

$$10^2 = 10 \times 10 = 100$$

and this is the beginning value.

Now that we have an understanding of exponents, we want to consider what happens when we put them into problems involving order of operations. Recall that the order of operations tells us to simplify the exponents after the parentheses, but before we do the multiplying and dividing. In the following example we will show, in detail, the steps needed.

Example

Simplify the following expression.

$$2 \times 3 + 5 - 2^3$$

In this example, we need to begin with simplifying the exponent. Two cubed is the same as $2 \times 2 \times 2$ or 8. This converts our expression to

$$2 \times 3 + 5 - 8$$

Next, we need to simplify the multiplication in our problem. Since 2×3 equals 6, our expression becomes

$$6 + 5 - 8$$

We now must add and subtract, moving from left to right as they appear. Thus, we add 6 and 5 together first. This gives

$$11 - 8$$

Finally, we are able to do the subtraction and get 3 as our final answer.

Drill: Cubes and Roots

Rewrite the following without using exponents.

1. 3^2

2. 2^4

Rewrite the following using exponents.

3. $5 \times 5 \times 5$

4. $2 \times 2 \times 2 \times 2 \times 2$

Find the square root of the following numbers.

5. 49

6. 81

Simplify the following expression.

7. $7 \times 2 - 6 - 2^3$

Answers to Drill Questions

1. 3×3

2. $2 \times 2 \times 2 \times 2$

3. 5^3

4. 2^5

5. 7

    $7 \times 7 = 49$

6. 9

    $9 \times 9 = 81$

7. 0

    $$(7 \times 2) - 6 - 2^3 = (7 \times 2) - 6 - 8$$
    $$= 14 - 6 - 8$$
    $$= 8 - 8$$
    $$= 0$$

MEASUREMENT

Working with figures is yet another important part of mathematics. Two common figures that we regularly deal with are **rectangles** and **squares**. A **square** is a rectangle with all the sides of the same length. As we move through this section, notice that in each problem the units are constant. This is very important when dealing with the units. If the measurements are not already the same, we want to convert them.

We can calculate a few measurements to learn a lot about an object. Some of these measurements are perimeter, area, and volume. We will discuss each of these in detail as we move through this section.

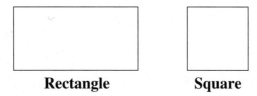

Rectangle   **Square**

The **perimeter** is the distance around the outside of the object. Imagine that we are able to walk around the object and measure the distance we travel. In a rectangle, the perimeter will be twice the length plus twice the width. Notice that if we add numbers together that have inches for units, our answer will also have inches for units. As a formula, we have

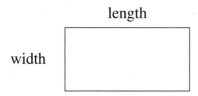

Perimeter = 2(length) + 2(width)

Example

Find the perimeter of a rectangle with the following dimensions.

length = 5 feet and width = 4 feet

Since we know the length and width of our rectangle, we can substitute these values into our formula. Notice that since our dimensions are given in feet, our answer will also have feet as a unit.

Perimeter = 2(length) + 2(width)

Perimeter = 2(5) + 2(4)

We can now do the multiplication and then the addition to get our answer.

Perimeter = 10 + 8 = 18 feet

We now want to consider what happens to our formula when we look at a square. Since all four sides have the same length, our perimeter will be determined by multiplying the measure of one side and 4 together. In the example below, you will see that our work is not much different than for a rectangle. As a formula, this would be

Perimeter = 4(side)

Example

Find the perimeter of the square with the following measurement on each side.

side = 5 inches

Since we know the measure of each side of our square, we can substitute this value into our formula. Notice that since our dimension is given in inches, our answer will also have inches as a unit.

Perimeter = 4(side)

Perimeter = 4(5)

We can now do the multiplication to get our answer.

Perimeter = 20 inches

Another useful measurement is the **area** of an object. This is the amount of space enclosed by the boundaries of the object. In a rectangle, the area is the length and width multiplied together. Notice that if we multiply two numbers together that have feet as units, our answer will have *square* feet as its unit. As a formula, we have

Area = (length) × (width)

Examples

Find the areas of rectangles with the following dimensions.

(a)   length = 2 inches and width = 3 inches

Since we know the length and width of our rectangle, we can substitute these values into our formula. Notice that since our dimensions are given in inches, our answer will have square inches as a unit.

Area = (length) × (width)

Area = (2) × (3)

We can now do the multiplication to get our answer.

Area = 6 inches^2

(b)   length = 5 feet and width = 2 feet

Since we know the length and width of our rectangle, we can substitute these values into our formula. Notice that since our dimensions are given in feet, our answer will have square feet as a unit.

Area = (length) × (width)

Area = (5) × (2)

We can now do the multiplication to get our answer.

Area = 10 feet^2

When dealing with a square, our area formula becomes a little bit easier. Since all sides have the same length, our formula becomes the measure of one side squared. Written as a formula, we get

Area = (side)^2

Examples

Find the areas of squares with the following measures on each side.

(a)   side = 9 inches

Since we know the measure of the sides of our square, we can substitute this value into our formula. Notice that since our dimension is given in inches, our answer will have square inches as a unit.

Area = (side)^2

Area = $(9)^2 = 9 \times 9$

We can now simplify this to get our answer.

Area = 81 inches^2

(b)   side = 6 feet

Since we know the measure of the sides of our square, we can substitute this value into our formula. Notice that since our dimension is given in feet, our answer will have square feet as a unit.

Area = (side)^2

Area = $(6)^2 = 6 \times 6$

We can now simplify this to get our answer.

Area = 36 feet^2

Now we want to consider a box. A useful measure here is the **volume**. The volume is the amount of stuff that can be placed into the object. We can find this measurement by multiplying the length, width, and height together. Notice that if we multiply three numbers together that have inches as their units, our answer will have units of *cubic* inches. As a formula, we have

Volume = (length) $\times$ (width) $\times$ (height)

Examples

Find the volumes of the following boxes.

(a)   length = 6 inches, width = 4 inches, and height = 2 inches

Since we know the measure of the length, width, and height of our box, we can substitute these values into our formula. Notice that since our dimensions are given in inches, our answer will have cubic inches as a unit.

Volume = (length) $\times$ (width) $\times$ (height)

Volume = $(6) \times (4) \times (2)$

We can now do the multiplication and get our answer.

Volume = $(24) \times (2) = 48$ inches^3

(b)   length = 1 foot, width = 2 feet, and height = 3 feet

Since we know the measure of the length, width, and height of our box, we can substitute these values into our formula. Notice that since our dimensions are given in feet, our answer will have cubic feet as a unit.

Volume = (length) $\times$ (width) $\times$ (height)

Volume = $(1) \times (2) \times (3)$

We can now do the multiplication and get our answer.

Volume = $(2) \times (3) = 6$ feet^3

Drill: Measurement

Find the perimeters of rectangles with the following dimensions.

1.   length = 1 foot and width = 6 feet

2.   length = 2 inches and width = 4 inches

Find the perimeters of squares with the following measure on each side.

3.   side = 3 inches

4.   side = 6 feet

Find the areas of rectangles with the following dimensions.

5.   length = 9 feet and width = 12 feet

6.   length = 11 inches and width = 6 inches

Find the areas of squares with the following distances on each side.

7.   side = 11 inches

8.   side = 2 feet

Find the volumes of the following box.

9.   length = 4 inches, width = 7 inches, and height = 3 inches

10.   length = 5 feet, width = 4 feet, and height = 6 feet.

Answers to Drill Questions

1.   14 feet

Perimeter = 2(width) + 2(length)

= 2(6) + 2(1)

12 + 2 = 14 feet

2. 12 inches

    Perimeter = 2(width) + 2(length)

    = 2(4) + 2(2)

    8 + 4 = 12 inches

3. 12 inches

    Perimeter = 4(side)

    4(3) = 12 inches

4. 24 feet

    Perimeter = 4(side)

    4(6) = 24 feet

5. 108 feet^2

    Area = length × width

    9 × 12 = 108 feet^2

6. 66 inches^2

    Area = length × width

    11 × 6 = 66 inches^2

7. 121 inches^2

    Area = side^2

    11^2 = 121 inches^2

8. 4 feet^2

    Area = side^2

    2^2 = 4 feet^2

9. 84 inches^3

    Volume = length × width × height

    4 × 7 × 3 = 84 inches^3

    4 × 7 = 28

    28 × 3 = 84

10. 120 feet^3

    Volume = length × width × height

    5 × 4 × 6 = 120 feet^3

    5 × 4 = 20

    20 × 6 = 120

V. PERCENTS

INTRODUCTION TO PERCENTS

Percents play an important role in our lives. It is hard to pick up a newspaper or listen to the news without hearing the word percent or seeing the symbol (%). Some examples of this are: "Crime Rate Up 32%," "Car Prices Increase 10%," and "Going Out of Business Sale—75% Off of Everything."

The easiest way to understand percents is to think of them as so many out of 100. If, at a 100 person party, 15 of the people are males, then we know that 15% of the people are male. Likewise, if 57% of the city voted for a school levy, then we know that out of every 100 people, 57 voted yes. If the city's population is 200 people, then 114 people voted for the levy. As we saw in the last example, we do not always have 100 people but, when working with percents, it is just easier to think in that format.

If we are given information about a situation where exactly 100 people are not involved, we can convert it to a percent by dividing the number of people that meet some type of requirement by the total group. This "answer" will come out as a decimal. In order to write this value using the percent symbol, we must move the decimal point two places to the *right*. Therefore, for example, 0.39 would represent 39%. Thus, out of every 100 people, 39 would act in a certain way.

Examples

Write the following decimals as percents.

(a) 0.24

In order to change this into a percent, we must move the decimal point two places to the right. Therefore, 0.24 would be 24%.

(b) 0.457

In order to change this into a percent, we must move the decimal point two places to the right. Therefore, 0.457 would be 45.7%.

(c) 1.52

In order to change this into a percent, we must move the decimal point two places to the right. Therefore, 1.52 would be 152%.

It is also helpful to be able to convert percentages to decimals. In order to change a percent into its decimal value, we must move the decimal point two places to the left. Therefore, 16% is the same as 0.16. As we will see in the next section, when working with a percent, we must remember to convert to a decimal before any calculations are done.

Examples

Write the following percents as decimals.

(a) 38%

In order to convert a percent into a decimal, we must move the decimal point two places to the left. Even though the original problem does not contain a decimal point, one is assumed to be after the last digit. This can be written as 38.%. Therefore, 38% would be 0.38.

(b) 61.3%

In order to convert a percent into a decimal, we must move the decimal point two places to the left. Therefore, 61.3% would be 0.613.

(c) 7%

In order to convert a percent into a decimal, we must move the decimal point two places to the left. Since we only have one digit here, it might be a good idea to place a zero in front of the seven so that we can see two positions. This gives us 07%. Therefore, 7% would be 0.07.

(d) 378%

In order to convert a percent into a decimal, we must move the decimal point two places to the left. Therefore, 378% would be 3.78.

As we mentioned before, we can find the percent of something by dividing. Another way to look at this is in a fractional form. The numerator contains the number of people who meet a certain requirement. The denominator contains the total number of people. In the examples below, we will see how easy it is to find the percent.

Examples

Find the percents in the following situations.

(a) 6 is what percent of 8?

In order to find the percent here, we place the 6 in the numerator and the 8 in the denominator. This division gives us 6/8 or 0.75. From our discussion, we know that this is 75%.

(b) 9 is what percent of 72?

In order to find the percent here, we place the 9 in the numerator and the 72 in the denominator. This division gives us 9/72 or 0.125. From our discussion, we know that this is 12.5%.

(c) 4 is what percent of 28?

In order to find the percent here, we place the 4 in the numerator and the 28 in the denominator. This division gives us 4/28 or 0.1428571. From our discussion, we know that this is 14.29%, rounded to two decimal places.

Drill: Introduction to Percents

Write the following decimals using the percent symbol.

1. 0.59

2. 7.04

3. 0.085

Write the following percents as decimals.

4. 38%

5. 17.4%

6. 5.2%

Find the percents in the following situations.

7. 5 out of 25

8. 2 out of 20

9. 45 out of 405

10. 28 out of 42

Answers to Drill Questions

1. 59%

   Move the decimal point two places to the right to convert from a decimal to a percent.

2. 704%

   Move the decimal point two places to the right to convert from a decimal to a percent.

3. 8.5%

   Move the decimal point two places to the right to convert from a decimal to a percent.

4. 0.38

   Move the decimal point two places to the left when converting a percent to a decimal.

5. 0.174

   Move the decimal point two places to the left when converting a percent to a decimal.

6. 0.052

   Move the decimal point two places to the left when converting a percent to a decimal.

7. 20%

$$5 \text{ out of } 25 \ = \frac{5}{25} = .2 = 20\%$$

8. 10%

$$2 \text{ out of } 20 \ = \frac{2}{20} = .1 = 10\%$$

9. $11.1\overline{1}\%$

$$45 \text{ out of } 405 \ = \frac{45}{405}$$
$$= .111\overline{1}$$
$$= 11.1\overline{1}\%$$

10. $66.6\overline{6}\%$

$$28 \text{ out of } 42 \ = \frac{28}{42}$$
$$= .666\overline{6}$$
$$= 66.6\overline{6}\%$$

PERCENT PROBLEMS

Now that we have an introduction to percents, we want to use them in problems. We have already discussed how to denote percents and convert decimals to percents, and how to find out what percent a number is of another number. Here we want to consider the other possibilities. In the example below, we will see how to find a certain percent of a number and how to solve increase and decrease problems. A basic formula for percents is:

Amount = percent × beginning

In most percent problems this formula can be manipulated into a form that will help us.

Examples

Simplify the following percent problems.

(a) 16% of 30

Here we are given the percent and the beginning amount. We are asked to find the final amount. When working with problems involving words, "of" normally means multiplication. Also, recall that when working with percents, we need to convert them into decimals. Therefore, this problem becomes

16% of 30 or 0.16×30

We are then able to do the multiplication and simplify this to 4.8. Thus, 4.8 is 16% of 30.

(b) 248% of 500

Here we are given the percent and the beginning amount. We are asked to find the final amount. When working with problems involving words, "of" normally means multiplication. Also, recall that when working with percents, we need to convert them into decimals. Therefore, this problem becomes

248% of 500 or 2.48×500

We are then able to do the multiplication and simplify this to 1,240. Thus, 1,240 is 248% of 500.

(c) 51.9% of 6

Here we are given the percent and the beginning amount. We are asked to find the final amount. When working with problems involving words, "of" normally means multiplication. Also, recall that when working with percents, we need to convert them into decimals. Therefore, this problem becomes

51.9% of 6 or 0.519×6

We are then able to do the multiplication and simplify this to 3.114. Thus, 3.114 is 51.9% of 6. If we round our answer to one decimal place we get 3.1.

Examples

Find the numbers described below.

(a) 25% of what number is 12?

In this problem, we are given the percent and the final amount, but not the beginning amount. We also know that we must change the percent to a decimal in order to work with it. To find our answer, we must divide the final amount by the percent. Here we have

$$\frac{12}{25\%} \text{ or } \frac{12}{0.25}$$

When we divide, we get 48. This tells us that 25% of 48 is 12.

(b) 17% of what number is 51?

In this problem, we are given the percent and the final amount, but not the beginning amount. We also know that we must change the percent to a decimal in order to work with it. To find our answer, we must divide the final amount by the percent. Here we have

$$\frac{51}{17\%} \text{ or } \frac{51}{0.17}$$

When we divide, we get 300. This tells us that 17% of 300 is 51.

Drill: Percent Problems

Simplify the following percent problems.

1. 31% of 50

2. 59% of 600

Find the numbers described below.

3. 12% of what number is 25?

4. 67% of what number is 46?

5. 89% of what number is 512?

Answers to Drill Questions

1. 15.5

   31% of $50 = 31\% \times 50 = .31 \times 50 = 15.5$

2. 354

   59% of $600 = 59\% \times 600 = .59 \times 600 = 354$

3. $208.3\overline{3}$

   The required number is

   $25 \div 12\% = 25 \div .12 = 208.3\overline{3}$

4. 68.656716

   The required number is

   $46 \div 67\% = 46 \div .67 = 68.656716$

5. 575.2809

   The required number is

   $512 \div 89\% = 512 \div .89 = 575.2809$

VI. ADVANCED TOPICS

PROBABILITY

Now that we have a good understanding of mathematics, we want to discuss some other topics that are a little bit more involved. The first of these topics is probability. Geometry and multi-step word problems will be covered later in this section.

In probability, we are studying the chance of something happening. This is called a **successful outcome**. In other words, we want to know what is the chance that a successful outcome will occur in a certain situation. Here we will be looking at results that are not under our control. That is, the outcome is random. We come across a lot of places where probability can be used. Two examples would be the state lottery and game shows.

The probability of an outcome is expressed between 0 and 1. Percents can also be used here. A probability of 0 (or 0%) denotes an impossibility. An event with 0% probability will never happen. A probability of 1 (or 100%) must happen. An event with 100% probability will always occur. All other probabilities lie somewhere between 0 and 1, that is, between 0% and 100% (if percentages are used). Below is the general formula that can be used to calculate the probability of an event occurring.

$$\text{Probability} = \frac{\text{Number of ways a successful outcome can occur}}{\text{Number of possible outcomes}}$$

Examples

Twenty marbles are placed in a can. Two are black, six white, five red, four blue, and three yellow. Without looking, one marble is drawn from the can. What is the probability of the following occurring?

(a)   What is the probability of drawing a blue marble?

Since our can contains four blue marbles, there are four ways for a successful outcome to occur. We have a total of 20 marbles in the can, and each has an equal chance of being drawn. Hence, there are 20 possible outcomes. We can now put this information into our formula and calculate the probability.

$$\text{Probability} = \frac{\text{Number of ways a successful outcome can occur}}{\text{Number of possible outcomes}}$$

$$\text{Probability} = \frac{4}{20} = 0.20$$

Therefore, the probability of drawing a blue marble is 0.2 or 20%.

(b)   What is the probability of drawing a black marble?

Since our can contains two black marbles, there are two ways for a successful outcome to occur. We have a total of 20 marbles in the can, and each has an equal chance of being drawn. Hence, there are 20 possible outcomes. We can now put this information into our formula and calculate the probability.

$$\text{Probability} = \frac{\text{Number of ways a successful outcome can occur}}{\text{Number of possible outcomes}}$$

$$\text{Probability} = \frac{2}{20} = 0.10$$

Therefore, the probability of drawing a black marble is 0.1 or 10%.

(c)   What is the probability of drawing a white marble?

Since our can contains six white marbles, there are six ways for a successful outcome to occur. We have a total of 20 marbles in the can, and each has an equal chance of being drawn. Hence, there are 20 possible outcomes. We can now put this information into our formula and calculate the probability.

$$\text{Probability} = \frac{\text{Number of ways a successful outcome can occur}}{\text{Number of possible outcomes}}$$

$$\text{Probability} = \frac{6}{20} = 0.30$$

Therefore, the probability of drawing a white marble is 0.3 or 30%.

(d)   What is the probability of drawing a red, white, or blue marble?

Since our can contains five red, six white, and four blue marbles, there are 15 ways for a successful outcome to occur. We have a total of 20 marbles in the can, and each has an equal chance of being drawn. Hence, there are 20 possible outcomes. We can now put this information into our formula and calculate the probability.

$$\text{Probability} = \frac{\text{Number of ways a successful outcome can occur}}{\text{Number of possible outcomes}}$$

$$\text{Probability} = \frac{15}{20} = 0.75$$

Therefore, the probability of drawing a red, white, or blue marble is 0.75 or 75%.

Drill: Probability

Fifteen marbles are placed in a can. Five are pink, six blue, two yellow, one orange, and one white. Without looking, one marble is drawn from the can. Find the probability of the following events occurring.

1. What is the probability of drawing an orange marble?

2. What is the probability of drawing a blue marble?

3. What is the probability of drawing a yellow or white marble?

4. What is the probability of drawing a pink marble?

5. What is the probability of drawing a pink, yellow, orange, or white marble?

Answers to Drill Questions

1. $6.6\overline{6}\%$

    Probability of drawing orange

    $$= \frac{1}{15} = 6.6\overline{6}\%$$

2. 0.4 or 40%

    Probability of drawing blue

    $$= \frac{6}{15} = 40\%$$

3. 0.2 or 20%

    Probability of drawing yellow or white

$$= \frac{2+1}{15} = \frac{3}{15} = 20\%$$

4. $0.\overline{3}$ or $33.\overline{33}\%$

Probability of drawing pink

$$= \frac{5}{15} = 33.\overline{3}3\%$$

5. 0.6 or 60%

Probability of drawing pink, yellow, orange, or white

$$= \frac{5+2+1+1}{15} = \frac{9}{15} = 60\%$$

GEOMETRY

A **circle** is an object where every point on the curve is an equal distance from a center point. We now need to introduce some terminology that is particular to circles. If we draw a straight line from one side of the circle, through the center, and then continue to the other side, this line is called the **diameter**. The formula for the diameter is

Diameter = 2 × radius. The **radius** is half of the diameter. The formula for the radius is

Radius = $\frac{1}{2}$ × diameter.

Examples

Find the radii of the following circles.

(a) Circle with diameter of 16 inches.

Since we know the diameter of this circle, we can calculate the radius easily.

Radius = $\left(\frac{1}{2}\right)$ × (diameter)

Radius = $\left(\frac{1}{2}\right)$ × (16) = 8

Therefore, the radius is 8 inches.

(b) Circle with diameter of 2 feet.

Since we know the diameter of this circle, we can calculate the radius easily.

Radius = $\left(\frac{1}{2}\right)$ × (diameter)

$$\text{Radius} = \left(\frac{1}{2}\right) \times (2), \text{ Radius} = 1 \text{ foot}$$

Therefore, the radius is 1 foot.

Examples

Find the diameters of the following circles.

(a) Circle with radius of 3 inches.

Since we know the radius, we can plug its value into our formula and calculate the diameter.

Diameter = (2) × (radius)

Diameter = (2) × (3)

Diameter = 6 inches

Therefore, the diameter of this circle is 6 inches.

(b) Circle with radius of 1.6 feet.

Since we know the radius, we can plug its value into our formula and calculate the diameter.

Diameter = (2) × (radius)

Diameter = (2) × (1.6)

Diameter = 3.2 feet

Therefore, the diameter of this circle is 3.2 feet.

Drill: Geometry

Find the radii of the following circles. If needed, round your answers to the hundredths place.

1. Circle with diameter of 13 inches.

2. Circle with diameter of 5 centimeters.

Find the diameters of the following circles. If needed, round your answer to the hundredths place.

3. Circle with radius of 7 feet.

4. Circle with radius of 12.6 inches.

5. Circle with radius of 2.25 centimeters.

Answers to Drill Questions

1. $6\dfrac{1}{2}$ or 6.5 inches

    Radius $= \left(\dfrac{1}{2}\right) \times$ (diameter)

    Radius $= \left(\dfrac{1}{2}\right) \times (13)$

    Radius $= \dfrac{13}{2} = 6\dfrac{1}{2}$ or 6.5 inches

2. $2\dfrac{1}{2}$ or 2.5 centimeters

    Radius $= \left(\dfrac{1}{2}\right) \times$ (diameter)

    Radius $= \left(\dfrac{1}{2}\right) \times (5)$

    Radius $= \dfrac{5}{2} = 2\dfrac{1}{2}$ or 2.5 centimeters

3. 14 feet

    Diameter $= (2) \times$ (radius)

    Diameter $= (2) \times (7)$

    Diameter $= 14$ feet

4. 25.2 inches

    Diameter $= (2) \times$ (radius)

    Diameter $= (2) \times (12.6)$

    Diameter $= 25.2$ inches

5. 4.5 centimeters

    Diameter $= (2) \times$ (radius)

    Diameter $= (2) \times (2.25)$

    Diameter $= 4.5$ centimeters

MULTI-STEP WORD PROBLEMS

Since we are now "experts" in mathematics, we want to discuss multi-step word problems. Throughout this section, we will be building upon ideas that we have already covered. In these examples, it is best to break the problem into different steps and then solve each of them separately.

The biggest area where this can be seen is when we spend money. Sometimes this is called Consumer Mathematics. A common question is how much money will we have left? To answer this question, we must first know how much we have and how much we spent. The following examples will show this in more detail.

Examples

Solve the following problems.

(a)   Kelli goes to the store to get a few groceries. She buys two loaves of bread for $2.19, some oranges for $1.99, a pound of ham for $3.99, and three candy bars for $1.70. If Kelli gives the clerk $10, how much change will she get back?

First, we must find out how much she spent. This can be done by adding everything together.

Spent = (Bread) + (Oranges) + (Ham) + (Candy)

Spent = (2.19) + (1.99) + (3.99) + (1.70)

Spent = $9.87

Now that we know that she spent $9.87, we can subtract this value from the amount she gave the clerk to find out how much change she will get back.

Change = (Total) – (Spent)

Change = $10.00 – $9.87

Change = $0.13

Therefore, she will have $0.13 (or 13 cents) left after her purchases.

(b)   George is buying furniture for his new home. He buys a couch and chair for $599, a television for $279, a bed for $978, and a table with chairs for $1,200. If the sales tax is $155 and George gives the salesperson $3,500, how much change will he get back?

First, we must find out how much he spent. This can be done by adding everything together.

Spent = (Couch & Chair) + (Television) + (Bed) + (Table & Chairs) + (Tax)

Spent = (599) + (279) + (978) + (1,200) + (155)

Spent = $3,211

Now that we know that he spent $3,211, we can subtract this value from the amount he gave the salesperson to find out how much change he will get back.

Change = (Total) – (Spent)

Change = $3,500 – $3,211

Change = $289

Therefore, he will have $289 left after his purchases.

Solving increase and decrease problems is a good example of how we can split problems into pieces. In most cases, percents are involved. We are looking to see what the final amount will be if the beginning amount is increased (or decreased) by a certain percent. The examples below will show this in more detail.

Examples

In the following problems, find the amount of increase and the new amount.

(a)   The price of a $30 book is increased by 10%. What will be the new price of the book?

In this problem, the increase will be 10% of the original price (or $30). By converting the percent into a decimal and multiplying, we can find the amount of the increase.

Increase = 10% of $30

Increase = $0.10 \times 30 = \$3$

By combining the increase with the original price, we can find the new price of the book easily. Therefore, the new price will be

(New Price) = (Old Price) + (Increase)

(New Price) = $30 + $3 = $33

Therefore, the new price will be $33.

(b)   The attendance at a football game increases by 37%. If 12,000 people normally attend, how many will be attending now?

In this problem, the increase will be 37% of the original attendance (or 12,000). By converting the percent into a decimal and multiplying, we can find the amount of the increase.

Increase = 37% of 12,000

Increase = $0.37 \times 12,000 = 4,400$ people

By combining the increase with the original attendance, we can find the new attendance at the football game easily. Therefore, the new attendance will be

(New Attendance) = (Old Attendance) + (Increase)

(New Attendance) = 12,000 + 4,400 = 16,400 people

Therefore, the new attendance will be 16,400 people.

(c)   A magazine normally contains 25 pages. If the number of pages increases by 145%, how many pages does it now have?

In this problem, the increase will be 145% of the original number of pages (or 25). By converting the percent into a decimal and multiplying, we can find the amount of the increase.

Increase = 145% of 25

Increase = $1.45 \times 25 = 36.25$ pages

By combining the increase with the original number of pages, we can find the new number of pages in the magazine easily. Therefore, the new number of pages will be

(New Number of Pages) = (Old Number of Pages) + (Increase)

(New Number of Pages) = 25 + 36.25 = 61.25

Therefore, the magazine will now have approximately 62 pages.

Examples

In the following problems, find the amount of decrease and the new amount.

(a)   A grocery store is having a sale on hot dogs (normally priced at $1.09). If, during the sale, the price is reduced by 83%, what is the sale price?

In this problem, the discount will be 83% of the original price (or $1.09). By converting the percent into a decimal and multiplying, we can find the amount of the discount.

Discount = 83% of $1.09

Discount = 0.83 × 1.09 = $0.9047

By combining the discount with the original price, we can find the new price of the hot dogs easily. Therefore, the new price will be

(New Price) = (Old Price) – (Discount)

(New Price) = $1.09 – $0.9047 = $0.1853

Therefore, during the sale, a package of hot dogs will sell for $0.19 (or 19 cents).

(b)   The attendance at a high school basketball game decreased by 17%. If 125 people normally attend, how many people will attend now?

In this problem, the decrease will be 17% of the original attendance (or 125). By converting the percent into a decimal and multiplying, we can find the amount of the decrease.

Decrease = 17% of 125

Decrease = 0.17 × 125 = 21.25 people

By combining the decrease with the original attendance, we can find the new attendance easily. Therefore, the new attendance will be

(New Attendance) = (Old Attendance) – (Decrease)

(New Attendance) = 125 – 21.25 = 103.75

Therefore, the new attendance at the basketball game will be approximately 104 people.

(c)   The weight of a package of cookies decreases by 26%. What is the weight of a new package if the old package weighed 16 ounces?

In this problem, the decrease will be 26% of the original weight (or 16). By converting the percent into a decimal and multiplying, we can find the amount of the decrease.

Decrease = 26% of 16

Decrease $= 0.26 \times 16 = 4.16$ ounces

By combining the decrease with the original weight, we can find the new weight easily. Therefore, the weight will become

(New Weight) = (Old Weight) – (Decrease)

(New Weight) $= 16 - 4.16 = 11.84$

Therefore, the new weight of the cookie package will be approximately 12 ounces.

Drill: Multi-Step Word Problems

Solve the following problems.

1. Sam goes to the store for groceries. He buys a turkey for $19.75, bread for $1.99, and peaches for $0.36. If he gives the cashier $30, how much will he get back?

2. Nancy is shopping at a craft store. If she has $10 and purchases styrofoam for $2.99, yarn for $1.99, glue for $0.99, and the sales tax is $0.36, how much will she get back?

3. Edith needs to send some flower arrangements. If she has $400 to spend and sends six arrangements at $39.90 each, how much will she have left?

    In the following problems, find the amount of increase and the new amount.

4. The price of a newspaper increases by 7%. If it originally cost $1.25, what would be the new price?

5. The attendance at a hockey game increases by 58%. If the original attendance is 37,000, what would be the new attendance?

6. The population of a town increased by 201%. If the original population was 47,123, what would be the new population?

7. The number of books published by REA increases by 2.572%. If they originally published 150 books, how many books do they now publish?

    In the following problems, find the amount of decrease and the new amount.

8. The population of a city decreases by 42%. If the original population was 152,967, what would be the new population?

9. A cookie is now 92% fat free. If the regular cookie contains 6.2 grams of fat, how much fat does the "fat free" cookie have?

10. The number of pages in a magazine decreases by 78%. If the original magazine contained 99 pages, how many pages will the magazine now have?

Answers to Drill Questions

1. $7.90

    $19.75
      1.99 $30.00
    +   .36   ⟶   − 22.10
    $22.10 total purchases $ 7.90 change

2. $3.67

      $2.99
       1.99
        .99 $10.00
    +   .36 ⟶ − 6.33
      $6.33 total $3.67 change

3. $160.60

    6 arrangements × $39.90 = 239.40 total
      $400.00
    − 239.40
      $160.60 left

4. $1.34

    New price = $1.25 + (.07 × $1.25) = $1.34

5. 58,460 people

    New attendance = 37,000 + (.58 × 37,000) = 58,460 people

6. 141,840 people

    New population = 47,123 + (2.01 × 47,123) = 141,840 people

7. 154 books

    Number of books = 150 + (.02572 × 150) = 154 books

8. 88,721 people

    New population = 152,967 − (.42 × 152,967) = 88,721 people

9. 0.496 grams

    Amount of fat = 6.2 − (.92 × 6.2) = .496 grams

10. 22 pages

    Number of pages = 99 − (.78 × 99) = 22 pages

COOP/ HSPT

CHAPTER 6

Quantitative Skills Review

Chapter 6

QUANTITATIVE SKILLS REVIEW

I. SERIES QUESTIONS
II. COMPARISON QUESTIONS
III. PRE-ALGEBRA QUESTIONS

Remember, there is no penalty for getting a wrong answer, so it is good test-taking practice to guess an answer if you cannot figure one out. While you are taking the test, guess the answers to questions you have trouble with, and check them on your question sheet. Then, if you have time at the end of the test, you can go back and look at them again. If you do skip questions, make sure you skip the corresponding spaces on the answer sheet. Check now and then during the test to be sure that the number on the answer sheet corresponds to the question you are answering.

In any case, there is a strong emphasis on questions that ask you to compare sizes, give sequences, and find numbers from word descriptions. If you had trouble with either the *Quantitative Skills* subtest of the HSPT or the *Sequences* test on the COOP, you'll need to take time and study one or more of the following areas:

- Sequences
- Geometric and nongeometric comparisons
- Number manipulations.

I. SERIES QUESTIONS

Series questions begin with the words: "Look at this series," followed by a list of integers. This is followed by the question "What numeral should come next?" or, less often, the question "What numeral should fill in the blank?"

Your goal is to find a pattern in the numbers and use the pattern to determine the missing number. The best way to figure out the pattern is to start at the beginning of the list and see how to get from the first number to the second number. Then, take the second number and see how to get from it to the third number. If you find the same method in both cases, you have probably discovered the rule for all the numbers. If the methods are different, continue on to the next two pairs of numbers and see if the pattern you discovered for the first two pairs is repeated. If it is, you have found the rule.

The four basic arithmetic operations — addition, subtraction, multiplication, and division — are used to get from number to number. In a majority of questions, only one operation is used, but many questions involve two operations.

TIP: Here is a good way to solve series problems.

Write the operation and number you use to get from one number in the series to the next directly on the question sheet. Write them between and slightly above each pair of numbers.

Example

Look at the series: 2, 3, 7, 8, 12,... What numeral should come next?

To answer, write on the question sheet as follows:

$$+1 \quad +4 \quad +1 \quad +4 \quad +1 = 13$$
$$2, \quad 3, \quad 7, \quad 8, \quad 12,...$$

The answer is the sum of 12 and 1, or 13.

Sometimes it is not clear what the rule is to get from one number to the next. Look at the next example.

Example

Look at the series: 2, 3, 6, 7, 14, 15,... What numeral should come next?

To answer, write on the question sheet as follows:

$$+1 \quad x2 \quad +1 \quad x2 \quad +1 \quad x2 = 30$$
$$+1 \quad +3 \quad +1 \quad +7 \quad +1 \quad +11?$$
$$2, \quad 3, \quad 6, \quad 7, \quad 14, \quad 15,...$$

The answer is the product of 15 and 2, or 30. Note that the rule is not always clear, so keep all four arithmetic operations in mind while answering series questions.

☞ Drill: Series

For questions 1 through 5, what numeral should come next?

1. 60, 68, 76, 84, 92,...

2. 96, 48, 24, 12, 6,...

3. 91, 87, 80, 76, 69,...

4. 4, 7, 11, 16, 22,...

5. 55, 50, 25, 20, 10,...

For question 6, what numeral should fill in the blank?

6. 14, 24, __, 41, 48, 54,...

Answers to Drill Questions

1. The correct answer is 100. To get from 60 to 68, add 8. To get from 68 to 76, add 8. The "add 8" rule applies to the next two numbers also. So, to get the last number, add 8 to 92, which yields 100.

$$+8 \quad +8 \quad +8 \quad +8 \quad +8 = 100$$

60, 68, 76, 84, 92,...

2. The correct answer is 3. To get from 96 to 48, you could subtract 48, divide by 2, or, what is the same thing, multiply by 1/2. To get from 48 to 24, you could subtract 24, or divide by 2. Since the rule "divide by 2" is repeated, we try it for the next two numbers. Since it works, the last number must be 6 divided by 2, which is 3.

$$\div2 \quad \div2 \quad \div2 \quad \div2 \quad \div2 = 3$$

-48   -24

96, 48, 24, 12, 6,...

3. The correct answer is 65. To get from 91 to 87, subtract 4. To get from 87 to 80, subtract 7. This is not a repeat of the "subtract 4" rule, so let's try the next two pairs of numbers. To get from 80 to 76, subtract 4, and from 76 to 69, subtract 7. Since the rules "subtract 4" and "subtract 7" repeat, we get the next number by subtracting 4, and 4 subtracted from 69 is 65.

$$-4 \quad -7 \quad -4 \quad -7 \quad -4 = 65$$

91, 87, 80, 76, 69,...

4. The correct answer is 29. To get from 4 to 7, add 3. To get from 7 to 11, add 4. This is not a repeat of the "add 3" rule, so let's try the next two pairs of numbers. To get from 11 to 16, add 5, and from 16 to 22, add 6. It appears that the number added goes up by one each time. So, to get the last number, we add 7 to 22 to get 29.

$$+3 \quad +4 \quad +5 \quad +6 \quad +7 = 29$$

4, 7, 11, 16, 22,...

5. The correct answer is 5. To get from 55 to 50, subtract 5. To get from 50 to 25, either subtract 25 or divide by 2. Let's try the next two pairs of numbers. To get from 25 to 20, subtract 5, and from 20 to 10, either subtract 10 or divide by 2. Since dividing by 2 is a repeat

rule, we would use it if we had to. However, we get the next number using the "subtract 5" rule, and 5 subtracted from 10 is 5.

$$-5 \quad \div 2 \quad -5 \quad \div 2 \quad -5 = 5$$

$$-5 \quad -25 \quad -5 \quad -10? \quad -5$$

$$55, \quad 50, \quad 25, \quad 20, \quad 10, ...$$

6.   The answer is 33. This question is somewhat harder because the missing number is in the middle, not at the end. To get from 14 to 24, add 10. We can't do the next two pairs, but to get from 41 to 48, add 7, and to get from 48 to 54, add 6. The number being added seems to be decreasing by 1. Let's try adding 9 to 24 to get the following number, 33. If we then add 8 to 33 we get 41, so the rule — add a number that drops by 1 each time — works for all the numbers. Therefore, the missing number is 33.

$$+10 \quad +9 \quad +8 \quad +7 \quad +6$$

$$14, \quad 24, \quad \_\_, \quad 41, \quad 48, \quad 54, ...$$

TIP: When you do series questions, first solve the problem, then look at the four choices. If you have done the problem correctly, you should find your answer on the list of choices. Then just mark it on the answer sheet. If you look at the choices first, you may confuse yourself and have trouble analyzing the series correctly.

II. COMPARISON QUESTIONS

Comparison questions begin either with words similar to, (1) "Examine (A), (B), and (C) and find the best answer," followed by three choices—(A), (B), and (C)—in picture form or numerical expression form, or the words, (2) "Examine the figure (or circle, or graph, etc.) and find the best answer," followed by 'a' geometric figure or graph. Most questions follow the "A, B, C" format, but a few follow the "examine the figure" format. All questions conclude with four statements comparing quantities in the pictures or expressions, and you must choose the statement that is true.

PICTURES AND GRAPHS

Pictures can represent any of the following: a number of items; a fraction or area; or a geometric figure. Graphs can be of different types, including picture graphs and bar graphs.

TIP: Here is a good way to solve comparison problems.

Write the quantity associated with each picture, graph, important part of the figure, or numerical expression directly on the question sheet. It will then be easier to choose the true statement at the end of the problem.

☞ Drill: Pictures and Graphs

DIRECTIONS: Choose the best answer.

Number of Items

1. Examine (*A*), (*B*), and (*C*) and find the best answer.

    (*A*)   (*B*)   (*C*)

    (A) *A* and *C* are equal.   (C) *B* and *C* are equal.

    (B) *B* is greater than *A*.   (D) *A* is greater than *B*.

Fraction or Area

2. Examine the equal rectangles (*A*), (*B*), and (*C*) and find the best answer regarding their shaded parts.

    (*A*)   (*B*)   (*C*)

    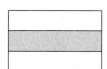

    (A) *A* is greater than *B*.   (C) *B* is greater than both *A* and *C*.

    (B) *A* is smaller than *C*.   (D) *A*, *B*, and *C* are equal.

Picture Graph

3. Examine *A*, *B*, and *C* and find the best answer.

     = 40 People   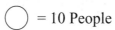 = 10 People

    (*A*)   (*B*)   (*C*)

    (A) *A* and *B* are equal.

(B) *A* plus *B* equals *C*.

(C) *C* is greater than *A* and *B* combined.

(D) *C* is less than *A* and *B* combined.

Geometric Figure

4.   Examine the circle with center *B* and find the best answer.

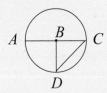

(A) *BC* is equal to *CD*   (C) *AC* is equal to *CD*

(B) *AB* is equal to *CD*   (D) *BD* is equal to *AB*

Bar Graph

5.

(A) *A* plus *B* equals *C* plus *D*

(B) *C* minus *D* equals *B* minus *A*.

(C) *C* minus *A* equals *B* minus *D*.

(D) *A* plus *D* equals *B* plus *C*.

ANSWERS TO DRILL QUESTIONS

1.   **(D)** The correct answer is (D). Count the circles in each part and write the numbers on the picture. You should have *A* = 12, *B* = 11, and *C* = 10. Then it is obvious that the only correct answer is that *A* is greater than *B*.

2.   **(D)** The correct answer is (D). Write the fraction represented by each picture. You should have *A* = 1/3, *B* = 1/3, and *C* = 3/9 which reduces to 1/3. Since all three fractions are equal, (D) is the correct answer.

3.   **(B)** The correct answer is (B). Writing the number represented by the picture in each part, you should get *A* = 10 people, *B* = 40 + 10 = 50 people, and *C* = 40 + (2 × 10) = 40 + 20 = 60 people. Since *A* (10 people) + *B* (50 people) = 60, (B) is the correct answer.

4.   **(D)** The correct answer is (D). *AB* is a radius of the circle, as is *BC* and *BD*. Since all radii are equal in length, (D) is the correct answer. Note that *CD* is longer than either *BD* or *BC* because it is the longest side in triangle *BCD*. On the other hand, *CD* cannot be as long as *AC* because *A* is the point on the circle that is farthest from *C*.

5.   **(B)** The answer is (B). Writing the height of each bar of the graph beside its label, you should get $A = 2$, $B = 4$, $C = 5$, and $D = 3$. Since $C - D = 2$, and $B - A = 2$, (B) is the correct answer.

NUMERICAL EXPRESSIONS

About half of the comparison questions involve numerical expressions. These are usually one of three kinds: grouping, numerals, or miscellaneous. The numerals may be in ratio, decimal, or percent form.

Remember: Write the number or simplified version of each part on the question sheet beside the expression.

☞ Drill: Numerical Expressions

<u>**DIRECTIONS:**</u> Choose the best answer.

Grouping

1.   Examine (*A*), (*B*), and (*C*) and find the best answer.

   (*A*) $(3 + 2) \times 4$

   (*B*) $3 + (2 \times 4)$

   (*C*) $(3 \times 4) + 2$

      (A)   *A* is greater than both *B* and *C*.

      (B)   *B* is greater than *C*.

      (C)   *C* is greater than *A*.

      (D)   *A*, *B*, and *C* are equal.

Numerals

2. Examine (*A*), (*B*), and (*C*) and find the best answer.

   (*A*) 5%

(B) 1/5

(C) .5

    (A) *A* is the largest number.

    (B) *B* is the largest number.

    (C) *C* is the largest number.

    (D) *A* and *C* are equal.

Miscellaneous

3.   Examine (*A*), (*B*), and (*C*) and find the best answer.

    (A) 2^3

    (B) 3^2

    (C) 3×2

    (A) *A* is greater than *B*.

    (B) *A* is equal to *B*.

    (C) *A* and *C* are equal.

    (D) *A* is greater than *C*.

Answers to Drill Questions

1. **(A)** Choice (A) is the correct answer. Evaluate each expression first, and write the answer on the question sheet beside the expression. Remember to do the expressions in parentheses first.

For *A*, $(3 + 2) = 5$, and $5 \times 4 = 20$.

For *B*, $(2 \times 4) = 8$, and $3 + 8 = 11$.

For *C*, $(3 \times 4) = 12$, and $12 + 2 = 14$.

Since 20 is greater than both 11 and 14, (A) is the correct answer.

2. **(C)** Choice (C) is the correct answer. Express each fraction in the same form. Let's try decimals.

For (*A*), $5\% = .05$.

For (*B*), $1/5 = .20$.

(*C*) is already expressed in decimal form, but let's write it to the same number of decimal places as (*A*) and (*B*), or $.5 = .50$.

408

Since .50 is greater than both .05 and .20, (C) is the correct answer.

3.   **(D)** Choice (D) is the correct answer.

For (*A*), $2^3 = 2 \times 2 \times 2 = 8$.

For (*B*), $3^2 = 3 \times 3 = 9$.

For (*C*), $3 \times 2 = 6$.

Since 9 is greater than 6, (D) is the correct answer.

TIP: To do comparison questions, you have to consider the four choices you are given and choose the best one. You might find it helpful to cross off wrong answers as you reject them. This way, you won't get confused about which choices you have considered already and which you haven't. Also, if you correctly eliminate three answers, the fourth answer must be the right one.

III. PRE-ALGEBRA QUESTIONS

Pre-algebra questions ask you to find a number from a word description. The questions begin with the words, "What number..." or an expression like, "1/2 of what number..." followed by information about the number or, in the second case, 1/2 of the number. After you determine the number from the information you have been given, you choose the letter associated with it from the list of four choices that follows the question.

In order to answer the questions, you must know the mathematical meanings of certain words or expressions. Examine the following table:

Expression	Word Meaning	Mathematical Notation	Example
1/2 of	1/2 times	$1/2 \times$	$1/2$ of $20 = 1/2 \times 20 = 10$
3 more than	add 3	$+3$	3 more than $12 = 12 + 3 = 15$
3 less than	subtract 3	-3	3 less than $12 = 12 - 3 = 9$
is, makes, leaves	equals	$=$	3 less than 12 makes $= 12 - 3 = 9$
4 squared	4 times itself	4^2 or 4×4	4 squared is $4^2 = 4 \times 4 = 16$
twice	2 times	$2 \times$	twice $7 = 2 \times 7 = 14$

There are two main ways to solve these questions. The first is to use algebra. If you have not studied algebra through simple linear equations, use the second method. The second is to do the calculation directly from the words of the question—the word method. Let's do an example using both methods. *(Note: We have called these questions "pre-algebra" questions because you do not need to know algebra to solve them.)*

Example

What number is 5 more than 1/4 of 36?

A. Algebra method. Translate the sentence into algebra. Use *x* for "what number."

$$x = (1/4 \times 36) + 5$$
$$x = 9 + 5$$
$$x = 14$$

B. Word method. First evaluate the expression after the word "equals," which is usually "is," "makes," or "leaves."

$$1/4 \text{ of } 36 = 1/4 \times 36 = 9$$
$$5 \text{ more than } 9 = 9 + 5 = 14$$

Then determine the number from the remaining information. In this example, the number is 14.

Now let's do a more difficult example.

Example

What number subtracted from 35 leaves 6 less than 1/3 of 42?

A. Algebra method. Translate into algebra.

$$35 - x = (1/3 \times 42) - 6$$
$$35 - x = 14 - 6$$
$$35 - x = 8$$

Subtracting 35 from both sides of the equation gives

$$-x = 8 - 35$$

So, $-x = -27$, and multiplying both sides by -1 gives

$$x = 27$$

B. Word method. Evaluate the expression to the right of "leaves" in the question.

$$1/3 \text{ of } 42 = 1/3 \times 42 = 14$$
$$6 \text{ less than } 14 = 14 - 6 = 8$$

If we subtract some number from 35 to get 8, the number must be 27 since $35 - 8 = 27$. So, the answer is 27.

TIP: If you are using the word method, you might want to use the process of elimination once you have evaluated the expression to the right of the word "equals." That is, try each of the four choices you are given until you find the right one.

For example, look at the problem we just did. It says, "What number subtracted from 35 leaves...," and you have figured out that it leaves 8. Assume that the question included the following four choices for answers: (A) 22; (B) 17; (C) 27; (D) 29. You could subtract each number from 35 until you get an answer of 8. Again, the obvious answer is (C) 27.

Try the following drill questions. Look at the table above if you are not sure what the words mean. Answers and explanations follow the questions. (Note that the four choices are not included here, but if you want to use the process of elimination method, you can practice it in the sample tests that follow this section.)

☞ Drill: Pre-Algebra

DIRECTIONS: Solve the following problems using the algebra method or word method.
---

1. What number is 7 less than 2/3 of 18?

2. What number divided by 6 leaves 8 more than 7?

3. What number added to 12 is twice the product of 3 and 1/2 of 14?

4. 1/4 of what number is 3 more than 2 squared?

5. What number multiplied by 4 makes 7 more than half of 26?

Answers to Drill Questions

1. The correct answer is 5.

    A. Algebra method. Translate the words into algebra.

$$x = (2/3 \times 18) - 7$$
$$x = 12 - 7$$
$$x = 5$$

    B. Word method. Evaluate the sentence after the word "is."

2/3 of 18 = 2/3 × 18 = 12

7 less than 12 = 12 − 7 = 5

2. The correct answer is 90.

    A. Algebra method.

$$x/6 = 7 + 8$$
$$x/6 = 15$$

Multiplying both sides of the equation by 6 yields

$$x = 90$$

    B. Word method.

8 more than 7 = 7 + 8 = 15

If a number divided by 6 equals 15, the number must be
6 times 15, which equals 90.

3. The correct answer is 30.

    A. Algebra method.

$$12 + x = 2 \times (3 \times (1/2 \times 14))$$

Do parentheses from the inside out.

$$12 + x = 2 \times (3 \times 7)$$

$12 + x = 2 \times 21$

$12 + x = 42$

Subtract 12 from both sides.

$x = 30$

B.   Word method.

$1/2$ of $14 = 1/2 \times 14 = 7$

the product of 3 and $7 = 3 \times 7 = 21$

twice $21 = 2 \times 21 = 42$

If a number is added to 12 to get 42, the number must be 42 minus 12, or 30.

4.   The correct answer is 28.

A.   Algebra method.

$1/4 \times x = (2 \times 2) + 3$

$1/4 \times x = 4 + 3$

$1/4 \times x = 7$

Multiply both sides by 4, which gives

$x = 28$

B.   Word method.

2 squared $= 2 \times 2 = 4$

3 more than $4 = 4 + 3 = 7$

$1/4$ of a number is 7, so the number must be 4 times 7, or 28.

5.   The correct answer is 5.

A.   Algebra method.

$4x = (1/2 \times 26) + 7$

$4x = 13 + 7$

$4x = 20$

Divide both sides by 4.

$x = 5$

B.   Word method.

half of $26 = 1/2 \times 26 = 13$

7 more than $13 = 13 + 7 = 20$

If the number multiplied by 4 makes 20, the number must be 20 divided by 4, or 5.

Point to Remember: There are three types of questions. If you like doing one type more than the other two, do that type first. You will gain confidence as you do them and will be more likely to succeed with the harder questions later. Similarly, if there is one type of question you don't like to do, save questions of that type for the end.

COOP/ HSPT

CHAPTER 7

Memory

Review

Chapter 7

MEMORY REVIEW

When you hear that you are going to have a vocabulary test, do you get nervous because you think you have a bad memory? Maybe you don't always do as well on tests as you would like, but that doesn't mean you have a bad memory. You probably remember the lyrics to some of your favorite songs, the phone numbers of some of your friends, and even which shows are on TV at which times. When you think about all of the things you have memorized already, you should realize that you do not have a bad memory. You are able to remember things, and with a few tricks, you can learn to memorize even more.

Memory is a skill, and like any other skill, it can improve with practice. But, people need to be taught the techniques and strategies that they can use to improve their memory. These strategies can be used when studying for a vocabulary quiz, a science test, or any other test that requires memorization. But, it's not just helpful with tests; memory techniques should be considered lifelong skills that you can use in many areas of your life! So, while reviewing the strategies explained for the *memory* test, keep these few points in mind:

•   You are able to remember many things.

•   Your memory will be even better once you learn some memory strategies and techniques.

•   The more you practice these memory tricks, the better you will become at using them, and the better your memory will be.

•   You will be able to use these important strategies in and out of school.

Think about it: What do you want to memorize? Your friends' birthdates; statistics about your favorite performers and sports stars; lyrics to your favorite songs; other school-, home-, and work-related information? Everyone can use memory techniques in many different ways. Your memory will be "tested" when you take the COOP exam, and the strategies you are about to learn will help you on this exam, as well as in many other areas of your life. (Part of the COOP memory test is based on "made up" words. The following examples will also use "made up" words.)

LEARNING THE STRATEGIES

Sometimes people think it's very difficult to memorize information and assume they just have bad memories. It may seem hard because they may not have been taught some of the techniques and "tricks" that can help them. Consider this example: Pat might not be able to change the oil in the car. That doesn't mean Pat is stupid or that he will never be able to change the oil in the car; it just means that Pat has never been taught to do it. Once someone shows Pat, it will be easy for him to change the oil. Likewise, once you learn a few strategies for improving your memory, you will be able to remember many, many things — especially new words.

PRACTICING THE STRATEGIES

Think about it: What is something that you do pretty well? Dance? Play a sport? Play an instrument? Ride a horse? Snowboard? Skate? Think about how you did when you first tried this activity. How did you get better? You probably took lessons or practiced frequently. Memory is like this. Not only do you need to be taught strategies to improve your memory, but you need to practice in order to improve your ability to remember things.

TECHNIQUES: ASSOCIATION AND VISUALIZATION

Have you ever been a member of an association or club? As part of a group, you have a **connection or link** to the other members. Maybe you've been told that you were "guilty by association" because you were nearby when trouble started. Even though you were innocent, you were **linked or connected** to the problem. Have you ever said, "I don't associate with him," about someone with whom you do not spend time? When you associate with someone, you are **connected or linked** to that person in some way.

In memory, an association is a connection or a link. Making "associations" will help you memorize words. New words will be easier to remember if you link them or associate them with something you already know or with which you are familiar. It is much easier to remember something you are familiar with, something known, rather than something unknown.

ASSOCIATION TECHNIQUE # 1

Does it **sound** like a **similar** word?

Does it remind you of another word that sounds the same?

EX: Meeline means cat.

How can you remember that meeline means cat? Ask yourself: Does it sound like a similar word? Does it remind me of another word I know already? Yes, it sounds like "feline," which I already know means cat. You can remember meeline means cat.

EX: Brockeer is a sport.

How can you remember that brockeer is a sport? Ask yourself: Does it sound like a similar word? Does it remind me of another word I already know? Yes, it sounds like "soccer," which I know is a sport. You can remember brockeer is a sport.

VISUALIZATION

What does it mean to visualize something? Notice the word "visual" at the beginning of the word visualize. If you didn't know the definition of visualization, you might be able to guess that it has something to do with visuals or vision. And you would be right. To visualize is to see an image in your mind. We call this your "mind's eye."

With memory, visualization is linking an unknown word with a picture or image of something known. When learning new words, it often helps to link a picture with the word. Create a picture that you can see in your mind's eye. You will learn a few different ways to do this.

VISUALIZATION TECHNIQUE # 1

Do you see part of the meaning in the word?

EX: Bapabea means bear.

Ask yourself: Do I see part of the meaning in the word? Yes, you see "bea" in the word. Seeing that will help you remember that bapa**bea** means **bear**. It's a visual clue.

EX: A weretelon is part of a flower.

Ask yourself: Do I see part of the meaning in the word? Yes, you see "wer" in the word. Seeing that will help you remember that **wer**etelon means flo**wer**. Use the visual clue to help you remember the meaning.

VISUALIZATION TECHNIQUE # 2

Can you picture the meaning of the word? Create a picture for your mind's eye so that you can "see" what the word means.

EX: Craftebloon means stage.

Ask yourself: Can I picture the word and the meaning? Yes, try to picture a stage with a person on it singing loudly, "craftebloon, craftebloon, craftebloon." You can remember craftebloon means stage when you see this image in your mind's eye.

EX: Flemistip is a new soda.

Ask yourself: Can I picture the word and the meaning? Yes, picture someone drinking a huge can of soda with the word Flemistip on it in big bright letters. They might even be saying, "Yum. I love Flemistip!" Now, you can remember Flemistip is a flavor of soda when you see this image in your mind's eye.

VISUALIZATION TECHNIQUE # 3

Can you create a picture out of the **shape** of a word?

EX: Tiltat means skyscraper.

Ask yourself: Can I create a picture out of the shape of the word? Yes, I can think of a skyscraper as a tall building, and when I look at the word "tiltat" I see the tall letters, the t's and the l, as the buildings or skyscrapers. Now, you can remember "tiltat" means skyscraper.

EX: Olo means face.

Ask yourself: Can I create a picture out of the shape of the word? Yes, I see the two o's as eyes and the I as a nose. When I look at the word "olo," I see the face. Now, you can remember olo means face.

COMBINING VISUALIZATION & ASSOCIATION

COMBINATION TECHNIQUE # 1

Does it **sound** like a familiar word? (with a different meaning, but a **similar sound**) Does it **remind** you of a familiar word? (with a different meaning, but a **similar sound**)

EX: Propold means to shout.

Ask yourself: Does propold sound like a familiar word with a different meaning? Or does propold remind me of a familiar word with a different meaning? Yes, prop<u>old</u> sounds like <u>gold</u>. I can picture a piece of gold **shouting** or someone finding gold and **shouting** "Gold! Gold!" Now, you will remember that prop<u>old</u> means <u>shout</u>.

COMBINATION TECHNIQUE # 2

Can you see a word that reminds you of the definition?

EX: Lopodots means peas.

Ask yourself: Do I see a word that reminds me of peas? Yes, dots reminds me of peas. Now, you can remember that lopo<u>dots</u> means peas.

HINTS FOR VISUALIZING

When you create pictures for your mind use exaggeration—try motion. Your pictures will be easier to remember. Make the pictures silly or exaggerated and they will stick in your mind better (like someone drinking an enormous can of Flemistip). Active images are also easier to remember (like the image of someone drinking Flemistip and saying, "I love Flemistip" rather than an image of just a can of Flemistip).

SUMMARY

Memory is important in test taking and in your daily life. Review and practice these techniques:

- Think of another word that **sounds similar** (brockeer = a sport).

- Look for part of the meaning in the word (bapa<u>bea</u> = <u>bear</u>).

- Picture the meaning of the word (craftebloon = stage).

- Create a picture out of the **shape** of a word (olo = face).

- Think of another word that is familiar (propold = gold = shouting).

- Look for a word that reminds you of the definition (lopo<u>dots</u> = peas).

And most of all, remember that with these tools, you can remember new words and information.

Memory Practice Drill 1

Using one of the techniques that we've learned, try to develop a way of remembering the following definitions:

1. Ebullient means enthusiastic.

2. Ingenuous means genuine.

3. Shimmer means to sparkle.

4. Hullabaloo means an uproar.

5. Penurious means stingy.

6. Tiff means a fight.

Detailed Answers:

1. Combination Technique # 2. Ask yourself: Do I see a word that reminds me of ebullient? Yes, a bull is something that is enthusiastic. Now, you can remember that ebullient means enthusiastic.

2. Visualization Technique #1. Do you see a part of the meaning in the word? Yes, you see "gen" in the word. This, in turn, will help you remember that ingenuous means genuine. This is a visual clue.

3. Association Technique #1. How can you remember that shimmer means to sparkle? Does it remind you of another word that you know? Yes, it sounds like glimmer which you know means to sparkle.

4. Visualization Technique #2. Try to picture the word and the meaning. Picture a large crowd of people yelling and protesting on the street and holding up signs that say "hullabaloo." When you picture this image in your mind's eye, you will know that "hullabaloo" means an uproar.

5. Combination Technique #1. Does it sound like a familiar word? Does it remind you of a familiar word? Yes, penurious sounds like furious. You can picture a man walking into a store and becoming furious because he is stingy and does not like the prices. Now, you will remember that penurious means stingy.

6. Visualization Technique #3. Ask yourself: Can I create a picture out of the shape of the word? Yes, I can picture the "t" and the "ff" as people who are in disagreement. Picture the "i" as the candle which indicates fire in between them and makes the "ff" people sway the other way. Now, you can remember that "tiff" means fight.

If you really think about it, you'll find that these techniques can be used no matter what the word. For example, if you changed "ebullient" to "tembullmient," combination technique #2 could still be used. Even if you changed the word "shimmer" to "vimmer" or "ingenuous" to "mingenist," the techniques can still be utilized. Since the COOP *Memory* test uses nonsensical words, making this connection is crucial.

Memory Practice Drill 2

With the last exercise in mind, try to use the same techniques on nonsensical words. The actual COOP test will use made up words to try and test your memory. You'll see how these techniques can be utilized no matter what the word.

1. Tillent means wealth.

2. Sillactur means sick.

3. Slendless means infinity.

4. Sirt means youthful.

5. Zive means happy.

6. Lool means eyeglasses.

Detailed Answers:

1. Combination Technique # 2. Ask yourself: Do I see a word that reminds me of wealth? Yes, a till is something that holds money. Now you can remember that "tillent" means wealth.

2. Visualization Technique #1. Do you see a part of the meaning in the word? Yes, you see "ill" in the word. This, in turn, will help you remember that "sillactur" means sick. This is a visual clue.

3. Association Technique #1. How can you remember that slendless means infinity? Does it remind you of another word that you know? Yes, it sounds like endless which you know means infinity.

4. Visualization Technique #2. Try to picture the word and the meaning. Picture a group of young kids on a carousel with hats on that say "sirt." When you picture this image in your mind's eye, you will know that "sirt" means youthful.

5. Combination Technique #1. Does it sound like a familiar word? Does it remind you of a familiar word? Yes, zive sounds like drive. You can picture a man walking into a car dealership and leaving with a brand new car. He becomes happy because he is driving a new car. Now, you will remember that "zive" means happy.

6. Visualization Technique #3. Ask yourself: Can I create a picture out of the shape of the word? Yes, I can picture the "oo" as glasses and the "l's" as part of the frames. Now, you can remember that "lool" means eyeglasses.

COOP/ HSPT

HSPT

Practice Test 2

Subtest 1: Verbal Skills

TIME: 16 Minutes
60 Questions

DIRECTIONS: Select the best answer choice.

---

1. Microscope is to cell as telescope is to _____

   (A) far.

   (B) heat.

   (C) star.

   (D) astronomer.

2. Key is to door as combination is to _____

   (A) numbers.

   (B) safe.

   (C) open.

   (D) window.

3. Best is to good as worst is to _____

   (A) better.

   (B) worse.

   (C) bad.

   (D) well.

4. Usher is to aisle as actor is to _____

   (A) theater.

   (B) stage.

   (C) play.

   (D) role.

5. Flexible is to gymnast as eloquent is to _____

   (A) editor.

   (B) speech.

   (C) orator.

   (D) articulate.

6. Incite is to provoke as inception is to _____

   (A) stimulus.

   (B) beginning.

   (C) end.

   (D) celebrate.

7. Exhausted is to tired as ecstatic is to _____

   (A) relieved.

   (B) peaceful.

   (C) smile.

   (D) happy.

8. Bench is to park as sofa is to _____

    (A) living room.   (C) couch.

    (B) church.   (D) furniture.

9. Expand is to contract as reveal is to _____

    (A) conceal.   (C) document.

    (B) secret.   (D) disclose.

10. Impartial is to prejudiced as exploit is to _____

    (A) use.   (C) expose.

    (B) protect.   (D) prevent.

11. To loiter is to

    (A) litter.   (C) hasten.

    (B) relapse.   (D) linger.

12. Inflammable is

    (A) inflammation.   (C) similar.

    (B) noncombustible.   (D) flammable.

13. To vindicate is to

    (A) clear.   (C) pose.

    (B) convict.   (D) blame.

14. A premonition is a

    (A) promotion.   (C) dream.

    (B) luxury.   (D) forewarning.

15. Soothe means to

    (A) warn.   (C) blacken.

    (B) comfort.   (D) strengthen.

16. Fervent most nearly means

    (A) hesitant.   (C) enthusiastic.

    (B) cool.   (D) warm.

17. Crucial means

    (A) technical.

    (B) experimental.

    (C) fundamental.

    (D) advanced.

18. To reprimand is to

    (A) praise.

    (B) return.

    (C) correct.

    (D) threaten.

19. Chastity is

    (A) purity.

    (B) correction.

    (C) religious.

    (D) familiarity.

20. Disrespectful means

    (A) careless.

    (B) rude.

    (C) valuable.

    (D) safe.

21. Contempt is

    (A) temptation.

    (B) fear.

    (C) commend.

    (D) scorn.

22. Agile most nearly means

    (A) wool.

    (B) limber.

    (C) unpredictable.

    (D) difficult.

23. Redeem means to

    (A) recover.

    (B) locate.

    (C) destroy.

    (D) research.

24. To pulverize is to

    (A) grind.

    (B) attempt.

    (C) pervert.

    (D) preserve.

25. To presume is to

    (A) swindle.

    (B) predict.

    (C) prosper.

    (D) assume.

26. To prevaricate most nearly means to

    (A) endanger.   (C) threaten.

    (B) lie.   (D) prevent.

27. Postmortem most nearly means

    (A) after death.   (C) stockade.

    (B) celebration.   (D) position.

28. Patty is five years older than Stephanie. Stephanie is two years older than Kerri. Kerri is seven years younger than Patty. If the first two statements are true, the third is

    (A) true.

    (B) false.

    (C) uncertain.

29. Sue is two inches taller than Lynn. Lynn is three inches taller than Kate. Kate is five inches shorter than Sue. If the first two statements are true, the third is

    (A) true.

    (B) false.

    (C) uncertain.

30. Jarret earned more money over the summer vacation than his brothers. Matthew and Brian are his brothers. Matthew made less money than Jarret and Brian. If the first two statements are true, the third is

    (A) true.

    (B) false.

    (C) uncertain.

31. Phyllis read more books over the summer vacation than any of her friends. Betty and Lorraine are her friends. Betty read fewer books than Phyllis and Lorraine. If the first two statements are true, the third is

    (A) true.

    (B) false.

    (C) uncertain.

32. Main Street is wider than Ocean Avenue. Lake Avenue is wider than Willow Road and the same width as Ocean Avenue. Main Street is narrower than Willow Road. If the first two statements are true, the third is

(A) true.

(B) false.

(C) uncertain.

33. Nicole can type faster than Michelle. Joanne can type faster than Nancy and the same speed as Michelle. Nicole types slower than Nancy. If the first two statements are true, the third is

(A) true.

(B) false.

(C) uncertain.

34. Jennifer takes ballet lessons five days a week. Maryann takes ballet lessons three days a week. Jennifer and Maryann take ballet lessons on the same day at least once a week. If the first two statements are true, the third is

(A) true.

(B) false.

(C) uncertain.

35. Joe plays basketball six days a week. Tony plays basketball four days a week. Joe and Tony play basketball on the same day at least three times a week. If the first two statements are true, the third is

(A) true.

(B) false.

(C) uncertain.

36. Broccoli costs more than carrots. Onions cost less than broccoli and lettuce. Carrots cost more than lettuce. If the first two statements are true, the third is

(A) true.

(B) false.

(C) uncertain.

37. Grapes cost more than plums. Peaches cost less than grapes and nectarines. Plums cost more than nectarines. If the first two statements are true, the third is

(A) true.

(B) false.

(C) uncertain.

38. Which word does <u>not</u> belong with the others?

    (A) Irritate   (C) Harass

    (B) Appease   (D) Pester

39. Which word does <u>not</u> belong with the others?

    (A) Vacant   (C) Spacious

    (B) Empty   (D) Unoccupied

40. Which word does <u>not</u> belong with the others?

    (A) Placid   (C) Calm

    (B) Chaotic   (D) Peaceful

41. Which word does <u>not</u> belong with the others?

    (A) Artery   (C) Vein

    (B) Capillary   (D) Circulatory

42. Which word does <u>not</u> belong with the others?

    (A) Hobo   (C) Exam

    (B) Ad   (D) Memo

43. Which word does <u>not</u> belong with the others?

    (A) Fiscal   (C) Perennial

    (B) Annual   (D) Temporal

44. Which word does <u>not</u> belong with the others?

    (A) Hinder   (C) Retard

    (B) Aid   (D) Impede

45. Which word does <u>not</u> belong with the others?

    (A) Cheerful   (C) Hopeful

    (B) Optimistic   (D) Desperate

46. Which word does <u>not</u> belong with the others?

    (A) Recover   (C) Regress

    (B) Relapse   (D) Backslide

47. Which word does <u>not</u> belong with the others?

    (A) Gloomy   (C) Dreary

    (B) Dismal   (D) Bright

48. Which word does <u>not</u> belong with the others?

    (A) Defendant   (C) Bailiff

    (B) Interrogate   (D) Plaintiff

49. Which word does <u>not</u> belong with the others?

    (A) Period   (C) Comma

    (B) Question mark   (D) Exclamation point

50. Which word does <u>not</u> belong with the others?

    (A) Precise   (C) Exact

    (B) Approximate   (D) Accurate

51. Which word does <u>not</u> belong with the others?

    (A) Simple   (C) Intricate

    (B) Complex   (D) Complicated

52. Which word does <u>not</u> belong with the others?

    (A) Diverse   (C) Uniform

    (B) Heterogeneous   (D) Varied

53. Which word does <u>not</u> belong with the others?

    (A) Dictionary   (C) Thesaurus

    (B) Nonfiction   (D) Encyclopedia

54. Which word does <u>not</u> belong with the others?

    (A) Itinerary   (C) Destination

    (B) Route   (D) Portfolio

55. Which word does <u>not</u> belong with the others?

    (A) Excrete   (C) Disburse

    (B) Discharge   (D) Expel

56. Presume means the opposite of

    (A) believe.   (C) suppose.

    (B) disprove.   (D) conclude.

57. Disdainful does not mean

    (A) arrogant.   (C) aloof.

    (B) proud.   (D) humble.

58. Infamous is the opposite of

    (A) notorious.   (C) prominent.

    (B) wicked.   (D) dishonorable.

59. Perpetual does not mean

    (A) constant.   (C) momentary.

    (B) eternal.   (D) enduring.

60. Imminent does not mean

    (A) proximate.   (C) past.

    (B) impending.   (D) close.

Subtest 2: Quantitative Skills

TIME: 30 Minutes
52 Questions

DIRECTIONS: Select the best answer choice.

---

61. What number is 12 less than $\frac{1}{3}$ of 60?

    (A) 4   (C) 6
    (B) 13   (D) 8

62. Look at this series: 33, 25, 17, 9,... What numeral should come next?

    (A) 1   (C) 5
    (B) 3   (D) 7

63. Look at this series: 98, 82, 75, 59, 52,... What numeral should come next?

    (A) 43   (C) 39
    (B) 36   (D) 38

64. Examine (a), (b), and (c) and find the best answer.

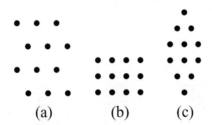

    (a)   (b)   (c)

    (A) (a) is equal to (b) which is equal to (c).

    (B) (a) is equal to (b) which is not equal to (c).

    (C) (b) is equal to (c) which is not equal to (a).

    (D) (a) is not equal to (b) which is not equal to (c).

65. Examine (a), (b), and (c) and find the best answer.

    (a) $(6 \times 1) + 2$

    (b) $(1 + 2) \times 6$

    (c) $(6 \times 2) + 1$

    (A) (a) is equal to (b) which is equal to (c).

    (B) (a) is greater than (b) and is greater than (c).

    (C) (b) is greater than (a) and is greater than (c).

    (D) (c) is greater than (a) and is greater than (b).

66. What number is 2 more than $\frac{3}{4}$ of 20?

    (A) 15   (C) 17

    (B) 7   (D) 11

67. What number is 9 less than $\frac{1}{2}$ of 32?

    (A) 9   (C) 13

    (B) 25   (D) 7

68. Look at this series: 52, 55, 60, 64, 70,... What numeral should come next?

    (A) 75   (C) 77

    (B) 76   (D) 78

69. Examine the equal squares (a), (b), and (c) and find the best answer regarding their shaded parts.

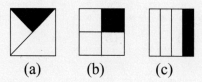

(a)   (b)   (c)

    (A) (a) is equal to (b) which is equal to (c).

    (B) (a) is greater than (b) which is equal to (c).

    (C) (a) is equal to (b) which is greater than (c).

    (D) (a) is equal to (b) which is less than (c).

70. What number added to 5 makes $\frac{5}{6}$ of 24?

    (A) 4   (C) 7

    (B) 5   (D) 15

71. Look at this series: 144, 140, 132, 120, 104,… What numeral should come next?

    (A) 96   (C) 84

    (B) 90   (D) 80

72. Look at this series: 72, 78, 83, 89, 94,… What numeral should come next?

    (A) 100   (C) 99

    (B) 96   (D) 97

73. What number is twice as much as 8 squared?

    (A) 32   (C) 96

    (B) 16   (D) 128

74. What number subtracted from 32 makes 6 more than 10?

    (A) 16   (C) 18

    (B) 4   (D) 12

75. Examine (a), (b), and (c) and find the best answer.

    (a) $\frac{2}{3}$ of 15

    (b) $\frac{2}{5}$ of 20

    (c) $\frac{3}{4}$ of 32

    (A) (c) is less than (a).   (C) (c) is less than (b).

    (B) (b) is less than (a).   (D) (a) is less than (b).

76. Examine the equal circles (a), (b), and (c) and find the best answer regarding their shaded parts.

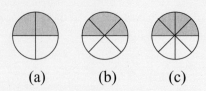

(a)   (b)   (c)

(A)   (a) is equal to (b) which is equal to (c).

(B)   (a) is equal to (b) which is not equal to (c).

(C)   (b) is equal to (c) which is not equal to (a).

(D)   (a) is not equal to (b) which is not equal to (c).

77. Look at this series: 1801, 1780, 1759, 1738,… What numeral should come next?

(A)   1720   (C)   1721
(B)   1719   (D)   1717

78. Look at this series: 42, 49, 56, __, 70, 77,… What numeral should fill in the blank?

(A)   83   (C)   63
(B)   84   (D)   35

79. What number added to 51 makes a number twice as large as 35?

(A)   16   (C)   28
(B)   21   (D)   19

80. Examine (a), (b), and (c) and find the best answer.

(a)   .08

(b)   8%

(c) $\dfrac{2}{25}$

(A)   (a) is equal to (b) which is equal to (c).

(B)   (b) is greater than (a).

(C)   (c) is greater than (a).

(D)   (c) is equal to (a) and not equal to (b).

81. What number subtracted from 96 makes 12 more than 11?

(A)   84   (C)   23
(B)   85   (D)   73

82. Examine the two connected squares and find the best answer.

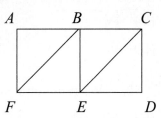

(A) *AC* is equal to *CE*.   (C) *FB* is equal to *EC*.

(B) *FA* is equal to *FD*.   (D) *BE* is equal to *BF*.

83. Look at this series: 250, 50, 10, 2,… What numeral should come next?

(A) 1   (C) .5

(B) .4   (D) .1

84. Look at this series: 100, 20, 25, 5, 10,… What numeral should come next?

(A) 1   (C) 5

(B) 2   (D) 10

85. What number added to 6 makes a number that is 8 less than 15?

(A) 7   (C) 9

(B) 2   (D) 1

86. Examine (a), (b), and (c) and find the best answer.

(a) $\dfrac{3}{4}$

(b) $\dfrac{2}{3}$

(c) $\dfrac{19}{24}$

(A) (a) is equal to (b) which is equal to (c).

(B) (a) is less than (b) and greater than (c).

(C) (b) is less than (c) and greater than (a).

(D) (a) is less than (c) and greater than (b).

87. Look at this series: XX, XVI, XII, VIII,... What numeral should come next?

    (A) X   (C) IV
    (B) VI   (D) II

88. Look at this series: 84, 79, 68, 63, 52,... What numeral should come next?

    (A) 47   (C) 41
    (B) 42   (D) 40

89. One half of what number is $\frac{2}{5}$ of 10?

    (A) 6   (C) 3
    (B) 4   (D) 8

90. Examine the circle with center E and find the best answer.

    (A) *AD* is equal to *AE*.   (C) *BC* is equal to *AD*.
    (B) *DC* is equal to *BD*.   (D) *AC* is equal to *AB*.

91. Look at this series: 18, 23, __, 37, 46, 51, 60,... What numeral should fill in the blank?

    (A) 69   (C) 35
    (B) 28   (D) 32

92. Look at this series: 5, 7, 14, 16, 32,... What numeral should come next?

    (A) 34   (C) 66
    (B) 64   (D) 40

93. Two-thirds of what number is 2 squared?

    (A) 12   (C) 6
    (B) 9   (D) 3

94. Examine (a), (b), and (c) and find the best answer.

(a) $(12 \times 2) \div 3$

(b) $(12 \times 3) \div 2$

(c) $3 \times (12 \div 2)$

(A)   (a) is equal to (b) which is equal to (c).

(B)   (a) is equal to (b) which is not equal to (c).

(C)   (a) is equal to (c) which is not equal to (b).

(D)   (b) is equal to (c) which is not equal to (a).

95. What number multiplied by 5 is $\dfrac{3}{4}$ of 40?

(A)   10   (C)   8

(B)   5   (D)   6

96. Look at this series: 29, 35, 26, 32, 23, 29,... What two numerals should come next?

(A)   35, 26   (C)   20, 26

(B)   35, 41   (D)   20, 11

97. Examine the three regions of the circle with center E and find the best answer.

(A)   (x) is greater than (y) and equal to (2).

(B)   (y) is greater than (x) and equal to (2).

(C)   (2) is greater than (y) and equal to (x).

(D)   (2) is equal to (y) plus (x).

98. What number added to 5 leaves 7 less than $\dfrac{2}{5}$ of 80?

(A)   16   (C)   25

(B)   20   (D)   32

99. Examine (a), (b), and (c) and find the best answer.

(a) $2(x + y)$

(b) $2x + 2y$

(c) $(x + y)2$

(A) (a) is equal to (b) which is equal to (c).

(B) (a) is equal to (b) but not equal to (c).

(C) (a) is not equal to (b) but is equal to (c).

(D) (a) is not equal to (b) and is not equal to (c).

100. What number subtracted from 50 leaves half the product of 10 and $\frac{2}{3}$ of 12?

(A) 1

(B) 4

(C) 8

(D) 10

101. Examine (a), (b), and (c) and find the best answer.

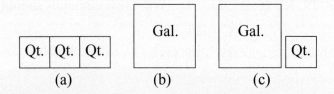

(A) (a) equals (b) which equals (c).

(B) (a) is greater than (b).

(C) (c) is greater than (a).

(D) (a) is equal to (b) but not equal to (c).

102. Examine (a), (b), and (c) and find the best answer.

(a) 1^6

(b) 6^1

(c) 12^0

(A) (a) is equal to (b) but is not equal to (c).

(B) (b) is equal to (c) but is not equal to (a).

(C) (c) is equal to (a) but is not equal to (b).

(D) (a) is not equal to (b) and is not equal to (c).

103. What number divided by 4 leaves 2 times $\frac{1}{3}$ of 3?

(A) 16   (C) 4

(B) 12   (D) 8

104. Examine the graph and find the best answer.

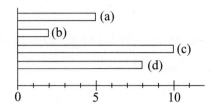

(A)   (a) minus (b) equals (d) minus (c).

(B)   (d) minus (a) equals (a) minus (b).

(C)   (c) plus (b) equals (a) plus (d).

(D)   (d) minus (b) equals (c) minus (a).

105. Look at this series: 98, 28, 103, 26, 108,… What numeral should come next?

(A) 24   (C) 21

(B) 22   (D) 20

106. Examine (a), (b), and (c) and find the best answer.

(a)   60% of 50

(b)   50% of 60

(c)   40% of 70

(A)   (a) is equal to (b) which is equal to (c).

(B)   (a) is equal to (b) but is not equal to (c).

(C)   (a) is equal to (c) but is not equal to (b).

(D)   (b) is equal to (c) but is not equal to (a).

107. Examine the rectangle and find the best answer.

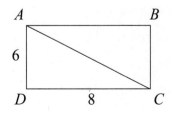

(A) The perimeter of the rectangle is 30.

(B) The perimeter of triangle *ABC* is 24.

(C) The area of triangle *ABC* is 48.

(D) The area of the rectangle is 60.

108. Look at this series: 60, 64, 16, 20, 5,… What numeral should come next?

(A) 1   (C) 9

(B) 2   (D) 10

109. Look at this series: 38, 34, 37, 31, 36, 28, 35,… What three numerals should come next?

(A) 26, 33, 24   (C) 25, 34, 22

(B) 27, 31, 23   (D) 23, 29, 20

110. What number subtracted from $\frac{1}{3}$ of 21 leaves $\frac{3}{8}$ of 16?

(A) 1   (C) 3

(B) 6   (D) 7

111. One-fifth of what number added to 5 makes 3 times $\frac{2}{3}$ of 18?

(A) 100   (C) 15

(B) 155   (D) 125

112. Look at this series: 32, 24, 27, 30, 22, 25,… What numeral should come next?

(A) 20   (C) 29

(B) 28   (D) 31

Subtest 3: Reading

TIME: 25 Minutes
62 Questions

Comprehension

DIRECTIONS: Read the following passages and then select the best answer choice.

Questions 113–117 are based on the following passage.

<u>Forgery</u> is a serious crime that can result in harsh prison sentences. In a recent case, a man was sent to jail for 15 years for committing forgery. He sold documents that he claimed were written by Abraham Lincoln. In fact, the man who sold them had written the documents himself. He was an antiques dealer and was very familiar with American history. He was able to make the documents look old, and he learned how to imitate Lincoln's handwriting based on real documents written by Lincoln that he had seen. He sold people letters, reports, and speeches that he claimed were Lincoln's.

He was caught when a woman who bought a letter from him took it to be analyzed in a laboratory. The people who examined it were experts on dating materials like paper and ink. It took them several weeks of careful investigation to discover that the paper the letter was written on was not more than 50 years old, so the letter could not possibly have been authentic. The woman alerted the police, who sent an undercover agent in to buy a document. When it too was shown to be a forgery, the antiques dealer was arrested.

At the sentencing, the judge told the man that he was "a liar who had betrayed the trust of his customers and distorted American history." In addition to jail time, the man must pay back all the money he earned from his fake documents.

113. According to the passage, the antiques dealer was arrested for

(A) stealing from his employers.

(B) selling forged documents.

(C) attacking a woman in his store.

(D) cheating on his taxes.

114. The word <u>forgery</u> as underlined and used in the passage most nearly means

(A) stealing.   (C) insulting.

(B) breaking.   (D) faking.

115. Based on the passage, which of the following is TRUE?

   (A) Forgery is not considered a serious crime.

   (B) It is easy to detect when a document has been forged.

   (C) The antiques dealer sold a forged document to an undercover police officer.

   (D) The antiques dealer was discovered to be a forger when he was caught in the act of writing a fake letter.

116. According to the passage, the antiques dealer was caught based on what evidence?

   (A) The kind of ink used on the letter had not existed when Lincoln was alive.

   (B) The handwriting was different than Lincoln's.

   (C) The letter contained many mistakes and errors.

   (D) The paper was not old enough to have been written on by Abraham Lincoln.

117. The punishment of the antiques dealer

   (A) includes only a 15 year prison sentence.

   (B) is 15 hours of community service.

   (C) was suspended by the judge.

   (D) includes both a jail sentence and an order to pay back the money he earned with his false documents.

Questions 118–122 are based on the following passage.

The employee turnover rate is a growing concern in the restaurant industry. Most employees in this business are young and part-time workers who end up doing some of the most important work in the company. They tend to want flexibility, a feeling of purpose, recognition, and good wages. The future success of restaurants depends on maintaining a strong base of long-term employees. This is possible through motivational techniques that will ultimately save restaurant owners money and allow their businesses to grow and prosper.

The average employee turnover rate last year was 70 percent. This can be very expensive for restaurant owners. Every time an employee leaves and is replaced, the restaurant must invest time and energy in training the new employee, while all the time and energy that went into training the departing one is lost. Restaurant owners need to develop motivational techniques to create an environment in which workers will be content and productive.

Such techniques could include: regular pay raises, recognition programs, like selecting an "Employee of the Month," and incentives such as movie passes or T-shirts for employees who demonstrate an excellent work record. Such programs will create a better atmosphere for workers and make them feel loyal to the company they work for, which will ultimately make the business more profitable.

118. The purpose of this passage is to

    (A) explain how employee turnover rates are calculated.

    (B) criticize employees for not remaining at one job for a long period of time.

    (C) warn restaurant owners that high employee turnover rates can be bad for their business and persuade them that motivational techniques will help keep employees happy with their jobs.

    (D) persuade restaurant owners to pay their employees less.

119. The word <u>motivational</u> as underlined and used in this passage, most nearly means

    (A) detrimental.   (C) encouraging.

    (B) harsh.   (D) discouraging.

120. According to the passage, high employee turnover rates are

    (A) beneficial to business owners.

    (B) harmful to business owners.

    (C) not a factor for business owners.

    (D) something that does not affect restaurants.

121. What is the tone of the author of this passage?

    (A) The author is impartial about employee turnover rates.

    (B) The author is mildly interested in trying to stop frequent turnover in restaurants.

    (C) The author feels that the danger of high employee turnover rates has been exaggerated.

    (D) The author strongly believes that high employee turnover rates is a matter that business owners should be concerned about.

122. Which of the following is NOT a motivational technique proposed in this passage?

    (A) Pay raises

    (B) Expense paid vacations

    (C) Incentives

    (D) Recognition programs

Questions 123–127 are based on the following passage.

Cubism is an <u>abstract</u> form of painting that emphasizes fracture, wildness, and irrationality at the expense of unity, control, and logic. This type of painting is the opposite of art forms that strive to represent the world as it actually appears to us. Some people object to it because it appears nonsensical and because it fails to conform to traditionally accepted ideals of "beautiful" art.

For instance, in his painting *Three Musicians*, Pablo Picasso (1881-1971), a Spanish artist and one of the most famous Cubists, offers us a look at three figures playing musical instruments, a seemingly ordinary scene. And yet in this painting the three musicians are hardly distinguishable from each other. They are drawn in such a way that each blends into the next. Their features are distorted so that they do not look like "real" people, and their hands and limbs are not in proper proportion to their bodies. The instruments they play bear only a passing resemblance to actual musical instruments, and, despite the work's title, it is not clear exactly how many figures are in the painting.

Despite its radical nature, Cubism has become one of the most important and powerful forms of artistic expression in the twentieth century. Cubism has had a formative influence on the modern consciousness, and its effects can be seen in many forms of art, design, and architecture.

123. The purpose of this passage is to

    (A) give a brief summary of Cubism.

    (B) give a biography of Pablo Picasso.

    (C) explain why Cubism is better than other styles of painting.

    (D) criticize Cubist painters.

124. Cubist paintings are all of the following EXCEPT

    (A) abstract.

    (B) unconventional.

    (C) irrational.

    (D) realistic.

125. The passage about the painting *Three Musicians* is intended to

    (A) show that Picasso was really a poor painter.

    (B) show that Picasso was the greatest painter of the twentieth century.

    (C) provide an example of a Cubist painting.

    (D) criticize the painting for being Cubist.

126. The word <u>abstract</u> as underlined and used in this passage most nearly means

    (A) good.

    (B) colorful

    (C) important.

    (D) difficult to understand.

127. The author contends that

    (A) Cubism is an important and influential style of painting.

    (B) Cubism has had little impact.

    (C) Cubism was very popular for a short time, but has since become unpopular.

    (D) Pablo Picasso was not really a Cubist.

Questions 128–132 are based on the following passage.

Millions of Americans do not have health insurance. This is a serious problem, but there is very little being done to address it. This is mostly due to a general feeling that any attempt to provide health care for people who don't have any would be too expensive. Lacking a plan to provide full health care costs to all Americans, we as a nation need at the very least to find a way to provide basic health care services.

Basic health care services would ensure that any American could visit a doctor of his or her choice for a diagnosis, medical counseling and advice, and preventative medicine, such as immunizations and screening for the early detection of illnesses. While this is not a full solution to the problem of rising health care costs, it is an immediate remedy for the millions of Americans who have nowhere to turn when they are feeling sick and have no access to medical advice when they have health questions. As a civilized and humane country, we need to continue to work toward finding a <u>comprehensive</u> solution, but for now we need to agree on providing basic health services for uninsured Americans.

128. The tone of this passage indicates that the author's purpose is to

    (A) convince readers that it is important to address the health needs of uninsured Americans.

    (B) give an impartial assessment of the problem.

    (C) teach readers about various diseases.

    (D) declare that he or she does not believe in providing health care to uninsured Americans.

129. According to the passage

    (A) there are many plans being put into effect to address health care problems.

    (B) health care reform is not very complicated.

    (C) not enough is being done to address health care problems.

    (D) Both A and B.

130. According to the author, providing basic health services

    (A) is a permanent solution to the problem of high medical costs.

    (B) is an idea that has been successfully tested in various cities.

    (C) would be too expensive.

    (D) is an important first step toward improving the health care system but not a permanent solution to its problems.

131. Which of the following would NOT be covered by the author's proposed basic health services?

    (A) Surgery

    (B) Medical advice

    (C) Immunizations

    (D) Health screenings

132. The word <u>comprehensive</u> as underlined and used in this passage most nearly means

    (A) incomplete.

    (B) complete.

    (C) unnecessary.

    (D) uninteresting.

Questions 133–137 are based on the following passage.

To the Shakers, perfection was found in the creation of an object that was both useful and simple. Their Society was founded in 1774 by Ann Lee, an Englishwoman from the working classes who brought eight followers to New York with her. "Mother Ann" established her religious community on the belief that worldly interests were evil.

To gain entrance into the Society, believers had to remain celibate, have no private possessions, and avoid contact with outsiders. The order came to be called "Shakers" because of the feverish dance the group performed. Another characteristic of the group was the desire to seek perfection in their work.

Shaker furniture was created to exemplify specific characteristics: simplicity of design, quality of craftsmanship, harmony of proportion, and usefulness. While Shakers did not create any innovations in furniture designs, they were known for their fine crafts-manship. The major emphasis was on function, and not on excessive or elaborate decorations that contributed nothing to the product's usefulness.

133. Based on the passage, how would you describe the lifestyle of the Shakers?

    (A) Decadent

    (B) Simple

    (C) Extravagant

    (D) Wasteful

134. According to the passage, the Shakers got their name from

(A)   a rival religious organization.

(B)   the town in which they built their community.

(C)   the dance they performed.

(D)   the Bible.

135. The Shakers were primarily

(A)   dancers.

(C)   a religious community.

(B)   furniture makers.

(D)   farmers.

136. Shaker furniture is characterized by

(A)   ornate designs.

(C)   its functional simplicity.

(B)   its uselessness.

(D)   its shoddy craftsmanship.

137. The purpose of this passage is

(A)   to provide a brief description of the Shakers.

(B)   to denounce the Shakers.

(C)   to advertise Shaker furniture.

(D)   to convert readers to the Shaker way of thinking.

Questions 138–142 are based on the following passage.

In 1975, Sinclair observed that it had often been supposed that the main factor in learning to talk is being able to imitate. Schlesinger (1975) noted that at certain stages of learning to speak, a child tends to imitate everything an adult says to him or her, and it therefore seems reasonable to accord to such imitation an important role in the acquisition of language.

Moreover, various investigators have attempted to explain the role of imitation in language. In his discussion of the development of imitation and cognition of adult speech sounds, Nakazema (1975) stated that although the parent's talking stimulates and accelerates the infant's articulatory activity, the parent's phoneme system does not influence the child's articulatory mechanisms. Slobin and Welsh (1973) suggested that imitation is the reconstruction of the adult's utterance and that the child does so by employing the grammatical rules that he has developed at a specific time. Schlesinger proposed that by imitating the adult, the child practices new grammatical constructions. Brown and Bellugi (1964) noted that a child's imitations resemble spontaneous speech in that they drop inflections, most function words, and sometimes other words. However, the word order of imitated sentences usually was preserved. Brown and Bellugi assumed that imitation is a function of what the child attended to or remembered. Shipley et al. (1969) suggested that repeating an adult's utterance assists the child's comprehension. Ervin (1964) and Braine (1971) found that a child's imitations do not contain more advanced structures than his or her spontaneous utterances; thus, imitation can no longer be regarded as the simple behavioristic act that earlier scholars assumed it to be.

138. The main purpose of this passage is to

    (A) encourage parents to read to their children.

    (B) discourage parents from letting their children imitate them.

    (C) put a stop to studies of language acquisition.

    (D) relate the findings of several experts in the field of language acquisition.

139. The tone of the passage is

    (A) informal.   (C) academic.

    (B) humorous.   (D) sad.

140. The author of this passage would agree with which of the following statements?

    (A) Children only imitate other children.

    (B) Language acquisition is a traumatic experience for children.

    (C) Language skills are easier for girls to master than boys.

    (D) Imitation is not a simple behavioristic act.

141. All of the following are said to be asserted by Brown and Bellugi EXCEPT

    (A) children are sensitive to harsh words.

    (B) a child's imitations often sound like spontaneous sounds.

    (C) the word order of imitated sentences is usually preserved.

    (D) imitation is a function of what the child remembered.

142. Based on this passage, it is clear that

    (A) language acquisition is a neglected field of study.

    (B) there has been a great deal of research done on language acquisition.

    (C) language acquisition was only really studied in the nineteenth century.

    (D) language acquisition is not considered a serious field of study.

Questions 143–147 are based on the following passage.

The Indians of California had five varieties of acorns, which they used as their principal source of food. This was a noteworthy accomplishment in technology since they first had to make the acorn edible. A process had to be developed for leaching out the poisonous tannic acid. They ground the acorns into a meal and then filtered it many times with water. This had to be done through sand or through tightly woven baskets. Early Indian campsites reveal the evidence of the acorn-processing labor necessary to provide enough food for their <u>subsistence</u>. The women patiently ground acorns into meal with stone pestles. The result, a pinkish flour that was cooked into a mush or thin soup, formed the bulk of their diet.

143. The main point of this passage is to

    (A)   encourage us to process food the way Indians did.

    (B)   study more early food processing techniques.

    (C)   convey information based on archaeological studies of Indians in California.

    (D)   criticize European treatment of Native Americans.

144. According to the passage, the early California Indians were the first people to

    (A)   weave baskets.   (C)   irrigate crops.

    (B)   live in California.   (D)   make the acorn edible.

145. We know about early Indian food processing techniques from

    (A)   drawings in caves.

    (B)   written documents.

    (C)   studies of tribes related to the early California Indians.

    (D)   archaeological studies of campsites.

146. Based on the passage, we know all of the following EXCEPT

    (A)   the early California Indians processed their food to make it edible.

    (B)   the early California Indians fought with other Indian tribes.

    (C)   acorns contain poisonous tannic acid.

    (D)   acorns were the principal food source for the early California Indians.

147. The word <u>subsistence</u> as underlined and used in this passage most nearly means

    (A)   survival.   (C)   religious worship.

    (B)   digestion.   (D)   starvation.

Questions 148–152 are based on the following passage.

Results of a study released by the College Board and the Western Interstate Commission for Higher Education show that in a year, the majority of California's high school graduates will be non-white and in two years, one-third of all the nation's students will be from minority groups. It is also predicted that nationally the total non-white and Hispanic student population for all grade levels will increase from 10.4 million to 13.7 million in about a decade. These figures suggest that now, more than ever, equal educational opportunities for all students must be our nation's number one priority.

148. An inference that can be made from this passage is that

    (A)   there are not enough teachers for California's high schools.

    (B)   the United States is becoming increasingly diverse.

    (C)   high schools are not providing an adequate education.

    (D)   many high school graduates cannot read very well.

149. The author of this passage would agree that

    (A)   schools should recruit more minority teachers.

    (B)   more money needs to be spent on sports programs.

    (C)   there are many unqualified teachers.

    (D)   the dropout rate is too high.

150. This passage uses what to help make its point?

    (A)   An anecdote   (C)   Threatening language

    (B)   Emotional language   (D)   Statistics

151. The author of the passage argues that

    (A)   American schools are sub-standard.

    (B)   European schools are better than American schools.

    (C)   equal opportunity in education is becoming increasingly important.

    (D)   minority students are enrolling in colleges at a greater rate than they were 10 years ago.

152. Based on this passage, we can infer that

    (A)   teaching high school is an excellent career.

    (B)   statistical findings can be the basis for formulating policy ideas.

(C) there is little evidence to suggest that there is discrimination against minority students.

(D) minority students are concentrated in certain areas of California.

Vocabulary

DIRECTIONS: Choose the word that means the same or about the same as the underlined word.

153. the <u>apex</u> of his career

(A) bottom (C) end

(B) beginning (D) peak

154. <u>compulsory</u> education

(A) required (C) private

(B) limited (D) optional

155. feel the <u>acute</u> pain

(A) slight (C) sharp

(B) recurring (D) steady

156. the <u>ambiguous</u> message

(A) understandable (C) foreign

(B) puzzling (D) illegible

157. the <u>eminent</u> scholar

(A) distinguished (C) unknown

(B) intelligent (D) confident

158. <u>scrutinize</u> the document

(A) forge (C) copy

(B) skim (D) examine

159. <u>convene</u> a discussion

(A) conclude (C) concentrate

(B) assemble (D) counterbalance

160. a <u>judicious</u> decision

    (A) biased   (C) sensible

    (B) reckless   (D) sensitive

161. a <u>ferocious</u> animal

    (A) tame   (C) wild

    (B) stubborn   (D) humorous

162. <u>obliterate</u> the evidence

    (A) examine   (C) create

    (B) conceal   (D) destroy

163. a <u>pallid</u> complexion

    (A) rosy   (C) sad

    (B) pale   (D) healthy

164. his <u>impetuous</u> decision

    (A) planned   (C) impulsive

    (B) recent   (D) wise

165. <u>mutinous</u> crewmen

    (A) cooperative   (C) changeable

    (B) quiet   (D) rebellious

166. the <u>placid</u> sea

    (A) deep   (C) stormy

    (B) calm   (D) large

167. the <u>replica</u> of the ship

    (A) copy   (C) original

    (B) forgery   (D) wreckage

168. two <u>conspicuous</u> characteristics

    (A) hidden   (C) noticeable

    (B) shady   (D) significant

169. an <u>abridged</u> story

   (A)   lengthened   (C)   shortened

   (B)   true   (D)   false

170. the <u>plausible</u> excuse

   (A)   unbelievable   (C)   believable

   (B)   praiseworthy   (D)   unforgivable

171. <u>thwart</u> an attack

   (A)   strengthen   (C)   accelerate

   (B)   repel   (D)   wage

172. a <u>discreet</u> remark

   (A)   hurtful   (C)   insensitive

   (B)   careful   (D)   polite

173. a <u>frugal</u> meal

   (A)   wasteful   (C)   abundant

   (B)   thrifty   (D)   leftover

174. <u>meager</u> accommodations

   (A)   lavish   (C)   inadequate

   (B)   large   (D)   healthy

Subtest 4: Mathematics

TIME: 45 Minutes
64 Questions

Concepts

DIRECTIONS: Select the best answer choice.

175. Round off 6.874 to the nearest hundredth.

    (A) 6.87

    (B) 6.88

    (C) 687

    (D) 68700

176. Add together: $5x - 3y + 12$ and $3y + 3x - 10$.

    (A) $8x + 2$

    (B) $8x - 2$

    (C) $8x + 6y$

    (D) $15x - 9y - 120$

177. Which of the points in the graph represents $(6, -3)$?

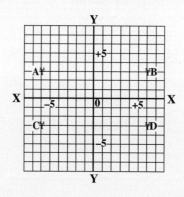

    (A) A

    (B) B

    (C) C

    (D) D

178. The sum of two consecutive even numbers is 74. What are the two numbers?

    (A) 35, 39

    (B) 36, 38

    (C) 37, 37

    (D) 34, 40

179. Simplify: $6\frac{2}{3} - 5\frac{1}{4}$.

(A) $\frac{5}{12}$

(C) $1\frac{11}{12}$

(B) $1\frac{5}{12}$

(D) $11\frac{11}{12}$

180. A perfect square number has 2 identical factors. Which of the following numbers is a perfect square?

(A) 12

(C) 16

(B) 14

(D) 18

181. In computing the area of a rectangle, Prince used the formula:

Area = length × width.

After calculating the areas of four rectangles, including three squares, Prince misplaced his homework notebook from which he copied the measures of the sides of the rectangles. Which of the following numbers does <u>not</u> represent the area of the square? [Hint: Remember that the length and width of the square are equal.]

(A) 24

(C) 36

(B) 25

(D) 64

182. Simplify: $\frac{3}{5} \times \frac{5}{6} + 21$.

(A) $21\frac{1}{2}$

(C) $21\frac{5}{6}$

(B) $21\frac{8}{11}$

(D) $21\frac{18}{25}$

183. Simplify: $5\frac{1}{4} \div 2\frac{1}{3}$.

(A) $12\frac{1}{4}$

(C) $1\frac{1}{2}$

(B) $2\frac{1}{4}$

(D) $\frac{4}{9}$

184. What number subtracted from 14 leaves $\frac{1}{7}$ of 77?

(A) 3   (C) 11

(B) 7   (D) 14

185. What percent of 80 is 200?

(A) 25%   (C) 120%

(B) 40%   (D) 250%

186. Rewrite $2\frac{3}{5}$ as a percent.

(A) 260%   (C) 26%

(B) 60%   (D) 2.6%

187. $x(-y + z) =$

(A) $-xy - xz$ (C) $xz - xy$

(B) $xy + z$ (D) $x - y + z$

188. Albert worked for five days, earning $460. What was his average daily income?

(A) $92   (C) $120

(B) $94   (D) $125

189. A parallelogram has two pairs of equal sides. Which of the following sets of sticks can be arranged to form a parallelogram?

(A)
3
4
5
6   (C)
4
6
6
4

(B)
4
4
6
8   (D)
3
5
7
9

190. The sum of the measures of the four interior angles of a quadrilateral is always 360 degrees. Which of the following sets of numbers represents the measures of interior angles of a quadrilateral?

(A) 25, 30, 60, 65   (C) 78, 85, 95, 102

(B) 80, 80, 90, 90   (D) 75, 95, 95, 105

191. What number is 45% of 2,000?

(A) 1,955   (C) 1,100

(B) 1,945   (D) 900

The graph below shows the attendance in a middle-school class for one week. Use the information in the graph to answer question 192.

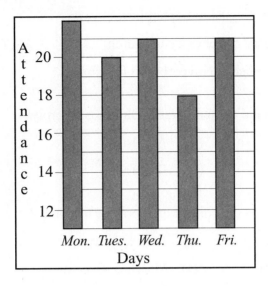

192. What was the average attendance from Wednesday to Friday?

(A) 18

(C) 20

(B) 19

(D) 22

The graph that follows is a record of the temperatures for each month of the year 1955 in Bluntsville, Kentucky. Use the information in this graph to answer questions 193-195.

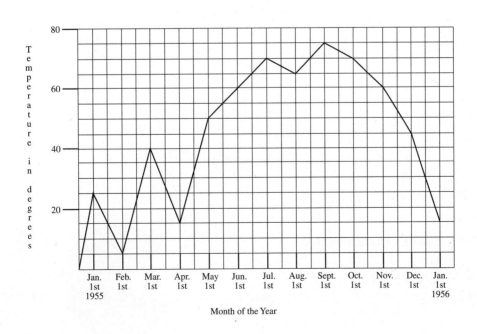

193. In which two months did the temperature rise the most steeply?

    (A)   February to March & April to May

    (B)   March to April & August to September

    (C)   January to February & February to March

    (D)   October to November & November to December

194. In which single month did the temperature fall most sharply?

    (A)   February   (C)   August

    (B)   April   (D)   December

195. In which two months was the coldest temperature the same?

    (A)   February & April   (C)   June & November

    (B)   May & December   (D)   March & December

196. The "7" in 465.2671 is in the thousandths place. In what place is the "7" in 472.625?

    (A)   hundreds   (C)   tenths

    (B)   tens   (D)   hundredths

197. Which of the following is an obtuse triangle?

    (A) 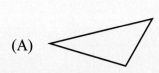   (C) 

    (B) 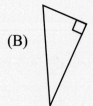   (D) 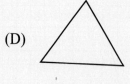

198. Find the value of x in the picture.

    (A)   55°   (C)   305°

    (B)   125°   (D)   360°

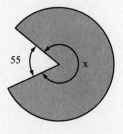

Problem-Solving

199. The simple interest, *I*, on *d* dollars for *y* years at the rate of *r*% per year is computed from the formula:

I = *d* ×*y*× r.

Use this formula to compute the simple interest on $4,500 invested for 1 year at 6% per year.

(A) $27   (C) $2,700

(B) $270   (D) $27,000

200. A welder joins 12 pipes together to make a flag pole. If each pipe measures 8.5 ft, what is the length of the flag pole?

(A) 1,020 ft   (C) 102 ft

(B) 205 ft   (D) 1,120 ft

201. One rainy day attendance in a school dropped from 400 to 336. What was the percent decrease in attendance?

(A) 1.6%   (C) 16%

(B) 1.9%   (D) 19%

202. Sandra broke a rectangular bathroom mirror. The mirror costs $2.60 per square foot. If the mirror that Sandra broke measures 2.5 feet by 6.4 feet, how much will it cost to replace this mirror?

Hint: To find the area of a rectangle, you may use the formula:

Area = length × width.

(A) $6.50   (C) $23.14

(B) $16.64   (D) $41.60

203. An ice cream machine pumps out 9 pints of ice cream in 6 seconds. At this rate, how many pints of ice cream would this machine pump out in 3 minutes?

(A) 18 pts.   (C) 162 pts.

(B) 27 pts.   (D) 270 pts.

204. Michael, Jason, and Alan share a sum of money. Michael takes $\frac{2}{7}$ of the money, while Jason takes $\frac{2}{5}$ of it. What fraction of the money is left for Alan?

(A) $\dfrac{24}{35}$ (C) $\dfrac{4}{11}$

(B) $\dfrac{11}{35}$ (D) $\dfrac{7}{11}$

205. The value of a computer decreases at the rate of 18% per year. If a new computer cost $1,500.00, what would be the value of this computer at the end of one year?

(A) $270   (C) $1,482

(B) $1,230   (D) $1,418

206. Damian won a television set in a raffle. But he decides to sell it for 22% less than its value of $375. How much does Damian sell the television set for?

(A) $457.50   (C) $292.50

(B) $353.00   (D) $82.50

207. To make a simple fence around her little rectangular flower garden, Jessica runs a rope around four pegs at the corners of the garden, as shown. What is the length of the rope?

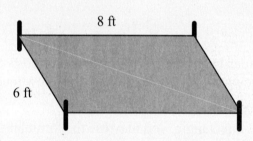

(A) 14 ft.   (C) 24 ft.

(B) 28 ft.   (D) 48 ft.

208. The leatherback turtle is 8 feet long while the common mud turtle is 5 inches long. What fraction of the leatherback turtle's length is the common mud turtle's length?

(A) $\dfrac{96}{5}$ (C) $\dfrac{8}{5}$

(B) $\dfrac{5}{96}$ (D) $\dfrac{5}{8}$

209. If the Indian lizard is 10 ft. long and the desertnight lizard is 5 in. long, what fraction of the Indian lizard's length is the desertnight lizard's length?

(A) $\dfrac{1}{2}$ (C) $\dfrac{1}{4}$

(B) $\dfrac{1}{24}$ (D) $\dfrac{5}{24}$

210. The anaconda may grow to 9 m long while an adult desert sidewinding viper measures only 25 cm. How many desert sidewinding vipers must be strung together, head to tail, to cover the length of one anaconda?

(A) 3.6   (C) 360

(B) 36   (D) 3,600

211. A few years ago Delaware had a population of 683,000 while Rhode Island had a population of 989,000. By how many people was the population of Rhode Island greater than that of Delaware?

(A) 36,000   (C) 306,000

(B) 206,000   (D) 316,000

212. There are 200 students in one small school. If 120 of these students are girls, what percent of them are boys?

(A) 80   (C) 60

(B) 70   (D) 40

213. Peter earned 84% by answering 63 questions correctly on a mathematics test. How many questions did he miss?

(A) 100   (C) 21

(B) 75   (D) 12

214. An ant can lift a weight up to 50 times its own body weight. If the weight-lifting power of a body builder is directly proportional to that of an ant, what weight should a man who weighs 175 lbs. be able to lift?

(A) 8,750 lb.   (C) 875 lb.

(B) 2,250 lb.   (D) 275 lb.

Use the diagram on the next page to answer questions 215 and 216.

215. What fraction of this rectangle is shaded?

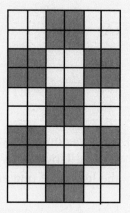

(A) $\dfrac{7}{15}$ (C) $\dfrac{5}{9}$

(B) $\dfrac{8}{15}$ (D) $\dfrac{4}{9}$

216. Approximately what percent of the rectangle is <u>not</u> shaded?

(A) 53%   (C) 7%

(B) 15%   (D) 17%

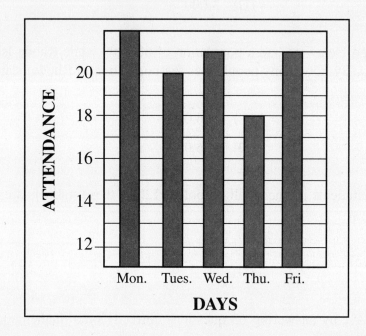

217. Observe that the attendance bar for Monday is "off the scale" (that is, the bar is too high to fit into the graph). If the average attendance for Monday and Tuesday was 23, what was the attendance on Monday?

(A) 30   (C) 23

(B) 26   (D) 20

218. Jeff's total score on 5 history tests was 395. When the teacher agreed to drop Jeff's lowest score, his total changed to 332. What was the test score that the teacher dropped?

(A) 63   (C) 82

(B) 79   (D) 85

219. The clear portions in this picture are half-circles. Find the area of the shaded region in the picture.

    The area of a circle may be computed from the formula:

    Area = $3.14 \times r^2$, where r = measure of radius of circle.

    (A) 86 cm^2 (C) 157 cm^2

    (B) 100 cm^2 (D) 243 cm^2

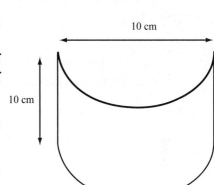

220. Mr. Stanley cuts off the top and bottom of a circular milk can. Then he slices the can vertically into two halves. The picture on the right shows one of the two halves of the can. If the can is 10 cm high, find the area of the half shown at the right.

    You may compute the circumference of a circle from the formula:

    Circumference = $3.14 \times d$, where d = measure of diameter of circle.

    (A) 314 cm^2 (C) 31.4 cm^2

    (B) 157 cm^2 (D) 15.7 cm^2

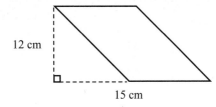

221. Find the area of the parallelogram below. ($a = b \times h$)

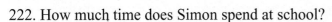

12 cm

15 cm

    (A) 90 cm^2 (C) 180 cm^2

    (B) 150 cm^2 (D) 360 cm^2

The circle graph shows how Simon spends the majority of his day, from 6:00 a.m. one morning to 6:00 a.m. the next morning. Use this information to answer questions 222 and 223 which follow.

222. How much time does Simon spend at school?

    (A) 15.4 hrs   (C) 8.6 hrs

    (B) 4.6 hrs   (D) 6.8 hrs

223. What percent of Simon's time does he spend on his homework?

    (A) 1%   (C) 2.4%
    (B) 10%   (D) 24%

224. Mrs. Patterson's dinner pot consisted of 8 oz. of black-eyed peas, 1/2 lb. of rice and 1 lb. of red beans. What percent of the food in this pot is rice?

    (A) 0.5%   (C) 50%
    (B) 18%   (D) 25%

225. The ratio of mid-sized cars to big cars in a parking lot is 63 to 37. If there are spaces for 189 mid-sized cars in a parking lot, how many spaces are there for big cars?

    (A) 100   (C) 111
    (B) 37   (D) 126

226. Sharon bought a dress and a pair of shoes. The price of the dress was originally $60 but was being sold at a 20% discount. The pair of shoes originally cost $80 but was discounted 15%. What was her discount on the entire purchase? (approximately)

    (A) 5%   (C) 25%
    (B) 17%   (D) 32%

227. Ten apples and one orange cost $2.70, whereas ten oranges and one apple cost $3.24. What is the cost of one apple and one orange?

    (A) .24   (C) .44
    (B) .34   (D) .54

228. Amy, Brenda, and Carol go to a restaurant for lunch. They decide that Amy will pay $\frac{1}{3}$ of the food bill; Brenda will pay $\frac{1}{5}$ of the bill, and Carol will pay the remainder of the bill. If Amy ends up paying $10.70, how much does Carol pay?

    (A) $19.26   (C) $14.98
    (B) $17.12   (D) $12.84

229. A basketball team wins 70% of the first 30 games it plays. If the team wins only half of the remaining games, it will have won 62% of all its games. What is the total number of games the team will have played?

(A) 56   (C) 44

(B) 50   (D) 38

230. Brian rides his bike from home to school, a distance of 3 miles. If his speed is 10 miles per hour for the first 6 minutes, how fast should he go in order for his trip to take a total of 12 minutes?

(A) 20 mi./hr.   (C) 12 mi./hr.

(B) 16 mi./hr.   (D) 10 mi./hr.

231. The rate of vibration of a string varies inversely depending on its length. A string 40 inches long will vibrate 100 times per second. What is the length of a string which vibrates 250 times per second?

(A) 16   (C) 64

(B) 25   (D) 100

232. At a particular party of 60 people, every person is talking, dancing, or both. 35 people are talking. If 27 people are both talking and dancing, how many people are dancing?

(A) 25   (C) 44

(B) 33   (D) 52

233. A square has a side of 6 inches and a rectangle has a length of 18 inches. If the perimeter of the rectangle is two and one-half times the perimeter of the square, what is the width of the rectangle?

(A) 15 inches   (C) 8 inches

(B) 12 inches   (D) 5 inches

234. One angle of an isosceles triangle is known to be 80°. Which one of the following could <u>not</u> be the measure of another angle in this triangle?

(A) 10°   (C) 50°

(B) 20°   (D) 80°

235. In a family of three people, the mother weighs 45 pounds more than the child, and the father weighs 3 times as much as the child. If their total weight is 370 pounds, what is the difference in weight between the father and the mother?

(A) 120 pounds   (C) 85 pounds

(B) 110 pounds   (D) 65 pounds

236. Two trains leave a station at the same time, traveling in opposite directions. After 5 hours, they are 560 miles apart. If one train's rate is 6 miles per hour faster than that of the other train, how many miles will the faster train cover in 3 hours?

(A) 159

(B) 168

(C) 177

(D) 186

237. A quiz contains only five multiple-choice questions. The first three questions have 5 choices each, and the last two questions are true-false only. If a student randomly guesses on each question, what is his probability of getting all five questions right?

(A) 1/30

(B) 1/216

(C) 1/500

(D) 1/972

238. Nine people are in an elevator, four men and five women. The average weight of the women is 130 pounds. If the total weight of the people is 1,350 pounds, what is the average weight of the men?

(A) 140 pounds

(B) 162 pounds

(C) 170 pounds

(D) 175 pounds

Subtest 5: Language Skills

TIME: 25 Minutes
    60 Questions

Punctuation, Capitalization, and Usage

> **DIRECTIONS:** Look for errors of punctuation, capitalization, or usage in the following sentences. If there are no mistakes, mark "D."

239. (A) My older brother is on the football team

    (B) When it became warm, I opened the window.

    (C) I forgot where I left my hat.

    (D) No mistakes.

240. (A) His uncle took him to the ball game.

    (B) The baby gurgled.

    (C) The dog brought me his bone.

    (D) No mistakes.

241. (A) The window on the front door was broken.

    (B) We went behind the house for the barbecue.

    (C) The present a music box was wrapped in purple paper.

    (D) No mistakes.

242. (A) Could you turn off the radio?

    (B) Congratulations on such an excelent job.

    (C) We walked over to where he was standing.

    (D) No mistakes.

243. (A) My grandmother sent a letter to my brother and I.

    (B) A storm was predicted for Wednesday.

    (C) Josh did not like that lunch.

    (D) No mistakes.

244. (A) We plan to go ice skating in february.

    (B) The books were too heavy to bring home.

    (C) We had my favorite dessert.

    (D) No mistakes.

245. (A) I tripped and hurt my knee.

    (B) He wandered in and said, "we wanted to do that."

    (C) Bowling can sometimes be fun.

    (D) No mistakes.

246. (A) We can't do that!

    (B) You doesn't have to help me.

    (C) Anne went home sick today.

    (D) No mistakes.

247. (A) Where did Marcia go?

    (B) My friends has a new baby sister.

    (C) Wait here for a minute.

    (D) No mistakes.

248. (A) I really can't help you.

    (B) I hope I have studied enough.

    (C) Isnt that your brother?

    (D) No mistakes.

249. (A) Mr Green wanted to hear me sing.

    (B) My neighbors started to laugh.

    (C) We walked in too soon.

    (D) No mistakes.

250. (A) We dove into the pool.

    (B) I hate shopping for new clothes.

    (C) We had a picnic outsides.

    (D) No mistakes.

251. (A) We carried the boxes out to the car.

     (B) Drawing are a fun course to take.

     (C) We met after school to discuss the election.

     (D) No mistakes.

252. (A) We ran, outside, quickly.

     (B) He doesn't understand the problem.

     (C) The car was unlocked, so we sat inside.

     (D) No mistakes.

253. (A) Could you please answer the telephone?

     (B) "Don't leave any lights on!" she said.

     (C) I waited for over an hour.

     (D) No mistakes.

254. (A) Are you sitting over there.

     (B) My favorite band is on the radio.

     (C) That is my favorite flavor.

     (D) No mistakes.

255. (A) That girl are making really funny faces.

     (B) "I'm going home now," she announced.

     (C) I have to help clean up.

     (D) No mistakes.

256. (A) We brought many cookie over to his house.

     (B) "You're standing on my foot!" I shrieked.

     (C) I had to start wearing glasses.

     (D) No mistakes.

257. (A) That book was very booring.

     (B) We were so tired that we slept until the afternoon.

     (C) I carried over the stereo, the books, and the chair.

     (D) No mistakes.

258. (A) I was looking for a large red car.

(B) Patty is going to meet us later.

(C) He had to mow the lawn before dinner.

(D) No mistakes.

259. (A) We went swimming in the lake.

(B) My friend moved to Arizona last year.

(C) Scott hurt his head he went to the doctor.

(D) No mistakes.

260. (A) The band sounded awful.

(B) We almost danced until midnight.

(C) I have to find a job.

(D) No mistakes.

261. (A) We waited for the football game to begin.

(B) John typed, read, and print out his report.

(C) Pat wants to come over later.

(D) No mistakes.

262. (A) Maxine is more better at math.

(B) We are going to the Mexican restaurant later.

(C) I fell asleep during the movie.

(D) No mistakes.

263. (A) "What time is it?" she asked.

(B) "Where are we going tonight" he wanted to know.

(C) "Look at the old car!"

(D) No mistakes.

264. (A) We see that television show last night.

(B) Joy wants to do that tomorrow.

(C) Our neighbor is building a pool in his backyard.

(D) No mistakes.

265. (A) For days from now I will be on vacation.

    (B) He spent last year in England.

    (C) Joe wants to be a teacher.

    (D) No mistakes.

266. (A) "Jack went in that direction," she said.

    (B) The game starts after school.

    (C) We left at the begining of the match.

    (D) No mistakes.

267. (A) Ian asked us to visit him later.

    (B) She warned That isn't such a good idea.

    (C) My aunt cooks for us on the holidays.

    (D) No mistakes.

268. (A) There were too many bugs near our campground.

    (B) He is reading The Adventures of Huckleberry Finn.

    (C) We gave my grandmother a watch for her birthday.

    (D) No mistakes.

269. (A) We drove quickly over the bridge.

    (B) The cat ate the fish.

    (C) I can't find my wallet

    (D) No mistakes.

270. (A) My birthday was last month.

    (B) We had hot dogs, hamburgers, and corn at the barbecue.

    (C) Henry was late for the meeting.

    (D) No mistakes.

271. (A) Its time to go home now.

    (B) Laura is not feeling well this evening.

    (C) We waited for over an hour.

    (D) No mistakes.

272. (A) Martin is washing the dishes.

    (B) He was so tired that he fell asleep in the car.

    (C) The mysterious dark car.

    (D) No mistakes.

273. (A) I used to sell cookies when I was younger.

    (B) we brought cupcakes, plates, and napkins over to her house.

    (C) The balloons were rising in the air.

    (D) No mistakes.

274. (A) My older brother carried the boxes out.

    (B) We walked quickly we thought someone was there.

    (C) Mike plays piano, guitar, and trumpet.

    (D) No mistakes.

275. (A) I don't think that I want to go.

    (B) What time does it start?

    (C) I through the ball at my sister.

    (D) No mistakes.

276. (A) Luke is afraid of planes.

    (B) I brought my lunch today.

    (C) My mom and dad likes to eat at restaurants.

    (D) No mistakes.

277. (A) The dogs jumped all over the couch.

    (B) I go to the store yesterday.

    (C) My cousin spends a lot of time using her computer.

    (D) No mistakes.

278. (A) I could not fall asleep last night.

    (B) Talking during the movie.

    (C) Sal has a lot of books to carry.

    (D) No mistakes.

Spelling

DIRECTIONS: Choose the sentence that contains a spelling error. If there are no errors, choose "D."

---

279. (A) The benefits outweigh the risks in his new business venture.

  (B) The speaker asked the group to complete a questionnaire.

  (C) Mrs. Blake's kindergarten class wore their Halloween costumes to school.

  (D) No mistakes.

280. (A) Boston is the capital of Massachusetts.

  (B) The newly married couple met with a financial advisor.

  (C) The atheletes are traveling to a basketball tournament.

  (D) No mistakes.

281. (A) The gardener was embarassed when he tripped over a hose.

  (B) The audience was fascinated when the tiger disappeared.

  (C) Nearly all of their possessions were destroyed in the hurricane.

  (D) No mistakes.

282. (A) Sharon's infection required immediate medical attention.

  (B) The desparate criminal hid in an abandoned factory.

  (C) The amateur photographer won first prize in the beach scene contest.

  (D) No mistakes.

283. (A) His physician urged him to eliminate sugar from his diet.

  (B) First impressions are not always accurate or lasting.

  (C) The child's frequent absenses are hindering her progress.

  (D) No mistakes.

284. (A) They planned an expedition to the ancient ruins of Mexico.

  (B) The maintainance crew was exhausted after the carnival.

  (C) The mayor's commitment to help immigrants is evident.

  (D) No mistakes.

285. (A) The scientist itemized the cost of new equipment for the laboratory.

(B) Congradulations on your successful completion of the program.

(C) I met my sisters-in-law in the theater lobby at intermission.

(D) No mistakes.

286. (A) Jim received many complements for his chocolate layer cake.

(B) The adolescent failed to consider the consequences of his actions.

(C) Katrina's interpersonal skills are a valuable asset on the job.

(D) No mistakes.

287. (A) Prioritizing tasks increases efficiency in the workplace.

(B) The yacht swerved off course in the turbulent waters.

(C) Studying a foreign language disciplines the mind.

(D) No mistakes.

288. (A) Whether to turn right or left at the intersection was a dilemma.

(B) Nearly all of their possessions were destroyed in the hurricane.

(C) The seniors were anxious to see their graduation date on the new school calender.

(D) No mistakes.

Composition

DIRECTIONS: Select the best answer choice.

289. Which of these best fits under the topic "Using Herbs to Season Food"?

(A) The flavor of herbs is most intense when they are fresh.

(B) Many kinds of herbs can grow easily from seed.

(C) Herbs should be protected from frost.

(D) None of these.

290. Which of these best fits under the topic "The Benefits of Vitamin C"?

(A) Vitamin C stays in the body for a short time and must be taken regularly.

(B) Strawberries and oranges are good sources of Vitamin C.

(C)   Vitamin C helps the body resist infections.

(D)   None of these.

291. Which of these best fits under the topic "Inventions of the 19th Century"?

(A)   Thomas Edison invented the phonograph in 1877.

(B)   In 1609, Galileo made a telescope and was the first to study the stars and planets.

(C)   Penicillin, the first antibiotic, was discovered by Alexander Fleming in 1928.

(D)   None of these.

292. Which of these best fits under the topic "Why Dinosaurs Became Extinct"?

(A)   The dodo and the mastodon are extinct.

(B)   Scientists learn about dinosaurs by studying fossils.

(C)   The Tyrannosaurus was a carnivore.

(D)   None of these.

293. Which topic is best for a one-paragraph theme?

(A)   Our Solar System   (C)   Travel Safety Tips

(B)   U. S. Presidents   (D)   None of these.

294. Which topic is best for a one-paragraph theme?

(A)   Telephone Etiquette

(B)   Trees of North America

(C)   Egyptian Art

(D)   None of these.

295. Where should the sentence, "**To protect itself, the oyster encloses the irritant in a sac,**" be placed in the selection below?

(1) A pearl forms in an oyster when a grain of sand, or another foreign substance, gets inside the oyster's shell. (2) The foreign substance irritates the oyster. (3) The oyster then secretes layers of mother-of-pearl, or nacre, around the sac to form a pearl.

(A)   The sentence does not fit in this paragraph.

(B)   after sentence 3

(C)   between sentences 1 and 2

(D)   between sentences 2 and 3

296. Where should the sentence, "**For example**, **when you press the letter 'M' on the keyboard**, **the letter 'M' appears on the monitor screen**," be placed in the selection below?

(1) The step by step process of operating a computer is a series of causes and effects. (2) When a computer is turned on, electricity surges through its internal parts. (3) This begins a chain reaction of causes and effects.

(A)   The sentence does not fit in this paragraph.

(B)   After sentence 3

(C)   Between sentences 1 and 2

(D)   Between sentences 2 and 3

297. Which sentence does not belong in this paragraph?

(1) A computer system is made up of both hardware and software. (2) Hardware is the name for the parts of the system that you can see and touch. (3) Many students find the smaller laptop computers very convenient. (4) Software is the name for the instructions, or programs, that tell the hardware what to do.

(A)   Sentence 1   (C)   Sentence 3

(B)   Sentence 2   (D)   Sentence 4

298. Which sentence does not belong in this paragraph?

(1) Monticello was the home of Thomas Jefferson, the third president of the United States. (2) Jefferson designed the home himself and lived there until his death in 1826. (3) Many tourists visit Monticello, which is located in Charlottesville, Virginia. (4) Jefferson was the governor of Virginia from 1779 to 1781.

(A)   Sentence 1   (C)   Sentence 3

(B)   Sentence 2   (D)   Sentence 4

STS HSPT

PRACTICE TEST 2

ANSWER KEY

Question Number	Correct Answer	If You Answered this Question Incorrectly, Refer to...

Subtest 1: Verbal Skills

1.	(C)	P. 194
2.	(B)	P. 194
3.	(C)	P. 194
4.	(B)	P. 194
5.	(C)	P. 194
6.	(B)	P. 194
7.	(D)	P. 190
8.	(A)	P. 191
9.	(A)	P. 190
10.	(B)	P. 190
11.	(D)	P. 197
12.	(D)	P. 197
13.	(A)	P. 197
14.	(D)	P. 197
15.	(B)	P. 197
16.	(C)	P. 197
17.	(C)	P. 197
18.	(C)	P. 197
19.	(A)	P. 197
20.	(B)	P. 197

21.	(D)	P. 197
22.	(B)	P. 197
23.	(A)	P. 197
24.	(A)	P. 197
25.	(D)	P. 197
26.	(B)	P. 197
27.	(A)	P. 197
28.	(A)	P. 186
29.	(A)	P. 186
30.	(C)	P. 186
31.	(C)	P. 186
32.	(B)	P. 186
33.	(B)	P. 186
34.	(A)	P. 186
35.	(A)	P. 186
36.	(C)	P. 186
37.	(C)	P. 186
38.	(B)	P. 195
39.	(C)	P. 195
40.	(B)	P. 195
41.	(D)	P. 195
42.	(A)	P. 195
43.	(A)	P. 195
44.	(B)	P. 195
45.	(D)	P. 195
46.	(A)	P. 195
47.	(D)	P. 195
48.	(B)	P. 195
49.	(C)	P. 195
50.	(B)	P. 195
51.	(A)	P. 195
52.	(C)	P. 195
53.	(B)	P. 195
54.	(D)	P. 195

55.	(C)	P. 195
56.	(B)	P. 196
57.	(D)	P. 196
58.	(C)	P. 196
59.	(C)	P. 196
60.	(C)	P. 196

Subtest 2: Quantitative Skills

61.	(D)	P. 409
62.	(A)	P. 401
63.	(B)	P. 401
64.	(A)	P. 404
65.	(C)	P. 407
66.	(C)	P. 409
67.	(D)	P. 409
68.	(A)	P. 401
69.	(A)	P. 404
70.	(D)	P. 409
71.	(C)	P. 401
72.	(A)	P. 401
73.	(D)	P. 409
74.	(A)	P. 409
75.	(B)	P. 407
76.	(A)	P. 404
77.	(D)	P. 401
78.	(C)	P. 401
79.	(D)	P. 409
80.	(A)	P. 407
81.	(D)	P. 409
82.	(C)	P. 404
83.	(B)	P. 401
84.	(B)	P. 401
85.	(D)	P. 409
86.	(D)	P. 407

87.	(C)	P. 401
88.	(A)	P. 401
89.	(D)	P. 409
90.	(C)	P. 404
91.	(D)	P. 401
92.	(A)	P. 401
93.	(C)	P. 409
94.	(D)	P. 407
95.	(D)	P. 409
96.	(C)	P. 401
97.	(D)	P. 404
98.	(B)	P. 409
99.	(A)	P. 407
100.	(D)	P. 409
101.	(C)	P. 404
102.	(C)	P. 407
103.	(D)	P. 409
104.	(B)	P. 404
105.	(A)	P. 401
106.	(B)	P. 407
107.	(B)	P. 404
108.	(C)	P. 401
109.	(C)	P. 401
110.	(A)	P. 409
111.	(B)	P. 409
112.	(B)	P. 401

Subtest 3: Reading Comprehension

113.	(B)	P. 272
114.	(D)	P. 282
115.	(C)	P. 272
116.	(D)	P. 272
117.	(D)	P. 272
118.	(C)	P. 270

119.	(C)	P. 282
120.	(B)	P. 272
121.	(D)	P. 280
122.	(B)	P. 274
123.	(A)	P. 270
124.	(D)	P. 274
125.	(C)	P. 275
126.	(D)	P. 282
127.	(A)	P. 280
128.	(A)	P. 270
129.	(C)	P. 272
130.	(D)	P. 280
131.	(A)	P. 274
132.	(B)	P. 282
133.	(B)	P. 275
134.	(C)	P. 272
135.	(C)	P. 272
136.	(C)	P. 272
137.	(A)	P. 270
138.	(D)	P. 270
139.	(C)	P. 275
140.	(D)	P. 280
141.	(A)	P. 274
142.	(B)	P. 275
143.	(C)	P. 270
144.	(D)	P. 272
145.	(D)	P. 272
146.	(B)	P. 274
147.	(A)	P. 282
148.	(B)	P. 275
149.	(A)	P. 280
150.	(D)	P. 272
151.	(C)	P. 280
152.	(B)	P. 275

Vocabulary

153.	(D)	P. 288
154.	(A)	P. 288
155.	(C)	P. 288
156.	(B)	P. 288
157.	(A)	P. 288
158.	(D)	P. 288
159.	(B)	P. 288
160.	(C)	P. 288
161.	(C)	P. 288
162.	(D)	P. 288
163.	(B)	P. 288
164.	(C)	P. 288
165.	(D)	P. 288
166.	(B)	P. 288
167.	(A)	P. 288
168.	(C)	P. 288
169.	(C)	P. 288
170.	(C)	P. 288
171.	(B)	P. 288
172.	(B)	P. 288
173.	(B)	P. 288
174.	(C)	P. 288

Subtest 4: Mathematics Concepts

175.	(A)	P. 354
176.	(A)	P. 409
177.	(D)	P. 404
178.	(B)	P. 315, 332
179.	(B)	P. 338
180.	(C)	P. 373
181.	(A)	P. 378
182.	(A)	P. 331, 334, 345

183.	(B)	P. 331, 350
184.	(A)	P. 341, 346
185.	(D)	P. 383
186.	(A)	P. 331, 382
187.	(C)	P. 409
188.	(A)	P. 371
189.	(C)	P. 377
190.	(C)	P. 315
191.	(D)	P. 385
192.	(C)	P. 452
193.	(A)	P. 404
194.	(D)	P. 404
195.	(D)	P. 404
196.	(B)	P. 354
197.	(A)	P. 391
198.	(C)	P. 391

Problem-Solving

199.	(B)	P. 385
200.	(C)	P. 377
201.	(C)	P. 396
202.	(D)	P. 378
203.	(D)	P. 320, 328
204.	(B)	P. 334
205.	(B)	P. 396
206.	(C)	P. 396
207.	(B)	P. 377
208.	(B)	P. 350
209.	(B)	P. 350
210.	(B)	P. 320, 323
211.	(C)	P. 317
212.	(D)	P. 382
213.	(D)	P. 393
214.	(A)	P. 320

215.	(A)	P. 328
216.	(A)	P. 328, 384
217.	(B)	P. 371
218.	(A)	P. 371
219.	(A)	P. 378, 391
220.	(B)	P. 391
221.	(C)	P. 378
222.	(C)	P. 328
223.	(B)	P. 328, 382
224.	(D)	P. 328, 382
225.	(C)	P. 345, 350
226.	(B)	P. 328, 382, 396
227.	(D)	P. 328, 353
228.	(C)	P. 334, 393
229.	(B)	P. 385, 395
230.	(A)	P. 320, 328
231.	(A)	P. 328, 320
232.	(D)	P. 315
233.	(B)	P. 377
234.	(A)	P. 391
235.	(C)	P. 315, 320
236.	(C)	P. 320, 323
237.	(C)	P. 388
238.	(D)	P. 371

Subtest 5: Language Skills
Punctuation, Capitalization, and Usage

239.	(A)	P. 228
240.	(D)	P. 217
241.	(C)	P. 232
242.	(B)	P. 251
243.	(A)	P. 217
244.	(A)	P. 244
245.	(B)	P. 246

246.	(B)	P. 212
247.	(B)	P. 212
248.	(C)	P. 237
249.	(A)	P. 228
250.	(C)	P. 249
251.	(B)	P. 212
252.	(A)	P. 229
253.	(D)	P. 239
254.	(A)	P. 228
255.	(A)	P. 212
256.	(A)	P. 204
257.	(A)	P. 251
258.	(D)	P. 210, 217
259.	(C)	P. 207
260.	(B)	P. 205
261.	(B)	P. 211
262.	(A)	P. 225
263.	(B)	P. 242
264.	(A)	P. 211
265.	(A)	P. 251
266.	(C)	P. 251
267.	(B)	P. 239
268.	(B)	P. 239, 245
269.	(C)	P. 228
270.	(D)	P. 211
271.	(A)	P. 238
272.	(C)	P. 206
273.	(B)	P. 245
274.	(B)	P. 206
275.	(C)	P. 211
276.	(C)	P. 212
277.	(B)	P. 211
278.	(B)	P. 206

Spelling

279.	(D)	P. 249
280.	(C)	P. 249
281.	(A)	P. 251
282.	(B)	P. 251
283.	(C)	P. 250
284.	(B)	P. 252
285.	(B)	P. 250
286.	(A)	P. 250
287.	(D)	P. 249
288.	(C)	P. 253

Composition

289.	(A)	P. 270
290.	(C)	P. 270
291.	(A)	P. 270
292.	(D)	P. 270
293.	(C)	P. 270
294.	(A)	P. 270
295.	(D)	P. 270
296.	(B)	P. 270
297.	(C)	P. 270
298.	(D)	P. 270

Subtest 1: Verbal Skills

DETAILED EXPLANATIONS OF ANSWERS

1. **(C)** A *telescope* is an instrument used to see things that are far away like *stars*; a *microscope* is an instrument used to make small things like *cells* appear larger. Both *telescope* and *microscope* are derived from the Greek root *scop*, which means *to look at*. The prefix *micro-* means *small*, while the prefix *tele-* means *far*.

2. **(B)** A *combination* unlocks a *safe* as a *key* unlocks a *door*.

3. **(C)** *Worst* is the superlative form of the adjective *bad* as *best* is the superlative form of the adjective *good*.

4. **(B)** An *actor* performs on a *stage* as an *usher* works in the *aisles* seating people.

5. **(C)** An *orator* can be described as *eloquent* as a *gymnast* can be described as *flexible*.

6. **(B)** *Inception* and *beginning* are synonyms, as are *incite* and *provoke*.

7. **(D)** *Ecstatic* means extremely *happy* as *exhausted* means extremely *tired*.

8. **(A)** A *sofa* is a seat for more than one person inside a house in a room such as a *living room*; a *bench* is a seat for more than one person in a *park*.

9. **(A)** *Reveal* and *conceal* are antonyms as are *expand* and *contract*.

10. **(B)** *Exploit* and *protect* are antonyms as are *impartial* and *prejudiced*.

11. **(D)** To *loiter* is to *pause*, *tarry*, *wait*, or *stay*. *Linger* (D) is the term which is closest to *loiter* in meaning. To *litter* (A) is to *scatter*, *strew*, or *disarrange*. Despite the similarity in spelling, the two words are not similar in meaning. Choice (A) is not appropriate. *Relapse* (B) means *deteriorate*, *regress*, or *decline*. The meaning of *relapse* is not related to the meaning of *loiter*. To *hasten* (C) is the opposite of to *loiter*; (C) is not the correct answer.

12. **(D)** *Inflammable* means *burnable*, *incendiary*, *combustible*, or *flammable* (D). The best choice of a synonym is *flammable* (D). The word *inflammation* (A) is similar in shape to *inflammable*, but it is not similar in meaning. An antonym of *inflammable* is *noncombustible* (B);

the directions do not indicate that the test-taker is to select an antonym. *Similar* (C) means *like, the same*. These words are not synonymous with *inflammable*. The test-taker should choose (D).

13. **(A)** To *vindicate* is to *acquit, absolve,* or *clear* (A). The antonym of *vindicate* is *convict* (B) or *condemn*. The test-taker, however, is not to choose an antonym. To *pose* (C) is to *assert, state,* or *profess*. Neither choice (B) nor (C) is the synonym for *vindicate* that the test-taker should select. Choice (D), or *blame*, is the opposite of *vindicate*.

14. **(D)** A *premonition* is a *forewarning* (D). It is not a *promotion* (A), or an *advancement*; neither is a *premonition* a *luxury* (B), a *comfort,* or a *frill*. A *premonition* may come in the form of a *dream* (C), but a *dream* is not synonymous with a *premonition*.

15. **(B)** *Soothe* means to *console* or to *comfort* (B). *Soothe* is not synonymous with *warn* (A) or *blacken* (C). *Warn* means to *advise* and *blacken* means to *darken*. The answer choice *strengthen* (D) is close to the meaning of *soothe* as in a kind of *encouragement*, but *comfort* (B) is the overall best answer.

16. **(C)** *Fervent* describes something of great *emotion* or *passion*; its best synonym would be the choice *enthusiastic* (C). Choices *hesitant* (A) and *cool* (B) are antonyms for this word. The answer choice *warm* (D) does not reflect the same degree of emotion that is displayed in *enthusiastic* (C).

17. **(C)** The word *crucial* means *of supreme importance*, and its best synonym would be the answer choice *fundamental* (C) which means *central* or *key*. The answer choice *technical* (A) means *pertaining to a process*; *experimental* (B) refers to something being *tried* or *tested*. Answer choice *advanced* (D) means *improved* or *promoted*. Therefore, *fundamental* (C) is the best answer.

18. **(C)** The word *reprimand* means to *scold* or *find fault with*. Its best synonym is *correct* (C) which means to *make right*. *Praise* (A) is the opposite of *reprimand*; it means to *speak highly of*. *Return* (B) means to *give back*, and *threaten* (D) means to *warn of danger or harm*. Therefore, the best answer choice is *correct* (C).

19. **(A)** *Chastity* is *purity* (A), *virtue,* or *honor*. *Correction* (B) is not the same as *chastity*. *Religious* (C) means *devout, pious,* and *holy*. *Religious* is not the best synonym for *chastity*. *Familiarity* (D), or *informality,* is not synonymous with *chastity*. Choices (B), (C), and (D) are not appropriate choices. Choice (A) is the best answer.

20. **(B)** The synonym for the word *disrespectful*, which means *having no appreciation*, is *rude* (B), which means *without manners or courtesy*. *Careless* (A) means *without thought or attention*. *Valuable* (C) means *having high worth or expensive qualities*. *Safe* (D) means *secure* and *without danger*. The best answer for a synonym for *disrespectful* is *rude* (B).

21. **(D)** *Contempt* is *scorn* (D) or *disdain*. *Temptation* (A) means *inducement, enticement,* and *lure*; it does not relate to or serve as a synonym for the word *contempt*. *Fear* (B), *horror,* and

dismay are not words with meanings similar to *contempt*. *Commend* (C) is to *laud, compliment,* or *applaud*; it is not a synonym for *contempt*.

22. **(B)**   *Agile* most nearly means *limber* (B), *nimble*, or *spry*. *Agile* does not mean *wool* (A). The test-taker who selects the word *wool* may have the word confused with *argyle*. *Unpredictable* (C) means *random, irregular,* or *unexpected*; choice (C) is not related to *agile*. *Difficult* (D) is not synonymous with *agile*. It is readily apparent that (A), (C), and (D) are not appropriate synonyms for *agile*.

23. **(A)**   *Redeem* means to *recover* (A), to *reclaim*, and to *restore*. *Redeem* is not a synonym for *locate* (B). *Locate* (B) means *find, search out, or discover*. There is no relationship between *redeem* and *destroy* (C), which means *demolish* or *obliterate*. Choice (D), *research,* means to *investigate* or *to study*. Choices (B), (C), and (D) are not the best choices for synonyms of *redeem*.

24. **(A)**   To *pulverize* is to *grind* (A) or to *crush*. To *attempt* (B) is to *try*, to *strive*, or to *venture*; this verb is not a synonym for *pulverize*. To *pervert* (C) is to *corrupt, entice,* or *allure*; it is not a synonym for *pulverize*. To *preserve* (D) or to *save* has the same beginning sound as *pulverize*, but it does not have the same meaning as *pulverize*. Choice (A) is the best word to select as a synonym.

25. **(D)**   To *presume* is to *assume*. The word *assume* (D) is the best synonym for *presume*. To *swindle* (A) means to *cheat* or to *take advantage of someone*. Choice (A) is not the best synonym for *presume*. To *predict* (B) is to *guess* or to *foresee*. Choice (B) is not an appropriate synonym. To *prosper* (C) is to *do well*, to *make advances*, or to *make gains*. Choice (C) is not the best term for a synonym of *presume*.

26. **(B)**   To *prevaricate* means most nearly to *lie* (B). Choice (B) is an acceptable substitute for *prevaricate*. Although it is sometimes *dangerous, unwise,* or *unsafe* to lie, to *endanger* (A)— to *put in danger*—is not the best choice as a synonym for *prevaricate*. To *threaten* (C) is to *torment* or to *scare*. To *prevent* (D) is to *impede*. This word (*prevent*) is not a synonym for *prevaricate*. It should be evident to the test-taker that (B) is the best answer.

27. **(A)**   *Postmortem* means *after death* (A). The prefix *post-* means *after*. The root word *mortem* refers to *death*. A *postmortem* is an autopsy performed after death. A *celebration* (B) is a gala or a joyful occasion. *Celebration* (B) is not a synonym for *postmortem*; choice (B) is therefore not an acceptable answer to this question. A *stockade* (C) is a *prison;* choice (C) is not an acceptable answer. *Position* (D) does not mean the same as *postmortem* since it refers to a place.

28. **(A)**   **True** is correct. If Patty is five years older than Stephanie, and Stephanie is two years older than Kerri, then Kerri is $5 + 2 = 7$ years younger than Patty.

29. **(A)**   **True** is correct. If Sue is two inches taller than Lynn, and Lynn is three inches taller than Kate, then Kate is $2 + 3 = 5$ inches shorter than Sue.

30. **(C)** **Uncertain** is correct. If Jarret earned more money than his brothers, Matthew and Brian, then we know for sure that Matthew made less money than Jarret, but we don't know if Matthew made more or less money than Brian.

31. **(C)** **Uncertain** is correct. If Phyllis read more books than any of her friends, and Betty and Lorraine are her friends, then we know for sure that Betty read fewer books than Phyllis, but we don't know if Betty read fewer or more books than Lorraine.

32. **(B)** **False** is correct. If the first two statements are true, then the opposite of the third statement is true: Main Street is *wider* than Willow Road.

33. **(B)** **False** is correct. If the first two statements are true, then the opposite of the third statement is true: Nicole types *faster* than Nancy.

34. **(A)** **True** is correct. Because there are seven days in a week, if Maryann takes ballet lessons five days a week, and Jennifer takes lessons three days a week, then they must take lessons on at least one of the same days. (5 + 3 = 8 − 7 = 1)

35. **(A)** **True** is correct. Because there are seven days in a week, if Joe plays basketball six days a week, and Tony plays basketball four days a week, then they must play basketball on at least three of the same days. (6 + 4 = 10 − 7 = 3)

36. **(C)** **Uncertain** is correct. We know that broccoli costs more than carrots and that onions cost less than broccoli and lettuce. However, the truth of the third statement is uncertain because we don't know the cost of carrots in relation to the cost of lettuce.

37. **(C)** **Uncertain** is correct. We know that grapes cost more than plums and that peaches cost less than plums and nectarines. However, the truth of the third statement is uncertain because we don't know the cost of plums in relation to the cost of nectarines.

38. **(B)** *Irritate*, *harass*, and *pester* have nearly the same meaning, while *appease* has the opposite meaning.

39. **(C)** *Vacant*, *empty*, and *unoccupied* have nearly the same meaning: *containing nothing*. Although *spacious* means a lot of space, the space is not necessarily empty.

40. **(B)** *Placid*, *calm*, and *peaceful* have nearly the same meaning, while *chaotic* has the opposite meaning.

41. **(D)** *Arteries*, *capillaries*, and *veins* are parts of the *circulatory* system.

42. **(A)** *Ad*, *exam*, and *memo* are "clipped words," words that have been shortened by common usage, while *hobo* is not. (*Ad: advertisement*; *exam: examination*; *memo: memorandum*)

43. **(A)** *Annual*, *perennial*, and *temporal* pertain to time; *fiscal* pertains to finances.

44. **(B)** *Hinder*, *retard*, and *impede* have nearly the same meaning, while *aid* has the opposite meaning.

45. **(D)** *Cheerful*, *optimistic*, and *hopeful* have nearly the same meaning, while *desperate* has the opposite meaning.

46. **(A)** *Relapse*, *regress*, and *backslide* have nearly the same meaning, while *recover* has the opposite meaning.

47. **(D)** *Gloomy*, *dismal*, and *dreary* have nearly the same meaning, while *bright* has the opposite meaning.

48. **(B)** A *defendant*, a *bailiff*, and a *plaintiff* are people in a courtroom, while *interrogate* is an action.

49. **(C)** A *period*, a *question mark*, and an *exclamation point* are end marks of punctuation; that is, they are used at the end of a sentence. A *comma* is not.

50. **(B)** *Precise*, *exact*, and *accurate* have nearly the same meaning, while *approximate* has a different meaning: *almost exact*.

51. **(A)** *Complex*, *intricate*, and *complicated* have nearly the same meaning, while *simple* has the opposite meaning.

52. **(C)** *Diverse*, *heterogeneous*, and *varied* have nearly the same meaning, while *uniform* has the opposite meaning.

53. **(B)** *Nonfiction* is a kind of prose, while a *dictionary*, a *thesaurus*, and an *encyclopedia* are reference books.

54. **(D)** Unlike *portfolio*, *itinerary*, *route*, and *destination* are words that relate primarily to travel.

55. **(C)** *Excrete*, *discharge*, and *expel* have nearly the same meaning, while *disburse* has a different meaning: *to pay out*.

56. **(B)** *Presume* means *believe* (A), *assume*, or *suppose* (C). *Presume* can also mean to *conclude* (D). It does not mean *disprove* (B) or *refute*. The opposite of *presume* is (B).

57. **(D)** *Disdainful* means *arrogant* (A), *aloof* (C), or *overconfident*. It can also mean *proud* (B) or *vain*. It does not mean *humble* (D), *modest*, *meek*, or *lowly*. The opposite or the antonym of *disdainful* is *humble* (D).

58. **(C)** *Infamous* means *notorious* (A), *wicked* (B), or *dishonorable* (D). *Infamous* does not mean *great*, *distinguished*, or *prominent* (C). The antonym of *infamous* is (C).

59. **(C)** *Perpetual* means *eternal* (B) or *enduring* (D). It also means *constant* (A) and *permanent*. *Perpetual* does not mean *fleeting* or *momentary* (C). Therefore, *momentary* (C) is the best choice for an antonym of *perpetual*.

60. **(C)** *Imminent* means *close* (D) or *impending* (B); it can mean *proximate* (A) or *soon*. It does not mean that which has already occurred or that which is *past* (C). Because the antonym is the answer needed, *past* (C) is the best choice as an antonym of *imminent*.

Subtest 2: Quantitative Skills

DETAILED EXPLANATIONS OF ANSWERS

For each problem, the answer will be given first. Then we will name the type of question—Series, Comparison, or Pre-algebra.

For Series questions, we will show the pattern on the list of numbers, state the rule, and get the answer.

For Comparison questions, we will give the quantities associated with (a), (b), and (c) or the picture, and, if necessary, explain how to get them. The correct choice of (A), (B), (C), or (D) will then be obvious.

For Pre-algebra questions, we will use the word method to arrive at the correct answer. Remember: you may want to use trial-and-error for some or all of the Pre-algebra questions.

61. **(D)**   8. Pre-algebra. $\frac{1}{3}$ of $60 = \frac{1}{3} \times 60 = 20$; 12 less than $20 = 20 - 12 = 8$.

62. **(A)**   1. Series.

$$
\begin{array}{ccccccc}
 & -8 & & -8 & & -8 & & -8 = \underline{1} \\
 \nearrow & & \searrow \nearrow & & \searrow \nearrow & & \searrow \nearrow \\
33 & & 25 & & 17 & & 9
\end{array}
$$

Rule: Subtract 8. $9 - 8 = 1$.

63. **(B)**   36. Series.

$$
\begin{array}{ccccccccc}
 & -16 & & -7 & & -16 & & -7 & & -16 = \underline{36} \\
 \nearrow & & \searrow \nearrow & & \searrow \nearrow & & \searrow \nearrow & & \searrow \nearrow \\
98 & & 82 & & 75 & & 59 & & 52
\end{array}
$$

Rule: Subtract 16; subtract 7. $52 - 16 = 36$.

64. **(A)**   (a) is equal to (b) which is equal to (c). Comparison. (a) = 12, (b) = 12, and (c) = 12. Count the circles.

65. **(C)**   (b) is greater than (a) and is greater than (c). Comparison. (a) = 6 + 2 = 8, (b) = 3 × 6 = 18, and (c) = 12 + 1 = 13. Do parentheses first.

66. **(C)** 17. Pre-algebra. $\frac{3}{4}$ of 20 = $\frac{3}{4} \times 20 = 15$; 2 more than 15 = 15 + 2 = 17.

67. **(D)** 7. Pre-algebra. $\frac{1}{2}$ of 32 = $\frac{1}{2} \times 32 = 16$; 9 less than 16 = 16 – 9 = 7.

68. **(A)** 75. Series.

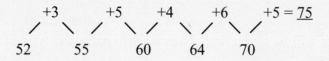

$$
\begin{array}{ccccccccc}
& +3 & & +5 & +4 & & +6 & & +5 = \underline{75} \\
52 & & 55 & & 60 & & 64 & & 70
\end{array}
$$

Rule: Add each time. The amount added goes up by 2, then down by 1. 70 + 5 = 75.

69. **(A)** (a) is equal to (b) which is equal to (c). Comparison. The shaded portion of each square represents $\frac{1}{4}$ of the whole square. So (a), (b), and (c) are all equal.

70. **(D)** 15. Pre-algebra. $\frac{5}{6}$ of 24 = $\frac{5}{6} \times 24 = 20$. The number added to 5 to give 20 is 20 – 5, or 15.

71. **(C)** 84. Series.

$$
\begin{array}{ccccccccc}
& -4 & & -8 & -12 & & -16 & & -20 = \underline{84} \\
144 & & 140 & & 132 & & 120 & & 104
\end{array}
$$

Rule: Subtract an amount that increases by 4 each time. 104 – 20 = 84.

72. **(A)** 100. Series.

$$
\begin{array}{ccccccccc}
& +6 & & +5 & +6 & & +5 & & +6 = \underline{100} \\
72 & & 78 & & 83 & & 89 & & 94
\end{array}
$$

Rule: Add 6, add 5. 94 + 6 = 100.

73. **(D)** 128. Pre-algebra. 8 squared = 8 × 8 = 64; twice as much as 64 = 2 × 64 = 128.

74. **(A)** 16. Pre-algebra. 6 more than 10 = 10 + 6 = 16. The number subtracted from 32 that yields 16 is 32 – 16, or 16.

75. **(B)**   (b) is less than (a). Comparison. (a) $= \frac{2}{3}$ of $15 = \frac{2}{3} \times 15 = 10$, (b) $= \frac{2}{5}$ of $20 = \frac{2}{5} \times 20 = 8$, and (c) $= \frac{3}{4}$ of $32 = \frac{3}{4} \times 32 = 24$.

76. **(A)**   (a) is equal to (b) which is equal to (c). Comparison. The shaded portion in each part represents half of the circle. (a) $= \frac{2}{4} = \frac{1}{2}$, (b) $= \frac{3}{6} = \frac{1}{2}$, and (c) $= \frac{4}{8} = \frac{1}{2}$. So all three fractions, or areas, are equal.

77. **(D)**   1717. Series.

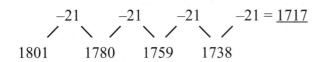

Rule: Subtract 21. $1738 - 21 = 1717$.

78. **(C)**   63. Series.

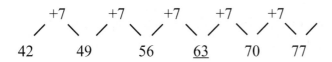

Rule: Add 7. $56 + 7 = 63$.

79. **(D)**   19. Pre-algebra. A number twice as large as $35 = 2 \times 35 = 70$. The number added to 51 to yield 70 is $70 - 51$, or 19.

80. **(A)**   (a) is equal to (b) which is equal to (c). Comparison. (a) $= .08$, (b) $= 8\% = .08$, (c) $= \frac{2}{25} = \frac{8}{100} = .08$. Convert all fractions to the same form, in this case, the decimal form. We could also use percent or ratio forms.

81. **(D)**   73. Pre-algebra. 12 more than $11 = 11 + 12 = 23$. The number subtracted from 96 to give 23 is $96 - 23$, or 73.

82. **(C)**   *FB* is equal to *EC*. Comparison. In a square, the diagonal is longer than a side and shorter than twice a side. Here is what each answer means: (A) twice a side equals a diagonal; (B) a side equals twice a side; (C) a diagonal equals a diagonal; and (D) a side equals a diagonal. Only (C) is true.

83. **(B)** .4 Series.

$$\div5 \quad \div5 \quad \div5 \quad \div5 = \underline{.4}$$
$$250 \quad 50 \quad 10 \quad 2$$

Rule: Divide by 5. $2 \div 5 = .4$.

84. **(B)** 2. Series.

$$\div5 \quad +5 \quad \div5 \quad +5 \quad \div5 = \underline{2}$$
$$100 \quad 20 \quad 25 \quad 5 \quad 10$$

Rule: Divide by 5, add 5. $10 \div 5 = 2$.

85. **(D)** 1. Pre-algebra. 8 less than $15 = 15 - 8 = 7$. The number added to 6 to give 7 is $7 - 6$, or 1.

86. **(D)** (a) is less than (c) and greater than (b). Comparison. (a) $= \dfrac{3}{4} = \dfrac{18}{24}$, (b) $\dfrac{2}{3} = \dfrac{16}{24}$, and (c) $= \dfrac{19}{24}$. Convert all fractions to fractions with the same denominator. In this case the smallest common denominator is 24.

87. **(C)** IV. Series.

$$-4 \quad -4 \quad -4 \quad -4 = 4 \text{ or } \underline{IV}$$
$$XX \quad XVI \quad XII \quad VIII$$

Rule: Subtract 4. $8 - 4 = 4$. In Roman numerals, $X = 10$, $V = 5$, and $I = 1$. Smaller numbers that follow bigger numbers are added; smaller numbers that come before bigger numbers are subtracted. So, $XX = 20$, $XVI = 16$, $XII = 12$, and $VIII = 8$. In Roman numerals, 4 is IV, which means 5 minus 1.

88. **(A)** 47. Series.

$$-5 \quad -11 \quad -5 \quad -11 \quad -5 = \underline{47}$$
$$84 \quad 79 \quad 68 \quad 63 \quad 52$$

Rule: Subtract 5, then subtract 11. $52 - 5 = 47$.

89. **(D)** 8. Pre-algebra. $\frac{2}{5}$ of $10 = \frac{2}{5} \times 10 = 4$. If $\frac{1}{2}$ of a number equals 4, the number is 2×4, or 8.

90. **(C)** *BC* is equal to *AD*. Comparison. The picture shows a square inside a circle. In a square, half of the diagonal is shorter than a side, which is shorter than the whole diagonal. Here is what the four answers mean: (A) a side equals half a diagonal; (B) a side equals a diagonal; (C) a side equals a side; (D) a diagonal equals a side. Clearly, (C) is the only choice that is true.

91. **(D)** 32. Series.

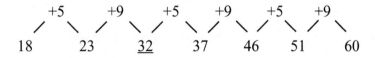

Rule: Add 5, then add 9. $23 + 9 = 32$.

92. **(A)** 34. Series.

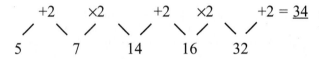

Rule: Add 2, multiply by 2. $32 + 2 = 34$.

93. **(C)** 6. Pre-algebra. 2 squared $= 2 \times 2 = 4$. If $\frac{2}{3}$ of a number is 4, $\frac{3}{2}$ of 4 must equal the number, or $\frac{3}{2} \times 4 = 6$.

94. **(D)** (b) is equal to (c) which is not equal to (a). Comparison. (a) $= 24 \div 3 = 8$, (b) $= 36 \div 2 = 18$, and (c) $= 3 \times 6 = 18$. Do the parentheses first.

95. **(D)** 6. Pre-algebra. $\frac{3}{4}$ of $40 = \frac{3}{4} \times 40 = 30$. If a number multiplied by 5 yields 30, the number is $30 \div 5$, or 6.

96. **(C)** 20, 26. Series.

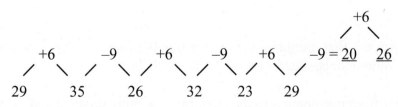

Rule: Add 6, then subtract 9. $29 - 9 = 20$; $20 + 6 = 26$.

97. **(D)** (2) is equal to (y) plus (x). Comparison. (2) takes up half of the circle, and (x) plus (y) takes up the other half. The two halves are equal.

98. **(B)** 20. Pre-algebra. $\frac{2}{5}$ of 80 = $\frac{2}{5} \times 80 = 32$. 7 less than 32 = 25. The number added to 5 that leaves 25 is 25 – 5, or 20.

99. **(A)** (a) is equal to (b) which is equal to (c). Comparison. This is a beginning algebra question. By the distributive property, (a) = $2(x + y) = 2x + 2y$. This is the same as (b). By the commutative property, (c) = $(x + y)2 = 2(x + y)$, which is the same as (a). So, all three expressions are equal.

100. **(D)** 10. Pre-algebra. $\frac{2}{3}$ of 12 = $\frac{2}{3} \times 12 = 8$. The product of 10 and 8 = $10 \times 8 = 80$, half of 80 = $\frac{1}{2}$ of 80 = $\frac{1}{2} \times 80 = 40$. The number subtracted from 50 that leaves 40 is 50 – 40, or 10.

101. **(C)** (c) is greater than (a). Comparison. There are 4 quarts in 1 gallon. So, in terms of quarts, the picture graphs represent the following amounts: (a) = 3 quarts, (b) = 4 quarts, and (c) = 5 quarts.

102. **(C)** (c) is equal to (a) but is not equal to (b). Comparison. The exponent tells the number of times you write the base number before multiplying. A zero exponent means the answer is 1 as long as the base number is not zero. (a) = $1^6 = 1 \times 1 \times 1 \times 1 \times 1 \times 1 = 1$, (b) = $6^1 = 6$, and (c) = $12^0 = 1$.

103. **(D)** 8. Pre-algebra. $\frac{1}{3}$ of 3 = $\frac{1}{3} \times 3 = 1$; 2 times $1 = 2 \times 1 = 2$. If the number divided by 4 leaves 2, the number is 4×2, or 8.

104. **(B)** (d) minus (a) equals (a) minus (b). Comparison. From the bar graph, (a) = 5, (b) = 2, (c) = 10, and (d) = 8. From these values, (B) is true and (A), (C), and (D) are false.

105. **(A)** 24. Series.

```
  ┌─── +5 ───┐┌─── +5 ───┐
98    28    103    26    108    24
      └─── -2 ───┘└─── -2 ───┘
```

Rule: Starting with the first number, every other number increases by 5. Starting with the second number, every other number decreases by 2. 26 – 2 = 24.

It is possible to go from one number to the next, but it is more complicated. If you subtract an amount to go from one number to the next, you add 5 more than that amount to get the next number, then subtract 2 more than that new amount to get the next number. Using this approach, the number list looks like this:

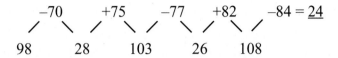

The next number is still 24.

106. **(B)**   (a) is equal to (b) but is not equal to (c). Comparison. (a) = 60% of 50 = .6 of 50 = .6 × 50 = 30, (b) = 50% of 60 = .5 of 60 = .5 × 60 = 30, and (c) = 40% of 70 = .4 of 70 = .4 × 70 = 28. To convert percents to decimals, move the decimal two places to the left. When multiplying, the number of decimal places in the answer is the sum of the decimal places in the numbers multiplied.

107. **(B)**   The perimeter of triangle *ABC* is 24. Comparison. We can get the length of *AC* using the Pythagorean Theorem. 6 + 8 = 36 + 64 = 100. 10 = 100, so *AC* = 10. Look at our choices. (A) The perimeter of the rectangle is the sum of the sides = 6 + 8 + 6 + 8 = 28, not 30. (B) The perimeter of triangle *ABC* is 6 + 8 + 10 = 24, so (B) is true. For completeness, look at (C) and (D). (C) The area of triangle *ABC* is half the base times the height, or half of 8 times 6, which is half of 48, or 24. (D) The area of the rectangle is the base times the height, or 8 times 6, which is 48.

108. **(C)**   9. Series.

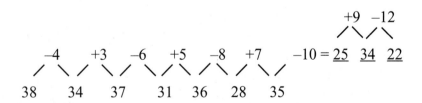

Rule: Add 4, then divide by 4. 5 + 4 = 9.

109. **(C)**   25, 34, 22. Series.

Rule: Subtract, then add. The amount you subtract increases by 2 each time. The amount you add is 1 less than the amount you last subtracted. 35 − 10 = 25, 25 + 9 = 34, 34 − 12 = 22. You could also do this by looking at every other number. Starting with the first number, you get the number after the next by subtracting 1. Starting with the second number, you get the one after the next by subtracting 3. The series of numbers would then look like this:

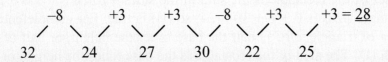

110. **(A)** 1. Pre-algebra. $\frac{3}{8}$ of 16 = $\frac{3}{8} \times 16 = 6$; $\frac{1}{3}$ of 21 = $\frac{1}{3} \times 21 = 7$. The number subtracted from 7 to leave 6 = 7 − 6, or 1.

111. **(B)** 155. Pre-algebra. $\frac{2}{3}$ of 18 = $\frac{2}{3} \times 18 = 12$; 3 times 12 = $3 \times 12 = 36$. A number added to 5 makes 36, so that number is 36 − 5, or 31. But 31 is $\frac{2}{3}$ of another number, and that number must be 5 times 31 = 5×31, or 155.

112. **(B)** 28. Series.

$$
\begin{array}{ccccccccccccc}
& -8 & & +3 & & +3 & & -8 & & +3 & & +3 = \underline{28} \\
& \diagup\diagdown & & \diagup\diagdown & & \diagup\diagdown & & \diagup\diagdown & & \diagup\diagdown & & \diagup \\
32 & & 24 & & 27 & & 30 & & 22 & & 25 &
\end{array}
$$

Rule: Subtract 8, add 3, add 3: 25 + 3 = 28.

Subtest 3: Reading

DETAILED EXPLANATIONS OF ANSWERS

Comprehension

113. **(B)**   The passage does not mention any employers (A), an attack (C), or taxes (D). The crime of forgery (B) is mentioned specifically in the second sentence and elaborated on throughout the passage.

114. **(D)**   The passage describes what the antiques dealer did: created documents that he claimed were written by someone else. Of the choices, "faking" (D) most closely expresses this.

115. **(C)**   The passage specifically refutes choices (A) and (B), while choice (D) represents a scenario not described at all. Choice (C) is supported explicitly.

116. **(D)**   Although analysis of ink (A) is mentioned as one way to detect forgery, it is not said to be the reason that the antiques dealer was caught. The passage specifically says that the antiques dealer had studied Lincoln's handwriting and reproduced it effectively, so choice (B) must be incorrect. Choice (C) is never stated in the passage—only choice (D) is supported by the passage.

117. **(D)**   The passage does say that the antiques dealer will get 15 years in jail, but it also gives additional information, so choice (A) is not the best answer. Choices (B) and (C) are clearly not supported by the passage, while choice (D) includes both the prisoner sentence and the order to make financial amends for his fraud.

118. **(C)**   The tone of this passage is argumentative and persuasive. It is not just imparting information. It is trying to convince its reader to take action on something. Only choice (C) reflects this purpose.

119. **(C)**   All the choices except (C) have a negative connotation. Choice (C) is in tune with the passage's message that workplaces need to be nicer atmospheres.

120. **(B)**   Choice (B) is supported throughout the passage very explicitly. The other choices tend toward contradicting the main point of the passage.

121. **(D)** As with question 118, the answer is dependent on your ability to detect the author's interest in writing this passage. By the word choice and things that are specifically said it is clear that the author is very invested in persuading the reader of the importance of taking this information seriously, which is supported only by choice (D).

122. **(B)** All the choices are explicitly mentioned except (B).

123. **(A)** While Picasso (B) is used as an example of a cubist painter, not enough is said about him to support calling this passage a biography of him. There is no attempt to compare Cubism (C) to other styles of painting or to critique Cubist painters (D). The passage is mainly concerned with giving some facts about Cubism and offering an example, supported by choice (A).

124. **(D)** The passage specifically mentions that Cubist paintings are NOT realistic (D).

125. **(C)** The painting is discussed in such a way to demonstrate some of the Cubist principles that have been mentioned. None of the other choices are supported by the passage.

126. **(D)** The passage makes it clear that Cubism is important (C), but choice (D) most accurately supports the usage of abstract here—particularly in the part about some objections to Cubism.

127. **(A)** The passage makes choice (A) explicit. The other choices are directly or indirectly refuted by the passage.

128. **(A)** The author is calling for specific action to be taken about a problem. The passage is clearly written to persuade rather than simply convey information. Therefore, choice (A) is best.

129. **(C)** The passage explicitly makes that clear while the topic is under discussion, it is not being addressed (C).

130. **(D)** The author is careful to emphasize that basic health services will not fix the problem of uninsured Americans. Choice (D) supports this.

131. **(A)** Surgery (A) is clearly not a basic health service; it is much more serious, time consuming, and expensive than the other proposals listed, and it is never mentioned in the passage.

132. **(B)** The context of the term indicates that its meaning most nearly means something wide-ranging or all-inclusive. The choice most like this is complete (B).

133. **(B)** Choices (A), (C), and (D) all mean nearly the same thing, while choice (B) expresses a much different concept that is supported by the passage.

134. **(C)**   There is specific mention of the origin of the Shaker name in their dance (C).

135. **(C)**   While the passage mentions dancing (A) and furniture making (B), the passage makes clear that the Shakers were primarily a religious community (C). There is no mention of farming (D).

136. **(C)**   The passage stresses that the Shakers believed in both simplicity and practicality. This is supported by choice (C).

137. **(A)**   The tone of the passage is descriptive rather than partial (D) or derogatory (B). Choice (A) is the most accurate way to characterize the passage.

138. **(D)**   The passage follows a format wherein several studies are presented to the reader, making choice (D) most accurate.

139. **(C)**   The inclusion of academic studies and the scientific tone of the passage make it very much opposed to the suggestions of choices (A), (B), and (D). Choice (C) is well supported by the passage.

140. **(D)**   Choice (D) is explicitly stated within the passage. None of the other choices are mentioned.

141. **(A)**   After Brown and Bellugi are mentioned, there is a listing of their findings, all of which appear in the choices except (A).

142. **(B)**   The amount of scholarship mentioned in just this brief passage suggests that (B) is the best answer. The other choices are not implied or mentioned specifically.

143. **(C)**   The tone of this passage is reminiscent of a textbook. There is no strong language that would suggest (D) or persuasive rhetoric that would suggest (A). While food processing is mentioned, the passage is about a specific kind of processing rather than about food processing in general (B). Choice (C) is the best answer.

144. **(D)**   Choice (D) is directly supported by the passage.

145. **(D)**   There is no mention of cave drawings (A), written documents (B), or studies of any other tribes (C). Choice (D) is supported by the passage.

146. **(B)**   There is no mention in the passage of any other Indian tribes or anything related to warfare (B), while all the other choices are supported by instances in the passage.

147. **(A)**   The passage deals with strategies employed by Indians to find foods that would sustain them. This is best supported by choice (A).

148. **(B)**   The statistics point toward an increasingly diverse nation (B) while none of the other choices are supported.

149. **(A)**   The author of this passage expresses a concern that schools may not at present be good atmospheres for minority students. Higher numbers of minority teachers (A) would no doubt make minority students feel more comfortable in California schools and be in line with the type of reform the author is advocating.

150. **(D)**   The author advances an argument based on numbers (D). None of the other choices are represented.

151. **(C)**   The final point made in the passage is supported by the assessment offered in choice (C).

152. **(B)**   One of the striking features of this passage is its use of statistics to advance an argument. This is clearly supported by choice (B) while the other choices are either inaccurate or not implied by the passage.

Vocabulary

153. **(D)**   The word *apex* means the height or *peak* (D). Answer choice (A), *bottom*, which means lowest or base, would be incorrect since it is the antonym of *apex*. Choice (B), *beginning*, which means start or inception, and (C), *end*, which means conclusion or finale, are opposites and have no connection with the word *apex*.

154. **(A)**   An education is *compulsory* when it is necessary or *required* (A). Answer choice (B), *limited*, which means inadequate, and (C), *private*, which means restricted, would both be incorrect. Answer choice (D), *optional*, means by choice and would also be incorrect because it is an antonym of *compulsory*.

155. **(C)**   The word *acute* means *sharp* (C) or intense. Answer choice (A), *slight*, which means small or insignificant, would be incorrect since it is the antonym of *acute*. *Recurring* (B) would be incorrect since it means frequent or repeated. *Steady* (D) would also be incorrect since it means constant or continuous.

156. **(B)**   A message would be *ambiguous* if it were *puzzling* (B). Answer choice (A), *under-standable*, which means comprehendible, would be the wrong answer choice since it is an antonym of *ambiguous*. *Foreign* (C), most commonly defined as exotic, might be chosen since it

could mean unknown, but *puzzling* (B) is a better answer choice. Be careful not to select choice (D), *illegible*, which means unreadable, as your answer choice—though it may appear correct; if something were *illegible* it could never be understood, yet if something were *ambiguous*, it could still be deciphered.

157. **(A)**   When a scholar becomes *eminent*, he/she becomes exalted or *distinguished* (A). Though intelligence would probably be necessary to become *eminent*, choice (B), *intelligent*, which means smart or keen, would not be a proper answer choice. Choice (C), *unknown*, which means unrevealed or hidden, would also be incorrect. Answer choice (D), *confident*, a possible result of becoming *eminent*, means assured or self-confident and would not be a correct answer choice.

158. **(D)**   When a person is told to *scrutinize* a document, he/she is to inspect and *examine* (D) it. He/she would not be asked to *forge* (A) it, which means counterfeit or duplicate falsely. Answer choice (B), *skim*, which means to browse or glance at, would be the antonym of *scrutinize* and therefore wrong. Nor would it mean answer choice (C), *copy*, which means to replicate or reproduce.

159. **(B)**   In order to *convene* a discussion, it will need to be *assembled* (B) or brought together. Answer choice (A), *conclude*, which means to close or end, would not be a correct answer choice. *Concentrate* (C), which means focus, could be mistaken for the correct answer since it could mean to collect; however, in this question, choice (B) would be the most preferable answer choice. Answer choice (D), *counterbalance*, means to equalize and would also not be the correct choice.

160. **(C)**   A *judicious* decision is a wise, rational, or *sensible* (C) decision. A *judicious* decision would probably not be made with *biased* (A) information, which means prejudiced or opinionated. *Reckless* (B) means rash or wild and would most likely be an antonym of *judicious* and incorrect. *Sensitive* (D), which means tense or unstable, would also not be a correct answer.

161. **(C)**   The word *ferocious* means savage, brutal, or *wild* (C). Choice (A), *tame*, means docile and gentle and would be incorrect since it is an antonym of *ferocious*. Though a *ferocious* animal may be *stubborn* (B), which means inflexible or persistent, it would be an incorrect answer choice. Choice (D), *humorous*, which means funny or amusing, would also be an incorrect choice.

162. **(D)**   To *obliterate* something means to eliminate or *destroy* (D) it. *Examine* (A), which means to study or analyze, would not be a correct choice. Likewise, *conceal* (B), which means to hide or cover, would also be incorrect. Choice (C), *create*, which means to produce or make, would be incorrect because it is *obliterate's* antonym.

163. **(B)**   A complexion that looks *pallid* is one that is sickly or *pale* (B). Answer (A), *rosy*, would be incorrect because it means healthy or flush, which is an antonym of *pallid*. A *pallid*

complexion may look gloomy or *sad* (C), but being gloomy and being pale are not synonymous. Choice (D), *healthy*, means hearty or robust and would be incorrect since it is also an antonym.

164. **(C)**   *Impetuous* decisions are made hastily or *impulsively* (C). The antonym of this word, however, would have allowed the decision to have been thought out and *planned* (A). The word *recent* (B) would not have been a correct choice since it means modern or contemporary. Choice (D), *wise*, would not have been a correct choice either since it means rational or intelligent.

165. **(D)**   *Mutinous* crewmen were known for their revolts and *rebellious* (D) deeds. This word's antonym, *cooperative* (A), means agreeing and is not the correct answer. *Quiet* (B), which means silent or stillness, would also be a wrong selection. Finally, if the crewmen had been *changeable* (D), which means adaptable or flexible, they would not be *rebellious*, which makes (D) incorrect.

166. **(B)**   A *placid* sea is still and *calm* (B). A *calm* sea could be *deep* (A), which means low, but low and *calm* are not synonymous words. Choice (C), *stormy*, means turbulent or wild and is an incorrect choice since it is *placid's* antonym. Choice (D), *large*, which means huge or massive, would be incorrect for the same reasons as choice (A).

167. **(A)**   A *replica* of something is a reproduction or *copy* (A). Be careful not to choose answer choice (B), *forgery*; even though it's a reproduction, (B) is an incorrect answer choice because it is done fraudulently. Answer choice (C), *original*, which means first or primary, would be incorrect since it is the antonym of *replica*. Choice (D), *wreckage*, means debris or remains and would also be an incorrect answer choice.

168. **(C)**   Things are *conspicuous* if they are seen or *noticeable* (C). Answer choice (A), *hidden*, which means concealed or unseen, would be incorrect since it is an antonym of *conspicuous*. Answer choice (B), *shady*, means questionable or notorious and would not be the correct answer choice. *Significant* (D) means critical or serious and would not be a correct answer choice.

169. **(C)**   A story is *abridged* if it is condensed or *shortened* (C). *Lengthened* (A), which means extended or made longer, would be incorrect since it is an antonym of *abridged*. Answer choice (B), *true*, which means authentic or accurate, would not be a correct answer choice. *False* (D), which means incorrect or wrong, would also be an incorrect answer choice.

170. **(C)**   An excuse is considered *plausible* if it is convincing or *believable* (C). Answer choice (A), *unbelievable*, would be incorrect since it is an antonym of *plausible*. *Praiseworthy* (B) means reputable or commendable and would not be a correct answer choice. *Unforgivable* (D) means inexcusable or unallowable and would be incorrect.

171. **(B)**   In order to *thwart* an attack, you must impede or *repel* (B) it. Answer choice (A),

strengthen, which means to intensify or fortify, would not be a correct answer choice. *Accelerate* (C) means to hasten or speed up and is incorrect. *Wage* (D) which means to undertake or carry on, is also not a correct choice.

172. **(B)** A *discreet* remark is made cautiously and *carefully* (B). If it were done with care, it would not be *hurtful* (A), which means insulting or offensive. Answer choice (C), *insensitive*, means ruthless or unkind and would not be correct. Choice (D), *polite*, means courteous or respectful and would also be incorrect.

173. **(B)** A *frugal* meal is economical or *thrifty* (B). *Wasteful* (A), means squandering or reckless and would be incorrect. Answer choice (C), *abundant*, means fruitful or plentiful and would also be incorrect. Answer choice (D), *leftover*, means remaining or extra and would be incorrect.

174. **(C)** *Meager* means inadequate or *insufficient* (C). *Large* (B) and *healthy* (D) are not correct. *Lavish* (A) means luxurious or excessive.

Subtest 4: Mathematics

DETAILED EXPLANATIONS OF ANSWERS

Concepts

175. **(A)** The digit that comes immediately after the hundredths place is 4, which is less than 5. So we leave the 7 in the hundredths place as it is: $6.874 \cong 6.87$.

176. **(A)** Arrange like terms vertically and add:

$$5x - 3y + 12$$
$$\underline{3x + 3y - 10}$$
$$8x + 0\ \ +2$$

Rearrange terms: $8x + 2$

177. **(D)** $(6, -3)$ is a point 6 spaces to the right of the Y-axis and 3 spaces below the X-axis. That is point D on the graph.

178. **(B)** Let n represent the smaller number, so the larger number must be $(n + 2)$. Then the sum of the two numbers must be: $n + (n + 2) = 2n + 2 = 74$. To solve this equation,

add -2 to both sides:
$$2n + 2 = 74$$
$$\underline{\quad -2\ \ -2}$$
divide both sides by 2: $\quad 2n\quad = 72 \quad n = 36$.

The smaller number is $n = 36$ and the larger number is $n + 2 = 36 + 2 = 38$.

179. **(B)** $6\dfrac{2}{3} - 5\dfrac{1}{4} = \dfrac{20}{3} - \dfrac{21}{4} = \dfrac{(20 \times 4) - (21 \times 3)}{12} = \dfrac{80 - 63}{12} = \dfrac{17}{12} = 1\dfrac{5}{12}$.

180. **(C)** One easy way to answer this question is to list the pairs of factors of the given numbers and then select the one that has a pair of identical factors:

$12 = 1 \times 6 = 3 \times 4$. (no pair of identical factors)
$14 = 2 \times 7$. (no pair of identical factors)
$16 = 2 \times 8 = 4 \times 4$. (1 pair of identical factors)
$18 = 2 \times 9 = 3 \times 6$. (no pair of identical factors)
So the answer is 16 because 16 has exactly one pair of identical factors.

181. **(A)** Since width of square = length of square, the number representing the area of a

square must be a perfect square number. That is, the number must have two identical factors. Here is one way to test for identical factors among the given numbers:

$24 = 2 \times 12 = 3 \times 8 = 4 \times 6$. (no pair of identical factors)
$25 = 5 \times 5$. (1 pair of identical factors)
$36 = 2 \times 18 = 3 \times 12 = 4 \times 9 = 6 \times 6$. (1 pair of identical factors)
$64 = 2 \times 32 = 4 \times 16 = 8 \times 8$. (1 pair of identical factors)
24 is the only number in the set that has no pair of identical factors. The answer must be 24.

182. **(A)** $\quad \dfrac{3}{5} \times \dfrac{5}{6} + 21 = \left(\dfrac{3}{5} \times \dfrac{5}{6}\right) + 21 = \dfrac{1}{2} + 21 = 21\dfrac{1}{2}.$

183. **(B)** $\quad 5\dfrac{1}{4} \div 2\dfrac{1}{3} = \dfrac{21}{4} \div \dfrac{7}{3} = \dfrac{21}{4} \times \dfrac{3}{7} = \dfrac{9}{4} = 2\dfrac{1}{4}.$

184. **(A)** $\quad$ First find $\dfrac{1}{7}$ of 77.

$\dfrac{1}{7} \times \dfrac{77}{1} = \left(7\dfrac{11}{77}\right) = \dfrac{1}{1} \times \dfrac{11}{1} = 11$. Then subtract eleven from fourteen to find the missing number. $14 - 11 = 3$.

185. **(D)** $\quad$ To express 200 as a percent of 80, write: $\dfrac{200}{80} \times \dfrac{100}{1} = 250\%.$

186. **(A)** $\quad 2\dfrac{3}{5} = 2.6$. So $2\dfrac{3}{5} = 2.6 \times 100 = 260\%$

187. **(C)** $\quad x(-y + z) = -xy + xz = xz - xy.$

188. **(A)** $\quad$ Albert's average daily earnings for the five days must be: $\$460 \div 5 = \dfrac{\$460}{5} = \$92.$

189. **(C)** $\quad$ We need 2 pairs of equal measures to form the opposite sides of the rectangle, which we find only in set c), namely 4 and 4; 6 and 6.

190. **(C)** $\quad$ If we add the four numbers in each set, in turn, we find that the only set that adds to exactly 360 is set c), $[(78 + 85 + 95 + 102) = 360]$.

191. **(D)** $\quad 45\%$ of $2,000 = \dfrac{45}{100} \times \dfrac{2,000}{1} = 900.$

192. **(C)** When we examine the graph, we see that the attendance on Wednesday was 21; on Thursday it was 18, and on Friday the attendance was 21 again. So the total attendance for the three days was 60. The average attendance for the three days must be 60 ÷ 3 = 20.

193. **(A)** First, observe that each space on the test score scale represents 5 degrees. By comparing the temperatures in February and in March, we observe that the temperature rose by 35 degrees. Similarly, we notice that the temperature rose by 35 degrees from April to May. These are the steepest monthly rises.

194. **(D)** The temperature fell from 45° at the start of December to 15° at the end of the month. This was a drop of 30° and represents the steepest drop on the graph.

195. **(D)** The lowest temperature was 15° at the end of March and December.

196. **(B)** The "7" in 4$\underline{7}$2.625 is in the tens position.

197. **(A)** "Obtuse" in this context means having an angle greater than 90°. In the pictures, the triangle in a) is the only one that has an obtuse angle.

198. **(C)** The measure of the total angle in a circle is 360°. The measure of the unshaded angle in the picture is 55°. The measure of the shaded angle is (360° − 55°) = 305°.

Problem-Solving

199. **(B)** Replace d with 4,500, y with 1 and r with 6:

$$I = \frac{4,500}{1} \times 1 \times \frac{6}{100} = \$270.$$

200. **(C)** The length of the flagpole is the sum of the measures of the 12 pieces of pipe. Since the 12 pipes are equal in length, we could simply multiply the length of one piece by 12: 8.5 × 12 = 102 ft.

201. **(C)** The decrease in attendance was (400 − 336) = 64. Express 64 to a percent of 400:

$$\frac{64}{400} \times \frac{100}{1} = 16\%.$$

202. **(D)** First, find the area of the mirror, using the given formula: Area = 2.5 × 6.4 = 16 ft². To find the cost of the new mirror, multiply the cost of 1 ft² by the area of the mirror: \$2.60 × 16 = \$41.60.

203. **(D)** First, convert 3 minutes to seconds, to make computation easier: 3 min. = 3 × 60 = 180 seconds. If in 6 seconds the pump pushes out 9 pts. of ice cream, then in 1 second it must push out $9 \div 6 = \frac{9}{6}$ pts. of ice cream. In 180 seconds, it must push out $\frac{9}{6} \times \frac{180}{1} = 270$ pts.

204. **(B)** Michael and Jason together have $\frac{2}{7} + \frac{2}{5} = \frac{10+14}{35} = \frac{24}{35}$

$\frac{35}{35} - \frac{24}{35} = \frac{11}{35}.$

205. **(B)** At the end of the year, the value of the computer decreases to $(100 - 18) = 82\%$. So we must find 82% of the value of a new computer: $\frac{82}{100} \times \frac{1,500}{1} = \$1,230.$

206. **(C)** With a deduction of 22%, Damian would have to accept only $(100 - 22) = 78\%$ of the marked price. 78% of \$375 = $\frac{78}{100} \times \frac{375}{1} = \$292.50$

207. **(B)** The task here is equivalent to finding the perimeter of the garden. In a rectangle the opposite sides are equal in measure. So there are two sides each measuring 8 ft. and two sides each measuring 6 ft. The four sides of the rectangle must add up to $(8 + 8) + (6 + 6) = 28$ ft.

208. **(B)** First, convert 8 ft to inches: 8 ft = $8 \times 12 = 96$ in. Now we can express 5 in. as a fraction of 96 in.: $\frac{5}{96}.$

209. **(B)** Begin by converting 10 ft to inches: 10 ft = $(10 \times 12) = 120$ in. Then express 5 in. as a fraction of 120 in: $\frac{5}{120} = \frac{1}{24}.$

210. **(B)** First, convert 9 m to cm: 9 m = $(9 \times 100) = 900$ cm. To figure out how many desert sidewinding vipers must be strung together to obtain the length of an anaconda, divide 900 cm by 25 cm: $900 \div 25 = 36.$

211. **(C)** The difference between the two populations is $(989,000 - 683,000) = 306,000.$

212. **(D)** Since 120 out of 200 students are girls, then there must be $(200 - 120) = 80$ boys in the school. To express 80 as a percent of 200, we write: $\frac{80}{200} \times \frac{100}{1} = 40\%.$

213. **(D)** 84% represents 63 questions. So 1% must represent $\frac{63}{84}$ questions and 100% must represent $\frac{63}{84} \times 100 = 75 - 63 = 12$ missed questions.

214. **(A)**   The task is simply to multiply 175 lb. by 50: $175 \times 50 = 8{,}750$ lb.

215. **(A)**   The rectangle has a total of $6 \times 10 = 60$ small squares, of which 28 are shaded. The fraction of the rectangle that is shaded is $\dfrac{28}{60} = \dfrac{7}{15}$.

216. **(A)**   32 of the 60 small squares are not shaded. This represents $\dfrac{32}{60} \times \dfrac{100}{1} = 53\%$.

217. **(B)**   If the average attendance for Monday and Tuesday was 23, then the total attendance for those two days must be $23 \times 2 = 46$. From the graph, we see that the attendance on Tuesday alone was 20. So the attendance on Monday must be $(46 - 20) = 26$.

218. **(A)**   Jeff's total dropped from 395 to 332. The difference is $(395 - 332) = 63$. This must be his score on the test that the teacher discarded.

219. **(A)**   The rectangle in the picture is a square, since each side measures $(10 + 10) = 20$ cm. The area of the square must be $20 \times 20 = 400$ cm^2. The area of each clear region is one-half of a full circle with the same radius. The area of such a full circle is $(3.14 \times 10^2) = 314$ cm^2. The area of each clear region (half circle) must be $314 \div 2 = 157$ cm^2. The combined areas of the two quarter circles must be $157 \times 2 = 314$ cm^2. The area of the unshaded region must be $400 - 314 = 86$ cm^2.

220. **(B)**   The half can is curved like a half circle, so the length of the curved edge is half the circumference of a circle of the same diameter. The circumference of a full circle with the same diameter would be $3.14 \times 10 = 31.4$ cm, and half of that is $31.4 \div 2 = 15.7$ cm. The area of the visible outer surface of the half can must be $15.7 \times 10 = 157$ cm^2.

221. **(C)**   The height of the parallelogram is clearly shown as 12 cm. The base of the parallelogram is 15 cm. So the area of the parallelogram must be $12 \times 15 = 180$ cm^2.

222. **(C)**   The total amount of time that Simon spends outside school is (2 hrs. + 2.4 hrs. + 3 hrs. + 8 hrs.) = 15.4 hr. So the time he spends in school is $(24 - 15.4) = 8.6$ hrs.

223. **(B)**   Simon spends 2.4 hrs. on his homework. Express this as a percent of 24 hrs.: $\dfrac{2.4}{24} \times \dfrac{100}{1} = 10\%$.

224. **(D)**   We first convert $\dfrac{1}{2}$ lb. and 1 lb. to ounces, to simplify computation: $\dfrac{1}{2}$ lb. $= \dfrac{1}{2} \times$

$\dfrac{16}{1}$ = 8 oz. and 1 lb. = 16 oz. Total amount of food in the pot = (8 oz. + $\dfrac{1}{2}$ lb. + 1 lb.) = (8 oz. +

8 oz. + 16 oz.) = 32 oz. Percent rice = $\dfrac{8}{32} \times \dfrac{100}{1}$ = 25%.

225. **(C)**   The ratio of mid-sized cars to big cars may be written as 63:37 or as $\dfrac{63}{37}$. Let n

represent the unknown number of big cars. Then we can write: $\dfrac{63}{37} = \dfrac{189}{n}$. So $63 \times n = 37 \times 189$

= 6,993 and $n = 111$.

226. **(B)**   Sharon paid (.80)($60) = $48 for the dress and (.85)($80) = $68 for the shoes. Her total cost was $116 after the discounts. Without the discounts, her total cost would have been $60 + $80 = $140. Now, $140 − $116 = $24, and $24/$140 ≈ 17%.

227. **(D)**   Let x = cost of one apple, y = cost of one orange. 10x + y = $2.70 and x + 10y = $3.24. Multiply the first equation by 10 to get 100x + 10y = $27.00 and then subtract the original second equation (x + 10y = $3.24) to get 99x = $23.76. So, x = .24. Substitute this value of x into the original first equation to get (10) (.24) + y = $2.70. Then y = .30. Finally, x + y = .54.

228. **(C)**   Carol's portion of the bill is $1 - \dfrac{1}{3} - \dfrac{1}{5} = \dfrac{7}{15}$. Since Amy paid $\dfrac{1}{3}$ of the bill, her

payment of $10.70 means the bill totaled ($10.70) (3) = $32.10. Thus, Carol paid $\left(\dfrac{7}{15}\right)$ ($32.10)

= $14.98.

229. **(B)**   Let x = number of remaining games. The team has already won (.70) (30) = 21 games. If the team wins one-half of the remaining games, its total number of wins will be 21 +

$\dfrac{1}{2}$x. The number of games played will be 30 + x. Then $\left(21+\dfrac{1}{2}x\right)$/(30 + x) = .62. Simplifying,

$21 + \dfrac{1}{2}$x = .62 (30 + x). Then, 2.4 = .12x, and x = 20. Finally, the number of games played = 50.

230. **(A)**   He has already traveled at 10 mi./hr. for 6 minutes, which means he covered 1 mile. He must travel 2 more miles in 6 minutes. Since 60 ÷ 6 = 10, Brian must travel (10) (2) = 20 mi./hr. for the remainder of the trip.

231. **(A)**   In this inverse relationship, rate of vibration times length of the string must be a constant. (40) (100) = 4,000. Then, 4,000 ÷ 250 = 16.

232. **(D)**   Let x = number of dancers only. Now 35 − 27 = 8 people who are drinking only, so

that $8 + 27 + x = 60$. This leads to $x = 25$, which represents the number of dancing only. The total number of dancing must be $27 + 25 = 52$.

233. **(B)** The perimeter of the square is (4) $(6) = 24$ inches. The rectangle's perimeter is $\left(2\frac{1}{2}\right)$ $(24) = 60$ inches. Since perimeter = (2) (length) + (2) (width), the length plus the width must be 30 inches for this rectangle. The width = $30 - 18 = 12$.

234. **(A)** If the other base angle is $80°$, the vertex angle = $180° - 80° - 80° = 20°$. If the vertex angle = $80°$, each base angle must be $(180° - 80°)/2 = 50°$. In either instance no angle of this triangle could be $10°$.

235. **(C)** Let x = weight of the child; $x + 45$ = weight of the mother, and $3x$ = weight of the father. Then, $x + (x + 45) + 3x = 370$. Simplifying, $5x + 45 = 370$, so $x = 65$. The mother's weight = $65 + 45 = 110$ pounds. The father's weight = (3) $(65) = 195$ pounds. Then $195 - 110 = 85$ pounds.

236. **(C)** Let x and $x + 6$ be the rates of the two trains. Then $5x + 5$ $(x + 6) = 560$. Solving, $x = 53$ and $x + 6 = 59$. The faster train goes (59) $(3) = 177$ miles.

237. **(C)** The student has a probability of $\frac{1}{5}$ to get any one of the first three questions correct. His probability of getting any one of the last two questions correct is $\frac{1}{2}$. The probability that he will correctly answer all 5 questions is $\left(\frac{1}{5}\right)\left(\frac{1}{5}\right)\left(\frac{1}{5}\right)\left(\frac{1}{2}\right)\left(\frac{1}{2}\right) = \frac{1}{500}$.

238. **(D)** The total weight of the women is (5) $(130) = 650$ pounds. The total weight of the men must be $1,350 - 650 = 700$ pounds. Finally, the men's average weight = $700/4 = 175$ pounds.

Subtest 5: Language Skills

DETAILED EXPLANATIONS OF ANSWERS

Punctuation, Capitalization, and Usage

239. **(A)** This sentence needs end punctuation, which in this case should be a period.

240. **(D)** There are no mistakes.

241. **(C)** The phrase containing extra information, "a music box," needs to be separated with a comma: "The present, a music box, was wrapped in purple paper."

242. **(B)** The word should be spelled "Excellent."

243. **(A)** The sentence should read "My grandmother sent a letter to my brother and me" since the subject of the sentence is "my grandmother" while "my brother and me" is the object.

244. **(A)** February is a proper noun and should be capitalized.

245. **(B)** Sentences that begin within quotation marks should begin with a capital letter: He wandered in and said, "We wanted to do that."

246. **(B)** For subject-verb agreement, the sentence should read "You don't have to help me."

247. **(B)** For subject-verb agreement, the sentence should read "My friend has a new baby sister" or "My friends have a new baby sister."

248. **(C)** The contraction for "Isn't" needs an apostrophe.

249. **(A)** The abbreviation for Mister requires a period: "Mr. Green."

250. **(C)** The word is spelled "outside" and not "outsides."

251. **(B)** For subject-verb agreement, the sentence should read "Drawing is a fun course to take."

252. **(A)** This sentence has too many commas. It should read "We ran outside quickly."

253. **(D)** There are no mistakes.

254. **(A)** This question needs to end in a question mark: "Are you sitting over there?"

255. **(A)** For subject-verb agreement, the sentence should read "That girl is making really funny faces."

256. **(A)** The word "many" means that there is more than one cookie; the sentence should read: "We brought many cookies over to his house."

257. **(A)** The word "booring" is spelled incorrectly. It should read "boring."

258. **(D)** There are no mistakes.

259. **(C)** This is a run-on sentence that should be separated into two sentences: "Scott hurt his head. He went to the doctor." It could also be combined with a conjunction: "Scott hurt his head, so he went to the doctor."

260. **(B)** The modifier "almost" is misplaced. The sentence should read "We danced until almost midnight."

261. **(B)** The verbs should be in the same tense, such as "John typed, read, and printed out his report."

262. **(A)** Better should not be preceded by "more"; it is an irregular comparative adjective. The sentence should read "Maxine is better at math."

263. **(B)** Since the speaker is asking a question, the sentence should have a question mark: "Where are we going tonight?" he wanted to know.

264. **(A)** The wrong verb tense is used in this example. The sentence should read: "We saw that television show last night."

265. **(A)** The word "four" should be used instead of "for."

266. **(C)** The word is spelled "beginning" and not "begining."

267. **(B)** The sentence is missing punctuation and quotation marks: "She warned, "That isn't such a good idea."

268. **(B)** The first and main words of book titles are capitalized and the entire title is italicized. He is reading *The Adventures of Huckleberry Finn*.

269. **(C)** This sentence needs end punctuation, such as "I can't find my wallet!"

270. **(D)** There are no mistakes.

271. **(A)** "It's" should have an apostrophe to mean "It is."

272. **(C)** This is a sentence fragment.

273. **(B)** The first word in a sentence should be capitalized.

274. **(B)** This is a run-on sentence that should be broken up: "We walked quickly. We thought someone was there." It could also be combined with a conjunction: "We walked quickly because we thought someone was there."

275. **(C)** The verb "threw" should be used instead of the word "through."

276. **(C)** For subject-verb agreement, the sentence should read: "My mom and dad like to eat at restaurants."

277. **(B)** The verb should be past tense since the action took place in the past: "I went to the store yesterday."

278. **(B)** This is a sentence fragment.

Spelling

279. **(D)** There are no mistakes.

280. **(C)** *The* **atheletes** *are traveling to a basketball tournament.* The correct spelling is **athletes**.

281. **(A)** *The gardener was* **embarassed** *when he tripped over the hose.* The correct spelling is **embarrassed**.

282. **(B)** *The* **desparate** *criminal hid in an abandoned factory.* The correct spelling is **desperate**.

283. **(C)** *The child's frequent* **absenses** *are hindering her progress.* The correct spelling is **absences**.

284. **(B)** *The* **maintainance** *crew was exhausted after the carnival.* The correct spelling is **maintenance**.

285. **(B)** **Congradulations** *on your successful completion of the program.* The correct spelling is **congratulations**.

286. **(A)** *Jim received many* **complements** *for his chocolate layer cake.* The correct spelling is **compliments**.

287. **(D)** There are no misspelled words.

288. **(C)** *The seniors were anxious to see the graduation date on the new school calender.* The correct spelling is **calendar**.

Composition

289. **(A)** Of the choices, ***The flavor of herbs is most intense when they are fresh***, is the only sentence that gives information about the topic.

290. **(C)** Of the choices, ***Vitamin C helps the body resist infections*** is the only sentence that states a benefit of vitamin C.

291. **(A)** Of the choices, ***Thomas Edison invented the phonograph in 1877*** is the only sentence that gives an example of a 19th-century invention.

292. **(D)** None of the choices gives information about the topic.

293. **(C)** ***Travel Safety Tips*** is the only topic that is narrow enough to be contained in one paragraph. The others are far too broad.

294. **(A)** ***Telephone Etiquette*** is the only topic that is narrow enough to be contained in one paragraph. The others are far too broad.

295. **(D)** The given sentence links sentences 2 and 3:

(2) The foreign substance irritates the oyster.

To protect itself, the oyster encloses the irritant in a sac

(3) The oyster then secretes layers of mother-of-pearl, or nacre, around the sac to form a pearl.

296. **(B)** The given sentence follows sentence 3 because it gives an example of a cause and effect:

(3) This begins a chain reaction of causes and effects.

For example, when you press the letter "M" on the keyboard, the letter "M" appears on the monitor screen.

297. **(C)** To choose the sentence that does not belong in the paragraph, you must first identify the topic sentence. The topic sentence states the controlling idea of the paragraph. Sentence 1 is the topic sentence of the paragraph: *A computer system is made up of both hardware and*

software. Sentences 2 and 4 both support the topic sentence by defining hardware and software. Although sentence 3, ***Many students find the smaller laptop computers very convenient***, does contain information about computers, it is not directly related to the topic sentence. Therefore, it does not belong in the paragraph.

298. **(D)**   To choose the sentence that does not belong in the paragraph, you must first identify the topic sentence. The topic sentence states the controlling idea of the paragraph. Sentence 1 is the topic sentence of the paragraph: *Monticello was the home of Thomas Jefferson, the third president of the United States*. Sentences 2 and 3 both support the topic sentence by giving additional information about Monticello. Sentence 3, ***Jefferson was the governor of Virginia from 1779 to 1781***, is not directly related to the topic sentence.

COOP/ HSPT

COOP

Practice Test 2

Test 1: Sequences

TIME: 15 Minutes
20 Questions

DIRECTIONS: Study the sequences and then choose the best answer from the choices given.

---

1. ○○○⦾|○○⦾⦾|○⦾⦾⦾| ___

    (A) ○⦾⦾○   (C) ○○⦾○

    (B) ⦾⦾⦾⦾   (D) ⦾⦾⦾○

2. ▨▨▨▨|▨▨▨▨|▨▨▨▨| ___

    (F) ▨▨▨   (H) ▨▨▨

    (G) ▨▨▨   (J) ▨▨▨

3. ○△△|△△○|△○△| ___

    (A) ○△△   (C) △△○

    (B) △○△   (D) ○△△

4. ▫▫▫▫| ▫▫▫▫| ▫▫▫▫|▫ ___

    (F) ▫▫▫   (H) ▫▫▫

    (G) ▫▫▫   (J) ▫▫▫

5. ▫▫|▫▫|▫▫| ___

    (A) ▫▫   (C) ▫▫

    (B) ▫▫   (D) ▫▫

6. ××+×|×+××| _____ |×××+

    (F) +×+×   (H) +×××

    (G) +++×   (J) ××+×

523

7. △○□ | ○□◇ | □◇○ | _____ | ○△□

   (A) □△○   (C) □○◇

   (B) ◇○△   (D) ◇△○

8. LPK | PKG | KGR | _____ | RSE

   (F) GKP   (H) GRE

   (G) GRS   (J) GKR

9. ADKX | BELY | _____ | DGNA

   (A) CGLZ   (C) CGMZ

   (B) CDKW   (D) CFMZ

10. HLM | PHL | CPH | _____ | XNC

    (F) PHN   (H) NCP

    (G) HXN   (J) NPC

11. TIKI | KIWI | _____ | LIPI

    (A) TIPI   (C) WILI

    (B) KIPI   (D) WIPI

12. $J_5 K_5 L_5$ | $J_5 K_5 L_4$ | $J_5 K_4 L_3$ | _____

    (F) $J_4 K_3 L_2$ (H) $J_4 K_4 L_3$

    (G) $J_5 K_4 L_4$ (J) $J_4 K_3 L_3$

13. $E_1 K_2 H_3$ | $E_2^1 K_3 H_2$ | _____ | $E_2^3 K_1^2 H_3^1$

    (A) $E_2^1 K_3^2 H_2^1$ (C) $E_3^1 K_2^2 H_1$

    (B) $E_2^1 K_3^2 H_2$ (D) $E_3^2 K_2^1 H_1$

14. $W_5 X_5 Y$ | $W_4 X_5 Y$ | $W_4 X_4 Y$ | _____ | $W_3 X_3 Y$

    (F) $W_3 X_5 Y$ (H) $W_5 X_4 Y$

    (G) $W_4 X_3 Y$ (J) $W_3 X_4 Y$

15. 3 12 18 | 4 16 22 | 6 24 __

(A) 28   (C) 32

(B) 30   (D) 36

16. 3 18 7 | 5 30 19 | 6 __ 25

(F) 36   (H) 30

(G) 40   (J) 42

17. 7 14 5 | 10 20 11 | 30 60 51 | 60 __ __

(A) 120 91   (C) 90 81

(B) 120 111   (D) 90 91

18. $6 \quad \frac{3}{5} \quad \frac{3}{10}$ | $8 \quad \frac{4}{5} \quad \frac{4}{10}$ | 12 ___ | $14 \quad \frac{7}{5} \quad \frac{7}{10}$

(F) $1\frac{1}{2}$ (H) $\frac{6}{5} \quad \frac{6}{10}$

(G) $\frac{5}{5} \quad \frac{5}{10}$ (J) $\frac{12}{5} \quad \frac{12}{10}$

19. 2 3 5 7 | 3 5 7 11 | 5 7 11 13 | __ __ __ __

(A) 7 11 13 15   (C) 7 11 13 17

(B) 7 11 13 19   (D) 7 11 13 21

20. 36 12 24 | 54 18 36 | 48 16 32 | 18 __ __

(F) 6 12   (H) 4 16

(G) 9 18   (J) 8 12

Test 2: Analogies

TIME: 7 Minutes
        20 Questions

DIRECTIONS: For numbers 1-20, choose the picture that would go in the empty box so that the bottom two pictures are related in the same way the top two are related.

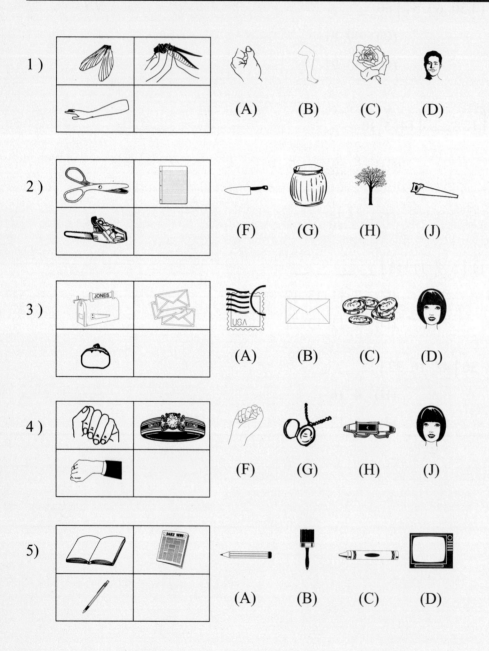

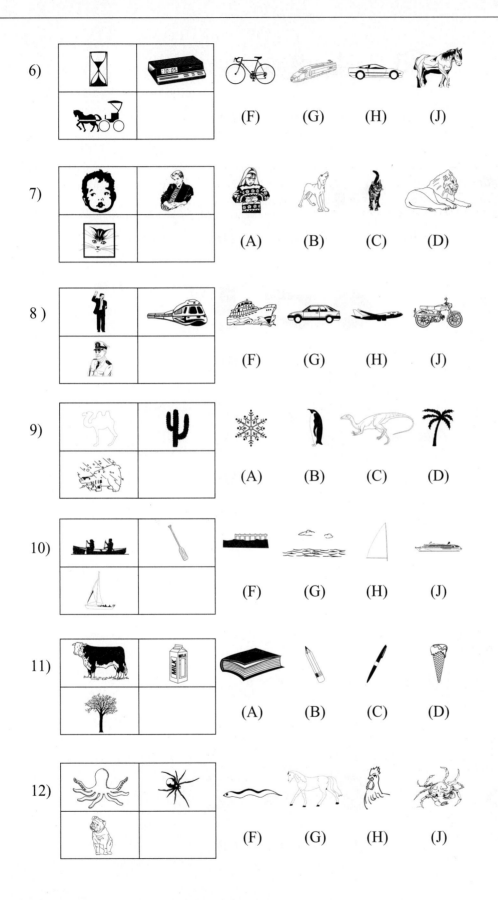

6) (F) (G) (H) (J)

7) (A) (B) (C) (D)

8) (F) (G) (H) (J)

9) (A) (B) (C) (D)

10) (F) (G) (H) (J)

11) (A) (B) (C) (D)

12) (F) (G) (H) (J)

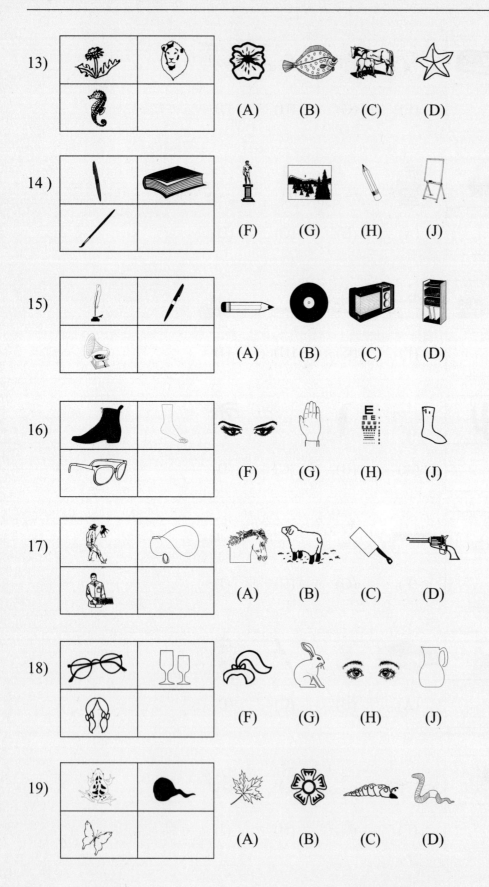

13)

(A) (B) (C) (D)

14)

(F) (G) (H) (J)

15)

(A) (B) (C) (D)

16)

(F) (G) (H) (J)

17)

(A) (B) (C) (D)

18)

(F) (G) (H) (J)

19)

(A) (B) (C) (D)

20)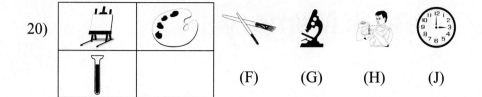

(F) (G) (H) (J)

Test 3: Memory

TIME: 17 Minutes
20 Questions

DIRECTIONS: Study the list below, then answer the questions that follow.

---

1. **Hemin** means quickly.
2. A **trelas** is a tree.
3. **Chanic** means greedily.
4. A **delmot** is a chair.
5. A **lation** is a small boat.
6. **Woggle** means to cry.
7. **Fumly** means clumsy.
8. A **bofot** is a fruit.
9. **Nedro** means weak.
10. A **pyrile** is an article of clothing.
11. A **quoth** is an insect.
12. A **mongrum** is a bowl.
13. **Thrats** are directions.
14. **Wrag** means to bother.
15. **Knute** means crazy.
16. **Azin** means cunning.
17. **Fupish** means to be annoying.
18. A **gortoken** is a kind of jewelry.
19. A **jucinthia** is a flower.
20. **Joib** means with care.

1. Which word means <u>a flower</u>?

   (A)   hemin

   (B)   delmot

   (C)   bofot

   (D)   nedro

   (E)   jucinthia

2. Which word means <u>quickly</u>?

   (F)   pyrile

   (G)   mongrum

   (H)   wrag

   (J)   knute

   (K)   hemin

3. Which word means <u>a small boat</u>?

    (A) thrats   (D) joib

    (B) fupish   (E) lation

    (C) gortoken

4. Which word means <u>clumsy</u>?

    (F) azin   (J) quoth

    (G) fumly   (K) chanic

    (H) woggle

5. Which word means <u>a bowl</u>?

    (A) bofot   (D) mongrum

    (B) delmot   (E) wrag

    (C) lation

6. Which word means <u>to bother</u>?

    (F) hemin   (J) quoth

    (G) trelas   (K) wrag

    (H) pyrile

7. Which word means <u>crazy</u>?

    (A) lation   (D) knute

    (B) chanic   (E) fupish

    (C) hemin

8. Which word means <u>to be annoying</u>?

    (F) joib   (J) thrats

    (G) nedro   (K) fupish

    (H) pyrile

9. Which word means <u>a kind of jewelry</u>?

    (A) delmot   (D) trelas

    (B) fumly   (E) gortoken

    (C) hemin

10. Which word means <u>with care</u>?

    (F) woggle   (J) joib

    (G) lation   (K) quoth

    (H) jucinthia

11. Which word means <u>an insect</u>?

    (A) azin   (D) hemin

    (B) bofot   (E) quoth

    (C) chanic

12. Which word means <u>weak</u>?

    (F) nedro   (J) delmot

    (G) pyrile   (K) mongrum

    (H) thrats

13. Which word means <u>a fruit</u>?

    (A) bofot   (D) jucinthia

    (B) wrag   (E) gortoken

    (C) thrats

14. Which word means <u>a chair</u>?

    (F) hemin   (J) joib

    (G) delmot   (K) nedro

    (H) pyrile

15. Which word means <u>to cry</u>?

    (A) trelas   (D) woggle

    (B) chanic   (E) mongrum

    (C) azin

16. Which word means <u>a tree</u>?

    (F) nedro   (J) trelas

    (G) quoth   (K) knute

    (H) thrats

17. Which word means <u>greedily</u>?

    (A) delmot

    (B) trelas

    (C) chanic

    (D) fumly

    (E) bofot

18. Which word means <u>directions</u>?

    (F) joib

    (G) thrats

    (H) wrag

    (J) knute

    (K) azin

19. Which word means <u>an article of clothing</u>?

    (A) chanic

    (B) hemin

    (C) delmot

    (D) pyrile

    (E) woggle

20. Which word means <u>cunning</u>?

    (F) nedro

    (G) fumly

    (H) azin

    (J) quoth

    (K) chanic

Test 4: Verbal Reasoning

TIME: 15 Minutes
     20 Questions

DIRECTIONS: For numbers 1-6, find the word that names a necessary part of the underlined word.

---

1. <u>pen</u>

    (A) paper   (C) ink

    (B) pencil   (D) crayon

2. <u>computer</u>

    (F) power   (H) printer

    (G) games   (J) CD-ROM

3. <u>ice</u>

    (A) snow   (C) water

    (B) sleet   (D) blue

4. <u>canine</u>

    (F) hound   (H) paws

    (G) cat   (J) collar

5. <u>coffee</u>

    (A) mug   (C) sugar

    (B) tea   (D) beans

6. <u>fork</u>

    (F) tine   (H) metal

    (G) spoon   (J) chopstick

DIRECTIONS: For numbers 7-12, the words in the top row are related in some way. The words in the bottom row are related in the same way. For each item, find the word that completes the bottom row of words.

---

7. whisper   talk   shout
   _____
   whimper   cry

   (A) sob   (C) yell

   (B) howl   (D) tears

8. sandals   bathing suit shorts
   _____
   boots   mittens

   (F) snow   (H) scarf

   (G) skis   (J) shirt

9. Empire State Building Mount Rushmore Golden Gate Bridge
   _____
   Colosseum   Leaning Tower of Pisa

   (A) the Vatican

   (B) the Great Wall of China

   (C) vacation

   (D) the Statue of Liberty

10. iris   retina   cornea
    _____
    lobe   drum

    (F) seeing   (H) body

    (G) canal   (J) hearing

11. patients   beds   medicine
    _____
    students   chalk

    (A) hospital   (C) study

    (B) doctors   (D) desks

12. man   worker   union
    boy   player

    (F) baseball   (H) team
    (G) batter   (J) catcher

DIRECTIONS: For numbers 13-17, find the statement that is true according to the given information.

13. Joey has 3 cats. He also has 2 dogs, but he doesn't have any birds.

    (A) Joey doesn't like birds.
    (B) Joey doesn't want any more pets.
    (C) Joey has at least 5 pets.
    (D) Joey's mother won't let him get any birds.

14. Bob's soccer team is in a special tournament. Once the team loses a game, they're out of the tournament. They had their first game today, and Bob is getting ready for tomorrow's game.

    (F) Bob's team won the game today.
    (G) Bob's team lost the game today.
    (H) Bob will be happy when the tournament is over.
    (J) Bob will play basketball when the soccer season is over.

15. In September, Jack went back to school and started 9th grade. The teacher asked all the students what book they had read last. Some students had read over the summer and some had not. Jack told the teacher the last book he had read was *Tom Sawyer* in 8th grade.

    (A) Jack was too busy to read during the summer.
    (B) Jack can't read.
    (C) Jack doesn't like to read.
    (D) Jack didn't read over the summer.

16. Jim, who had always been a little chubby, took his favorite pants out of the closet. He hadn't worn them since last fall because they were a little tight. He put them on and they were a little loose. This made Jim smile.

    (F) Jim lost weight.
    (G) Jim likes baggy pants.
    (H) Jim recently bought several new pairs of pants.
    (J) Jim gained weight over the winter.

17. When the waiter brought the pizza to the table, the cheese was sizzling and bubbling. It smelled and looked so good that Mark couldn't wait to take a bite. As he bit into it, he yelled and spit out the pizza.

    (A) Mark will never eat pizza again.

    (B) Mark doesn't like pizza.

    (C) The waiter brought the wrong kind of pizza to Mark's table.

    (D) Mark burnt his mouth.

DIRECTIONS: For numbers 18-20, find the correct answer.

---

18. Here are some words translated from an artificial language.

Speffblik means taller.

Reftblik means shorter.

Speffmrepl means tallest.

Which word means shortest?

    (F) speffreft   (H) speffrement

    (G) reftmrepl   (J) reftrement

19. Here are some words translated from an artificial language.

Ablahhamen means anytime.

Weskinhamen means sometime.

Ablahheronni means anywhere.

Which word means somewhere?

    (A) weskinheronni   (C) weskinweskin

    (B) weskinhamen   (D) ablahweskin

20. Here are some words translated from an artificial language.

Maskerintinni means sailboat.

Maskeringruse means yacht.

Abaerntinni means house.

Which word means mansion?

    (F) maskerabaern   (H) abaerngruse

    (G) tinniabaern   (J) tinnigruse

Test 5: Reading Comprehension

TIME: 40 Minutes
40 Questions

DIRECTIONS: Each passage is followed by questions based on its content. After reading the passage, choose the best answer to each question. Answer all questions based on what is indicated or implied in that passage.

Questions 1–4 are based on the following passage.

To the Shakers, perfection was found in the creation of an object that was both useful and simple. Their Society was founded in 1774 by Ann Lee, an English-woman from the working classes who brought eight followers to New York with her. "Mother Ann" established her religious community on the belief that worldly interests were evil.

To gain entrance into the Society, believers had to remain celibate, have no private possessions, and avoid contact with outsiders. The order came to be called "Shakers" because of the feverish dance the group performed. Another character-istic of the group was the desire to seek perfection in their work.

Shaker furniture was created to exemplify specific characteristics: simplicity of design, quality of craftsmanship, harmony of proportion, and usefulness. While Shakers did not create any innovations in furniture designs, they were known for fine craftsmanship. The major emphasis was on function and not on excessive or elaborate decorations that contributed nothing to the product's usefulness.

1. The Shakers were

    (A) a religious community.

    (B) a furniture company.

    (C) a dance troupe.

    (D) an English family.

2. The group came to be called the Shakers because

    (F) they made Shaker furniture.

    (G) they were from the working class.

    (H) they did a shaking dance.

    (J) they avoided contact with outsiders.

3. Shaker furniture is known for its

    (A) elaborate decoration.

    (B) high quality and simplicity.

    (C) high cost.

    (D) low cost.

4. The main purpose of this passage is

    (F) to convince people to join the Shakers.

    (G) to explain why the Shakers no longer exist.

    (H) to talk about Shaker quilts and furniture.

    (J) to tell about the Shakers and their furniture.

Questions 5–8 are based on the following passage.

Teachers should be cognizant of the responsibility they have for the development of children's competencies in basic concepts and principles of free speech. Freedom of speech is not merely the utterance of sounds into the air; rather, it is couched in a set of values and legislative processes that have developed over time. These values and processes are a part of our political conscience as Americans. Teachers must provide ample opportunities for children to express themselves effectively in an environment where their opinions are valued. Children should have ownership in the decision-making process in the classroom and should be engaged in activities where alternative resolutions to problems can be explored. Because teachers have such tremendous power to influence in the classroom, they must be careful to refrain from presenting their own values and biases that could "color" their students' belief systems. If we want children to develop their own voices in a free society, then teachers must support participatory democratic experiences in the daily workings of the classroom.

5. This passage is most likely written for

    (A) students.   (C) parents.

    (B) teachers.   (D) substitute teachers.

6. The word "cognizant," as used in the first line of the passage, means

    (F) proud.   (H) fearful.

    (G) aware.   (J) ignorant.

7.   Which of the following is the main idea of the paragraph?

   (A)   Teachers should let children make the classroom rules.

   (B)   Teachers should have the children solve their own arguments.

   (C)   Teachers should talk to children about voting.

   (D)   Teachers must help children develop the ability to exercise free speech.

8.   From the passage, it can be inferred that free speech

   (F)   is an idea that never changes.

   (G)   is an idea that changes and develops over time.

   (H)   exists only in the United States.

   (J)   cannot be taught in the classroom.

Questions 9–12 are based on the following passage.

   Experienced lawyers know that most lawsuits are won or lost before they are ever heard in court. Thus, successful lawyers prepare their cases carefully, undertaking exhaustive research and investigation prior to going to court. Interviews and statements allow one to ascertain those who are likely to be called as witnesses for the other side. This is the time for strategy planning in the building of the case: decisions to be made about expert witnesses to be called (such as doctors, chemists, or others who have special knowledge of the subject matter); books and articles to be read pertaining to the subject matter of the case; and meetings with witnesses to prepare them for possible questions by the opposing lawyers and to review the case. Finally, in preparing the case, a trial memorandum of law is handed to the judge at the outset of the trial. As a result of this thorough preparation, experienced lawyers know their strong and weak points and can serve their clients well.

9.   Drawing an inference from the passage, why are most cases won or lost before they are heard in court?

   (A)   It is easy to tell who is going to win most cases.

   (B)   The judge gets the trial memorandum before hearing the case.

   (C)   Research is the most important part of a case.

   (D)   Lawyers have strong and weak points, and picking the best lawyer is the most important part of the trial.

10.   The primary purpose of this passage is to illustrate

   (F)   that the legal system is biased against women.

(G)   that the legal system is biased against the poor.

(H)   the work lawyers do before they go to court.

(J)   the work lawyers do to present their cases in court.

11.   To build a case, lawyers do all of the following EXCEPT

(A)   read books and articles that relate to the case.

(B)   meet with witnesses.

(C)   meet with the judge.

(D)   consider calling expert witnesses.

12.   This passage was probably intended for an audience

(F)   of lawyers.

(G)   of judges.

(H)   of people involved in a lawsuit.

(J)   of people without any specialized knowledge of lawsuits.

Questions 13–16 are based on the following passage.

There is an importance of learning communication and meaning in language. Yet the use of notions such as communication and meaning as the basic criteria for instruction, experiences, and materials in classrooms may misguide a child in several respects. Communication in the classroom is vital. The teacher should use communication to help students develop the capacity to make their private responses become public responses. Otherwise, one's use of language would be in danger of being what the younger generation refers to as mere words, mere thoughts, and mere feelings.

Learning theorists emphasize specific components of learning: behaviorists stress behavior in learning; humanists stress the affective domain in learning; and cognitivists stress cognition in learning. All three of these components occur simultaneously and cannot be separated from each other in the learning process. In 1957, Festinger referred to dissonance as the lack of harmony between what one does (behavior) and what one believes (attitude). Attempts to separate the components of learning either knowingly or unknowingly create dissonances wherein language, thought, feeling, and behavior become diminished of authenticity. As a result, ideas and concepts lose their content and vitality, and the manipulation and politics of communication assume prominence.

13. The word "dissonance" as used in the passage means

    (A) happiness.   (C) disagreement.

    (B) anger.   (D) agreement.

14. According to the passage, humanist learning theorists consider which of the following most important?

    (F) The affective domain

    (G) Behavior

    (H) Cognition

    (J) Dissonance

15. This passage is probably aimed toward

    (A) learning theorists.   (C) teachers.

    (B) language theorists.   (D) students.

16. From the tone of the passage, the author

    (F) is not really interested in the topic.

    (G) is confused about what teachers should do.

    (H) feels strongly about the topic.

    (J) does not have a strong opinion.

Questions 17–20 are based on the following passage.

In 1975, Sinclair observed that it had often been supposed that the main factor in learning to talk is being able to imitate. Schlesinger (1975) noted that at certain stages of learning to speak, a child tends to imitate everything an adult says to him or her, and it therefore seems reasonable to accord to such imitation an important role in the acquisition of language.

Moreover, various investigators have attempted to explain the role of imitation in language. In his discussion of the development of imitation and cognition of adult speech sounds, Nakazema (1975) stated that although the parent's talking stimulates and accelerates the infant's articulatory activity, the parent's phoneme system does not influence the child's articulatory mechanisms. Slobin and Welsh (1973) suggested that imitation is the reconstruction of the adult's utterance and that the child does so by employing the grammatical rules that he has developed at a specific time. Schlesinger proposed that by imitating the adult, the child practices new grammatical constructions. Brown and Bellugi (1964) noted that a child's imitations resemble spontaneous speech in that they drop inflections, most function words, and sometimes other words. However, the word order of imitated sentences usually was preserved. Brown and Bellugi assumed that imitation is a function of what the child attended to or remembered. Shipley et al. (1969) suggested that repeating an adult's utterance assists the child's comprehension. Ervin (1964) and Braine (1971) found that a child's imitations do not contain more advanced structures than his or her spontaneous utterances; thus, imitation can no longer be regarded as the simple behavioristic act that earlier scholars assumed it to be.

17. The main topic of this passage is

   (A) how children learn to talk.

   (B) children's first words.

   (C) the role imitation plays in learning to talk.

   (D) how to teach a child to talk.

18. The author wrote this paragraph to

   (F) tell parents how to teach their children to talk.

   (G) tell teachers how to teach their classes to read.

   (H) explain that children shouldn't imitate their parents.

   (J) explain how imitation works for a child who is learning to talk.

19. Researchers have changed their minds about the importance of imitation because

   (A) a child doesn't think about what he/she imitates.

   (B) a child can only imitate grammar that he/she already knows.

   (C) a child only imitates what he/she does not understand.

   (D) a child's imitations are spontaneous.

20. Researchers included in the passage have found all of the following EXCEPT

   (F) a child's imitation often adds new words to what the adult has said.

   (G) a child's imitation is the reconstruction of an adult's speech.

   (H) a child's imitations resemble spontaneous speech.

   (J) a child's imitations help him or her understand what the adult has said.

Questions 21–25 are based on the following passage.

Beginning readers, and those who are experiencing difficulty with reading, benefit from assisted reading. During assisted reading the teacher orally reads a passage with a student or students. The teacher fades in and out of the reading act. For example, the teacher lets his or her voice drop to a whisper when students are reading on their own at an acceptable rate and lets his or her voice rise to say the words clearly when the students are having difficulty.

Students who are threatened by print, read word-by-word, or rely on grapho-phone-mic cues, will be helped by assisted reading. These students are stuck on individual language units which can be as small as a single letter or as large as phrases or sentences. As Frank Smith (1977) and other reading educators have noted, speeding up reading, not slowing it down, helps the reader make sense of a passage. This strategy allows students to concentrate on meaning as the short-term memory is not overloaded by focusing on small language units. As the name implies, assisted reading lets the reader move along without being responsible for every language unit; the pressure is taken off the student. Consequently, when the reading act is sped up, it sounds more like language, and students can begin to integrate the cuing systems of semantics and syntax along with grapho-phonemics.

21. According to the passage, assisted reading

   (A) hurts slow readers because they don't get to figure it out on their own.

   (B) helps slow readers understand what they are reading.

   (C) hurts slow readers because it doesn't give them time to understand what they are reading.

   (D) helps slow readers by putting more pressure on them.

22. Assisted reading is

   (F) when the reader gives out definitions of hard words in the passage.

   (G) when the teacher reads out loud with the students, getting louder or quieter depending on the students' abilities.

   (H) when the passage has pictures to help students understand it.

   (J) when the teacher reads to the student.

23. The passage says all of the following about assisted reading EXCEPT that

   (A) it speeds up reading.

   (B) it takes pressure off of the students.

(C) it lets the students concentrate on what the passage means.

(D) it makes the students responsible for every language unit.

24. According to the passage, a beginning reader can most easily make sense of a reading by

(F) reading slowly.

(G) concentrating on every word.

(H) speeding up and concentrating on the meaning.

(J) focusing on small language units.

25. As used in the passage, "individual language units" means

(A) small parts of language such as letters, phrases, or sentences.

(B) big pieces of language like paragraphs.

(C) a unit in a language textbook.

(D) an entire story or book.

Questions 26–30 are based on the following passage.

The First Amendment to the Constitution of the United States guarantees that Congress shall not make a law prohibiting the free exercise of religion or respecting an establishment of religion. Many voices in the country offer conflicting ideas. A Chief Justice of the Supreme Court of the United States described the separation of church and state as a wall based on bad history, a guide which is useless to judging, and a metaphor which should be discarded. A contemporary, prominent church pastor viewed this enforced separation of civil and religious authority as the result of the work of an infidel. A religious leader of the colonial period reaffirmed this amendment by asking that government continue to let people speak as they please and worship freely whether it be none, one, or 20 gods. In the modern context, then, it seems that threats to religious freedom still exist. Separation of church and state is not universally accepted.

26. The First Amendment prohibits

(F) the free exercise or establishment of religion.

(G) laws which prohibit freedom of religion.

(H) free speech.

(J) the free exercise or establishment of organizations.

27. According to the passage, critics of the First Amendment

    (A) believe the Constitution is useless.

    (B) believe it is the work of an infidel.

    (C) believe that religious leaders should rewrite the Constitution.

    (D) believe that churches have the final authority over the United States government.

28. In the passage, the word "reaffirmed" means

    (F) agreed with.   (H) ignored.

    (G) disagreed with.   (J) celebrated.

29. According to the passage, a Supreme Court Justice believes the First Amendment is all of the following EXCEPT

    (A) a useless guide.

    (B) a barrier based on a misinterpretation of history.

    (C) a clear guide.

    (D) a metaphor.

30. The main purpose of this passage is

    (F) to show that the separation of church and state is under attack.

    (G) to show that everyone believes in the separation of church and state.

    (H) to show that no one pays attention to the separation of church and state anymore.

    (J) to prove that the government should control religion.

Questions 31–35 are based on the following passage.

The first child labor laws were enacted in England through the efforts of those members of Parliament whose hearts were wrung by the condition of the little parish apprentices bound out to the early textile manufacturers of the north. Through the long years they were required to build up the code of child labor legislation which England now possesses: knowledge of the conditions has always preceded effective legislation. The efforts of that small number in every community who believe in legislative control have always been reinforced by the efforts of trade unionists rather than by the efforts of employers. This is partly because the employment of workingmen in the factories brings them in contact with the children who tend to earn lower wages and demoralize their trades and partly because workingmen have no money or time to spend for alleviating philanthropy, and must seize upon agitation and legal enactment as the only channel of redress which is open to them.

We may illustrate by imagining a row of people seated in a moving streetcar into which darts a boy of eight, calling out the details of the last murder, in the hope of selling an evening newspaper. A comfortable-looking man buys a paper from him with no sense of moral shock; he may even be a trifle complacent that he has helped along the little fellow, who is making his way in the world. The philanthropic lady sitting next to him may perhaps reflect that it is a pity that such a bright boy is not in school. She may make up her mind in a moment of compunction to redouble her efforts for various newsboys' schools and homes, that this poor child may have better teaching. Next to her sits a workingman trained in trade union methods. He knows that the boy's natural development is arrested, and that the abnormal activity of his body and mind uses up the force which should go into growth, moreover, that this premature use of his powers has but a momentary and specious value. He is forced to those conclusions because he has seen many a man, entering the factory at eighteen and twenty, so worn out by premature work that he was "laid on the shelf" within ten or fifteen years. He knows very well that he can do nothing in the way of ameliorating the lot of this particular boy; his only possible chance is to agitate for proper child-labor laws, to regulate, and if possible prohibit, street-vending by children, in order that the child of the poorest may have his school time secured to him and may have at least his short chance for growth.

31. The primary purpose of the passage is to show

   (A) that the only way to end child labor is through law.

   (B) that children learn more by working than they would in school.

   (C) that children can work full time and study at night.

   (D) that schools should teach children job skills.

32. Trade unionists agitate for laws against child labor because

   (F) they work in factories and they see the harm factories do to children.

   (G) factory owners pay everyone less when they hire children.

   (H) they know that the only way to end child labor is with child labor laws.

   (J) All of the above.

33. The author of the passage is against child labor because

   (A) she believes children are not responsible enough to work.

   (B) she believes the United States should follow England's lead in making laws against child labor.

(C)   she believes children should have the chance to go to school.

(D)   All of the above.

34.   The author makes all of the following arguments against child labor EXCEPT that

(F)   it stunts children's growth.

(G)   it demoralizes the trades.

(H)   it takes away jobs from adults.

(J)   England has already abolished child labor.

35.   In the last sentence of the passage, the word "ameliorating" is used to mean

(A)   calling attention to.

(C)   showing.

(B)   improving.

(D)   understanding.

Questions 36–40 are based on the following passage.

The primary aim of comedy is to amuse us with a happy ending; although comedies can vary according to the attitudes they project, which can be broadly identified as either high or low, terms having nothing to do with an evaluation of the play's merit. Generally, the amusement found in comedy comes from an eventual victory over threats or ill fortune. Much of the dialogue and plot development might be laughable, yet a play need not be funny to be comic. In fact, some critics in the Renaissance era thought that the highest form of comedy should elicit no laughter at all from its audience. A comedy that forced its audience into laughter failed in the highest comic endeavor, whose purpose was to amuse as subtly as possible. Note that Shakespeare's comedies themselves were often under attack for their appeal to laughter.

Farce is low comedy intended to make us laugh by means of a series of exaggerated, unlikely situations that depend less on plot and character than on gross absurdities, sight gags, and coarse dialogue. The "higher" a comedy goes, the more natural the characters seem and the less boisterous their behavior. The plots become more sustained, and the dialogue shows more weighty thought. As with all dramas, comedies are about things that go wrong. Accordingly, comedies create deviations from accepted normalcy, presenting problems which we might or might not see as harmless. If these problems make us judgmental about the involved characters and events, the play takes on the features of satire, a rather high comic form implying that humanity and human institutions are in need of reform. If the action triggers our sympathy for the characters, we feel even less protected from the incongruities as the play tilts more in the direction of tragicomedy. In other words, the action determines a figurative distance between the audience and the play. Such factors as characters' personalities and the plot's predictability influence this distance. The farther away we sit, the more protected we feel and usually the funnier the play becomes. Closer proximity to believability in the script draws us nearer to the conflict, making us feel more involved in the action and less safe in its presence.

36. According to the passage, a play is called a comedy if it

    (F) is funny.   (H) is absurd.

    (G) has a happy ending.   (J) has funny characters.

37. A comedy is called a farce if it

    (A) is exaggerated.   (C) makes people think.

    (B) is high comedy.   (D) is funny.

38. A comedy is called a satire if it

    (F) is high comedy.

    (G) is low comedy.

    (H) criticizes humanity and human institutions.

    (J) is predictable but funny.

39. According to the passage, the more believable a comedy is

    (A) the funnier it is.

    (B) the more involved and less safe the audience feels.

    (C) the more harmless it is to the audience.

    (D) the closer to Shakespeare's comedies it is.

40. The main purpose of this passage is

    (F) to explain the different types of comedies and how they work.

    (G) to argue that comedies are more enjoyable than tragedies.

    (H) to prove that Shakespeare' s comedies are the best ever written.

    (J) to explain figurative distance.

Test 6: Mathematics Concepts and Applications

TIME: 35 Minutes
40 Questions

DIRECTIONS: Select the best answer choice.

---

1. What is the value of q in the equation $4q + 8 = 16$?

   (A) 24   (C) 6

   (B) 8   (D) 2

2. Mr. Matthews worked for five days in a week. He earned $125 on Monday, $115 on Tuesday, $118 on Wednesday, and $123 on Thursday. If he earned a total of $591 for the week, how much was he paid on Friday?

   (F) $125   (H) $110

   (G) $120   (J) $100

3. Mary's average score on 5 tests was 88. If she scored 82 on test 1, 93 on test 2, 79 on test 3, and 90 on test 4, what was her score on test 5?

   (A) 96   (C) 86

   (B) 90   (D) 82

4. Rudy divided a certain number by 15 and the answer was 7.56. What is the value of the 6?

   (F) 6 tens   (H) 6 tenths

   (G) 6 singles   (J) 6 hundredths

5. Instead of dividing a certain number by 100, Martha multiplied it by 100. If Martha wrote 8.47265 as the answer, what should be the correct answer?

   (A) 84726.5   (C) 0.0847265

   (B) 847.265   (D) 0.00084726

6. Dwayne added 34 to a certain number when the teacher told him to subtract 34 from the

number. Dwayne wrote the answer as 15. If he had done what the teacher said, what should have been the correct answer?

(F) −53   (H) 49

(G) 19   (J) 83

7. Arrange the following quantities in order, from <u>largest to smallest</u>:

$\sqrt{36}$ 36   3.6

(A) 36, 3.6, $\sqrt{36}$ (C) 36, $\sqrt{36}$, 3.6

(B) $\sqrt{36}$, 3.6, 36   (D) 3.6, $\sqrt{36}$, 36

8. Tamara works for 20 hours at $4.75 an hour. How much does she earn for the 20 hours?

(F) $950.00   (H) $24.75

(G) $95.00   (J) $9.50

9. If $u = 5$ and $v = 3$, what is the value of $-2u + 3v$?

(A) −19   (C) 1

(B) −1   (D) 19

10. If $x = -3$ and $y = 2$, find the value of $(3xy)^2$.

(F) 324   (H) −36

(G) 36   (J) −324

11. Raymond's order of books arrived in 6 boxes of 9 books each and one box of 2 books. How many books did Raymond receive?

(A) 63   (C) 54

(B) 56   (D) 52

12. From the school's store room, Mrs. White collected 7 full boxes of marbles for her 12 students. If each full box holds 15 marbles, what is the minimum number of additional marbles that Mrs. White must collect in order to give her students exactly the same number of marbles?

(F) 3   (H) 84

(G) 9   (J) 105

13. The sum of two consecutive multiples of 7 is 1 less than the square of 6. Find the larger of the two multiples of 7?

(A) 42

(B) 35

(C) 21

(D) 14

14. In the figure, $\overline{AB}$ is a straight line. Find the value of x.

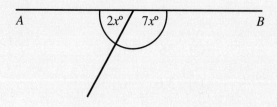

(F) 20

(G) 40

(H) 45

(J) 60

15. Find the value of v in the figure.

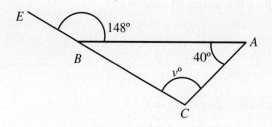

(A) 32

(B) 72

(C) 108

(D) 148

16. What is the value of y in the figure?

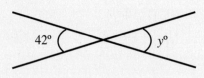

(F) 42

(G) 58

(H) 52

(J) 138

17. Two sets of straws are shown with the measures of their lengths. Which straw in set 2 would you combine with the two straws in set 1 so they can be joined end-to-end to form a triangle?

—————————— 26 cm
——— 11 cm   Set 1

(A) ——————— 14 cm

(B) ——————— 18 cm   Set 2

(C) ——————— 13 cm

(D) ———————————— 37 cm

18. Two sets of sticks are shown with the measures of their lengths. Which stick in set 2 would you combine with the two sticks in set 1 so they can be joined end-to-end to form a right triangle?

————— 8 cm   Set 1
——— 6 cm

(F) ——————— 8 cm

(G) ——————— 10 cm   Set 2

(H) ——— 6 cm

(J) ———————————— 37 cm

19. Sally says, "If you double a certain number, *n*, and then add 7 to the result, you obtain 35." Which one of the following equations accurately expresses Sally's original statement?

(A) $2n + 7 = 35$

(B) $2n - 7 = 35$

(C) $n + 7 \times 2 = 35$

(D) $2(n + 7) = 35$

20. There are 17 students in Mr. Anderson's class. 16 of these students are the same age and the 17th student is 9 years old. Let *y* represent the age of the 16 students. Which one of the following expressions best describes the total age of the students in Mr. Anderson's class?

(F) $17y + 9$

(G) $17(y - 9)$

(H) $16(y + 9)$

(J) $16y + 9$

21. What is the product of $4x - 1$ and $2x + 5$?

(A) $8x^2 + 18x - 5$

(B) $8x^2 + 22x - 5$

(C) $8x^2 - 18x - 5$

(D) $8x^2 - 20x - 5$

22. Simplify: $(3 + 5) \times 15 - 3$.

    (F) 120   (H) 78
    (G) 117   (J) 75

23. Multiply 35% of 140 by 16% of 50.

    (A) 560   (C) 39.2
    (B) 392   (D) 56

24. What is 135% of 80?

    (F) 10.8   (H) 1,080
    (G) 108   (J) 10,800

25. Pencils are sold in boxes of 24. Mrs. Archibald needs 6 pencils for each of her 22 students. What is the minimum number of boxes that Mrs. Archibald must buy?

    (A) 144   (C) 6
    (B) 132   (D) 5

Information for questions 26 to 29

Seven athletes took part in a broad jump. Each athlete competed in two rounds. Here are the distances they jumped in inches.

Athlete's name	Round 1	Round 2
Emelda	88	88
Frank	92	87
George	87	90
Linda	75	67
Maria	83	88
Tricia	79	82
Victor	91	93

26. Which one of the athletes improved the most, from the first to the second round?

    (F) George   (H) Tricia
    (G) Maria   (J) Victor

27. On the average, which one of the athletes jumped the longest distance?

(A) Frank   (C) Maria

(B) George   (D) Victor

28. What was the average score for the seven athletes in the first round?

(F) 90   (H) 85

(G) 87   (J) 82

29. If Linda's score in the second round were dropped, by how many inches would the average score for the remaining 6 athletes improve?

(A) 88   (C) 5

(B) 75   (D) 3

30. Brenda took 5 tests in the first semester, scoring an average of 64 points. During the second semester, she took 3 tests and scored an average of 55 points. During the third semester, Brenda took 4 tests, scoring an average of 59 points. Approximately what was Brenda's average score per test for the three semesters?

(F) 55   (H) 60

(G) 59   (J) 62

31. If 1 cm³ of loose snow weighs 0.125 gram, how many grams would 1,000,000 cm³ of loose snow weigh?

(A) 1,250,000   (C) 125

(B) 125,000   (D) 0.000000125

32. Solve for y: $5y + 6 = 51$.

(F) 8   (H) 45

(G) 9   (J) 57

33. Find the slope of the line in the graph.

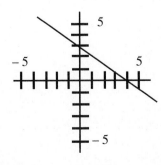

(A) $\dfrac{3}{4}$ (C) $-\dfrac{4}{3}$

(B) $-\dfrac{3}{4}$ (D) $\dfrac{4}{3}$

34. *ABCDEF* in the figure is a regular hexagon (it has 6 congruent sides and 6 congruent angles). Find the sum of all the interior angles of hexagon *ABCDEO*, in thick lines. These angles are marked 1, 2, ..., 6. (*Hint: You may use the dotted lines as a clue.*)

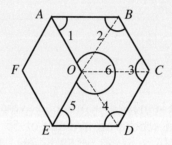

(F) 720°   (H) 480°

(G) 540°   (J) 360°

35. Find the total area of the 3 <u>visible faces</u> of the cube shown below.

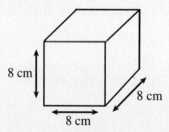

(A) 512 cm²   (C) 256 cm²

(B) 384 cm²   (D) 192 cm²

36. The formula for the area of a circle is πr^2, where *r* represents the radius of the circle. Find the area of the shaded region in the figure below, if $\pi = 3.14$.

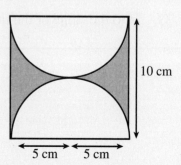

(F) 78.5 cm²

(G) 60.75 cm²

(H) 39.25 cm²

(J) 21.5 cm²

37. One mile equals 1.6 kilometers. If a car travels for 400 miles, how many kilometers were traveled?

    (A) 640

    (B) 250

    (C) 64

    (D) 25

38. On a map 1.5 in. represent 45 miles. What is the actual road distance, in miles, between two cities represented by 30 in. on the same map?

    (F) 20

    (G) 900

    (H) 1,350

    (J) 9,000

Information for questions 39 and 40

Adrian participated in a weight exercise program for a period of time. The graph below shows how Adrian's weight changed between January and August of the same year.

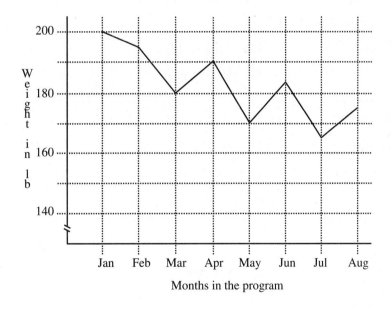

Months in the program

39. What was Adrian's overall weight loss between January and August?

    (A) 25 lbs.

    (B) 35 lbs.

    (C) 40 lbs.

    (D) 60 lbs.

40. What was Adrian's average weight loss between February and July?

    (F) 30 lbs.

    (G) 25 lbs.

    (H) 9 lbs.

    (J) 6 lbs.

Test 7: Language Expression

TIME: 30 Minutes
40 Questions

DIRECTIONS: For numbers 1-6, choose the answer that best completes the sentence.

---

1. After Mrs. Howard returned from her shopping trip, she _____ to the kitchen to make herself a cup of tea.

   (A) have gone   (C) went

   (B) had went   (D) has gone

2. I really didn't enjoy that horror book I just finished. _____, I am never going to read another book by the same author.

   (F) Regardless   (H) As a result

   (G) Because   (J) However

3. Those roses are the _____ flowers I have ever seen.

   (A) most beautiful   (C) as beautiful

   (B) more beautiful   (D) less beautiful

4. _____ I am your father, it is my responsibility to take care of you and keep you safe.

   (F) Besides   (H) Even though

   (G) However   (J) Because

5. I want to compliment _____ new hairstyle. It looks lovely on you.

   (A) you're   (C) your

   (B) you are   (D) yore

6. _____ he had been given his allowance on Friday, Matt still didn't have enough money for the movie.

   (F) Although   (H) Since

   (G) Because   (J) If

> **DIRECTIONS**: Choose the sentence that is complete and that is written correctly.

7. (A)   The tornado approached slowly houses and trees were torn up in its path.

    (B)   Tearing up houses and trees in its path, the tornado approached slowly.

    (C)   Slowly approaching as it tore up houses and trees in its path.

    (D)   The tornado slowly approaching tearing up houses and trees in its path.

8. (F)   Giving me lots of energy in the morning, I enjoy a big breakfast.

    (G)   Having a big breakfast in the morning gives me lots of energy.

    (H)   A big breakfast in the morning giving me lots of energy.

    (J)   I eat a big breakfast in the morning it gives me lots of energy.

9. (A)   For her birthday, a puppy will be given to Sandi because she is old enough now.

    (B)   Sandi is getting a puppy for her birthday, she is old enough to take care of it now.

    (C)   Getting a puppy because Sandi is old enough to take care of it now.

    (D)   Now that she is old enough to take care of it, Sandi is getting a puppy for her birthday.

10. (F)   When it is time for it to spawn and die, the salmon will swim against the current to the stream where it was born.

    (G)   The salmon swimming upstream will spawn and die it was born in that stream.

    (H)   Swimming against the current and spawning and dying in the stream where it was born.

    (J)   Swimming against the current to spawn and die, the salmon.

11. (A)   Every Memorial Day and Veterans' Day my grandmother puts up our flag my grandfather fought in World War II.

    (B)   Since my grandfather fought in World War II and my grandmother puts out the flag every Veterans' Day and Memorial Day.

    (C)   By putting out the flag every Veterans' Day and Memorial Day, my grandmother remembers my grandfather, who fought in World War II.

    (D)   Putting out the flag on Veterans' Day and Memorial Day, and remembering my grandfather who fought in World War II.

12. (F)   Street hockey is our favorite game in my neighborhood since we live on a dead-end street with a paved circle at the end.

(G)   Living on a dead-end street with a paved circle at the end and playing street hockey.

(H)   We play street hockey on our dead-end street we have a paved circle.

(J)   Since we live on a paved dead-end street and play our favorite game; street hockey.

DIRECTIONS: For numbers 13-17, choose the sentence that uses verbs correctly.

---

13. (A)   Even though the television was still on, I can hear the radio clearly.

(B)   Hugh wanted his cat to come inside, so he puts cat food by the door.

(C)   Terry will be leaving this afternoon after she got back from the movies.

(D)   As a result of an error by the airline, his luggage will be arriving on a later plane.

14. (F)   Angie plays tennis with Mark every Saturday, but this week he can't come.

(G)   The saxophone had a stuck key so Mr. Kady fixes it before the concert.

(H)   If we are going jogging this morning, you need to got dressed soon.

(J)   Eve says you shouldn't have took her new jeans from her closet yesterday.

15. (A)   I wish Gene and Val would have helped with the dishes and brang in the newspaper.

(B)   The Nelson's turtle often climbs on the rocks and knocks over its water dish.

(C)   You shouldn't of given her my phone number without my permission.

(D)   Jessie and I were going to meet the new boy at the museum, but he doesn't see us there.

16. (F)   Dad picked up the new book from the library, and I taked it to school with me.

(G)   After Karen takes her brother to his music lesson, she stopped by the gym.

(H)   Lennie has been away on vacation since Friday and is expected home next Wednesday.

(J)   Before Nick gets back from wrestling, I returned his radio to his room.

17. (A)   Mr. Post says you should of handed in your term paper yesterday.

(B)   My kitten loved to play with ribbon, but she gets tired easily and needs to sleep.

(C)   Bluefish can be broiled or baked, but it cooks fast and gets tough if you overcook it.

(D)   For the last few weeks the weather has been terrible, and my mother's arthritis been bothering her.

DIRECTIONS: For numbers 18-21, choose the underlined part that is the simple subject of the sentence.

---

18. <u>After</u> the <u>party</u>, <u>Howie</u> drove us home in his new pickup <u>truck</u>.
    F   G   H   J

19. My <u>house</u> is the best <u>place</u> to meet and decide <u>who</u> will be our <u>chairman</u>.
       A   B   C   D

20. During the <u>war</u>, many <u>soldiers</u> were wounded by <u>metal</u> fragments from hand <u>grenades</u>.
            F   G   H   J

21. The <u>mailman</u> expects to <u>deliver</u> the <u>mail</u> and leave without getting bitten by my <u>dog</u>.
      A   B   C   D

DIRECTIONS: For numbers 22-25, choose the underlined part that is the simple predicate (verb) of the sentence.

---

22. As you <u>leave</u> the main doors, please <u>notice</u> the No <u>Smoking</u> sign on <u>your</u> right.
         F   G   H   J

23. My brother and I <u>sat</u> <u>quietly</u> at a table <u>placed</u> right by the stage <u>entrance</u>.
                   A   B   C   D

24. A wizard <u>dressed</u> all in white <u>waved</u> his wand in the <u>direction</u> of a dove in a <u>cage</u>.
            F   G   H   J

25. <u>Bicycling</u> <u>is</u> one of the best types of <u>exercise</u> for people who are <u>behind</u> a desk all day.
     A   B   C   D

DIRECTIONS: For numbers 26-28, read the underlined sentences. Choose the sentence that best combines those sentences into one.

---

26. <u>Matty left for the party after dinner. He took the Jeep and money for gas.</u>

    (F)   Matty took the Jeep and money for gas and then ate dinner and left for the party.

    (G)   After finishing dinner, Marty took money for gas and left for the party in the Jeep.

    (H)   When Marty left for the party in the Jeep, he ate dinner and took money for gas.

(J) Eating dinner and taking money for gas, Marty left for the party while driving the Jeep.

27. Five of the kids in her algebra class went to Cara's house to study for the big test. They brought a pizza with them so they wouldn't get hungry.

(A) Arriving at Cara's house to study for the big test, five kids from her algebra class went out for pizza.

(B) Picking up a pizza so they wouldn't get hungry, Cara had five kids from her algebra class over to study for the big test.

(C) Stopping to pick up pizza on their way so they wouldn't get hungry, five kids from Cara's algebra class went to her house to study for the big test.

(D) Five kids from Cara's algebra class went to her house to study for the big test and also they brought pizza so they wouldn't get hungry.

28. Many people travel to New Orleans for Mardi Gras. They love the colorful costumes, the parades, and the wonderful food.

(F) Because they love the colorful costumes, the parades, and the wonderful food, many people travel to New Orleans for Mardi Gras.

(G) Although many people travel to New Orleans for Mardi Gras, they enjoy the colorful costumes, the parades, and the wonderful food.

(H) Many people enjoy the colorful costumes, the parades, and the wonderful food, and they also travel to New Orleans for Mardi Gras.

(J) When they enjoy the colorful costumes, the parades, and the wonderful food, many people travel to New Orleans for Mardi Gras.

DIRECTIONS: In numbers 29-31, choose the topic sentence that best fits the paragraph.

---

29. _____. The northern states wanted to extend the power of the federal government, while the southern states wanted to reserve as many rights as possible for the states. The North wanted federal money for projects such as railroads, canals, and roads, while the South had no need for these projects. The North favored the prohibition of slavery in the western states as they entered the union, while the South hoped to increase the number of slave states so as to ensure slavery's future.

(A) The Civil War was a result of many opposing points of view between the North and the South.

(B) The Civil War was the only war in which Americans fought themselves.

(C) Slavery was the main cause of the Civil War.

(D) The Civil War was a tragic and brutal war that caused misery for both the North and the South.

30. _____. Averaging 1.5 gallons in the typical adult, and comprising less than 10% of our total weight, blood carries all the nutrients and oxygen to the cells of our bodies through its vast circulatory system. It picks up oxygen from the lungs and nutrients from the digestive tract and carries them to the cell membranes, where it exchanges them for waste products that are then carried to the kidneys. In addition, blood carries heat produced by the muscles to all the other organs of the body.

   (F) Blood is composed of water and red and white blood cells.

   (G) Blood is important to our health.

   (H) Blood is our body's internal transportation system.

   (J) If we didn't have blood, we would die.

31. _____. Some poisonous plants such as bittersweet or nightshade can cause death or injury if leaves or berries are swallowed by animals. Other plants such as poison ivy and poison oak need only be touched to transfer their poisons. Still others, including some fungi, spread airborne toxins that are inhaled. Scientists believe that the purpose of all of these poisons, called biotoxins, is to defend plants against plant-eating animals.

   (A) Plants have many ways to defend themselves.

   (B) Poisonous plants use several different methods to ward off predators.

   (C) Plants can be dangerous and should be handled carefully.

   (D) Many botanists study poisonous plants.

DIRECTIONS: In numbers 32-34, choose the answer that best develops the topic sentence.

---

32. Bees perform several valuable services for people.

   (F) They are usually docile and will not sting unless their hive or their queen is threatened.

   (G) The queen bee does not leave the hive to collect nectar, but produces eggs that will develop into the workers of tomorrow.

   (H) As each bee settles on a flower to collect its nectar, tiny hairs on the legs of the bee collect pollen, which is in turn carried to the next flower, resulting in the pollination crucial to the development of fruit.

   (J) Bees are industrious insects, working tirelessly for the good of the hive.

33. The word democracy derives from two Greek words that contain its entire meaning: *demos*, which means "the people," and *kratos*, which means "rule."

(A) A democracy is a superior form of government to a monarchy or a dictatorship.

(B) In a monarchy, power is handed down from one generation of rulers to the next by right of birth.

(C) In a true democracy, the people choose their leaders, have equal rights under the law, and make the decisions that govern their lives.

(D) The Revolutionary War was fought against the British because the colonies wanted a democracy.

34. Three thousand years before Christ was born, the Egyptians were a highly civilized people.

(F) Archaeologists can tell that Tutankhamen was an important pharaoh of ancient Egypt by his intricate golden throne.

(G) They had learned to navigate the known world, had built intricate structures, and had developed a written language.

(H) Many of the relics of these ancient people have been preserved by the dry climate of the desert in which they lie.

(J) Egypt is the birthplace of many later cultures that have greatly influenced history.

DIRECTIONS: In numbers 35-37, choose the sentence that does not belong to the paragraph.

35. 1. Even before the Europeans brought horses to North America, Indians of the plains were able to supply their tribes with meat and skins by hunting buffalo. 2. Herds that were spread out allowed hunters to creep softly between the animals and kill several without frightening the others. 3. Buffalo could be stampeded over a cliff and would be killed by the fall or killed with clubs when they hit the bottom. 4. Dried and powdered buffalo meat mixed with fat and berries was called pemmican and was used by warriors as concentrated high energy food.

(A) Sentence 1   (C) Sentence 3

(B) Sentence 2   (D) Sentence 4

36. 1. Egyptians built their pyramids to protect their remains from robbers, since their remains and possessions would be needed in the other world after death. 2. They were built on the west bank of the Nile River so as to be closer to the land of the dead, which was toward the setting sun. 3. The Great Pyramid was the largest ever built, covering 13 acres. 4. The passages leading down to the burial chambers were sealed with heavy stones to further protect the precious remains.

(F) Sentence 1   (H) Sentence 3

(G) Sentence 2   (J) Sentence 4

37. 1. The principle of buoyancy is said to have first been recognized by the famous scientist Archimedes when climbing into his bath one day. 2. The legend states that he watched the water run over the side as he sat down, and he suddenly understood that there was a relationship between his volume and the amount of water. 3. From this understanding of displacement, he experimented until he could confidently state that an object immersed in a fluid would lose as much in weight as the weight of the fluid it displaced. 4. Large ships weighing many tons can float in water because of the vast amount of water that they displace.

(A) Sentence 1   (C) Sentence 3

(B) Sentence 2   (D) Sentence 4

DIRECTIONS: In numbers 38-40, read the paragraph. Choose the sentence that best fills the blank in the paragraph.

---

38. Grown in countries too cold for sugar cane, sugar beets run through a series of stages in a processing plant before they yield sugar for the table. _____. They are then washed and sliced, and the slices are washed with hot water to remove the beet juice. The juice is purified with lime and carbon dioxide, and then it is filtered. After boiling in a vacuum, its crystals are separated by centrifuge and cannot be distinguished from cane sugar.

(F) When they arrive from the field, beets are weighed and loaded on conveyor belts.

(G) The white sugar beets are harvested, and their roots have the tops cut off and shipped to farmers for cattle feed.

(H) Each sugar beet yields 14 teaspoons of sugar.

(J) Only cane sugar, however, yields the molasses that is used to make rum.

39. Beginning as a secret society during the potato famine in Ireland in 1843, the Molly Maguires came to the United States with other Irish immigrants. They became particularly active in Pennsylvania, where immigrant mine workers were poorly paid for dangerous and exhausting work. _____. The Molly Maguires committed acts of terrorism, including the killing of a mine owner and the destruction of property, but they were infiltrated by a detective from the Pinkerton Detective Agency. They were tried in 1885-1887, and 10 members were hanged for their crimes.

(A) The Molly Maguires were named for an Irish widow who had been abused by a wealthy landlord and had died.

(B) Arthur Conan Doyle wrote his work "The Valley of Fear," featuring Sherlock Holmes, about the Molly Maguires.

(C) The mine owners encouraged debt to the company store as an additional way to profit from their miserable workers and to ensure that they could not quit.

(D) The potato famine drove many Irish families to the United States in the hopes of work and a better standard of living.

40. Cubism, a form of abstract art where the forms of objects are reduced to their simplest fundamental shapes, was the style of choice for Pablo Picasso. In his painting "Three Musicians," Picasso not only simplified shapes, but flattened them, rearranged them, and eliminated shading as a way to show depth or dimension. _____. The result was a great sense of the relationship between figures and objects.

    (F) Although he was born in Spain, Picasso lived and worked most of his life in France.

    (G) Instead, he used the placement of the objects in relation to one another, as well as texture, to give life to the painting.

    (H) Cubism also influenced the paintings of Henri Matisse and Marc Chagall.

    (J) In all forms of abstract art, only certain qualities of the subjects are used in the finished picture.

COOP

PRACTICE TEST 2

ANSWER KEY

Question Number	Correct Answer	If You Answered this Question Incorrectly, Refer to...

Test 1: Sequences

1.	(B)	P. 401
2.	(H)	P. 401
3.	(A)	P. 401
4.	(J)	P. 401
5.	(A)	P. 401
6.	(H)	P. 401
7.	(B)	P. 401
8.	(G)	P. 401
9.	(D)	P. 401
10.	(H)	P. 401
11.	(C)	P. 401
12.	(F)	P. 401
13.	(D)	P. 401
14.	(J)	P. 401
15.	(B)	P. 401
16.	(F)	P. 401
17.	(B)	P. 401
18.	(H)	P. 401
19.	(C)	P. 401
20.	(F)	P. 401

Test 2: Analogies

1.	(D)	P. 189
2.	(H)	P. 189
3.	(C)	P. 189
4.	(H)	P. 189
5.	(A)	P. 189
6.	(H)	P. 189
7.	(C)	P. 189
8.	(F)	P. 189
9.	(B)	P. 189
10.	(H)	P. 189
11.	(A)	P. 189
12.	(G)	P. 189
13.	(C)	P. 189
14.	(G)	P. 189
15.	(D)	P. 189
16.	(F)	P. 189
17.	(C)	P. 189
18.	(G)	P. 189
19.	(C)	P. 189
20.	(G)	P. 189

Test 3: Memory

1.	(E)	P. 415
2.	(K)	P. 415
3.	(E)	P. 415
4.	(G)	P. 415
5.	(D)	P. 415
6.	(K)	P. 415
7.	(D)	P. 415
8.	(K)	P. 415
9.	(E)	P. 415
10.	(J)	P. 415
11.	(E)	P. 415

12.	(F)	P. 415
13.	(A)	P. 415
14.	(G)	P. 415
15.	(D)	P. 415
16.	(J)	P. 415
17.	(C)	P. 415
18.	(G)	P. 415
19.	(D)	P. 415
20.	(H)	P. 415

Test 4: Verbal Reasoning

1.	(C)	P. 198
2.	(F)	P. 198
3.	(C)	P. 198
4.	(H)	P. 198
5.	(D)	P. 198
6.	(F)	P. 198
7.	(A)	P. 189
8.	(H)	P. 189
9.	(A)	P. 189
10.	(G)	P. 189
11.	(D)	P. 189
12.	(H)	P. 189
13.	(C)	P. 275
14.	(F)	P. 275
15.	(D)	P. 275
16.	(F)	P. 275
17.	(D)	P. 275
18.	(G)	P. 189
19.	(A)	P. 189
20.	(H)	P. 189

Test 5: Reading Comprehension

1.	(A)	P. 272
2.	(H)	P. 272
3.	(B)	P. 272
4.	(J)	P. 270
5.	(B)	P. 275
6.	(G)	P. 282
7.	(D)	P. 270
8.	(G)	P. 275
9.	(C)	P. 275
10.	(H)	P. 270
11.	(C)	P. 270
12.	(J)	P. 275
13.	(C)	P. 282
14.	(F)	P. 272
15.	(C)	P. 275
16.	(H)	P. 280
17.	(C)	P. 270
18.	(J)	P. 270
19.	(B)	P. 272
20.	(F)	P. 274
21.	(B)	P. 272
22.	(G)	P. 272
23.	(D)	P. 274
24.	(H)	P. 272
25.	(A)	P. 282
26.	(G)	P. 272
27.	(B)	P. 272
28.	(F)	P. 282
29.	(C)	P. 274
30.	(F)	P. 270
31.	(A)	P. 270
32.	(J)	P. 272
33.	(C)	P. 280

34.	(H)	P. 274
35.	(B)	P. 282
36.	(G)	P. 272
37.	(A)	P. 272
38.	(H)	P. 272
39.	(B)	P. 272
40.	(F)	P. 270

Test 6: Mathematical Concepts and Applications

1.	(D)	P. 409
2.	(H)	P. 315, 317
3.	(A)	P. 371
4.	(J)	P. 354, 409
5.	(D)	P. 363, 409
6.	(F)	P. 315, 317
7.	(C)	P. 353, 374
8.	(G)	P. 360
9.	(B)	P. 409
10.	(F)	P. 369, 409
11.	(B)	P. 320
12.	(F)	P. 320, 323
13.	(C)	P. 320, 373
14.	(F)	P. 391
15.	(C)	P. 391
16.	(F)	P. 391
17.	(B)	P. 377
18.	(G)	P. 377
19.	(A)	P. 409
20.	(J)	P. 409
21.	(A)	P. 409
22.	(G)	P. 369, 409
23.	(B)	P. 320, 385
24.	(G)	P. 385
25.	(C)	P. 320

26.	(G)	P. 317
27.	(D)	P. 371
28.	(H)	P. 371
29.	(D)	P. 371
30.	(H)	P. 371
31.	(B)	P. 360
32.	(G)	P. 409
33.	(B)	P. 409
34.	(F)	P. 391
35.	(D)	P. 377
36.	(J)	P. 377, 391
37.	(A)	P. 360
38.	(G)	P. 320
39.	(A)	P. 404
40.	(J)	P. 371

Test 7: Language Expression

1.	(C)	P. 211
2.	(H)	P. 233
3.	(A)	P. 225
4.	(J)	P. 233
5.	(C)	P. 238
6.	(F)	P. 233
7.	(B)	P. 229
8.	(G)	P. 212
9.	(D)	P. 229
10.	(F)	P. 229
11.	(C)	P. 229
12.	(F)	P. 233
13.	(D)	P. 211
14.	(F)	P. 211
15.	(B)	P. 211
16.	(H)	P. 211
17.	(C)	P. 211

18.	(H)	P. 204
19.	(A)	P. 204
20.	(G)	P. 204
21.	(A)	P. 204
22.	(G)	P. 210
23.	(A)	P. 210
24.	(G)	P. 210
25.	(B)	P. 210
26.	(G)	P. 207, 229
27.	(C)	P. 207, 229
28.	(F)	P. 233
29.	(A)	P. 270
30.	(H)	P. 270
31.	(B)	P. 270
32.	(H)	P. 270
33.	(C)	P. 270
34.	(G)	P. 270
35.	(D)	P. 270
36.	(H)	P. 270
37.	(D)	P. 270
38.	(F)	P. 270
39.	(C)	P. 270
40.	(G)	P. 270

Test 1: Sequences

DETAILED EXPLANATIONS OF ANSWERS

1. **(B)** The number of double-rings increases from the right in each set.

2. **(H)** The figures in the first and third sets move clockwise from left to right. The second set figures move counterclockwise. The fourth set figures are counterclockwise.

3. **(A)** The first figure becomes the last; the other figures move one position to the left.

4. **(J)** The dots in each set move clockwise.

5. **(A)** The sets alternate between one dot outside a square and both dots inside the squares.

6. **(H)** The plus sign moves one position to the left, then starts on the far right.

7. **(B)** The first figure in each set is removed; the second and third figures move one position to the left; a new figure becomes the third.

8. **(G)** The first letter in each set is removed; the second and third letters move one position to the left; a new letter becomes the third.

9. **(D)** Each letter in a set becomes the next letter in the alphabet.

10. **(H)** The last letter in each set is removed; the first and second letters move one position to the right; a new letter becomes the first.

11. **(C)** The second and fourth letters are always I; the third letter becomes the first letter.

12. **(F)** The subscripts decrease by one, from right to left, one at a time.

13. **(D)** The subscripts move clockwise around the letters.

14. **(J)** The subscripts decrease by one, from left to right, one at a time.

15. **(B)** The second number in each set is 4 times the first number; the third number is 6 more than the second number.

16. **(F)** The second number in each set is 6 times the first number; the third number is 11 less than the second number.

17. **(B)** The second number in each set is 2 times the first number; the third number is 9 less than the second number.

18. **(H)** The second number in each set is the first number divided by 10; the third number is the second number divided by 2.

19. **(C)** Each set is made up of consecutive prime numbers. The first number of a set is the second number of the previous set.

20. **(F)** The second number in each set is the first number divided by 3; the third number is 2 times the second number.

Test 2: Analogies

DETAILED EXPLANATIONS
OF ANSWERS

1.   **(D)**   A wing is part of an insect, just as an arm is part of a person (D). Choices (A), hand, and (B), leg, are parts of a person, but the relationship is concerned with the part and then the whole entity. If (A) or (B) were selected, the analogy would be listing two parts, which does not match the first pair of pictures. Choice (C), flower, may be associated with insects, but it has nothing to do with an "arm."

2.   **(H)**   Scissors are used to cut paper, just as a chainsaw is used to cut down trees (H). Choice (F), knife, and (J), saw, are additional objects which may be used in cutting, but they are not the objects cut primarily by chainsaws. Choice (G), barrel, is also an incorrect answer choice.

3.   **(C)**   A mailbox holds letters, just as a change purse holds coins (C). Answer choices (A), stamp, and (B), envelope, are associated with the first pair of pictures, but they have nothing to do with change purse. Choice (D), woman, may carry a change purse, but the relationship is carrier/contents, not carrier/user.

4.   **(H)**   A finger is where one wears a ring, just as a wrist is where one wears a watch, choice (H). Choice (F), hand, would be incorrect since the picture would need to be an object, what is being worn. Answer choice (G), necklace, is not worn on the wrist; it is worn on the neck. Lastly, choice (J), person, would be incorrect since the picture that is required should relate to ring (which, again, is an object).

5.   **(A)**   Both books and newspapers are read, just as both pens and pencils (A) are used for writing. Choice (B), a paintbrush, is used for painting, not writing, and should not be paired with a pen. Choice (C), a crayon, is generally used for drawing or coloring, also not writing. Lastly, a television, choice (D), is watched, it is not used as a writing tool.

6.   **(H)**   An hour glass is an old-fashioned method of telling time, and a digital clock is a modern method of telling time, just as a horse and buggy is an old-fashioned method of transportation and an automobile (H) is a modern method. Choices (F), bicycle, and (J), horse, are both methods of transportation, but they are not modern methods—at least not in comparison to the automobile. A train, choice (G), is a relatively modern mode of transportation, yet notice the picture that it would be compared to—a horse and buggy. Automobile would be a better choice than train in this analogy since automobiles transport nearly the same number of people as horse

and buggies did. Trains are for public transportation, and the selection would be incorrect since they carry a greater number of people.

7. **(C)**   A baby is a newborn human being, just as a kitten is a cat which has recently been born. Answer choice (A), the picture of the girl, is not how you would picture a grown kitten; this choice is incorrect. Choice (B), dog, would only be correct if the first picture were a puppy, but since it is a kitten, this selection is wrong. Do not let choice (D), lion, confuse you. Lions are cats, but a newborn lion would be pictured as a cub—not a kitten.

8. **(F)**   A train conductor operates a train, just as a captain controls a ship (F). Answer choice (G), car, would not be a correct answer choice since the person who ordinarily operates a car is the driver. Answer choice (H), airplane, would also be incorrect since the person who operates an airplane is the pilot. Lastly, motorcycles, answer choice (J), are normally operated by drivers, not captains.

9. **(B)**   A camel and a cactus are living things associated with a desert climate, just as a polar bear and a penguin (B) are living things associated with a polar climate. Answer choice (A), snowflake, can be associated with the polar climate; however, snowflakes are inanimate objects. The picture that completes the analogy would need to be a living thing. Answer choices (C), lizard, and (D), palm tree, are both associated with warmer weather and would not relate with polar bear (which is of a polar climate).

10. **(H)**   A canoe moves through the water by using paddles, just as a sailboat moves through the water by using a sail (H). Answer choices (F), dock, and (G), water, are places that are associated with boats; these two answer choices take no part in the actual movement of the boat through the water. Answer choice (J), yacht, would be incorrect since it is just another type of boat.

11. **(A)**   Just as milk is made directly from cows, a book is made up of paper which is taken from a tree. (D), a branch is part of a tree and (B) and (C) are not made directly from trees.

12. **(G)**   An octopus has eight legs and a spider has eight legs just as a dog has four legs and a horse (G) has four legs. Answer choices (F), eel, (H), rooster, and (J), crab, are all incorrect since none of these animals has four legs like a dog.

13. **(C)**   Just as a lion is found in the name of the flower dandelion, horse is found within the name seahorse. Answer choice (A), flower, would be incorrect since it is not found within the word seahorse. Though similar to the seahorse, answer choices (B), fish, and (D), starfish, would be incorrect since their names are not found in the word seahorse. Be careful not to think that any of these incorrect answers are correct simply because they might be closely associated with the words listed.

14. **(G)**   An author uses a pen to write a book, just as an artist uses a paintbrush to create a painting. Answer choice (F), sculpture, is not usually made with a paintbrush. Artists who make sculptures usually use chisels or other such tools. Answer choice (H), pencil, could be used by both an author and artist; however, the missing picture needs to be what the first picture (the

tool) helps in creating. Answer choice (J), easel, would be incorrect for the same reason; it might also be a tool for an artist, but the picture needs to be the product.

15. **(D)**   A feather pen is an old-fashioned writing implement and a pen is a modern writing implement just as a phonograph is an old-fashioned piece of equipment for playing music and a stereo (D) is a modern piece of equipment for playing music. Answer choice (A), pencil, is incorrect since the missing picture should be an updated version of the first picture. A record, answer choice (B), is an old way of recording music. This answer choice is incorrect since the missing picture needs to be both contemporary and an updated version of the first picture. An old radio, answer choice (C), would be incorrect since the missing second picture needs to be a more contemporary version of the first picture.

16. **(F)**   A boot is placed on a foot just as glasses are placed on the eyes (F). Answer choice (G), hand, would be incorrect since the picture that would complete the analogy needs to be the corresponding place where people put their glasses. Answer choice (H), eye chart, is used to determine whether glasses are needed or not, but it is also not where a person places glasses. Answer choice (J), sock, is associated with boots and feet, but is again, not a location where people normally place their glasses.

17. **(C)**   Just as a cowboy uses a lasso to do his job herding animals, so does a butcher use a cleaver (C) to cut meat and do his job. Answer choice (A), horse, is the usual animal a cowboy rides to herd animals but it is not used by butchers. Answer choice (B), sheep, are a kind of meat to be cut, but, they are not used by butchers as a tool. Lastly, answer choice (D), gun, is incorrect because butchers do not use guns.

18. **(G)**   Glasses for the eyes sounds the same as glasses for drinking, just as the hair on top of a person's head sounds the same as the animal hare (rabbit). Answer choice (F), pony tail, is something someone can do with hair; it is not a homonym for hair. Answer choice (H), eyes, are what glasses are used for, but it is also not a homonym for hair. A pitcher, answer choice (J), is made of glass, but it also does not have anything to do with hair, nor is it a homonym of it.

19. **(C)**   In the same way that a frog is an adult tadpole, a butterfly is an adult caterpillar. Answer choices (A), leaf, and (B), flower, are incorrect since they do not complete the analogy of the butterfly. The missing picture would need to be a young butterfly, or a caterpillar, answer choice (C). Answer choice (D), worm, is a different type of invertebrate.

20. **(G)**   An easel and a paint pallet would be found in an artist's studio just as a test tube and a microscope (G) would be found in a scientist's lab. Answer choice (F), paintbrush, would be found in the art studio, but the picture that is needed to complete the analogy should be science-related. A scientist, answer choice (H), would be found in a laboratory, but the pictures listed in this analogy need to be objects found in the art studio and laboratory, not the people who work there. Answer choice (J), clock, is not the best answer choice because it is too vague of an object. A microscope is a more specific piece of equipment for a science lab, so it is the better choice.

Test 3: Memory

DETAILED EXPLANATIONS OF ANSWERS

1.   **(E)**   Jucinthia means a flower. One way that you may have connected the word jucinthia with its definition is to associate the word jucinthia with the name of a flower that it sounds like. An example would be the flower hyacinth.

2.   **(K)**   Hemin means quickly. One way that you may have connected the word hemin with its definition is to associate the first letter of **h**emin with the first letter of the word hurry. The connection is that if a person is hurrying, he or she is probably doing something quickly.

3.   **(E)**   Lation means small boat. For strategies on how to connect the word lation to its definition, refer to the techniques presented in the Memory Review.

4.   **(G)**   Fumly means clumsy. One way that you may have connected the word fumly with its definition is to connect the words by their similarity of sound. The -umly of **fumly** and -lumsy of **clumsy** sound a bit alike.

5.   **(D)**   Mongrum means a bowl. For strategies on how to connect the word mongrum to its definition, refer to the techniques presented in the Memory Review.

6.   **(K)**   Wrag means to bother. For strategies on how to connect the word wrag to its definition, refer to the techniques presented in the Memory Review.

7.   **(D)**   Knute means crazy. One way that you may have connected the word knute with its definition is to associate the first three letters of **knu**te with the word knucklehead. The connection being that the nickname **knu**cklehead is often given to a person who is thought of as crazy.

8.   **(K)**   Fupish means to be annoying. One way that you may have connected the word fupish with its definition is to associate some of the words in **fupish** with the word **fresh**. The connection is that people who are fresh (or rude) are annoying.

9.   **(E)**   Gortoken means a kind of jewelry. One way that you may have connected the word gortoken with its definition is to find the word token within gor**token**. The connection being that husbands often give a gift of jewelry to their wives as a **token** of their affection.

10. **(J)**   Joib means with care. For strategies on how to connect the word joib to its definition, refer to the techniques presented in the Memory Review.

11. **(E)**   Quoth means an insect. One way that you may have connected the word quoth with its definition is to find a name of an insect that sounds like quoth. A good example would be the insect name moth.

12. **(F)**   Nedro means weak. For strategies on how to connect the word nedro to its definition, refer to the techniques presented in the Memory Review.

13. **(A)**   Bofot means a fruit. For strategies on how to connect the word bofot to its definition, refer to the techniques presented in the Memory Review.

14. **(G)**   Delmot means a chair. For strategies on how to connect the word delmot to its definition, refer to the techniques presented in the Memory Review.

15. **(D)**   Woggle means to cry. One way that you may have connected the word woggle with its definition is to take the first letter of the word **w**oggle and associate it with the word weep. The connection is that to **w**eep is the same as to cry.

16. **(J)**   Trelas means a tree. One way that you may have connected the word trelas to its definition is to match the first three letters in the words **tre**las and **tre**e.

17. **(C)**   Chanic means greedily. For strategies on how to connect the word chanic to its definition, refer to the techniques presented in the Memory Review.

18. **(G)**   Thrats means directions. Perhaps one way that you may have connected the word thrats to its definition is to take the exclamation RATS! from th**rats**. The connection is that if a driver did not have directions and got lost, he'd most likely exclaim, "Rats!!"

19. **(D)**   Pyrile means an article of clothing. For strategies on how to connect the word pyrile with its definition, refer to the techniques offered in the Memory Review.

20. **(H)**   Azin means cunning. For strategies on how to connect the word azin with its definition, refer to the techniques offered in the Memory Review.

Test 4: Verbal Reasoning

DETAILED EXPLANATIONS
OF ANSWERS

1.   **(C)**   Ink. A pen is useless without ink; ink is a necessary part of a pen. Paper (A) is what a pen writes on, but it is not a necessary part to a pen. A pencil and a crayon (B) and (D) are just other writing implements; they are not a part of a pen.

2.   **(F)**   Power. A person cannot use a computer without power; power is a necessary part of a computer. Some computers have game software (G) on them, others do not. Even though some people love computer games, they're not a necessary part of a computer. A computer is useful in many ways, even without a printer (H). A CD-ROM (J) is a good thing to have, but not all computers have one.

3.   **(C)**   Water. Ice is frozen water. Without water there could be no ice; water is a necessary part of ice. Snow and sleet (A) and (B) are different forms of precipitation. They are often associated with ice, but they are not a part of ice. Sometimes ice looks blue (D), but it is not a necessary part of ice.

4.   **(H)**   Paws. Canines have paws; paws are a part of a canine. A hound (F) is a type of canine. They are the same thing, not parts. A cat (G) is just another type of animal; it is not a part of a canine. Some canines wear collars (J), but some do not. There are canines without collars; a collar might be a part of a canine, but it is not a necessary part of a canine.

5.   **(D)**   Beans. Coffee is made from beans; without the beans there would be no coffee. A mug (A) is a coffee container. It is used to hold coffee, but it is not part of the coffee itself. Tea is just another type of beverage; it is not a part of coffee (B). Some people put sugar in their coffee, but one can have coffee without sugar; it is not a necessary part of coffee (C).

6.   **(F)**   Tine. A fork is composed of a few tines. Tines are a necessary part of a fork. A spoon (G) is another type of utensil. It is commonly associated with a fork, but it is not a part of a fork. Some forks are made of metal (H), but not all are, so metal is not a necessary part of a fork. Like the spoon, a chopstick is just another type of utensil, not a part of a fork (J).

7.   **(A)**   Sob. The relationship between whisper/talk/shout is that they show an increasing intensity of the same action. Talk is louder than whisper, and shout is louder than talk. Whimper/cry/sob show the same increase in intensity. Howl and yell, (B) and (C), are other types of actions that a person can do, but they are not the same as whimpering and crying, so they do not show an increase in intensity. Tears (D) are what one would shed when crying or sobbing. This

analogy contains actions or verbs of increasing intensity, not nouns used or produced during the actions.

8. **(H)** Scarf. The relationship between sandals/bathing suit/shorts is that they are summer apparel. Boots/mittens/scarf are winter apparel. All of the items are connected based on their season of use. It may snow during the season one uses boots and mittens, but all of the items need to be clothing items (F). Skis are equipment one uses in the winter; they are not apparel (G). It's true that a shirt is an item of apparel that one wears in the winter, but one wears a shirt in the summer, spring, and fall also, so it is not the best choice for a winter apparel item (J).

9. **(A)** The Vatican. The relationship between the Empire State Building/Mount Rushmore/the Golden Gate Bridge is that they are all famous landmarks in the United States. Likewise, the Colosseum, the Leaning Tower of Pisa, and the Vatican are all famous landmarks in Italy. The Great Wall of China (B) is a famous landmark, but it is not located in the same country as the other two items. The Empire State Building, Mount Rushmore, and the Golden Gate Bridge are all located in the same country, so the second set of words should also have the same relationship. One might take a vacation (C) to all of these places, but the location is a more specific connection. The Statue of Liberty (D) is located in the United States, making a good connection with the first three landmarks, but it is not a match with the Colosseum and the Leaning Tower of Pisa.

10. **(G)** Canal. The relationship between the iris/retina/cornea is that they are all parts of the eye. Lobe/drum/canal are all parts of the ear. All of these things are connected as parts of specific parts of the body. Seeing is what the eye does (F), and hearing is what the ear does (J), but they are not parts. In this analogy, one is looking for parts of the same whole, not the function of the parts. The parts of the eye and the parts of the ear are parts of the body (H), but this is too broad. Canal, a specific part of the ear, like lobe and drum, is a much better answer.

11. **(D)** Desks. The relationship between patients/beds/medicine is that they are things found in a specific place—a hospital. Students/chalk/desks are all things found in a specific place—a school. A hospital (A) is the place where the first 3 items are found; it has nothing to do with the second set of words. Doctors (B) are found in a hospital (with the first set of words), not a school, like the second set of words. Study (C) is an action that students should do in school, but the words listed are items or nouns, not verbs.

12. **(H)** Team. The relationship between man/worker/union is of one's role. A man can become a worker and join a union. A boy can be a player and join a team. Baseball (F) might be one type of team, but the question is of what can the boy be a part? A boy can be part of a team just as the worker can be a part of a union. (G) and (J), batter and catcher, are types of players, but again the answer needs to be what the player can join, not what type of player he might be.

13. **(C)** Joey has at least 5 pets. If you add up the 3 cats and the 2 dogs, you see Joey has at least 5 pets. Even though he doesn't have any birds, he might have more pets, but we know he has at least those 5. The fact that he doesn't have any birds doesn't mean he doesn't like birds (A). There is nothing indicating whether Joey wants more pets (B). He may or may not. Joey's mom is not mentioned, and we have no idea why Joey doesn't have any birds (D).

14. **(F)** Bob's team won the game today. If they hadn't won, they would be out of the tournament, and there would be no reason for Bob to get ready for another game. If they had lost, they would be out of the tournament, and there would be no game to get ready for the next day (G). There is nothing indicating whether Bob enjoys playing (H). We have no reason to suspect that he wants the tournament to end. Basketball is not mentioned, and we have no idea what Bob plans to do in the future, other than play tomorrow's game (J).

15. **(D)** Jack didn't read over the summer. Jack hasn't read anything since 8th grade. It's now September, so he must not have read anything over the summer. We have no idea why Jack didn't read over the summer. We only know that he did not (A). Nothing is mentioned to explain why (B). Also, if he read *Tom Sawyer*, he is able to read (C).

16. **(F)** Jim lost weight. Since the pants that were tight before are loose now and Jim is smiling, it seems likely that he lost some weight. Since Jim was always chubby, and he hadn't worn his favorite pants for a while and was trying them now, it would seem that he was trying them because he hoped they would fit better. He might not like pants that are too tight, but we don't know if he really likes baggy pants (G). There is nothing indicating whether Jim bought any new pants. There is no mention of new pants at all (H). If Jim last wore the pants in the fall because they were too tight, and now they are a little loose, we know he lost weight. We have no reason to suspect that he gained weight (J). Although it is possible that he gained and then lost, there is nothing suggesting this, so it is not the best choice for an answer.

17. **(D)** Mark burnt his mouth. Since the pizza was sizzling and bubbling, we can guess by his reaction that it was too hot and Mark burnt his mouth. There is nothing indicating whether Mark will ever eat pizza again (A). Although it is possible, we have no reason to suspect that he will not eat pizza again. Both (B) and (C) might be true, but the sizzling and bubbling cheese make (D) a stronger choice for an answer. Also, there isn't really anything suggesting the waiter made a mistake.

18. **(G)** Reftmrepl. Look at speffblik meaning taller and reftblik meaning shorter. Blik must represent "er." That leaves speff to mean tall and reft to mean short. Look at speffmrepl meaning tallest. Mrepl must represent the suffix meaning "est," since speff means tall. So reftmrepl must mean shortest.

19. **(A)** Weskinheronni. Look at ablahhamen meaning anytime and weskinhamen meaning sometime. Hamen must mean time. That leaves ablah to mean any and weskin to mean some. Look at ablahhamen, meaning anytime, and ablahheronni, meaning anywhere. Ablah must mean any. That leaves herronni to mean where. So weskinheronni must mean somewhere.

20. **(H)** A sailboat is a smaller boat and a yacht is a larger boat, but they are both boats. If maskerintinni means sailboat and maskeringruse means yacht, maskerin must be the root meaning of a type of boat. Tinni is a suffix indicating a smaller form of the root, a smaller boat or sail boat. Gruse is a suffix indicating a larger form of the root, a larger boat or yacht. Therefore, if an abaertinni is a house, or a smaller form of a place to live, abaerngruse must be a larger form of the root, or a larger place to live, a mansion.

Test 5: Reading Comprehension

DETAILED EXPLANATIONS
OF ANSWERS

1. **(A)**   The last sentence of the first paragraph says that the Shakers were a religious community. Although the Shakers made furniture they were not a furniture company (B). They did a shaking dance but were not a dance troupe (C). Although the founders came from England and called the leader "Mother Ann," they weren't a family (D).

2. **(H)**   The second paragraph explains that the group was called the Shakers because of the dance they did. Shaker furniture is called that because it was made by the Shakers (F), not the other way around. Both (G) and (H) are true but are unrelated to the name Shakers.

3. **(B)**   The last paragraph discusses Shaker furniture and its emphasis on quality and simplicity. The passage states that Shaker furniture was not elaborately decorated (A). The passage does not mention cost (C) and (D).

4. **(J)**   The passage discusses the Shakers and their furniture. It doesn't try to recruit new members (F), or explain why the Shakers no longer exist (G). Although the passage talks about furniture, it does not mention quilts (H).

5. **(B)**   The author seems to have a strong interest in advising teachers; many sentences and clauses in the passage begin with "Teachers must..." and "Teachers should..." The passage does not address students (A) or parents (C). Because the passage is advising teachers on how to run their classrooms, the advice does not really apply to substitute teachers (D), who don't have their own classes.

6. **(G)**   "Cognizant" means aware. Ignorant (J) is the opposite of cognizant. Choices (F) and (H) are unrelated.

7. **(D)**   In this passage the author is arguing that teachers should help their students develop their powers of free speech. The passage does say that children should be involved in the decisions and problem solving of the classroom, but children making the classroom rules (A) and solving their own arguments (B) are not the main focus of the passage. The passage does not mention voting (C).

8. **(G)**   In the second sentence of the passage the author states that free speech has devel-

oped over time, not the opposite (F). The author doesn't say that free speech only exists in the U.S. (H). The entire passage argues that free speech can be taught in the classroom (J).

9. **(C)** The first two sentences of the passage establish that research and investigation are the most important parts of a case. There is no evidence for choice (A) in the passage. The judge does receive a trial memorandum (B), but this has nothing to do with the winning or losing of a case. The passage does mention strong and weak points (D), but this is not why cases are won or lost before court.

10. **(H)** This passage discusses the work done by lawyers before they present the case. It does not mention biases of the legal system (F) and (G), nor does it cover the work lawyers do once they are in court (J).

11. **(C)** The passage does not say that lawyers meet with the judge before the case is in court. The passage does describe reading books and articles (A), meeting with witnesses (B), and considering calling expert witnesses (D).

12. **(J)** This passage is for the average public because it explains, in non-technical language, what lawyers do to prepare a case. Lawyers (F) and judges (G) would not need this process explained to them. The passage does not give advice or instructions to the reader, making it unlikely that the passage is intended for those involved in lawsuits (H).

13. **(C)** "Dissonance" most nearly means disagreement. Agreement (D) is the opposite. Happiness (A) and anger (B) are unrelated to dissonance.

14. **(F)** The first sentence of the second paragraph lists learning theorists and what they stress: humanists stress the affective domain (F), behaviorists stress behavior (G), and cognitivists stress cognition (H). Dissonance (J), discussed a few lines later, is not a type of learning theorist.

15. **(C)** This passage is probably aimed at teachers because it explains different theories while assuming some knowledge of the subject. It also gives advice on what the teacher should do. Learning theorists (A) would not need the explanations in this paragraph. This passage would not be for language theorists (B) because it discusses learning theory, not language theory. The reading level of this passage is too difficult for students (D), and it also describes what teachers should do to help students, not what the students themselves should do.

16. **(H)** The author seems to feel quite strongly about the ideas he or she is presenting in the passage. The first paragraph is about how important this topic is, and this importance is stressed in the second paragraph as well. The author of this paragraph is arguing for a certain kind of teaching; therefore, he or she is interested in the topic (F), has a strong opinion about it (J), and has definite ideas about how teachers should teach (G).

17. **(C)** The author gives the topic of the passage from the very first sentence. The passage

is about the role of imitation in learning to talk, but does not describe how children learn to talk (A), first words (B), or how to teach a child to talk (D).

18. **(J)** The author wrote this passage to explain how imitation works for a child learning to talk. The passage does not give directions to parents (F) or teachers (G). We can infer from the passage that it is very important that children do imitate their parents; therefore, (H) is incorrect.

19. **(B)** The last sentence of the passage says that a child only imitates structures that he or she has already come up with on her or his own. Thus, imitation is not as simple a behavior as researchers had thought. It seems that a child must know or understand a structure to imitate it; therefore, (A) and (C) are false. In the last sentence, spontaneous speech is set up as the opposite of imitation (D).

20. **(F)** The passage does not say that a child adds to what an adult has said. Slobin and Welsh call the imitation a reconstruction (G). Brown and Bellugi say that imitation resembles spontaneous speech (H). Shipley says that imitation aids the child's comprehension (J).

21. **(B)** The second paragraph explains that assisted reading makes slow readers read faster and lets them concentrate on figuring out the meaning of the reading and does not hurt slow readers (A). It does give them time to understand what they are reading (C). Assisted reading eases slow readers and does not put pressure on them (D).

22. **(G)** Assisted reading is defined in the first paragraph. The teacher does not give definitions (F) or read to the students (J). Readings with illustrations (H) are not called assisted readings.

23. **(D)** The second paragraph says that "assisted reading lets the reader move along without being responsible for every language unit." Assisted reading does speed up reading (A), take, pressure off the students (B), and let, the students concentrate on meaning (C).

24. **(H)** The passage says that beginning readers can make sense of a reading by speeding up the reading so that it sounds more like language. Reading slowly (F), concentrating on every word (G), and focusing on small language units (J) are all problems for the beginning reader.

25. **(A)** The second sentence of the second paragraph gives the definition of "individual language units." Paragraphs (B) and stories and books (D) are the opposite of individual language units. A unit in a language textbook (C) is unrelated to the topic.

26. **(G)** The answer to this question is found in the very first sentence of the passage: the First Amendment outlaws any laws which prohibit freedom of religion. Outlawing freedom of religion is the opposite (F). Choices (H) and (J) are wrong because they are about free speech, not freedom of religion.

27. **(B)** The passage states that one critic of the First Amendment has called it the work of an infidel. The statements in choices (A), (C), and (D) are not included in the passage.

28. **(F)** "Reaffirmed" most nearly means "agreed with". "Disagreed with" (G) is the opposite and "ignored" (H) and "celebrated" (J) are unrelated.

29. **(C)** The statement by the Supreme Court Justice calls the First Amendment a metaphor (D), a barrier (B), and a useless guide (A), which is the opposite of a clear guide (C).

30. **(F)** The second to last sentence states that threats to religious freedom still exist (F). Choice (G) is disproved in the last sentence, which says that not everyone accepts the separation of church and state. This passage shows that there is still interest in the separation of church and state (H) and it is against government control of religion (J).

31. **(A)** The passage concentrates on showing that child labor will only be ended through protest and legal enactment, not by employers or philanthropists. The passage argues that children should be given the chance to go to school (B). The passage does not mention night school (C) or what schools should teach children (D).

32. **(J)** All of the statements about why trade unionists agitate for child labor laws are in the passage (F), (G), and (H).

33. **(C)** The passage mentions several times that children should be in school, and it is clearly stated in the last sentence of the passage. The passage does not say that children are irresponsible (A). Although one of the arguments the author uses in her case against child labor in America is that England has already abolished it, this is not her reason for trying to end child labor (B).

34. **(H)** The author does not say that child laborers take jobs away from adults, but she does say that it demoralizes the trades that employ children (G). She says that it takes energy away from growth (F) and that the U.S. should abolish child labor as England has (J).

35. **(B)** "Ameliorating" means improving or bettering. Choices (A), (C), and (D) are unrelated.

36. **(G)** The first sentence of the passage defines comedy as having a happy ending. A comedy may be funny (F), absurd (H), or have funny characters (J), but it doesn't have to in order to be a comedy.

37. **(A)** The first sentence of the second paragraph says a farce is a low comedy (B) that depends upon exaggeration (A). A farce does not have to make people think (C) or be funny (D).

38. **(H)** Satire is defined in the second paragraph of the passage as implying that humanity and human institutions need to be reformed. Although a satire is a form of high comedy, a high comedy is not necessarily a satire (F). Low comedies (G) and predictable comedies (J) are not called satires.

39. **(B)** The last few sentences of the passage explain that the more believable a comedy is,

the less distanced from it an audience feels. Therefore, the audience feels more involved in the action and less protected from the conflicts on stage. The more an audience cares about what happens to the characters, the less funny (A) and less harmless (C) the play seems to the audience. The passage does not discuss the "believability" of Shakespeare's comedies (D).

40. **(F)**   This passage names different types of comedies and explains what defines them and how they function for the audience. The passage does not measure the enjoyability of comedies and tragedies (G). The passage points out that Shakespeare's comedies have been criticized for their appeal to laughter (H). Although the passage explains the concept of figurative distance (J), this is not the passage's main purpose.

Test 6: Mathematics Concepts and Applications

DETAILED EXPLANATIONS OF ANSWERS

1. **(D)** Subtract 8 from both sides of the equation: $4q + 8 - 8 = 16 - 8$; so $4q = 8$. Divide both sides by 4: $\frac{4q}{4} = \frac{8}{4}$; so $q = 2$.

2. **(H)** Mr. Matthews' total earnings for the first 4 days was ($125 + $115 + $118 + $123) = $481. His earnings for Friday must be $591 - $481 = $110.

3. **(A)** Mary's total test score for the 5 tests is $88 \times 5 = 440$. The subtotal for the first 4 tests is $(82 + 93 + 79 + 90) = 344$. The missing score must be $440 - 344 = 96$.

4. **(J)** The 6 is two places to the right of the decimal point. So it is in the hundredths position, that is, 6 hundredths.

5. **(D)** In order to recover the original number, we must undo the effect of multiplication, by dividing $8.47265 \div 100 = 0.0847265$. Now we must perform the division that Martha should have performed: $0.0847265 \div 100 = 0.000847265$.

6. **(F)** In order to recover the original number, let us undo the effect of addition: $15 - 34 = -19$. Now we can perform the subtraction, which Dwayne should have performed: $-19 - 34 = -53$.

7. **(C)** First, find $\sqrt{36}$: $\sqrt{36} = 6$. The correct order is 36, $\sqrt{36}$, 3.6.

8. **(G)** Tamara's total earnings for the 20 hours is $4.75 \times 20 = 95.

9. **(B)** $-2u + 3v = -2(5) + 3(3) = -10 + 9 = -1$.

10. **(F)** $(3xy)^2 = 3^2 x^2 y^2 = 9(-3)^2(2)^2 = 9 \times 9 \times 4 = 324$.

11. **(B)** The number of books in the 6 full boxes is $6 \times 9 = 54$. The total number of books that Raymond received is $54 + 2 = 56$.

12. **(F)** The total number of marbles in the 7 full boxes is $7 \times 15 = 105$. Each of the 12

students would receive $105 \div 12 = 8$, remainder 9. The number of additional marbles that Mrs. White must collect is $12 - 9 = 3$.

13. **(C)** Let n represent the smaller of the two multiples of 7. Then the next larger multiple of 7 must be $n + 7$, and the sum of these two multiples of 7 is $n + (n + 7)$ or $2n + 7$. The square of 6 is $6 \times 6 = 36$. Since $2n + 7$ is 1 less than 36, then: $2n + 7 = 36 - 1$ or $2n + 7 = 35$. Let us add -7 to both sides of the equation: $2n + 7 - 7 = 35 - 7$, or $2n = 28$. Divide both sides by 2: $\dfrac{2n}{2} = \dfrac{28}{2}$. So the smaller multiple of 7 is $n = 14$ and the larger one is $n + 7 = 14 + 7 = 21$.

14. **(F)** The whole angle below $\overline{AB}$ measures $180°$. So $2x + 7x = 180$, or $9x = 180$. (We can safely ignore the degree sign.) Divide both sides of the equation by 9: $\dfrac{9x}{9} = \dfrac{180}{9}$, which shows that $x = 20$.

15. **(C)** The sum of the measures of the exterior angle ABE and the (unmarked) interior angle ABC is $180°$. (Angles ABE and ABC are supplementary.) So the measure of interior angle ABC is $180° - 148° = 32°$. The sum of interior angles BAC, ACB, and ABC is $40° + v° + 32° = 180°$. So $v + 72 = 180$ (we shall ignore the degree sign). Add -72 to both sides: $v + 72 - 72 = 180 - 72$, or $v = 108$.

16. **(F)** When two straight lines intersect at one point, the vertically opposite angles so formed are congruent. Hence, $y = 42$.

17. **(B)** Recall that the sum of the measures of any two sides of a triangle must be greater than the measure of the third side. The straw shown in (B) is the only one that can be combined with the two in set 1 to meet this requirement. (D) 37 cm would be too big for the triangle.

18. **(G)** Pythagoras' theorem states that the sum of the squares of the measures of the two shorter sides of a right triangle equals the square of the measure of the longest side. The stick in (G) is the only one that can be grouped with the two in set 1 to meet this requirement.

19. **(A)** If we doubled n and added 7 to the result, you would obtain $2n + 7$. So $2n + 7 = 35$.

20. **(J)** The total age of the first 16 students is $16 \times y = 16y$. The total age of the 17 students is $16y + 9$.

21. **(A)** Multiply each term in $4x - 1$ by each term in $2x + 5$, and collect terms: $(4x - 1)(2x + 5) = 8x^2 + 18x - 5$.

22. **(G)** $(3 + 5) \times 15 - 3 = 8 \times 15 - 3 = 120 - 3 = 117$.

23. **(B)** First calculate 35% of 140: $\dfrac{35 \times 140}{100} = 49$. Next, calculate 16% of 50: $\dfrac{16 \times 50}{100} = 8$. Finally, multiply 49 by 8: $49 \times 8 = 392$.

24. **(G)**   135% of 80 is $\dfrac{135 \times 80}{100} = 108$.

25. **(C)**   The total number of pencils needed is $22 \times 6 = 132$. At 24 pencils per full box, the number of boxes that will hold 132 pencils must be $132 \div 24 = 5.5$. Since pencils are sold only in full boxes, Mrs. Archibald must buy 6 boxes.

26. **(G)**   First, calculate the improvement for each athlete (all figures are in inches): George—$90 - 87 = 3$, Maria—$88 - 83 = 5$, Tricia—$82 - 79 = 3$, and Victor—$93 - 91 = 2$. From these figures, we see that Maria showed the most improvement.

27. **(D)**   Begin by computing the athlete's total scores (all figures are in inches): Frank—$92 + 87 = 179$, George—$87 + 90 = 177$, Maria—$83 + 88 = 171$, and Victor—$91 + 93 = 184$. These figures indicate that Victor jumped the longest distance. (Notice that it was not necessary to compute the actual averages, since the ranking would remain unchanged if we divided all the totals by 2 to find the averages.)

28. **(H)**   The average score for the 7 athletes in the first round is $(88 + 92 + 87 + 75 + 83 + 79 + 91) \div 7 = 595 \div 7 = 85$.

29. **(D)**   First calculate the average score, with Linda's score included, for the second round: $(88 + 87 + 90 + 67 + 88 + 82 + 93) \div 7 = 595 \div 7 = 85$. Next, compute the average score, without Linda's score: $(88 + 87 + 90 + 88 + 82 + 93) \div 6 = 528 \div 6 = 88$. (Remember that, without Linda, there are only 6 athletes.) So the increase in the average score is $88 - 85 = 3$ in.

30. **(H)**   Begin by computing the total score for each semester: total score for semester 1 — $64 \times 5 = 320$, total score for semester 2 — $55 \times 3 = 165$, and total score for semester 3 — $59 \times 4 = 236$. The total score for semesters 1, 2, and 3 is $320 + 165 + 236 = 721$. Since Brenda took $5 + 3 + 4 = 12$ tests, her average score for the 3 semesters is $721 \div 12 = 60.083$, which can be rounded to 60.

31. **(B)**   Multiply 0.125 by 1,000,000: $0.125 \times 1,000,000 = 125,000$.

32. **(G)**   Add -6 to both sides of the equation: $5y + 6 - 6 = 51 - 6$, so $5y = 45$. Divide both sides by 6: $\dfrac{5y}{5} = \dfrac{45}{5}$, so $y = 9$.

33. **(B)**   The graph intersects the y-axis at 3 points from the 0 position and the x-axis at 4 points from the 0 position. Observing that the line is left-inclined (running from upper left to lower right), we see that the slope of the line is $-\dfrac{3}{4}$. (The slope is negative because the line is left-inclined.)

34. **(F)**   (The numbering of the angles only serves to indicate precisely which angles to focus on, and the information that *ABCDEF* is a regular hexagon is irrelevant.) It would be wise,

however, to make use of the <u>hint</u>, which reminds us that concave hexagon *ABCDEO* consists of the 4 triangles *AOB*, *BOC*, *COD*, and *DOE*. The sum of the measures of the interior angles of hexagon *ABCDEO* must equal the sum of the measures of the interior angles of triangles *AOB*, *BOC*, *COD*, and *DOE*. Remember that the sum of the measures of the three interior angles of any triangle is 180°. So the sum of the interior angles of these 4 triangles is 180° × 4 = 720°.

35. **(D)**   Since the 6 faces of any cube are congruent, their areas must also be congruent. So, to compute the area of the three visible faces of a cube, we need only to compute the area of one face and multiply it by 3: The area of 1 face is 8 cm × 8 cm = 64 cm². So the area of 3 faces is 3 × 64 cm² = 192 cm².

36. **(J)**   The boundary of the composite picture is a rectangle and the unshaded regions are semicircles. Compute the area of the whole rectangle: The total width of the rectangle is 5 cm + 5 cm = 10 cm. So the area of the rectangle is 10 cm × 10 cm = 100 cm². The radius of each semicircle is 5 cm. The combined areas of the two semicircles would be equal to the area of one full circle with the same radius. Thus, the combined areas of the semicircles is πr^2 = 3.14 × 5² = 3.14 × 25 = 78.5 cm². Hence, the area of the shaded region is 100 cm² – 78.5 cm² = 21.5 cm².

37. **(A)**   If 1 mile equals 1.6 kilometers, then 400 miles = 1.6 × 400 = 640 kilometers.

38. **(G)**   If 1.5 in. represents 45 miles, then 30 in. must represent $\dfrac{30 \times 45}{1.5}$ = 900 miles.

39. **(A)**   The quickest way to compute Adrian's weight loss between January and August is to subtract his weight in August from his weight in January: 200 lbs. – 175 lbs. = 25 lbs. (Of course, we could also find the overall weight loss by subtracting the intermediate losses and adding the intermediate gains. You can verify that this would yield the same result but waste time.)

40. **(J)**   The fastest way to compute Adrian's average weight loss between February and July is to subtract his weight in July from his weight in February and divide by 5: (195 lbs. – 165 lbs.) ÷ 5 = 30 ÷ 5 = 6 lbs. To check this shortcut, do this (ignore the pound sign; make gains + and losses –):

Period	*Weight change*
February to March	195 – 180 = – 15
March to April	180 – 190 = + 10
April to May	190 – 170 = – 20
May to June	170 – 185 = + 15
June to July	185 – 165 = – 20
Total weight change	– 30

So, the average weight loss = 30 lbs. ÷ 5 = 6 lbs., as obtained by the shortcut method.

Test 7: Language Expression

DETAILED EXPLANATIONS OF ANSWERS

1. **(C)**   The verb must be past tense to agree with "returned."

2. **(H)**   The relationship is cause and effect.

3. **(A)**   The statement implies more than two flowers being compared.

4. **(J)**   The relationship is cause and effect.

5. **(C)**   The pronoun "your" is used for possession.

6. **(F)**   The sentence implies that the outcome was not to be expected, so "although" is the correct choice.

7. **(B)**   (A) is a run-on sentence; (C) and (D) are not sentences.

8. **(G)**   (F) is impossibly awkward, (H) is not a sentence, and (J) is a run-on sentence.

9. **(D)**   (A) is impossibly awkward, (B) is a comma splice, and (C) is not a sentence.

10. **(F)**   (G) is a run-on sentence; (H) and (J) are not sentences.

11. **(C)**   (A) is a run-on sentence; (B) and (D) are not sentences.

12. **(F)**   (G) and (J) are not sentences, and (H) is a run-on sentence.

13. **(D)**   (A), (B), and (C) have conflicting tenses within the sentence.

14. **(F)**   (G) has conflicting tenses; (H) contains "to got," and (J) contains "have took."

15. **(B)**   (A) contains "brang," (C) contains "shouldn't of," and (D) has conflicting tenses.

16. **(H)**   (F) contains "taked," and (G) and (J) have conflicting tenses.

17. **(C)**   (A) contains "should of," and (B) and (D) contain conflicting tenses.

18. **(H)**   "Howie" is the simple subject.

19. **(A)**   "House" is the simple subject.

20. **(G)** "Soldiers" is the simple subject.

21. **(A)** "Mailman" is the simple subject.

22. **(G)** "Notice" is the simple predicate.

23. **(A)** "Sat" is the simple predicate.

24. **(G)** "Waved" is the simple predicate.

25. **(B)** "Is" is the simple predicate.

26. **(G)** (F) is in the wrong sequence; (H) sounds as if he is eating and driving, as does (J).

27. **(C)** (A) is in the wrong sequence; (B) sounds as though Cara bought the pizza, and (D) rambles.

28. **(F)** (G) infers an exception; (H) gives no cause and effect, and (J) makes no sense.

29. **(A)** The paragraph contrasts the concerns of the northern and southern states.

30. **(H)** The paragraph stresses that the circulatory system carries things through the body.

31. **(B)** The focus is only on poisonous plants, and it stresses self-defense.

32. **(H)** Only (H) focuses on service to people.

33. **(C)** Only (C) explores the meaning of the Greek words that form democracy.

34. **(G)** Only (G) addresses behaviors that separate civilized from uncivilized people.

35. **(D)** The focus of the paragraph is ways to kill buffalo, and sentence 4 is on uses for the meat.

36. **(H)** The focus of the paragraph is reasons for the pyramid's structure and placement, and sentence 3 simply states dimensions.

37. **(D)** The focus of the paragraph is Archimedes and his discoveries, while sentence 4 is on a modern application of buoyancy.

38. **(F)** Only (F) is related to what happens at the processing plant.

39. **(C)** The focus of the paragraph is the emergence of the Molly Maguires in the United States and on their involvement in mines. (A) and (B) are interesting but unrelated facts, and (D) is out of chronological sequence.

40. **(G)** (F) and (H) are unrelated to Picasso's use of cubism in the indicated painting. (J) is too general and poorly related to this paragraph.

COOP/
HSPT

HSPT

Optional Tests

HSPT OPTIONAL TESTS

Depending on the school to which you are applying, you may or may not have to take one of three optional tests on the HSPT. These tests include a wide range of questions which test your knowledge in Science, Mechanics, or the Catholic Religion. It is important to remember that you will only have to take one of these.

While your score on the optional test is not included on your exam score as a whole, your school will receive a report which explains your overall performance on the exam, be it the Science, Mechanical Aptitude, or Catholic Religion exam. Additionally, this information can be used in class placement or curriculum development.

COOP/ HSPT

CHAPTER 8

General Science Review

Chapter 8

GENERAL SCIENCE REVIEW

    I.   **LIFE SCIENCE**

   II.   **PHYSICAL SCIENCE**

  III.   **EARTH SCIENCE**

General Science, as its name implies, is a broad survey of the most important concepts from the three basic fields of science: life science, physical science, and earth science. This review is not meant as a textbook or comprehensive study of any given topic; rather, its purpose is to remind readers of topics and concepts that are normally taught in science courses in junior and senior high school science classes.

Each of the basic science fields contains major specializations, as follows:

life science—biology, ecology, human health

physical science—measurement, chemistry, physics

earth science—astronomy, geology, meteorology, oceanography

I. LIFE SCIENCE

BIOLOGY

Biology is the study of living things. Living things are differentiated from nonliving things by the ability to perform all the following life activities at some point in a normal life span:

Life Activity	Function
food getting	procurement of food through eating, absorption, or photosynthesis
respiration	exchange of gases
excretion	elimination of wastes
growth and repair	increase in size over part or all of a life span, repair of damaged tissue
movement	willful movement of a portion of a living thing's body, or direction of growth in a particular direction
response	reaction to events or things in the environment
secretion	production and distribution of chemicals that aid digestion, growth, metabolism, etc.
reproduction	the making of new living things similar to the parent organism(s)

It is important to note that living things *must*, during a typical life span, be able to perform all these activities. It is quite common for non-living things to perform one or more of these activities (for example, robots—movement, response, repair; crystals—growth).

Cells

Cells are the basic structural units of living things. A cell is the smallest portion of a living thing that can, by itself, be considered living. Plant cells and animal cells, though generally similar, are distinctly different because of the unique plant structures, cell walls, and chloroplasts.

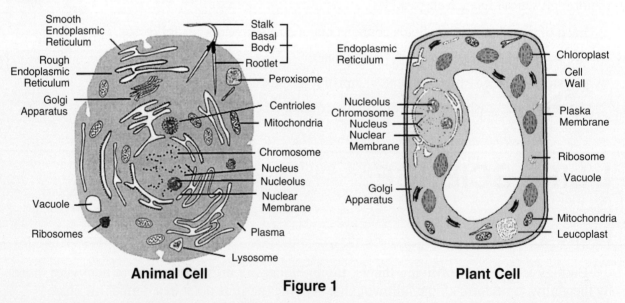

Figure 1

Cells are made of several smaller structures, called organelles, which are surrounded by cell fluid, or cytoplasm. The function of several cell structures, including organelles, is listed below:

Cell Structure	Function
cell membrane	controls movement of materials into and out of cells
cell wall	gives rigid structure to plant cells
chloroplast	contains chlorophyll, which enables green plants to make their own food
cytoplasm	jellylike substance inside of a cell
mitochondrion	liberates energy from glucose in cells for use in cellular activities
nucleus	directs cell activities; holds DNA (genetic material)
ribosome	makes proteins from amino acids
vacuole	stores materials in a cell

There are many processes that cells perform to maintain essential life activities. Several of these processes, related to cell metabolism, are described below:

Process	Organelle	Life Activity
diffusion	cell membrane	food getting, respiration, excretion
osmosis	cell membrane	food getting, excretion
phagocytosis	cell membrane	food getting
photosynthesis	chloroplasts	food getting
respiration (aerobic)	mitochondria	provides energy
fermentation	mitochondria	provides energy

(Metabolism is the sum of chemical processes in living things.)

Cells need to move materials into their structures to get energy and to grow. The cell membrane allows certain small molecules to flow freely across it. This flow of chemicals from areas of high concentration to areas of low concentration is called diffusion. Osmosis is diffusion of water across a semipermeable membrane. Particles too large to be passed through the cell membrane may be engulfed by the cell membrane and stored in vacuoles until they can be digested. This engulfing process is called phagocytosis.

All cells need energy to survive. Sunlight energy can be made biologically available by converting to chemical energy during photosynthesis. Photosynthesis is carried out in the chloroplasts of green cells. Chlorophyll, the pigment found in chloroplasts, catalyzes (causes or accelerates) the photosynthesis reaction that turns carbon dioxide and water into glucose (sugar) and oxygen.

$$6CO_2 + 6H_2O \xrightarrow[\text{chlorophyll}]{\text{sunlight}} C_6H_{12}O_6 + 6O_2$$

carbon dioxide   water   glucose   oxygen

Sunlight and chlorophyll are needed for the reaction to occur. Chlorophyll, because it is a catalyst, is not consumed in the reaction and may be used repeatedly.

The term "respiration" has two distinct meanings in the field of biology. Respiration, the life activity, is the exchange of gases in living things. Respiration, the metabolic process, is the release of energy from sugars for use in life activities. Respiration, the metabolic process, occurs on the cellular level only. Respiration, the life activity, may occur at the cell, tissue, organ, or system level, depending on the complexity of the organism involved.

All living things get their energy from the digestion (respiration) of glucose (sugar). Respiration may occur with oxygen (aerobic respiration) or without oxygen (anaerobic respiration or fermentation). When respiration is referred to, it generally means aerobic respiration.

$$\text{aerobic respiration: } C_6H_{12}O_6 + 6O_2 \longrightarrow 6CO_2 + 6H_2O + \text{energy}$$

$$\text{fermentation: } C_6H_{12}O_6 \longrightarrow CO_2 + \text{alcohol} + \text{energy}$$

Aerobic respiration occurs in most plant and animal cells. Fermentation occurs in yeast cells and other cells in the absence of oxygen. Fermentation by yeast produces the alcohol in alcoholic beverages and the gases that make yeast-raised breads light and fluffy.

Classification

All known living things are grouped in categories according to shared physical traits. The process of grouping organisms is called classification. Carl Linné, also known as Linneaus, devised the classification system, binomial nomenclature, used in biology today. In the Linneaus system, all organisms are given a two-word name (binomial). The name given consists of a genus (e.g., Canis) and a species (e.g., lupus) designation. Genus designations are always capitalized and occur first in the binomial. Species designations usually start with a lowercase letter and occur second. Binomials are usually underlined or italicized, e.g., *Genus species,* or *Homo sapiens,* or *Canis lupus*.

There exists just one binomial for each organism throughout the scientific community. Similar genera of organisms are grouped into families. Families are grouped into orders, orders are grouped into classes, classes are grouped into phyla, and phyla are grouped into kingdoms. The seven basic levels of classification, listed from the largest groupings to the smallest, are: kingdom, phylum, class, order, family, genus, species.

Most biologists recognize five biological kingdoms today, the Animals, Plants, Fungi, Protists, and Monerans. Most living things are classified as plants or animals.

Monerans (e.g., bacteria, blue-green algae) are the simplest life forms known. They consist of single-celled organisms without a membrane-bound cell nucleus. Blue-green algae make their own food by photosynthesis; bacteria are consumers or parasites.

Protists (e.g., protozoa, single-celled algae) are single-celled organisms having cell nuclei. Protozoa (e.g., amoeba, paramecia) are predators or decomposers. Algae (e.g., Euglena, diatoms) are producers and utilize photosynthesis.

Fungi (e.g., molds, mushrooms, yeast) are multicellular decomposers that reproduce through spores. (Yeast constitute an exception to the multicellular makeup of most fungi in that they are single-celled and reproduce through budding.) Fungi are the only multicellular decomposers that are not mobile.

Plants

Plants are multicellular organisms that make their own food through photosynthesis. Plants are divided into two phyla, the Bryophyta and Tracheophyta.

Bryophytes are nonvascular plants. They lack true roots and woody tissues. Bryophytes (e.g., moss, liverworts, and multicellular algae) live in water or in damp areas and reproduce by spores. Bryophytes do not grow very tall because they lack the structural support of vascular tissue.

Tracheophytes are vascular plants. They have woody tissues and roots. The woody tissues in vascular plants enable them to grow quite large. The roots of vascular plants enable them to find water even in soils that are dry at the surface.

Tracheophytes are divided into three classes, Filicinae, Gymno-spermae, and Angiospermae. Filicinae are ferns. They reproduce by spores. Gymnosperms (e.g., spruce, pines) are plants whose seeds form in cones. The seeds are unprotected. Angiosperms (e.g., apple trees, grass) are plants whose seeds are protected by fruits or other structures. Angiosperms are further divided into monocots or dicots, based on seed structure. Cotyledons are food storage structures in seed embryos. Monocots (e.g. grasses, bananas) have one cotyledon per seed. Dicots (e.g. oak trees, pumpkins) have two cotyledons per seed.

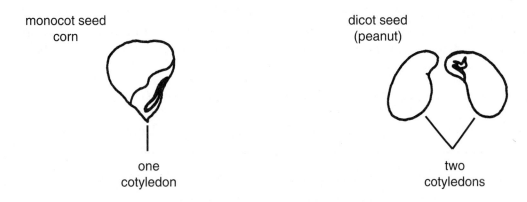

monocot seed
corn

one
cotyledon

dicot seed
(peanut)

two
cotyledons

Figure 2

Animals

Animals are multicellular organisms that cannot make their own food but can move themselves about. The animal kingdom is split into 26 phyla. Some of the phyla are listed below:

Phylum	Examples	Traits
Porifera	sponges	no organs, pores in body let water flow through, bringing food and taking away wastes
Coelenterata (Cnidaria)	jelly fish, corals, hydra	no organs, body sac-like, stinging cells to capture prey
Platyhelminthes	flatworms, flukes, tapeworms	single opening to body, true organs, often parasitic to humans
Aschelminthes (Nematoda)	roundworms	two openings to body, may be parasitic
Mollusca	snails, octopus, clams	gills, open circulatory system, produce shells (internal or external)
Annelida	earthworms, leeches	closed circulatory system
Arthropoda	spiders, insects, crabs	jointed exoskeletons, jointed legs
Echinodermata	starfish, sea urchins	plate-like internal skeleton, tube feet, spiny or knobby surface
Chordata	fish, birds, mammals, reptiles	notochord (primitive cartilaginous spine) and gills present at some point in development, hollow dorsal nerve cord

The arthropod and chordate phyla deserve special note. The arthropods include ten classes, which include the arachnidae, insecta, and crustaceae. Arachnids include spiders and ticks. These animals have two body regions and eight legs. Insects have three body regions and six legs. They include an incredible variety of animals; for example, grasshoppers, flies, beetles, and butterflies are typical insects. Crustaceans have two body regions and ten legs and live mostly in water. Crabs, crayfish, and lobsters are all crustaceans.

The chordate phylum has three subphyla, one of which is the vertebrata, or vertebrates. Vertebrates have an internal skeleton which includes a spine made up of vertebrae. The spine protects the dorsal nerve cord (spinal cord). Animals without spines (all phyla except Chordata) are called invertebrates.

Vertebrates

Eight classes of vertebrates exist, though four are often spoken of collectively as "fish."

Class	Examples	Traits
Agnatha	jawless fish, no scales, cartilaginous skeleton	lampreys, hagfish
Placodermi	hinged jaws	extinct
Chondrichthyes	cartilaginous skeleton, no scales, jaws	sharks, skates, rays

(continued)

	Osteichthyes	bony skeleton, scales, jaws	bass, trout, goldfish
F	Amphibia	aquatic eggs and larvae, terrestrial adults	frogs, toads, salamanders
I	Reptilia	terrestrial eggs and adults, cold-blooded	turtles, snakes, lizards
S			
H	Aves	feathers, warm-blooded, external egg development	eagles, ducks, pigeons
	Mammalia	fur, milk-producing, internal egg development, warm-blooded	rats, horses, humans

Most vertebrates are cold-blooded. Their bodies do not generate heat, so their body temperature is determined by their environment. Fish are cold-blooded animals with gills for respiration and fins for movement. Reptiles are cold-blooded animals with lungs for respiration and legs for movement (except for snakes). Amphibians are cold-blooded animals that start life with gills and fins, but then change. The change in form that amphibians undergo as they mature is called metamorphosis. Adult amphibians have lungs and legs.

Birds (Aves) and mammals are warm-blooded. Their bodies generate heat. Birds and mammals can also sweat to lower body temperature. Birds are covered with feathers and have eggs that develop outside the mother's body. Mammals are covered with fur and have eggs that develop within the mother's body.

Mammals are divided into 17 orders, based on body structure. Some of the more familiar orders are listed below.

Order	Examples	Traits
Marsupials	kangaroos, opossums	pouches in mothers for carrying young
Rodents	mice, rats, beaver, squirrels	gnawing teeth
Carnivores	dogs, bears, cats, skunks	meat eaters
Cetaceans	whale, dolphin, porpoises	aquatic, flippers for limbs
Primates	monkeys, apes, humans	opposable thumbs, erect posture, highly developed brains
Ungulates (2 orders)	horses, camels, buffalo	grass chewers

Viruses

Most biologists recognize viruses as a third kind of being. Viruses are organic particles that are capable of causing diseases in living things, such as smallpox, rabies, and influenza. Viruses are sometimes classified as living things because they contain genetic material and create off-spring similar to themselves. Viruses are often not classified as living things because they have no ability to synthesize or process food, and cannot reproduce without the help of other organisms. Viruses are parasitic. Their basic structure is a protein shell surrounding a nucleic acid core.

ECOLOGY

Ecology is the study of the relationship between living things and their environment. An environment is all the living and nonliving things surrounding an organism.

Populations and Communities

A population is a group of similar organisms, like a herd of deer. A community is a group of populations that interact with one another. A pond community, for example, is made of all the plants and animals in the pond. An ecosystem is a group of populations that share a common pool of resources and a common physical/geographical area. A beech-oak-hickory forest ecosystem, for example, is made of populations in the forest canopy, on the forest floor, and in the forest soil.

Each population lives in a particular area and serves a special role in the community. This combination of defined role and living areas is the concept of niche. The niche of a pond snail, for example, is to decompose materials in ponds. The niche of a field mouse is to eat seeds in fields. When two populations try to fill the same niche, competition occurs. If one population replaces another in a niche, succession occurs. Succession is the orderly and predictable change of communities as a result of population replacement in niches.

A climax community is a community in which succession no longer occurs. Climax communities are stable until catastrophic changes, such as forest fires, hurricanes, or human clearing of land, occur. Each ecosystem type is defined by its climax communities, for example, beech-oak-hickory forests in the American Northeast or prairies in the American Midwest.

Food and Energy

Energy enters ecosystems through sunlight. Green plants turn this energy into food in the process of photosynthesis. Organisms that make their own food are called producers. Animals that get their food energy from eating plants or other animals are called consumers. Consumers that eat plants are herbivores; those that eat animals are carnivores; those that eat plants and animals are called omnivores. Animals that eat other organisms are called predators; the organisms that get eaten are called prey. Organisms that get their food energy from dead plants or animals are called decomposers.

As energy moves from one organism to another, it creates a pattern of energy transfer known as a food web.

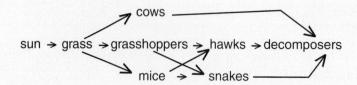

Arrows represent energy transfer in a food web. At each energy transfer (arrow), some energy is lost. Energy is lost because organisms use energy to grow, move, and live.

Many nutrients, such as nitrogen and phosphorus, are routinely cycled through the bodies of living things. These nutrient cycles are disrupted when humans remove parts of the ecosystem or add excess materials to an ecosystem.

Pollution is any material added to an ecosystem that disrupts its normal functioning. Typical pollutants are excess fertilizers and industrial emissions. Conservation is the practice of using natural areas without disrupting their ecosystems. Conservationists try to limit the amounts of pollution entering ecosystems.

HUMAN HEALTH

The Human Body

A human is a very complex organism. This complexity requires individual cells to become specialized at certain tasks. Groups of specialized cells form tissues, such as muscles, skin, or blood. Tissues are specialized to perform specific tasks. Groups of tissues form organs, such as the heart, kidney, or brain. Systems are groups of organs working together to perform the basic activities of life, such as excretion or reproduction. The human body has several systems in it.

The skeleton supports the body and gives it shape. The skeletal system is composed of bones, cartilage, and ligaments. The human body has 206 bones in it. The areas where two or more bones touch one another are called joints. Five types of joints exist in the human body: fixed joints (skull bones), hinge joints (elbow or knee), pivot joints (neck bones), sliding joints (wrist bones), and ball-and-socket joints (shoulder or hip). Bone surfaces in joints are often covered with cartilage, which reduces friction in the joint. Ligaments hold bones together in a joint.

The muscular system controls movement of the skeleton and movement within organs. Three types of muscle exist: striated (voluntary), smooth (involuntary), and cardiac. Cardiac muscle is found only in the heart and is involuntary. Smooth muscle is found in organs and cannot be consciously controlled (involuntary). Striated muscle is attached to a skeleton and its actions can be controlled at will, or voluntarily. Tendons attach muscles to bone. Muscles perform work by contracting. Skeletal muscles work in pairs. The alternate contraction of muscles within a pair causes movement in joints.

The digestive system receives and processes food. The digestive system includes the mouth, stomach, large intestine, and small intestine. Food is physically broken down by mastication, or chewing. Food is chemically broken down in the stomach, where digestive enzymes break the food down into simple chemicals. The small intestine absorbs nutrients from food. The large intestine absorbs water from solid food waste.

The excretory system eliminates wastes from the body. Excretory organs include the liver, kidneys, bladder, large intestine, rectum, and skin. The kidneys filter blood and excrete wastes, mostly in the form of urea. The bladder holds liquid wastes until they can be eliminated via the urethra. The large intestine absorbs water from solid food waste, and the rectum stores solid waste until it can be eliminated. The skin excretes waste through perspiration. The lungs excrete gaseous waste.

The circulatory system is responsible for internal transport in the body. It is composed of the heart, blood vessels, lymph vessels, blood, and lymph. The heart is a muscular four-chambered pump. The upper chambers are called atria and the lower chambers are called ventricles. Blood flows from the body to the (1) right atrium, to the (2) right ventricle, to the lungs, then to the (3) left atrium, to the (4) left ventricle, and back to the body.

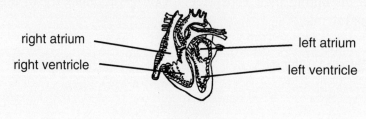

Figure 4

The heart chambers contract to expel the blood they contain. Blood flows in one direction through the heart because of valves within the heart and blood vessels. The closing of valves during heart contractions creates an audible heartbeat. An adult human heart normally contracts 60–80 times per minute.

There are three types of blood vessels: arteries, veins, and capillaries. Arteries have thick, muscular walls and carry oxygenated blood away from the heart. Veins have thin walls and carry de-oxygenated blood to the heart. Capillaries have extremely thin walls and connect arteries to veins.

Blood is always under pressure in the arteries. Blood pressure increases when the heart is contracting. Blood pressure during heart contraction is systolic pressure. Blood pressure during heart relaxation is diastolic pressure. Human blood pressure is always reported as a ratio of systolic pressure/diastolic pressure. Typical blood pressure for adults is 140 mm Hg/90 mm Hg. Pressures ranging far above or below these values indicate illness.

The fluid portion of blood is called plasma. The solid material in blood includes red blood cells, white blood cells, and platelets. Red blood cells carry oxygen to cells and carry carbon dioxide away from cells. White blood cells fight infections and produce antibodies. Platelets cause the formation of clots.

The lymphatic system drains fluid from tissues. Lymph nodes filter impurities in the lymph fluid, and often become swollen during infections.

The respiratory system exchanges oxygen for carbon dioxide. The respiratory system is composed of the nose, trachea, bronchi, lungs, and diaphragm. Air travels from the nose through the trachea and bronchi into the lungs. The air is drawn in by the contraction of the diaphragm, a muscle running across the body below the lungs. Gas exchange occurs in the lungs across air sacks called alveoli. Air is then pushed back toward the nose by relaxation of the diaphragm.

The nervous system controls the actions and processes of the body. The nervous system includes the brain, spinal cord, and nerves. Electrical impulses carry messages to and from the brain across the spinal cord and nerves. Nerves extend to every portion of the body. The spinal cord is protected by the back bone.

The three principal regions of the brain are the cerebrum, cerebellum, and brain stem. The cerebrum occupies 80% of the brain's volume and is responsible for intelligence, memory, and thought. The cerebellum is located at the lower rear portion of the brain, and it controls balance and coordination. The brain stem connects the brain to the spinal cord and is found at the lower central portion of the brain. The brain stem controls autonomic (involuntary) body functions and regulates hormones.

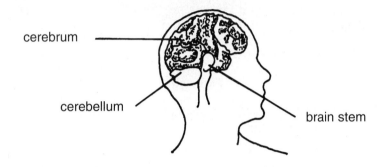

Figure 5

The endocrine system controls activities in the body through chemical agents called hormones. It is composed of many ductless glands throughout the body which excrete hormones into the bloodstream. The brain controls production and release of hormones.

Listed below are several major endocrine glands and the most important hormones they produce:

Gland	Hormone	Action
hypothalamus	oxytocin	stimulates labor in childbirth and production of milk in females
pituitary	growth hormone	stimulates growth
thyroid	thyroxin	controls rate of cellular respiration
parathyroid	parathormone	controls amount of calcium in the blood
thymus	thymosin	helps to fight infections
adrenals	adrenalin	helps during stress and shock, activates flight-or-fight response
pancreas	insulin	regulates blood sugar
ovaries (female)	estrogen, progesterone	controls female maturing process, maintains pregnancy
testes (male)	testosterone	controls male maturing process

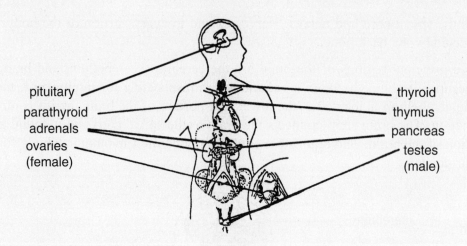

Figure 6

The reproductive system produces eggs in women and sperm in men which can combine to create an embryo. The female reproductive system includes the ovaries, fallopian tubes, uterus, and vagina. One egg each month is released from one of the ovaries and then travels down the fallopian tubes. If it is fertilized, it then becomes implanted in the lining of the uterus, where a baby begins to form. When sufficiently grown, the baby leaves the uterus and its mother's body through the vagina, or birth canal.

The male reproductive system consists of the testicles, vas deferens, urethra, and penis. Sperm are produced in the testicles. They move through the vas deferens from the testicles to the urethra. During intercourse, sperm pass through the penis (via the urethra) and into a woman's vagina. In a woman's body, sperm pass through the cervix into the uterus and up the fallopian tubes, where fertilization of an egg may take place.

Nutrition

Nutrition is the study of how living things utilize food substances. Food provides energy and raw materials for growth, repair, and metabolism. Energy (calories) is derived chiefly from carbohydrates, but also from fats and proteins. Raw materials for life processes come chiefly from protein, but also from carbohydrates (starches and sugars), fats, minerals, and vitamins. Fiber in the diet helps in elimination of wastes.

Listed below are several vitamins important to human health.

Vitamin	Principal Source	Deficiency Symptom(s)
A	green and yellow vegetables	night blindness, dry, brittle skin
B_1	cereals, yeast	beriberi (muscular atrophy and paralysis)
B_2	dairy products, eggs	eye problems
B_{12}	liver and meat	anemia
C	citrus fruits, tomatoes	scurvy
		(continued)

D	fortified milk, eggs	rickets (malformed bones)
E	meat, oils, vegetables	male sterility, muscular problems
K	green vegetables	impaired blood clotting

Foods can be placed in one of four basic food groups. A healthy diet is one that includes food from each of these groups daily, as shown on the following page.

Food Group	Importance	Examples
Meat, Fish, and Eggs	protein	steak, trout
Dairy	fats, calcium, protein	milk, cheese
Fruits and Vegetables	fiber, minerals, vitamins	apples, carrots
Grains and Cereals	starch (for energy), protein, fiber	bread, pasta

Human Genetics

The study of genetic material and inheritance is called genetics. Each of the cells in a living thing has a specific structure and role in the organism. The structure of a cell and its function are determined, to a large degree, by the genes within a cell. Genes are code units found on chromosomes within the nucleus of a cell. Genes give instructions about the structure and function of a cell.

Cells age and die. Organisms continue to live despite the death of individual cells because cells reproduce. Mitosis is the process of cell reproduction through cell division; one cell divides to become two new cells. During mitosis, the genetic material (genes) in the parent cell are copied so each of the offspring gets the same instructions (genes). The passing of genetic material from one generation to the next is called inheritance.

Most cells in the human body have 46 chromosomes. Some special cells, called eggs and sperm, have only 23 chromosomes. Egg and sperm cells get 23 chromosomes through meiosis, a process of cell division that reduces the number of chromosomes in a cell. Most cells in the human body reproduce quite often. Egg and sperm cells (sex cells) cannot reproduce until they join with another sex cell. The process of an egg and sperm cell joining is called fertilization.

A fertilized human sex cell has 46 chromosomes, 23 from the mother and 23 from the father. This fertilized sex cell will multiply to form a new organism. The genes of the new organism are a mixture of genes from both parents, so the new organism will be unique from each parent. The process of combining genetic materials from two parent organisms to form a unique offspring is called sexual reproduction.

During sexual reproduction an organism receives two genes for each trait, one from each parent. Sometimes one trait will mask another, as is the case with eye color. If a person has one gene for brown eyes and one gene for blue eyes, the person will always have brown eyes. A genetic trait that masks another, like the gene for brown eyes, is called a dominant trait. A gene that can be masked, like the gene for blue eyes, is called a recessive trait.

Understanding dominance helps us to figure out the genetic configuration of an individual. An individual with blue eyes must have two genes for blue eyes, since it is a recessive trait. Recessive traits are shown by lowercase letters, so the genetic symbol for blue eyes is "bb." An individual with brown eyes must have at least one gene for brown eyes, which is dominant. Dominant genes are shown by uppercase letters, so the genetic symbol for brown eyes could be "Bb" or "BB."

An individual with two different genes (e.g., Bb) for a trait is called heterozygous for that trait. An individual with two similar genes (e.g., BB or bb) for a trait is called homozygous for that trait.

When the parents' genetic type is known, the probability of the offspring showing particular traits can be predicted using the Punnett Square. A Punnett Square is a large square divided into four small boxes. The genetic symbol of each parent for a particular trait is written alongside the square, one parent along the top and one parent along the left side.

Each gene symbol is written in both boxes below or to the right of it. This results in each box having two gene symbols in it. The genetic symbols in the boxes are all the possible genetic combinations for a particular trait of the offspring of these parents. Each box has a 25% probability of being the actual genetic representation for a given child.

The genetic symbol "AA" in the example has a 25% probability of occurring. If a genetic symbol occurs in more than one box, the genetic probabilities are added. The genetic code "Aa" in the example has a 50% probability of occurring because it is shown in two boxes of the Punnett Square.

The Punnett Square shows how two parents can have a child with traits different from either parent. Two parents heterozygous for brown eyes (Bb), have a 25% probability of producing a child homozygous for blue eyes (bb), as shown in the example.

Human sex type is determined by genetic material in sperm. The genetic sex code for human females is XX. The genetic sex code for human males is XY. Eggs carry only X genes. Sperm carry X or Y genes. The probability of a fertilized human egg being male, or XY, is 50%.

Human blood type is determined genetically. Genes for blood type may be one of three kinds, *i*, I^A, or I^B. The *i* gene is recessive. Blood type O is caused by *ii* genetic code. The I^A and I^B genes are dominant. They may be represented by $I^A i$ or $I^A I^A$ and $I^B i$ or $I^B I^B$, respectively. Blood type AB has genetic code $I^A I^B$. Blood types fit the Punnett Square model.

II. PHYSICAL SCIENCE

MEASUREMENT

The physical characteristics of an object are determined by measurements. Measured characteristics include mass, volume, length, temperature, time, and area. There are two common measurement systems, English and metric.

Characteristic	English System	Metric System
mass/weight	pound	kilogram
volume	quart	liter
length	foot	meter
temperature	°Fahrenheit	°Celsius
time	second	second

The English system, used most often in the United States, does not have a consistent system of conversion factors between units.

EXAMPLE

1 yard = 3 feet, 1 foot = 12 inches, 1 yard = 36 inches

The metric system, used most often in science, has conversion factors between units based on multiples of 10.

EXAMPLE

1 kilometer = 1,000 meters
1 meter = 100 centimeters = 1,000 millimeters

Prefixes in the metric system indicate the number of multiples of the base units, so it is simple to determine the conversion factors between units.

Prefix	Multiplication Factor	Unit Symbols
kilo	× 1,000	km, kg, kl
no prefix (base unit)	× 1	m, g, l
deci	× 0.1	dm, dg, dl
centi	× 0.01	cm, cg, cl
milli	× 0.001	mm, mg, ml

A third measurement system, the International System of Units, or SI, is based on the metric system. SI differs from the metric system by using the Kelvin temperature scale. The size of a degree in the Celcius and Kelvin scale are the same, but "0°" is different. 0° Kelvin = – 273°Celsius. 0° Kelvin, also known as absolute zero, is the temperature at which, theoretically, all molecular movement ceases.

To convert from °Celsius to °Fahrenheit, use the following equation:

$$°C = {}^5/_9 \; (°F - 32°).$$

To convert from °Celsius to Kelvin, use the following equation:

$$°C + 273° = K.$$

CHEMISTRY

Matter is everything that has volume and mass. Water is matter because it takes up space. Light is not matter because it does not take up space.

States of Matter

Matter exists in three states, as follows:

State	Properties	Example
solid	definite volume, definite shape	ice
liquid	definite volume, no definite shape	water
gas	no definite volume, no definite shape	water vapor or steam

Thermal or heat energy causes molecules or atoms to vibrate. As vibration of particles increases, a material may change to a different state; it may melt or boil. Decreasing energy in a material may cause condensation or freezing. Temperature is a measure of the average kinetic energy, or vibration, of the particles of a material. For most materials, the boiling point and freezing point are important. The boiling point of water is 100°C, and its freezing point is 0°C.

State Change	Process Name	Heat Change
solid $\longrightarrow$ liquid	melting	heat added
liquid $\longrightarrow$ gas	evaporation or boiling	heat added
gas $\longrightarrow$ liquid	condensation	heat removed
liquid $\longrightarrow$ solid	freezing	heat removed

Structure of Matter

Atoms are the basic building blocks of matter. Atoms are made of three types of subatomic particles, which have mass and charge. Protons and neutrons are found in the nucleus, or solid center of an atom. Electrons are found in the outer portion of an atom. This outer portion is mostly made of empty space. Under most conditions, atoms are indivisible. Atoms may be split or combined to form new atoms during atomic reactions. Atomic reactions occur deep inside the sun, in nuclear power reactors and nuclear bombs, and in radioactive decay.

Subatomic Particle	Mass	Charge	Location
proton	1 amu	+1	nucleus
neutron	1 amu	0	nucleus
electron	0 amu	−1	outside nucleus

Most atoms have equal numbers of protons and electrons, and therefore no net charge. Atoms with unequal numbers of protons and electrons have net positive or negative charges. Charged atoms are called ions. Atomic mass is determined by the number of protons and neutrons in an atom. The way to express atomic mass is in atomic mass units (amu).

A material made of just one type of atom is called an element. Atoms of an element are represented by symbols of one or two letters, such as C or Na. Two or more atoms may combine to form compounds.

Atoms of the same element have the same number of protons in their nuclei. An atom is the smallest particle of an element that retains the characteristics of that element. Each element is assigned an atomic number, which is equal to the number of protons in an atom of that element.

The Periodic Table lists all the elements in order according to their atomic number. The elements are grouped vertically in the Periodic Table according to their chemical properties. The Periodic Table is a reference tool used to summarize the atomic structure, mass, and reactive tendencies of elements.

Molecules are two or more atoms bonded together covalently. Molecules form, decompose, or recombine during chemical reactions. Materials made of one type of molecule are called compounds. Compounds may be represented by formulas using atomic symbols and numbers (e.g., H_2SO_4). The numbers show how many atoms of each type are in the compound. For example, the symbol for water, H_2O, shows that a molecule of water contains two hydrogen atoms and one oxygen atom. Atomic symbols without subscript numbers represent just one atom in a molecule.

Chemical compounds containing carbon are called organic, because these materials are often made by living things. The chemistry of organic compounds is complex and distinct from that of other compounds. Therefore, organic chemistry is a large and distinct discipline. Compounds without carbon are called inorganic.

Mixtures are materials made of two or more compounds or elements. They can be separated by physical means, such as sifting or evaporation. Liquid or gas mixtures are called suspensions, colloids, or solutions. Suspensions have particles that settle out unless the mixture is stirred. Dust in air is a suspension. Colloids have particles large enough to scatter light, but small enough to remain suspended without stirring. Milk is a colloid; it is opaque because its particles scatter light. Solutions have particles so small they do not scatter light. They are transparent to light and particles do not settle out.

A substance that dissolves another to form a solution is called the solvent. Chemicals that are dissolved in solutions are called solutes. In a salt water solution, water is the solvent. Not all chemicals can function as solvents. Some solvents (like gasoline) are able to dissolve only certain solids. Water is sometimes called the "universal solvent" because it is able to dissolve so many chemicals.

Concentration is a measure of how much solute is in a solution. A given amount of solvent is able to dissolve only a limited amount of solute. This amount may be increased if the solution is heated or pressure on the solution is increased. Dilute solutions have relatively little solute in solution. Concentrated solutions have a lot of solute in solution.

Solutions that are able to dissolve more solute are called unsaturated. Solutions that cannot dissolve more solute are called saturated. Solutions that are saturated at high temperature or high pressure may become super-saturated at lower temperatures or pressures. Supersaturated solutions contain more dissolved solute than normally is present in a saturated solution. These solutions are unstable, and solute may crystallize out of the solution easily.

Chemical Reactions

Matter may undergo chemical and physical changes. A physical change affects the size, form, or appearance of a material. These changes include melting, bending, or cracking. Physical changes do not alter the molecular structure of a material. Chemical changes do alter the molecular structure of matter. Examples of chemical changes are burning, rusting, and digestion.

Under the right conditions, compounds may break apart, combine, or recombine to form new compounds. This process is called a chemical reaction. Chemical reactions are described by chemical equations, such as $NaOH + HCl \longrightarrow NaCl + H_2O$. In a chemical equation, materials to the left of the arrow are called reactants and materials to the right of the arrow are called products. In a balanced chemical equation, the number of each type of atom is the same on both sides of the arrow.

$$\text{unbalanced: } H_2 + O_2 \longrightarrow H_2O$$

$$\text{balanced: } 2H_2 + O_2 \longrightarrow 2H_2O$$

There are four basic types of chemical reactions: synthesis, decomposition, single replacement, and double replacement. A synthesis reaction is one in which two or more chemicals combine to form a new chemical.

Examples

(A) Synthesis Reaction

$$A + B \longrightarrow AB, \text{ or } 2H_2 + O_2 \longrightarrow 2H_2O$$

A decomposition reaction is one in which one chemical breaks down to release two or more chemicals.

(B) Decomposition Reaction

$$AB \longrightarrow A + B, \text{ or } 2H_2O \longrightarrow 2H_2 + O_2$$

A single replacement reaction involves a compound decomposing and one of its constituent chemicals joining another chemical to make a new compound.

(C) Single Replacement Reaction

$$AB + C \longrightarrow A + BC, \text{ or } Fe + CuCl_2 \longrightarrow FeCl_2 + Cu$$

A double replacement reaction is one in which two compounds decompose and their constituents recombine to form two new compounds.

(D) Double Replacement Reaction

$$AB + CD \longrightarrow AC + BD, \text{ or } NaOH + HCl \longrightarrow NaCl + H_2O$$

Acids and Bases

Acid and base are terms used to describe solutions of differing pH. The concentration of hydrogen ions in a solution determines its pH, which is based on a logarithmic scale.

Solutions having pH 0–7 are called acids and have hydrogen ions (H+) present. Common acids include lemon juice, vinegar, and battery acid. Acids are corrosive and taste sour.

Solutions pH 7–14 are called bases (or alkaline), and have hydroxide ions (OH⁻) present. Bases are caustic and feel slippery in solution. Common bases include baking soda and lye. Solutions of pH 7 are called neutral and have both ions present in equal, but small, amounts.

The reaction created when an acid and base combine is a double replacement reaction known as a neutralization reaction. In a neutralization reaction, acid + base $\longrightarrow$ water + salt.

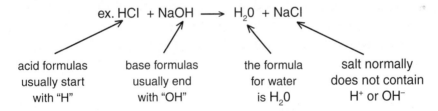

ex. HCl + NaOH $\longrightarrow$ H$_2$0 + NaCl

acid formulas usually start with "H" / base formulas usually end with "OH" / the formula for water is H$_2$0 / salt normally does not contain H⁺ or OH⁻

PHYSICS

Motion

Moving objects can be measured for speed or momentum. Speed is the distance an object travels per unit of time. Cars measure speed in miles or kilometers per hour.

$$\text{Speed } (v) = \frac{\text{distance } (d)}{\text{time } (t)} \qquad v = \frac{d}{t}$$

Example

If a car travels 3.5 km in 7 minutes, it has a speed of 3.5 km/7 min, or 0.5 km/min.

Momentum is the tendency of an object to continue in its direction of motion. The amount of momentum is a product of its mass and velocity.

Momentum = mass × speed

The heavier a moving object is, or the faster it is moving, the harder it is to stop the object or change its direction.

Energy and Work

Energy is the ability to do work. Energy comes in many different forms; examples include heat, light, and sound. All energy can be described as potential or kinetic. Potential energy is stored through chemical structure, position, or physical configuration. Kinetic energy is energy of motion. Light, sound, and heat are kinetic energy, as is the energy possessed by a moving object.

Energy can be transformed from one type to another, but it never is created or destroyed. The potential chemical energy in a peanut butter sandwich is transformed through digestion and metabolism into the kinetic energy of heat and motion. The potential energy of a book sitting on a shelf is turned into the kinetic energy of motion, sound, and heat as the book falls and hits the floor.

Heat is an important type of energy. Heat may travel through three paths: conduction, convection, and radiation. Conduction occurs when a hot material comes in contact with a cold one. Heat moves from a hot material into a cold material until the temperature of both is equal. An example of conduction is the heating of a metal spoon when it is used to stir a cup of hot tea.

Convection is based on a density change caused by heating. As materials, especially gases and liquids, are heated, they become less dense. Warm air, which is less dense, rises, while cold air, which is more dense, sinks. In a room or other enclosed space, this rising and falling of materials of different density creates a current of air (or other heated material). As heat is added to the space, from a source like a stove or sunny window, the current carries the heat through the space.

Radiation is heat that spreads out from a very hot source into the surrounding material. Radiant heat energy is carried by electromagnetic waves, just like the light given off by a hot light bulb filament. Radiant heat energy travels in straight lines in all directions from its source. Sources of radiant heat include wood stoves and light bulbs in homes.

Insulators are materials that slow down or prevent the movement of heat. Air is a good insulator. Most commercial insulation consists of a material with many pockets of air. Conductors are materials that transmit heat well. Metals are excellent heat conductors.

Work occurs when a force (push or pull) is applied to an object, resulting in movement.

Work = force × distance $W = f \times d$

The greater the force applied, or the longer the distance traveled, the greater the work done. Work is measured in newton-meters or foot-pounds. One newton-meter equals one joule.

Mass is a measure of the amount of matter in an object. Weight is the gravitational force on an object. Mass is a constant; it never changes with location. Weight varies with the pull of gravity. Objects weigh less on the moon than on Earth. In space, where there is no gravity, objects are weightless (but they still have the same mass).

Power is work done per unit time.

$$\text{Power} = \frac{\text{work done}}{\text{time interval}} \qquad P(\text{watt}) = \frac{W}{T} \ (\text{Joules}/\text{seconds})$$

If someone moves an object weighing 5 newtons over a distance of 10 meters in 30 seconds, they use the power of 1.7 watts.

= 1.7 n-m/sec, or 1.7 watts

1 watt = 1n-m/sec

Machines change the direction or strength of a force. Simple machines are used throughout our lives.

Simple Machine	Examples
inclined plane	ramp, wedge, chisel
screw	threads on bolts, cork screws, jar lids
lever	seesaw, crowbar, automobile jack
wheel and axle	doorknob, bicycle
pulley	fan belt, elevator

In designing machines, 100% efficiency is the goal. Efficiency is the ratio of work output to work input.

$$\% \text{ efficiency} = \frac{\text{work done}}{\text{energy used}} \times 100.$$

One hundred percent efficiency can never be achieved because some energy is always lost through friction or heat production.

Wave Phenomena

Sound and light are wave phenomena. Waves are characterized by wavelength, speed, and frequency. Wavelength is the distance between crests or troughs of waves.

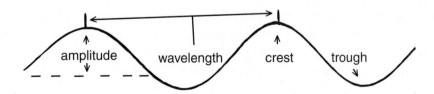

Speed is how fast a wave crest or trough moves. If a wave moves 4 meters in 2 seconds, its speed is 2 m/sec.

$$\text{speed} = \frac{\text{distance}}{\text{time}} = \frac{4m}{2 \text{ sec}} = 2m/sec$$

Frequency is the number of crests or troughs that move past a point per second. Frequency is measured in Hertz. One wave moving past a point per second equals one Hertz.

$$\text{Frequency} = \frac{\text{speed}}{\text{wavelength}}.$$

Sound is caused by the vibration of objects. This vibration of objects creates waves of disturbance that can travel through air and most other materials. If these sound waves hit your eardrum, you perceive sound.

Sound is characterized by its pitch, loudness, intensity, and speed. Pitch is related to frequency. High pitches (e.g., high music notes) have high frequencies. Loudness is related to wave amplitude. Loud sounds have big amplitudes. Sound intensity is measured in decibels. Intensity is related to amplitude and frequency of sound waves. Loud, high-pitched music has a much greater intensity than quiet, low-pitched music.

The speed of sound waves is related to their medium. Sound travels more quickly through more dense materials (solids, liquids) than less dense materials (gases). Sound does not travel through a vacuum.

Light is a type of electromagnetic wave. The chief types of electromagnetic waves, listed according to their relative frequency and wavelength, are shown on the following page.

Low frequency ← — — — — — — — — → high frequency

| radio waves | micro waves | infrared light | visible light | ultraviolet light | x-rays | gamma rays |

long wavelength ← — — — — — — — — → short wavelength

Light travels much more quickly (300,000 km/sec) than sound does (330 m/sec). It can pass through a vacuum. As light passes through a material, it travels in a straight path. When light moves from one material to another, it may be transmitted, absorbed, reflected, or refracted.

Transparent materials (e.g., water, glass) allow light to pass directly through them. This passing through is called transmission. Opaque objects (e.g., wood) absorb light. No light comes out of them. Mirrors reflect light. They re-emit light into the medium it came from. Light rays going into a mirror are called incident rays. Light rays going out of a mirror are called reflected rays.

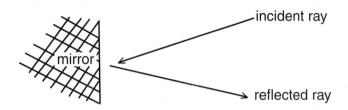

Refraction is the bending of light. Light may be refracted when it moves from one material to another (e.g., air ⟶ water). Mirages are formed when light refracts while moving from cool air to warm air.

Sometimes, during refraction, sunlight is broken into the colors that form it, causing a spectrum. The colors in a spectrum are red, orange, yellow, green, blue, indigo, and violet. A rainbow is a spectrum caused when light passes from dry air into very humid air.

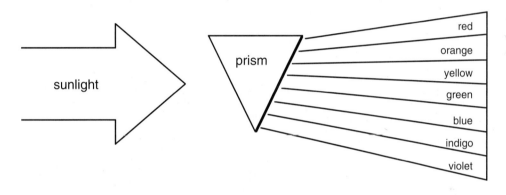

Figure 12

Lenses are transparent materials used to refract light. The shape of a lens determines how light passing through it will be bent.

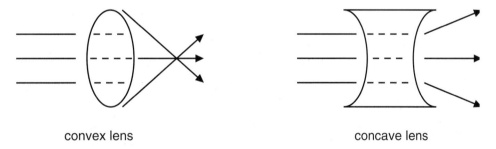

Figure 13

Basic Electricity

All matter is made of atoms. All atoms contain positively charged particles, called protons, and negatively charged particles, called electrons. Protons are tightly bound to atoms and cannot move much. Electrons are loosely attached to atoms, and may leave one atom to join another.

Atoms may carry electrical charges. A neutral atom has equal numbers of protons and electrons in it. The charges of the protons and electrons cancel each other, so the atom has no net charge. If an atom has more electrons than protons, the extra electrons give the atom a negative charge. If an atom has less electrons than protons, the missing electrons leave the atom with a positive charge.

Electrons may not be destroyed. If two objects are rubbed together, however, electrons may move from one object to another, leaving both charged. Electrons may also flow through certain materials. The flow of electrons produces an electric current. Conductors are materials that let electrons flow freely (e.g., metals, water). Insulators are materials that do not let electrons flow freely (e.g., glass, rubber, air).

Electricity (electric current) flows from areas of many electrons to areas of few electrons. The path along which electrons flow is called a circuit. In a direct current (DC) circuit, electrons flow in one direction only. In an alternating current, the current changes direction many times per second. Alternating current (AC) is the type of current supplied over power lines.

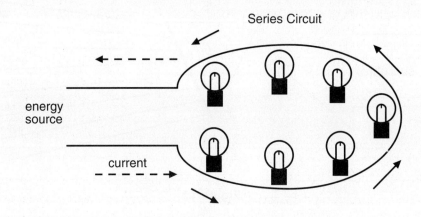

Figure 14

Circuits may be described as being in series or in parallel. Series circuits are made of a single pathway, through which all currents must flow. If any part of a series circuit breaks, the circuit is "opened," and the flow of the current must stop. Some sets of Christmas tree lights are designed in series. If one bulb in the string of lights burns out, none of the lights in the string will work, because the current is disrupted for the entire string.

Parallel circuits provide more than one pathway for current to flow. If one of the pathways is opened, so that current cannot flow in it, the current will continue to move through the other paths. Most circuits, for example those in our homes, are wired in parallel, so that burned out light bulbs and turned off television sets do not disrupt electricity used in other parts of our homes.

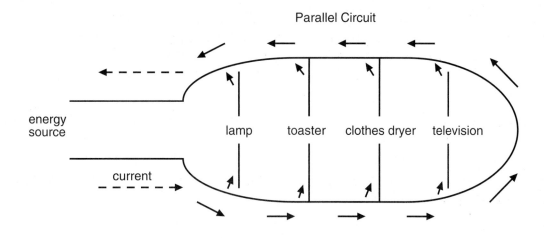

Figure 15

Wires (lines) are limited in the amount of current they can safely carry. If too much current passes through them, they may heat up and melt or cause a fire. Current passing through lines increases with each appliance added to the circuit.

Fuses and circuit breakers are safety devices that limit the current flow in a circuit. Fuses work by passing current through a thin metal ribbon. When the current exceeds the capacity of the fuse, the metal ribbon melts, leaving an open circuit, which cannot carry current. Circuit breakers use magnets and bimetallic strips to open circuits if the current becomes too great. Fuses must be replaced after they "blow," or melt. Circuit breakers may simply be reset to be used again.

Volts measure the work done as electrons move from one point to another within a circuit. Battery "strength," or ability to do work, is measured by volts. Amperes measure the current, or flow of charge through a circuit. Ohms measure the resistance to the flow of electrons.

Volts = amperes × ohms $V = IR$

Watts measure electrical power consumption. Electrical appliances and light bulbs are rated by their wattages so consumers can compare power consumption before purchasing these products. One watt equals one joule per second of power (one newton-meter per second). One watt of energy can lift an object weighing one newton over one meter in one second. A kilowatt-hour is the amount of energy used in one hour by one kilowatt of power.

Power = current × voltage, or 1 Watt = 1 ampere × 1 volt

$P = VI$

Magnetism

Magnets are solids that attract iron. Naturally occurring magnets are called lodestones. Magnetic forces make magnets attract or repel each other. Magnetic forces are created by regions in magnets called magnetic poles. All magnets have a north and a south pole. The north pole of one magnet will repel the north pole of another magnet; the same holds true for south poles. The south pole of one magnet will attract the north pole of another magnet.

A magnetic field is the area affected by magnetic force. A magnetic field surrounds both poles of a magnet. A magnetic field can be created by an electric current. Electromagnets create large magnetic fields with electric current. Similarly, if a wire is moved through a magnetic field, a current is produced. Electric generators make electricity by passing wires through a magnetic field.

The Earth has a magnetic field. Compasses are magnets that align themselves with the Earth's magnetic field.

III. EARTH SCIENCE

Earth science is the study of the earth and its place in the universe. Earth science has many subgroups, including, but not limited to, astronomy, geology, meteorology, and oceanography.

ASTRONOMY

Astronomy is the study of celestial bodies and their movements.

The Earth is one of nine planets in our solar system. A solar system is composed of a star and the objects that move about it. The largest objects moving about a star are called planets. The planets in our solar system, beginning at the sun and moving away from it, are Mercury, Venus, Earth, Mars, Jupiter, Saturn, Uranus, Neptune, and Pluto.

Many objects smaller than planets exist in our solar system. If one of these smaller objects reaches the atmosphere of Earth, it is called a meteor or "shooting star." The glow of a meteor is caused by its burning as it passes through our atmosphere. Meteors that reach the Earth's surface are called meteorites.

The Earth's path around the sun is called its orbit. The Earth's orbit around the sun, called a revolution, is completed in $365^1/_4$ days. An axis is an imaginary line passing through the poles of the earth. The Earth spins on its axis, and each spin is called a rotation. One rotation takes 24 hours. Rotation causes the alternation of day and night on Earth.

The Earth revolves about the sun. Its axis is tilted $23^1/_2°$ from perpendicular to the plane of Earth's orbit. This tilt results in differing proportions of day and night on Earth throughout the year, and also causes the seasons. Day and night are of equal length only twice each year, at the autumnal equinox and vernal equinox (the first day of autumn and the first day of spring).

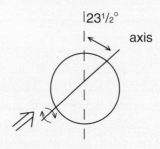

The moon is a satellite of Earth. It moves in orbit about Earth, and one revolution takes $27^{1}/_{3}$ days. The moon reflects sunlight, which causes it to glow. When the Earth blocks sunlight from reaching the moon, it creates a shadow on the moon's surface, known as a lunar eclipse. If the moon blocks sunlight from hitting the Earth, a solar eclipse is created. The moon has a gravitational pull on Earth which causes tides, or periodic changes in the depth of the ocean.

GEOLOGY

Geology is the study of the structure and composition of the Earth.

The Earth is composed of three layers, the crust, mantle, and core. The core is the center of the Earth; the inner core is made of solid iron and nickel. It is about 7,000 km in diameter. The mantle is the semi-molten layer between the crust and core, and is about 3,000 km thick. The crust is the solid outermost layer of the Earth, ranging from 5–40 km thick. It is composed of bedrock overlaid with mineral and/or organic sediment (soil).

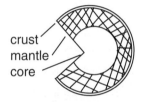

Large pieces of the Earth's crust, called plates, move at times, creating earthquakes, volcanoes, faults, and mountains. The study of these movements is called plate tectonics. Faults are cracks in the crust formed when plates move. Faults gape open when plates move apart and are closed when plates slide past one another. Earthquakes occur when plates slide past one another abruptly. Earthquakes may also be caused by volcanoes. The magnitude of earthquakes is measured by seismograph on the Richter scale.

Volcanoes can form from plates colliding which lets magma reach the crust's surface. Magma is molten rock beneath the Earth's crust. Lava is molten rock on the Earth's surface. Mountains are formed by volcanic activity or the collision of plates, which causes the crust to buckle upward.

Rocks are naturally occurring solids found on or below the surface of the Earth. Rocks are made of one or more minerals. Minerals are pure substances made of just one element or chemical compound. Rocks are divided into three groups, based on the way they are formed.

1. **Igneous**—rocks formed by cooling of magma or lava (e.g., granite, obsidian).
2. **Sedimentary**—rock formed from silt or deposited rock fragments by compaction at high pressures and/or cementation (e.g., shale, limestone).
3. **Metamorphic**—rocks formed from igneous or sedimentary rock after exposure to high heat and pressure (e.g., marble, slate).

Weathering is the breaking down of rock into small pieces. Rock is weathered by acid rain, freezing, wind abrasion, glacier scouring, and running water. Erosion is the transportation of rock or sediment to new areas. Agents of erosion include wind, running water, and glaciers.

METEOROLOGY

Meteorology is the study of the atmosphere and its changes.

The atmosphere is a layer of air surrounding the Earth. Air is a mixture of gases, the most common being nitrogen and oxygen. The atmosphere is studied because (1) it protects (insulates) the Earth from extreme temperature changes, (2) it protects the Earth's surface from meteors, and (3) it is the origin of weather.

The atmosphere can be divided into several layers. The troposphere is the layer closest to Earth. Almost all life and most weather activity is found there. The stratosphere is the chief thermally insulating layer of the atmosphere. It contains the ozone layer and jet stream. The stratosphere is the region where ozone is produced. The thermosphere causes meteors to burn up by friction as they pass through. This layer reflects radio waves. The exosphere is the outer layer of the atmosphere. It eventually blends into the vast region we call "space."

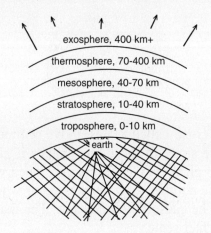

Weather is the local, short-term condition of the atmosphere. The two factors that affect weather most are the amounts of energy and water present. Most of the energy that affects weather comes from the sun. As solar (sun) energy hits the Earth, most of it is scattered or reflected by the atmosphere. The solar energy that gets through the atmosphere warms the Earth's crust which, in turn, warms the atmosphere. The Earth does not absorb solar energy uniformly; the equator absorbs more than the poles do. This difference in energy (heat) absorption causes, in part, wind.

Water covers about 70 percent of the Earth's surface. As that water slowly evaporates, some of the vapor is held in the atmosphere. It is the water vapor in our atmosphere that causes humidity, fog, clouds, and precipitation.

An air mass is a huge area of air that has nearly uniform conditions of temperature and moisture. When two air masses meet, the boundary between them is called a front. Fronts are the location of most stormy weather.

Warm air is less dense than cold air. That means, a given volume of warm air weighs less than an equal volume of cold air. Air masses push down on the earth below them, causing air pressure. Warm air masses, because they are less dense, push down less and cause low pressure areas. Cold air masses, which are more dense, cause high air pressure. Air moves from high pressure to low pressure areas, causing wind.

Different aspects of the weather may be measured using special instruments:

Weather Aspect	Instrument
wind speed	anemometer
air pressure	barometer
humidity	hygrometer
temperature	thermometer

Clouds can be used to predict the weather.

Cloud Type	Appearance	Weather
stratus	flat, broad	light colored—stable weather conditions dark colored—rain expected soon
cumulus	fluffy, solid-looking	light colored—good weather dark colored—heavy rains, perhaps thunderstorms
cirrus	thin, wispy	fair weather and changes in weather in near future

Climate is the general atmospheric condition of a region over a long period of time.

OCEANOGRAPHY

Oceanography is the study of the ocean.

Sea water differs from fresh water in its salinity, or saltiness. Fresh water, the water we drink, has relatively few dissolved solids in it and has low salinity. Ocean water has a lot of dissolved material in it and therefore has a high salinity. Many materials are dissolved in sea water, but the most abundant dissolved material is common salt, sodium chloride.

Ocean waters move through tides, waves, and currents. Tides are periodic changes in ocean depth. They are caused by the gravitational attraction among the moon, Earth, and sun. Most waves are caused by winds. Some ocean currents are caused by density differences in sea water. Currents are like rivers within the ocean. The swift-moving water in currents can transport material over large distances very quickly.

HSPT

Optional Test: General Science

Time: 30 Minutes
   40 Questions

DIRECTIONS: Select the best answer choice.

---

1. A hypothesis explains and relates

   (A) conclusions.   (C) theories.

   (B) facts.   (D) guesses.

2. Body cells, such as muscle or bone cells, reproduce by

   (A) osmosis.   (C) diffusion.

   (B) mitosis.   (D) meiosis.

3. According to the cell theory,

   (A) all living things are composed of cells.

   (B) the number of cells in an organism is set before birth.

   (C) cell activity is controlled by the nucleus.

   (D) eukaryotic cells have a cell wall for protection.

4. Maintaining a balanced internal control is called

   (A) homeostasis.   (C) diffusion.

   (B) osmosis.   (D) pump balance.

5. An organic molecule is any molecule

   (A) containing carbon.   (C) found in dead organisms.

   (B) containing phosphorus. (D) that is naturally grown.

6. Mitosis results in

(A) offspring cells exactly like the parent cell.

(B) offspring cells different from the parent cell.

(C) new combinations of mother cells.

(D) none of the above.

7. An example of a fungus is

(A) mushroom.   (C) penicillium.

(B) bread mold.   (D) All of the above.

8. The circulatory system is responsible for all of the following EXCEPT

(A) the distribution of oxygen.

(B) carrying nutrients.

(C) removing urea from the body.

(D) stopping the flow of blood after an injury.

9. The type of muscle tissue found in the walls of many internal organs is identified as

(A) striated.   (C) skeletal.

(B) smooth.   (D) cardiac.

10. Infectious diseases are caused by

(A) bacteria, fungi, and protozoans.

(B) bacteria only.

(C) fungi only.

(D) protozoans only.

11. The atomic theory states that all matter is composed of

(A) carbon.   (C) molecules.

(B) atoms.   (D) compounds.

12. Chemical action may involve all of the following EXCEPT

(A) combining of atoms of the elements to form a molecule.

(B) separation of the molecules in a mixture.

(C) breaking down compounds into elements.

(D) reacting a compound and an element to form an element and a new compound.

13. All chemical changes involve

    (A) a decreased stability in a solution.

    (B) an increased stability in a solution.

    (C) breaking of bonds and forming new ones.

    (D) formation of ion reactants.

14. Which of the following involves a chemical change?

    (A) The rusting of iron

    (B) The evaporation of water

    (C) The melting of ice

    (D) An ice cube floating in a glass of water

15. Combustion is a(n)

    (A) reaction where things are broken down to products with less potential energy.

    (B) reaction where things are combined together to form a more complex product.

    (C) endothermic reaction.

    (D) exothermic reaction.

16. A chemical formula will

    (A) describe the organization and composition of a substance.

    (B) tell the rate of the chemical reaction.

    (C) show when equilibrium is reached.

    (D) describe the physical properties of each element involved.

17. In a chemical reaction at equilibrium, which of the following changes will always increase the amount of the product?

    (A) Add a catalyst

    (B) Increase pressure

    (C) Increase temperature

    (D) Increase concentration of reactant

18. Chemical action may involve all of the following EXCEPT

    (A) combining of atoms of elements to form a molecule.

    (B) separation of the molecules in a mixture.

    (C)   reacting a compound and an element to form a new compound and a new element.

    (D)   combusting a compound to form a new substance.

19. Acceleration is defined as the

    (A)   change in position divided by the time needed to make that change.

    (B)   change in velocity divided by the time needed to make that change.

    (C)   time it takes to move from one speed to another speed.

    (D)   time it takes to move from one place to another place.

20. The ability of a body to change shapes when a force is applied and then return to its original shape when that force is removed is

    (A)   elasticity.   (C)   springforce.

    (B)   compression.   (D)   girders.

21. Energy can

    (A)   not be created.   (C)   be changed in form.

    (B)   not be destroyed.   (D)   All of the above.

22. Friction acts parallel to the surfaces that are sliding over one another and in the

    (A)   same direction as the motion.

    (B)   opposite direction of the motion.

    (C)   contact line and circular motion.

    (D)   direction of the sliding force.

23. When refraction occurs, part of a wave

    (A)   is bent more than another part.

    (B)   slows down before another part.

    (C)   is pushed to one side.

    (D)   is closer together than it appears.

24. The greater the mass of an object, the greater the force necessary

    (A)   to change its position.

    (B)   to change its force.

    (C)   to change its rate of motion.

    (D)   to change its shape.

25. The two factors that determine the amount of work done are

    (A) the magnitude of the force exerted and the weight of the object moved.

    (B) the distance of the object moved in the time required.

    (C) the displacement of the object and the magnitude of the force in the direction of the displacement.

    (D) the magnitude of the force in the direction of the displacement and the time required.

26. Machines may be used

    (A) to divide the force.

    (B) to multiply speed.

    (C) to divide force and speed simultaneously.

    (D) to keep the direction of the force constant.

27. Heat transfer occurs

    (A) from an object of a lower temperature to one of higher temperature.

    (B) from an object of a higher temperature to one of a lower temperature.

    (C) when electrons bump into each other.

    (D) when the temperature rises.

28. Specific heat is related to the amount of heat

    (A) a specific object has.

    (B) one molecule contains.

    (C) transferred by one molecule.

    (D) needed to change the temperature of one gram of a substance by one degree Celsius.

29. When the Earth passes between the sun and the moon, this causes the occurrence of a(n)

    (A) phase.   (C) darkness.

    (B) ellipse.   (D) eclipse.

30. Which planet is the closest to the sun?

    (A) Earth   (C) Mercury

    (B) Mars   (D) Pluto

31. Meteoroids are chunks of iron resulting from collisions between

(A) asteroids.

(B) planetoids.

(C) stars.

(D) meteorites.

32. An axis is

(A) a connecting line at the equator.

(B) a connecting line between the poles.

(C) a connecting line between orbits.

(D) a pole.

33. The cause of the Earth's magnetic field is

(A) enormous currents.

(B) space satellites.

(C) a lost secret.

(D) in the Earth's crust.

34. An odorless, colorless mixture of gases that surrounds the Earth is commonly called

(A) nitrogen.

(B) oxygen.

(C) carbon dioxide.

(D) air.

35. The source of evaporation is the

(A) movement of air.

(B) atmosphere.

(C) sunlight.

(D) currents.

36. Crude oil, natural gas, and coal are called

(A) nuclear energy sources.

(B) alternate energy sources.

(C) natural sources.

(D) None of the above.

37. Hurricanes occur over

(A) land.

(B) water.

(C) land during the day.

(D) water and land.

38. Fog is

(A) the same as smog.

(B) caused when cold air moves over warm air.

(C) a collection of minute water droplets.

(D) associated with a tornado.

39. An instrument that measures humidity is called a(n)

    (A) thermometer.   (C) hygrometer.

    (B) anemometer.   (D) barometer.

40. A cell structure which stores materials in a cell is called a

    (A) ribosome.   (C) cell wall.

    (B) vacuole.   (D) cell membrane.

HSPT

Optional Test: General Science

ANSWER KEY

Question Number	Correct Answer	If You Answered this Question Incorrectly, Refer to...
1.	(B)	P. 601
2.	(B)	P. 613
3.	(A)	P. 602
4.	(A)	P. 603
5.	(A)	P. 617
6.	(A)	P. 613
7.	(D)	P. 605
8.	(C)	P. 610
9.	(B)	P. 609
10.	(A)	P. 607
11.	(B)	P. 624
12.	(B)	P. 618
13.	(C)	P. 618
14.	(A)	P. 618
15.	(A)	P. 618
16.	(A)	P. 618
17.	(D)	P. 618
18.	(B)	P. 618
19.	(B)	P. 619
20.	(A)	P. 619
21.	(D)	P. 619

22.	(B)	P. 619
23.	(B)	P. 622
24.	(C)	P. 621
25.	(C)	P. 621
26.	(B)	P. 621
27.	(B)	P. 620
28.	(D)	P. 620
29.	(D)	P. 627
30.	(C)	P. 626
31.	(A)	P. 626
32.	(B)	P. 626
33.	(C)	P. 626
34.	(D)	P. 628
35.	(C)	P. 628
36.	(D)	P. 608
37.	(D)	P. 628
38.	(C)	P. 628
39.	(C)	P. 629
40.	(B)	P. 735

DETAILED EXPLANATIONS
OF ANSWERS

1.   (**B**)   By definition a hypothesis is an educated guess based upon a set of facts. Further experiments, or more facts, are used to determine whether the hypothesis is true or false.

2.   (**B**)   Body cells reproduce by mitosis. Mitosis is a form of cell division whereby each of two daughter cells receives the same genetic material as the parent cell. Mitosis is responsible for growth, regeneration, and cell replacement in multicellular organisms.

3.   (**A**)   According to cell theory, all living things are composed of cells. Some cells are total living organisms, while other cells are the basic units of structure of other living things, such as tissues and organs.

4.   (**A**)   The definition of homeostasis is the ability to maintain the balance of internal control. Homeostasis accounts for all the movement into and out of the cell. While the cell can adjust to a wide range of environmental needs and wants, there is a limit to the extent of adjustment.

5.   (**A**)   By definition any molecule that contains carbon is organic. Molecules that do not contain carbon are referred to as inorganic.

6.   (**A**)   Mitosis is the process of cell division by which each of the two daughter nuclei receives the same chromosome, and thus genetic material, as the parent nucleus. Therefore, in mitosis the offspring cells are exactly like the parent cell.

7.   (**D**)   A fungus is a eukaryote, mainly a multicellular organism, that has structures that are rootlike, caps of filaments, and reproductive. Fungi reproduce by asexual and sexual methods. The functions of the structures are digestive-like, respiration, and reproductive. Examples of fungi include mushrooms, bread mold, and penicillium, which is a specific type of bread mold.

8.   (**C**)   The main function of the circulatory system is to distribute oxygen and nutrients to all the organs. An auxiliary portion of the circulatory system, the lymphatic system, drains excess tissue fluids back into the circulatory system and carries white blood cells which destroy harmful microorganisms. The circulatory system does not remove urea from the blood; the renal system does.

9.   (**B**)   Of the three human muscles, striated, smooth, and cardiac, the smooth muscle is found in the linings of the body such as the digestive system and internal organs. Smooth muscles are generally involuntary muscles.

10. **(A)** By definition, an infectious disease can be caused by bacteria, fungi, or protozoans. Infectious diseases are spread from one person to another.

11. **(B)** According to the atomic theory, proposed by Thomas Dalton, all matter is composed of small indivisible particles, or atoms.

12. **(B)** By definition, in a chemical action a substance is changed to a new substance which has different properties. The act of separating molecules in a mixture is a physical change. The separated molecules do not have different properties.

13. **(C)** All chemical changes involve the breaking of bonds and forming new ones. Changes that do not break bonds are known as physical changes.

14. **(A)** During the rusting of iron, the iron metal is changed to iron oxide. In the other examples, the water in the beginning of the process is still water at the end of the process, although it may be in a different state of matter, i.e., liquid or vapor.

15. **(A)** Combustion is a reaction where things are broken down into products with less potential energy than the reactants. An example of combustion is the burning of wood. A combustion reaction may be exothermic or endothermic.

16. **(A)** A chemical formula is a detailed description of how the elements are organized in the compound. The formula will not reveal the hidden structure of the substance, or tell how the substance will react.

17. **(D)** In a chemical reaction at equilibrium, changing the temperature, pressure, or amount of catalyst will result in a new equilibrium state, but may not increase the amount of product. The only way to increase the amount of product is to increase the concentration of reactants.

18. **(B)** By definition, in a chemical action, a substance is changed to a new substance which has different properties. The act of separating molecules in a mixture is a physical change. The separated molecules do not have different properties.

19. **(B)** Acceleration is equal to the change in speed, or velocity, divided by the time interval. Acceleration is directly proportional to the acting force and inversely proportional to mass.

20. **(A)** The ability of a body to change shapes when a force is applied and then return to its original shape when the force is removed is the definition of elasticity. Objects that do not return to their original shapes are said to be inelastic.

21. **(D)** According to the Law of Conservation of Energy, energy can neither be created nor destroyed, but it may change form.

22. **(B)** Friction is a force that acts between materials that are moving past each other. Friction is a result of irregularities in the surfaces. When two surfaces are sliding over one another, the frictional force acts in the opposite direction of motion.

23. **(B)** Refraction is the bending of waves toward the direction of the slower wave velocity. Part of the wave slows down before the other part.

24. **(C)** The greater the mass of an object, the greater the force necessary to change its rate of motion or acceleration. This is stated in Newton's second law, $F = ma$. As m increases, F must increase if the acceleration, a, is to remain the same.

25. **(C)** Work is the distance an object has been moved multiplied by the force used to move the object. Time is not needed to determine the amount of work done.

26. **(B)** Machines are devices by which energy can be transferred from one place to another or from one form to another. Machines can be used to multiply the speed at which the work is done.

27. **(B)** Heat is a form of energy that is created by the motion of molecules making up the object. Heat transfer always occurs between an object of high temperature and one of a lower temperature.

28. **(D)** Specific heat is defined as the quantity of heat required to raise the temperature of a unit of mass of a substance by one degree. Specific heat is dependent upon the chemical composition of the substance.

29. **(D)** Eclipses are observed when the Earth passes between the sun and the moon, or when the moon passes between the sun and the Earth.

30. **(C)** Mercury is the planet closest to the sun. It is followed by Venus and Earth. Pluto is the planet farthest from the sun.

31. **(A)** Meteoroids are chunks of iron resulting from collisions between asteroids. Asteroids are small irregularly shaped objects orbiting between Jupiter and Mars.

32. **(B)** An axis is defined as a line connecting two poles. The Earth has an axis connecting the North Pole and the South Pole.

33. **(C)** The Earth acts through its center as a large magnet. Scientists are not sure what produces the enormous magnetic currents that are deep within the Earth and responsible for the Earth's magnetic field.

34. **(D)** Air is the odorless, colorless gas that surrounds the Earth and extends approximately 1,000 miles above the surface. Air is made up of 78% nitrogen, 21% oxygen, and argon, water vapor, dust particles, and other gases make up the remaining 1%.

35. **(C)**   Sunlight is the source of energy for temperature change, evaporation, and currents for water movement through the atmosphere.

36. **(D)**   Most of today's energy is supplied from fossil fuels, such as crude oil, natural gas, and coal. Fossil fuels are from natural sources.

37. **(D)**   Hurricanes occur when the atmospheric conditions, tail movements, winds, and pressure change severely. Hurricanes can move from water to land; a tornado results from the wind force when the hurricane moves further inland.

38. **(C)**   Fog is a hydrometer which consists of a visible collection of minute water droplets suspended in the atmosphere near the earth's surface. It is caused by the atmospheric humidity and warm temperature layer being transported over a cold body of water or land surface.

39. **(C)**   A hygrometer measures humidity. A thermometer (A) measures temperature, an anemometer (B) calculates wind speed, and a barometer (D) tracks air pressure.

40. **(B)**   Ribosomes (A) make proteins from amino acids, a cell wall (C) gives rigid structure to plant cells, and a cell membrane (D) controls movement of materials into and out of cells. Answer choice (B) vacuole, is a membrane bound structure contained within the cell.

COOP/ HSPT

CHAPTER 9

Mechanical Aptitude Review

MECHANICAL APTITUDE REVIEW

I. Introduction

Mechanics is the branch of Physics dealing with the motions or states of material bodies. The mechanical aptitude test items require qualitative rather than quantitative reasoning. However, research studies have shown that three abilities are important in achieving high-score results on mechanical aptitude tests. These abilities are described as follows: (1) the ability to correctly identify which attributes (characteristics) of a system are relevant to its mechanical function, (2) the ability to use rules or concepts consistently, and (3) the ability to quantitatively combine information about two or more relevant attributes. Most practical or everyday physical processes we experience can be explained using the fundamental concepts and laws of Physics. This section reviews some of the basic scientific concepts and laws that are most important in understanding mechanical systems and their principles of operation.

II. Measurement

GEOMETRY

The angle between two straight lines is defined by drawing a circle with its center at the point of intersection. The magnitude of angle A is proportional to the fraction of a complete circle which lies between the two lines. Angles are measured in degrees.

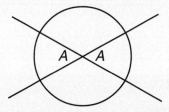

When two straight lines meet so that the angle between them is a right angle (90°), they are said to be perpendicular. Line CA is perpendicular to BD.

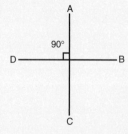

Two straight lines are said to be parallel if the extension of their sides will never intersect. As shown below, line AB is parallel to line CD.

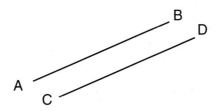

The application of geometry usually requires only a few general rules. Three of the most important are as follows:

Rule 1: When two straight lines intersect, they form opposing angles which are equal.

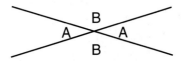

Rule 2: When a straight line intersects (cuts across) two parallel lines, the alternate interior angles are equal.

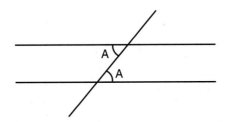

Rule 3: For any triangle, the sum of the interior angles is equal to 180º.

$$\angle A + \angle B + \angle C = 180º$$

MEASUREMENT OF PERIMETER

The perimeter of a closed geometric figure is a measure of the distance around the figure or the sum of its sides.

The perimeters of a rectangle and a triangle are shown below.

Rectangle

Perimeter = 2L + 2W

Triangle

Perimeter = a + b + c

The perimeter of a circle is called its circumference and is given by the following formula:

C = 2 πr = πd
r = radius
d = 2r = diameter
π = 3.14

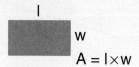

MEASUREMENT OF AREA

Area is a measure of the surface inside of a geometric figure. The area of a rectangle is found by multiplying the length by the width.

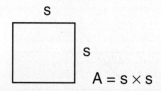

A = l×w

Since a square is a rectangle with all sides of equal length, its area is given by:

$$A = s \times s$$

The area of a circle is expressed in terms of the constant π and the radius of the circle as shown below:

$$A = \pi r^2$$

MEASUREMENT OF VOLUME

Volume can be thought of as the amount of space occupied by a particular solid figure, or as the space occupied by a fluid in a solid container. The volume of a rectangular solid is found by multiplying its length, height, and width.

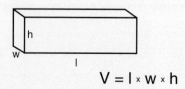

$$V = l \times w \times h$$

A rectangular solid in which all edges are of equal length is called a cube.

The volume of a cube is:

$V = l \times w \times h$

Two other commonly encountered solid shapes are the right circular cylinder and the sphere. These solid figures are shown below along with the formulas for computing their volume.

Right Circular Cylinder

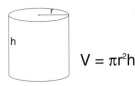

$V = \pi r^2 h$

Sphere

$V = 4/3 \pi r^3$

III. Vectors and Forces

VECTOR ADDITION

Measurable quantities that have magnitude and direction are called vectors. Two important vector quantities are displacement and force. Displacement is defined as a motion in a particular direction and a specified distance. A force is any push or pull exerted on an object. A vector quantity is completely specified by giving its magnitude and direction. Vector quantities can be added the way displacements are added. How do we add displacements? Suppose we walk 30 meters to the east. We have now given the magnitude, 30 meters, and a direction, to the east. This is conveniently represented graphically by a vector, an arrow drawn to a suitable scale in the correct direction as shown below:

North

West ———————→ East
            30 meters

South

If this displacement is now followed by a displacement of 40 meters to the north, the new displacement is represented by using the same scale for BD:

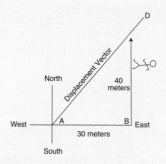

The resultant displacement is the vector AD.

NOTE: Some physical quantities can be described by just a number and a unit or dimension and are called scalar quantities. An example of a scalar quantity is: 12cm^2. Scalar quantities, which are measured in the same units, may be added or subtracted in the usual way. For example,

$$14 \text{ mm} + 13 \text{ mm} = 27 \text{ mm}$$

$$20 \text{ ft}^2 - 14 \text{ ft}^2 = 6 \text{ ft}^2$$

Forces

A force is a vector quantity because it has magnitude and direction— e.g., 5 pounds acting westward.

Concurrent forces are two or more forces acting simultaneously on the same point of an object. We are often concerned about getting the combined effect of these forces. The resultant of two or more forces is a single force which produces the same effect as these forces (and can therefore be used to replace them). For example, if a 4 lb. force and a 3 lb. force act in the same direction, their resultant is a 7 lb. force in the same direction. If they act in opposite directions (at an angle of 180°), their resultant is the difference between the two forces, a 1 lb. force in the direction of the 4 lb. force.

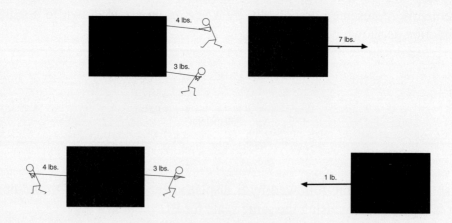

Conversely, a single force may be replaced by two or more other forces — its components. Usually, we use two components at right angles to each other. For example, if, as shown, a box is pulled along flat ground by means of a rope making an angle of 30° with the horizontal, the 5 lb. force applied to the end of the rope is equivalent to a horizontal force of 4 lb. and a vertical force of 3 lb. We get the value of these components by constructing a rectangle as shown in the figure.

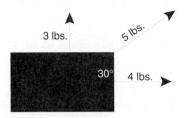

The following diagrams are several additional examples of the effects of forces acting at an angle and the effects of balanced forces.

IV. Equilibrium

We know from experience that a stationary object remains at rest unless some outside force acts on it. A suspended weight will hang until it is released. A can of oil will stay on a workbench until someone tips it over. We know that a force is necessary to cause an object to move if it is originally at rest.

NEWTON'S LAWS

Less obvious is the fact that an object in motion will continue in motion until an outside force changes the motion. For example, a steel bar that slides on a floor soon comes to rest because of its interaction with the floor. This same bar would slide much farther on ice before stopping. This is because the horizontal interaction, called friction, between the floor and the bar is much greater than the friction between the ice and the bar (the greater the friction, the sooner the object will stop). This leads to the idea that a sliding bar on a perfectly frictionless horizontal plane would stay in motion forever. These ideas are part of Newton's first law of motion.

Newton's First Law: A body at rest remains at rest, and a body in motion remains in uniform motion in a straight line unless acted on by an external, unbalanced force.

There can be no force unless two bodies are involved. When a hammer strikes a nail, it exerts an "action" force on the nail. But the nail must also "react" by pushing back against the hammer. In all cases there must be an acting force and a reacting force. Whenever two bodies interact, the force exerted by the second body on the first (the reaction force) is equal in magnitude and opposite in direction to the force exerted by the first body on the second (the action force). This principle is stated in Newton's third law.

Newton's Third Law: To every action there must be an equal and opposite reaction.

Objects at rest or in motion with constant speed are said to be in equilibrium. We know from Newton's first law that all forces must be balanced in such cases. Otherwise, there would be a change in the state of rest or motion. At least one condition for equilibrium, therefore, must be that the resultant force acting on an object is equal to zero.

Consider the following diagram of a 200 lb. object suspended from a ceiling by means of a rope. Since the object is at rest, it is in equilibrium. Therefore, Newton's first law applies and the resultant of all forces acting on it is zero. The earth supplies a 200 lb. force acting downward (called weight). An equal and opposite force must be applied to the object by the rope. This pull of the rope is referred to as the tension in the rope. The tension in the rope must be 200 lb to counter balance the downward force.

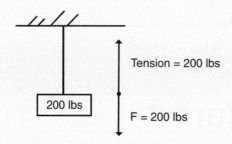

MOTION

Speed is distance covered per unit time. Velocity of an object is its speed in a given direction. Speed is a scalar quantity, while velocity is a vector quantity. The velocity changes if either the speed or the direction of motion, or both, change. You can think of direction as being given by the points of a compass. You can then readily see that if an object is moving at constant speed around a horizontal circle, its direction, and therefore its velocity, are constantly changing. One instant, the object may be moving towards the north, and a little later it will be moving towards the south.

Uniform motion is motion in which the velocity is constant. If the velocity changes, the motion is said to be accelerated. Acceleration is defined as the rate of change of velocity. Uniformly accelerated motion is motion with constant acceleration. If an object is allowed to fall freely near the surface of the earth (that is, its initial velocity is zero and no forces other than gravity act on it during its fall) the acceleration of the object remains constant and is independent of the mass of the object. If an object is projected into the air in some direction other than vertical, air resistance being negligible, the path is a parabola, as shown on the next page.

An object that is thrown or shot is known as a projectile. Projectile motion can be thought of as a combination of two separate motions: a horizontal motion in which the velocity remains constant, and a vertical motion due to gravity. If the object is projected horizontally, the vertical motion is the same as in free fall. Examples of projectiles are a ball that has been thrown, an arrow that has been shot from a bow, and a rocket after it has burnt all of its fuel.

ROTATIONAL EQUILIBRIUM

If two equal and opposite parallel forces (non-concurrent) are applied to an object, their resultant force is zero, but the object will rotate unless some other forces are properly applied. The torque or moment of force is the effectiveness of a force in producing or tending to produce rotation. The magnitude of this torque is the product of the applied force times the length of the moment arm (the tendency of a force to produce rotation of an object is called the moment of the force—or torque). The length of the moment arm is the perpendicular from the fulcrum or pivot to the direction of the force. In general, the moment arm, and therefore the torque, are the greatest when the force is perpendicular to the object. Torques can be clockwise or counterclockwise in direction. The diagram below illustrates how the unbalanced force F has no rotational effect at point A but becomes increasingly effective as the moment arm gets longer.

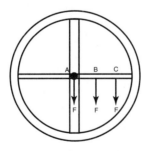

If we are to ensure that rotational effects are also balanced, to achieve rotational equilibrium, we must require that there be no resultant torque. The algebraic sum of all the torques about any axis must be zero. Thus, the clockwise torques are exactly equal in magnitude to the counterclockwise torques.

Every particle on the earth has at least one force in common with every other particle—its weight. Regardless of the shape and size of an object, there exists a point at which the entire weight of the body may be considered to be concentrated. This point is called the center of gravity of the body. The center of gravity of an object is that point at which the entire weight of a body may be considered as acting and produces the same resultant torque. If the mass of a body is uniformly distributed and if the body has a regular shape, such as a sphere, cylinder, rectangle, or cube, then its center of gravity will be located at its geometric center. Some objects such as a hollow square, a circular hoop, and a carpenter's square all have centers of gravity outside the material of the body.

Equilibrium is further classified as being stable or unstable. The terms describe the behavior of objects when they are disturbed slightly from their equilibrium positions. An object in stable equilibrium will tend to return to its equilibrium position when slightly disturbed. When an object is slightly disturbed and a displacing torque causes it to topple or fall over, the object is said to be in unstable equilibrium. These equilibrium conditions are illustrated below:

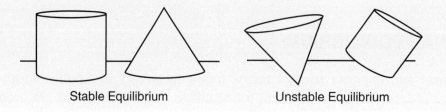

Stable Equilibrium   Unstable Equilibrium

Symmetry

Symmetry of objects can be explained and illustrated as follows: two points P1 and P2 in a plane are symmetric with respect to a line S. In other words, P1 and P2 are reflections of each other with respect to line S. In this case line S is an axis of symmetry. This axial symmetry is shown below:

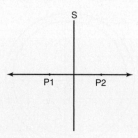

For example, a circle is symmetric with respect to any diameter, and an isosceles triangle is symmetrical with respect to the altitude to its base.

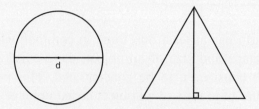

V. Simple Machines

Machines are an arrangement of materials that enable us to do work with less effort, force, or with greater speed. A machine is a device which will transfer a force from one point of application to another for some practical advantage. For example, we may want to lift a flag to the top of a pole. It is inconvenient to climb to the top of the pole each day and pull the flag up. Instead, we keep a pulley at the top of the pole and, with the aid of a rope, apply a downward force at A and produce an upward force on the flag at B, as shown in the diagram.

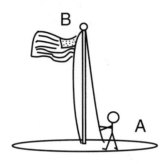

TYPES OF SIMPLE MACHINES

There are six types of simple machines: pulley, lever, wheel and axle, inclined plane, screw, and wedge.

The force that we apply to the machine in order to do the work (such as at A in the above case) is known as the effort. The force which we have to overcome (such as the weight at B) is known as the resistance.

Mechanical advantage is the advantage gained from machines. An ideal machine would be a machine that was completely frictionless. The actual mechanical advantage (AMA) of a machine is the ratio of the resistance to the effort (AMA = $\frac{R}{E}$). The ideal mechanical advantage (IMA) of a machine is equal to the ratio of the distance the input force moves to the distance the output force moves.

Levers

When we use crowbars, bottle openers, or oars, we are using the simple machine known as the lever. A lever is a rigid bar free to turn about a fixed point known as the fulcrum or pivot. The things we said about torques previously, apply to the lever. As shown in the diagram, the oar can rotate around P. We pull on the oar handle at A and, as a result, a push is exerted on the water at B by the oar blade.

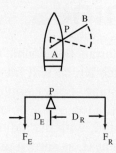

The three classes of levers are shown in the pictures and diagrams below. Also, the ideal mechanical advantage (IMA) of a lever depends on where the fulcrum is located with respect to the points where the effort and resistance, respectively, are applied.

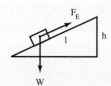

Inclined Planes

When heavy objects have to be raised to a platform or put into a truck, it is often found to be convenient to slide these objects up along a board. An inclined plane is a flat surface one end of which is kept at a higher level than the other, as shown in the diagram.

The input work, or work done by the effort, equals F_E times the length of the plane, l. The work output equals the height of the object W times the height of the plane, h. The ideal mechanical advantage of the inclined plane is the ratio of the weight of the object to the ideal effort or the ratio of length of the plane to the height of the plane.

Pulley

When heavy objects have to be lifted through a considerable distance, the pulley is a convenient, simple machine for the job. The pulley is a wheel mounted to a frame so that it may turn readily around the axis through the center of the wheel. If the frame and wheel move through space as the pulley is used, we have a movable pulley. Otherwise, we say we have a fixed pulley. For many common pulley arrangements, the ideal mechanical advantage can be determined visually by counting the number of rope segments supporting the movable pulley(s). Some typical pulley arrangements are shown on the following page.

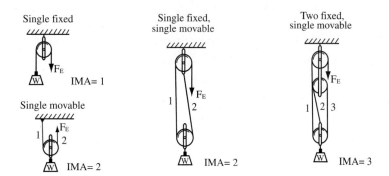

Wheel and Axle

A wheel and axle consists of a wheel or crank rigidly attached to an axle which turns with it as shown in the following diagram:

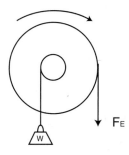

Applications of this are found in the steering wheel of an automobile (the shaft is the axle), the screwdriver, and a doorknob. In the diagram, a wheel and axle are used to lift a weight, W. This represents the resistance and is attached to the rim of the axle. The effort, F_E, is applied to a rope connected to the rim of the wheel. The ratio of the circumference of the wheel to the circumference of the axle is the ideal mechanical advantage.

Screws

The diagram below shows a jackscrew, which illustrates the principle of the screw.

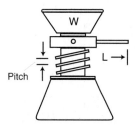

The effort, F_E, may be applied at the end of a rod of length L. As the effort is applied through a circumference, $(2\pi L)$ the screw advances the distance between two adjacent threads and moves the weight through the same distance. This distance is known as the pitch of the screw. The weight represents the resistance.

Wedges

The wedge may be thought of as a double inclined plane. It is used in devices like an axe to split wood. It is easy to use when the length is large compared with the thickness.

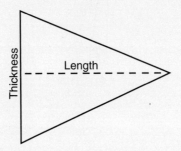

Torque

In most mechanical applications, work is done by transmitting torque from one drive to another. For example, the belt drive transmits the torque from a driving pulley to an output pulley as shown in the following diagram.

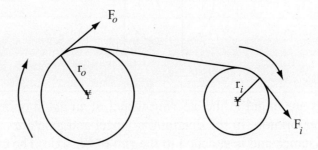

Gears

We must also consider the application of gears. A gear is simply a notched wheel that can transmit torque by meshing with another notched wheel as shown in the following spur gears.

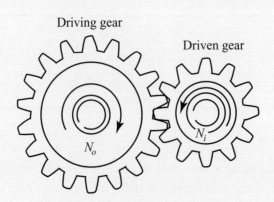

A pair of meshing gears differs from a belt drive only in the sense that the gears rotate in opposite directions. The use of gears avoids the problem of slippage, which is common with belt drives. It also conserves space and allows for a greater torque to be transmitted. Examples of other types of gears are shown in the following figures.

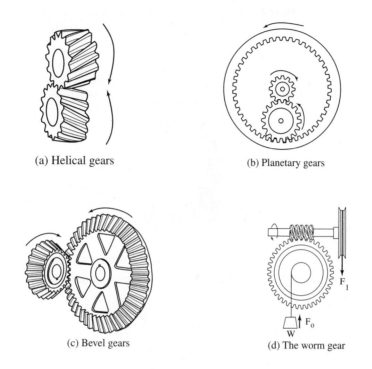

(a) Helical gears

(b) Planetary gears

(c) Bevel gears

(d) The worm gear

VI. Fluids

The term fluid refers to both gases and liquids. A solid has definite shape and volume. A liquid has definite volume, but it takes the shape of its container. A gas has neither definite shape nor volume, and it expands to fill any container into which it is put. A cubic foot of concrete weighs more than a cubic foot of water; therefore, we say the concrete is denser than the water. The density of a substance is the mass of a unit volume. A solid tends to sink in a liquid of lesser density and to float in one of greater density. Instead of speaking about the density of a substance, it has been found more convenient to speak about its relative density, or density compared to a standard. This is its specific gravity. The specific gravity of liquids can be found by using a hydrometer. The higher the hydrometer floats, the denser the liquid.

PRESSURE

Fluids push against the container in which they are placed. Pressure is the amount of force exerted by a substance per unit area. Liquid inside a container exerts a force on the bottom and sides of the container because of its weight. The pressure due to a liquid is equal to the height of the liquid (h) times its density (d) and "g" (the acceleration due to gravity). This is true not only on the bottom of the container but also on the sides at any depth of the liquid. Liquid pressure is independent of the size or shape of the container; it depends only on the depth and density of the liquid.

Gases have weight, but their densities are less than those of liquids and solids. Gases also exert pressure. The Earth's atmosphere is a mixture of gases. Atmospheric pressure is not constant. It decreases with altitude and can be measured using a mercury barometer as shown below:

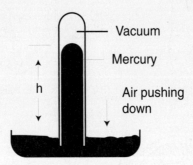

Pressure applied to a confined fluid is transmitted throughout the liquid without loss and acts perpendicularly on the surface of the container. For example, consider the hydraulic press shown.

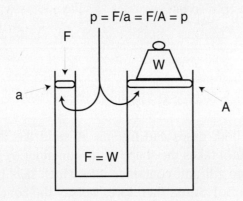

PASCAL'S PRINCIPLE

A small force (F) is applied to the piston of small area (a). This produces a pressure (p) on the enclosed fluid and this same pressure is transmitted by the fluid to act on the underside of the large piston, whose area is A. The resulting force (F=pA) is larger than F and is able to support the large weight (W). This is known as Pascal's Principle.

ARCHIMEDES' PRINCIPLE

The apparent loss in weight of an object immersed in a fluid equals the weight of the displaced fluid. When an object is placed in a fluid, some of the fluid is pushed out of the way — that is, some of the fluid is displaced. This is so because no two objects can occupy the same space at the same time. In the case of an object that is fully submerged, like object A in the diagram,

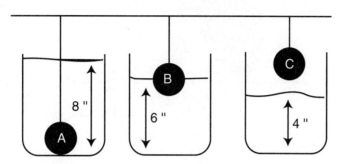

the volume of fluid displaced equals the volume of the object. A stone held in water appears lighter than when held in air. The apparent loss in weight equals the weight of the displaced fluid. This is a statement of Archimedes' Principle.

The upward push of a fluid on an object immersed in it is the buoyant force of the fluid, or its buoyancy. The apparent loss in weight equals the buoyancy. The apparent loss in weight due to the buoyant effect of gases can usually be neglected. However, the rising of balloons depends on this. The lifting force of the gases in a balloon is equal to the weight of the air displaced by the balloon minus the weight of the gas in the gas bags.

FLUIDS IN MOTION

In studying fluids in motion, we shall assume that all fluids in motion exhibit streamline flow. Streamline flow is the motion of a fluid in which every particle in the fluid follows the same path (past a particular point) as that followed by previous particles.

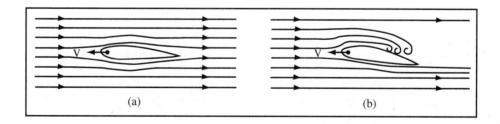

(a) (b)

If the speed of a fluid is increased, its pressure is decreased. This principle is made use of in the design of airplane wings to give the plane lift. The wing is designed so that the air will move faster over the top of the wing than across the bottom. As a result, the air pressure on top of the wing is less than on the bottom, with the consequence that the upward push of the air on the wing is greater than the downward push. The figure below shows a method you can use to demonstrate the decrease in pressure that results from an increase in speed. This method consists of blowing air past the top surface of a paper. The pressure in the airstream above the paper will be reduced. This allows excess pressure on the bottom to force the paper upward.

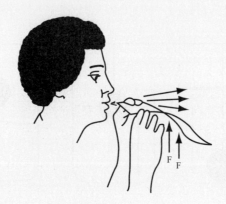

VII. Temperature

One way of defining temperature is to say that it is the degree of heat or coldness of an object.

Most solids expand when heated and contract when cooled. The same lengths of different solids expand in different amounts when heated through the same temperature change. For example, brass expands more than iron. This difference is made use of in thermostats, where a bimetallic strip is used. When heated, the bimetallic strip bends with the brass forming the outside of the curve, as shown in the picture.

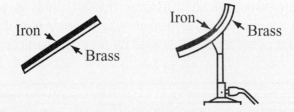

When a solid expands, it expands not only in length but also in width and thickness.

Most liquids expand when heated and contract when cooled. Different liquids expand in different amounts when heated through the same temperature change.

If the pressure on a gas is kept constant, heating the gas will result in an increase in its volume. Another important relationship for gases is if the temperature of a gas is kept constant, the volume of the gas varies inversely with its pressure (i.e., an increase in volume results in a decrease in pressure and the reverse is also true). Also, at constant volume, heating a gas will result in an increase in pressure.

VIII. Heat

Heat can be defined as a form of energy which flows between two objects because they are at different temperatures. It is energy in transit.

METHODS OF HEAT TRANSFER

Sometimes, we want heat to escape; sometimes, we want to keep it from escaping. In the case of heat engines, such as the gasoline engine, only some of the heat can be used to do work. It is necessary to get rid of the excess heat or the engine would rapidly overheat. In the case of heating a home, we want the heat to get from the furnace to the room, but we may want to keep the heat from getting out of the house. The three methods of heat transfer are conduction, convection, and radiation.

Conduction

Conduction is the process in which heat is transferred by molecular collisions through a medium (a solid, a liquid, or a gas). The medium itself does not move. For example, if we heat one end of a copper rod, the other end gets hot too. The energy transfer in metallic conductors is chiefly by means of direct particle interaction. In general, metals are good conductors; good conductors of heat are also good conductors of electricity. Silver is the best metallic conductor of heat and electricity. Copper and aluminum are also very good. Liquids and gases, as well as non-metallic solids (e.g. glass and wood), are poor conductors of heat. Poor conductors are known as insulators.

Convection

Convection is the process of transferring heat in a fluid which involves the motion of the heated portion to the cooler portion of the fluid. The heated portion expands, rises, and is replaced by cooler fluid, thus giving rise to so-called convection currents. This may be observed over a tall radiator. Radiators heat rooms chiefly by convection.

Radiation

Radiation is the process of transferring heat which can take place in a vacuum. It takes place by a wave motion similar to light. The wave is known as an electromagnetic wave. The most obvious source of radiant energy is our sun. The higher the temperature of an object, the greater the amount of heat it radiates.

Black objects radiate more heat from each square centimeter of surface than light-colored objects at the same temperature. The vacuum bottle (thermos bottle) is designed with the three methods of heat transfer in mind. Examples of all three methods of heat transfer are shown in the pictures below.

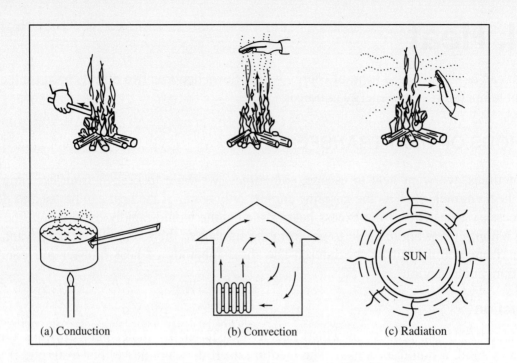

(a) Conduction (b) Convection (c) Radiation

IX. Rotational Motion

Uniform circular motion is motion in which there is no change in speed, only a constant change in direction. An example of uniform circular motion is afforded by swinging a toy in a circular path with a string. As the toy revolves with constant speed, the inward force of the tension in the string constantly changes the direction of the toy, causing it to move in a circular path. If the string should break, the toy would fly off at a tangent perpendicular to the radius of its circular path. This is shown in the picture below.

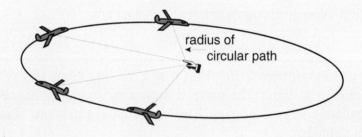

radius of circular path

CENTRIPETAL FORCE

The inward force necessary to maintain uniform circular motion is defined as the centripetal force. This inward force will increase with a larger mass or a higher speed, but will decrease with a larger radius of the circular path.

When an automobile is driven around a sharp turn on a perfectly level road, friction between the tire and the road provides centripetal force. If this centripetal force is not adequate, the car may slide off the road. The maximum value of the force of friction determines the maximum speed with which a car can negotiate a turn of a given radius.

We can now consider the effects of banking a turn to eliminate the need for a friction force. Refer to the pictures below. The horizontal component of the normal force (weight of the automobile) provides the necessary centripetal force.

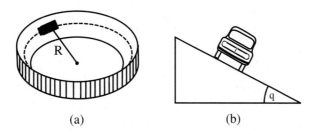

(a)   (b)

Thus, a banking angle is required to negotiate a turn without the need for a friction force. This required banking angle is larger with higher speed and smaller with a larger radius of circular path.

ANGULAR DISPLACEMENT

Another type of circular motion exists when an entire body rotates about an axis. For example, wheels, drive shafts, and fly wheels all use rotational effects to accomplish work. In such cases, it is often necessary to measure the amount of rotation, which is called angular displacement. To understand what is meant by angular displacement, consider the rotating disk shown in the following figure.

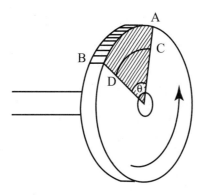

Angular displacement, θ, is indicated by the shaded portion of the disk. The angular displacement is the same from C to D as it is from A to B, for a rigid body.

The time rate change in angular displacement is called the angular velocity. Thus, if an object rotates through an angle θ in a time, t, its angular velocity is given by the angular displacement divided by the time.

The axis of rotation of a rigid rotating object can be defined as that line of particles which remains in a fixed position during rotation. This may be a line through the body, as with a spinning top, or it may be a line through space, as with a rolling hoop. In any case, the farther a particle is from the axis of rotation, the greater its linear speed. Hence, the linear speed can be expressed as a function of the angular speed; the linear speed equals the product of angular speed times the radius of the circular path.

X. Properties of Solids

We define an elastic body as one which returns to its original size and shape when a deforming force is removed. The quicker a body returns to its original shape, the more elastic the body is. Rubber bands, diving boards, footballs, and springs are common examples of elastic bodies. Putty, dough, and clay are examples of inelastic bodies. For elastic materials, Hooke's Law applies: The deformation or distortion of an elastic object is proportional to the distorting force. For example, if a 10g object suspended from a spring stretches the spring 2 cm, a 20g object will stretch it 4 cm. The uniform elongation of a spring is shown in the following diagram:

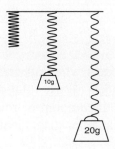

Other types of deformations are tensile stress and compressive stress. Tensile stress (stress is defined as force per a unit of area) occurs when equal and opposite forces are directed away from each other. A compressive stress occurs when equal and opposite forces are directed toward each other. In the case of a tensile or compressive stress, the strain may be considered a change in length per unit length. The effectiveness of any force producing a stress is highly dependent upon the area over which the force is distributed. A force distributed over a larger area is generally less effective than a force over a smaller area.

XI. Electricity

Two types of electric charges exist, a positive (+) charge and a negative (−) charge. Like charges repel and unlike charges attract. A conductor (discussed earlier under heat transfer) is a material through which charge can easily be transferred. An insulator is a material which resists the flow of charge.

The flow of electric charge constitutes an electric current. The electric current is the rate of flow of charge past a given point in an electric conductor. If a copper wire is connected to the terminals of a battery or generator, charge will go through the wire from the negative terminal to the positive terminal. This is usually taken as the direction of the current in the wire. A device with the ability to maintain a voltage or potential difference between two points is called a source of electromotive force (emf). The most familiar sources of emf are batteries and generators. Batteries convert chemical energy to electrical energy and generators transform mechanical energy into electrical energy. Batteries have two terminals: one positive, the other negative.

Resistance is defined as opposition to the flow of electric charge. Although most metals are good conductors of electricity, all offer some opposition to the surge of electric charge through them. Electrical resistance is independent of the applied emf and the current passing through it. The resistance of most metallic conductors goes up when the temperature goes up. Also, the greater the length of conductor wire, the higher the resistance. The greater the resistance, the smaller the current for a given voltage. Also, at a given temperature, the greater the voltage, the larger the current.

An electric circuit consists of any number of conductors joined so that at least one closed path is provided for current. Two or more elements (for example, light bulbs) in a circuit are said to be in series if they have only one point in common that is not connected to some third element. Current can follow only a single path through the elements in series. The following figure shows a battery circuit with three resistances (light bulbs) connected in series.

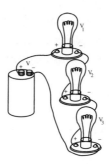

There are several limitations in the operation of series circuits. If a single element in a series circuit fails to provide a conducting path, the entire circuit is opened and current stops. More-over, each element in a series circuit adds to the total resistance of the circuit, thereby limiting the total current which can be supplied. These problems can be overcome by providing alternate paths for electric current. Such a connection, in which current can be divided between two or more elements, is called a parallel connection. A parallel circuit is one in which two or more components are connected to two common points in the circuit. The following figure shows a battery circuit with three light bulbs (resistances) connected in parallel.

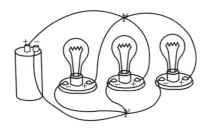

The relationship of voltage, currents, and resistance is shown in Ohm's law:

$$\text{Current} = \frac{\text{voltage}}{\text{resistance}}$$

Also, electrical power in a circuit is measured in terms of the product of the voltage times the current.

XII. Magnetism

All substances are either magnetic or non-magnetic. A magnetic substance is one that can be attracted by a magnet. Magnetic materials include iron, nickel, cobalt, and alloys of iron. Non-magnetic substances are only feebly affected by a magnet, for example, glass, wool, brass. When a bar magnet is freely suspended, the magnet comes to rest in a north-south position. A magnetic pole is the region of a magnet where its strength is concentrated; every magnet has at least two poles. The end pointing toward the Earth's north is called the north-seeking pole or the north (N) pole of the magnet. The opposite, south-seeking end is called the south (S) pole. A compass consists of a light-weight, magnetized needle pivoted on a support. The north and south poles of a magnet are different and this can be demonstrated by the law of magnetic forces. This law states that like magnetic poles (N-N or S-S) repel each other, and unlike magnetic poles (N-S) attract each other. These results have been found through experimentation.

XIII. Wave Motion

One of the most important ways of transferring energy is through wave motion. Energy can be distributed from one point to other points without physical transfer of the material between the points. We are all familiar with water waves, which carry a disturbance through water, but the same principle can be applied to much more complicated events. Mechanical waves, which involve local disturbances in a mass medium, are the basis for the transmission of sound. Electromagnetic waves carry energy in the forms of light, heat, and radio waves through empty space. A mechanical wave is a physical disturbance in an elastic medium (solid, liquid, or gas).

PERIODIC MOTION

Periodic motion is motion which is repeated over and over again. The motion of a pendulum is periodic. As long as its arc of swing is small, the time required for a back-and-forth swing is constant. This time is called its period and the period depends on the length of string of the pendulum. The longer the string, the longer the period of the pendulum.

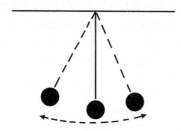

The pendulum consists of a bob of small mass swinging back and forth through a small angle at the end of a string or wire. The motion of tuning fork prongs is also periodic.

SOUND WAVES

When we speak about sound, we usually mean the sound wave. Sound waves can travel in solids, liquids, or gases. They are produced by vibrating objects (such as tuning forks). Sound cannot be transmitted through the vacuum of empty space. During a thunderstorm, we observe the flash of lightning before we hear the thunder. Even though both light and sound travel at measurable speeds, the speed of light is so much greater in comparison that the transmission of light can be considered instantaneous. At 27°C, the speed of sound is approximately 343 m/sec, or 1,127 ft/sec. The higher the temperature, the faster sound waves travel. In general, sound travels faster in liquids and solids than in air.

XIV. Light

In many ways, light behaves like a wave. For example, it is possible to have two light beams interfere with each other so that their combination is dimmer than either beam alone. Heat and light are transferred through practically empty space to earth from the sun. Radio waves also travel through empty space. These are examples of self-sustaining waves called electromagnetic waves.

The speed of light is fantastically high. In empty space, it is about 3×10^8 m/sec, or 186,000 miles/sec. In air, the speed of light is only slightly less. Also, in transparent liquids and solids the speed of light is considerably less than in air.

A luminous body is one that emits light of its own. An incandescent object is one that emits light because it has been heated. The filament in our electric light bulbs is incandescent; the firefly is luminous, but not incandescent. An illuminated object is one that is visible by the light that it reflects.

One of the most important properties of light is the fact that it travels in a straight line. It is convenient to use the ray to represent the direction in which the light travels and to think of light as traveling in a straight line as long as the medium doesn't change. When light hits a surface, usually some of the light is reflected. The normal for this light is the line drawn perpendicular to the surface at the point where the light ray touches the surface. The light that goes towards the surface is known as incident light and is represented by the incident ray. Light also travels millions of miles of space from the sun and other stars. Light, unlike sound, travels through vacuums. Refer to the following diagram.

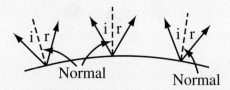

The angle of incidence (i) is the angle between the incident ray and its normal. The reflected light is represented by the reflected ray; the angle of reflection (r) is the angle between the reflected ray and its normal. The law of reflection states that, when a wave is reflected, the angle at incidence equals the angle of reflection, and the incident ray, the normal, and the reflected ray lie in a common plane. This law applies not only to light but also to other waves, and this is true of smooth and rough surfaces.

Any dark-colored object absorbs light, yet a black object absorbs nearly all the light it receives. Light that is not absorbed upon striking a surface is either reflected or transmitted. If all the light upon an object is reflected or absorbed, the object is said to be opaque. Since light cannot pass through an opaque body, a shadow will be produced in space behind the object, as illustrated in the following picture.

Look at the shadow of your hand held in front of an electric lamp. It has a fuzzy edge. The shady border exists because the source of light is spread out over an area. In the dark central shadow, called the umbra, light from the source is blocked completely by the object. But light from part of the source reaches the fuzzy shadow region, called the penumbra. Thus, if light did not travel in straight lines, there would be no shadows.

XV. Optics

Optics is the study of the generation, manipulation, and deflection of light. It is also concerned with the interaction of light with matter and a variety of systems (scientific, commercial, etc.).

PLANE MIRROR

A plane mirror is a perfectly flat mirror. The characteristics of an image produced by such a mirror can be determined by means of a ray diagram, as shown in the following diagram.

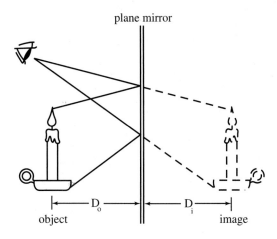

Image in a Plane Mirror

The image is found by ray tracing and the law of reflection. From this diagram, we can determine the characteristics of an image in a plane mirror:

1. The image is the same size as the object.

2. The image is upright (if the object is upright).

3. The image is as far behind the mirror as the object is in front.

4. The image is virtual. This means that the image is formed by rays which do not actually pass through it; if a screen were placed at the position of the image, no image would be seen.

5. The image is laterally reversed. This can be thought of in terms of two people shaking hands: their arms extend diagonally between them. When a person holds his hand out to the mirror, the arm of his image comes out straight at him.

SPHERICAL SURFACES

Spherical surfaces are commonly used as the reflecting surfaces of curved mirrors. This provides two types of spherical mirrors: concave mirrors and convex mirrors. For a concave mirror, the reflecting surface is inside of the spherical surface. (Like a cave, a concave mirror is recessed.) For a convex mirror, the reflecting surface is the outer portion of the spherical surface. In particular, all the images for a convex mirror are virtual, upright, and reduced in size, as illustrated in the diagram.

Images with Convex Mirrors

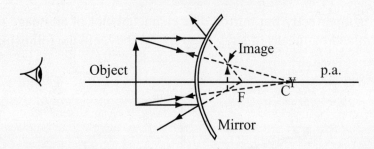

Note: We are able to see a virtual image in a mirror because the real image of the object is formed on the retina "screen" of our eye.

The following two ray diagrams show that with a concave mirror we can get both real and virtual images. Notice that the kind of image produced is based on the location of the object. In ray diagram (A) a real image is produced since the object π is placed beyond the focal point (F). In ray diagram (B), a virtual image is produced, since the object π is placed between the focal point (F) and the mirror. Notice also that the virtual image (ray diagram [B]) produced with a concave mirror is larger than the object.

Images with Concave Mirrors

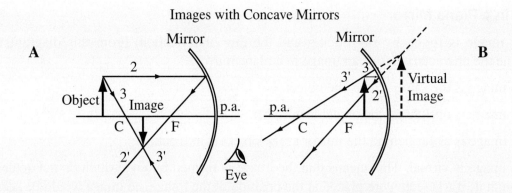

XVI. Standard Time Zones

Time zones for the boundaries of the United States are shown in the figure on the next page.

The boundaries change in some areas when daylight saving time is adopted from April through October each year. The major (eastern part) of Alaska and the Hawaiian Islands are two hours ahead of Pacific Standard Time. Alaska's western coast and the Aleutian Islands are three hours ahead of Pacific Standard Time. When you travel west into a different time zone, the time kept by your watch will be one hour past or ahead of the standard time of the westward zone; therefore, you must move the hour hand back one hour if the watch is to maintain the correct time. This process will be necessary as you continue west through additional time zones.

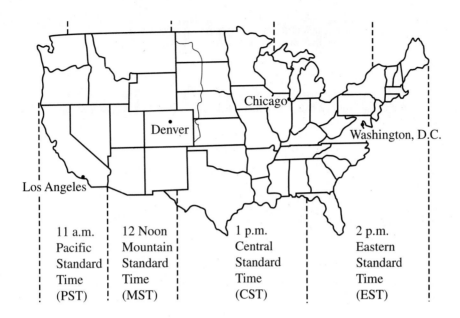

11 a.m.
Pacific
Standard
Time
(PST)

12 Noon
Mountain
Standard
Time
(MST)

1 p.m.
Central
Standard
Time
(CST)

2 p.m.
Eastern
Standard
Time
(EST)

Optional Test:

Mechanical Aptitude

Time: 30 Minutes
40 Questions

DIRECTIONS: Select the best answer choice.

---

1. Which person must pull hardest to lift the weight?

    A. 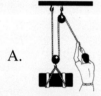   C.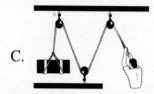

    B.   D. No difference exists.

2. Which car is less likely to roll?

    A. 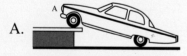   C.

    B.    D. No difference exists.

3. Which is the hardest way to carry the hammer?

A.

C.

B.

D. No difference exists.

4. In which picture are the books more likely to knock over the bookend?

A.

C.

B.

D. No difference exists

5. When the right-hand gear turns in the direction shown, which way does the top gear turn? (NOTE: The gears are interlocked.)

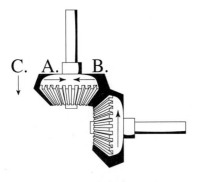

D. The top gear will not move at all.

6. In which picture can the ferry cross the river more quickly?

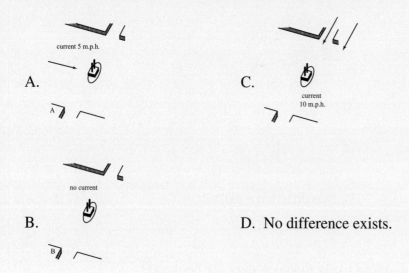

B.   D. No difference exists.

7. Which shaft will turn most slowly?

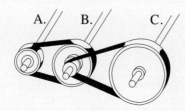

    D. All turn with the same speed.

8. For the balloon to stay up, the gas in the bag must be:

    A. Heavier than the surrounding air.

    B. Lighter than the surrounding air.

    C. The same weight as the surrounding air.

    D. The same temperature as the surrounding air.

9. Which is the best way for an astronaut to signal her companion on the moon?

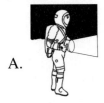

A.

C.

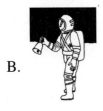

B.

D. No difference exists.

10. Which truck will turn over more easily?

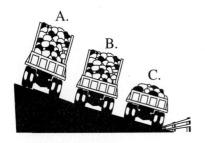

D. No difference exists.

11. In which picture can the woman see what is happening behind her?

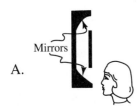

A.

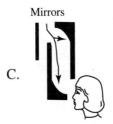

C.

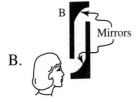

B.

D. Each woman can see behind her.

12. In which picture are the magnets placed so as to attract each other?

A.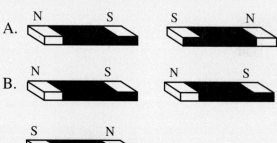

B.

C.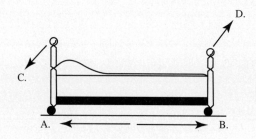

D. Both A and C.

13. Which way has this bed just been rolled if its wheels are able to rotate?

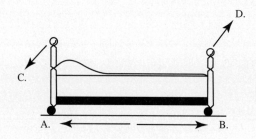

14. Which picture shows how this wooden circle will stand?

A.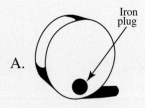

C.

B.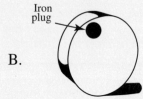

D. None of them.

15. Which box weighs more?

A.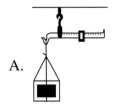

C.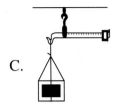

B.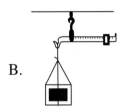

D. All the boxes are equal in weight.

16. Which one piece of cable will give this pole the best support?

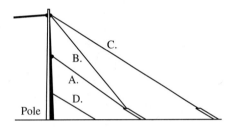

17. Which dam is stronger?

A.

C.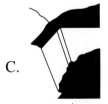

B.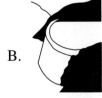

D. No difference exists.

18. Which way will the hands of this clock seem to turn when seen in the mirror?

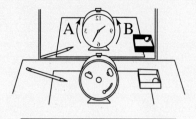

C. It depends on the time of day.

D. Inconclusive due to picture

19. Which picture shows the timer ticking the slowest?

A.

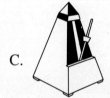

C.

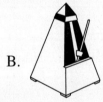

B.

D. No difference exists.

20. Which part of the refrigerator is coldest?

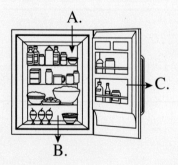

D. All parts are the same temperature.

21. Which drawing shows how a bomb actually falls from the plane?

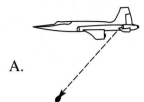

A.

C.

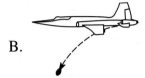

B.

D. All of them.

22. Which container would hold the most water?

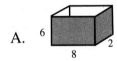

A.   6   8   2

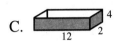

C.   4   12   2

B.   8   6   2

D. All hold the same amount of water.

23. At which point was the basketball moving the slowest?

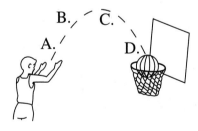

24. Which shelf could support the most weight?

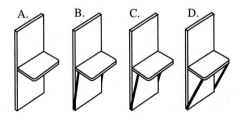

25. In the example given below, the amount of gas in each balloon is the same. The atmospheric pressure outside the balloon is highest on which balloon?

A. B. C.

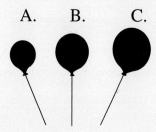

D. The pressure is equal on all the balloons.

26. Which picture shows the lamps connected to give the most light?

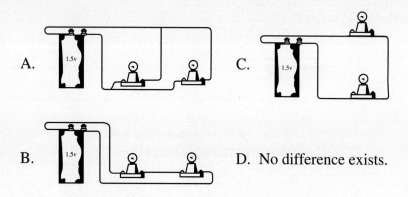

A.

C.

B.

D. No difference exists.

27. After it hits the black ball, which way will ball "X" go?

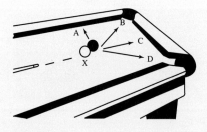

28. Which object is least likely to tip over?

A.

C.

B.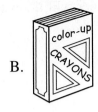

D. All are equally likely to tip over.

29. If it is 8:00 A.M. Eastern Standard Time in Miami, Florida, what is the correct standard time in San Diego, California?

A. 8:00 P.M.

B. 11:00 A.M.

C. 6:00 A.M.

D. None of these.

30. Which figure is not symmetrical?

A.

C.

B.

D. All are symmetrical.

31. Three bricks of the same weight and dimensions are placed on a table top as shown. Which brick exerts the greatest pressure on the table top?

A.

C.

B.

D. All the bricks exert the same pressure.

32. All three steel containers hold the same volume of water. In which container will the water heat up the quickest?

A.
4 cm

C.
6 cm

B.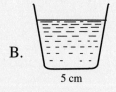
5 cm

D. No difference exists.

33. Which perimeter is the longest?

A.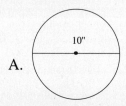

C.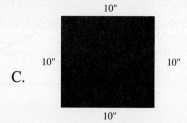

B.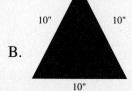

D. All are the same length.

34. Which angle is the smallest?

A.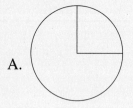

C.

B.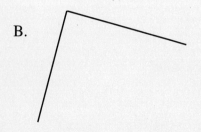

D. All are the same size.

35. What level in the can must the water reach in order to start pouring out of the tube?

    D. The water will pour out at any level.

36. With which of the following is it hardest to lift the weight?

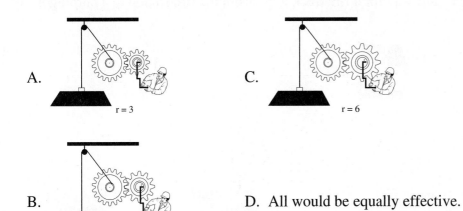

    D. All would be equally effective.

37. Which of the three lettered shadows represents the place where the shadow would actually appear?

    D. None of these places.

38. As the wheel turns on its axle, which of the three lettered points will be moved the slowest?

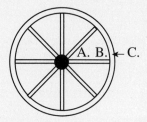

   D. All turn at the same rate.

39. Which would be the fastest way for a fire truck to go from the fire station to a burning house?

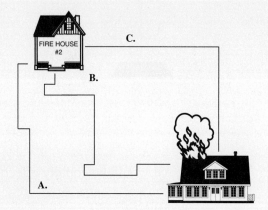

   D. All the routes are equally fast.

40. Which liquid is the heaviest?

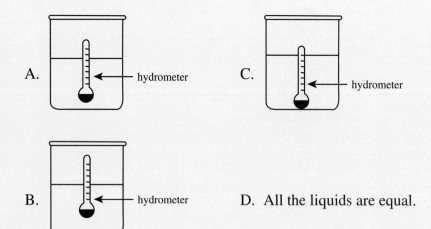

   D. All the liquids are equal.

HSPT

Optional Test: Mechanical Aptitude

ANSWER KEY

Question Number	Correct Answer	If You Answered this Question Incorrectly, Refer to...
1.	(B)	P. 656
2.	(A)	P. 656
3.	(A)	P. 658
4.	(B)	P. 651
5.	(A)	P. 658
6.	(B)	P. 650
7.	(C)	P. 658
8.	(B)	P. 661
9.	(A)	P. 669
10.	(A)	P. 665
11.	(A)	P. 671
12.	(B)	P. 668
13.	(B)	P. 657
14.	(A)	P. 651
15.	(C)	P. 658
16.	(C)	P. 656
17.	(A)	P. 660
18.	(B)	P. 671
19.	(A)	P. 668
20.	(B)	P. 662
21.	(B)	P. 652
22.	(D)	P. 649

23.	(C)	P. 652
24.	(D)	P. 658
25.	(A)	P. 660
26.	(A)	P. 667
27.	(D)	P. 651
28.	(A)	P. 651
29.	(D)	P. 673
30.	(C)	P. 655
31.	(B)	P. 650
32.	(C)	P. 663
33.	(C)	P. 648
34.	(D)	P. 646
35.	(B)	P. 659
36.	(A)	P. 658
37.	(B)	P. 670
38.	(D)	P. 657
39.	(C)	P. 648
40.	(B)	P. 661

Detailed Explanations of Answers

1.   **(B)**   Person in B has only one fixed pulley. The person in A has one fixed and one movable pulley and the person in C has three fixed pulleys. Both A and C have greater mechanical advantages than B.

2.   **(A)**   Both cars B and C sit on inclined plane surfaces. Due to their weights (and also the friction between the tires and surface), the cars are more likely to roll down the incline. Car A rests only on the edge of a platform.

3.   **(A)**   The farther the hammer head is away from the person's shoulder (pivot point), the greater the torque (force times distance) and the harder it would be to carry the hammer. Pictures B and C show the hammer heads closer to the person's shoulder.

4.   **(B)**   The bookend in picture B has to support all the weight of the books. Also, the position of the bookend will cause it to tip over more easily due to unstable equilibrium. The bookends in A and C are in more stable equilibrium positions and only have to support the lower weight distribution of the books.

5.   **(A)**   This is an example of bevel gears. As the right-hand gear turns upward, the top gear must turn towards the right. Response C indicates the top gear moving downward, which is not indicated by the mechanical nature of the gears.

6.   **(B)**   Pictures A and C indicate the presence of current which would slow down the actual speed of the ferry. One can also analyze this problem using some simple vector diagrams as follows:

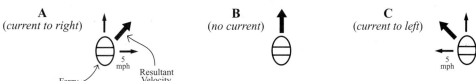

7.   **(C)**   Pulley C has the largest diameter compared to the others. Also, we assume the belt does not slip; thus, the belt will move with the same linear velocity around each pulley. Recall that V=(Insert Greek Letter), thus (Insert Equations) where i = input and o = output for each pulley. Hence, as the diameters of the pulleys become larger, the angular speeds of the shafts are reduced to maintain this constant linear velocity.

8.   **(B)**   Apply the concept of densities here. The lighter or less dense the gas is inside the balloon compared to the atmosphere gas (air), the higher the balloon will rise. The temperature of the gas inside the bag does not have to be equal to the outside air, since warm or hot gas can be added to the balloon to make it rise.

9.   **(A)**   The light (flashlight) can be seen through the helmet of the astronaut, while the sound

of the ringing bell (B) may not be heard through the helmet. Choice (C) is incorrect since no air is present in space to carry sound waves.

10. **(A)** Apply the banking angle principle and center of gravity to the trucks. Truck A has a higher center of gravity and a larger banking angle compared to the other trucks (B and C). Thus, the entire weight of the truck acts at this center of gravity and increases the likelihood of tipping over.

11. **(A)** Observe that in picture A, the top mirror faces outward, which enables the person to see the reflection of the image in the top mirror (object behind her) using the bottom mirror, which she is looking into. In Picture B, the top mirror faces inward which will give no image of the object(s) behind the woman. The following ray diagram illustrates this concept using mirror A.

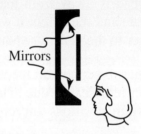

Mirrors

12. **(B)** Apply the law of magnets, which states that opposite ends or poles of a magnet attract each other (N-S).

13. **(B)** Observe the rollers on the bottom of the bed. They are straight and to the left, which indicate that the bed must have been rolled to the right.

14. **(A)** The iron plug (due to its weight) in all the circles would cause the circles to rotate and achieve a state of equilibrium. This would occur only in picture A where the iron plug is at the bottom.

15. **(C)** Apply the concept of torques. Specifically, the sum of the torques in the clockwise direction must equal the sum of the torques in the counterclockwise direction. In picture C, the weight on the right side is the farthest from the pivot or balance point (the hook). Recall that the applied force or weight times the distance is the torque, which is the greatest here.

16. **(C)** Cable C is attached to the highest point on the pole and it makes the largest angle. Cable B is attached at the same point as cable C, but it makes a smaller angle, and thus gives less support. Cables A and D are attached at lower points on the pole, which would give less support.

17. **(A)** The dam in picture A would be the strongest since it is bent inward, or concave, which would provide more support for the weight of the water. Dam B is bent convex, or in the direction the water could flow; while in dam C, the wall is straight. Although stronger than dam B, C would be weaker than dam A.

18. **(B)** Imagine looking straight at the clock; the hands would move in direction A or clockwise. But when looking at its image in the mirror, the hands would seem to move counterclockwise, or direction B.

19. **(A)** Apply the principle of periodic motion and the pendulum set-up. The period (timing) of a pendulum is proportional to the length of the stick on the timer. The longer the stick, the greater its period. In timer A, the weight is at a higher point compared to the other timers. The length is longer; thus, the timer pendulum moves at a smaller or slower period. Refer to the diagram below:

20. **(B)** The cold air in the refrigerator is at the bottom, since cold air sinks while the warmer air rises to the top. Cold air is more dense, since the mass of particles occupies a smaller volume than warmer air. Recall that density is mass per unit volume and for warm air, the particles occupy a larger volume and thus are less dense or lighter.

21. **(B)** Recall that as the plane is moving in a specific direction, or forward. The released bomb, which is now a projectile, follows a parabolic type path (picture B). Picture A shows a straight line path, which is not physically realistic. Picture C shows a parabolic path, but inverted. This is not true since the motion of the plane (direction) and of the bomb would be the same.

22. **(D)** All the volumes of the rectangular containers are the same since all the dimensions are identical. The containers are just oriented differently. The volume of a rectangular solid figure is given by the product l×w×h.

23. **(C)** Use the concept of projectile motion to answer the question. At the highest point of the trajectory of a projectile, the ball's speed is zero, or the slowest motion. This occurs at point C.

24. **(D)** Apply the concept of torque. For shelf D, the supporting edge of the brace under the shelf is at the extreme forward edge. Thus, there is no length of arm (distance) for a downward force to produce a torque. This production of torque (as in shelves A, B, and C) would cause the shelf to collapse.

25. **(A)** If all the balloons contain the same amounts of gas, then the atmospheric pressure must be the greatest on balloon A. The increased outside pressure reduces the volume of the

balloon. Apply Boyle's Law: increasing the pressure of a gas reduces its volume.

26. **(A)** The most light would be given by picture or circuit A, since it is a parallel circuit of lamps. Both pictures B and C are series circuits. Each lamp in a series circuit adds to the total resistance of the circuit, thereby limiting the total current which can be supplied. Apply Ohm's Law: current is proportional to voltage. A lowering of current would indicate a reduced voltage and less power at each lamp. This results in less light.

27. **(D)** Once ball "X" hits the black ball, it would proceed in the right, or "D," direction. The "X" ball hits the black ball on the right and will continue in that direction.

28. **(A)** Use the center of gravity and equilibrium concepts. The briefcase has the lowest center of gravity, which provides the most stable equilibrium. The briefcase is constructed heavier at the bottom.

29. **(D)** None of these times gives the correct time. San Diego, California, is in the Pacific Standard time on the West Coast. The time should be 5:00 A.M. in San Diego.

30. **(C)** For an object to be symmetrical, the right half of the object should be identical to its left half in reference to the axis of symmetry (dotted line). For picture A, the hexagon, and picture B, the star, this symmetry occurs. But in the triangle (picture C), the right sides are longer than the left sides.

31. **(B)** Recall that pressure is defined as the applied force or weight per unit area. Since all the bricks have the same weight, the pressure exerted on the tabletop would depend on how (which side of the tabletop) the brick is placed. The same weight applied over a smaller area, as in picture B, gives a greater pressure.

32. **(C)** Surface area of the container (and water) exposed to the heat from the stove is the key difference here. Container C has the greatest area of water exposed to the heat. Thus, more water molecules are heated faster.

33. **(C)** Recall that the perimeter of a geometric figure is the distance around the figure. The figure with the longest perimeter would be the square in picture C. For the circle in picture A, the circumference is equal to π (3.14) times the diameter (10"). The perimeter is 10" times 3 sides or 30" for the triangle, and 10" times 4 sides or 40" for the square.

34. **(D)** These angles are all the same size. Notice that the angles are formed from two perpendicular lines which form right angles (90°).

35. **(B)** Observe that the level of water inside the can must reach at least the top of the spout. This will occur first at level B, at which point the water will start pouring out of the spout (tube).

36. **(A)** The circumference of the crank on the pulley is actually the wheel and axle machine.

Apply the mechanical advantage of the wheel and axle to this set-up. The smaller the radius of the wheel, the smaller the circumference. The circumference of the wheel in this set-up is the circular rotation of the crank. The smaller the circumference, the lower the mechanical advantage; hence; the crank in picture A would be the hardest to lift the weight.

37. **(B)** The source of light here is the sun. Parts of the tree will be opaque and form a shadow in the space behind the tree. This shadow would be at B in the picture based on the position of the sun.

38. **(D)** The angular velocity ω is the same for all points on the wheel. As shown in the diagram below, each point travels the same angular distance, Θ, in the same amount of time.

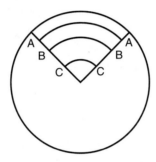

39. **(C)** The shortest distance between two points (or locations) is a straight line or the least number of straight lines. When a certain distance is traveled, a turn or change of direction occurs. This involves a reduction in speed. This slowdown also involves more time. Routes A and B have two or more turns, while route C has only one change of direction.

40. **(B)** Apply the concept of finding the specific gravity of liquids by using a hydrometer. The hydrometer floats higher in denser liquids. The further down in a liquid the hydrometer goes, the less dense the liquid. You can also use the principle of density and Archimedes' principle; lighter objects are buoyed upwards more than heavier objects. The hydrometer in container B floats the highest.

COOP/ HSPT

CHAPTER 10

Catholic Religion Review

Chapter 10

CATHOLIC RELIGION REVIEW

I. BEGINNINGS OF CHRISTIANITY

II. THE SACRAMENTS

III. PRAYER

IV. THE TEN COMMANDMENTS

V. MARIAN LIFE

VI. THE WHO'S WHO OF THE CATHOLIC CHURCH

VII. THE CHRISTIAN LIFESTYLE

For almost two thousand years there has been a unique following in the world. This following has attracted millions of people from all walks of life who come together for one common purpose, who work towards one common goal, who seek to know and understand God and neighbor. These people come together to worship as a community, to work towards salvation, and to know Jesus Christ. This following is known as Christianity.

Christianity has its foundations in the preaching of Jesus Christ and his call to repentance. Since the time of Jesus Christ, his work and his message have been carried on by many people. Christians throughout the world today share in the same faith as that of the early Christians. The faith of the Christian people has survived for nearly 2000 years and continues to be a testimony and a sign of faith in God and his Son.

The Roman Catholic church stands at the forefront of Christianity today. Catholicism is both rich in tradition and responsive to today's modern world. There are many aspects of the Roman Catholic church; the moral life, the biblical life, the worship and sacramental life, the ecumenical life, the Marian life, the modern life of the church, and many others. In these next pages we will explore various aspects of the life of the church and how they relate to those of us living in the present. These next pages will also serve as an overview of the Catholic church, as we look at some of its basic teachings and traditions.

I. BEGINNINGS OF CHRISTIANITY

Prior to Christianity there existed the Jewish faith. The Jews were God's chosen people, led out of slavery in Egypt by Moses and into the Promised Land.

> God also said to Moses, "I am the LORD. As God the Almighty I appeared to Abraham, Isaac and Jacob, but my name, LORD, I did not make known to them. I also established my covenant with them, to give them the land of Canaan, the land in which they were living as aliens. And now that I have heard the groaning of the Israelites, whom the Egyptians are treating as slaves, I am mindful of my covenant. Therefore, say to the Israelites: I am the LORD. I will free you from the forced labor of the Egyptians and will deliver you from their slavery. I will rescue you by my outstretched arm and with mighty acts of judgement. I will take you as my own people, and you shall have me as your God. You will know that I, the LORD, am your God when I free you from the labor of the Egyptians and bring you into the land which I swore to give to Abraham, Isaac and Jacob. I will give it to you as your own possession—I, the LORD!" (Exodus 6:2-8)

God established with the people of Israel an ancient covenant that he would free them, which he did through Moses. This is why the Israelites were referred to as "God's chosen people."

It is in the people of Israel, the Jewish people, that we can find our roots, the roots of Christianity. Mary and Joseph, the mother and foster father of Jesus Christ, were Jewish. Jesus Christ therefore was born as a Jew, lived as a Jew, and died as a Jew. However, he came into the world in order to reveal more fully his Father in heaven. He came into the world so that the gates of heaven (those that had been closed by the sins of our ancestors) would be opened and so that the sins of humankind would be forgiven. He came to establish a new commandment of love. However, anytime something new is introduced, there will be those who will reject it. This is what happened in the time of Christ. Many people would not recognize Jesus as the Son of God and ultimately, because of this, he was put to death. However, when Christ ascended into heaven he had finished his work on Earth and had challenged and charged others to continue his saving mission.

Christ's ministry here on Earth can best be described in a four-fold fashion. Christ came to preach, to teach, to heal, and to love. Looking at these four aspects of Christ will help us to better understand how the Catholic church uses them in ministering to today's society. We will also be able to better understand how Christ lived and worked amongst his people.

THE PREACHING CHRIST

"Stop judging and you will not be judged. Stop condemning and you will not be condemned. Forgive and you will be forgiven. Give and gifts will be given to you." (Luke 6:37-38)

Here we find a very simple message of Jesus Christ and a very good example of his style of preaching. Jesus preached so that others would understand what he was saying. His message in the passage above was simple: do not do something that you would not want done unto you and do things that you would want done unto you. Sound familiar? How often do we hear that today from parents, friends, guardians, teachers? A lot of times we just need to put ourselves in other people's places and think about how we would feel if we were that person. The same message that Jesus preached two thousand years ago rings true today. Think about it. The words of a man who lived so long ago have an impact on your life today! The Catholic church does exactly the same thing. When a priest preaches at mass, he relates the scriptures to modern times. Jesus Christ preached to the people of his time and so the Church today preaches to the people of its time. From the beginning until today the message is still the same.

THE TEACHING CHRIST

"A sower went out to sow his seed. And as he sowed, some seed fell on the path and was trampled, and the birds of the sky ate it up. Some seed fell on rocky ground, and when it grew, it withered for lack of moisture. Some seed fell among thorns, and the thorns grew with it and choked it. And some seed fell on good soil, and when it grew, it produced fruit a hundredfold." After saying this, he called out, "Whoever has ears to hear ought to hear." (Luke 8:5-8)

Jesus taught his people through the use of parables. Parables were stories through which people would be able to relate to what Christ was saying and better understand his message. In the parable above, Jesus is talking about how people hear the Word of God and respond to it. Think of the seeds as people. The seeds that fell on the rocky ground represent those people who hear the message but don't understand what it means. These people may be overcome by other things that seem more interesting than the Word of God. The seeds that fell into the thorns represent those who have so many other things happening in their lives they don't pay attention to the Word. And finally, the seeds that fell on the good soil represent those who hear the Word, know what it means, and live it. This is the way Jesus chose to teach. He related ordinary things of the lives of his people, such as planting and farming, to the message of his Father. Through this the people came to know Christ and follow him.

THE HEALING CHRIST

One day as Jesus was teaching, Pharisees and teachers of the law were sitting there who had come from every village of Galilee and Judea and Jerusalem, and the power of the Lord was with him for healing. And some men brought on a stretcher a man who was paralyzed; they were trying to bring him in and set [him] in his presence. But not finding a way to bring him in because of the crowd, they went up on the roof and lowered him on the stretcher through the tiles into the middle in front of Jesus. When he saw their faith, he said, "As for you, your sins are forgiven." (Luke 5:17-20)

There are many times in the Gospel when we find stories of Jesus healing people in need. We will find one common characteristic among these healing stories. Jesus Christ healed people because of their faith. People who wanted to be healed needed to put their faith in Christ and believe that, indeed, he did have the power to heal.

The Catholic church today carries on Christ's healing mission through the sacraments of reconciliation and the anointing of the sick, through which someone enters into a healing relationship with Christ. More explanation of these two sacraments will be given later in this text.

THE LOVING CHRIST

> It was now about noon and darkness came over the whole land until three in the afternoon because of an eclipse of the sun. Then the veil of the temple was torn down the middle. Jesus cried out in a loud voice, "Father, into your hands I commend my spirit"; and when he had said this he breathed his last. (Luke 23:44-46)

If there ever was an ultimate example of the love of Christ for his people, it was his death on the cross. The Catholic faith teaches us that it was for our sins that Christ was sacrificed on the cross. Imagine yourself in the place of Christ. You know exactly what kind of death you will suffer. You know exactly the pain that will be involved and the humiliation that will result. You have the power to stop your death from happening, yet you let yourself be tortured and nailed to a cross. The love that Jesus showed us is an unconditional, timeless love. It is a love that is given to us no matter what we do or who we are.

II. THE SACRAMENTS

Think for a moment of some special celebrations that you have had in your life. Maybe it was a birthday party, maybe a graduation party, or an anniversary. Whatever the occasion, it probably marked a special event in your life. In the same way the Church has special celebrations to mark important events in the life of a Catholic Christian. These seven special events are called sacraments.

The traditional definition of a sacrament is an outward sign given to us by God to give grace. Let's try and look at that in a different way to gain a better understanding of what a sacrament is. A sacrament is a sign that we can see and know, that comes to us from God, through which we are able to become aware of God's life and love in us and in the world around us.

BAPTISM

When you hear the word "water," what do you think of? Maybe you think of a lake, or the ocean, or something that is life-giving. It is a well known fact that water is indeed life-giving. People can last for weeks without food, but only days without water. People, plants, and animals all need water to survive. Water is a symbol of life, and is therefore fitting to be used as the main symbol of baptism, as well as the main symbol of new life.

In the sacrament of baptism we receive new life in Christ. We are "born again" in the waters of baptism. Baptism is the sacrament through which a person is first initiated into the Catholic church. It is the first of the three sacraments of initiation. The other two are communion and confirmation. We will talk a little bit more about those later on.

There are a few other symbols of the sacrament of baptism. During the rite of baptism, a person is anointed with the oil of catechumens and the sacred chrism. The word "catechumen" refers to someone who is seeking entrance and preparing to come into the faith; therefore, the oil is a symbol of the beginning of the person's journey of faith.

A lighted candle is presented to the person who has been baptized or to the parents of the person (depending on the person's age) as a reminder of the light which is Jesus Christ.

After the baptism, the person is clothed in a white garment as a symbol of his or her purity and new life in Jesus Christ.

EUCHARIST

The Sacrament of the Eucharist is the reception of the Body and Blood of Jesus Christ. At a certain time in the life of Catholics, they will receive their first Holy Communion. After that, Catholics are welcome to receive communion as often as they want to as long as they are not in the state of serious sin.

Jesus Christ gave us the Eucharist as an everlasting reminder of his sacrifice. One thing, however, must be clear. Catholics believe that the Eucharist is the real presence of the Body and Blood of Christ. It is not merely a symbol, but a sacrament. During the mass, bread and wine become Christ's Body and Blood. The priest who is presiding at the mass calls upon the Holy Spirit "to make them (the gifts of bread and wine) holy by the power of your Spirit, so that they may become for us the Body and Blood of Jesus Christ."

Later on in the Eucharistic Prayer, the priest will pray the words that Christ prayed at the Last Supper: "Take this all of you and eat it, this is my body which will be given up for you. Take this all of you and drink of it, for this is the cup of my blood, the blood of the new and everlasting covenant, which will be shed for you and for all so that sins may be forgiven. Do this in memory of me." The Catholic church believes that it was at the Last Supper that Christ instituted the Eucharist and commanded us to carry it on.

Of the seven sacraments, the Eucharist is the one which is the most important.

> The Eucharist is "the source and summit of the Christian life....The other sacraments, and indeed all ecclesiastical ministries and works of the apostles, are bound up with the Eucharist and are oriented toward it. For in the blessed Eucharist is contained the whole spiritual good of the Church, namely Christ himself, our Pasch." (*Catechism of the Catholic Church*).

The word "communion" means to be in union with someone or something. When we receive Christ in the Eucharist we enter into a union with him. We become one in Christ. After we have eaten Christ's body and have drunk his blood, we have Jesus within us and are at that point in a most perfect union with Him.

CONFIRMATION

> When the time for Pentecost was fulfilled, they were all in one place together. And suddenly there came from the sky a noise like a strong driving wind, and it filled the entire house in which they were. Then there appeared to them tongues as of fire, which parted and came to rest on each one of them. And they were all filled with the holy Spirit and began to speak in different tongues, as the Spirit enabled them to proclaim. (Acts 2:1-4)

The sacrament of confirmation completes the process of Catholic Initiation. It is the sacrament in which someone is sealed with the gift of the Holy Spirit and is enabled to, by the full graces of baptism, live as a mature Christian. The reception of confirmation seals someone's membership in the Catholic Church. The sacrament is a testimony of the recipient's desire to live a Christian lifestyle and to be dedicated to the service of God and his Church.

The passage above from the Acts of the Apostles describes the events of Pentecost which took place after the death, resurrection, and ascension of Jesus Christ. Prior to Pentecost, the apostles were hiding in an upper room because they were afraid that they would be put to death because of their relationship with Jesus. The Holy Spirit came upon the apostles so that they would be enabled to go forth and preach his message of salvation to the world. The apostles went about this mission by using all that had been revealed to them by Christ. In the same way, through the sacrament of confirmation, the Holy Spirit allows us to be witnesses to the gospel message of Christ.

Jesus knew that he would not be on Earth as a human being forever. He also did not want to leave his people alone. He promised that he would send them the Holy Spirit so that his presence would always be with them. *The Catechism of the Catholic Church* describes this promise and its effect on the apostles and on all who received the Spirit.

Christ desired that the Spirit that was within him be shared with many people. The promised Spirit of Pentecost would come as a source of strength and assistance for all who received it. Those who received the Spirit became proclaimers of the mission of Christ. Indeed Christ's desire was fulfilled. His Spirit filled the hearts of all who desired it. It is through confirmation that we receive that same Spirit that Christ wants for all who believe.

RECONCILIATION

There is a question that many people ask about the sacrament of reconciliation (also known as penance or confession), "Why do I have to tell my sins to a priest to be forgiven? Why can't I just sit in my home and talk to God and tell him that I am sorry?" Good questions! But there are even better answers!

The Catholic church believes that when someone sins, they sin not only against God but also against the community. Those who approach the sacrament of penance obtain pardon from God's mercy for the offense committed against him, and are, at the same time, reconciled with the Church, which they have wounded by their sins, that by charity, by example, and by prayer, labors for their conversion. Sin can best be described as choosing to turn away from God and others. God gave us free will and sometimes we choose to act in opposition to the will of God. When a priest says the words of absolution (the time when someone's sins are forgiven), he is forgiving those sins in the name of God and in the name of the Catholic community.

The Church also believes that Jesus gave the apostles (those who followed him and who became the first priests and bishops) the authority to forgive sins. "Only God forgives sins. Jesus says of himself, 'The Son of Man has authority on Earth to forgive sins' and exercises this divine power: 'Your sins are forgiven.' Further, by virtue of his divine authority he gives this power to men to exercise in his name." (*Catechism of the Catholic Church*) "The disciples were filled with joy at seeing the Lord. Jesus said to them again, 'Peace be with you. As the Father sent me, so I send you.'"

> And when he had said this, he breathed on them and said to them, "Receive the holy Spirit. Whose sins you forgive are forgiven them, and whose sins you retain are retained." (John 20:20-23)

Today a priest carries on the mission of the apostles, which Christ gave them by absolving people from their sins, in the name of God and the community.

The sacrament of reconciliation provides an opportunity for people to talk to someone with whom they will be able to confide. It provides a time for people to seek the healing and the comfort of their God and their Church. It is through the sacrament of reconciliation that a Catholic knows there will always be a place to go to; there will always be a place to turn and seek the mercy of our heavenly father despite our sinfulness.

When someone approaches the sacrament of reconciliation, that person must be truly sorry for the sins that he or she has committed and must seek forgiveness. It is through this sacrament of healing that we are reminded of God's endless mercy.

The sacrament of reconciliation is a sacrament of conversion. When someone converts, that person is beginning anew. In a sense, he or she is starting a new life all over again. Once we have received the graces of the sacrament of reconciliation, we are challenged to go forth and bring the love and mercy of God to all we meet.

ANOINTING OF THE SICK

> Is anyone among you suffering? He should pray. Is anyone in good spirits? He should sing praise. Is anyone among you sick? He should summon the presbyters of the church, and they should pray over him and anoint [him] with oil in the name of the Lord, and the prayer of faith will save the sick person, and the Lord will raise him up. If he has committed any sins, he will be forgiven. (James 5:13-15)

The above passage from the book of James in the New Testament best describes the reason for the anointing of the sick. When a Catholic is ill, a priest may anoint that person with the oil of the sick. This oil, blessed by the bishop, will help the person in both their physical and spiritual healing.

The anointing of the sick is available to any ill person who desires to receive it, no matter what condition that person is in. The sacrament is no longer only administered when a person is close to death. Many older Catholics may remember the term "last rites" which is now referred to as the anointing of the sick. The term "last rites" is no longer used, as the sacrament itself is not always the last sacramental act a person may receive. That is not to say that someone who is close to death may not receive the sacrament. The important point to remember is that the anointing of the sick may be received by any sick person at any time. Someone who has reached a point of old age may receive the sacrament along with someone who may be preparing to undergo an operation.

The sacrament may be received more than once. For example, if Mr. Smith had a heart attack in January, was anointed, and recovered, and then had another serious illness in May, he could be anointed again. Someone can also be anointed again if their condition worsens during their illness.

So what does the sacrament do? The anointing of the sick is a profound source of healing, and brings the ill into a unique union with God. The effects of the sacrament can be felt both physically and spiritually. The sacrament provides a sense of peace, a source of grace, and a spirit of wholeness.

Of the two healing sacraments, this sacrament stands as a testimony to the healing mission of Christ. Christ commanded for the sick to be healed. The Church today lives out that commandment through anointing. However, like the people Christ healed, those who are anointed must want to be healed, and be people of faith. Remember that when Christ healed someone, he always reminded the person that it was his or her faith that had healed them.

MARRIAGE

"The matrimonial covenant, by which a man and a woman establish between themselves a partnership of the whole of life, is by its nature ordered toward the good of the spouse and the procreation and education of offspring; this covenant between baptized persons has been raised by Christ the Lord to the dignity of a sacrament." (*Catechism of the Catholic church*).

The sacrament of matrimony is one of the two sacraments of service, the other being holy orders, which we will discuss in the next section of this text. Matrimony is a sacrament of service because, in the union between man and woman, a spirit of service must exist. The couple are in service to each other, their children, the Church, and community. "In service to each other" does not mean that one of the partners dominates over the other. Marriage is a two-way street and each partner must recognize the equality of the other and be willing to help, strengthen, and comfort that person when needed. In the same way, the couple serves their children by raising them with a solid Christian background and by being with them in times of need. The couple is called to explore their talents and gifts and see how they might best be able to help the Church and community.

Throughout the Bible, marriage is one of the central themes. This shows the importance of the union between man and woman and eventually Man and God.

For Catholics, marriage is not simply a legal union, but a holy union. When a couple approaches the sacrament of matrimony, they have chosen to come before God and the Church's minister (a priest or deacon) to have their union blessed and consecrated by God. When the couple assumes the duties of the sacrament of marriage, they are assuming a duty to themselves and to God. They promise to accept children from God with love and raise them in the faith. The couple lives out their married life in the presence of God through their involvement in the Church community.

Marriage can be described in one way as a covenant (an agreement between two people). When the couple professes their marriage vows, they enter into a sacred covenant. It is a covenant, like that promised by God to the people of Israel and the new covenant made through the blood of Christ. It is a covenant that will involve sacrifice, good times and bad times, happiness and sorrow, but a covenant that will ultimately lead to a life of grace, joy, and peace.

HOLY ORDERS

"Holy orders is the sacrament through which the mission entrusted by Christ to his apostles continues to be exercised in the Church until the end of time: thus it is the sacrament of apostolic ministry. It includes three degrees: episcopate, presbyterate, and diaconate." (*Catechism of the Catholic Church*).

When Christ was ending his mission on Earth, he knew that he would need others to continue the work that he had begun. He charged his apostles with this work and commissioned them as the first priests of the Church. The sacrament of holy orders continues this important work begun by Christ. It is through this sacrament that a man is ordained a bishop, priest, or deacon. (This is what episcopate, presbyterate, and diaconate mean.)

Let's take a look at each of the three callings within the sacrament of holy orders.

The Call to Be a Deacon

Within the Catholic church there are two different kinds of deacons. There is a transitional deacon and a permanent deacon. A transitional deacon is a man in a stage of progression and will one day be ordained a priest. He is usually ordained a transitional deacon six months to a year before he will be ordained a priest. A permanent deacon is a man who feels that God is calling him to service in the church in an ordained capacity, although he still feels he is being called to married life.

A deacon may serve the church in many different ways. The deacon may baptize, officiate at a marriage ceremony, be a minister of communion, proclaim the gospel during mass, and preach the homily. A deacon may not be the minister of reconciliation, preside at mass, or anoint the sick. These functions are reserved for a priest.

The Call to Be a Priest

The call to priesthood is a very special and unique calling. It is a vocation that calls a man to a deep union with Christ and to a life of sacrificial giving to the people of God. When someone becomes a priest, they do so because they feel that God has called them to ordained ministry for the church in a most special way. When a man accepts this calling, he is dedicating his life to

God and God's people, and, when ordained, will accept the vows of chastity, obedience, and for some priests, poverty. A man who feels called to a religious priesthood (for example: Franciscan, Salesian, etc.) will live in community and not own any material things. A man who feels called to diocesan priesthood, meaning he will serve a specific geographical area, such as the Archdiocese of Los Angeles or the Diocese of Charleston, will most likely live in a community setting, will receive a paycheck, and may own material things. All of the vows that a man takes at ordination are sacred and symbolize the great desire he has to serve God.

The priest is called upon to preside at the celebration of mass, be the minister of reconciliation, officiate at a wedding ceremony, anoint the sick, lead the people of God in a parish setting, school setting, seminary setting, mission setting, and many other places. The priest is called to give his whole self to God and his people. The will of God must be at the forefront of his life.

The Call to Be a Bishop

From time to time there are priests who are called by God to be raised to the order of bishop. Bishops are priests who have shown extraordinary leadership and dedication to the people of God. Bishops share in many different roles in the church, and are considered shepherds, leaders of flocks. A bishop's primary job is to preach the gospel of Jesus Christ. Some bishops serve as the leader of a diocese or Archdiocese (here they hold the title of Archbishop). Some bishops serve as auxiliary bishops and assist another bishop with the work of leading a diocese. Other bishops are called to work in Rome, the center of the Roman Catholic Church. Here, they work with different committees and organizations who help to lead the church at a worldwide level.

Holy orders is indeed a sacrament of service. Like marriage, the person who enters into the sacrament is entering into a covenant with God and other people. It is a covenant that dedicates itself to a life of love, service, and holiness.

III. PRAYER

Prayer and worship are at the very heart of the life of the Catholic church. Prayer is a form of communication with God, Jesus, the Holy Spirit, and the saints. It is through prayer that believers can communicate needs, desires, praise, and thanks. Prayer takes on many different forms and is communicated in many different ways. It can be both private and public. We pray in the privacy of our homes, in our cars, and in public places like a church. When we pray we may say prayers that we learned as a child, such as the Hail Mary or Our Father, or we may pray by just telling God our feelings, fears, or desires, without needing any set formula to pray by.

Prayer is essential for the life of any Christian.

> Prayer and *Christian life* are *inseparable*, for they concern the same love and the same renunciation, proceeding from love; the same...loving conformity with the Father's plan of love; the same transforming union in the Holy Spirit who conforms us more and more to Christ Jesus; the same love for all men, the love with which Jesus has loved us.

The *Catechism of the Catholic Church* tells us here that it is through prayer that we are able to love Christ all the more. It is through prayer that we come into union with the Holy Spirit, which brings us into a more perfect union with God. Whether we stop in a chapel during the day to say an Our Father, kneel at our bedside before going to sleep, or come together as a community at mass, our prayers make a difference in our lives and the lives of those around us.

THE LITURGICAL YEAR

As the secular year is separated into seasons, so the Church year is separated into seasons. The seasons help us to distinguish the different times of the Church year and help to emphasize the special celebrations and observances that take place throughout the year. The seasons of the liturgical year are: Advent, Christmas, Ordinary Time, Lent, and Easter.

Advent

The Church year begins with the celebration of Evening Prayer I on the first Sunday of Advent. Advent is the four weeks before Christmas when we prepare for the coming of Jesus Christ into the world as a human being. Advent is mainly a preparational season and not a penitential season, as is Lent. During Advent we recall the words of the Prophet Isaiah and of John the Baptist who spoke of he who was to come. The two spoke of the Messiah, meaning "anointed one." From the days of Isaiah to John the Baptist (the cousin of Christ who went before him to prepare people for his coming by calling them to repentance from their sins), the coming of Christ was anticipated. There was always a need for preparation. It is for this reason that the Church today sets aside four weeks for the faithful to prepare for the birth of Christ. We prepare for Christ's birth by looking at our lives and seeing how we can improve them, by praying and asking the Lord to enter our lives and by trying to live a good Christian life.

Christmas

Now this is how the birth of Jesus Christ came about. When his mother Mary was betrothed to Joseph, but before they lived together, she was found with child through the holy Spirit. Joseph her husband, since he was a righteous man, yet unwilling to expose her to shame, decided to divorce her quietly. Such was his intention when, behold, the angel of the Lord appeared to him in a dream and said, "Joseph, son of David, do not be afraid to take Mary your wife into your home. For it is through the holy Spirit that this child has been conceived in her. She will bear a son and you are to name him Jesus, because he will save his people from their sins." All this took place to fulfill what the Lord had said through the prophet:

"Behold, the virgin shall be with child and bear a son, and they shall name him Emmanuel," which means "God is with us."

When Joseph awoke, he did as the angel of the Lord had commanded him and took his wife into his home. Jesus was born in Bethlehem of Judea. (Matthew 1:18-24, 2:1)

The season of Advent leads to the season of Christmas. The Christmas season begins with Evening Prayer I on Christmas Eve and ends with the feast of the Baptism of the Lord a week after Epiphany. For Catholics, Christmas is not merely a one day celebration. We celebrate the birth of Christ, his Holy Family, the Epiphany (the visit of the wise men), and the Baptism of Christ. All of these celebrations are part of the Christmas miracle. The passage above from the gospel of Saint Matthew describes how the birth of Christ came about. Jesus entered the world as you and I entered the world. Jesus experienced a human birth as you and I did. Catholic teaching tells us that Jesus Christ was both human and divine. He was human like us in all ways except that he never sinned since, at the same time, Jesus was the Son of God.

The Christmas story is one of wonder, amazement, and joy. Mary, the mother of Christ, became pregnant with Jesus through the power of the Holy Spirit. Mary did not become pregnant by a man, but by the power of God. Mary was a virgin when she gave birth to Christ and remained such. Jesus Christ, the savior of the world, the Son of God, was born from a virgin in a stable. This is how our king entered the world. God became man, word became flesh.

Ordinary Time

The season that follows Christmas and Easter is called "Ordinary Time." It is named such because there are no major celebrations during this time. However, Ordinary Time is no less important than any of the other seasons of the Church year. During Ordinary Time we are called to reflect upon the ordinary events of our lives and to see how Christ is present within those events. Ordinary Time can in fact become an extraor-dinary time because of our call to look at these ordinary events of our lives and see them in a different way. "While the other liturgical seasons have their own distinctive character and celebrate a specific aspect of the mystery of Christ, the weeks of Ordinary Time—especially the Sundays—are devoted rather to the mystery of Christ in all its aspects. Ordinary Time enables the Church to appreciate more fully the ministry and message of Christ." What does all that mean? Basically, it says that Ordinary Time helps us to come to know: (1) what Christ is all about, and (2) the mystery of his life and death.

Lent

Lent begins on Ash Wednesday and ends on Holy Thursday. Ash Wednesday is the day on which Catholics come together as a community to receive ashes on their foreheads as a reminder of our need to turn back to Christ and to follow his ways. The ashes also serve as a reminder of the fact that we are mortal and will some day die. "The custom of imposing ashes, a symbol of ancient penitential practice, is a symbolic act signifying human mortality ('Remember that you are dust and into dust you shall return') and total human dependence on the graciousness and mercy of God. It is a fitting act to begin the prayer and purification that is proper to Lent." (*Catechism of the Catholic church*). Catholics are called upon to observe Ash Wednesday as a day of fast and abstinence (not eating meat and having only one full meal) as a means of self-denial for the sake of the Kingdom of God.

Lent is seen as a penitential season. Lent is a forty day period, during which the church prepares for the death and resurrection of Jesus Christ. It is a time to recall our sinfulness and to seek the Lord's mercy and forgiveness.

The Easter Triduum

The Easter Triduum begins on Holy Thursday and includes the days of Good Friday and Holy Saturday. These three days are among the most important of the entire church year. It is in these three sacred days that the whole mystery of Jesus' suffering, death, and resurrection are revealed.

The Evening Mass of the Lord's Supper on Holy Thursday recalls how Jesus washed the feet of his apostles, and also recalls Christ sharing the Last Supper with them. At the Last Supper Christ desired to celebrate one last meal with his friends before he left them. It was at this supper that Jesus instituted the Eucharist. The mass on Holy Thursday ends with the transfer of the Eucharist to a place of reservation. The sanctuary area of the church is cleared of all cloths and decorations and the church is kept in darkness. This serves to remind us of the fate of Christ. In most churches, the Eucharist, the Body of Christ, is reserved for veneration by the people until midnight at which time it is reserved in a private place.

On Good Friday the Church recalls the passion and death of Jesus Christ. Mass is not celebrated on this day. However, the Church celebrates a service of the Passion of the Lord with the distribution of the Eucharist that has been consecrated at mass the evening before. During the service on Good Friday we listen to and participate in the reading of the passion of Christ, which recalls how Christ was condemned to death, stripped of his clothes, nailed to a cross, and how he died. During the service the people present are invited to venerate or kiss the cross as an action of their love for Christ. Good Friday is a day of sorrow and celebration. We are sad at the death of Christ but at the same time we celebrate the fact that Jesus Christ died for our sins and it is through his death that we might live.

The evening of Holy Saturday holds the most important liturgical event of the Church's year, the Easter Vigil. It is during this celebration that the Easter Sacraments of Baptism, Confirmation, and Eucharist are celebrated. It is here that Catechumens (adults preparing to receive all the sacraments of initiation) and Candidates (those preparing to receive communion, confirmation, or to make a profession of faith) reach the high point of their journey in the R.C.I.A. (Rite of Christian Initiation of Adults) program. The Easter Vigil begins outside of the church with the lighting of the Easter fire and the paschal candle, which is a symbol of Christ our light. The Easter Vigil celebrates the resurrection of Christ three days after his death.

The celebration of Easter is not just one day (Easter Sunday) but an entire season. It is a season of celebration and joy. The Easter season calls for all the people of God to reflect upon the resurrection of Christ and how his resurrection became a triumph over death. The Easter season concludes with the celebration of Pentecost, where the Holy Spirit descended upon the Apostles.

THE CELEBRATION OF MASS

The mass is the most important liturgical celebration for the Church. It is during the mass that we hear the word of God and receive Jesus Christ in the Eucharist. The mass is a celebration by people with faith in and love for God and his church. The mass has four basic parts to it, each of them having its respective distinction in helping us to come to know and love our God even more.

The mass begins with the introductory rites. The introductory rites are just that, an introduction. The priest, who is the principal celebrant of the mass, introduces the celebration of that day and then calls us to bring to mind our sins and ask for God's forgiveness. This recollection of sins is called the penitential rite. The penitential rite may, at some times, be replaced by a rite of sprinkling with holy water which recalls our baptism. At some masses the Gloria may be spoken or sung followed by the opening prayer of the mass.

The mass continues with the Liturgy of the Word. The first reading is proclaimed by a lector and is usually taken from the Old Testament. The Responsorial Psalm follows and is either sung or spoken. The second reading comes from the New Testament, usually from a letter of St. Paul. The Gospel Acclamation follows, which announces that the words of Jesus Christ are about to be proclaimed in the gathered assembly. The priest or deacon then proclaims the gospel which is taken from one of the four gospel authors Matthew, Mark, Luke, or John. The homily then follows in which the priest or deacon takes the scriptures that have been proclaimed that day and applies them to our modern lives. Next is the profession of faith. It is in this profession, which is either the Nicene or Apostles Creed, that we state our beliefs as have been given to us by the Church. The Prayers of the Faithful follow. It is during this time that we pray for the needs of our Church, world, and community.

The Liturgy of the Eucharist follows the collection and the preparation of the altar and gifts. It is during the Liturgy of the Eucharist that the Eucharistic Prayer is given and the priest calls down the Holy Spirit upon the gifts of bread and wine and asks that they become the Body and Blood of Jesus Christ. Later, the priest will pray the words that Jesus prayed at the Last Supper and at this point he will consecrate the bread and the wine and they will become the Body and Blood of Jesus Christ. After the Eucharistic Prayer we pray together the words that Christ taught us in the Our Father. Having finished the Our Father, we share with each other a sign of the peace of Christ. It is in this expression that we join Christ in spreading a message of peace to all we know. The Lamb of God is then sung or said in which we ask Jesus, who is the "Lamb of God," to have mercy on us. We then receive the Body and Blood of our Lord in the Eucharist. After receiving our Lord, we thank him for the gift of his Body and Blood. A communion song and/or meditation song may be sung at this point.

The concluding rites follow, during which the priest gives the closing prayer and then prays a blessing over those gathered for the celebration. After this the priest dismisses the community and sends us forth to live our faith and love others as God has loved us.

For many people the mass ends when they leave the church. However, the point is that the mass has to be lived every day of our lives. We do not stop living our faith when we leave the church. We do not stop recalling the life and death of Christ when we leave the church. We must live the words we hear in the scriptures at mass and live as a person who has received Jesus Christ.

The basic message: Be Jesus to others, love others, forgive others, and help others.

CELEBRATION OF COMMUNION OUTSIDE OF THE MASS

There are celebrations in the Church in which people receive communion that do not take place within the context of mass. These are typically called "communion services." Many times a communion service is celebrated when a priest is not available to celebrate mass. This happens frequently in parishes that are located in rural areas where there are not many priests available. A deacon or Eucharistic Minister may preside at a service of communion.

A service of communion begins as mass would with a greeting, introduction, and penitential rite, followed by the opening prayer. The Liturgy of the Word follows as is described in "The Celebration of the Mass" section of this text. Following the Prayer of the Faithful, the people gathered for the service join in praying the Our Father. Afterwards, the minister may bring the Eucharist from the tabernacle (the place of repose where the Body of Christ is kept) and distribute Jesus to those gathered there. The service ends with the closing prayer, a prayer of blessing, and dismissal.

OTHER LITURGICAL CELEBRATIONS

There are liturgical celebrations in the Church that do not involve the distribution of the Eucharist. Among these celebrations are reconciliation services and The Liturgy of the Hours.

Reconciliation services often take place during the seasons of Advent and Lent. Though they occur throughout the liturgical year, it is during those seasons that Catholics prepare themselves for Christ's coming and death. A communal service of reconciliation is basically a gathering of Catholics together to hear the word of God and to come to the sacrament of reconciliation. A service may consist of readings, a homily, and prayers. Time for individual confessions usually follows the service.

The liturgy of the hours is the ancient prayer of the Church that was traditionally prayed by priests, sisters, and brothers. Today, however, there is an emphasis on the importance of lay people (those not ordained or professed to religious life) to pray the liturgy of the hours. Also known as praying the breviary, the liturgy of the hours includes prayers for morning, daytime, evening, night, and the office of readings. The liturgy of the hours serves to unite the universal church in prayer and to allow anyone an opportunity to maintain a close relationship with their God through a structured, daily form of prayer.

IV. THE TEN COMMANDMENTS

Earlier in this text, it was mentioned that God had handed down to Moses the Ten Commandments. The Ten Commandments are a set of moral guidelines given by God for his people to live by. The Church today still looks to the Ten Commandments as a basis for its moral teaching and as a basis for Catholics to judge their actions.

The Ten Commandments are:

1. I, the LORD, am your God, who brought you out of the land of Egypt, that place of slavery. You shall not have other gods beside me.

2. You shall not take the name of the LORD, your God, in vain.

3. Remember to keep holy the Sabbath day.

4. Honor your father and your mother.

5. You shall not kill.

6. You shall not commit adultery.

7. You shall not steal.

8. You shall not bear false witness against your neighbor.

9. You shall not covet your neighbor's house.

10. You shall not covet your neighbor's wife, nor his male or female slave, nor his ox or ass, nor anything else that belongs to him.

Each of these commandments help us to choose right from wrong. God gave us these ten basic moral lessons so that we would be able to know how God wanted us to act. Let's take a look at each one of the commandments.

FIRST COMMANDMENT

I, the LORD, am your God, who brought you out of the land of Egypt, that place of slavery. You shall not have other gods beside me.

It is in this commandment that God tells his people that they are not to adore or have any devotion to any false gods. Our faith tells us that there is one God. It was especially common in the days of the Israelites for there to be worship of false gods. Our God wanted to make sure that his people clearly understood that there was only one God and worship of any other gods was to no purpose. The same applies to you and I today. We are called to worship only one God, the true God. There are people in the world who worship animals or objects as gods. We are called upon to reject such false worship and put our faith, hope, and trust in God our Father. Remember that God chose Moses to lead the Israelites out of slavery in Egypt and into the promised land. It is for this reason that God said "I am the LORD your God who brought you out of slavery."

SECOND COMMANDMENT

You shall not take the name of the LORD, your God, in vain.

Like people of thousands of years ago, people of today tend to use the name of God in a way that is opposite to the meaning of the name of God. At times, people use the title "God" when they are frustrated and angry and might place blame on God when things go wrong. They might even use God's name along with a curse word. This does not make any sense. God stands for all that is good, all that is sacred. At the same time we must also show respect for the name of our God. We therefore are called to only use God's name as it should be used. When we use the name of God in a way that is wrong or improper, we are disrespecting God. At all times we must be aware of our language and try to only use the name of God as it should be used.

THIRD COMMANDMENT

Remember to keep holy the Sabbath day.

The people of Israel took seriously their responsibility to keep the Sabbath day holy. This was a day to go to the temple and worship and a day during which no work was done. There were laws in the Jewish faith which prohibited the Jews from doing any sort of manual labor or working activity on this most special day. Jesus himself was criticized by the Pharisees for healing on the Sabbath day. Jesus, however, challenged these people and warned them against not interpreting this law with severe strictness. Jesus wanted to show people that the Sabbath was a day for thanking God and remembering all of his gifts. In the same way we as Catholics are called to set aside a special day to worship our God and call to mind all of the many gifts that he has given to us, and thank him for his presence within our lives.

Catholics observe the third commandment by coming together each Sunday and celebrating mass. It is important to gather together each week to pray because as a community we can help one another and share our experiences of faith and hope with each other. As discussed earlier in this text, for Catholics the mass is the most important public form of worship. We mark the Sabbath day each week with a most fitting celebration. Catholics are obligated to come together each week to celebrate mass. It is in this way that we may hear the word of God and receive him in the Eucharist. This is one way through which we live in the true spirit of the Sabbath day. In the mass, we thank our God, we celebrate our God, we love our God, and we praise our God. However, we must remember to practice the teachings given at mass in our homes, workplaces, and all aspects of our lives throughout the rest of the week.

FOURTH COMMANDMENT

Honor your father and your mother.

Parents are very important people in our lives. It is because of them, through the blessings of God, that we are able to be a part of the human race. It is because they have given us the gift of life and because they have been entrusted with our care that we are called upon to treat our mother and father with honor.

There are many ways that we can live out our call of honoring our parents. One way that we can do this is by being respectful to our parents. It is hard at times to do things that our parents ask us to do. Whether it is taking out the garbage, walking the dog, cleaning our room, or taking care of our little brother and sister, there is probably a good reason as to why mom or dad may ask us to do these things. Sometimes, we just need to say, "Sure I'll do it." There may also be reasons why we cannot do what they ask. When this happens we need to speak to our parents with respect and explain the situation to them. This may be a better way of approaching the situation than getting mad and maybe saying something to our parents that we might regret later. We can honor our parents also by thanking them for all they do and letting them know that they are appreciated for giving us life and raising us.

FIFTH COMMANDMENT

You shall not kill.

"You have heard that it was said to your ancestors, You shall not kill; and whoever kills will be liable to judgment." (Matthew 5:21-22)

At the outset this commandment seems pretty clear. However, we need to look at it from the standpoint of respect for life at all stages. It is the belief of the Catholic church that every human life is sacred. This includes babies inside their mothers, the jailed prisoner, or the elderly person. People do not have the right to "play God" and decide when a human life should be ended. Whether a criminal is killed in capital punishment or an unwanted baby is aborted—these instances are just as similar to the cold-blooded murderer people equate with this commandment. Life is only given by God and only he has the right to take it. Life begins at the point of conception in the womb of the mother and ends when God calls that person to him. People who commit murder decide to interfere with the plan of God and destroy a life before it is time for that life to be ended. When we gain an understanding of how we must respect everyone, no matter what point of their life they are in, we can start to live out the true meaning of the fifth commandment. For our purposes remember this: every life has been created by God and is therefore sacred and must be respected.

SIXTH COMMANDMENT

You shall not commit adultery.

The sixth commandment speaks of sexuality. It is a call to sexual responsibility. Our world today is one whose norms reject Christian teaching about sex. Our world is one that wishes to say that "anything goes" when it comes to sex. As young Christians, we must reject the views of most of our modern world and accept a sexual responsibility. We must be aware of the consequences of our actions and be ready to accept them, both in one's relationship and to one's self.

Our bodies are temples of the Holy Spirit, and we must treat them as such. The Catholic church tells us that sex is reserved for marriage. It is in marriage that a man and a woman join togther in a sacred union and it is through their sexual relations that they express a most intimate love for each other and share in the life-creating process with God.

SEVENTH COMMANDMENT

You shall not steal.

The seventh commandment forbids unjustly taking or keeping the goods of one's neighbor, or wronging him in any way with respect to his goods. It commands justice and charity in the care of earthly goods and the fruits of men's labor. For the sake of the common good, it requires for the universal destination of goods and respect for the right to private property. Christian life strives to order this world's goods to God and to fraternal charity. (*Catechism of the Catholic Church*).

This commandment calls us to have respect for the property of our neighbor. The message of the commandment is distinctly clear: do not take what is not yours. This command, given by God to the people of Israel so many years ago, still has the same meaning for you and I today. Whether it be someone's video game, clothes, car, or watch, we have a responsibility to respect others' possessions and not take them as our own. It is not important whether something is worth five cents or five thousand dollars, the property of others must be respected.

Many times it is hard to resist the temptations of this world when it comes to stealing. We may see something that we find very alluring and really want to own. It is in times like these that we should put ourselves in the place of the person or persons from whom we would be stealing the item. How would you feel if your bike, money, or favorite game was taken? You would probably be angry and want the item back. This is one way to resist the temptation to steal and to follow the seventh commandment of God.

EIGHTH COMMANDMENT

You shall not bear false witness against your neighbor.

"The duty of Christians to take part in the life of the church impels them to act as *witnesses of the gospel* and of the obligations that flow from it. This witness is a transmission of the faith in words and deeds. Witness is an act of justice that establishes the truth or makes it known." *The Catechism of the Catholic church* states here that as Christians we must be people who live the words found in the gospel. We must be witnesses to the words and teachings of Jesus Christ. Therefore, we are called to be people who are truthful. As people of the gospel, we are living examples of the truth of Christ.

There are so many times in our lives when it is very hard to tell the truth. We might find ourselves in a situation where telling a lie seems like the easiest way out. The truth, however, is that many times when we tell one lie it will lead to another lie and then a snowball effect will take place where we just get ourselves deeper and deeper into trouble. There is an old phrase that says "honesty is the best policy." This phrase is very true and very real. Telling the truth may mean that we will be in trouble, but we will have the satisfaction of knowing that we have been truthful and that we can be honest people.

Many times when we lie we wind up hurting other people. Statements that we make, or gossip that spreads as a result of our lies leads to people getting the wrong image about someone or something. Here's a story to explain this point. John was a boy who was about eleven years old. John loved to play baseball. Every chance he got, he would be outside in his backyard playing catch or hitting the baseball around the yard. John's mother many times warned him about not hitting the baseball towards the house because he might break a window. One day John was hitting the ball around in the backyard, in the direction of the house, when he accidentally broke the kitchen window. When John's mom found the broken window, she asked John if he knew what had happened. John said that his neighbor, Jimmy, had been playing outside and that he had broken the window. John's mother called Jimmy's father and told him what happened. Jimmy denied having broken the window, but he was punished for it anyway. When Jimmy's punishment was over, he saw John again and ignored him, because he knew that John had told a lie. John started feeling really guilty and soon told his mom what really happened. John's mother and John both apologized to Jimmy, and John finally faced up to what he had done.

If John had just told the truth at the outset of the whole problem, he would have avoided the situation with Jimmy and not have lost some of his mom's confidence in him. When we lie about something we did or about others, we hurt people and, in the end, people's trust in us decreases.

NINTH COMMANDMENT

You shall not covet your neighbor's wife (or husband).

The ninth commandment deals with desires of the flesh. This commandment from God warns against lustful desires of someone else's wife or husband, and goes back to the temptation issue that was discussed earlier in this text. There is also a call in this commandment to purity. God tells us that we must strive to be pure beings, resisting the temptations of the flesh. This is not an easy task. Although sexual attraction is almost always present and prevalent in society, as well as deemed acceptable, God is asking that we resist such sexual tendencies. It is important to keep in mind the teachings of Jesus on this subject.

TENTH COMMANDMENT

You shall not covet your neighbor's house, nor his male or female slave, nor his ox or ass, nor anything else that belongs to him.

In the tenth and final commandment, we are confronted with the issues of greed and envy. This commandment warns against wanting things which are not yours. This is not the same as the seventh commandment which warns against stealing things. You could think of the tenth commandment as a preface to the seventh.

There are times when we will find ourselves desiring other people's goods or being jealous because someone has something that we do not have. God calls us to overcome these desires by thinking about that which we do have. We are called in these situations to count our blessings and become aware of all we have received and should be thankful for.

Today, the Roman Catholic church continues to call people to a moral responsibility. It is in the moral teaching of the Church that issues such as those we have discussed in this review of the ten commandments are emphasized. The Church calls her members to live a moral lifestyle and knows that we are not perfect people; we are sinners. Yet there exists a continual call to think before we act, to look to God and his church for strength and guidance in the midst of confusion and conflict when it comes to handling moral issues.

V. MARIAN LIFE

The Roman Catholic church holds Mary, the Mother of God, in great veneration. Catholics honor Mary as the Mother of God and mother of the Church. It should be clearly understood that Catholics do not worship Mary. Catholics worship the one true God. Mary is held in high esteem as the Mother of God and therefore deserves the utmost respect and honor. She, however, is not a god and is not to be worshipped.

MARY AS THE MOTHER OF GOD

Mary is the "Mother of God" since she is the mother of the Son of God, who is God himself. The Holy Spirit in Mary fulfilled the plan of the Father's loving goodness. Through the Holy Spirit, Mary conceived and gave birth to the son of God. By the Holy Spirit's power and her faith, her virginity became uniquely fruitful. (*Catechism of the Catholic Church*).

The Catholic church professes Mary to be the Mother of God. As the above passage explains, Mary is the Mother of God since she is the mother of Jesus Christ, who is God made flesh. As Catholics, we believe in one God in three divine persons—the Blessed Trinity. We believe in God the Father, God the Son, and God the Holy Spirit. God the Father, he who has always existed, sent God the Son into the world through Mary so that he might live among us and be our savior. God the Holy Spirit dwells amongst us as an everlasting presence of his love. It was through the power of the Holy Spirit that Mary conceived Jesus.

God chose Mary from the time of her conception to be the mother of Christ. It was for this reason that the Roman Catholic church believes Mary was immaculately conceived. This means that Mary was kept free from the stain of original sin so that she could bear the son of God in complete purity. (When the Church speaks of the "Immaculate Conception," it is of Mary's conception and not of Christ's.)

The Son of God became present in the womb of Mary by the power of the Holy Spirit. Mary had no sexual relations with Joseph, her husband. The Angel Gabriel appeared to Mary and announced to her that she would conceive a child by the power of the Spirit. Mary accepted this announcement and let it be done unto her as God willed. The Church professes that Mary remained a virgin for her entire life. "Mary 'remained a virgin in conceiving her Son, a virgin in giving birth to him, a virgin in carrying him, a virgin in nursing him at her breast, always a virgin' with her whole being she is 'the handmaid of the Lord.'" (*Catechism of the Catholic Church*).

As the Mother of Christ, Mary was entrusted with the task of raising the Son of God. She was chosen by God the Father to watch over Jesus until the time came when he could be on his own and fulfill his father's plan. Mary's dedication to the will of God is an example of the great love that Mary has for all God's people. The love that she showed for Jesus Christ is the same love that she shows to all the followers of Christ.

MARY AS THE MOTHER OF THE CHURCH

All Catholics are members of "The Mystical Body of Christ." By our baptism we are born into this body. It is through our baptism that we become one in Christ and for this reason that Mary is called the Mother of the Church. Mary is the Mother of Christ and is therefore the mother of all who are baptized into Christ. Mary is the guardian, watching over the whole Body of Christ, as she watched over Jesus himself. It is through the protection and intercession of the Blessed Virgin Mary that the Church becomes stronger and grows closer to the one, true, living God.

MARIAN PRAYER

Many Catholics have a special devotion to the Mother of God because of her great role in the mystery of our salvation. Catholics honor Mary in one special way–through the praying of the rosary. The rosary is a repetitious series of prayer which looks at the life of Christ through the eyes of Mary. The Our Father precedes each decade of Hail Marys. There are three different sets of mysteries to the rosary, each reflecting upon different periods of the life of Mary and her son. There are the joyful—The Annunciation, The Visitation, The Birth of Jesus, The Presentation, and The finding of the child Jesus; sorrowful—The agony in the garden, The scourging, The crown of thorns, The carrying of the cross, and The crucifixion; and glorious mysteries— The Resurrection, The Ascension, The descent of the Holy Spirit, The Assumption, and The Coronation. It is through these mysteries that we come to gain a greater understanding of Mary's special role in the life of the Church.

VI. THE WHO'S WHO OF THE CATHOLIC CHURCH

In the section of this text entitled "The Sacramental Life of the Church: Holy Orders," an explanation was given about the life of a priest, of a deacon, and of a bishop. We will now discuss some of the other roles that people fulfill in the Church.

RELIGIOUS SISTER OR BROTHER

A religious sister or brother is someone who has received a calling to pursue a full-time vocation. After thinking and praying about his or her decision, he or she professes service in the Church. A sister or brother has three vows: poverty, chastity, and obedience. By taking these vows, sisters and brothers state that they will not own many material possessions, not engage in romantic relationships or be married, and be obedient to their superior when accepting assignments.

Religious sisters and brothers can be members of many different religious orders. Some orders include Dominicans, Franciscans, and Salesians. Each order has a different purpose or mission. Some religious orders have the sole mission of teaching, healthcare, retreat work, or missionary work. Religious sisters and brothers commit themselves to the service of God's people in a very special way. They choose to live their lives for others and to live out the message of the gospel.

SEMINARIAN

A seminarian is a man who has felt a call by God to serve him and his Church as a priest. A seminarian goes to school to learn theology and takes various classes that will help him in his ministry as a priest. A seminarian may also spend time working in parishes, hospitals, nursing homes, and many other places that will help him to gain an understanding of the life that he will be living as a priest. The seminarian uses his time of preparation for the priesthood not only for studying but also for discernment. During his course of study, the seminarian may find that he might need more time to think about his calling or may feel that God wants him to serve the Church in another way.

ROLES OF THE LAITY

The laity are those people in the Church who are not ordained or professed to religious life. The laity share in the call to be servants by filling many roles within the Church. In the Church of today, the priest no longer does everything. Since Vatican II, the meeting of many bishops from around the world in the early 1960s, there has been an emphasis for the laity to be actively involved in the life of the church. Being an active member of a parish no longer means just coming to mass on Sunday. It means being involved in various ministries and organizations within the parish. The following include some of the ways in which the laity may serve the parish. It should be noted that sometimes religious brothers and sisters may also be serving in these roles.

Lector

A lector is a person who proclaims the first and second readings during the Liturgy of the Word and may sometimes read the responsorial psalm if it is not sung by a cantor. A lector has been trained in the various skills needed to proclaim the Word of God. A lector does not simply "read" the scriptures, but proclaims them with enthusiasm and meaning. A lector may also read the prayer of the faithful.

Eucharistic Minister

The eucharistic minister is called upon to distribute the Body and Blood of Christ at mass and also to bring Christ's body to the sick and those who are elderly and not able to come to mass. A eucharistic minister is a Catholic, selected by the local pastor and parish staff, who is in good standing with the Church and has received all of the sacraments of initiation. The eucharistic minister receives training and is approved by the local bishop.

Minister of Music

The minister of music is the person in the parish or gathered congregation who is responsible for coordinating all of the music programs of the parish. This may include directing choirs, playing musical instruments, and planning music for various celebrations.

Cantor

A cantor is a person who works with the parish music ministry program. This person leads the congregation in song during liturgical celebrations. The cantor fulfills an important role because music enhances our worship and adds so much to the celebration.

Minister of Hospitality

The minister of hospitality, sometimes known as an usher, greets people as they arrive for worship, helps with seating people, and assists with the collection of the offertory money.

Sacristan

The sacristan is responsible for setting up all the needed items for mass and assisting the priest and other ministers with various preparations.

Director of Religious Education

The director of religious education, sometimes called director of faith development, is responsible for coordinating all of the educational aspects of the parish. This may include religious education for children (CCD), education of adults, and education of those considering entering the church community (R.C.I.A.).

Depending on the size of the parish or gathered congregation, there may be other ministries that take place within that specific place.

VII. THE CHRISTIAN LIFESTYLE

This review has offered information about Roman Catholics and the Roman Catholic Church. This review has given an outline of the early beginnings of the Church, to the sacramentals, worship, and moral life of the Church, to the role of Mary and the people who lead the Church. All of these are practical tools for understanding the Church and its mission. However, all of this information does no good if we do not live what we learn. Living the Christian lifestyle means taking what we hear, learn, and know about Jesus Christ and his Church and putting it into practice in our everyday lives. This is not an easy task. It requires hard work and dedication. It means taking to heart the words of Jesus Christ and being Jesus Christ to others. This, after all, is at the core of the gospel. Christ preached unconditional love to everyone he met. When we can take his message to heart, then we know that we have heard Jesus Christ and have accepted the challenge to live as followers of him.

We can live as followers of Jesus Christ by our words, deeds, and actions. We can show that we love Jesus and want to live as he lived by sharing our possessions, helping a friend or parent, saying "thank you," or kind words to people we meet. We could surprise our parents and do the dishes or clean our room one night when we are not asked. This is what faith in Christ is all about. Remember the golden rule...do unto others as you would have them do unto you.

Jesus Christ established what was to become the Roman Catholic church upon the foundation of St. Peter, apostle of Christ and the first pope. Jesus knew that Peter would be able to handle this important mission of spreading the good news to the world. Today, we are called to be like St. Peter in being a strong foundation of the mission of Jesus Christ. We are called to bring his message to the world. St. Peter went around the world and told people about Jesus and his wonderful message of peace and love for all people. This is the mission of the Church today and the mission of each Catholic: proclaim Jesus Christ as Savior; proclaim his love for all people and live the gospel as a servant of God.

HSPT

Optional Test: Catholic Religion

Time: 30 Minutes
40 Questions

DIRECTIONS: Select the best answer choice.

---

1. The people chosen by God to be led out of slavery in Egypt and into the promised land were the

   (A) Canaanites.   (C) Saducees.

   (B) Israelites.   (D) Pharisees.

2. The person God chose to lead the Israelites out of Egypt was

   (A) Noah.   (C) Moses.

   (B) Jonah.   (D) John.

3. The mother and surrogate father of Jesus were

   (A) Mary & Joseph.   (C) Mary & Peter.

   (B) Mary & John.   (D) Mary & Paul.

4. When Jesus healed people, he healed them because they had

   (A) faith.   (C) doubt.

   (B) anger.   (D) None of the above.

5. The ultimate act of love by Christ for his people was

   (A) the Wedding at Cana.

   (B) the healing of the blind man.

   (C) Jesus' death on the cross.

   (D) None of the above.

6. An outward sign of God's life and love in the world is called a

   (A) parable. (C) gospel.

   (B) sin. (D) sacrament.

7. The first sacrament of Christian initiation is

   (A) baptism. (C) confirmation.

   (B) reconciliation. (D) communion.

8. Water is one of the main symbols of baptism because it is a sign of

   (A) new life. (C) hurt.

   (B) sin. (D) hate.

9. When we receive Jesus Christ in the Eucharist, we receive the Body and Blood of Christ which is

   (A) only a symbol of Jesus.

   (B) a memento of Jesus' love.

   (C) the real presence of Jesus.

   (D) just bread and wine.

10. Christ instituted the Eucharist

    (A) at his Baptism.

    (B) when Moses received the Ten Commandments.

    (C) at the Wedding at Cana.

    (D) at the Last Supper.

11. The apostles received the Holy Spirit at

    (A) the crucifixion.

    (B) Pentecost.

    (C) the Last Supper.

    (D) the crowning with thorns.

12. Jesus Christ sent the Holy Spirit to the apostles so that they would be able to

    (A) go forth and preach the message of salvation to all the world.

(B) have a pet bird.

(C) know Mary better.

(D) find their way to Nazareth.

13. Choosing to turn away from and not love God and others is known as

(A) baptism.

(B) Pentecost.

(C) grace.

(D) sin.

14. When a priest says the words of absolution during the sacrament of reconciliation, he is forgiving sins

(A) in the name of himself.

(B) in the name of God and in the name of the community.

(C) in the name of the person being forgiven.

(D) in the name of society.

15. The effects of the anointing of the sick may be felt

(A) only physically.

(B) only spiritually.

(C) both physically and spiritually.

(D) None of the above.

16. The anointing of the sick may be received

(A) only once.

(B) twice.

(C) three times.

(D) as many times as necessary.

17. The sacrament of matrimony is a sacrament of

(A) healing.

(B) service.

(C) initiation.

(D) None of the above.

18. Marriage can best be described as a covenant which means

(A) an agreement between two people.

(B) a separation between people.

(C) a life of frustration.

(D) an annulment.

19. Marriage is one of the sacraments of service, the other sacrament of service is

    (A) holy orders.   (C) communion.

    (B) baptism.   (D) confirmation.

20. The most important work of a bishop is

    (A) running a diocese.

    (B) paying the bills.

    (C) preaching the gospel message of Jesus Christ to the world.

    (D) assigning priests to parishes.

21. The liturgical year is divided into

    (A) chapters.   (C) seasons.

    (B) verses.   (D) None of the above.

22. The Advent season is _____ weeks long.

    (A) five   (C) two

    (B) six   (D) four

23. The word "Messiah" means

    (A) holy one.   (C) restricted one.

    (B) anointed one.   (D) mystical one.

24. Jesus experienced a

    (A) human birth.   (C) Both (A) and (B).

    (B) nonhuman birth.   (D) Neither (A) nor (B).

25. The liturgical season following Christmas is called

    (A) Lent.   (C) Ordinary Time.

    (B) Advent.   (D) Easter.

26. Ash Wednesday begins the season of

    (A) Easter.   (C) Advent.

    (B) Christmas.   (D) Lent.

27. The Easter Triduum includes the days of

    (A) Holy Thursday, Good Friday, and Holy Saturday.

    (B) Holy Thursday, Easter Sunday, and Holy Saturday.

    (C) Holy Thursday, Ash Wednesday, and Good Friday.

    (D) Holy Thursday, Easter Sunday, and Good Friday.

28. The Church celebrates the Evening Mass of the Lord's Supper on

    (A) Holy Saturday.   (C) Holy Thursday.

    (B) Easter Sunday.   (D) Good Friday.

29. The celebration of Christ's death takes place on

    (A) Good Friday.   (C) Holy Saturday.

    (B) Holy Thursday.   (D) (A) and (B).

30. Catechumens are baptized during the

    (A) Evening Mass of the Lord's Supper.

    (B) celebration of the Lord's Passion.

    (C) Mass of the Easter Vigil.

    (D) None of the above.

31. The most important liturgical celebration for the Church is

    (A) the mass.   (C) Advent.

    (B) confession.   (D) Lent.

32. The commandment that speaks about worshipping only the Lord God is the

    (A) tenth.   (C) third.

    (B) first.   (D) fourth.

33. Catholics can obey the third commandment by

    (A) not working unnecessarily on Sunday.

    (B) spending time with their families.

    (C) gathering together to worship the Lord.

    (D) All of the above.

34. Human life begins at

    (A) birth.

    (B) death.

    (C) middle-age.

    (D) conception.

35. The commandment which speaks about greed and envy is the

    (A) first.

    (B) tenth.

    (C) third.

    (D) fourth.

36. The Catholic church professes Mary to be both the Mother of God and the Mother of the

    (A) Earth.

    (B) Church.

    (C) death.

    (D) guilty.

37. The Trinity refers to

    (A) God, Mary, and the Pope.

    (B) God the Father, God the Son, and God the Holy Spirit.

    (C) Jesus, Peter, and Paul.

    (D) Both (A) and (B).

38. The "Immaculate Conception" refers to

    (A) the birth of Jesus.

    (B) the birth of Mary.

    (C) the conception of Jesus.

    (D) the conception of Mary.

39. The word "laity" refers to

    (A) the ordained.

    (B) the non-ordained.

    (C) Both (A) and (B).

    (D) None of the above.

40. Jesus Christ established the Roman Catholic church upon the foundation of Saint

    (A) John.

    (B) Paul.

    (C) Peter.

    (D) Mark.

Optional Test: Catholic Religion

ANSWER KEY

Question Number	Correct Answer	If You Answered this Question Incorrectly, Refer to...
1.	(B)	P. 698
2.	(C)	P. 698
3.	(A)	P. 698
4.	(A)	P. 699
5.	(C)	P. 700
6.	(D)	P. 700
7.	(A)	P. 700
8.	(A)	P. 700
9.	(C)	P. 701
10.	(D)	P. 701
11.	(B)	P. 702
12.	(A)	P. 702
13.	(D)	P. 703
14.	(B)	P. 703
15.	(C)	P. 703
16.	(D)	P. 704
17.	(B)	P. 704
18.	(A)	P. 704
19.	(A)	P. 704
20.	(C)	P. 706
21.	(C)	P. 707
22.	(D)	P. 707
23.	(B)	P. 707

24.	(A)	P. 707
25.	(C)	P. 707
26.	(D)	P. 708-709
27.	(A)	P. 708-709
28.	(C)	P. 708-709
29.	(A)	P. 709-710
30.	(C)	P. 709-710
31.	(A)	P. 709-710
32.	(B)	P. 711
33.	(D)	P. 711
34.	(D)	P. 713
35.	(B)	P. 717
36.	(B)	P. 717
37.	(B)	P. 717
38.	(D)	P. 717
39.	(B)	P. 719
40.	(C)	P. 720

DETAILED EXPLANATIONS OF ANSWERS

1.   **(B)**   The Israelites were the people chosen by God. It was because of this covenant that the Israelites became known as "God's chosen people." The Canaanites (A) were merchants in Old Testament times. Saducees (C) were a very conservative class of priests in the Old Testament, and Pharisees (D) were an Old Testament group who were separated from everything that was impure and defiled.

2.   **(C)**   Moses was the person who God chose to lead the Israelites out of slavery in Egypt and into the promised land. Noah (A) was the person who God told to put two of every creature in an ark before the great flood. Jonah (B) was the person who spent three days and nights in the belly of the whale, and John (D) was the gospel writer.

3.   **(A)**   Mary was chosen by God to give birth to Jesus Christ. Joseph, who was engaged to Mary at the time of her pregnancy, was chosen by God to be the surrogate father of Jesus. John (B) was the gospel writer, Peter (C) was a disciple chosen by Christ to be the first Pope, and Paul (D) was the New Testament writer who was converted to Christianity after years of persecuting Christians.

4.   **(A)**   It is written many times in the gospels that Jesus healed people because they had faith. In order for someone to be healed, they needed to believe that they indeed could be healed by the grace of God. Anger (B) and doubt (C) are both contrary to the reason why people would be healed.

5.   **(C)**   Christ's dying on the cross was the ultimate act of love by Jesus for his people because it showed a love that was unconditional as well as sacrificial. The Wedding at Cana (A) was the site of the first miracle of Christ when he changed water into wine. The healing of the blind man (B) was one of the many miracles Jesus performed because of the faith the people had in him.

6.   **(D)**   A sacrament is an outward sign instituted by Christ to give grace. It is through the sacraments that we come to know our God better and the mysteries of his kingdom are revealed to us. A parable (A) is a story through which Jesus taught people. Sin (B) is our consciously choosing to turn away from God and others.

7.   **(A)**   It is in baptism that we are welcomed as members of God's church. Reconciliation (B) is the sacrament through which we are forgiven of our sins. Confirmation (C) is the sacrament in which we complete our Christian initiation. Communion (D) is the sacrament in which we receive the Body and Blood of Jesus Christ.

8.   **(A)**   It is through the use of water that life is sustained in people, animals, and plants. It

is for this reason that God chose water as a symbol of the new life we receive in baptism. Sin (B) is our turning away from God and others and is by no means a symbol of new life. Hurt (C) is a result of sin and therefore cannot be the answer. Hate (D) is a form of sin.

9.   **(C)**   The Catholic church professes that the Eucharist is the real presence of Jesus Christ. The Body and Blood of Christ is not a symbol (A), but a sacrament. Therefore, the Eucharist is not a memento (B) or only bread and wine (D). During the words of consecration, the bread and wine become the Body and Blood of Jesus Christ.

10.   **(D)**   Christ gathered with his apostles at the Last Supper to celebrate with them this one last meal. This was where Jesus told them to "take and eat for this is my body" and to "take and drink for this is my blood." It is from this that the Eucharistic celebration comes. Christ was baptized (A) by John the Baptist as a sign of the need for all people to repent. Moses received the Ten Commandments (B) in the days of the Old Testament and this has nothing to do with the Eucharist. The Wedding at Cana (C) was when Jesus performed his first miracle of turning water into wine.

11.   **(B)**   It was at Pentecost that the apostles received the Holy Spirit. The apostles were hiding in an upper room after the crucifixtion of Christ because they were scared that they too would be put to death for their association with Jesus. At Pentecost, the Holy Spirit came upon the apostles and gave them the courage to go forth and make disciples of all nations. The crucifixion (A) was when Jesus died, while the Last Supper (C) was when Jesus celebrated the Eucharist with his apostles. The crowning with thorns (D) occurred after Jesus was arrested and condemned to death. Roman guards put a crown made of thorns on Jesus' head to mock him because he was referred to as the "King of the Jews."

12.   **(A)**   Jesus sent the Holy Spirit to the Apostles so that they would be able to go forth and preach the message of salvation to all the world. The apostles needed the Holy Spirit because it rid them of their fear. Though the Holy Spirit is often represented as a dove, the Holy Spirit is actually a part of the Trinity of God and not an animal (B). The apostles already knew Mary (C) pretty well as she had been with them for a while. The apostles already knew their way to Nazareth (D).

13.   **(D)**   When we choose to reject God and others, we choose to sin. Sin is an act that we commit that we know is wrong, but do anyway. Grace (C) is God's life and love in us and in our world. Pentecost (B) is the day on which the Holy Spirit descended upon the apostles. Baptism (A) is when we become members of the Mystical Body of Christ and the Church.

14.   **(B)**   When a priest prays the words of absolution during the sacrament of reconciliation he is absolving sins in the name of God and in the name of the community. The priest does not absolve in his name (A) because he is a mediator between God and the person being forgiven. The supplicant (C) is asking for forgiveness, therefore this cannot be the answer. Finally, although the person being forgiven may have commited sins against society (D), that person is seeking to be reconciled with God also.

15. **(C)**   It is through the anointing of the sick that someone may be healed both physically and spiritually. This healing process can come about through the person's faith in God and through the intercessory prayers and anointing. The key word in this question is *may*. A person may only be healed spiritually (B), meaning that through faith and the grace of God, they come to be at peace. If someone is healed physically (A) through the sacrament, a spiritual healing has taken place also.

16. **(D)**   A person may receive the anointing of the sick as many times as necessary. The person may receive the sacrament when they learn of their initial illness and may receive it if their condition gets worse or if they are about to have surgery.

17. **(B)**   Through the sacrament of matrimony, the couple enters into a life of service to each other and to their children. Matrimony is unlike the sacraments of reconciliation and confirmation in that these two sacraments deal especially with healing (A). Baptism, communion, and confirmation mark specific points in the initiation (C) of a Catholic. Marriage is not part of the initiation process into the church.

18. **(A)**   When a couple enters into marriage, they enter into a covenant or an agreement between two people. It is in this agreement that the couple promises to love, honor, and respect each other. A covenant is by no means a separation (B). Although there are hard times in marriages, the living out of a covenant is not a total period of frustration (C). An annulment (D) is a declaration that states that a marriage never took place because there were conditions which either one or both members of the couple were unaware of prior to the ceremony, and invalidates the bond.

19. **(A)**   Holy orders is a sacrament of service stating that a deacon, priest, or bishop pledges a life of service to God and his people. Baptism (B) is a sacrament of initiation along with communion (C) and confirmation (D).

20. **(C)**   The most important work of a bishop is to preach the gospel message of Jesus Christ to the world. This is his most important role because the bishop is seen as the primary teacher and preacher in a diocese or in whatever capacity that bishop is serving. Many bishops have the responsibility of running a diocese (A), however the bishop must keep the preaching of the gospel at the forefront of his work. Paying the bills (B) is important, however this job is often left to someone who can give more attention to it. The bishop takes into consideration where priests will be assigned (D), but he has people who help him in this process.

21. **(C)**   Seasons make up the liturgical year. The seasons help us to focus on the particular celebration taking place during that part of the year. Chapters (A) deal with parts of a book while verses (B) deal with scripture, quotes, or parts of a song.

22. **(D)**   During the four weeks of Advent we prepare for the coming of our Lord at Christmas. Therefore (A), (B), and (C) are wrong.

23. **(B)**   Sacred Scripture had promised the Jews a "Messiah" to lead them to glory and be

their Savior. This is where the meaning of "Messiah" as "anointed one" (B) comes from. Jesus was holy (A), but this is not the meaning of the word "Messiah." Messiah does not mean restricted (C) or mystical (D).

24. **(A)** Jesus Christ entered the world through the means of a human birth. Although Jesus is divine, meaning he is the Son of God, he entered the world as a human. Therefore choices (B), (C), and (D) are wrong.

25. **(C)** The season of Ordinary Time follows the Christmas season. Lent (A) is the 40 day season before Holy Thursday when we repent and prepare for Christ's suffering, death, and resurrection. Advent (B) is the four weeks of preparation before Christmas, while Easter (D) is the season during which we celebrate the resurrection of Christ.

26. **(D)** Ash Wednesday begins the season of Lent (D). It is during this season that a preparation for the passion of Christ takes place. Easter (A) is the season of joyful celebration of Christ's resurrection. Christmas (B) is the season during which we celebrate the birth of Christ and includes the feast of the Holy Family, the Epiphany, and the Baptism of the Lord. Advent (C) is a preparatory season before Christmas.

27. **(A)** It is during the Easter Triduum that we celebrate the days of Holy Thursday, Good Friday and Holy Saturday (A). Easter Sunday (B) is a celebration after the Triduum, while Ash Wednesday (C) begins the season of Lent. (For D, see B)

28. **(C)** The night on which the Church celebrates the Evening Mass of the Lord's Supper is Holy Thursday. This is the night when Christ gathered one last time with his apostles and established the Sacrament of the Eucharist. On Holy Saturday (A) we celebrate the Mass of the Easter Vigil, during which the Easter Sacraments are received by the catechumens and candidates. Easter Sunday (B) is the day on which we celebrate Christ's resurrection from the dead. Good Friday (D) is a celebration of the death of Christ.

29. **(A)** It is on Good Friday (A) that the Church remembers and celebrates Christ's death. Holy Thursday (B) is when the Evening Mass of the Lord's Supper is celebrated. It is on Holy Saturday (C) that the Easter Vigil is celebrated.

30. **(C)** During the Mass of the Easter Vigil (C), catechumens, those seeking baptism and the other sacraments of initation, are baptized. The Evening Mass of the Lord's Supper (A) is on Holy Thursday while the Celebration of the Lord's Passion (B) is on Good Friday.

31. **(A)** The mass (A) is the most important liturgical celebration for the Church because it is in the mass that we hear the Word of God and then receive Jesus Christ in the Eucharist. Confession (B) is an important aspect in the life of a Catholic, however, the mass stands before confession in importance. Advent (C) and Lent (D) are liturgical seasons.

32. **(B)** It is in the first (B) commandment that God requires us to avoid worshipping false gods. We know that there is only one true God and it is he that we give worship to. For this reason, (A), (C), and (D) are wrong.

33. **(D)** All of these answers are living the third commandment. It is important that people avoid unnecessary work (A) unless their responsibility to their family requires them to. Spending time together as a family (B) can establish loving bonds among parents and children, as well as between the family and God. Gathering together, Christians can find strength and personal support as they glorify the Lord on Sundays (C).

34. **(D)** Human life begins at the moment of conception. At conception, a human being begins to form. Weeks, days, or months do not matter. Our earthly human life ends at death (B). Although some people may think their life is over at middle age (C), this is not true. At birth (A) the child has already been experiencing life in the womb of his or her mother.

35. **(B)** In the tenth (B) commandment, God warns us against being greedy or envious of other people's possessions. Therefore, (A), (C), and (D) are wrong. It is important to be thankful for what we already have!

36. **(B)** It is because Mary is the Mother of God that she is also the Mother of the Church. Since we profess the Church to be the Mystical Body of Christ, then Mary serves as the Mother of that body. Therefore (A), (C), and (D) are wrong answers.

37. **(B)** God the Father, God the Son, and God the Holy Spirit make up the Trinity. It is through these three divine persons in one that we find God. Therefore (A), (C), (D) are incorrect.

38. **(D)** God chose Mary from the time of her conception to be the Mother of Christ. God chose to keep her pure and holy, free from the stain of Original Sin. It is for this reason that we refer to Mary's conception (D) as the "Immaculate Conception." The birth of Jesus (A) does not refer to a conception, neither does the birth of Mary (B). The conception of Jesus was a miracle, but the term "Immaculate Conception" refers to Mary.

39. **(B)** The non-ordained are the laity. The ordained (A), a bishop, priest, or deacon have taken vows to God and the Church to serve in a special way and are therefore no longer "lay" people. Therefore, (C) and (D) are wrong.

40. **(C)** Christ chose St. Peter (C) to be the first pope. Christ knew that a leader would be needed for the early church, and so he chose Peter because of his great faith and devotion. John (A) was the gospel writer, while Paul (B) never met Christ but converted to Christianity after years of persecuting the church. Mark (D) is another gospel writer.

The High School Tutors®

The **HIGH SCHOOL TUTOR** series is based on the same principle as the more comprehensive **PROBLEM SOLVERS**, but is specifically designed to meet the needs of high school students. REA has revised all the books in this series to include expanded review sections and new material. This makes the books even more effective in helping students to cope with these difficult high school subjects.

If you would like more information about any of these books,
complete the coupon below and return it to us or go to your local bookstore.

"The ESSENTIALS" of LANGUAGE

Each book in the **LANGUAGE ESSENTIALS** series offers all the essential information of the grammar and vocabulary of the language it covers. They include conjugations, irregular verb forms, and sentence structure, and are designed to help students in preparing for exams and doing homework. The **LANGUAGE ESSENTIALS** are excellent supplements to any class text or course of study.

The **LANGUAGE ESSENTIALS** are complete and concise, with quick access to needed information. They also provide a handy reference source at all times. The **LANGUAGE ESSENTIALS** are prepared with REA's customary concern for high professional quality and student needs.

Available Titles Include:

French   *Italian*

German   *Spanish*

If you would like more information about any of these books, complete the coupon below and return it to us or visit your local bookstore.

MAXnotes®

REA's Literature Study Guides

MAXnotes® are student-friendly. They offer a fresh look at masterpieces of literature, presented in a lively and interesting fashion. **MAXnotes®** offer the essentials of what you should know about the work, including outlines, explanations and discussions of the plot, character lists, analyses, and historical context. **MAXnotes®** are designed to help you think independently about literary works by raising various issues and thought-provoking ideas and questions. Written by literary experts who currently teach the subject, **MAXnotes®** enhance your understanding and enjoyment of the work.

Available **MAXnotes®** include the following:

Absalom, Absalom!
The Aeneid of Virgil
Animal Farm
Antony and Cleopatra
As I Lay Dying
As You Like It
The Autobiography of
    Malcolm X
The Awakening
Beloved
Beowulf
Billy Budd
The Bluest Eye, A Novel
Brave New World
The Canterbury Tales
The Catcher in the Rye
The Color Purple
The Crucible
Death in Venice
Death of a Salesman
Dickens Dictionary
The Divine Comedy I: Inferno
Dubliners
The Edible Woman
Emma
Euripides' Medea & Electra
Frankenstein
Gone with the Wind
The Grapes of Wrath
Great Expectations
The Great Gatsby
Gulliver's Travels
Handmaid's Tale
Hamlet
Hard Times
Heart of Darkness

Henry IV, Part I
Henry V
The House on Mango Street
Huckleberry Finn
I Know Why the Caged
    Bird Sings
The Iliad
Invisible Man
Jane Eyre
Jazz
The Joy Luck Club
Jude the Obscure
Julius Caesar
King Lear
Leaves of Grass
Les Misérables
Lord of the Flies
Macbeth
The Merchant of Venice
Metamorphoses of Ovid
Metamorphosis
Middlemarch
A Midsummer Night's Dream
Moby-Dick
Moll Flanders
Mrs. Dalloway
Much Ado About Nothing
Mules and Men
My Antonia
Native Son
1984
The Odyssey
Oedipus Trilogy
Of Mice and Men
On the Road

Othello
Paradise
Paradise Lost
A Passage to India
Plato's Republic
Portrait of a Lady
A Portrait of the Artist
    as a Young Man
Pride and Prejudice
A Raisin in the Sun
Richard II
Romeo and Juliet
The Scarlet Letter
Sir Gawain and the
    Green Knight
Slaughterhouse-Five
Song of Solomon
The Sound and the Fury
The Stranger
Sula
The Sun Also Rises
A Tale of Two Cities
The Taming of the Shrew
Tar Baby
The Tempest
Tess of the D'Urbervilles
Their Eyes Were Watching God
Things Fall Apart
To Kill a Mockingbird
To the Lighthouse
Twelfth Night
Uncle Tom's Cabin
Waiting for Godot
Wuthering Heights
Guide to Literary Terms

Available at your local bookstore or order directly from us by sending in coupon below.

REA's Test Preps
The Best in Test Preparation

- REA "Test Preps" are **far more** comprehensive than any other test preparation series
- Each book contains up to **eight** full-length practice tests based on the most recent exams
- **Every** type of question likely to be given on the exams is included
- Answers are accompanied by **full** and **detailed** explanations

REA publishes over 60 Test Preparation volumes in several series. They include:

Advanced Placement Exams(APs)
Biology
Calculus AB & Calculus BC
Chemistry
Computer Science
Economics
English Language & Composition
English Literature & Composition
European History
Government & Politics
Physics B & C
Psychology
Spanish Language
Statistics
United States History

College-Level Examination Program (CLEP)
Analyzing and Interpreting Literature
College Algebra
Freshman College Composition
General Examinations
General Examinations Review
History of the United States I
History of the United States II
Human Growth and Development
Introductory Sociology
Principles of Marketing
Spanish

SAT II: Subject Tests
Biology E/M
Chemistry
English Language Proficiency Test
French
German

SAT II: Subject Tests (cont'd)
Literature
Mathematics Level IC, IIC
Physics
Spanish
United States History
Writing

Graduate Record Exams (GREs)
Biology
Chemistry
Computer Science
General
Literature in English
Mathematics
Physics
Psychology

ACT - ACT Assessment

ASVAB - Armed Services Vocational Aptitude Battery

CBEST - California Basic Educational Skills Test

CDL - Commercial Driver License Exam

CLAST - College Level Academic Skills Test

COOP & HSPT - Catholic High School Admission Tests

ELM - California State University Entry Level Mathematics Exam

FE (EIT) - Fundamentals of Engineering Exams - For both AM & PM Exams

FTCE - Florida Teacher Certification Exam

GED - High School Equivalency Diploma Exam (U.S. & Canadian editions)

GMAT CAT - Graduate Management Admission Test

LSAT - Law School Admission Test

MAT- Miller Analogies Test

MCAT - Medical College Admission Test

MTEL - Massachusetts Tests for Educator Licensure

MSAT- Multiple Subjects Assessment for Teachers

NJ HSPA - New Jersey High School Proficiency Assessment

NYSTCE: LAST & ATS-W - New York State Teacher Certification

PLT - Principles of Learning & Teaching Tests

PPST- Pre-Professional Skills Tests

PSAT - Preliminary Scholastic Assessment Test

SAT

TExES - Texas Examinations of Educator Standards

THEA - Texas Higher Education Assessment

TOEFL - Test of English as a Foreign Language

TOEIC - Test of English for International Communication

USMLE Steps 1,2,3 - U.S. Medical Licensing Exams

U.S. Postal Exams 460 & 470

RESEARCH & EDUCATION ASSOCIATION
61 Ethel Road W. • Piscataway, New Jersey 08854
Phone: (732) 819-8880   **website: www.rea.com**

Please send me more information about your Test Prep books

Name _____

Address _____

City _____ State _____ Zip _____

REA's Books Are The Best!
(a sample of the <u>hundreds of letters</u> REA receives each year)

" I am writing to congratulate you on preparing an exceptional study guide. In five years of teaching this course I have never encountered a more thorough, comprehensive, concise and realistic preparation for this examination. "
Teacher, Davie, FL

" I have found your publications, *The Best Test Preparation...* to be exactly that. "
Teacher, Aptos, CA

" I am writing to thank you for you test preparation... your book helped me immeasurably and I have nothing by praise for your GRE Preparation "
Student, Benton Harbor, MI

" Your *GMAT* book greatly helped me on the test. Thank you. "
Student, Oxford, OH

" I recently got the *French SAT II* Exam book from REA. I congratulate you on first-rate French practice tests. "
Instructor, Los Angeles, CA

" The *REA LSAT* Test Preparation guide is a winner! "
Student, Montgomery, AL

" This book is great. Most of my friends that used the REA AP book and took the exam received 4's or 5's (mostly 5's which is the highest score!!) "
Student, San Jose, CA